Fodor's 2010

ARIZONA & THE GRAND CANYON

Fodor's Travel Publications   New York, Toronto, London, Sydney, Auckland
www.fodors.com

W9-ANC-460

Be a Fodor's Correspondent

Your opinion matters. It matters to us. It matters to your fellow Fodor's travelers, too. And we'd like to hear it. In fact, we *need* to hear it.

When you share your experiences and opinions, you become an active member of the Fodor's community. That means we'll not only use your feedback to make our books better, but we'll publish your names and comments whenever possible. Throughout our guides, look for "Word of Mouth," excerpts of your unvarnished feedback.

Here's how you can help improve Fodor's for all of us.

Tell us when we're right. We rely on local writers to give you an insider's perspective. But our writers and staff editors—who are the best in the business—depend on you. Your positive feedback is a vote to renew our recommendations for the next edition.

Tell us when we're wrong. We're proud that we update most of our guides every year. But we're not perfect. Things change. Hotels cut services. Museums change hours. Charming cafés lose charm. If our writer didn't quite capture the essence of a place, tell us how you'd do it differently. If any of our descriptions are inaccurate or inadequate, we'll incorporate your changes in the next edition and will correct factual errors at fodors.com *immediately*.

Tell us what to include. You probably have had fantastic travel experiences that aren't yet in Fodor's. Why not share them with a community of like-minded travelers? Maybe you chanced upon a beach or bistro or B&B that you don't want to keep to yourself. Tell us why we should include it. And share your discoveries and experiences with everyone directly at fodors.com. Your input may lead us to add a new listing or highlight a place we cover with a "Highly Recommended" star or with our highest rating, "Fodor's Choice."

Give us your opinion instantly at our feedback center at www.fodors.com/feedback. You may also e-mail editors@fodors.com with the subject line "Arizona Editor." Or send your nominations, comments, and complaints by mail to Arizona Editor, Fodor's, 1745 Broadway, New York, NY 10019.

You and travelers like you are the heart of the Fodor's community. Make our community richer by sharing your experiences. Be a Fodor's correspondent.

Happy Traveling!

Tim Jarrell, Publisher

FODOR'S ARIZONA & THE GRAND CANYON 2010

Editor: Cate Starmer

Editorial Contributors: Andrew Collins, Carrie Frasure, JoBeth Jamison, Cara LaBrie, Mara Levin

Production Editor: Evangelos Vasilakis

Maps & Illustrations: Mark Stroud, David Lindroth, *cartographers*; Bob Blake, Rebecca Baer, *map editors*; William Wu, *information graphics*

Design: Fabrizio La Rocca, *creative director*; Guido Caroti, Siobhan O'Hare, *art directors*; Tina Malaney, Chie Ushio, Ann McBride, Jessica Walsh, *designers*; Mèlanie Marin, *senior picture editor*

Cover Photo: (Colorado River, Grand Canyon National Park): Marjorie McBride/ Alamy

Production Manager: Angela McLean

COPYRIGHT

ISBN 978-1-4000-0856-8

ISSN 1559-6230

SPECIAL SALES

This book is available at special discounts for bulk purchases for sales promotions or premiums. Special editions, including personalized covers, excerpts of existing books, and corporate imprints, can be created in large quantities for special needs. For more information, write to Special Markets/Premium Sales, 1745 Broadway, MD 6-2, New York, New York 10019, or e-mail specialmarkets@randomhouse.com.

AN IMPORTANT TIP & AN INVITATION

Although all prices, opening times, and other details in this book are based on information supplied to us at press time, changes occur all the time in the travel world, and Fodor's cannot accept responsibility for facts that become outdated or for inadvertent errors or omissions. So **always confirm information when it matters,** especially if you're making a detour to visit a specific place. Your experiences—positive and negative— matter to us. If we have missed or misstated something, **please write to us.** We follow up on all suggestions. Contact the Arizona & the Grand Canyon editor at editors@fodors. com or c/o Fodor's at 1745 Broadway, New York, NY 10019.

PRINTED IN CHINA

10 9 8 7 6 5 4 3 2 1

CONTENTS

Fodor's Features

MAPS

ABOUT
THIS BOOK

Our Ratings

Sometimes you find terrific travel experiences and sometimes they just find you. But usually the burden is on you to select the right combination of experiences. That's where our ratings come in.

As travelers we've all discovered a place so wonderful that its worthiness is obvious. And sometimes that place is so experiential that superlatives don't do it justice: you just have to be there to know. These sights, properties, and experiences get our highest rating, **Fodor's Choice**, indicated by orange stars throughout this book.

Black stars highlight sights and properties we deem **Highly Recommended**, places that our writers, editors, and readers praise again and again for consistency and excellence.

By default, there's another category: any place we include in this book is by definition worth your time, unless we say otherwise. And we will.

Disagree with any of our choices? Care to nominate a place or suggest that we rate one more highly? Visit our feedback center at www.fodors.com/feedback.

Budget Well

Hotel and restaurant price categories from ¢ to $$$$ are defined in the opening pages of each chapter. For attractions, we always give standard adult admission fees; reductions are usually available for children, students, and senior citizens. Want to pay with plastic? **AE, D, DC, MC, V** following restaurant and hotel listings indicate if American Express, Discover, Diners Club, MasterCard, and Visa are accepted.

Restaurants

Unless we state otherwise, restaurants are open for lunch and dinner daily. We mention dress only when there's a specific requirement and reservations only when they're essential or not accepted—it's always best to book ahead.

Hotels

Hotels have private bath, phone, TV, and air-conditioning and operate on the European Plan (aka EP, meaning without meals), unless we specify that they use the Continental Plan (CP, with a Continental breakfast), Breakfast Plan (BP, with a full breakfast), or Modified American Plan (MAP, with breakfast and dinner) or are all-inclusive (AI, including all meals and most activities). We

always list facilities but not whether you'll be charged an extra fee to use them, so when pricing accommodations, find out what's included.

Listings
★	Fodor's Choice
★	Highly recommended
✉	Physical address
✢	Directions or Map Coordinates
✆	Mailing address
☎	Telephone
🖷	Fax
⊕	On the Web
✍	E-mail
✑	Admission fee
☉	Open/closed times
Ⓜ	Metro stations
▭	Credit cards

Hotels & Restaurants
🏨	Hotel
↵	Number of rooms
✧	Facilities
�	Meal plans
✕	Restaurant
⌕	Reservations
↘	Smoking
፼	BYOB
✕🏨	Hotel with restaurant that warrants a visit

Outdoors
🏌	Golf
⛺	Camping

Other
☾	Family-friendly
⇨	See also
✉	Branch address
☞	Take note

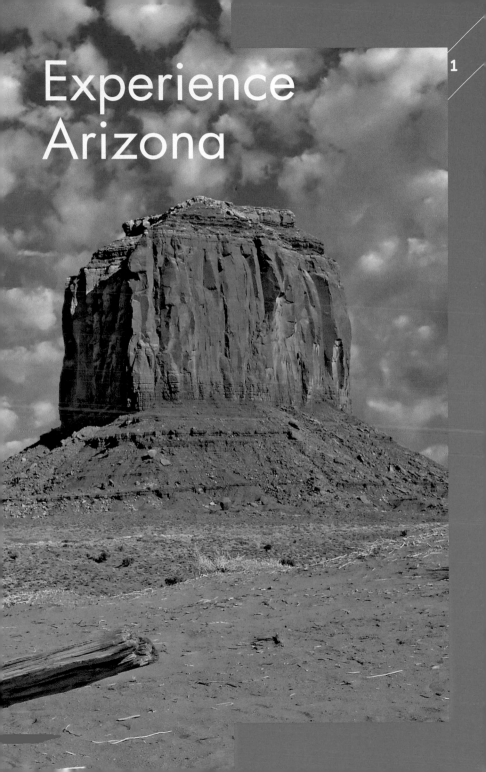

Experience
Arizona

WHAT'S WHERE

The following numbers refer to chapters.

2 Phoenix, Scottsdale, and Tempe. Rising where the Sonoran Desert butts up against the Superstition Mountains, the Valley of the Sun is filled with resorts and spas, shops and restaurants, more than 200 golf courses, and nearby mountains and trails.

3 Grand Canyon National Park. One of nature's longest-running works in progress, with the popular South Rim or the more remote North Rim. Don't just peer over the edge—take the plunge into the canyon on a mule train, on foot, or on a raft trip.

4 North-Central Arizona. Cool, laid-back towns here are as bewitching as the high desert landscape they inhabit. There are quaint escapes like Prescott and Jerome, New Age Sedona with its red-rock buttes, and the vibrant university town of Flagstaff.

5 Northeast Arizona. This remote area includes the stunning surroundings of Monument Valley. Alongside today's Navajo and Hopi communities, the breathtaking Canyon de Chelly and Navajo National Monument are reminders of how ancient peoples lived with the land.

6 Eastern Arizona. Summer visitors flock to the lush, green White Mountains and the warm colors of the Painted Desert. Nearby Petrified Forest National Park protects trees that stood when dinosaurs walked the earth.

7 Tucson. The history of Arizona begins here, where Hispanic, Anglo, and Native American cultures became intertwined in the 17th century and still are today. Farther out, city slickers enjoy horseback rides at some of the region's many guest ranches, or luxury pampering at world-class spas.

8 Southern Arizona. Splendid mountain and desert scenery evokes the romanticized spirit of the Wild West. Enduring pockets of westward expansion are the largest draw today: infamous Tombstone and the mining boomtown Bisbee.

9 Northwest Arizona and Southeast Nevada. This under-explored corner of Arizona includes Lake Havasu City and its bit of Britannia in the form of London Bridge; old-fashioned Americana around Kingman, a hub on legendary Route 66; and Hoover Dam and Laughlin's casinos, just a short jaunt away in Nevada.

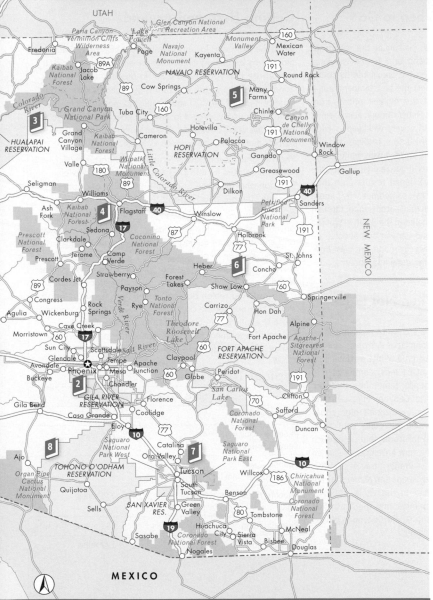

ARIZONA PLANNER

When to Go

High season at the resorts of Phoenix and Tucson is winter, when the snowbirds fly south. Expect the best temperatures—and the highest prices—from December through March, when nearly every weekend is filled with outdoor festivals and the air is scented with orange blossoms. If you're on a budget, the posh desert resorts drop their prices—sometimes by more than half—from June through September. The South Rim of the Grand Canyon and Sedona are busy year-round, but least busy during the winter months.

When Not to Go

For a statewide excursion, keep in mind that Arizona's climate is extreme. While a winter visit might be most comfortable in Phoenix, remember that the Grand Canyon, Flagstaff, and Sedona—Arizona's high country—will be quite cold then. Also take note that areas such as eastern Arizona are designed for summer travelers, thus many shops and restaurants are closed in the winter months. Remember that the North Rim of the Grand Canyon is closed in winter.

Getting Here and Around

Since the state was largely developed when the United States was beginning its fascination with the open road, it's no surprise that you'll need a car to properly explore Arizona. Deceptively vast, Arizona is the nation's sixth largest state at nearly 114,000 square mi. No matter where you start your journey, expect to spend a good portion of your time in the car. Fortunately, Arizona offers an attractive canvas that ranges from desert to forest.

Phoenix and Tucson have international airports; smaller, regional carriers fly into Flagstaff. Amtrak lines service Flagstaff and Tucson. Car rental is available at airports in Phoenix, Tucson, and Flagstaff.

Road conditions vary by season and location, so expect anything: you can start your day in 100°F heat in Phoenix and end it in near-freezing temperatures in the Grand Canyon. Be sure to plan accordingly for the weather: if driving in the desert during the summer, keep bottled water in the car; in winter in the high country be prepared for icy roads. And remember that violent flash floods and dust storms can pepper the area during the summer monsoons. Storms usually pass quickly. For road information, the Arizona Department of Transportation has a travelers' assistance line. Just dial 511 from any phone.

Typical Travel Times

	Hours by Car	Distance
Phoenix–Flagstaff	2½	145 miles
Phoenix–Grand Canyon South Rim	4½	175 miles
Phoenix–Lake Mead/Hoover Dam	4½	260 miles
Phoenix–Monument Valley	6	275 miles
Phoenix–Yuma	3	185 miles
Tucson–Phoenix	2	120 miles

What to Pack

Thanks to extreme climates and Western informality, you can go almost anywhere in Arizona in a pair of jeans.

■ Bring layers for trips north or east, particularly when temperatures dip after the sun sets.

■ For formal dining, call ahead for attire requirements. In most places, a shirt and dress slacks will be more than sufficient.

■ Depending on your desired level of activity, you will need to pack different gear: golf shoes, hiking boots, or flip-flops.

■ No matter your plans, be prepared with hats and sunscreen for sun protection. The desert heat can be intense and quite deceptive.

Tribal Lands

Arizona has 22 Native American reservations, each with its own government and culture. Most tribes have Web sites or phone-information lines, and it's best to contact them for information before a trip. Many require a permit for hiking or biking in scenic areas. Always be respectful of individual cultures and traditions.

Did You Know . . .

With the exception of the Navajo Nation in the northeast corner of the state, Arizona does not observe daylight saving time. Arizona is in the Mountain Standard Time zone.

How's the Weather?

1

Phoenix averages 325 sunny days and 7 inches of precipitation annually. The high mountains see about 25 inches of rain. The Grand Canyon is usually cool at the rim and about 20°F warmer on the floor. The North Rim is generally about 10 degrees cooler than the South Rim, which is open year-round. Temperatures in valley areas like Phoenix and Tucson average about 60°F to 70°F in the daytime in winter and between 100°F and 115°F in summer. Flagstaff and Sedona stay much cooler, dropping into the 30s and 40s in winter and leveling off at 80°F to 90°F in summer.

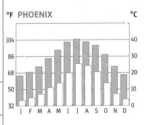

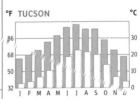

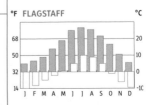

ARIZONA TOP ATTRACTIONS

The Grand Canyon

(A) Discover Mother Nature's creativity firsthand with a visit to this natural wonder. When it comes to visiting Grand Canyon National Park, there are statistics and there are sights, and both are sure to leave you in awe. With an average width of 10 mi, a length of 277 mi, and a depth of 1 mi, the enormity of the canyon is nearly impossible to fathom. You can view the spectacle from the South Rim, but the North Rim is the rim less traveled. Whether exploring the area on foot, by mule, by raft, or by plane, the journey is one worth savoring.

Petrified Forest and the Painted Desert

(B) Arizona's diverse and historic landscape shows off some of its most magnificent achievements here. The Painted Desert takes on hues that range from blood-red to the purest pink throughout the day. View a forest of trees that stood with dinosaurs at the Petrified Forest, as well as ancient dwellings and fossils. You can enjoy the entire national park in less than a day and take in a bit of nostalgia with Route 66's vestiges in nearby Holbrook along the way.

Sedona

(C) Loved for its majestic red rocks, its spiritual energy, and its fantastic resorts and spas, Sedona is unlike any other town in America. The fracturing of the western edge of the Colorado Plateau created the red-rock buttes that loom over Sedona, and this landscape has attracted artists, entrepreneurs, and New Age followers from all over. Take the active route and explore Oak Creek Canyon and the surrounding area on foot or by bike or Jeep; or indulge in the luxe life at a world-class spa or restaurant.

Scottsdale

(D) The West's most Western town, modern Scottsdale is equal parts kitsch and overt opulence. Resorts, spas, and golf can easily absorb an entire vacation. Stroll through art galleries and Western boutiques in Old Town during the day, and discover chic nightlife and fine cuisine at night. Scottsdale is part of the Valley of the Sun, along with Phoenix, Tempe, and some 20 other communities.

The Heard Museum

(E) One of Phoenix's jewels, the Heard proudly features one of the most comprehensive collections of Native American art in the world. Interactive art-making exhibits are alongside a staggering amount of Southwestern pottery, jewelry, kachinas, and textiles. Plus, the museum gift shop is one of the best places in town to find authentic souvenirs worth treasuring.

Monument Valley

(F) One of the most familiar sights of Arizona—thanks to dozens of Hollywood productions and the keen eye of Ansel Adams—the fantastic sculpted buttes, mesas, and rock formations of Monument Valley are yet another reminder of the abundance of nature's handiwork in the state. Take a Navajo–guided tour to appreciate the nuances of the area.

Desert Botanical Garden

(G) While there are stellar museums and preserves across Arizona, none is like the Desert Botanical Garden, 150 acres in Phoenix dedicated to the diversity of the desert. With more than 4,000 species of cacti, trees, and flowers, visitors discover the variety and breadth of this mysterious landscape—all in the comfort of America's fifth-largest city.

QUINTESSENTIAL ARIZONA

Road Trips

Arizona is the place to take a road trip. Get in the car, pick a destination, and go take a look. For optimal enjoyment, avoid the interstate highways and take the state routes instead. Stop at every roadside historic marker (well, OK, you can skip some if you want) and at any place with a sign that reads PIE. Go to Bisbee. Go to Jerome. Go to Oatman. Go to Greer. Travel AZ 260 from Payson to Show Low or historic Route 66 from Ash Fork to Topock; take AZ 60 through the Salt River Canyon, or U.S. 191 from Springerville to Clifton; take AZ 88, the Apache Trail, from Apache Junction to Roosevelt Dam. Wherever you go, roll down the windows, turn up the radio, inhale deeply, and enjoy the ride. Regardless of your destination, the wide-open spaces of Arizona entice and amaze anew with every bend in the road.

Salsa and Margaritas

You're in Arizona, so join the quest to find your favorite salsa and margaritas. No two salsas are the same, and every city and town boasts its own local favorite. Spicy and chunky? Tangy and juicy? Tear-inducing? They run the gamut.

You'll find the flavors change regionally, from mesquite-imbued concoctions in the East, inspired by Tex-Mex cuisine, to fresh-from-the-garden medleys in southern Arizona that are authentically Mexican.

And who needs water when you can complement the flavors even better with perfectly salty-and-sour margaritas? They can take the sting away from a particularly robust salsa, all while washing down a delightful Mexican feast.

Arizona is known for its magnificent natural landmarks, its rich history, and its captivating cuisine. Here are some easy ways to get to know the lay of the land and start thinking like an Arizonian.

The Night Sky

Away from the metropolitan areas of Phoenix and Tucson, where the by-products of urban life obscure the firmament, the night sky is clear and unpolluted by lights or smog. In December in the desert, the Milky Way stretches like a chiffon scarf across the celestial sphere. Lie on your back on the hood of your car at night, allow your eyes time to adjust to the darkness, and you'll see more stars than you could possibly have imagined.

For a closer look, you can visit Lowell Observatory on Mars Hill, in Flagstaff or the Kitt Peak National Observatory in southwest Arizona (outside of Tucson) and look at celestial objects through large telescopes.

Rodeo

People take rodeo seriously in Arizona, whether it's a holiday extravaganza like those in Prescott or Payson (which draw top cowboys from around the country), a bull-riding competition at Camp Verde, or a bunch of working cowboys gathered for a team roping contest in Williams.

These days, particularly with the emergence of bull riding as a stand-alone event—and the crowds often cheer as much for the bulls as the cowboys—rodeos are no longer the hayseed and cowpokey events Arizona grandpas might have enjoyed. Rock-and-roll rodeo has arrived and there is frequently live music as well as roping. So, if you see a flyer posted in a shop window advertising a rodeo, take a walk on the wild side and check out the fine arts of riding and roping. You might be surprised how graceful it is.

IF YOU LIKE

Hiking

Arizona has a wealth of awe-inspiring natural landmarks. So you can hike in and out, up and down, or just around beautiful and varied landscapes, into canyons, to a mountain summit, or just along a meandering trail through a desert or a forest.

Wherever you go, make sure you're well prepared with water, food, a good hat, and a camera to capture your achievement.

From the long-heralded trails such as Bright Angel in the Grand Canyon to iconic Camelback Mountain in Phoenix, there's a summit or path in every corner of the state waiting for you.

If waterfalls are your thing, check out **Havasu Canyon**, an 8-mi hike that descends 3,000 feet to splashing pools of turquoise water.

The highest of the four peaks that comprise San Francisco Peaks is **Mount Humphreys**, the ultimate goal for hikers seeking the best view in the state. Timing an ascent can be tricky, though, as the snow doesn't melt until mid-July, and by then the summer rains and lightning come almost daily in the afternoon. Go early in the morning and pay attention to the sky.

For some archaeology with your hiking, **Walnut Canyon National Monument** has a paved and stepped trail descending 185 feet into an island of stone where you can explore prehistoric cliff dwellings. There are steps and handrails, but the climb out is strenuous.

Water Sports

You don't miss the water until it's not there, but Arizonians do their best to ensure that the well doesn't go dry. Dams and canal systems help to fill vast reservoirs, and the resulting rivers and lakes provide all manner of water-sport recreation. You can have it easy, you can have it rough, or you can have it fast.

Easy is a week on a **houseboat** on a lake. Houseboats are available for rent on major lakes along the Colorado River, as well as on Lake Powell, Lake Mead, and Lake Havasu. On smaller lakes motorized boats are prohibited, but kayaks and canoes make for an enjoyable excursion along the pine-covered shorelines. You can even take a rowboat out on Tempe Town Lake.

Rough is a **river raft trip**. There are nearly two-dozen commercial rafting companies offering trips as short as three days or as long as three weeks through the Grand Canyon. Options include motorized rafts or dories rowed by Arizona's version of the California surfer—the Colorado River boatman. The Hualapai Tribe, through the Hualapai River Runners headquartered in Peach Springs, offers one-day river trips. Don't let the short duration fool you: the boatmen take you through several rapids, and thrills abound.

Fast involves a **speedboat** and water skis or Jet Skis. Both are popular on major lakes and along the Colorado River. You can go from dam to dam along the Colorado, and on lakes the size of Powell and Mead you can ski until your legs give out.

Desert

Arizona has a desert for you; actually, it has more than one. The trouble is, any desert is inhospitable to life forms unaccustomed to its harsh realities. People die in the desert here every year, from thirst, exposure, and one inexplicable trait—stupidity. Using good sense, you can explore any stretch of desert in April and May and experience a landscape festooned with flowers and blooming cacti.

To experience the desert without running the risk of leaving your bones to bleach in the sun, there are two exceptional alternatives: the **Desert Botanical Garden** in Phoenix is a showcase of the ecology of the desert with more than 4,000 different species of desert flora sustained on 150 acres. A walk through here is wonderfully soothing.

There's also the **Arizona-Sonora Desert Museum** in Tucson, which isn't really a museum but a zoo and a botanical garden featuring the animals and plants of the Sonoran Desert. If you want to see a diamondback rattlesnake without jumping out of your shoes, this is the place.

And, of course, there are long drives in which you can see the wide expanses from the comfort of your car. Early spring brings the flaming-red blossoms of the ocotillo and the soft yellow-green branches of the paloverde, and the desert will be carpeted with ephemeral flowers of pink, blue, and yellow.

Along U.S. Highway 93, south of Wikieup in northwest Arizona, you can see the desert in its most abundant display, but there are countless other places, as well.

Native American Culture

John Ford Westerns and the enduring myths of the Wild West pale in comparison to the experience of seeing firsthand the Native American cultures that thrive in Arizona. You can stop at a trading post and see artisans demonstrating their crafts, visit one of Arizona's spectacular Native American museums, or explore an ancient Native American dwelling.

Hubbell Trading Post and **Cameron Trading Post** are on Navajo reservations, while **Keam's Canyon Trading Post** is on the Hopi Reservation. The **Navajo Village Heritage Center** in Page offers an opportunity to understand life on the reservation.

The **Heard Museum,** in Phoenix, houses an impressive array of Native American cultural exhibits. The **Museum of Northern Arizona,** in Flagstaff, has collections related to the natural and cultural history of the Colorado Plateau, an extensive collection of Navajo rugs, and an authentic Hopi kiva (men's ceremonial chamber). The **Colorado River Museum,** in Bullhead City, focuses on the history of the area and includes information and artifacts pertaining to the Mohave Indians. **Chiricahua Regional Museum and Research Center,** in Willcox, focuses on Apache culture.

The **Montezuma Castle National Monument** is one of the best-preserved prehistoric ruins in North America. **Tuzigoot National Monument** is not as well preserved as Montezuma Castle, but more impressive in scope. The **Casa Grande National Monument** is a 35-foot-tall structure built by the Hohokam Indians who lived in the area.

FLAVORS OF ARIZONA

Despite the fact that it has become a culinary melting pot, Arizona has long been lumped into the spicy Southwest category of cuisine. But by pairing all of neighboring and global influences with diverse Native cultures and regional history and local agriculture, creative chefs and entrepreneurs have started to earn Arizona its own star on the food walk of fame.

The Native Palate

From flash-flood farming in the south to sustained agriculture in the Verde Valley, to livestock ranching in the state's northernmost reaches, Native American food customs are becoming customary off the reservations. Gourds, desert beans, mesquite pods, tree nuts, cactus fruit, agave nectar, and local game like quail and elk are buzz words on award-winning menus. And Navajo fry bread, a tradition born from the worst of times, is one of the state's most sought-after treats.

■ **Kai,** Chandler. Using the Pima word for seed, this elegant and scenery-studded restaurant on the Gila Indian Reservation plants the seeds of blending local food traditions of the Tohono O'odham people with fine dining.

■ **Cameron Trading Post,** Cameron. If you're headed to Lake Powell, Monument Valley, or the North Rim, there's no better place to stop and try a Navajo taco, made from fry bread.

■ **Hopi Cultural Center Restaurant,** Third Mesa, Hopi Reservation. One of the only places to find authentic piki (paper-thin blue-corn bread) and Hopi stew, with lamb, hominy, and chiles.

Spice of Life

Arizona has long been defined by its heat. With a natural affection for everything from Mexican jalapeños to New Mexican Hatch green chilies, local food artists

have given recipes ranging from chips and salsa to chicken mole and chilaquiles a most memorable flair. But this kind of love doesn't have to hurt.

■ **Café Poca Cosa,** Tucson. This hip, family-owned eatery changes its menus daily but consistently maintains its authentic approach to Mexican cuisine.

■ **Los Dos Molinos,** Phoenix. Talk about burning love. For those who like it hot, this is the state's reigning restaurant. Signature dishes like Shrimp Veracruz, drenched in New Mexico red chili, summon tears of joy and pain.

■ **The Mission,** Scottsdale. A modern twist on old-school Mexican food like Pollo a la Brasa, chilaquiles, and avocado margaritas.

Fruits of the Desert

Arizona's local-grown wine industry is also not to be overlooked. What began as an experiment in 1973 has become a booming business in southern Arizona's Santa Cruz Valley where, as it turns out, the soil in many areas is nearly identical to that of Burgundy.

■ **Callaghan Wineries,** Elgin. Producing bold Spanish reds and a delicate white, this southeastern Arizona vineyard and winery has established itself as a favorite on area wine-tasting tours.

■ **Keeling Schaeffer Vineyards,** Pearce. Featuring fruity Chardonnays, sold-out Grenaches and Syrahs, this vineyard with Mary Jane Colter–inspired architecture offers tastings and tours by appointment only.

■ **Page Springs Cellars,** Cornville. Taking a gamble on the high-desert soil of the Verde Valley has paid off for winemaker Eric Glomski and his Southern Rhone varietals.

LODGING PRIMER

Gone are the days when Arizona's acclaimed accommodations were reserved for the East Coast elite who traveled across the country by train to winter at rustic dude ranches and healing desert hot springs. The state is still a destination for sun and Western fun, but today it accommodates everyone, as does the veritable boom of lodging options—more comfortably than ever before. *See more information on Accomodations in Travel Smart.*

Resorts and Spas

Building on its tradition of being the ultimate winter escape, Arizona's desert communities have built some of the world's most renowned, award-winning luxurious retreats. From the exclusive **Canyon Ranch** in Tucson to Scottsdale's **Phoenician**, the **Four Seasons at Troon North** and Paradise Valley newcomer **Montelucia**, to Sedona's **Enchantment Resort** and Mii amo spa, this onetime one-horse state has become a Mecca for exclusive, restorative overnight experiences.

Dude Ranches

While golf carts have seemingly replaced the saddled steed as the vacation transportation of choice, the call of the Old West remains alive and well here, and is answered by a number of authentic dude ranches in central and southern Arizona. Dude ranches like Wickenburg's **Kay El Bar Ranch, X Diamond Ranch** in the White Mountains, and Tucson's **White Stallion Ranch** offer uniquely Western experiences, great for families, couples, and friends. The more luxury oriented **Rancho de los Caballeros** near Wickenburg offers the best of both destination-travel worlds with a golf course *and* horses. Giddy-up!

Luxury with Local Flair

In its transition from territorial to high-tech times, Arizona has managed to keep some of its historic charm while infusing modern amenities. Tucson's Hacienda del Sol, a former parochial school, has become of one of the area's most prized luxury getaways while maintaining its Old World appeal. **Wigwam Resort**, once a bastion of the Goodyear Tire empire, remains an authentic piece of history, even after an multimillion dollar renovation, as does Winslow's **La Posada**. And **El Tovar Lodge** has been a beautifully preserved, architectural masterpiece perched for prime accommodations atop the Grand Canyon since 1905.

Quaint and Cozy

There are a variety of wonderful bed-and-breakfasts, locally owned inns, and cabins that operate around the state. Southern Arizona is a haven of locally owned bird-watcher retreats. The White Mountains, Sedona, and Verde Valley area host a sweet cache of **riverside cabins** and **romantic inns**. Even the big cities boast places to have a small-town experience. Check out ⊕www.bnbfinder.com or ⊕www.bedandbreakfast.com.

Strange Bedfellows

If you're looking for a truly unusual experience, you're in luck. Arizona's got plenty of them. Bisbee is home to the **Shady Dells**, a court of vintage Airstreams, all done in different decor. More literal than the Goodyear resort is Holbrook's **Wigwam Motel**, where the rooms are actual Indian teepees. Jerome's **Grand Hotel** and Flagstaff's **Hotel Monte Vista**, among others, are renowned for their resident ghosts. The only scary thing would be to miss out on the fun.

TOP EXPERIENCES

Grand Canyon Hiking

You could spend the rest of your life hiking the Grand Canyon and never cover all the trails. There are hiking and walking trails aplenty, for all levels of fitness. Bright Angel Trail is the most famous, but it's tough: with an elevation change of more than 5,000 feet, don't try to hike to the Colorado River and back in one day. Less strenuous is the 9-mi Rim Trail, a paved, generally horizontal walk. Other outstanding choices are the South Kaibab Trail and the Hermit Trail.

Jeep Tours

Why explore Arizona on foot when open-air four-wheeling is available, complete with guide and driver? Jeep tours abound in the Grand Canyon State, whether it's a rough ride on a Pink Jeep tour in the red rocks of Sedona or a Lavender Jeep tour in historic Bisbee, a weeklong excursion or an afternoon adventure. Some of these companies have special permits that provide access to national forests, and an up-close view of Native American communities.

Colorado River-Rafting

Hiking too boring? Jeep tours not enough? True thrill-seekers take the plunge when they visit Arizona. There are nearly two-dozen commercial river-rafting companies in Arizona that offer trips as short as a day or as long as three weeks through the Grand Canyon. These rough-riding trips are popular with travelers, so be sure to make reservations very early.

Personal Pampering

If roughing it in the great outdoors isn't your vacation style, head to one of Arizona's world-class spas for a day of complete relaxation. Enjoy a standard mani-and-pedi afternoon, or further indulge in a specialty treatment, such as a creek-side massage at L'Auberge de Sedona, or a Native American–inspired session at the Golden Door Spa at the Boulders Resort in Carefree. Finish the day with a decadent meal at your resort's restaurant.

Biltmore Golfing

One of Phoenix's most historic hotels is also home to some of the Valley's most heralded golf courses. The Arizona Biltmore, Arizona's first resort, set the standard in 1929. The Biltmore has two 18-hole championship courses. Arizona's climate is particularly hospitable to golfers, so greens fees are especially pricey in winter and spring. Early risers can find slightly more affordable fees in the wee hours of the morning during the summer. Other premier Phoenix-area courses where you can play like a pro include the Phoenician and Troon North.

Native American Traditions

Westerns and the enduring myths of the Wild West pale in comparison to the experience of seeing firsthand the Native American cultures that thrive in Arizona. Stop at a trading post on a reservation to see artisans demonstrating their crafts. Visit one of Arizona's fantastic Native American museums, such as the Heard Museum in Phoenix or the Museum of Northern Arizona in Flagstaff. At spectacular national monuments, such as Montezuma Castle near Camp Verde, visitors can see 600-year-old preserved dwellings.

GREAT ITINERARIES

1

HIGHLIGHTS OF ARIZONA

PHOENIX AND THE VALLEY OF THE SUN: 1–2 Days

The metropolitan Phoenix area is the best place to begin your trip to Arizona, with a wealth of hotels and resorts. Reserve a day in the Valley and visit the Heard Museum and Desert Botanical Garden. Select one of the area's popular Mexican restaurants for dinner. If time permits, stroll through Old Town Scottsdale's tempting art galleries. Depending on your remaining time in the Valley, you can escape to a spa for a day of pampering, get out your clubs and hit the links, or—if the season is right ⇒ catch a major-league baseball spring-training game.

Logistics: Sky Harbor International Airport is located at the center of the city and is 20 minutes away from most of the Valley's major resorts. Plan on driving everywhere in the greater Phoenix area, as public transportation is nearly nonexistent. Phoenix is a remarkably simple area to navigate. Designed on a grid, numbered streets run north–south and named streets (Camelback Road, Glendale Avenue) run east–west. Grand Avenue, running about 20 mi from downtown to Sun City, is the only diagonal. If you need to know which direction you're facing, you can see South Mountain, conveniently looming up in the south, from nearly any point in the city.

GRAND CANYON SOUTH RIM: 1–2 Days

The sight of the Grand Canyon's immense beauty has taken many a visitor's breath away. Whatever you do, though, make sure you catch a sunset or sunrise view of the canyon. A night, or even just dinner at the grand El Tovar Hotel won't disappoint, but book your reservation early (up to 6 months ahead). Outdoors enthusiasts will want to reserve several days to hike and explore the canyon; less ambitious travelers can comfortably see the area in one or two days.

Logistics: Arizona is a large state; the drive north from Phoenix to the Grand Canyon will take several hours, so budget at least a half-day to make the 225-mi trip. Take Interstate 17 north from Phoenix into Flagstaff. The best way to reach the South Rim of the canyon is via U.S. 180 northwest from Flagstaff. It's best to travel to the canyon from the city during the week—Interstate 17 fills with locals looking to escape the heat on Friday and Saturday. If you have specific plans, whether it's a mule ride and rafting trip or dining and lodging, be sure to book early for the canyon—reservations are necessary.

RED ROCKS AND SPECTACULAR SIGHTS: 3–4 Days

Option 1: Sedona and Surrounding Area

The unusual red-rock formations in Sedona are sole destinations for most visitors to Arizona, and it's no wonder. Spend at least a day exploring the town and its beauty, whether on a calm stroll or a thrilling Jeep tour. The surrounding area includes Flagstaff, a college town with a love for the outdoors and the stars; Prescott, with its Whiskey Row and Victorian homes; and Jerome, a charming artists' community that thrives more with every passing year.

Logistics: If possible, visit Sedona midweek, before the city folk fill the streets on the weekend. If Sedona is too pricey for your stay, consider the nearby towns of Flagstaff or Prescott, which have ample motels and budget hotels.

Option 2: Landmarks of Indian Country

The majestic landscapes in Monument Valley and Canyon de Chelly are among the biggest draws to Arizona. Made famous by countless Westerns and photographs, the scenes are even more astounding firsthand. This northeast corner of the state is worth several days of exploration. The famous Four Corners, where Arizona, New Mexico, Colorado, and Utah meet, are within a short drive. For a brief trip, make Monument Valley and Canyon de Chelly the priorities. With added days, you can visit a Native American trading post, Lake Powell and Glen Canyon, and the Four Corners. On your drive toward Interstate 40, be sure to spend an hour or two at Petrified Forest National Park, where you'll see a prehistoric forest.

Logistics: Approximately 100 mi from Sedona, the fascinating sites of northeast Arizona are a destination unto themselves. Don't be fooled: this is a remote area and will take hours to reach, whether you're coming from Phoenix, Sedona, or the Grand Canyon. Most travelers view this corner of the state as a road-trip heaven, as the highways offer one scenic drive after the other. Plan on making one of the main towns—Tuba City, Page, Window Rock—your base, and take day trips from there. No matter what your itinerary, plan ahead and make reservations early: the best way to see these popular sites is via guided tour.

ROAD TRIP TIPS

■ If your budget permits, renting a four-wheel-drive vehicle will allow you to take advantage of side trips to remote areas.

■ Climate extremes, both heat and cold, make Arizona traveling hazardous, so heed the advice of locals. If somebody tells you it's a "little warm" to be poking around in those hills, they're probably correct.

■ Carry plenty of water, and if your vehicle should break down, put the hood up and stay with the vehicle.

■ Arizona's distances can be surprisingly vast. The drive from Phoenix to the Grand Canyon takes at least a half day.

SCENIC DRIVES AND HISTORIC TOWNS: 2–4 Days
Option 1: The White Mountains of Eastern Arizona

If nature walks and hiking are still tops on your itinerary, consider spending a few days in the White Mountains before returning to Phoenix. The breathtaking White Mountains area of eastern Arizona is a favorite for anglers and cross-country skiers. The White Mountains Trails System near Pinetop-Lakeside is considered one of the best in the nation, and can accommodate all fitness levels. Creek-side resorts with private cabins are common in the towns of the White Mountains.

Logistics: The most scenic route back to Phoenix is via the Salt River Canyon on U.S. 60 to Globe. The landscape transforms from ponderosa pine forests to high desert along the journey, marking an ideal transition from one extreme to the other. Or you can travel to Tucson from the White Mountains on one of the

most scenic routes in the United States (if a bumpy and wild ride is your style). The Coronado Trail, U.S. 191 from Springerville to Clifton, is one of the world's curviest roads. The trip, which includes steep stretches and plenty of turns, will take at least four hours. Once in Clifton, you can continue south to Willcox, where Interstate 10 will take you to Tucson.

Option 2: Tucson, the Old West, and Historic Sites

If culture and shopping are a bit more attractive, consider spending time in Tucson and visiting its neighboring historic communities. Spend at least a day in Tucson proper, visiting Mission San Xavier del Bac, Saguaro National Park, and the Arizona-Sonora Desert Museum. If hiking is your game, don't miss Sabino Canyon, which offers gorgeous views of the area. With Tucson as your hub, take a day trip just a bit farther south to historic Tombstone and Bisbee. On the way back to the interstate, stop by Kartchner Caverns State Park for a view of the series of spectacular wet caves. Hour-long guided tours are available by reservation.

Logistics: Phoenix is two hours away via Interstate 10, a relatively unscenic drive. Casa Grande is the midway point between the two cities, and is a good place to stop for a rest. History buffs may want to stop at Picacho Peak, site of the westernmost battle of the Civil War.

THE STORY OF THE
COLORADO RIVER
THE GRAND CANYON, HOOVER DAM,

By Carrie Frasure

High in Colorado's Rocky Mountains, the Colorado River begins as a catch-all for the snowmelt off the mountains west of the Continental Divide. By the time it reaches the Grand Canyon it has become a raging river, red with silt as it sculpts spectacular landscapes. Even though it's partially tamed by a network of dams, the Colorado is still a mighty river.

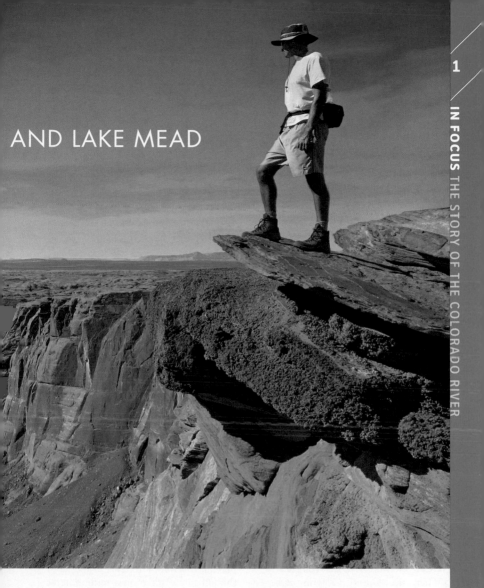

AND LAKE MEAD

As the primary artery of the Colorado River Basin, the Colorado River provides a vital lifeline to the arid southwest. Its natural course runs 1,450 miles from its origin in Colorado's La Poudre Pass Lake to its final destination in the Gulf of Colorado. Along the way it gathers strength and speed from a multitude of tributaries. In northern Arizona, it's known as the primary sculptor of the Grand Canyon, where it now flows 4,000 to 6,000 feet below the rim. The river takes a lazy turn at the Arizona–Nevada border, where Hoover Dam creates the reservoir at Lake Mead. The river continues at a relaxed pace along the Arizona–California border, bringing energy and irrigation to people in Arizona, California, and Nevada before flowing into northwestern Mexico.

CREATION OF THE GRAND CANYON

Considered one of the seven natural wonders of the world, the Grand Canyon stretches along 277 miles of the Colorado River, ranging in width from 4 to 18 miles. Nearly 2 billion years of geologic history is revealed in exposed layers cut up to a mile deep in the Colorado Plateau. As uplift raised the plateau, the river and its tributaries slowly cut into the canyon's layers. Under the sculpting power of wind and water, the shale layers eroded into slopes and the harder sandstone and limestone layers created terraced cliffs, resulting in the canyon profiles seen today.

ENVIRONMENTAL CONCERNS

When the Grand Canyon achieved national park status in 1919, only 44,173 people made the grueling overland trip to see it. Today, the park receives nearly 5 million visitors a year. The construction of Lake Powell's Glen Canyon Dam and the tremendous increase in visitation has greatly impacted the fragile ecosystems. Air pollution has affected visibility, non-native plants and animals threaten the extinction of several native species, wildfire suppression has led to the dangerous overgrowth of forest landscapes, and the constant buzz of aerial tours has disturbed the natural solitude. ■TIP➜ Help ease the South Rim's congestion by taking the free shuttles, which have comprehensive routes along both Hermit Road and Desert View Drive as well as throughout Grand Canyon Village.

WHO LIVES HERE

Paleo-Indian artifacts show that humans have inhabited the Grand Canyon for more than 12,000 years. The plateau-dwelling Hualapai ("people of the tall pines") live on a million acres along 108 miles of the Colorado River in the West Rim. The Havasupai ("people of the blue green water") live deep within the walls of the 12-mile-long Havasu Canyon—a major side canyon connected to the Grand Canyon at the Colorado River—as they have for nearly 1,000 years.

Above and right, views of Colorado River in Grand Canyon from Toroweap.

BEST CANYON VIEWS

■ Hopi Point, South Rim

■ Yavapai Point, South Rim

■ Lipan Point, South Rim

■ Grandview Point, South Rim

■ Bright Angel Point, North Rim

■ Cape Royal, North Rim

■ Point Sublime, North Rim

HOOVER DAM

HISTORY

Hoover Dam was built in 1935 and was the world's largest hydroelectric power plant and tallest dam. It has since lost these titles; however, it's still the tallest solid concrete arch-gravity dam in the western hemisphere. The dam was completed two full years ahead of the six year construction schedule during the Great Depression.

ENVIRONMENT VERSUS ECONOMY

Prior to the dam's construction, the river, swollen by snowmelt, flooded the lowlands along the California-Arizona border each spring before drying up so drastically that water levels were too low to divert for crops each summer. The dam tamed the mighty river and today provides a stable, year-round water supply for 18 million people and more than one million acres of farmland. However, the lack of flooding and the controlled waters have negatively affected the backwater riparian habitats bringing several native fish species to the brink of extinction.

WHAT'S IN A NAME?

Even though it was located in the Black Canyon, the Hoover Dam was originally referred to as the Boulder Dam Project. The dam was officially named

ARTISTIC LEANINGS

Hoover Dam is an engineering marvel *and* a work of art. The design features the flowing lines of Modernism and Art Deco used by architect Gordon B. Kaufmann, designer of the Los Angeles Times Building. Artist Allen True, whose murals are prominent in the Colorado State Capitol, used Native American geometric designs in the terrazzo floors. But it's the pair of 30-foot bronze statues—*Winged Figures of the Republic*—that dominate the dam. The striking figures were sculpted by Oskar J.W. Hansen, who also created the five bas-reliefs on the elevator towers and the bronze plaque memorial for the 96 workers who died during the construction.

after Herbert Hoover in 1931. When Hoover lost his bid for re-election to Franklin D. Roosevelt in 1932, Harold Ickes took the office of the Secretary of the Interior and immediately issued notice to the Bureau of Reclamation to refer to the structure as Boulder Dam. In 1947, Hoover was vindicated when the naming controversy was settled with a resolution signed by President Harry S. Truman, restoring the name to Hoover Dam—much to the retired Ickes' indignation.

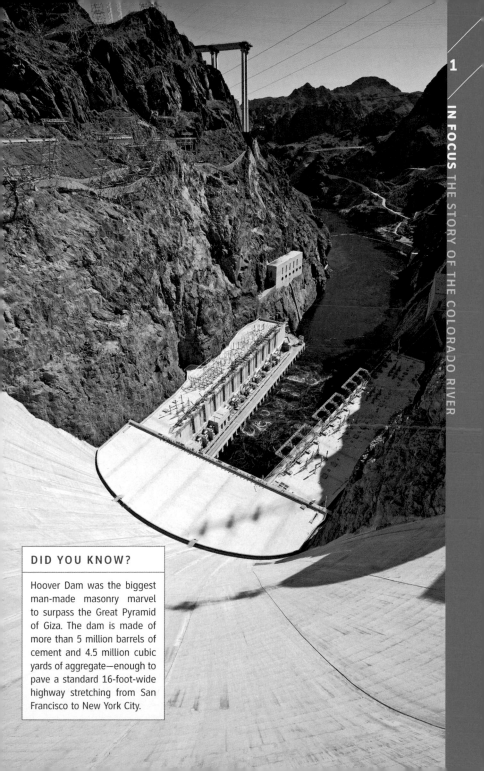

DID YOU KNOW?

Hoover Dam was the biggest man-made masonry marvel to surpass the Great Pyramid of Giza. The dam is made of more than 5 million barrels of cement and 4.5 million cubic yards of aggregate—enough to pave a standard 16-foot-wide highway stretching from San Francisco to New York City.

LAKE MEAD

HISTORY

Prior to the construction of Hoover Dam, the canyon lands and river valleys along this western section of the Colorado River were home to settlements including the towns of St. Thomas and Kaolin as well as hundreds of Native American archaeological sites. After the dam was built, these towns and sites became submerged by Lake Mead.

ENVIRONMENT

The lakes's cool waters are surrounded by the stark drama of the Mojave Desert—North America's hottest and driest. Nearly 96% of its water comes from snowmelt in Colorado, New Mexico, Utah, and Wyoming. This means the water level is at its highest in early spring and late fall. Levels drop in summer when agricultural demands are at their highest and the surrounding desert heats up.

TODAY

Construction of Hoover Dam created Lake Mead's 100-mile long reservoir, which was named after Bureau of Rec-lamation Commissioner Elwood Mead. This enormous reservoir became the United States' first National Recreation Area in 1964. Today, more than 9 million people visit this wonderland each year.

TOMORROW

Over the last few years, Lake Mead's water levels have dropped drastically. As one of the largest reservoirs in the world, it provides water to residents and farmers in Arizona, California, Nevada and northern Mexico. An extended drought and the increased demand for this critical resource have exceeded the amount of water deposited into the lake by the Colorado River. Already the dramatic drop in the lake's water level has led to the exposure of parts of St. Thomas, as well as a series of islands in Boulder Basin. A recent study by the Scripps Institution of Oceanography shows that if the current conditions continue, there's a 50% chance that Lake Mead may be dry by 2021.

Above, Lake Mead. Opposite, sailing on the lake.

SPORTS IN THE AREA

Water recreation dominates the placid waters of Lake Mead. The dramatic scenery of the surrounding Mojave Desert just adds to the year-round draw. Some of the favorite sporting activities at this far-reaching reservoir include:

■ fishing for striped bass and rainbow trout

■ relaxing on a houseboat

■ exploring hidden coves by canoe or kayak

■ swimming at Boulder Beach

■ hitting the wakes on water skis

■ scuba diving at North Boulder Beach's Dive Park

GEOLOGY FIELD GUIDE

Some of Arizona's greatest assets are the unique landscapes and bizarre geological features you'll see.

Arch

This type of window in a rock wall forms either through erosion, when wind and sand wear away the rock face, or through the freezing action of water. When water enters spaces or joints in a rock and freezes there, the expansion of the ice can crack off chunks of rock.

Bridge

If a window through a rock is created by water flowing beneath it, it is called a bridge. You can see many natural bridges in canyon country, such as Rainbow Bridge near Lake Powell.

Butte

A butte is what remains when a mesa erodes. You can see good examples of this formation in Monument Valley.

Canyon

A canyon forms when water and wind erode soft layers of the Earth's rock crust. The hardness of the rock determines the shape of the canyon: A narrow, or slot, canyon generally results when the rock is the same composition all the way down and water runs through the crack. A step-like canyon such as the Grand Canyon forms when alternating soft and hard layers are eroded by wind and water, with a river cutting a narrow groove in the bottom of the canyon.

Caves

Caves—natural underground chambers that open to the surface—give you an opportunity to descend below the Earth's surface and learn about the forces of heat and water upon rocks and minerals. Kartchner Caverns, south of Tucson, is an immense wet "live" cave system.

Mesa

A mesa, or hill with a smooth, flat, table-like top (mesa means "table" in Spanish), is a clear example of how hard rock stands higher and protects the soft rock beneath. A single mesa may cover hundreds of square miles of land. There are many mesas in the Hopi Reservation, including the villages of First, Second, and Third Mesa.

Monument

This general term applies to geologic formations that are much taller than they are wide, or to formations that resemble man-made structures. You can see many monuments in Monument Valley.

Petrified Wood

If you want to know what the desert Southwest used to look like, picture the Florida Everglades populated with giant dragonflies and smaller species of dinosaurs. Arizona's Petrified Forest offers a glimpse of the once lush, tropical world. Stumps and logs from the ancient woodland are now turned to rock because they were immersed in water and sealed away from the air, so normal decay did not occur. Instead, the preserved wood gradually hardened as silica, or sand, filtered into its porous spaces, almost like cement.

Spire

As a butte erodes, it may become one or more spires. There are many buttes and spires in the Chiracahua National Monument.

Window

One of the more intriguing landforms you will encounter while touring canyon country are large openings in solid rock walls. These are known as arches or bridges, depending on what created the opening. Together, the two types of forms are called windows.

Phoenix, Scottsdale, and Tempe

WORD OF MOUTH

"There are activities galore in the Phoenix area . . . There is untold shopping, great hiking . . . The Phoenix Art Museum is near the Heard Museum, both [are] great stops. One that I think is a must-see is Frank Lloyd Wright's Taliesin West in Scottsdale . . . Also, Carefree is a charming town, Old Town Scottsdale is fun."

—1515c

WELCOME TO PHOENIX, SCOTTSDALE, AND TEMPE

TOP REASONS TO GO

★ **Resort spas:** With dozens of outstanding desert spas, Phoenix has massaged and wrapped its way to the top of the relaxation destinations list.

★ **The Heard Museum:** This small but world-renowned museum elegantly celebrates Native American people, culture, art, and history.

★ **Shopping and Dining:** From Old Town Scottsdale to the Fashion Squares, the Valley of the Sun is a retail mecca, as well as a melting pot of fine and funky dining establishments.

★ **The Great Outdoors:** Sure there's urban sprawl, but Phoenix also has cool and accessible places to get away from it all, like the Desert Botanical Garden, Papago Park, Tempe Town Lake, and mountain and desert preserves.

★ **Golf:** All year long links lovers can take their pick of top-rated public and private courses—many with incredibly spectacular views.

1 Downtown and Central Phoenix. As the site of Arizona's government operations and the state's largest concentration of skyscrapers, this area used to be strictly business. Nowadays it's home to some of the Valley's major museums, performance venues, and sports arenas, plenty of high-rise homeowners, and a new light rail system that's changing the face of the city.

2 Greater Phoenix. Here is an unusual mix of attractions ranging from hip, historic neighborhoods to acres of mountain preserves, to cultural and ethnic centers and corridors of modern commercial enterprise. Hike a couple of peaks, peek at the animals in the Phoenix Zoo, zoom on over to the Phoenix Art and Heard museums, then relax at a luxury mountainside resort—all in one day.

2

GETTING ORIENTED

It can be useful to think of Phoenix as a flower with petals (other communities) growing in every direction from the bud of Sky Harbor Airport. The East Valley includes Scottsdale, Paradise Valley, Ahwatukee, Tempe, Mesa, Fountain Hills, and Apache Junction. To the southeast are Chandler and Gilbert. The West Valley includes Glendale, Sun City, Peoria, and Litchfield Park. Central Avenue, which runs north and south through the heart of Downtown Phoenix, is the city's east–west dividing line. Everything east of Central is considered the East Valley and everything west of Central is the West Valley. Phoenix has grown around what was once a cluster of independent towns in Maricopa County, but the gaps between communities that were open desert space just a few short years ago have begun to close in and blend the entire Valley into one large, sprawling community.

3 Scottsdale. Once an upscale Phoenix sibling, it now flies solo as a top American destination. A bastion of high-end and specialty shopping, historic sites, elite resorts, restaurants, and spas, and more golf than even Tiger can shake a club at, Scottsdale can easily absorb an entire vacation.

4 Tempe and Around. The home of Arizona State University and a creative melting pot of residents, Tempe is equal parts party and performance, especially along its main artery, Mill Avenue, where commerce and culture collide.

PHOENIX, SCOTTSDALE, AND TEMPE PLANNER

How's the Weather?

It's a common misconception that Phoenix forever hovers around 100°F. That may hold true from May to October, but the winter months have been known to push the mercury down to 35°F. The city has also experienced consecutive days of nonstop rain. Such instances are rare, but it's good to be prepared and check weather reports before you pack.

Arizona can get pretty darn hot in the summer, so plan your outdoor activities for the cooler parts of the day and save the air-conditioned stuff for when it's needed: the Heard Museum is not only a must-see, it's inside, as are the nearby Phoenix Art Museum and many other popular attractions.

Visitor Information

Most Valley cities have tourism centers where you can get maps or excursion suggestions; Phoenix's Visitors Bureau has locations all over town. For planning information contact, **Greater Phoenix Convention & Visitors Bureau** (☎ 602/254–6500   ⊕ www. phoenixcvb.com) and **Scottsdale Convention & Visitors Bureau** (☎ 800/782–1117 ⊕ www.scottsdalecvb.com).

Getting Here and Around

To get around Phoenix, *you will need a car*. Only the major downtown areas (Phoenix, Scottsdale, Tempe, and Glendale) are pedestrian-friendly. Don't expect to nab a rental car without a reservation, however, especially in the high season from January to April.

Many accidents in the Valley are a result of confusion in the left-turn lanes. Weekdays from 6 AM to 9 AM and 4 PM to 6 PM the center and left-turn lanes on the major surface arteries of 7th Street and 7th Avenue become one-way traffic-flow lanes between McDowell Road and Dunlap Avenue. These specially marked lanes are dedicated mornings to north–south traffic (into downtown) and afternoons to south–north traffic (out of downtown).

Phoenix **Sky Harbor International Airport (PHX)** (☎ 602/273–3300   ⊕ www.phxskyharbor.com) is served by most major airlines. The blue vans of **SuperShuttle** (☎ 602/244–9000 or 800/258–3826   ⊕ www.super shuttle.com) each take up to seven passengers to their individual destinations. Fares are $13 to Downtown Phoenix, around $20 to most places in Scottsdale, and $33 or more to places in far North Scottsdale or Carefree.

Amtrak (☎ 602/253–0121 or 800/872–7245   ⊕ www. amtrak.com) provides train service to Flagstaff and Tucson with bus transfers to Phoenix.

The Valley's new light rail system spans 20 miles from central Phoenix to Mesa. It's most convenient for exploring the downtown museums or Mill Avenue near Arizona State University. Fares are $2.50/day and multi-day passes are available. Phoenix runs a free Downtown Area Shuttle (DASH), and the city of Tempe operates the Free Local Area Shuttle (FLASH). **Valley Metro** (☎ 602/262–7433   ⊕ www. valleymetro.org) has more public transit information.

Taxi fares are unregulated in Phoenix, except at the airport. The 800-square-mi metro area is so large that one-way fares in excess of $50 are not uncommon. Except within a compact area, such as Central Phoenix, travel by taxi is not recommended. Taxis charge about $3 for the first mile and $1.50 per mile thereafter (not including tips). Try **Checker/ Yellow Cab** (☎ 602/252–5252   ⊕ www.aaayellowaz. com) or **Courier Cab** (☎ 602/232–2222).

Making the Most of Your Time

Three to five days is an optimal amount of time to spend in Phoenix if you want to relax, get outside to hike or golf, and see the main sites like the Heard Museum and Scottsdale. Extra time will allow you to make some interesting side trips to nearby places like Arcosanti, Wickenburg, Cave Creek, and Carefree.

Remember that the Valley of the Sun is sprawling, so planning ahead will help you save time and gas. If you're heading to the Heard Museum downtown, for instance, you might want to visit the nearby Arizona Science Center and/or the Phoenix Art museum, too, both of which are close to the light rail line. If you're going to Taliesin West, do so before or after spending time in Scottsdale.

Phoenix to Grand Canyon Timing Tip

If you're driving to the Grand Canyon from Phoenix, allow at least two full days, with a minimum drive time of four hours each way. You can always anticipate slow-moving traffic on Interstate 17, but in the afternoon and evening on Friday and Sunday lengthy standstills are almost guaranteed, something to remember if your plans involve getting back to Sky Harbor Airport to catch a flight out.

Sightseeing Tours

If you'd like a break from driving, consider a tour to see the Valley's top attractions. Reservations are a must all year.

Gray Line Tours (☎ *602/437–3484* or *800/777–3484* ⊕ *www.graylinephoenix.com*) gives seasonal, 3-hour narrated tours including Downtown Phoenix, the Arizona Biltmore hotel, Camelback Mountain, Papago Park, and Scottsdale's Old Town; the price is about $52.

Open Road Tours (☎ *602/997–6474* or *800/766–7117* ⊕ *www.openroadtours.com*) offers excursions to Sedona and the Grand Canyon, Phoenix city tours, and Native American–culture trips to the Salt River Pima–Maricopa Indian Reservation. Local tours cost about $49.

Vaughan's Southwest Custom Tours (☎ *602/971–1381* or *800/513–1381* ⊕ *www.southwesttours.com*) gives a 4½-hour city tour for 11 or fewer passengers in custom vans, stopping at the Pueblo Grande Museum, the Arizona Biltmore, and the state capitol for $50. Vaughan's will also take you east to the Apache Trail.

Festivals and Events

Jan. FBR Open. Formerly the Phoenix Open, this golf tournament is "The Greatest Show on Grass." ☎ *602/870–0163* ⊕ *www.fbropen.com.*

PF Chang's Rock & Roll Marathon. Live bands line the course and a concert follows the 26.2-mi race. ☎ *800/311–1255* ⊕ *www.rnraz.com.*

Mar. Indian Fair & Market. More than 600 Native American artists and artisans are showcased at the Heard Museum. ☎ *602/252–8848* ⊕ *www.heard.org.*

Tempe Music Festival. Top acts from a variety of genres perform on multiple stages in Tempe. ⊕ *www.tempemusicfestival.com.*

The Parada del Sol Parade and Rodeo. "The World's Largest Horse Drawn Parade," features cowboys, cowgirls, horses, and floats. ☎ *480/990–3179* ⊕ *www.paradadelsol.org.*

Scottsdale Arts Festival. This is jam-packed with arts and crafts— and music. ☎ *480/994–2787* ⊕ *www.scottsdaleperformingarts.org.*

Ostrich Festival. A weekend of music, entertainment, and (of course) ostrich races in Chandler. ☎ *866/993–2477* ⊕ *www.ostrichfestival.com.*

Apr. Scottsdale Culinary Festival. This weekend-long festival makes mouths water. ☎ *480/945–7193* ⊕ *www.scottsdaleculinaryfestival.org.*

Updated by
Cara LaBrie
and Jo Beth
Jamison

The Valley of the Sun, otherwise known as metro Phoenix (i.e., Phoenix and all its suburbs, including Tempe and Scottsdale), is named for its 325-plus days of sunshine each year. Although many come to Phoenix for the golf and the weather, the Valley has much to offer by way of shopping, outdoor activities, and nightlife. The best of the latter is in Scottsdale and the East Valley with their hip dance clubs, old-time saloons, and upscale wine bars.

The Valley marks the northern tip of the Sonoran Desert, a prehistoric seabed that extends into northwestern Mexico with a landscape offering much more than just cacti. Palo verde and mesquite trees, creosote bushes, brittle bush, and agave dot the land, which is accustomed to being scorched by temperatures in excess of 100°F for weeks at a time. Late summer brings precious rain as monsoon storms illuminate the sky with lightning shows and the desert exudes the scent of creosote. Spring sets the Valley blooming, and the giant saguaros are crowned in white flowers for a short time in May—in the evening and cool early mornings—and masses of vibrant wildflowers fill desert crevices and span mountain landscapes.

EXPLORING THE VALLEY OF THE SUN

DOWNTOWN AND CENTRAL PHOENIX

Updated by
Cara La Brie

Changes in the Valley over the past two decades has meant the emergence of a real downtown in Phoenix, where people hang out: there are new apartments and loft spaces, cultural and sports facilities—including Chase Field (formerly known as Bank One Ballpark and still affectionately referred to by many locals as BOB) and the US Airways Center, and large areas for conventions and trade shows. It's retained a mix of past and present, too, as restored homes in Heritage Square, from

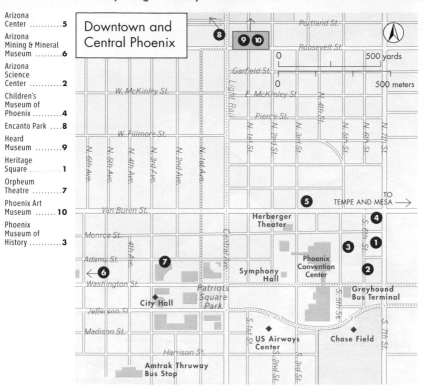

the original townsite, give an idea of how far the city has come since its inception around the turn of the 20th century. Many locals refer to parts of downtown, particularly around the sports venues, as Copper Square. Local "ambassadors" are located on some street corners and provide directions and advice like mobile concierges. You can spot them by their bright orange T-shirts.

GETTING HERE
AND AROUND
There are lots of parking options downtown, and they're listed on the free map provided by Downtown Phoenix Partnership, available in many local restaurants (⊕*www.coppersquare.com*).Many downtown sites are served by DASH (Downtown Area Shuttle), a free bus service, or by light rail.

TIMING
Art Link's First Fridays & Art Detour (☎602/256–7539 ⊕*www.artlink-phoenix.com*) is an excellent way to check out the Phoenix arts scene: galleries stay open late and crowds converge to view the work of emerging and established artists, listen to live music, and see impromptu street performances.

Numbers in the margin correspond to numbers on the Downtown and Central Phoenix map.

TOP ATTRACTIONS

④ **Children's Museum of Phoenix.** Opened in the summer of 2008, the new Children's Museum of Phoenix is a playground for kids of all ages, featuring hands-on exhibits where children learn by playing. Venture through the "noodle forest," relax in the book loft, or get a crash course in economics by role-playing at the on-site market. ⊠ *215 N. 7th St., Downtown Phoenix* ☎ *602/253–0501* ⊕ *www.childrensmuseumof phoenix.org* ⊡ *$9. Free on First Friday evenings* ☉ *Tues.–Sun. 9 AM–4 PM; Fri. 6–10 PM for First Fridays. Closed Mon.*

❾ **Heard Museum.** Pioneer settlers Dwight and Maie Heard built a Spanish colonial–style building on their property to house their collection of Southwestern art. Today the staggering collection includes such exhibits as a Navajo hogan, an Apache wickieup (a temporary Native American structure, similar to a lean-to, constructed from branches, twigs, and leaves, sometimes covered with hides), and rooms filled with art, pottery, jewelry, kachinas, and textiles. The Heard also actively supports Indian artists and displays their work. A fabulous long-term exhibition called "Home: Native People in the Southwest," opened in 2005. Annual events include the Guild Indian Fair & Market and the World Championship Hoop Dance Contest. Children enjoy the interactive art-making exhibits. ■ **TIP➜** The museum also has an incredible gift shop with authentic, high-quality goods purchased directly from Native American artists. There's a museum satellite branch in Scottsdale that has rotating exhibits, and another in the West Valley featuring some of the Heard's permanent collection as well as rotating exhibits. ⊠ *2301 N. Central Ave., Central Phoenix* ☎ *602/252–8848* ⊕ *www.heard. org* ⊡ *$10* ☉ *Mon.–Sat. 9:30–5, Sun. 11–5* ⊠ *Heard Museum West: 16126 N. Civic Center Plaza, West Valley, Surprise* ☎ *623/344–2200* ⊡ *$5* ☉ *Tues.–Sun. 10–5* ⊠ *Heard Museum North: 32633 N. Scottsdale Rd., North Scottsdale* ☎ *480/488–9817* ⊡ *$3* ☉ *Mon.–Sat. 10–5, Sun. 11–5.*

❶ **Heritage Square.** In a parklike setting from 5th to 7th streets between Monroe and Adams streets, this city-owned block contains the only remaining houses from the original Phoenix townsite. On the south side of the square, along Adams Street, stand several houses built between 1899 and 1901. The Bouvier Teeter House has a Victorian-style tearoom, and the Thomas House and Baird Machine Shop are now Pizzeria Bianco, one of the area's most popular eateries. The one-story brick Stevens House holds the **Arizona Doll and Toy Museum** (⊠ *602 E. Adams St., Downtown Phoenix* ☎ *602/253–9337* ⊡ *$3* ☉ *Tues.–Sat. 10–4, Sun. noon–4. Closed Mon. and Aug.*). **Rosson House,** an 1895 Victorian in the Queen Anne style, is the queen of Heritage Square. Built by a physician who served a brief term as mayor, it's the sole survivor among fewer than two-dozen Victorians erected in Phoenix. It was bought and restored by the city in 1974. ⊠ *6th and Monroe Sts.,*

Downtown Phoenix ☎*602/262–5070* ⊕*www.rossonhousemuseum. org* ☞*$5* ⊙ *Wed.–Sat. 10–3:30, Sun. noon–3:30.*

⑩ Phoenix Art Museum. This museum is one of the most visually appealing pieces of architecture in the Southwest. Basking in natural light, the museum makes great use of its modern, open space by tastefully fitting more than 17,000 works of art from all over the world—including sculptures by Frederic Remington and paintings by Georgia O'Keeffe, Thomas Moran, and Maxfield Parrish—within its soaring concrete walls. The museum hosts more than 20 significant exhibitions annually. Complete your tour with lunch at Arcadia Farms, the in-house café that serves some of the best homemade fare in town. ✉*1625 N. Central Ave., Central Phoenix* ☎*602/257–1222* ⊕*www.phxart.org* ☞*$10; free Tues. 3–9* PM *and during First Fridays evenings* ⊙ *Wed.– Sat. 10–5, Tues. 10–9; First Fridays evenings 6–10.*

WORTH NOTHING

⑤ Arizona Center. Amid dramatic fountains, sunken gardens, and towering palm trees stands this two-tier, open-air structure: downtown's most attractive shopping venue. The center has about 50 shops and restaurants, open-air vendors, a large sports bar, and a multiplex cinema. ✉*400 E. Van Buren St., Downtown Phoenix* ☎*602/271–4000* ⊕*www.arizonacenter.com.*

⑥ Arizona Mining and Mineral Museum. Arizona's phenomenal wealth and progress has had a lot to do with what lies beneath the actual land, namely the copper, gold, silver, and other earthbound deposits. This museum offers a mother lode of information and features more than 3,000 rocks, minerals, fossils, and mining equipment, including a 43-foot-tall Boras mine headframe and an 1882 baby-gauge steam train locomotive. ✉*1502 W. Washington, Downtown Phoenix* ☎*602/771–1611* ⊕*www.mines.az.gov* ☞*$2* ⊙ *Weekdays 8–5, Sat. 11–4.*

② Arizona Science Center. With more than 300 hands-on exhibits, this is
Ⓒ the venue for science-related exploration. You can pilot a simulated air-
★ plane flight, travel through the human body, navigate your way through the solar system in the Dorrance Planetarium, and watch a movie in the giant, five-story film theater. ✉*600 E. Washington St., Downtown Phoenix* ☎*602/716–2000* ⊕*www.azscience.org* ☞*Museum $12; combination museum, theater, and planetarium $20* ⊙ *Daily 10–5.*

⑧ Encanto Park. Urban Encanto (Spanish for "enchanted") Park covers 222
Ⓒ acres at the heart of one of Phoenix's oldest residential neighborhoods. There are many attractions, including picnic areas, a lagoon where you can paddleboat and canoe, a municipal swimming pool, a nature trail, the Enchanted Island amusement park, fishing in the park's lake, and two public golf courses. ✉*1202 W. Encanto Blvd., Central Phoenix* ☎*602/261–8993 or 602/254–1200* ⊕*www.enchantedisland.com* ☞*Park free, Enchanted Island rides $1 each* ⊙ *Park daily 6–midnight; Enchanted Island hrs vary by season and weather.*

**NEED A
BREAK?** The Victorian-style tearoom in the **Bouvier Teeter House** (✉ *622 E. Adams St., Downtown Phoenix* ☎ *602/252–4682* ⊕ *www.theteeterhouse.com*),

Phoenix History: A City Grows in the Desert

As the Hohokam (the name comes from the Piman word for "people who have gone before") discovered 2,300 years ago, the miracle of water in the desert can be augmented by human hands. Having migrated from northwestern Mexico, Hohokam cultivated cotton, corn, and beans in tilled, rowed, and irrigated fields for about 1,700 years, establishing more than 300 mi of canals—an engineering miracle when you consider the limited technology available. They constructed a great town upon whose ruins modern Phoenix is built, and then vanished. Drought, long winters, and other causes are suggested for their disappearance.

MODERN BEGINNINGS

From the time the Hohokam left until the Civil War the once fertile Salt River valley lay forgotten, used only by occasional small bands of Pima and Maricopa Indians. Then in 1865 the U.S. Army established Fort McDowell in the mountains to the east, where the Verde River flows into the Salt River. To feed the men and the horses stationed there, a former Confederate Army officer reopened the Hohokam canals in 1867. Within a year, fields bright with barley and pumpkins earned the area the name Pumpkinville. By 1870 the 300 residents had decided that their new city would arise from the ancient Hohokam site, just as the mythical phoenix rose from its own ashes.

A CITY ON THE RISE

Phoenix would grow indeed. Within 20 years it had become large enough—its population was about 3,000—to wrest the title of territorial capital from Prescott. By 1912, when Arizona was admitted as the 48th state, the area,

irrigated by the brand-new Roosevelt Dam and Salt River Project, had a burgeoning cotton industry. Copper was mined elsewhere but traded in Phoenix, and cattle were raised elsewhere but slaughtered and packed here in the largest stockyards outside of Chicago.

Meanwhile, the climate, so long a crippling liability, became an asset. Desert air was the prescribed therapy for the respiratory ills rampant in the sooty, factory-filled East; Scottsdale began in 1901 as "30-odd tents and a half dozen adobe houses" put up by health-seekers. By 1930 travelers looking for warm-winter recreation as well as rejuvenating aridity filled the elegant San Marcos Hotel and Arizona Biltmore, the first of the many luxury retreats for which the area is now known worldwide. The 1950s brought residential air-conditioning, an invention that made the summers bearable for the growing workforce of the burgeoning technology industry.

PHOENIX TODAY

The Valley is very much a work still in progress, and historians are quick to point out that never in the world's history has a metropolis grown from "nothing" to attain the status of Phoenix in such a short period of time. At the heart of all the bustle, though, is a way of life that keeps its own pace: Phoenix is one of the world's largest small towns—where people dress informally and where the rugged, Old West spirit lives on in many of the Valley's nooks and crannies despite the sprawling growth. And if the summer heat can be overwhelming, at least it has the restorative effect of slowing things down to an enjoyable pace.

2

which was built as a private home in 1899, serves authentic teatime fare; there are also heartier sandwiches and salads.

⑦ Orpheum Theatre. This Spanish-colonial movie palace has been an architectural focal point of downtown since it was built in 1929. The eclectic ornamental details of the interior have been meticulously restored, and the Orpheum is still a venue for live performances, from Broadway shows to ballet to lectures. ⊠ *203 W. Adams St., Downtown Phoenix* ☎ *602/534–5600* ⊕ *www.friendsoftheorpheumtheatre.org* ⊗ *Tours by appointment only.*

③ Phoenix Museum of History. This striking glass-and-steel museum offers exhibits on regional history from the 1860s (when Anglo settlement began) through the 1930s. Interactive exhibits are designed to help visitors appreciate the city's multicultural heritage as well as its tremendous growth. ⊠ *105 N. 5th St., Downtown Phoenix* ☎ *602/253–2734* ⊕ *www.pmoh.org* ☜ *$6* ⊗ *Tues.–Sat. 10–5.*

GREATER PHOENIX

While suburban towns are popping up all around Phoenix, the city's core neighborhoods just outside downtown Phoenix maintain the majority of its history and appeal. There are options aplenty to take you out hiking in the hills, or inside to some of the country's most interesting cultural sites.

TOP ATTRACTIONS

⑮ **Desert Botanical Garden.** Opened in 1939 to conserve and showcase the ecology of the desert, these 150 acres contain more than 4,000 different **Fodor'sChoice** species of cacti, succulents, trees, and flowers. A stroll along the ½-mi-★ long "Plants and People of the Sonoran Desert" trail is a fascinating lesson in environmental adaptations; children enjoy playing the self-guiding game "Desert Detective." Specialized tours are available at an extra cost; check the Web site for times and prices. ■**TIP**➔ The Desert Botanical Garden stays open late, to 8 PM year-round, and it's particularly lovely when lighted by the setting sun or by moonlight, so you can plan for a cool, late visit after a full day of activities. ⊠ *1201 N. Galvin Pkwy., Papago Salado* ☎ *480/941–1225* ⊕ *www.dbg.org* ☜ *$15* ⊗ *Oct.–Apr., daily 8–8; May–Sept., daily 7–8.*

⑯ **Hall of Flame.** Retired firefighters lead tours through more than 100 restored fire engines and tell harrowing tales of the "world's most dangerous profession." The museum has the world's largest collection of fire-fighting equipment, and children can climb on a 1916 engine, operate alarm systems, and learn fire safety lessons from the pros. Helmets, badges, and other firefighting-related articles dating from as far back as 1725 are on display. ⊠ *6101 E. Van Buren St., Papago Salado* ☎ *602/275–3473* ⊕ *www.hallofflame.org* ☜ *$6* ⊗ *Mon.–Sat. 9–5, Sun. noon–4.*

⑲ **Huhugam Heritage Center.** Built to harmonize with the land, the Huhugam ★ Heritage Center mixes cool modern architecture with red earth, and as a whole is an impressive new way of looking at the past. Named for the tribe from which the modern-day Akimel O'odham (Pima) and Pee Posh (Maricopa) tribes descended, the small museum and education center is

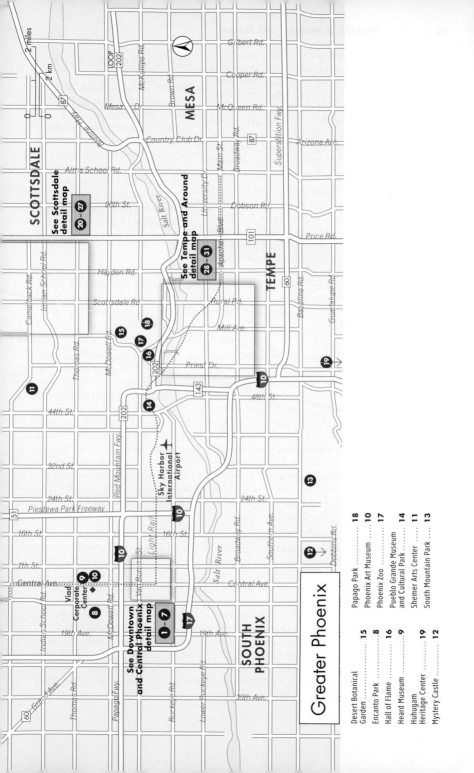

Greater Phoenix

a celebration and collection of arts, culture, and history of the native people of the Gila River. It's about a 45-minute drive from Downtown Phoenix and worthwhile for those interested in Native American culture. ⊠*4759 N. Maricopa Rd., The Gila River Indian Community* ☎*520/796–3500* ⊕*www.huhugam. com* ☞*$5* ⊙ *Wed.–Fri. 10–4.*

PAPAGO SALADO

The word Papago, meaning "bean eater," was a name given by 16th-century Spanish explorers to the Hohokam, a vanished native people of the Phoenix area. Farmers of the desert, the Hohokam lived in central Arizona from about AD 1 to 1450, when their civilization abandoned the Salt River (Rio Salado) valley, leaving behind the remnants of their villages and also a complex system of irrigation canals.

12 🔄 ★ **Mystery Castle.** At the foot of South Mountain lies a curious dwelling built from desert rocks by Boyce Gulley, who came to Arizona to cure his tuberculosis. Full of fascinating oddities, the castle has 18 rooms with 13 fireplaces, a downstairs grotto tavern, a roll-away bed with a mining railcar as its frame, and some original pieces of Frank Lloyd Wright–designed furniture. The pump organ belonged to Elsie, the "Widow of Tombstone," who buried six husbands under suspicious circumstances. ⊠*800 E. Mineral Rd., South Phoenix* ☎*602/268–1581* ☞*$5* ⊙ *Oct.–June, Thurs.–Sun. 11–4. Call to confirm hrs.*

14 🔄 Fodor'sChoice ★ **Pueblo Grande Museum and Cultural Park.** Phoenix's only national landmark, this park was once the site of a 500-acre Hohokam village supporting about 1,000 people and containing homes, storage rooms, cemeteries, and ball courts. Three exhibition galleries hold displays on the Hohokam culture and archaeological methods. View the 10-minute orientation video before heading out on the ½-mi Ruin Trail past excavated sites that give a hint of Hohokam savvy: there's a building whose corner doorway was perfectly placed for watching the summer-solstice sunrise. Children particularly like the hands-on, interactive learning center. Guided tours by appointment only. ⊠*4619 E. Washington St., Papago Salado* ☎*602/495–0901* ⊕*www.pueblogrande.com* ☞*$5* ⊙ *Oct.–Apr., Mon.–Sat. 9–4:45, Sun. 1–4:45; May–Sept., Tues.–Sat. 9–4:45. Closed Sun. and Mon.*

WORTH NOTING

18 🔄 **Papago Park.** An amalgam of hilly desert terrain, streams, and lagoons, this park has picnic ramadas (shaded, open-air shelters), a golf course, a playground, hiking and biking trails, and even largemouth bass and trout fishing. (An urban fishing license is required for anglers age 15 and over. Visit ⊕*www.azgfd.gov* for more information.) The hike up to landmark **Hole-in-the-Rock**—a natural observatory used by the native Hohokam to devise a calendar system—is steep and rocky, and a much easier climb up than down. **Governor Hunt's Tomb,** the white pyramid at the top of Ramada 16, commemorates the former Arizona leader and provides a lovely view. ⊠*625 N. Galvin Pkwy., Papago Salado* ☎*602/262–4881* ⊕*www.papagosalado.org* ☞*Free* ⊙ *Daily 5 AM–11 PM.*

② **Phoenix Zoo.** Four designated trails wind through this 125-acre zoo,
replicating such habitats as an African savanna and a tropical rain
forest. Meerkats, warthogs, desert bighorn sheep, and the endangered
Arabian oryx are among the unusual sights. The Forest of Uco is home
to the endangered spectacled bear from South America. Harmony Farm
on the Discovery Trail introduces youngsters to small mammals, and a
stop at the Big Red Barn provides a chance to groom a horse or milk
a cow. The Butterfly Pavilion is also enchanting. The 30-minute narrated safari train tour costs $3 and provides a good orientation to the
park. ■TIP➔In December the zoo stays open late (6–10 PM) for the popular "ZooLights" exhibit that transforms the area into an enchanted forest
of more than 225 million twinkling lights, many in the shape of the zoo's
residents. Starry Safari Friday Nights in summer are fun, too. ⊠ 455 N.
Galvin Pkwy., Papago Salado ☎ 602/273–1341 ⊕ www.phoenixzoo.
org ⊠ $16 ⊙ Hours vary by month and weather. Check Web site for
more details. Generally, Oct.–May, daily 9–4; May–Oct., daily 7–2.
ZooLights extends holiday hours until 10.

⑪ **Shemer Arts Center.** Near the Phoenician Resort, the Shemer Arts Center
features revolving exhibits of current Arizona artists who have agreed
★ to donate one of their pieces to the center's permanent collection. The
collection is largely contemporary, and exhibits change every month or
so in this former residence. ⊠ 5005 E. Camelback Rd., Camelback Corridor ☎ 602/262–4727 ⊕ www.phoenix.gov/shemer ⊠ Free ⊙ Tues.
10–9, Wed.–Fri. 10–5, Sat. 10–1. Closed Sun. and Mon.

⑬ **South Mountain Park.** This desert wonderland, the world's largest city
park (almost 17,000 acres), offers a wilderness of mountain-desert trails
★ for hikers, bikers, and horseback riders—and a great place to view
sunsets. The Environmental Center has a model of the park as well as
displays detailing its history, from the time of the ancient Hohokam
people to gold-seekers. Roads climb past picnic ramadas constructed
by the Civilian Conservation Corps, winding through desert flora to the
trailheads. Look for ancient petroglyphs, try to spot a desert cottontail
rabbit or chuckwalla lizard, or simply stroll among the desert vegetation. Maps of all scenic drives as well as hiking, mountain biking, and
horseback trails are available at the Gatehouse Entrance just inside the
park boundary (see Outdoors below). ⊠ 10919 S. Central Ave., South
Phoenix ☎ 602/495–0222 ⊕ www.phoenix.gov/parks ⊠ Free ⊙ Daily
4:30 AM–10:30 PM; Environmental Education Center: Fri.–Sat. 9–3.

**NEED A
BREAK?**
If hiking at South Mountain Park has piqued your appetite, or you're looking for some unique picnic fixings, stop at nearby **Carolina's** (⊠ 1202 E.
Mohave St., South Phoenix ☎ 602/252–1503 ⊕ carolinasmexicanfood.
com) for what might be the best flour tortillas you've ever eaten. A burrito
is the best way to try 'em out, and you can eat in or get takeout.

SCOTTSDALE

Nationally known art galleries, souvenir shops, and funky Old Town fill
downtown Scottsdale—the third-largest artist community in the United States. Fifth Avenue is known for shopping and Native American

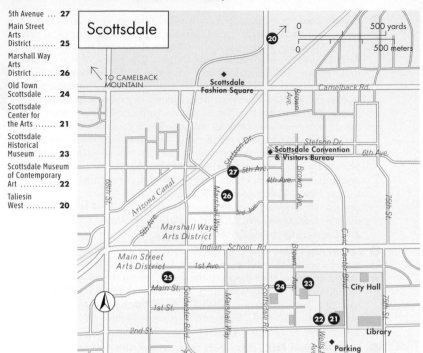

jewelry and crafts stores, while Main Street and Marshall Way are home to the international art set with galleries and interior-design shops.

GETTING HERE AND AROUND Although your tour of downtown can easily be completed on foot, the Ollie the Trolley service operates a trolley with regular service through Scottsdale (☎480/970–8130 information).

TIMING If you have limited time in the area, spend a half-day in downtown Scottsdale and the rest of the day at Taliesin West.

Art Walk (⊕ *www.scottsdalegalleries.com*), every Thursday 7–9 PM year-round (except Thanksgiving), is perfect for checking out the Scottsdale galleries: locals and tourists browse Main Street and Marshall Way, the two major gallery strips, and the atmosphere is a party.

Numbers in the margin correspond to numbers on the Scottsdale map.

TOP ATTRACTIONS

27 **5th Avenue.** Whether you seek handmade Native American arts and crafts, casual clothing, or cacti, you'll find it here—at such landmark shops as Gilbert Ortega and Kactus Jock. ⊠*5th Ave. between Civic Center Rd. and Stetson Dr., Old Town* ⊕*www.scottsdale5thave.org.*

2

The Sugar Bowl Ice Cream Parlor (⊠ *4005 N. Scottsdale Rd., Old Town*
☎ *480/946–0051* ⊕ *www.sugarbowlscottsdale.com*) transports you back
in time to a 1950s malt shop. In business in the same building since 1958,
the Sugar Bowl serves great burgers and lots of yummy ice-cream confec-
tions. Valley resident Bill Keane, creator of the comic strip "Family Circus,"
has often used this spot as inspiration for his cartoons, many of which are
on display here.

㉕ ★ **Main Street Arts District.** Gallery after gallery displays artwork in myriad
styles—contemporary, Western realism, Native American, and traditional. Several antiques shops are also here; specialties include porce-
lains and china, jewelry, and Oriental rugs. ⊠ *Bounded by Main St. and
1st Ave., Scottsdale Rd. and 69th St., Old Town.*

㉖ **Marshall Way Arts District.** Galleries that exhibit predominantly contemporary art line the blocks of Marshall Way north of Indian School Road,
and upscale gift and jewelry stores can be found here, too. Farther north
on Marshall Way across 3rd Avenue are more art galleries and creative
stores with a Southwestern flair. ⊠ *Marshall Way, from Indian School
Rd. to 5th Ave., Old Town.*

㉔ **Old Town Scottsdale.** "The West's Most Western Town," this area has
rustic storefronts and wooden sidewalks; it's touristy, but the closest
you'll come to experiencing life here as it was 80 years ago. High-quality
jewelry, pots, and Mexican imports are sold alongside kitschy souvenirs.
⊠ *Main St. from Scottsdale Rd. to Brown Ave., Old Town.*

㉒ **Taliesin West.** Ten years after visiting Arizona in 1927 to consult on designs for
the Biltmore hotel, architect Frank Lloyd Wright chose 600 acres of rugged
Sonoran Desert at the foothills of the McDowell Mountains as the site for his
permanent winter residence. Today the site is a National Historic Landmark
and still an active community of students and architects. Wright and appren-
tices constructed a desert camp here using organic architecture to integrate
the buildings with their natural surroundings. In addition to the living quarters, drafting studio, and small apartments of the Apprentice Court, Taliesin
West has two theaters, a music pavilion, and the Sun Trap—sleeping spaces
surrounding an open patio and fireplace. Five guided tours are offered, ranging from a one-hour "panorama" tour to a three-hour behind-the-scenes
tour, with other tours offered seasonally; all visitors must be accompanied by
a guide. ■ **TIP→** Wear comfortable shoes for walking. The half-hour drive from
downtown Scottsdale is very worthwhile. Drive north on the 101 Freeway to
Frank Lloyd Wright Boulevard. Follow Frank Lloyd Wright Boulevard for
a few miles to the entrance at the corner of Cactus Road. ⊠ *12621 Frank
Lloyd Wright Blvd., North Scottsdale* ☎ *480/860–2700* ⊕ *www.franklloyd
wright.org* 🖅 *$27–$60* ☉ *Daily 8:30–5, with evening tours starting at 6:30
most days. Call to confirm.*

Fodor'sChoice ★

WORTH NOTING

㉑ **Scottsdale Center for the Peforming Arts.** Galleries within this cultural and
entertainment complex rotate exhibits frequently, but they typically
emphasize contemporary art and artists. You might be able to catch a
comical, interactive performance of the long-running "Late Night Cat-
echism," or an installation of modern dance. The acclaimed Scottsdale

Frank Lloyd Wright's Taliesen West

More than just an artist's retreat and workshop, Taliesin West and the surrounding desert still inspire both visitors and architects who study here. Frank Lloyd Wright once said "The desert abhors the straight, hard line." Though much of Wright's most famed work is based on such lines, this sprawling compound takes its environment into consideration like few desert structures do. Taliesin West mirrors the jagged shapes and earthen colors of its mountain backdrop and desert surroundings. Even Wright's interior pieces of "origami" furniture assume the mountain's unpredictable shapes.

ARIZONA INSPIRATION

Write first came to Phoenix from Wisconsin in 1927 to act as a consultant to architect Albert Chase McArthur on the now famed Arizona Biltmore. Later Write was also hired to design a new hotel in what is currently Phoenix South Mountain Park. Wright and his working entourage returned to the Valley and, instead of residing in apartments, they built a camp of asymmetrical cabins with canvas roofs that maximized but pleasantly diffused light, and blended into the rugged mountain backdrop.

When the hotel project failed due to the stock market crash of 1929, Wright and his crew returned to Taliesin, his Wisconsin home and site of his architectural fellowship, and the camp was disassembled and carted away. But the concept of his humble worker village would remain in Wright's creative consciousness and a decade later the renowned architect found an appropriate plot of land north of Scottsdale.

NATURAL CONSTRUCTION

Built upon foundations of caliche, known as nature's own concrete, and painted in crimson and amber hues that highlight the "desert masonry," the buildings seem to adhere naturally to the landscape. The asymmetrical roofs resemble those of Wright's South Mountain camp and were covered with canvas for many years before Wright added glass. Supported by painted-steel-and-redwood beams, they face the sun-filled sky like the hard shell of a desert animal that seems to be comfortable here despite all the odds against its survival.

ARCHITECTURAL LEGACY

The over 70-year-old property and its structures, which Wright envisioned as a "little fleet of ships," are perhaps some of the best non-native examples of organic architecture. They also serve as desert building blocks for future generations of Wright protégés—some perhaps schooled on these very grounds—to balance man and Mother Nature.

WORD OF MOUTH

Travelers at Fodors.com recommend the following tours and tips for your visit:

"The 90 minute tour [was] a great introduction to Wright's life, architectural philosophy and school, and to the desert landscape." —sms73

"I highly recommend reading *Loving Frank* [by Nancy Horan] to gain insight into this man." —DebitNM

"If they are offering a night tour, take that one. The place is magical at night and you can get a glimpse of what it was like when the complex was WAY out in the desert all alone." —starrs

Taliesin West was Frank Lloyd Wright's winter residence. The original Taliesin in Wisconsin was his summer home.

㉒ Arts Festival is held annually in March. The **Scottsdale Museum of** **Contemporary Art** (⊠*7374 E. 2nd St., Old Town* ☎*480/994–2787* ⊕*www.scottsdalearts.org* ⊠*$7, free Thurs.* ☉*Hrs vary.*), a "museum without walls," is on-site, and there's also a good museum store for unusual jewelry and stationery, posters, and art books. New installations are planned every few months, with an emphasis on contemporary art, architecture, and design. Free docent-led tours are conducted on Thursday at 1:30. Kids can visit the Young at Art gallery. ⊠*7380 E. 2nd St., Old Town* ☎*480/994–2787* ⊕*www.scottsdalearts.org* ⊠*Free* ☉*Call for performance info.*

㉓ **Scottsdale Historical Museum.** Scottsdale's first schoolhouse, this redbrick building houses a reconstruction of the 1910 schoolroom, as well as photographs, original furniture from the city's founding fathers, and displays of other treasures from Scottsdale's early days. ⊠*7333 Scottsdale Mall, Old Town* ☎*480/945–4499* ⊕*www.scottsdalemuseum.com* ⊠*Free* ☉*Oct.–May, Wed.–Sun. 10–5; June–Sept., Wed.–Sun. 10–2.*

TEMPE AND AROUND

Tempe is the home of Arizona State University's main campus and a thriving student population. A 20-minute drive from Phoenix, the tree- and brick-lined Mill Avenue is the main drag, filled with student hangouts, bookstores, boutiques, eateries, and a repertory movie house. There are always things to do or see, and plenty of music venues and fun, casual dining spots. This is one part of town where the locals actually hang out, stroll, and sit at the outdoor cafés.

The inverted pyramid that is Tempe City Hall, on 5th Street, one block east of Mill Avenue, was constructed by local architects Rolf Osland and Michael Goodwin not just to win design awards (which they have), but also to shield city workers from the desert sun. The pyramid is built mainly of bronzed glass and stainless steel, and the point disappears in a sunken courtyard lushly landscaped with jacaranda, ivy, and flowers, out of which the pyramid widens to the sky: stand underneath and gaze up for a weird fish-eye perspective.

The banks of the Rio Salado in Tempe are the site of a new commercial and entertainment district, and Tempe Town Lake—a 2-mi-long waterway created by inflatable dams in a flood control channel—which is open for boating. There are biking and jogging paths on the perimeter.

GETTING HERE AND AROUND
Street parking is hard to find, especially amid all the construction, but you can park in the public garage at Hayden Square, just north of 5th Street and west of Mill Avenue. Get your ticket stamped by a local merchant to avoid paying parking fees. The FLASH (Free Local Area Shuttle) (☎602/253–5000) does a loop around Arizona State University, with stops at Mill Avenue and Sun Devil Stadium. Light rail also stops at Third Street and Mill Avenue.

TIMING
The **Tempe Festival of the Arts** on Mill Avenue is held twice a year (in early December and March–April); it has all sorts of interesting arts and crafts (⊕*www.tempefestivalofthearts.com*).

Numbers in the text correspond to numbers on the Tempe & Around map.

EXPLORING

🟑 **Arizona State University.** What began as the Tempe Normal School for Teachers—in 1886 a four-room redbrick building and 20-acre cow pasture—is now the 750-acre Tempe campus of ASU, the largest university in the Southwest. The university now has four campuses located across the Valley. The **ASU Memorial Union** (✉*1290 S. Normal Ave.* ☎*480/965–5728*) has maps of a self-guided walking tour of the Tempe campus—it's a long walk from Mill Avenue, so you might opt for the short version suggested here. You'll wind past public art and innovative architecture—including a music building that bears a strong resemblance to a wedding cake, designed by Taliesin students to echo Frank Lloyd Wright's Gammage Auditorium, and a law library shaped like an open book—and end up at the 71,706-seat **Sun Devil Stadium** (✉*ASU Campus, 5th St.* ☎*480/965–9011*), home to the school's Sun Devils. One of the most outstanding stadiums in the country, it has a spectacular setting. It's literally carved out of a mountain and cradled between the Tempe buttes. While touring the west end of campus, stop into the **Arizona State University Art Museum** (✉*Mill Ave. and 10th St.* ☎*480/965–2787* ⊕*www.asuartmuseum.asu.edu* ☜*Free* ☉*Sept.–Apr., Tues. 11–8, Wed.–Sat. 11–5; May–Aug., Tues.–Sat. 11–5. Closed Sun.–Mon.*). It's in the gray-purple stucco Nelson Fine Arts Center, just north of Gammage Auditorium. For a relatively small museum, it has an extensive collection, including 19th- and 20th-century painting and sculpture by masters such as Winslow Homer, Edward Hopper, Georgia

2

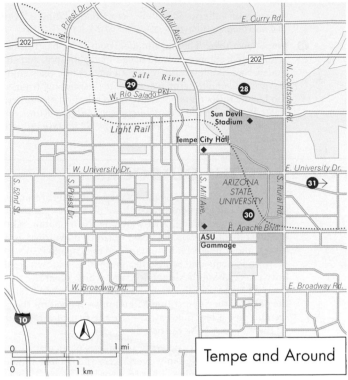

Tempe and Around

O'Keeffe, and Rockwell Kent. Works by faculty and student artists are
also on display, and there's a gift shop. In Matthews Hall, the **Northlight
Gallery** (⊠ *Matthews Hall, Mill Ave. and 10th St.* ☎ *480/965–6517*
⊕ *www.art.asu.edu* ✉ *Free Tues.–Thurs. 10:30–4:30, Sat. 12:30–4:30.
Closed Mon., Fri.–Sat.*) exhibits works by both renowned and emerging photographers.

**NEED A
BREAK?**

The outdoor patio of the **Coffee Plantation** (⊠ *680 S. Mill Ave.* ☎ *480/
829-3919*), a popular café near the ASU campus, is a lively scene—students
studying, locals chatting over coffee, and poets and musicians presenting
their latest works.

㉛ **Arizona Museum of Natural History.** Kids young and old get a thrill out of
the largest collection of dinosaur fossils in the state at this large museum
where you can also pan for gold and see changing exhibits from around
the world. ⊠ *53 N. Macdonald St., Mesa* ☎ *480/644–2230* ⊕ *www.
azmnh.org* ✉ *$10* ⊙ *Tues.–Fri. 10–5, Sat. 11–5, Sun. 1–5.*

㉙ **Tempe Center for the Arts.** This award-winning arts center at the edge
of Tempe Town Lake has become a great source of local pride since it
opened in 2007. Visual art, music, theater, and dance, featuring local,
regional, and international talent are showcased in a state-of-the-art,
600-seat proscenium theater, a 200-seat studio theater, and a 3,500

square-foot gallery. ✉*700 W. Rio Salado Pkwy.* ☎*480/350–2822* ⊕*www.tempe.gov/arts.*

㉘ Tempe Town Lake. The man-made Town Lake has turned downtown
☾ Tempe into a commercial and urban-living hot spot, and attracts college
students and Valley residents of all ages. Little ones enjoy the Splash
Playground, and fishermen appreciate the rainbow trout–stocked lake.
Rio Lago Cruises rents boats and has a selection of short cruise options.
✉*80 W. Rio Salado Pkwy., between Mill and Rural Aves. north of
Arizona State University* ☎*480/350–8625, 480/517–4050* ⊕*www.
riolagocruises.com.*

SPORTS AND THE OUTDOORS

The mountains surrounding the Valley of the Sun are among its greatest
assets, and outdoors enthusiasts have plenty of options within the city
limits to pursue hiking, bird-watching, or mountain-biking passions.
Piestewa (formerly Squaw) Peak, north of downtown, is popular with
hikers, and Camelback Mountain and the Papago Peaks are landmarks
between Phoenix and Scottsdale. South of downtown are the much less
lofty peaks of South Mountain Park, which separates the Valley from
the rest of the Sonoran Desert. East of the city, beyond Tempe and Mesa,
the peaks of the Superstition Mountains—named for their eerie way of
seeming just a few miles away—are the first of a range that stretches
all the way into New Mexico.

Central Arizona's dry desert heat imposes particular restraints on outdoor endeavors—even in winter hikers and cyclists should wear lightweight opaque clothing, a hat or visor, and high-UV-rated sunglasses,
and should carry a quart of water for each hour of activity. The intensity
of the sun makes strong sunscreen (SPF 15 or higher) a must, and don't
forget to apply it to your hands and feet. ■**TIP➔From May 1 to October 1
you shouldn't jog or hike from one hour after sunrise until a half hour before
sunset.** During these times the air is so hot and dry that your body will
lose moisture at a dangerous, potentially lethal rate. And keep your
eyes peeled in natural desert areas; rattlesnakes and scorpions could
be on the prowl.

BALLOONING

A sunrise or sunset hot-air-balloon ascent is a remarkable desert sightseeing experience. The average fee—there are more than three-dozen
Valley companies to choose from—is $150 per person, and hotel pickup
is usually included. Since flight paths and landing sites vary with wind
speeds and directions, a roving land crew follows each balloon in flight.
Time in the air is generally between 1 and 1½ hours, but allow three
hours for the total excursion.

Adventures Out West and Unicorn Balloon Company (☎*480/991–3666 or
800/755–0935* ⊕*www.adventuresoutwest.com*) has horseback riding,
jeep tours, and hot-air-balloon flights that conclude with complimentary champagne, a flight certificate, and video. **The Hot Air Balloon Company** (☎*623/847–1511 or 800/843–5987* ⊕*www.arizonaballooning.
com*) offers private and group sunrise and sunset flights with sparkling

beverages and fresh pastries served on touchdown. **Hot Air Expeditions** (☎*480/502–6999 or 800/831–7610* ⊕*www.hotairexpeditions.com*) is the best ballooning in Phoenix. Flights are long, the staff is charming, and the gourmet snacks, catered by the acclaimed Vincent restaurant, are out of this world.

BICYCLING

There are plenty of gorgeous areas for biking in the Phoenix area, but riding in the streets isn't recommended, as there are few adequate bike lanes in the city. **Phoenix Parks and Recreation** (☎*602/262–6861* ⊕*www. ci.phoenix.az.us/parks*) has detailed maps of Valley bike paths. Note that the desert climate can be tough on cyclists, so make sure you're prepared with lots of water.

Pinnacle Peak (✉ *26802 N. 102nd Way, 25 mi northeast of downtown Phoenix* ☎*480/312–0990* ⊕*scottsdaleaz.gov/parks*) is a popular place to take bikes for the ride north to Carefree and Cave Creek, or east and south over the mountain pass and down to the Verde River, toward Fountain Hills. **Scottsdale's Indian Bend Wash** (✉*Along Hayden Rd., from Shea Blvd. south to Indian School Rd.* ☎*480/312–7275* ⊕*scottsdaleaz. gov/parks*) has paths suitable for bikes winding among its golf courses and ponds. **South Mountain Park** (*see above*) is the prime site for mountain bikers, with its 40-plus mi of trails—some of them with challenging ascents and all of them quiet and scenic. **Tempe Town Lake** (✉*Southwest corner of Mill Ave. and Washington St.* ☎*480/350–8625* ⊕*Tempe.gov/ lake*) has 5 mi of paths for skating, running, bicycling, and walking. **Trail 100** runs throughout the Phoenix Mountain preserve (✉*Enter at Dreamy Draw park, just east of the intersection of Northern Ave. and 16th St.* ☎*602/262–6696* ⊕*Phoenix.gov/parks*); it's just the thing for mountain bikers.

Several area adventure-tour outfits will pick you up at your hotel, supply the bikes, and take you out for excursions at different levels. **ABC/Desert Biking Adventures** (☎*602/320–4602 or 888/249–2453* ⊕*www.desertbikingadventures.com*) offers 2-, 3-, and 4-hour mountain-biking excursions through the McDowell Mountains and the Sonoran Desert. **AOA Adventures** (☎*480/945–2881 or 866/455–1601* ⊕*www.aoa-adventures.com*) leads half-day, full-day, and multiple-day adventures, with their extremely knowledgeable and personable staff. **Wheels N' Gear** (✉*16447 N. 91st St., North Scottsdale, Scottsdale* ☎*480/945–2881*) rents bikes by the day or the week.

FOUR-WHEELING

Taking a jeep or a wide-track Humvee through the backcountry has become a popular way to experience the desert's saguaro-covered mountains and curious rock formations. Prices start at around $100 per person.

Arrowhead Desert Jeep Tours (✉*2734 W. Michelle Dr. 85053* ☎*602/942–3361* ⊕*www.azdeserttours.com*) offers gold panning on a private claim, cookouts, cattle drives, river crossings, and Native American dance demonstrations. **Desert Dog Hummer Adventures** (✉*17212 E. Shea Blvd., Fountain Hills* ☎*480/837–3966* ⊕*www.azadventures.com*) heads out on half- and full-day Hummer tours to the Four Peaks Wilderness

Area in Tonto National Forest and the Sonoran Desert. U-Drive desert cars and ATV tours are also available. **Desert Storm Hummer Tours** (✉*15525 N. 83rd Way, No. 8, Scottsdale 85260* ☎*480/922–0020 or 866/374–8637* ⊕*www.dshummer.com*) conducts 4-hour nature tours, climbing 4,000 feet up the rugged trails of Tonto National Forest via Hummer. **Wayward Wind Tours** (✉*2418 E. Danbury St., Phoenix 85032* ☎*602/867–7825 or 800/804–0480* ⊕*www.waywardwindtours.com*) ventures down to the Verde River on its own trail and offers wilderness cookouts for large groups. **Wild West Jeep Tours** (✉*7127 E. Becker La., Suite #74, Scottsdale 85254* ☎*480/922–0144* ⊕*www.wildwestjeep tours.com*) has special permits that allow it to conduct four-wheeler excursions in the Tonto National Forest and to visit thousand-year-old Indian sites listed on the National Register of Historic Places.

GOLF

Arizona has more golf courses per capita than any other state west of the Mississippi River, making it one of the most popular golf destinations in the United States. The sport is also one of Arizona's major industries, and green fees can run from $35 at a public course to more than $500 at some of Arizona's premier golfing spots. New courses seem to pop up monthly: there are more than 200 in the Valley (some lighted at night), and the PGA's Southwest section has its headquarters here. Call well ahead for tee times during the cooler months. During the summer, fees drop dramatically and it's not uncommon to schedule a round before dawn. ■**TIP→** Some golf courses offer a discounted twilight rate— and the weather is often much more amenable at this time of day. Check course Web sites for discounts before making your reservations. Also, package deals abound at resorts as well as through booking agencies like **Scottsdale Golf Adventures** (☎*800/398-8100* ⊕*www.scottsdalegolfadventures.com*), who will plan and schedule a nonstop golf holiday for you. If you're looking for a little more pampering, try **Scottsdale Swing** (☎ *888/807–9464* ⊕*www.scottsdaleswing.com*), who will arrange a complete golf holiday, complete with access to the area's best night spots. For a copy of the *Arizona Golf Guide,* contact the **Arizona Golf Association** (☎*602/944–3035 or 800/458–8484* ⊕*www.azgolf.org*).

MUNICIPAL COURSES FodorśChoice ★ **ASU Karsten Golf Course** (✉*1125 E. Rio Salado Pkwy., Tempe* ☎*480/921– 8070* ⊕*www.asukarsten.com* ⚑*. 18 holes. Par 70. Green fees: $40–$108.* ☞*Facilities: Driving range, putting green, golf carts, rental clubs, pro shop, lessons, restaurant, bar*) is the Arizona State University 18-hole golf course where NCAA champions train.

Encanto Park (✉*2775 N. 15th Ave., Central Phoenix* ☎*602/253–3963* ⊕*phoenix.gov/sports* ⚑*. 18 holes. Par 72. Green fees: $24–$46.* ☞*Facilities: Driving range, putting green, golf carts, rental clubs, pro shop, restaurant, bar.*) has attractive, affordable public 9- and 18-hole courses.

Papago Golf Course (✉*5595 E. Moreland St., Papago Salado, Phoenix* ☎*602/275–8428* ⊕*phoenix.gov/SPORTS/papago.html* ⚑*. 18 holes. Par 72. Green fees: $30–$109* ☞*Facilities: Driving range, putting green, golf carts, rental clubs, pro shop, restaurant, bar*) is a low-priced 18 holes and Phoenix's best municipal course; it debuted a new design in late 2008.

PUBLIC COURSES FodorśChoice ★ **Gold Canyon Golf Club** (✉*6100 S. King's Ranch Rd., Gold Canyon* ☎*480/982–9090 or 800/827–5281* ⊕*www.gcgr.com* ⚑*. Dinosaur Mountain: 18 holes. Par 72. Sidewinder: 18 holes. Par 72. Green fees: $40–$210* ☞*Facilities: Driving range, putting green, golf carts, rental* clubs, pro shop, lessons, restaurant, bar), near Apache Junction in the East Valley, offers fantastic views of the Superstition Mountains and challenging golf.

★ **Grayhawk Country Club** (✉ *8620 E. Thompson Peak Pkwy., North Scottsdale, Scottsdale* ☎ *480/502–1800* ⊕ *www.grayhawk.com* ⛳ *Talon: 18 holes. Par 72. Raptor: 18 holes. Par 72. Green fees: $255–$350* ⛳ *Facilities: Driving range, putting green, golf carts, rental clubs, pro shop, lessons, restaurant, bar*), a 36-hole course, has beautiful mountain views. Summer green fees are much lower.

Hillcrest Golf Club (✉ *20002 Star Ridge Dr., Sun City West* ☎ *623/584–1500* ⊕ *www.hillcrestgolfclub.com* ⛳ *18 holes. Par 70. Green fees: $22–$59* ⛳ *Facilities: Driving range, putting green, golf carts, rental clubs, pro shop, lessons, restaurant, bar*) is the best course in the Sun Cities development, with 18 holes on 179 acres of well-designed turf.

Raven Golf Club at South Mountain (✉ *3636 E. Baseline Rd., South Phoenix* ☎ *602/243–3636* ⊕ *www.ravenatsouthmountain.com* ⛳ *18 holes. Par 72. Green fees: $35–$180* ⛳ *Facilities: Driving range, putting green, golf carts, rental clubs, pro shop, lessons, restaurant, bar*) has thousands of Aleppo pines and Lombardy poplars, making it a cool, shady 18-hole haven for summertime golfers. Call or visit the Web site for other Raven golf properties.

SunRidge Canyon (✉ *13100 N. SunRidge Dr., Fountain Hills* ☎ *480/837–5100* ⊕ *www.sunridgegolf.com* ⛳ *18 holes. Par 72. Green fees: $35–$190* ⛳ *Facilities: Driving range, putting green, golf carts, rental clubs, pro shop, lessons, restaurant, bar*), east of Scottsdale, is a great 18-hole course for both the low handicapper and those who score above 100. The incredible mountain views are almost distracting.

Fodor's Choice **Troon North** (✉ *10320 E. Dynamite Blvd., North Scottsdale, Scottsdale*
★ ☎ *480/585–7700* ⊕ *www.troonnorthgolf.com* ⛳ *Monument: 18 holes. Par 72. Pinnacle: 18 holes. Par 71. Green fees: $75–$295* ⛳ *Facilities: Driving range, putting green, golf carts, rental clubs, pro shop, lessons, restaurant, bar*) is a challenge for the length alone (7,008 yards). The million-dollar views add to the experience at this perfectly maintained 36-hole course.

RESORT **Arizona Biltmore Country Club** (✉ *Arizona Biltmore Resort & Spa, 24th*
COURSES *St. and Missouri Ave., Camelback Corridor* ☎ *602/955–9655* ⊕ *www. arizonabiltmore.com* ⛳ *Adobe: 18 holes. Par 71. Links: 18 holes. Par 71. Green fees: $49–$185* ⛳ *Facilities: Driving range, putting green, golf carts, rental clubs, pro shop, lessons, restaurant, bar*), the granddaddy of Valley golf courses, has two 18-hole PGA championship courses, lessons, and clinics.

Lookout Mountain Golf Club (✉ *Pointe Hilton at Tapatio Cliffs, 1111 N. 7th St., North Phoenix* ☎ *602/866–6356* ⊕ *www.pointehilton.com* ⛳ *18 holes. Par 71 Green fees: $79–$149* ⛳ *Facilities: Driving range, putting green, golf carts, rental clubs, pro shop, lessons, restaurant, bar*) has one 18-hole, par-72 course.

Marriott's Camelback Golf Club (✉ *Marriott's Camelback Inn, 7847 N. Mockingbird La., Paradise Valley* ☎ *480/596–7050* ⊕ *www.*

The Valley of the Sun is a popular destination for golfing with more than 200 courses in the area.

camelbackinn.com 🏌 *Indian Bend: 18 holes. Par 72. Padre: 18 holes. Par 72. Green fees: $40–$145* ⚐ *Facilities: Driving range, putting green, golf carts, rental clubs, pro shop, lessons, restaurant, bar*) has two 18-hole courses. Summer twilight green fees are $ $40.

Ocotillo Golf Resort (✉ *3751 S. Clubhouse Dr., Chandler* ☎ *480/917–6660* ⊕ *www.ocotillogolf.com* 🏌 *27 holes (three 9-hole courses) Blue/Gold: Par 72. White/Gold: Par 71. Blue/White: Par 71. Green fees: $175* ⚐ *Facilities: Driving range, putting green, golf carts, rental clubs, pro shop, lessons, restaurant, bar*) is designed around 95 acres of man-made lakes; there's water in play on nearly all 27 holes. Summer twilight green fees are $35.

★ **The Phoenician Golf Club** (✉ *The Phoenician, 6000 E. Camelback Rd., Camelback Corridor* ☎ *480/423–2449* ⊕ *www.thephoenician.com* 🏌 *27 holes. Oasis: 9 holes. Par 35. Desert: 9 holes. Par 35. Canyon: 9 holes. Par 35. Green fees: $35–$200* ⚐ *Facilities: Driving range, putting green, golf carts, rental clubs, pro shop, lessons, restaurant, bar*) has a 27-hole course. Summer fees after 11 AM start at $35.

★ **Tournament Players Club of Scottsdale** (✉ *Fairmont Scottsdale Princess Resort, 17020 N. Hayden Rd., North Scottsdale, Scottsdale* ☎ *480/585–4334 or 888/400–4001* ⊕ *www.tpc.com* 🏌 *Champions: 18 holes. Par 71. Stadium: 18 holes. Par 71. Green fees: $47–$272* ⚐ *Facilities: Driving range, putting green, golf carts, rental clubs, pro shop, lessons, restaurant, bar.*), a 36-hole course by Tom Weiskopf and Jay Morrish, is the site of the PGA FBR Open, which takes place in January.

Wigwam Golf and Country Club (✉ *Wigwam Resort, 300 Wigwam Blvd., Litchfield Park* ☎ *623/935–3811* ⊕ *www.wigwam*

resort.com ♨*Blue: 18 holes. Par 70. Gold: 18 holes. Par 72. Red: 18 holes. Par 72. Green fees: $64–$172* ✆*Facilities: Driving range, putting green, golf carts, rental clubs, pro shop, lessons, restaurant, bar)* is the home of the famous Gold Course, as well as two other 18-hole courses.

HIKING

One of the best ways to see the beauty of the Valley of the Sun is from above, so hikers of all calibers seek a vantage point in the mountains surrounding the flat Valley.

The Phoenix Mountain Preserve Council (✉*Box 26121, Phoenix 85068* ☎*602/390–6086* ⊕*www. phoenixmountains.org*) administers the city's **Phoenix Mountain Preserve System**, a series of mountainous regions that surround the city. The group has its own park rangers who can help plan your hikes. It also publishes a book, *Day Hikes and Trail Rides in and around Phoenix*.

■TIP➜No matter the season, be sure to bring sunscreen, a hat, plenty of water, and a camera to capture a dazzling sunset. It's always a good idea to tell someone where you'll be and when you plan to return.

The wonderful folks at **AOA Adventures** (☎*480/945–2881* or *866/455–1601* ⊕*www.aoa-adventures.com*) cater to hikers at different levels of expertise on their half-day, full-day, and multiple-day hikes. The guides are extremely knowledgeable about local flora and fauna.

★ **Camelback Mountain and Echo Canyon Recreation Area** (✉*Tatum Blvd. and McDonald Dr., Paradise Valley* ☎*602/256–3220 Phoenix Parks & Recreation Dept.*) has intermediate to difficult hikes up the Valley's most outstanding central landmark.

⟳ **The Papago Peaks** (✉*Van Buren St. and Galvin Pkwy., Papago Salado, Scottsdale* ☎*602/256–3220 Phoenix Parks & Recreation Dept. Eastern and Central District*) were sacred sites for the Tohono O'odham. The soft-sandstone peaks contain accessible caves, some petroglyphs, and splendid views of much of the Valley. This is a good spot for family hikes.

Piestewa Peak (✉*2701 E. Piestewa Peak Dr., Phoenix* ☎*602/262–7901 North Mountain Preserves Ranger Station*), just north of Lincoln Drive, has a series of trails for all levels of hikers. It's a great place to get views of downtown. Allow about 1½ hours for each direction. **Pinnacle Peak Trail** (✉*26802 N. 102nd Way, 1 mi south of Dynamite and Alma School Rds., North Scottsdale, Scottsdale* ☎*480/312–0990*) is a well-maintained trail offering a moderately challenging 3½-mi round-trip hike—or horseback experience for those who care to round

2

PERFECT YOUR GOLF SWING

Feel like you need to swing like a Tiger before you take on the Valley's premier golf courses? Troon North has a solution: the **Callaway Golf Performance Center** (☎*480/585–5300* ⊕*www. troonnorthgolf.com*) is a state-of-the-art facility that analyzes your swing and fits your clubs with 3-D imagery and software designed by the experts at Callaway. Golf greats like Tiger Woods and Phil Mickelson use similar technologies to perfect their games—why shouldn't you? With only 10 such facilities in the country, it's definitely worth checking out.

up a horse at the local stables. Interpretive programs and trail signs along the way describe the geology, flora, fauna, and cultural history of the area. **Lost Dog Wash Trail** (⊠*12601 N. 124th St., north of Shea Blvd., North Scottsdale, Scottsdale ⊕www.scottsdaleaz.gov/preserve ☎480/312–7013)*, part of the continually expanding McDowell-Sonoran Preserve (⊕*www.mcdowellsonoranconservancy.com)*, is a mostly gentle 4.5-mile round trip that will get you away from the bustle of the city in a hurry. The trailhead has restrooms and a map that shows a series of trails for varying skill levels.

★ **South Mountain Park** (⊠*10919 S. Central Ave., South Phoenix ☎602/495– 0222)* is the jewel of the city's Mountain Park Preserves. Its mountains and arroyos contain more than 60 mi of marked and maintained trails— all open to hikers, horseback riders, and mountain bikers. It also has three car-accessible lookout points, with 65-mi views. Rangers can help you plan hikes to view some of the 200 petroglyph sites.

☾ **Waterfall Trail** (⊠*13025 N. White Tank Mountain Rd., Waddell ☎623/935– 2505)* is a short and easy trail. Part of the 25 mi of trails available at the White Tanks Regional Park, it's kid-friendly, and strollers and wheelchairs roll along easily to Petroglyph Plaza, which boasts 1,500-year-old boulder carvings—dozens are in clear view from the trail. From there the trail takes a rockier but manageable course to a waterfall, which, depending on area rainfall, can be cascading, creeping, or completely dry. Stop at the visitor center to view desert reptiles such as the king snake and a gopher snake in the aquariums.

HORSEBACK RIDING

More than two dozen stables and equestrian-tour outfitters in the Valley attest to the saddle's enduring importance in Arizona—even in this auto-dominated metropolis. Stables offer rides for an hour, a whole day, and even some overnight adventures. Some local resorts can arrange for lessons on-site or at nearby stables.

Cowboy College (⊠*30208 N. 152nd St., North Scottsdale, Scottsdale ☎480/471–3151 or 888/330–8070 ⊕www.cowboycollege.com)* has wranglers who will teach you everything you need to know about ridin', ropin', and ranchin'.

MacDonald's Ranch (⊠*26540 N. Scottsdale Rd., North Scottsdale, Scottsdale ☎480/585–0239 ⊕www.macdonaldsranch.com)* offers 1- and 2-hour trail rides and guided breakfast, lunch, and dinner rides through desert foothills above Scottsdale.

★ **OK Corral & Stable** (⊠*2655 E. Whiteley St., Apache Junction ☎480/982– 4040 ⊕www.okcorrals.com)* offers 1-, 2-, and 4-hour horseback trail rides and steak cookouts as well as 1- to 5-day horse-packing trips. Ron Feldman, an authority on the history and secrets of the Lost Dutchman Mine, is the guide for historical pack trips through the Superstition Mountains.

Ponderosa Stables (⊠*10919 S. Central Ave., South Phoenix ☎602/268– 1261 ⊕www.arizona-horses.com).* To enjoy your South Mountain experience from a higher perch, consider renting horses at this nearby stables. This private company rents its land from the city of Phoenix, and will take you on an excursion, or send you on one of your own. Rentals cost $30 per person, per hour.

RAFTING

Cimarron Adventures and River Co. (☎*480/994–1199* ⊕*www.cimarron adventures.com*) arranges half-day float trips down the Salt and Verde rivers; trips cost about $45 per person. **Desert Voyagers** (☎*480/998–7238* ⊕*www.desertvoyagers.com*) specializes in raft and kayak trips.

SAILPLANING–SOARING

Turf Soaring School (⊠*8700 W. Carefree Hwy., Carefree* ☎*602/439–3621* ⊕*www.turfsoaring.com*) gives scenic sailplane rides that last from 20 to 30 minutes. Costs are from $109 per person.

TENNIS

With all the blue sky and sunshine in the Valley, it's a perfect place to play tennis or watch the pros. The recently opened Surprise Tennis and Racquet Complex, a public facility in Surprise, is the place to watch big-time tournaments such as the Fed Cup. Most major resorts, such as the Radisson, Phoenician, Wigwam, Fairmont Princess, and JW Marriott Desert Ridge (and many smaller properties), have tennis courts. Granted, tennis plays second fiddle to golf here—but many of the larger resorts offer package tennis deals. If you're not staying at a resort, there are more than 60 public facilities in the area.

Surprise Tennis and Racquet Complex (⊠*14469 W. Paradise La., Surprise* ☎*623/222–2400* ⊕*www.surpriseaz.com/tennis*) features 25 public courts where you can play for 90 minutes on their state-of-the-art lighted courts for only $4. **Kiwanis Park Recreation Center** (⊠*6111 S. All America Way, Tempe* ☎*480/350–5201* ⊕*www.tempe.gov/kiwanis*) has 15 lighted premier-surface courts (all for same-day or one-day-advance reserve). **Mountain View Tennis Center** (⊠*1104 E. Grovers Ave., Phoenix* ☎*602/534–2500* ⊕*www.phoenix.gov/sports*), just north of Bell Road, has 20 lighted courts and group lessons. Court fees are $1.50 per person for 90 minutes. **Phoenix Tennis Center** (⊠*6330 N. 21st Ave., West Phoenix* ☎*602/249–3712* ⊕*www.phoenix.gov/sports*) is a city facility with 22 lighted hard courts. **Scottsdale Ranch Park** (⊠*10400 E. Via Linda, Scottsdale* ☎*480/312–7774* ⊕*www.scottsdaleaz.gov/parks*) is a city facility with 12 lighted courts. Lessons are available here, too.

TOURS

Arizona Outback Adventures (☎*480/945–2881 or 866/455–1601* ⊕*www.aoa-adventures.com*) leads hiking, biking, and rafting tours around the state.

TUBING

The Valley may not be known for its wealth of water, but locals manage to make the most of what there is. A popular summer stop is the northeast side of the Salt River, where sun worshippers can rent an inner tube and float down the river for an afternoon. Tubing season runs from May to September. Several Valley outfitters rent tubes. Make sure you bring lots of sunscreen, a hat, water—and a rope for attaching your cooler to a tube.

Salt River Recreation (✉ *Usery Pass and Power Rds., Mesa* ☎*480/984–3305* ⊕*www.saltrivertubing.com*), offers shuttle-bus service to and from your starting point and rents tubes for $15 (cash only) for the day.

WHERE TO EAT

Updated by
JoBeth Jamison

Phoenix and its surroundings have metamorphosed into a melting pot for every type of cuisine imaginable, from northern to Tuscan Italian; from mom-and-pop to Mexico City Mexican; from low-key Cuban to high-end French- and Greek-inspired Southwestern; from Japanese- and Spanish-style tapas to kosher food and American classics with subtle ethnic twists.

Just as the Valley of the Sun has attracted visitors from around the world, it has also been attracting a record number of worldly residents. Fortunately for everyone, many of those people are skilled chefs and/or restaurateurs who have opted to share their gifts with the public.

Eateries like La Grande Orange Grocery and Vincent's Touch of Provence market are revolutionizing Phoenix's "fast-food" concept with gourmet pay-and-take meals, while tapas-style restaurants like Lola, Tapino, and See Saw are usurping the traditional sit-down dinner by offering mouthwatering mini-entrées in a casually hip, community-oriented atmosphere. Four-star cuisine, some concocted by celebrity chefs, also awaits all over the Valley, from Kai in Chandler to Scottsdale's Bourbon Steak, along with Binkley's and Café Bink in Cave Creek. Dotted with massive strip malls, Phoenix outskirts are becoming a haven of corporate eateries, but don't worry, there's plenty of divine, independent dining for all tastes and all trends in between.

Many of the best restaurants in the Valley are in resorts, camouflaged behind courtyard walls, or tucked away in shopping malls. Newer, upscale eateries are clustered along Camelback Corridor—a veritable restaurant row, running west to east from Phoenix to Scottsdale—and in Scottsdale itself. Great Mexican food can be found throughout the Valley, but the most authentic spots are in the Hispanic neighborhoods of South Phoenix.

PLANNING INFORMATION

Restaurants change hours, locations, chefs, prices, and menus frequently, so it's best to call ahead to confirm. Show up without a reservation during tourist season (October through mid-May), and you may have to head for a fast-food drive-through window to avoid a two-hour wait for a table. All listed restaurants are open for lunch and dinner unless otherwise specified.

WHAT IT COSTS					
	¢	$	$$	$$$	$$$$
At Dinner	under $8	$8–$12	$13–$20	$21–$30	over $30

Prices are per person for a main course. The final tab will include sales tax of 8.1% in Phoenix, 7.95% in Scottsdale.

BEST BETS FOR PHOENIX, SCOTTSDALE, AND TEMPE DINING

With hundreds of restaurants to choose from, how will you decide where to eat? Fodor's writers and editors have selected their favorite restaurants by price, cuisine, and experience in the Best Bets lists below. In the first column, Fodor's Choice properties represent the "best of the best" in every price category. You can also find specific details about a restaurant in the full reviews, listed by neighborhood then alphabetically in the following pages.

Fodor'sChoice★

AZ 188, p. 83

Chelsea's Kitchen, p. 68

Noca, p. 73

La Grande Orange, p. 69

Lon's at the Hermosa, p. 77

FEZ, p. 69

Pane Bianco, p. 70

The Mission, p. 84

Rancho Pinot Grill, p. 82

Sea Saw, p. 84

T. Cook's at the Royal Palms, p. 74

Best By Price

¢

Carolina's, p. 77

Fry Bread House, p. 69

La Grande Orange, p. 69

Mrs. White's Golden Rule Café, p. 71

Kashman's Place, p. 85

Pepe's Taco Villa, p. 79

$

Pane Bianca, p. 70

Via Delosantos, p. 77

$$

Basis, p. 76

$$$

Medizona, p. 81

L'Ecole, p. 81

Rancho Pinot Grill, p. 82

Sea Saw, p. 84

Sens, p. 72

True Food, p. 75

$$$$

Binkley's, p. 129

Bourbon Steak, p. 84

Kai, p. 87

Best By Cuisine

BEST LOCAL EATS

La Grande Orange, p. 69

Mrs. White's Golden Rule Café, p. 71

Via Delosantos, p. 77

BEST MARGARITAS

Carlsbad Tavern, p. 79

Los Dos Molinos, p. 78

Pepe's Taco Villa, p. 79

Via Delosantos, p. 77

Best By Experience

BEST BREAKFAST

La Grande Orange, p. 69

Matt's Big Breakfast, p. 71

Original Pancake House, p. 82

BEST HOTEL DINING

Bistro 24 at the Ritz-Carlton Hotel, p. 72

Bourbon Steak at the Fairmont Scottsdale Princess, p. 84

elements at Sanctuary on Camelback Mountain, p. 77

Kai at Sheraton Wild Horse Pass Resort, p. 87

Lon's at the Hermosa, p. 77

T. Cooks at the Royal Palms Resort, p. 74

BEST SPECIAL OCCASION

Kai, p. 87

Binkley's, p. 129

T. Cook's at the Royal Palms, p. 74

GREAT VIEW

elements, p. 77

Lon's at the Hermosa, p. 77

T. Cook's at the Royal Palms, p. 74

BEST PATIO WINING AND DINING

Chelsea's Kitchen, p. 68

Olive & Ivy, p. 81

AZ 188, p. 83

elements, p. 77

House of Tricks, p. 88

Rosa's Mexican Grill, p. 88

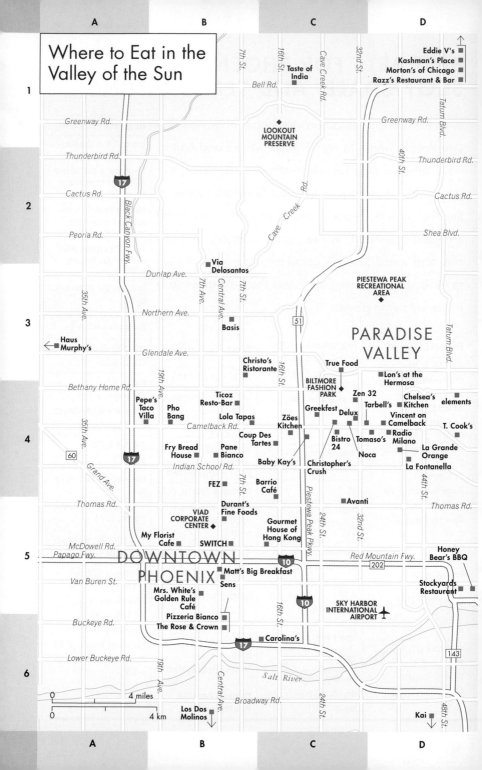

Where to Eat in the Valley of the Sun

A   B   C   D

1

Eddie V's
Kashman's Place
Morton's of Chicago
Razz's Restaurant & Bar

7th St.
16th St.
Cave Creek Rd.
32nd St.
Tatum Blvd.

Taste of India
Bell Rd.

Greenway Rd.   Greenway Rd.

LOOKOUT MOUNTAIN PRESERVE

Thunderbird Rd.   Thunderbird Rd.

40th St.

17

Cactus Rd.   Cactus Rd.

2

Peoria Rd.   Shea Blvd.

Cave Creek

Black Canyon Fwy.

Dunlap Ave.
Via Delosantos

PIESTEWA PEAK RECREATIONAL AREA

35th Ave.
7th Ave.
Central Ave.
7th St.

Northern Ave.

3

Basis

51

PARADISE VALLEY

← Haus Murphy's

Glendale Ave.

Christo's Ristorante

True Food

Tatum Blvd.

19th Ave.

Bethany Home Rd.

BILTMORE FASHION PARK

Lon's at the Hermosa

Pepe's Taco Villa

Ticoz Resto-Bar

Greekfest   Zen 32   Tarbell's   Chelsea's Kitchen   elements

Pho Bang

Lola Tapas

Zöes Kitchen   Delux   Vincent on Camelback

Camelback Rd.

16th St.

T. Cook's

4

35th Ave.

60

Coup Des Tartes

Bistro 24   Tomaso's   Radio Milano

La Grande Orange

17

Fry Bread House

Pane Bianco

Baby Kay's

Noca

La Fontanella

Indian School Rd.

Christopher's Crush

44th St.

FEZ

Barrio Café

Avanti

Thomas Rd.

Grand Ave.

Thomas Rd.

VIAD CORPORATE CENTER

Durant's Fine Foods

Piestewa Peak Pkwy.

24th St.

32nd St.

My Florist Cafe

Gourmet House of Hong Kong

Honey Bear's BBQ

SWITCH

McDowell Rd.

5

Papago Fwy.

DOWNTOWN PHOENIX

10

Red Mountain Fwy.   202

Stockyards Restaurant

Van Buren St.

Matt's Big Breakfast

16th St.

10

Mrs. White's Golden Rule Café

Sens

SKY HARBOR INTERNATIONAL AIRPORT

143

Buckeye Rd.

Pizzeria Bianco

The Rose & Crown

17   Carolina's

Lower Buckeye Rd.

48th St.

19th Ave.

Central Ave.

Salt River

24th St.

6

0   4 miles

0   4 km

Los Dos Molinos

Broadway Rd.

Kai

A   B   C   D

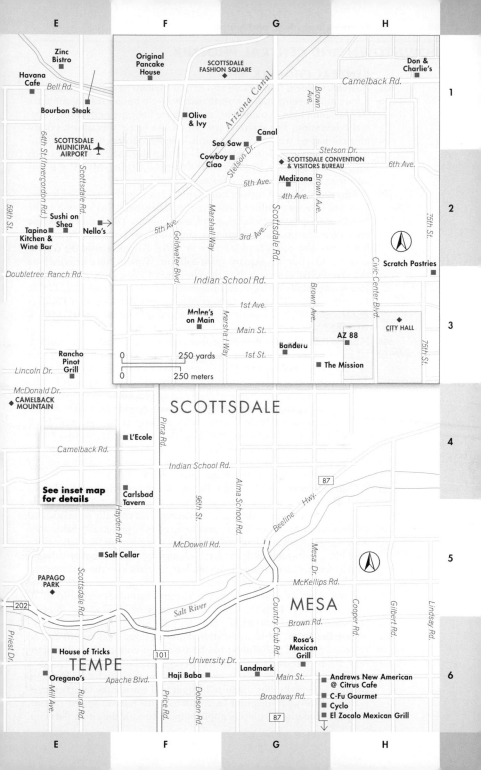

DOWNTOWN AND CENTRAL PHOENIX

CENTRAL PHOENIX

$$$ ✕**Avanti.** Owners Angelo Livi and Benito Mellino have been welcoming
ITALIAN guests to this romantic, yet aesthetically lively Italian restaurant since
1974. Candlelight, a piano bar, and a dance floor are perfect for a spe-
cial celebration. For starters, try one of the house specialties: potato
gnocchi paired with spinach ravioli. The veal dishes, such as saltim-
bocca or osso buco, are particularly memorable. ⊠*2728 E. Thomas
Rd., Central Phoenix* ☎*602/956–0900* ▤*AE, D, DC, MC, V* ⊕*www.
avanti-az.com* ⊙*No lunch weekends* ✛*C5.*

$$ ✕**Baby Kay's.** Named for the Louisiana native who brought her know-
CAJUN how and love for creole creations to the Valley, Baby Kay's is one of the
few Phoenix places specializing in Cajun cuisine. You'll find authentic
takes on red beans and rice, gumbo, jambalaya, po'boys, catfish, and the
house specialty: spicy crawfish stew *étouffée.* Baby Kay sold the restaurant in 2006, but her piquant spirit rolls on. Worthwhile extras include
the green-olive coleslaw. For the cholesterol conscious, grilled items
and spring salads with creole vinaigrette will do in a pinch. ⊠*2119 E.
Camelback Rd., Town and Country Shopping Center, Central Phoenix*
☎*602/955–0011* ⊕*www.babykayscajunkitchen.com* ▤*AE, MC, V*
⊙*Closed Sun.* ✛*C4.*

$$$ ✕**Barrio Cafe.** Owners Wendy Gruber and Silvana Salcido Esparza have
MEXICAN taken Mexican cuisine to a new level. Expect guacamole made to order
at your table and modern Mexican specialties such as *cochinita pibil,*
12-hour slow-roasted pork with red achiote and sour orange, and *chiles
en Nogada,* a delicious traditional dish from central Mexico featuring a
spicy poblano pepper stuffed with fruit, chicken, and raisins. The flavor-
packed food consistently draws packs of people, but you can drink
in the intimate atmosphere—and a specialty margarita or *aqua fresca*
(fruit water)—while you wait for a table. ⊠*2814 N. 16th St., Central
Phoenix* ☎*602/636–0240* ⊕*www.barriocafe.com* ⚖*Reservations not
accepted* ▤*AE, MC, V* ⊙*Closed Mon.* ✛*C4.*

$$ ✕**Chelsea's Kitchen.** With its hip, Pacific Northwest–chic interior and a
AMERICAN patio that feels more like a secret garden, Chelsea's Kitchen can easily
Fodor's Choice make you forget you're dining in the desert. This casually sophisticated
★ establishment insists on the freshest ingredients (especially fish), used
with equally fresh and flavorful ideas that complement the restaurant's
cool but comfortable style. Specials change frequently, and are always
worth steering away from the menu, but regulars love the shrimp cevi-
che, burgers , signature tacos with tortillas and corn chips made on-site,
and red velvet cake for dessert. On Sundays brunch is served from 10
to 3. ⊠*5040 N. 40th St., Central Phoenix* ☎*602/957–2555* ⊕*www.
chelseaskitchenaz.com* ▤*AE, MC, V* ✛*D4.*

$$$ ✕**Coup Des Tartes.** Tables are scattered among three small rooms and an
FRENCH enclosed patio of a charming old house at this country French restau-
rant. It's BYOB, and there's an $8 corkage fee, but all's forgiven when
you taste the delicate cuisine prepared in the tiny kitchen. The menu
changes seasonally, but if you're lucky it will feature the utterly unfor-
gettable Moroccan-inspired lamb shank with harissa-spiced ragout,
the pork tenderloin with pineapple maple glaze, or the citrus fettucini.

The banana brûlée tarte is their signature dessert, but seasonal offerings like the four berry tarte remind mouths why they put the mind through all the guilt. ⊠*4626 N. 16th St., Central Phoenix* ☎*602/212–1082* ⊕*www.nicetarts.com* ⌂*Reservations essential* ▭*AE, D, MC, V* ⌂*BYOB* ⊗*Closed Sun. and Mon. No lunch* ⊹*C4.*

$$$$
STEAK
✕**Durant's Fine Foods.** Durant's has endured since 1950 in the same location with the same menu and even many of the original waitstaff, making it one of Phoenix's legendary eating establishments. Supreme steaks, chops, and fresh seafood, including Florida stone crab and oysters Rockefeller, dominate here; when the restaurant once tried to update its menu, regulars protested so furiously the idea was shelved. Durant's is not à la carte, like many Valley steakhouses,which means their entrée prices include soup or salad and a side dish. Those in the know enter through the kitchen door and frequent the Rat Pack–style bar for jumbo martinis fit for ol' Blue Eyes himself. ⊠*2611 N. Central Ave., at Virginia, Central Phoenix* ☎*602/264–5967* ⊕*www.durants finefoods.com.* ▭*AE, D, DC, MC, V* ⊹*B5.*

$–$$
ECLECTIC
Fodor's Choice
★
✕**FEZ.** From its sleek interior to its central location and diverse clientele, right down to its affordable lunch, happy hour, dinner, Sunday brunch, and late-night menus, FEZ covers everything. "American fare with a Moroccan flair" means bold culinary leaps, with choices like the FEZ Burger, *kisras* (flatbread pizza), and the signature crispy rosemary pomegranate chicken—but it all lands safely on the taste buds. Potables include specialty martinis and margaritas and a formidable wine list. The owners also run the SWITCH and Ticoz restaurants. ⊠*3815 N. Central Ave., Central Phoenix* ☎*602/287–8700* ⊕*www.fezoncentral. com* ▭*AE, MC, V* ⊹*B4.*

¢
SOUTHWESTERN
✕**Fry Bread House.** Indian fry bread, a specialty of the Native American culture, is a delicious treat—pillows of deep-fried dough topped with sweet or savory toppings and folded in half. Local fry-bread fanatics get their fix from chef-owner Cecelia Miller of the Tohono O'odham Nation. Choose from culture-crossing combinations like savory shredded chili beef with cheese, beans, green chiles, veggies, and sour cream, or try the sweeter synthesis of honey and sugar, or chocolate with butter. ⊠*4140 N. 7th Ave., Central Phoenix* ☎*602/351–2345* ▭*D, MC, V* ⊗*Closed Sun.* ⊹*B4.*

$$
ITALIAN
✕**La Fontanella.** Quality and value are a winning combination at this outstanding neighborhood restaurant. The interior is reminiscent of an Italian villa, with antiques, crisp table linens, fresh flowers, and windows dressed in lace curtains, and chef-owner Isabelle Bertuccio turns out magnificent food, often using recipes from her Tuscan and Sicilian relatives. The escargots and herb-crusted rack of lamb top the list. Homemade pasta is served with Sicilian semolina bread and homemade sausages or meatballs. For dessert, Isabelle's husband Berto creates sumptuous gelato. ⊠*4231 E. Indian School Rd., Central Phoenix* ☎*602/955–1213* ▭*AE, D, DC, MC, V* ⊗*No lunch* ⊹*D4.*

¢
AMERICAN
Fodor's Choice
★
✕**La Grande Orange.** This San Francisco–inspired store and eatery sells artisanal nosh and novelty items, along with a formidable selection of wines. Valley residents flock to LGO, as they call it, to see and be seen, and to feast on mouthwatering sandwiches, pizzas, salads, and decadent

breads and desserts. The small tables inside fill up quickly at breakfast and lunch, but there's also seating on the patio. Try the Commuter Sandwich on a homemade English muffin, the open-faced Croque Madame or the delicious French pancakes with a sweet Spanish latte. ⊠*4410 N. 40th St., Central Phoenix* ☎*602/840–7777* ⊕*www.lagrandeorangegrocery. com* ⌔*Reservations not accepted* ☰ *AE, MC, V* ✛*D4.*

$ ✕**Lola Tapas.** The menu at this tiny tapas bar is about as big as the res-
SPANISH   taurant itself, but both focus on a delicious and delightful community-oriented dining experience. A long central table and two smaller ones tightly accommodate the steady stream of folks who come for the snug, ambient Latin atmosphere and the sensible portions of sensational food like garbanzo beans with garlic and sautéed spinach, the tortilla de patatas, or the grilled steak with seasoned butter. If you can find a space at the tiny bar in back, settle in with what may be the Valley's best sangria, white and red, while you wait. By day Lola transforms into a delicious Spanish-style coffeehouse. ⊠*800 E. Camelback Rd., Central Phoenix* ☎*602/265–4519* ⊕*www.lolatapas.com* ⌔*Reservations not accepted* ☰*AE, MC, V* ⊙*Closed Sun. and Mon. No lunch* ✛*B4.*

$ ✕**Pane Bianco.** Chef-owner Chris Bianco spends his evenings turning out
AMERICAN some of the Valley's best pizza at his downtown Pizzeria Bianco, and
Fodor'sChoice his days creating to-die-for take-out sandwiches at this minimalist shop.
★   Order at the counter, pick up your brown-bagged meal (which always includes a piece of candy), and dine outside at a picnic table. The menu only has a few sandwich selections (the tuna with red onion, gaeta olives, and arugula is an excellent choice), but each features wood-fired-oven focaccia stuffed with farm-fresh ingredients. Afterward, pop in to Lux next door and cleanse your palate with a cup of the Valley's best coffee, then hop on the light rail just out front and hit the town. ⊠*4404 N. Central Ave., Central Phoenix* ☎*602/234–2100* ⊕*www.pizzeriabianco. com* ☰*AE, MC, V* ⊙*Closed Sun. and Mon. No dinner* ✛*B4.*

$$ ✕**Radio Milano.** One of the many eateries conceived by the wildly suc-
ITALIAN   cessful team behind La Grande Orange (LGO), Radio Milano is a sleek
☺   and casual Italian-inspired experience with simple, but simply fantastic food. Radio serves unusual but tasty fare like Italian fresh-fish sashimi, deviled eggs, and celery Caesar salad for starters, and simple but standout pasta dishes and entrées like hand-made pappardelle with goat cheese, corn, asparagus, and tomatoes, and pork roast "prime rib" with baby spinach and potato. Kids eat free noodles, meatballs, and minipizza until 7 PM. Adults will enjoy a small but great selection of wine and beer along with cool, crisp Italian-inspired cocktails like blood-orange champagne or limoncello. Leave room for the olive-oil cake. ⊠*3950 E. Campbell Ave., Central Phoenix* ☎*602/956–6600* ⊕*www.radiomilanobar.com* ☰*AE, MC, V* ✛*D4.*

$ ✕**Ticoz Resto-Bar.** The slogan "Urban. Latin. Sexy. Chill" fits this place
LATIN AMERICAN like a stiletto heel. The colorful but dark interior is sleek and cool, the fare has just the right spice, and the happy-hour mojitos have just the right price, making this a hot Central Phoenix haunt. The bar and patio are great for sipping, dining, and people-watching, but for a more intimate experience the restaurant offers an elegant retreat. Try the Ticoz lettuce wraps, the empanadas, the sweet-corn tamales, or *barbacoa*

(simmered) beef. ✉*5114 N. 7th St., Central Phoenix* ☎*602/200–0160* ⊕*www.ticozofarizona.com* ☐*AE, MC, V* ✛*B4.*

DOWNTOWN PHOENIX

$ ✗**Gourmet House of Hong Kong.** Traditional Chinatown specialties like
CHINESE *chow fun* (thick rice noodles) are excellent at this simple, diner-style place: try the assorted-meat version, with chicken, shrimp, pork, and squid. Dishes with black-bean sauce are among the menu's best. Delights such as five-flavor frogs' legs, duck feet with greens, and beef tripe casserole are offered, if you're feeling adventurous. ✉*1438 E. McDowell Rd., Downtown Phoenix* ☎*602/253–4859* ⊕*www.gourmethouseof hongkong.com* ☐*DC, D, MC, V* ✛*C5.*

¢ ✗**Matt's Big Breakfast.** Fresh, filling, and simply fantastic, the food at
AMERICAN this itty-bitty, retro hip diner is a great way to start any day, especially
Fodor's Choice when you have time to walk or sleep it off afterward. Ingredients like
★ hearty bacon strips, jams, and whole-grain breads come from local sources, and each one is of the highest quality. Build your own omelet with a side of crispy hash browns or indulge in a Belgian waffle, but let it be known that Matt's fat pancakes are legendary. Lunch options include sandwiches and chili, or breakfast, again. Be prepared to wait, or call ahead for take out. ✉*Downtown Phoenix* ☎*602/254–1074* ⊕*www.mattsbigbreakfast.com* ⌕*Reservations not accepted* ☐*AE, MC, V* ☾*Closed Mon. No dinner* ✛*B5. 602/254–1074*

¢ ✗**Mrs. White's Golden Rule Café.** This lunch spot, located in a plain yellow
SOUTHERN building downtown, has been the best place in town for true Southern cooking for decades. The humble lunch counter and few surrounding tables are the setting in which to enjoy rich entrées—from fried chicken to catfish and pork chops. Each of the six entrées comes with corn bread and peach cobbler, all of which fill, not just the belly, but the soul. ✉*808 E. Jefferson St., Downtown Phoenix* ☎*602/262–9256* ⊕*www.mrswhitesgoldenrulecafe.com* ⌕*Reservations not accepted* ☐*No credit cards* ☾*Closed Sun.* ✛*B5.*

$ ✗**My Florist Café.** Cool, classic, and supremely stylish, My Florist is a
CAFÉ stunning pacesetter for the future of food and fun in the downtown Phoenix area. The sleek, high-ceiling interior, a wall of windows, hardwood floors, and a pristine jazz piano welcome enlightened locals who know good taste and great-tasting food—the menu consists of gourmet salads and sandwiches made with phenomenal breads baked fresh daily at the adjoining Willo Bakery. ✉*534 W. McDowell Rd., Downtown Phoenix* ☎*602/254–0333* ⊕*www.myfloristcafe.com.* ☐*AE, DC, MC, V* ✛*B5.*

$ ✗ **Pizzeria Bianco.** Brooklyn native Chris Bianco makes pizza with a
PIZZA passion in this small establishment on Heritage Square. His wood-fired-oven thin-crust creations incorporate the finest and freshest ingredients (including homemade mozzarella cheese). The brick oven was imported from Italy. Bar Bianco next door is a good place to relax with a beverage while you wait for your table. ■TIP➔Arrive a few minutes before they open at 5 PM to avoid the long wait, especially on Friday and Saturday nights. ✉*623 E. Adams St., Downtown Phoenix* ☎*602/258–8300* ⊕*www.pizzeriabianco.com* ☐*AE, MC, V* ☾*Closed Sun. and Mon. No lunch* ✛*B5.*

$ ✕ **The Rose & Crown.** Next to two of the Valley's major sports com-
BRITISH plexes, this American restaurant can't deny its European roots. The
Rose & Crown offers good, hearty, traditional, English pub grub—
fish-and-chips, bangers and mash, and shepherd's pie—with equally
hearty beers to wash it down. The atmosphere in the historic home is
comfortable and inviting, and without the decades of stale smoke, ale,
and grease. Expect a wait on game and special-event nights. ✉628 E.
Adams St., at 7th St., Downtown Phoenix ⊕*www.theroseandcrown
pub.org* ☎602/256–0223 ⌦*Reservations not accepted* ⊟*AE, D, DC,
MC, V* ✛*B5.*

$$$ ✕**Sens.** After irreconcilable differences with the landlord of downtown's
ASIAN favorite Asian food destination, it was the destiny of Hong Kong–born
chef-owner Johnny Chu to close up Fate and open Sens just down the
road. This Asian tapas and sake bar is dimly lit and cozy, but fast-paced
and hip. You'll see Chu behind the bar preparing the fusion fare that
has built him a cult following. Favorites include the papaya mango
salad, claypot-steamed clams, the volcano flamed beef (seared on a hot
stone), and the must-try soup gyoza (dumplings with the soup inside).
Chu's famed sweet and spicy wok dishes from Fate are served at lunch.
There are more than 40 kinds of sake, including Junmai, Ginjo, Daig-
injo, and unfiltered Nigori. Dinner is served until 2 AM on weekends,
accompanied by a DJ spinning tunes. ✉*705 N. 1st St., Suite 120,
Downtown Phoenix* ☎602/254–6424 ⊕*www.sensake.com* ⊟*MC,
V* ◷*Closed Sun.* ✛*B5.*

$ ✕**SWITCH.** Determined to make their mark on Central and Downtown
AMERICAN Phoenix, the creators of eclectic FEZ and latin Ticoz opened another
carefully conceived restaurant in 2007—SWITCH. The interior is dark,
making it a cool way to beat the summer heat, and the atmosphere is
perfect for enjoying lighthearted conversation and a meal before hit-
ting the museums or after taking in a show. The unique menu features
fresh sandwiches, healthful salads, a fabulous cheese platter, gourmet
burgers, steaks, seafood, baked goods, and crepes, along with pre-
mium beer, wine, and cocktails served in a sleek, modern setting with
couch conversation pits and one of downtown's best patios, free from
direct sunlight and traffic noise. ✉*2603 N. Central Ave., Downtown
Phoenix* ☎602/264–2295 ⊕*www.switchofarizona.com* ⊟*AE, D,
MC, V* ✛*B5.*

GREATER PHOENIX

CAMELBACK CORRIDOR

$$$$ ✕**Bistro 24.** Smart and stylish, with impeccable service, the Ritz's Bistro
FRENCH 24 has a parquet floor, colorful murals, an elegant bar, and an outdoor
patio. Take a break from shopping at nearby Biltmore Fashion Park
and enjoy the largest Cobb salad in town. For dinner, try classic French
steak au poivre with *frites*, grilled fish, or sushi. Happy hour is every day
from 5 to 7 in the bar. Sunday brunch is a local favorite. ✉*Ritz-Carlton
Hotel, 2401 E. Camelback Rd., Camelback Corridor* ☎602/952–2424
⊕*www.ritzcarlton.com* ⊟*AE, D, DC, MC, V* ◷*Closed Sun. and Mon.
evenings* ✛*C4.*

2

$$$
FRENCH
Fodor'sChoice
★

✕**Christopher's Crush.** Upon total renovation of the Biltmore Fashion Park, Chef Christopher Gross and wife Paola took their wildly successful Fermier Brasserie and Wine Bar from one end of the complex and reinvented it on the other in 2008. New, incredibly hip, and even better than their last incarnation, Crush delivers casual, contemporary elegance with a social, exhibition-kitchen bar, an open dining area, a private table, and an intimate lounge. The menu ranges from good-value wood-fired-oven pizzas and outstanding burgers and creative bar nosh to the pricier French inspirations. Gross is famous for dishes like the smoked truffle-infused filet mignon and stunning new masterpieces. Don't forget the Gruyère mashed potatoes on the side, and the Grande Marnier soufflé to finish. ✉*Biltmore Fashion Park, 2502 E. Camelback Rd., Camelback Corridor* ☎*602/522–2344* ⊕*www.chirstophersaz. com* ▭*AE, MC, V* ✛*C4.*

$
AMERICAN

✕**Delux.** Cool tones of blue and gray are accented by a granite-topped bar and a long candlelit communal table in the center of this small, hipster burger joint, Delux serves delicious salads, sandwiches, and burgers made with all-natural Harris Ranch beef—try the Delux Burger, with Maytag blue and Gruyère cheeses and caramelized onions. Sweet-potato or regular, crispy fries arrive in a fun mini shopping cart. Open every night until 2 AM, this is a great place to grab a late-night bite. Leave room for something cool and creamy at the Gelato Spot across the parking lot. ✉*3146 E. Camelback Rd., Camelback Corridor* ☎*602/522–2288* ⊕*www.deluxburger.com* ⚘*Reservations not accepted* ▭*AE, D, DC, MC, V* ✛*C4.*

$$$
GREEK

✕**Greekfest.** This informal but elegant restaurant is lovingly decorated with whitewashed walls, hardwood floors, and imported Greek artifacts. Search the menu's two pages of appetizers for *taramosalata* (caviar blended with lemon and olive oil) and *saganahi* (cheese flamed with brandy and extinguished with a squirt of lemon). The moussaka (lamb casserole) is wonderful, and don't forget dessert (try *galaktoboureko*, warm custard pie baked in phyllo). If all you seek is a sweet treat and some genuine Greek coffee, visit the adjoining Cafestia European dessert and coffeehouse. ✉*1940 E. Camelback Rd., Camelback Corridor* ☎*602/265–2990* ▭*AE, D, DC, MC, V* ⊕*www.thegreekfest.com* ✖*Closed Sun.* ✛*C4.*

$$
AMERICAN
Fodor'sChoice
★

✕**Noca.** This small, hidden strip-mall establishment went from grand opening to celebrated Valley restaurant in record time since it's July 2008 opening. Not only is it a hip place to see, be seen, and to sample everything, owner Eliot Wexler wants to see everyone happy. The waitstaff are veteran fine-dining servers, and the chefs manage to turn even cotton candy into a culinary work of art. Different nights of the week offer daily specials like the lauded Japanese wagyu cheesesteak with Kobe beef on Thursdays and a fried chicken dinner on Sundays. For starters, try their bacon and eggs (crispy poached egg with pork-belly confit, onion jam, and maple syrup) or the duck confit with a huckleberry waffle, dates, and vinaigrette. Sound a lot like breakfast? Wait until you try the doughnut holes for dessert. ✉*3118 E. Camelback Rd., Camelback Corridor* ☎*602/956–6622* ⊕*www.restaurantnoca. com* ▭*AE, MC, V* ✖*No lunch* ✛*C4.*

Many restaurants are tucked into strip malls, but some resorts have great restaurants, like T. Cook's at the Royal Palms.

$$$–$$$$
MEDITERRANEAN
Fodor's Choice
★

✗**T. Cook's at the Royal Palms.** One of the finest restaurants in the Valley, T. Cook's oozes romance, from the floor-to-ceiling windows with dramatic views of Camelback Mountain to its 1930s-style Spanish-colonial architecture and decor. The Mediterranean-influenced menu includes grilled "fireplace" fare like bone-in beef short rib with carrot risotto cake, paella, and a changing variety of enticing entrées. Desserts and pastries are works of art. For special-occasion meals, call on the services of the resort's Director of Romance. ✉*Royal Palms Resort & Spa, 5200 E. Camelback Rd., Camelback Corridor* ☎*602/840–3610* ⊕*www.royalpalmshotel.com* ⚓*Reservations essential* ▭*AE, D, DC, MC, V* ✛*D4.*

$$$
ITALIAN

✗**Tomaso's.** In a town where restaurants can come and go almost overnight, Tomaso's has been a favorite since 1977, and for good reason. Chef Tomaso Maggiore learned to cook at the family's restaurant in Palermo, Sicily, and honed his skills at the Culinary Institute of Rome. The result is authentic Italian cuisine that's consistently well prepared and delicious. The house specialty, *osso buco* (braised veal shank), is outstanding. Other notables include risotto and cannelloni. The Phoenix location has long been an unpretentious favorite, nestled into the northeast corner of a small, upscale shopping center in the heart of Camelback Corridor. Meanwhile, the elegant but enormous Chandler location is all about the party, with a large main dining room and lounge as well as a number of private rooms that accommodate parties of 10 to 120. ✉*3225 E. Camelback Rd., Camelback Corridor* ☎*602/956–0836* ▭*AE, D, DC, MC, V* ⊗*Closed Sun.* ⊗*No lunch weekends* ⊕*www.tomasos.com* ✛*D4.*

The Phoenix area dining scene is hot, and not just because of the many spicy Southwestern and Mexican ingredients.

$$$
AMERICAN
✕**True Food.** Renovated Biltmore Fashion Park is filled with new faces, like this unique collaboration of Fox Restaurant Concepts and natural health guru Dr. Andrew Weil. Weil has long promoted an "anti-inflammatory" diet comprised of healthy fats (olive and canola oils), gluten-free carbohydrates, hormone- and antibiotic-free meats—all drawn from organic, local, and sustainable sources—and very little dairy. Fox has taken Weil's teachings and turned them into one of Camelback Corridor's most fashionable eateries. The idea, and it works, is guilt-free dining in the purest sense, from the sustainable salmon and spelt pizzas to the butternut squash ravioli with yogurt filling. Even the wines and vodkas are organic. ✉*Biltmore Fashion Park, 2502 E. Camelback Rd., Ste. 135., Camelback Corridor* ☎*602/774–3488* ⊕*www.foxrestaurantconcepts.com/true_food_kitchen.html* ▤*AE, D, DC, MC, V* ✛*C4.*

$$$–$$$$
SOUTHWESTERN
✕**Vincent on Camelback.** Chef Guerithault is best known for creating French food with a Southwestern touch. You can make a meal of his famous appetizers: corn ravioli with white-truffle oil, or shrimp beignets with lavender dressing. The dessert menu overflows with intoxicating soufflés. The multiroom interior is intimate and elegant, but the service can be gruff. Better known among locals is the market held in the parking lot on Saturdays during the cooler months. ✉*3930 E. Camelback Rd., Camelback Corridor* ☎*602/224–0225* ⊕*www.vincentoncamelback.com* ♨*Reservations essential* ▤*AE, D, DC, MC, V* ☿*Closed Sun. No lunch Sat.* ✛*D4.*

$$
SEAFOOD
✕**Zen 32.** In the ebb and flow of central Phoenix, Zen 32 has managed to stay afloat while just about every other sushi restaurant has sunk—the convenient location, casually chic atmosphere, and

consistently creative rolls make it easy to understand why. The soft-shell crab, rainbow, and caterpillar rolls, and the succulent citrus yellowtail are favorites from the sushi menu, while the grill produces plenty of tasty nonfish fare. The covered patio faces the zoom and vroom of 32nd Street, but the soothing mist and meditation music create a tranquil, yes, even Zen-like atmosphere. ✉ *3160 E. Camelback Rd., Camelback Corridor* ☎ *602/954–8700* ⊕ *www.zen32.com* ⊟ *AE, MC, V* ⊘ *No lunch weekends* ✛ *C4.*

GLENDALE

$$ ✕ **Haus Murphy's.** On weekends you
GERMAN   can kick back with the accordionist at this charming storefront restaurant. Schnitzel is a specialty, not surprisingly, especially the spicy paprika version teamed with crispy chunks of fried potatoes and green beans. Sauerbraten, paired with tart red cabbage and two huge potato dumplings, is not for the faint of appetite. Wash everything down with a German beer—there are eight on tap—and save room for the homemade apple strudel and Black Forest torte. ✉ *5739 W. Glendale Ave., Glendale* ☎ *623/939–2480* ⊕ *www.hausmurphys.com* ⊟ *AE, D, MC, V* ⊘ *No lunch on Mon.* ✛ *A3.*

NORTH CENTRAL PHOENIX

$$ ✕ **Basis.** Fortunately, enough people have known about this little strip-
AMERICAN   mall secret to keep it going since 2003, but it's high time the gossip got
Fodor's Choice   out. In a bright, contemporary and tasteful space the menu is a great
★   mix of American creations with a splash of Southwestern and Cajun accents, including crisp calamari with vinaigrette, seared (to perfection) ahi tuna salad, a shrimp po'boy sandwich with chipotle aioli, blackened jumbo scallops and tenderloin medallions, or Basis mac and cheese. The staff is friendly, knowledgeable, and adept at pairing the perfect wine from their distinctive selection with their unusual dishes. Leave room for the guajillo squash flan or an ancho-chile brownie. ✉ *410 E. Thunderbird Rd., North Central Phoenix* ☎ *602/843–3689* ⊕ *www. basisnewamerican.com* ⊟ *AE, MC, V* ✛ *B3.*

$$ ✕ **Christo's Ristorante.** Don't judge this book by its cover. Cozy and unas-
ITALIAN   suming in a Phoenix strip mall, Christo's keeps its tables filled with loyal customers who enjoy fine Italian cuisine. Attentive servers ensure that your water glass never empties, and folks rave about the fresh seafood dishes, the roasted rack of lamb, the veal, and the delicious pasta dishes. Start with the delicious, panfried calamari. Dinner's main courses come with soup and salad. Before or after dinner, enjoy a cocktail in the piano bar or spend your evening snacking to the music from the bar menu.

A TOUCH OF PROVENCE MARKET

On Saturday from 9 AM to 1 PM, October through May, some of the Valley's tastiest creations, from crepes to paella to *panini*, can be found in the parking lot of Vincent on Camelback (⊕ *www.vincenton camelback.com*), at the Touch of Provence market. Overseen by the restaurant, young Vincent protégés cook up custom orders and people are encouraged to "custom tip" into jars labeled with creative causes such as "Saving for MIT" or "Honeymoon Fund." Touch of Provence also features a wine vendor and sellers of independent culinary curios like fresh pesto, honey, jam, and wines.

2

✉6327 N. 7th St., North Central Phoenix ☎602/264–1784 ⊕www. christos1.com ☰AE, D, DC, MC, V ⊙Closed Sun. ✛B3.

$ ✕**Taste of India.** This perennial favorite in the Valley specializes in north-
INDIAN ern Indian cuisine. Breads here—bhatura, naan, paratha—are superb, and vegetarians enjoy wonderful meatless specialties, including the eggplant-based benghan bhartha and bhindi masala, a tempting okra dish. Just about every spice in the rack is used for the lamb and chicken dishes, so be prepared to guzzle extra water—or an English beer. If your server says that a dish is spicy, trust them. ✉1609 E. Bell Rd., Ste. B4, North Central Phoenix ☎602/788–3190 ⊕www.tasteofindiaaz.com ☰AE, MC, V ✛C1.

$ ✕**Via Delosantos.** The family-owned restaurant looks a little rough
MEXICAN around the edges outside, but it's what's inside that counts—an accom-
Fodor'sChoice modating staff, an enormous and authentic Mexican menu, and one of
★ the best-tasting and best-priced house margaritas in town. Entrées are ample, and include more than just tired combinations of beef, beans, and cheese. Try the fajitas calabacitas with a yellow- and green-squash succotash; or the delicious chicken delosantos, a cheesy chicken breast and tortilla concoction. Expect to wait on weekends, either at the bar or outside, but the experience will be worth it. ✉9120 N. Central Ave., North Central Phoenix ☎602/997–6239 ⌲Reservations not accepted ☰AE, D, DC, MC, V ✛B3.

PARADISE VALLEY

$$$ ✕**elements.** Perched on the side of Camelback Mountain at the Sanctu-
ECLECTIC ary Resort, this stylish modern restaurant offers breathtaking desert-sunset and city-light views. There's a cordial community table where you can sit and order such appetizers as the trilogy of duck, wild escargot wontons, and fried calamari with miso-scallion vinaigrette. Seasonal specials and entrées are excellent; among the best is the bacon-wrapped fillet of beef with blue cheese and merlot demi-glace. ✉Sanctuary on Camelback Mountain, 5700 E. McDonald Dr., Paradise Valley ☎480/607–2300 ⊕www.sanctuaryoncamelback.com ⌲Reservations essential ☰AE, D, DC, MC, V ✛D4.

$$$ ✕**Lon's at the Hermosa.** In an adobe hacienda hand-built by cowboy artist
AMERICAN Lon Megargee, this romantic spot has sweeping vistas of Camelback Mountain and the perfect patio for after-dinner drinks under the stars. Megargee's art and cowboy memorabilia decorate the dining room, while Chef Michael Rusconi's creations decorate the tables. The menu changes seasonally, but includes appetizers like short ribs. Wood-grilled, melt-in-your-mouth filet mignon over Gorgonzola mashed potatoes, and more exotic dishes like cactus pear–lacquered duck breast are main-course options. Phoenicians love the Sunday brunch. ✉Hermosa Inn, 5532 N. Palo Cristi Dr., Paradise Valley ☎602/955–7878 ⊕www.lons. com ☰AE, D, DC, MC, V ⊙No lunch Sat. ✛D3.

SOUTH PHOENIX

¢ ✕**Carolina's.** This small, nondescript restaurant in South Phoenix makes
MEXICAN the most delicious, thin-as-air flour tortillas imaginable. In-the-know locals and downtown working folk have been lining up at Carolina's for years to partake of the homey, inexpensive Mexican food, so it makes sense that she expanded to let a little more of the Valley in on the action

The tacos, tamales, burritos, flautas, and enchiladas are served on paper plates. You can buy tortillas to take away, but good luck getting home with a full bag. There also a branch in North Central Phoenix at 2126 E. Cactus Rd. ✉*1202 E. Mohave St., South Phoenix* ☏*602/252–1503* ☐*AE, D, DC, MC, V* ⊘*Closed Sun. Dinner on weekdays only until 7:30 PM and Sat. until 6 PM* ⊕*www.carolinasmex.com* ✛*C6.*

$ ✗**Honey Bear's BBQ.** Honey Bear's motto—"You don't need no teeth to
SOUTHERN   eat our meat"—may fall short on grammar, but this place isn't packed with folks looking to improve their language skills. In 1986 childhood friends Mark Smith and Gary Clark expanded from a catering business to their first wildly succesful Honey Bear's restaurant on East Van Buren Street; today they are in demand all across the Valley. This is Tennessee-style barbecue, which means smoky baby back ribs basted in a tangy sauce. The sausage-enhanced "cowbro" beans and scallion-studded potato salad are great sides, and, teeth or no teeth, finishing off with a no-frills but tasty piece of sweet-potato pie will put a smile on your face. All three locations feel like neighborhood joints; branches are at 2824 Central Avenue in Phoenix and 7670 South Priest Drive in Tempe. ✉*5012 E. Van Buren St., South Phoenix* ☏*602/273–9148* ⊕*www.honeybearsbbq.com* ◁*Reservations not accepted* ☐*AE, D, MC, V* ✛*D5.*

$ ✗**Los Dos Molinos.** In a hacienda that belonged to silent-era movie star
MEXICAN   Tom Mix, this fun restaurant focuses on New Mexican–style Mexican food. That means *hot.* New Mexico chiles form the backbone and fiery breath of the dishes, and the green-chile enchilada and beef taco are potentially lethal. The red salsa and enchiladas with egg on top are excellent, as is the popular shrimp Veracruz with red chile sauce. This adobe building is in a largely Hispanic neighborhood in the South Mountain foothills, and features a funky courtyard where you can sip potent margaritas while waiting for a table. Fodors.com users agree that this is a must-do dining experience if you want authentic New Mexican–style food, but be prepared to swig lots of water. There are less authentic experiences at the Downtown Phoenix and Mesa locations. ✉*8646 S. Central Ave., South Phoenix* ☏*602/243–9113* ◁*Reservations not accepted* ☐*AE, D, DC, MC, V* ⊘*Closed Sun. and Mon.* ⊕*www.losdosmolinos.com* ✛*B6.*

$$$$ ✗**Stockyards Restaurant.** If you're looking for a hearty meal, "Arizona's
STEAK   Original Steak House" is the place to go. Succulent, signature prime rib, immensely thick steaks, fresh seafood, and poultry are complemented by rib-sticking side dishes such as whiskey-sweet-potato mash, cowboy beans with chorizo, and roasted corn. The handsome dining-room decor features Old West heavy wood, etched glass, and pressed-tin ceilings without a hint of hokeyness. A beautiful hand-carved mahogany bar and huge cut-glass chandelier adorn the 1889 Saloon in back. ✉*5009 E. Washington, South Phoenix* ☏*602/273–7378* ⊕ *www. stockyardsrestaurant.com* ☐*AE, D, DC, MC, V* ⊘*No lunch weekends.* ✛*D5.*

WEST PHOENIX

¢–$ ✗ **Pepe's Taco Villa.** The neighborhood's not fancy, and neither is this
MEXICAN restaurant, but in a town with a lot of gringo-ized south-of-the-border
FodorśChoice fare, this is the real friendly, real deal. Tacos *rancheros*—spicy, shred-
★ ded pork pungently lathered with adobo paste—are a dream. So are
the green-corn tamales and authentic imported *machacado* (air-dried
beef). The chiles rellenos may be the best in the state. All are perfect
with a margarita from the full bar. Don't leave without trying the sensational mole, a rich sauce fashioned from chiles and chocolate. ✉ *2108
W. Camelback Rd., West Phoenix* ☎ *602/242–0379* ⊕ *www.pepestaco
villa.com* ▭ *AE, D, MC, V* ⊙ *Closed Tues.* ✛ *A4.*

¢–$ ✗ **Pho Bang.** While this little hole-in-the-wall restaurant has gotten
VIETNAMESE renewed mileage as senator John McCain's favorite pho stop, at the end
of the day it's all about simplicity and freshness of the food, pho sure.
The house specialty is *tom va bo nuong vi* (#35 on the menu): the server
brings three plates, one with transparently thin slices of marinated beef
and raw shrimp; another with piles of mint, lettuce, cilantro, pickled
leeks, cucumber, and carrot; and the last with rice paper. You fire up
the portable grill and cook the beef and shrimp. When they're done,
combine with the veggies, fold into rice paper, and start dunking. The
cha gio eggrolls are a delicious pho starter. ✉ *1702 W. Camelback Rd.,
Suite 14, West Phoenix* ☎ *602/433–9440* ▭ *MC, V* ✛ *B4.*

SCOTTSDALE

CENTRAL SCOTTSDALE

$$$$ ✗ **Canal.** It's flashy, loud, expensive, and hip. Welcome to Canal, and
ECLECTIC just about every other restaurant located near the Scottsdale Waterfront.
While Canal may not suit everyone's taste, it does appeal to quite a few
taste buds in ways that other hot spots do not. If you go, save up for the
30 Dollar Sandwich, which seems to be the one item that lives up to its
price tag. This meaty creation is stacked on buttery challah with Boursin
cheese, mushrooms, heirloom tomatoes, watercress, and asparagus—all
topped with a batter-fried lobster claw. Enjoy it on the patio looking
out over the waterfront. For a mellower atmosphere, arrive before peak
dinner hours on the weekend or go during the week. ✉ *7144 E. Stetson
Dr., Ste. 250, Central Scottsdale* ☎ *480/949–9000* ⊕ *www.canalaz.com*
▭ *AE, D, DC, MC, V* ⊙ *Closed Sun* ✛ *G2.*

$$ ✗ **Carlsbad Tavern.** A mix of cavern meets tavern, this longtime local
MEXICAN favorite is aptly named, as it attracts a seemingly nocturnal and not-too-
picky crowd. Best loved for happy-hour and late-night snacks, this busy
New Mexico–style eatery also serves big portions of such tasty dishes
as a half pound habanero cheeseburger, green-chile mashed potatoes,
chipotle barbecue baby back ribs, and *carne adovada*, a spicy, slow-
roasted pork specialty. They'll custom mix your margarita with fresh
lime and lemon juice and blend it with your choice of some 35 tequilas.
There's a late-night menu for the after-10 PM crowd. ✉ *3313 N. Hayden
Rd., Central Scottsdale* ☎ *480/970–8164* ⊕ *www.carlsbadtavern.com*
▭ *AE, D, MC, V* ✛ *F4.*

$$ ✗ **Don & Charlie's.** Attention sports fans! This hangout is a favorite
STEAK with major-leaguers in town for spring training, playoff, or Superbowl

LOCAL CHAINS WORTH A TASTE

The Valley of the Sun has some good reliable chain restaurants, particularly good for large groups (and large portions). Here are the most popular:

Elephant Bar. The predominantly Pacific Rim, elephant-size menu at this large chain offers some pleasant Cajun (catfish and jambalaya) and plain old American (New York steak, lemon herb chicken) entrées. Pacific Rim specialties include Miso Yaki fire-grilled salmon and the delicious Pan-Asian vegetable and noodle soup with teriyaki chicken skewers. The portions are large, so consider sharing dessert—try the giant cookie ice-cream sandwich. ⊕ *www.elephantbar.com*

Garduño's. This gargantuan Mexican restaurant has several equally ample locations in Glendale, Chandler, and Central Phoenix, all made to accommodate large parties in the mood to eat and be entertained. Try the unusually good green-chile clam chowder or the fresh guacamole made table-side for starters, and experience a grilled chimichanga or fajitas for your main course. ⊕ *www.gardunosrestaurants.com*

Morton's of Chicago. The Windy City chain is famous for exceptional service, immense steaks, and entertaining table-side presentations, but most of all for consistency. Its business-formal atmosphere, menus, and operations are replicated at the Camelback Road and North Scottsdale locations. If you've been hankerin' for a great, aged prime steak, you won't go wrong here. The monstrous 24-ounce porterhouse or 14-ounce double-cut fillet can satisfy the hungriest cowpoke. ⊕ *www.mortons.com*

Nello's. Leave it to two brothers from Chicago to come up with the motto "In Crust We Trust," and Nello's excels in both thin-crust and deep-dish pies. Try traditional varieties heaped with homemade sausage and mushrooms, or go vegetarian with the spinach pie. Pasta entrées are very good, too, and the family-style salads are inventive and fresh. Each of the five Valley locations has its own neighborhood feel: The original Tempe parlor hosts plenty of regulars, while the Old Town Scottsdale location offers more of an upscale, art-clad pizza experience. ⊕ *www.nellosscottsdale.com*

Oregano's. Huge portions are an understatement at this eight-branch casual Chicago-theme eatery. Come hungry and feast on fresh salads, tasty baked sandwiches, pizza (deep-dish, thin crust, or stuffed), and pasta dishes. The young, friendly staff and kitschy 1950s decor create a fun and comfortable, family-friendly vibe. Save room for the famous pizza cookie: a half-pound of chocolate-chip or white-chocolate macadamia-nut cookie dough baked on a 6-inch pizza pan and topped with three scoops of vanilla-bean ice cream. ⊕ *www.oreganos.com*

Zoe's Kitchen. Cool, clean, fast, inexpensive, and nutritious, this link in a national chain is worth noticing. Hit the Camelback area spas or downtown museums and galleries, then have a light but filling, Greek-inspired meal without the guilt. Each location is uniform in its bright, modern cafeterialike setting, where first you order, then you sit. Make sure to try the Greek chicken pita or Greek salad, and the coleslaw with feta cheese. ⊕ *www.zoeskitchen.com*

games. A venerable chophouse, D&C specializes in "American comforts" with prime-grade steak and sports memorabilia—the walls are covered with pictures, autographs, and uniforms. The spacious and Cheers-like interior, friendly staff. and New York sirloin, prime rib, and double-thick lamb chops are a hit; sides include au gratin potatoes and creamed spinach. ⊠7501 E. Camelback Rd., Central Scottsdale 480/990–0900 ⊕www.donandcharlies.com ⊟AE, D, DC, MC, V ⊗No lunch ✛H1.

$$$
FRENCH
✕**L'Ecole.** You won't regret putting yourself in the talented hands of the student chefs at the Valley's premier cooking academy. Choose from an extensive list of French-inspired entrées or the four-course prix-fixe menu, available for lunch ($30) and dinner ($35). The fine-dining atmosphere is designed to give students (who fill each restaurant position) and customers the impression of the real thing, which is why customers keep coming back. The menu changes seasonally, but expect inventive appetizers such as lobster gratin, stuffed rabbit saddle, ricotta gnocchi, and entrées such as filet mignon. ⊠Scottsdale Culinary Institute, 8100 E. Camelback Rd., Central Scottsdale 480/425–3111 ⊕www.dine withsci.com ⌖Reservations essential ⊟AE, D, DC, MC, V ⊗Closed weekends ✛F4.

ECLECTIC
$$$
Fodor'sChoice
★
✕**Medizona.** The daring (and pricey) combination of Mediterranean-meets-New Mexican cuisine has been pleasing renowned critics and foodies from across the country and all over town for a decade. Though it appears somewhat lackluster from the outside, the inside is intimate and charming, with Saltillo-tile floors and a mix of brick and yellow walls with accents of dark blue and white that create a pleasant background for the restaurant's marriage of ethnic fare. Where else have you ever had tantalizing rabbit baklava, or achiote-rubbed panfried salmon with crayfish-corn risotto and morel mushroom–baby clam sauce, or Moroccan-spiced chicken with black-bean saffron couscous and cilantro yogurt sauce, or prickly-pear tiramisu to top off such a palette-puzzling meal? For something more casual, enjoy the new adjoining wine lounge and tapas bar. ⊠ 7217 E. 4th Ave., Central Scottsdale 480/947–9500 ⊕www.medizonarestaurant.com ⊟AE, MC, V ⊗Closed Sun. ✛G2.

$$$
MEDITERRANEAN
✕**Olive & Ivy.** Tucked into the south side of the high-traffic, high-priced Scottsdale Waterfront complex, Olive & Ivy is a pleasant surprise. The contemporary restaurant fronts a long, elegant bar with endless bottles of alcohol. By day the light comes from the wall of windows that look out onto the ample patio with cozy couches and fire pits, as well as the man-made waterway for which the complex is named. By night the giant space becomes intimate with dim, designer lighting. A full dinner menu, featuring a mix of fish and meat creations with Italian and Mediterranean twists like white-shrimp risotto and veal and spinach ravioli is available, but the delicious variety of appetizers, like bacon-wrapped Medjoul dates, beet salad with goat-cheese dressing, and flatbreads make for a good meal. Wash them down with something from their ample wine list or one of their unique, not-too-sweet peach hibiscus margaritas. ⊠7135 E. Camelback Rd., Ste. 195, Central Scottsdale 480/715–2200 ⊕www.foxrrc.com/olive_ivy.html ⌖Reservations not accepted ⊟AE, D, DC, MC, V ✛F1.

$
AMERICAN

✗**Original Pancake House.** The flapjacks here inspire worship from locals, who wait patiently for a table on weekends. The signature apple pancake is made from homemade batter poured over sautéed apples, then baked to perfection and glazed with cinnamon sugar. Other varieties, such as the Dutch Baby—oven-baked and served with whipped butter and powdered sugar—trump any chain-variety flapjacks. Some Fodors.com users claim that the atmosphere is a bit worn, but perhaps that's because

everything is made from scratch. Bring plenty of cash; their access to technology is as dated as the decor. ⊠*6840 E. Camelback Rd., Central Scottsdale* 🖀*480/946–4902* ⊕*www.originalpancakehouse.com* 🖚*Reservations not accepted* ▤*No credit cards* ⊘*No dinner* ✛*F1.*

$$$
ECLECTIC
Fodor's Choice
★

✗**Rancho Pinot Grill.** The attention to quality paid by the husband-and-wife proprietors here—he manages, she cooks—has made this one of the town's most lauded dining spots. Though the high ceilings ask for drama while the minimalist cowboy decor cries out for something cozier, thoughts of the ambivalent atmosphere and almost secret-handshake location are completely forgotten upon the first bite of food and replaced with taste-bud heaven. Chef Chrysa Robertson's inventive menu changes daily, depending on what's fresh. If you're lucky, you'll get a crack at the flatiron steak with arugula and salsa verde, the succulent short ribs with posole-style hominy and cojita cheese, or Nonni's Sunday chicken with toasted polenta. Organic and locally grown and raised ingredients are used whenever possible, which is just another reason why you'll want to return as many times as possible. ⊠*6208 N. Scottsdale Rd., northwest of Trader Joe's in Lincoln Village Shops, Central Scottsdale* 🖀*480/367–8030* ⊕*www.ranchopinot. com* ▤*AE, D, DC, MC, V* ⊘*Closed Sun. and Mon. mid-May–Nov. No lunch* ✛*E3.*

$$$
SEAFOOD

✗**Salt Cellar.** It's rare to find a restaurant in a cellar, especially in the desert. Originally a hamburger joint frequented by Arizona State University students, the South Scottsdale space has been transformed with crisp linen tablecloths and nautical decor. The kitchen dishes out straightforward, fresh—very fresh—seafood, and a friendly waitstaff serves it up. There's a reason this place has been in business since 1971. For starters, try Chesapeake Bay crab cakes, oysters Rockefeller, or turtle soup. Move on to such entrées as Idaho trout, Yakimono Hawaiian ahi, or charcoal-broiled king salmon. If you're really hungry, splurge on the 5-pound Maine lobster. If the main menu is a bit pricey for your taste, try the Oyster Bar menu, discounted from 4 to 7 PM and 10 PM to 1 AM. ⊠*550 N. Hayden Rd., South Scottsdale* 🖀*480/947–1963* ⊕*www.saltcellarrestaurant.com* ▤*AE, MC, V* ⊘*No lunch* ✛*E5.*

2

$ ✕**Scratch Pastries.** Duc and Noelle Liao are a model couple, literally.
CAFÉ The two met in Paris where Duc worked as a fashion photographer
Fodor'sChoice and Noelle as a model. Now, the two are the hottest pair in pastry
★ making. A graduate of Le Cordon Bleu, Duc Liao conjures up sublime
creations, both salty and sweet, from a savory duck-breast sandwich
and a mouthwatering mushroom quiche to perfectly flaky croissants
and a delicately sweet, parfaitlike mont blanc dessert. Don't let the
pastry shop's location in a strip mall fool you; this is a flavor trip all
the way to France. Expect crowds during peak lunch hours. ✉*7620
E. Indian School Rd., Ste. 103, Central Scottsdale* ☎*480/947–0057*
⊕*www.scratchpastries.com* ⌖*Reservations not accepted* ☰*AE, MC,
V* ⊗*No dinner* ✛*H3.*

OLD TOWN

$ ✕**AZ 188.** Prime for beautiful people–watching, this sleek, window-
AMERICAN walled restaurant serves some of the Valley's best (and biggest) cocktails
Fodor'sChoice and food at affordable prices. Large portions of tasty salads, sandwich-
★ es, sumptuous burgers (try the Au Poivre II), and perfectly poured cos-
mopolitans never fail to satisfy. The room is open and the atmosphere
is lively, just like the mixed clientele that jam-packs it every weekend.
If you're seeking quiet, dine outside on the beautiful patio overlooking
Scottsdale Mall. It's a great stop before and after an Old Town event
or a night of partying, Scottsdale style. ✉*7353 E. Scottsdale Mall,
Old Town* ☎*480/994–5576* ⊕*www.az88.com* ⌖*Reservations not
accepted* ☰*AE, D, DC, MC, V* ⊗*No lunch weekends* ✛*H3.*

$$ ✕**Bandera.** For a tasty dinner, try this casual, high-volume spot. The
AMERICAN rotisserie chicken is wonderfully moist and meaty; you'll see the birds
spinning in the window before you even walk through the door. Salads,
fresh fish, prime rib, and meat loaf are also on the menu, but the mashed
potatoes and grilled artichoke are divine. If you get here during prime
eating hours, especially on weekends, be prepared to wait. ✉*3821
N. Scottsdale Rd., Old Town* ☎*480/991 3524* ⊕*www.hillstone.com*
⌖*Reservations not accepted* ☰*AE, DC, MC, V* ⊗*No lunch* ✛*G3.*

$$$ ✕**Cowboy Ciao.** Looking for a culinary kick in Old Town Scottsdale?
ECLECTIC This kitchen, clad in pleasing cowboy cupid murals, weds Southwestern
fare and Italian flair, and it's no shotgun wedding. The menu changes frequently, but offers standby favorites such as espresso-rubbed filet mignon
and slow-roasted short ribs. The bread pudding creations are must-tries.
The wine list represents more than 40 countries and features 225 grape
varietals. Too much to choose from? Ask for the *Nifty Fifty,* a one-page
list of guest favorites. ✉*7133 E. Stetson Dr., Old Town* ☎*480/946–3111*
⊕*www.cowboyciao.com* ☰*AE, D, DC, MC, V* ✛*G2.*

$$ ✕**Malee's on Main.** This cozy but fashionable, casual eatery in the heart
THAI of Scottsdale's Main Street Arts District serves sophisticated, Thai-
inspired fare. Try the best-selling, crispy *pla:* flash-fried whitefish fillets
with fresh cilantro and sweet jalapeño garlic sauce. The spicy garlic
sautéed spinach is a must, along with curries made to order with tofu,
chicken, beef, pork, or seafood. You specify the spiciness—from mild to
flaming—but even "mild" dishes have a bite. ✉*7131 E. Main St., Old
Town* ☎*480/947–6042* ⊕*www.maleesthaibistro.com* ⌖*Reservations
essential* ☰*AE, DC, MC, V* ✛*F3.*

$$$
SOUTHWESTERN
Fodor'sChoice
★

✗ **The Mission** This new Scottsdale hot spot will take your taste buds to new levels. Not only is the food to live for, the dark and sophisticated space is also adjacent to an historic Catholic mission. Whether the savvy staff is explaining Spanish phrases on the menu or guiding you through the intricacies of tequila tasting, it's clear they like this place as much as the customers. Sit at the elegant bar or fireside on the patio and enjoy an avocado margarita with supreme starters or sides like table-side-crafted guacamole; Mission fries with lemon, chile, and cumin; or grits with chipotle and honey. House favorites include the pecan- and mesquite-grilled pork shoulder, grass-fed Uruguayan rib eye, and scallops with smoked tomato and Serrano ham. The weekend brunch menu alone could keep this place afloat with its *pollo a la brasa y waffles* (chicken waffles) and bacon-infused maple syrup, *chilaquiles* (like a spicy Spanish lasagna), and outstanding corn-and-crab pancakes with smoked Oaxacan pasilla crema. ⊠ *3815 N. Brown Ave., Old Town* ☎ *480/636–5005* ⊕ *www.themissionaz.com* ☐ *AE, MC, V* ⊹ *G3.*

$$$
JAPANESE
Fodor'sChoice
★

✗ **Sea Saw.** Chef Nobu Fukada is creating some of the Valley's most interesting food at this small, simple eatery. "Tapanese" cuisine—small plates of Japanese tapas such as baked black cod marinated in miso, allow you to sample lots of different tastes. Other delights include the whitefish carpaccio (served warm) and the sushi foie gras. If you're feeling really adventurous, try the "Omakase Menu," a 10-course dinner created from what's fresh that day. The few tables and bar seats fill up quickly, so if you have to wait, do as the locals do—indulge in a glass of wine next door at Kazimierz wine bar. ⊠ *7133 E. Stetson Dr., Old Town* ☎ *480/481–9463* ⊕ *www.seasaw.net* ⌁ *Reservations essential* ☐ *AE, D, DC, MC, V* ⊙ *No lunch* ⊹ *G1.*

NORTH SCOTTSDALE

$$$$
STEAK

✗ **Bourbon Steak.** Formerly the site of the once-renowned Marquesa restaurant, this upscale steak restaurant was opened in February 2008 by top-rated chef Michael Mina, and has been living up to the royal reputation of the Scottsdale Princess. Its severe but stunning stone-and-glass entry lets people know that they are in for something serious—seriously good. Its modern elegance is as tasty to the eyes as the food is to the palate. Select from American-grade or Japanese Kobe beef. The flaming doughnuts Foster makes a perfect finish to a fine meal. ⊠ *Fairmont Scottsdale Princess Resort, 7575 E. Princess Dr., North Scottsdale* ☎ *480/585–4848* ⊕ *www.Fairmont.com/Scottsdale* ⌁ *Reservations essential* ☐ *AE, D, DC, MC, V* ⊙ *Closed Mon. and Tues. Brunch only Sun. No lunch* ⊹ *E1.*

$$$
AMERICAN

✗ **Eddie V's.** The DC Ranch area is booming with great restaurants to keep the north Valley locals happy, including this one. By night Eddie V's appears almost too sophisticated for its upscale-mall location. Sleek lighting filters through massive panes of tinted glass, revealing an elegant, contemporary interior clad in crisp linens. Specializing in fresh seafood done right (try the Hong Kong–style Chilean sea bass or the broiled scallops), grilled meats, and fine wines, the place is great for fine dining. But with its inviting bar and lounge area and succulent appetizers like kung pao–style calamari and a variety of fresh oysters, Eddie's is also enormously popular (and slightly more affordable) as a happy-hour spot. ✉ *20715 N. Pima Rd., Ste. F1, North Scottsdale* ☎ *480/538–8468* ⊕ *www.eddiev.com* ▭ *AE, D, DC, MC, V* ✛ *D1.*

$$
LATIN AMERICAN
✕ **Havana Cafe.** Tapas are marvelous at this local chain of cozy Cuban-style cantinas. The rich, toucan- and banana-inspired café atmosphere allows guests to step into a tropical, culinary vacation. While sampling authentic Cuban creations like shrimp pancakes, ham and chicken croquettes, Cuban tamales, and paella heaped with a whole Maine lobster, diners can shed the stresses of an arid metropolis. New Puerto Rican menu items include stuffed green plantains and plantains with pork cracklings. There's something special for vegetarians, too: *cho cho*, a fresh chayote squash stuffed with loads of veggies and topped with a Jamaican curry sauce, and the new rice with pigeon peas. Two other locations are in Camelback Corridor and Ahwatukee. ✉ *6245 E. Bell Rd., North Scottsdale* ☎ *480/991–1496* ⊕ *www.havanacafe-az.com* ▭ *AE, D, DC, MC, V* ⊘ *No lunch Sun.* ✛ *E1.*

¢
AMERICAN
✕ **Kashman's Place.** This local duo of Jewish delis came all the way from Brooklyn, and brought a wealth of other influences with it. Nancy and Steve Kashman's original North Scottsdale location was so wildly popular that they decided to spread the love around with one more. They serve sumptuous omelets with crisp home fries, creatively blended salads, and piled-high sandwiches (like the Pennsylvania baked ham and Brie with champagne mustard on baguette) to a large following of locals and Fodors.com fans. Everything is deliciously fresh, and portions are generous. New York bagels (including the not-so-traditional multigrain, protein "power" bagel) are done the authentic way—boiled and baked on the premises using filtered water duplicated from New York City water samples. The matzo-ball soup is award-winning. Expect lines on weekends. ✉ *32531 N. Scottsdale Rd., at Ashler Hills, North Scottsdale* ☎ *480/488–5274* ✉ *23425 N. Scottsdale Rd., Ste. 6, Pinnacle Peak, North Scottsdale* ☎ *480/585–6221* ⊕ *www.kashmansplace.net* ▭ *AE, D, DC, MC, V* ⊘ *No dinner* ✛ *D1.*

$$$
ECLECTIC
✕ **Razz's Restaurant and Bar.** There's no telling what part of the globe chef-proprietor and maestro of fusion Erasmo "Razz" Kamnitzer will use for culinary inspiration on any given day, but his creations give dormant taste buds a wake-up call: black-bean paella is a twist on a Spanish theme; South American bouillabaisse is a fragrant fish stew stocked with veggies; and *bah mie goreng* teams noodles with fish, meat, and vegetables, perked up with dried cranberries and almonds. Count on it—Razz'll dazzle. ✉ *10315 N. Scottsdale Rd., North Scottsdale* ☎ *480/905–1308* ⊕ *www.razzrestaurant.com* ▭ *AE, D, DC, MC, V* ⊘ *Closed Sun. and Mon. and June–Aug. No lunch* ✛ *D1.*

$$–$$$
JAPANESE
✕ **Sushi on Shea.** You may be in the middle of the desert, but the sushi here will make you think you're at the ocean's edge. Fresh yellowtail, toro, shrimp, scallops, freshwater eel, and even monkfish liver pâté are among the long list of delights. *Nabemono* (hot pot or meals-in-a-bowl) are prepared at your table. The best dish? Maybe it's the *una-ju* (broiled freshwater eel with a sublime smoky scent) served over sweet rice. The fact that some people believe eel is an aphrodisiac only adds to its charm. The bento box is a good way to sample a variety of menu offerings. ✉ *7000 E. Shea Blvd., North Scottsdale* ☎ *480/483–7799* ⊕ *www.sushionshea.com* ▭ *AE, D, DC, MC, V* ✛ *E2.*

$$–$$$ ✗ **Tapino Kitchen & Wine Bar.** In the dining chaos of one of Scottsdale's
AMERICAN busiest intersections, this sleek, award-winning kitchen and wine bar
is a savory sight for overwhelmed eyes and under-whelmed taste buds.
Pick a quiet corner table or head into the highly social Vino Lounge
and take a seat on one of the stark white couches with the rest of the
hip crowd. Or if you're feeling adventurous, take a seat at the curved
central bar and let the personable, food- and wine-savvy bartenders
make up your mind. Wherever you sit, you can enjoy a vast menu of
unusual tapas including beef carpaccio with garlic aioli, petite lobster corn dogs with fancy ballpark dipping sauces, ricotta fondue with
elephant garlic and crostini, plenty of cheese plates, and a host of fine
wines. A late-night menu is served until 2 AM. ✉ *7000 E. Shea Blvd.,
Ste. 1010, North Scottsdale* ☎ *480/991–6887* ▭ *AE, D, DC, MC, V*
☿ *Closed Mon.–Wed. No lunch* ✛ *E2.*

$$$ ✗ **Zinc Bistro.** No detail was overlooked at this replica of a Parisian bis-
FRENCH tro, from the zinc-top bar and linen-draped tables topped with butcher
paper to the sidewalk café seating and mirrored walls. A Valley local,
chef-owner Matt Carter, who recently invested his time, money, and tal-
ents into the Mission in Old Town, prepares traditional French cuisine
almost as if he were a native Frenchman, though some Fodors.com users
claim that the waitstaff go a bit too far in emulating discourteous French
waiters. Bistro classics such as the flatiron steak, cassoulet with duck
confit, and the omelet piled high with pommes frites are excellent. Also
recommended are the roasted Dungeness crab and mushroom crepes,
and the onion soup. The wine list offers a good selection of reasonably
priced French wines. ✉ *15034 N. Scottsdale Rd., Kierland Commons,
North Scottsdale* ☎ *480/603–0922* ⊕ *www.zincbistroaz.com* ✍ *Res-
ervations not accepted* ▭ *AE, DC, MC, V* ✛ *E1.*

TEMPE AND AROUND

CHANDLER

$$$ ✗ **Andrew's New American @ Citrus Cafe.** Chef Andrew Parpadelle took
ECLECTIC the helm in 2008 to give this small, elegant yet casual, restaurant the
menu lift it needed. Though it was a longstanding Chandler tradition of
French food, to some the ritual was wearing a bit thin. Instead of just
French, the culinary offerings now cover a variety of cross-country and
overseas ethnicities. The romantic candlelit dining room is the perfect
setting for lovely items like the Arizona chopped salad, grilled corn-
bread with mole buttermaple-glazed quail, and merlot braised Black
Angus rib eye. Guests can greet Parpadelle as he scans the restaurant
and shares his expertise with a team of understudy chefs. ✉ *2330 N.
Alma School Rd., Chandler* ☎ *480/899–0502* ▭ *AE, D, DC, MC, V*
☿ *Closed Mon. No lunch* ✛ *G6.*

$–$$ ✗ **C-Fu Gourmet.** This is serious Chinese food, the kind you'd expect to
CHINESE find on Mott Street in New York City's Chinatown or Grant Avenue
in San Francisco. The large restaurant is generally loud and chaotic,
but there's a good reason why tons of Valley residents will endure long
drives and wait times to be part of it. C-Fu's specialty is fish, and you can
watch several species swimming around the big holding tanks. Shrimp
are fished out of the tank, steamed, and bathed in a potent garlic sauce.

Clams in black-bean sauce and tilapia in a ginger-scallion sauce also hit all the right buttons. If you don't find what you're looking for on the menu, tell them what you want and they'll make it. There's a daily dim sum brunch, too. ✉ *2051 W. Warner Rd., Chandler* ☎ *480/899–3888* ⊕ *www.cfugourmet.com* ▤ *AE, D, DC, MC, V* ✛ *G6.*

$ ✗ **Cyclo.** It's always exciting to find
VIETNAMESE an outstanding one-of-a-kind restaurant in a town that has more than its fair share of chain establishments, and Cyclo is just that. The friendly and gracious owner Justina Dwong is as much a draw as the well-prepared Vietnamese food. Try the *bánh xéo,* a crispy, turmeric-yellow crepe filled with juicy bites of pork and shrimp, or crispy *cha gío,* a spicy lemongrass chicken. A French-inspired, jasmine-scented crème brûlée provides a perfect ending to the meal in a lovely setting. ✉ *1919 W. Chandler Blvd., Chandler* ☎ *480/963–4490* ⊕ *www.cycloaz.com* ▤ *MC, V* 🍴 *BYOB* ⊘ *Closed Sun. and Mon.* ✛ *G6.*

$$ ✗ **El Zocalo Mexican Grill.** A positively caliente experience that might be
MEXICAN one of the key reasons to put Chandler on your map. With high ceilings, plenty of open space, and a modern twist, El Zocalo is a far cry from the typical Mexican cantina. Enjoy a huge selection of Mexico's finest tequilas and sip on Spanish wines while savoring some authentic Mexican fare out on the inviting, courtyard-style patio. As the night marches on, push your table aside and put on your dancing shoes for some fantastic salsa music performed live by a top-notch local band. ✉ *28 S. San Marcos Pl., Chandler* ☎ *480/722–0303* ⊕ *www.elzocalo. com* ▤ *AE, D, DC, MC, V* ⊘ *Closed Sun. and Mon.* ✛ *G6.*

$$$$ ✗ **Kai.** Innovative Southwestern cuisine at the prestigious and award-
SOUTHWESTERN wining, yet oddly earthy Kai ("seed" in the Pima language) uses indigenous ingredients from local tribal farms. The seasonal menu reflects the restaurant's natural setting on the Gila River Indian Community. Standout appetizers include lobster tail on Indian fry bread and sea urchin in piquillo pepper fondue. Entrées like loin of Rocky Mountain elk with pumpkin, and the Cheyenne River buffalo tenderloin are excellent. The restaurant is adorned with Native American artifacts and has huge windows that showcase gorgeous mountain and desert views. ✉ *Sheraton Wild Horse Pass Resort & Spa, 5594 W. Wild Horse Pass Blvd., Chandler* ☎ *602/225–0100* ⊕ *www.wildhorsepassresort. com* 🍴 *Reservations essential* 👔 *Jacket required* ▤ *AE, D, DC, MC, V* ⊘ *Closed Sun. and Mon.* ✛ *D6.*

MESA

$$$ ✗ **Landmark.** In a 1908 building that was originally a Mormon church,
AMERICAN this family-run restaurant serves all-American home cooking. The traditional but dated dining room is decorated with lace curtains, chandeliers, loads of wallpaper, and white linens, and the food is straightforward

and comfy—roast turkey, prime rib, fried chicken, steak, and seafood dishes. The real draw, though, is the salad *room,* probably the largest salad bar you'll ever see, featuring nearly 100 choices including soups, breads, salad fixings, and hot dishes. Save room for Landmark ice-cream pie. ⊠*809 W. Main St., Mesa* ☎*480/962–4652* ⊕*www. landmarkrestaurant.com* ⊟*AE, D, MC, V* ⊹*G6.*

¢   ✕**Rosa's Mexican Grill.** This festive, family-friendly restaurant summons
MEXICAN   up images of a Baja beach taqueria. The tacos are Rosa's true glory:
ⓒ   beef, pork, and chicken are marinated in fruit juices and herbs for 12 hours, slowly oven-baked for another 10, then shredded and charbroiled. The fish taco is the best in Phoenix, in a class by itself. Spoon on one of Rosa's five fresh homemade salsas, but beware the fiery habanero version—it might be able to strip the enamel off your teeth. ⊠*328 E. University Dr., Mesa* ☎*480/964–5451* ⊕*www.rosasmexicangrill.com* ⊟*AE, D, DC, MC, V* ☾*Closed Sun.* ⊹*G6.*

TEMPE

¢–$ ✕**Haji Baba.** This casual Tempe treasure is a local, hole-in-the-wall Mid-
MIDDLE EASTERN   dle Eastern favorite that gets consistent rave reviews. The reasonably priced menu includes hummus, *labni* (fresh cheese made from yogurt), fabulous falafel gyros, shawarma, and kebab plates, all served up by a friendly and efficient staff. The adjoining store stocks an ample selection of imported Middle Eastern, Mediterranean, Indian, and European foods including everything from delicious cured olives, fava beans, and grape leaves to chocolate-covered halvah bars, rose water, and countless other hard-to-find specialties. ⊠*1513 E. Apache Blvd., Tempe* ☎*480/894–1905* ⊕*www.haji-baba.com* ⌫*Reservations not accepted* ⊟*AE, D, MC, V* ☾*Takeout only on Sun.* ⊹*F6.*

$$$ ✕**House of Tricks.** There's nothing up the sleeves of Robert and Robin
ECLECTIC   Trick, who work magic on the ever-changing eclectic menu that emphasizes the freshest available seafood, poultry, and fine meats, as well as vegetarian selections, keeping up with the changing tastes of ASU attendees and visitors. One of the Valley's most unusual dining venues, the restaurant encompasses a completely charming 1920s home and a separate brick- and adobe-style house originally built in 1903, adjoined by an intimate wooden deck and outdoor patio shaded by a canopy of grapevines and trees. Dinner serves up entrées like cider-roasted chicken on chorizo cornbread stuffing. At lunch you can't go wrong with the quiche of the day. ⊠*114 E. 7th St., Tempe* ☎*480/968–1114* ⊕*www. houseoftricks.com* ⊟*AE, D, MC, V* ☾*Closed Sun.* ⊹*E6.*

WHERE TO STAY

The Valley of the Sun now offers locals and visitors some of the country's best choices when it comes to funky, high-fashion accommodations.

Developers and hoteliers have taken advantage of the Valley's wide-open spaces to introduce super-size, luxury resorts like the Westin Kierland and the Marriott Desert Ridge Resort offering everything from their own golf courses and water parks to four-star restaurants and shopping villages. Places like the retro-hip Hotel Valley Ho, the Hollywood-chic Mondrian Scottsdale, and the sleek, mountainside Sanctuary have

BEST BETS FOR PHOENIX, SCOTTSDALE, AND TEMPE LODGING

Fodor's offers a selective listing of lodging at every price range, from the city's best budget motel to its most sophisticated luxury hotel. Here we've compiled our top picks by price and experience. The very best properties—those that provide a particularly remarkable experience in their price range—are designated with the Fodor's Choice logo.

2

Fodor's Choice★

Arizona Grand Resort, p. 101

Boulders Resort, p. 130

FireSky Resort, p. 101

Four Seasons at Troon North, p. 103

JW Marriott Desert Ridge, p. 99

Mondrian Hotel, p. 102

Rancho de los Caballeros, p. 133

Royal Palms, p. 95

Sanctuary on Camelback, p. 100

Westin Kierland, p. 104

Best by Price

¢
Noftsger Hill Inn, p. 140

$
Best Western Inn Suites, p. 99
Comfort Inn, p. 103
Hotel Highland, p. 94

$$
aloft, p. 108
Crowne Plaza San Marcos, p. 108
Wingate Inn & Suites, p. 105

$$$
Hermosa Inn, p. 100
Hotel Indigo, p. 102
Pointe Hilton at Piestewa Peak, p. 99

$$$$
Four Seasons at Troon North, p. 103
JW Marriott Camelback Inn Resort, p. 100
The Phoenician, p. 102
Royal Palms, p. 95

Best by Experience

BEST LARGE RESORTS

Arizona Biltmore, p. 91
Montelucia Resort & Spa, p. 100
JW Marriott Desert Ridge, p. 99
The Phoenician, p. 102
Westin Kierland, p. 104

BEST SMALL RESORTS

Hermosa Inn, p. 100

Sanctuary on Camelback Mountain, p. 100
Wigwam Resort, p. 98

BEST GOLF RESORTS

Fairmont Scottsdale Princess, p. 103
Four Seasons at Troon North, p. 103
The Phoeniclan, p. 102

GREAT VIEW

The Buttes Marriott Resort, p. 109
JW Marriott Camelback Inn Resort, p. 100
CopperWynd, p. 98
Sanctuary on Camelback Mountain, p. 100

BEST REMOTE RETREATS

Boulders Resort, p. 130
CopperWynd, p. 98
Four Seasons at Troon North, p. 103
Rancho de Los Caballeros, p. 133

BEST URBAN HOTSPOT HOTELS

aloft, p. 108
FireSky, p. 101
Hotel Valley Ho, p. 105
Mondrian Hotel, p. 102
W Scottsdale, p. 95

brought Arizona to the forefront of luxury-hotel style. Regal resorts like the Phoenician, the Four Seasons, the romantic Royal Palms Resort, and the new Spanish-inspired Intercontinental Montelucia keep lodging grounded in traditional, unsurpassed elegance, while plenty of boutique and business hotels keep it grounded in price.

Downtown Phoenix properties tend to be the business hotels, close to the heart of the city and the convention centers—and often closer to the average vacationer's budget. Many properties here cater to corporate travelers during the week but lower their rates on weekends to entice leisure travelers, so ask about weekend specials when making reservations. With more than 55,000 hotel rooms in the metro area, you can take your pick of anything from a luxurious resort to a guest ranch to an extended-stay hotel. For a true Western experience, guest-ranch territory is 60 mi northwest, in the town of Wickenburg.

PLANNING INFORMATION
Many people flee snow and ice to bask in the warmth of the Valley, so winter is the high season, peaking January through March. Summer season—mid-May through the end of September—is giveaway time, when a night at a resort often goes for half of the winter price, but be forewarned: in the height of summer it can be too hot to do anything outside your air-conditioned room.

WHAT IT COSTS					
	¢	$	$$	$$$	$$$$
For 2 People	under $100	$100–$150	$151–$225	$226–$350	over $350

Prices are for a standard double in high season.

DOWNTOWN AND CENTRAL PHOENIX

CENTRAL PHOENIX
$$$ ⊞ **Hilton Suites.** This practical hotel is a model of excellent design within tight limits. It sits off Central Avenue, 2 mi north of downtown amid a cluster of office towers. The marble-floor, pillared lobby opens into an 11-story atrium with palm trees, natural boulder fountains, glass elevators, and a lantern-lit café. The hotel offers a full breakfast, and if you're up for more than a drink at the inviting lounge bar or dinner at the on-site chain restaurant, you can take the free shuttle service to other area eats and attractions. **Pros:** spacious updated rooms with flat-screen TVs, great business amenities, nicest and largest hotel serving this pocket of central Phoenix. **Cons:** expensive parking ⊠10 E. Thomas Rd., Central Phoenix 🕾602/222–1111 ⊕www.phoenixsuites. hilton.com ⤶226 suites �ð In-room: Internet, Wi-Fi. In-hotel: restaurant, room service, bar, pool, gym, concierge, laundry facilities, laundry service, parking (paid), no-smoking rooms, some pets allowed, public Wi-Fi ⊟AE, D, DC, MC, V ⦿BP ⊹B5.

DOWNTOWN PHOENIX

$$ ⊡ **Hotel San Carlos.** Built in 1927 in an Italian Renaissance design, the seven-story San Carlos is the only historic hotel still operating in Downtown Phoenix. Among other distinctions, it was the Southwest's first air-conditioned hotel, and suites bear the names of such movie-star guests as Marilyn Monroe and Spencer Tracy. Big-band music, wall tapestries, Austrian crystal chandeliers, shiny copper elevators, and an accommodating staff transport you to a more genteel era. The rooms are snug by modern standards but have attractive period furnishings. An off-site fitness center accommodates guests for a small fee. **Pros:** a distinctive, recently updated, character-filled spot for a downtown stay. **Cons:** old-time charm may not translate well to those used to modern spaciousness and amenities. ⊠ *202 N. Central Ave., Downtown Phoenix* ☎*602/253–4121 or 866/253–4121* ⊕*www.hotelsancarlos.com* ⌂*109 rooms, 12 suites* ♿*In-room: Wi-Fi. In-hotel: restaurant, pool, room service, laundry service, parking (paid), public Wi-Fi, no-smoking rooms* ⊟*AE, D, DC, MC, V* ♿*B5.*

$$$ ⊡ **Hyatt Regency Phoenix.** This convention-oriented hotel efficiently handles the arrival and departure of hundreds of business travelers each day. The seven-story atrium has huge sculptures, colorful tapestries, potted plants, and comfortable seating areas. The revolving restaurant has panoramic views of the Phoenix area. Rooms are spacious, but the atrium roof blocks east views on floors 8 through 10. **Pros:** business amenities, views from restaurant. **Cons:** will be undergoing renovations through 2010; tricky area to navigate; parking gets pricey. ⊠ *122 N. 2nd St., Downtown Phoenix* ☎*602/252–1234* ⊕*www.hyatt.com* ⌂*712 rooms, 25 suites* ♿*In-room: Wi-Fi. In-hotel: 4 restaurants, bars, pools, gym, concierge, parking (paid), no-smoking rooms* ⊟*AE, D, DC, MC, V* ♿*B5.*

$$$ ⊡ **Wyndham Phoenix.** This Wyndham has an appealing mix of classic comfort and modern accommodations. Ideally situated for all things downtown (but little else), the hotel stands, with very little competition, in the center of bustling Copper Square. Recently updated, spacious rooms with subtle Southwestern tones are designed for the business traveler, and are relatively quiet and well lit, with large desks and ergonomic desk chairs, but they're also kid-friendly, comfortable, and convenient for pro baseball and basketball fans as well as theater- and concertgoers. **Pros:** prime location for light-rail travel, on-site Starbucks for coffee junkies. **Cons:** despite being family-friendly, this property is primarily oriented to business travelers. ⊠ *50 E. Adams St., Downtown Phoenix* ☎*602/333–0000 or 800/359–7253* ⊕*www.wyndhamphx. com* ⌂*532 rooms, 108 suites* ♿*In-room: refrigerator (some), Internet, Wi-Fi. In-hotel: restaurant, room service, bar, pool, gym, laundry service, parking (paid), no-smoking rooms* ⊟*AE, D, DC, MC, V* ♿*B5.*

GREATER PHOENIX

CAMELBACK CORRIDOR

$$$$ ⊡ **Arizona Biltmore Resort & Spa.** Designed by Frank Lloyd Wright's colleague Albert Chase McArthur, the Biltmore has been Phoenix's premier resort since it opened in 1929. The lobby, with its stained-glass

Where to Stay in the Valley of the Sun

A · B · C · D

1
2
3
4
5
6

7th St.
16th St.
Cave Creek Rd.
32nd St.
Tatum Blvd.

Bell Rd.

Greenway Rd.
Greenway Rd.

LOOKOUT
MOUNTAIN
PRESERVE

Thunderbird Rd.
40th St.
Thunderbird Rd.

Cactus Rd.
Cactus Rd.

Black Canyon Fwy.
Cave Creek Rd.
Cave Creek
Shea Blvd.

Peoria Rd.

Dunlap Ave.

7th Ave.
Central Ave.
7th St.

Best Western Inn
Suites Hotel

PIESTEWA PEAK
RECREATIONAL
AREA

Northern Ave.

51

Paradise
Valley

35th Ave.
19th Ave.

Glendale Ave.

Pointe Hilton
at Piestewa
Peak

JW Marriott's
Camelback Inn

Intercontinental
Montelucia
Resort & Spa

Bethany Home Rd.
Bethany Home Rd.

16th St.

BILTMORE
FASHION PARK

Courtyard
Phoenix
Camelback

Arizona
Biltmore

Hermosa
Inn

Sanctuary on
Camelback
Mountain

Tatum Blvd.

35th Ave.
Camelback Rd.

Homewood
Suites

The Ritz-Carlton

Phoenix
Inn Suites

Hotel
Highland

Royal
Palms
Resort &
Spa

44th St.

60

17

Indian School Rd.

Piestewa Peak Pkwy.
24th St.
32nd St.

Thomas Rd.

Grand Ave.

Wigwam
Resort

Hilton
Suites

7th St.

Thomas Rd.

VIAD
CORPORATE
CENTER

McDowell Rd.

Papago Fwy.

DOWNTOWN
PHOENIX

10

Red Mountain Fwy.

202

Van Buren St.

Hotel
San Carlos

Wyndham Phoenix

Hyatt
Regency
Phoenix

16th St.

10

SKY HARBOR
INTERNATIONAL
AIRPORT

Buckeye Rd.

17

19th
Ave.
Central Ave.
24th St.
48th St.
143

Lower Buckeye Rd.

Salt River

0   4 miles
0   4 km

Broadway Rd.

The Buttes
Marriot Resort

Sheraton
Wild Horse Pass
Resort & Spa

Arizona Grand Resort

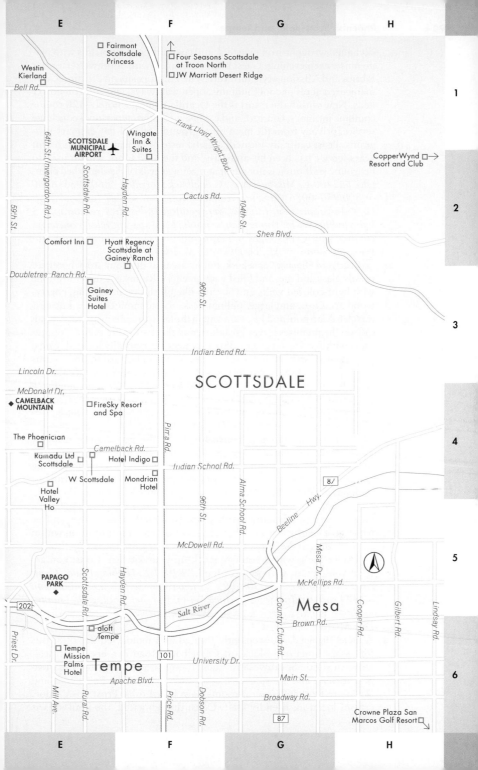

skylights, wrought-iron pilasters, and cozy sitting alcoves, fills with piano music each evening. Guest rooms are large, with Southwestern-print fabrics and Mission-style furniture. The Biltmore sits on 39 impeccably manicured acres of cool fountains, open walkways, and colorful flower beds. New within the resort is the Ocatilla boutique hotel—120 rooms combine intimacy, comfort, and exclusivity, offering personal concierge service, privacy from the main hotel grounds, and all-day culinary programs. **Pros:** centrally located; stately, historic charm. **Cons:** in recent years service has been hit-and-miss, and the food is not what it used to be; young staff often is not adept at meeting needs of distinguished clientele. ⊠*2400 E. Missouri Ave., Camelback Corridor* ☎*602/955–6600 or 800/950–0086* ⊕*www.arizonabiltmore.com* ↘*787 rooms, 72 villas* &*In-room: safe, Internet, refrigerator. In-hotel: 5 restaurants, 3 bars, public Wi-Fi, tennis courts, pools, gym, spa, bicycles, concierge, children's programs (ages 6–12), laundry service, parking (paid), no-smoking rooms* ☐*AE, D, DC, MC, V* ⊹*C4.*

$$ 🖥 **Courtyard Phoenix Camelback.** Public areas in this four-story hotel are mostly glass and tile, and filled with greenery. Rooms are tastefully done with light-colored walls and accents like plush down bedding, cherrywood armoires, and large, pullout desks to accommodate the business traveler. A lap pool and Jacuzzi await in the landscaped courtyard. A small café on the premises serves breakfast, and there are more than 50 restaurants within a 1½-mi radius. **Pros:** great value; centrally located. **Cons:** tucked into a strip mall–looking property, it can be hard to find; rooms facing parking garage may be noisy. ⊠*2101 E. Camelback Rd., Camelback Corridor* ☎*602/955–5200 or 800/321–2211* ⊕*www.camelback courtyard.com* ↘*155 rooms, 12 suites* &*In-room: refrigerator (some), Internet. In-hotel: restaurant, pool, gym, laundry facilities, laundry service, parking (free)* ☐*AE, D, DC, MC, V* ⊹*C4.*

$$$ 🖥 **Homewood Suites Phoenix–Biltmore.** This all-suites chain is a major value, especially considering its location in the heart of the upscale Biltmore District and Camelback Corridor. Suites have a spacious living and working area with a sleeper sofa and one or two separate bedrooms; each has a full kitchen. Every Monday to Thursday evening there is a complementary "Welcome Home" reception featuring anything from a taco bar to baked potatoes with all the trimmings. Guests also get free passes to a nearby fitness club, free breakfast, and transportation within a 5-mi radius of the hotel. **Pros:** great location, within walking distance of Trader Joe's, where you can stock up your kitchen. **Cons:** you get what you pay for with the free food. ⊠*2001 E. Highland Ave., Camelback Corridor* ☎*602/508–0937* ⊕*www.homewoodsuites.hilton.com* ↘*124 suites* &*In-room: kitchen, Wi-Fi. In-hotel: pool, gym, laundry facilities, laundry service, public Wi-Fi, no-smoking rooms* ☐*AE, D, DC, MC, V* ⍾*BP* ⊹*C4.*

$ 🖥 **Hotel Highland.** Conveniently located and remodeled in 2008, this four-story hotel one block off Camelback Road is a heck of a deal. Done in subtle Southwestern hues, rooms are designed for the business traveler and are spacious, cool, and comfortable. Local calls and Wi-Fi are free, and several rooms have jetted tubs. **Pros:** great value; central location; friendly staff. **Cons:** though gated, the pool area is

2

exposed to parking lot and street. ✉*2310 E. Highland Ave., Camelback Corridor* ☎*602/956–5221 or 800/956–5221* ⊕*www.hotelhighland.us.com* ⇆*120 rooms* ⚕*In-room: refrigerator, microwave, Wi-Fi. In-hotel: restaurant, bar, room service, pool, gym, laundry facilities, public Wi-Fi, no-smoking rooms* ▤*AE, D, DC, MC, V* ⊙*CP* ✢*C4.*

$$$$ 🏨 **The Ritz-Carlton, Phoenix.** Behind the sand-color facade and out-of-place architecture hides a graceful luxury hotel known for impeccable service. The lobby and public rooms are elegantly inviting, decorated with 18th- and 19th-century European paintings. Guest rooms and suites are spacious enclaves of luxury with premium mattresses and pillows, Egyptian-cotton sheets, and downy duvets that are even more inviting after the nightly turndown service, complete with fine chocolate. The staff is conscientious and attentive, and the central location means dining, shopping, and entertainment are within strolling distance. Mountain and city vistas can be appreciated from the second-floor terrace, where there is also a heated pool. **Pros:** impeccable service, a walkway (under Camelback Road) gives guests easy access to the recently renovated Biltmore Fashion Park. **Cons:** right on the corner of one of the busiest intersections in town, expect noise and exhaust when patio dining. ✉*2401 E. Camelback Rd., Camelback Corridor* ☎*602/468–0700 or 800/241-3333* ⊕*www.ritzcarlton.com/hotels/phoenix* ⇆*267 rooms, 14 suites* ⚕*In-room: safe, refrigerator, Internet, Wi-Fi. In-hotel: restaurant, room service, bar, pool, gym, children's programs (ages 5–12), laundry service, public Wi-Fi, executive floor, parking (paid), no-smoking rooms* ▤*AE, D, DC, MC, V* ✢*C4.*

$$$$
Fodor's Choice
★ 🏨 **Royal Palms Resort & Spa.** Once the home of Cunard Steamship executive Delos T. Cooke, this Mediterranean-style resort has a stately row of the namesake palms at its entrance, courtyards with fountains, and individually designed rooms. Deluxe suites, casitas and villas (including the newly added Montevista accommodations) are all different, though they follow one of three elegant styles—trompe-l'oeil, romantic retreat, or Spanish colonial. The restaurant, T. Cook's, is renowned, and the open-air Alvadora Spa seems like it has every imaginable amenity, including an outdoor rain shower. **Pros:** a favorite among Fodors.com users in search of romantic getaways; houses a cozy cigar lounge. **Cons:** expensive. ✉*5200 E. Camelback Rd., Camelback Corridor* ☎*602/840–3610 or 800/672–6011* ⊕*www.royalpalmsresortandspa.com* ⇆*43 rooms, 27 suites, 44 casitas, 5 villas* ⚕*In-room: safe, refrigerator, Internet, Wi-Fi. In-hotel: restaurant, room service, bar, pool, gym, spa, bicycles, laundry service, parking (paid), no-smoking rooms* ▤*AE, D, DC, MC, V* ✢*D4.*

$$$$ 🏨 **W Scottsdale.** If you're looking for cowboy comforts or a true feel for the Southwest, you may want to keep moseying down the list. But

RESORTS IN THE VALLEY OF THE SUN

	HOTEL NAME	Worth Noting	Location	Rooms	Restaurants	Bars	Pools	Spa	Golf Courses	Shopping	Near Major Venues
	Arizona Biltmore	Quiet and sophisticated	Camelback Corridor	811	4	2	8	yes	2	yes	
★	Arizona Grand Resort	Great for families	South Phoenix	640	6	4	7		1	yes	
	Best Western Inn Suites	Well priced, convenient north-central location	North Central Phoenix	109			1			yes	
	Boulders Resort	Spectacular desert setting, remote	Carefree	160	4	2	4	yes	2	yes	
	Buttes Marriott Resort	Hillside resort near ASU	Tempe	353	2	3	1	yes		yes	yes
	Comfort Inn	Affordable Scottsdale location	North Scottsdale	124			1			yes	
	CopperWynd Resort and Club	Quiet, breathtaking Fountain Hills views	Fountain Hills	40	2	1	2	yes			
	Courtyard Phoenix Camelback	Great location, Marriott amenities	Camelback Corridor	167	1		1			yes	
	Crowne Plaza San Marcos Golf Resort	Historic golf resort	Chandler	295	2	2	1	yes	1	yes	
	Fairmont Scottsdale Princess	Home of TPC golf course and 6,300-seat tennis stadium	North Scottsdale	651	5	6	5	yes	2	yes	yes
★	FireSky Resort & Spa	Unique, upscale family fun	Central Scottsdale	204	1	2	3	yes		yes	yes
★	Four Seasons at Troon North	Remote but luxurious desert mountain getaway	North Scottsdale	232	3	1	3	yes	1		yes
	Gainey Suites Hotel	Chic boutique hotel	North Scottsdale	162			1			yes	

Hermosa Inn	A cozy getaway	Paradise Valley	35	1	1	1			yes	
Hilton Suites	Comfortable, central location	Central Phoenix	226	1	1	1			yes	yes
Homewood Suites Phoenix-Biltmore	Residential living, great location	Camelback Corridor	124			1			yes	
Hotel Highland	Great location	Camelback Corridor	120	1	1	1			yes	
★ JW Marriott Desert Ridge	Desert setting filled with water features	North Central Phoenix	950	9	5	5	yes	2	yes	
★ Mondrian Hotel Scottsdale	Hollywood Haute Hotel	Central Scottsdale	194	1	3	1	yes		yes	yes
★ The Phoenician	Luxury with a fabulous location	Central Scottsdale	755	6	2	10		3	yes	yes
Pointe Hilton at Piestewa Peak	Unique, inner-city mountain resort	North Central Phoenix	562	3	3	2	yes		yes	
Rancho de los Caballeros	Remote, luxury guest-ranch	Wickenburg	79	1	1	1	yes	1		
The Ritz-Carlton, Phoenix	In the heart of the Valley, across from Biltmore Fashion Park	Camelback Corridor	281	1	1	1			yes	
★ Royal Palms Resort & Spa	Gorgeous foothill location	Camelback Corridor	182	1	1	1	yes		yes	
★ Sanctuary on Camelback	Modern amenities, spectacular views	Paradise Valley	98	1	1	3	yes		yes	
Sheraton Wild Horse Pass Resort & Spa	Award-winning accommodations and dining	Chandler	500	4	3	4	yes	2	yes	yes
★ Westin Kierland Resort & Spa	Central to fine shopping and dining	North Scottsdale	827	8	6	4	yes	1	yes	yes
Wigwam Resort	Historic West Valley charm	Litchfield Park	331	2	2	2	yes	3		yes
Wingate Inn & Suites	Scottsdale Airpark convenience, class, and comfort	North Scottsdale	117	1	2	1			yes	yes
Wyndham Phoenix	Prime downtown location	Downtown Phoenix	640	1	1	1			yes	yes
W Scottsdale	Modern Scottsdale Hot Spot	Camelback Corridor	224	1	3	1	yes		yes	yes

if you'd like to hang your hat somewhere modern, hip and downright fabulous, look no further. A taste of youthful but sophisticated New York elegance, this hotel/hot spot, located in the heart of Scottsdale's shopping and social scene, caters to the wants and needs of the fashionable but fickle traveler with "Whatever/Whenever" service that provides guests with anything they want ("as long as it's legal!"). Live like a celebrity in the variety of top-notch bars and lounges, including the Living Room Lounge and Roku, the property's fine-dining sushi restaurant; or lie low with stunning mountain views at Wet, the exclusive pool and waterside experience—all things that make this a metropolitan desert oasis. **Pros:** unpretentious elegance right across from Scottsdale Fashion Square. **Cons:** decor can be an acquired taste for some. The staff's mandatory use of words that begin with "W" is annoying. ⊠ *7277 E. Camelback Rd., Camelback Corridor* ☎ *480/970–2100* ⊕ *www.whotels. com/scottsdale* ⬎ *197 rooms, 27 suites* ⬧ *In-room: safe, refrigerator, Internet, Wi-Fi. In-hotel: restaurant, room service, bars, pool, spa, gym, laundry service, Wi-Fi, parking (paid), no-smoking rooms* ☰ *AE, D, DC, MC, V* ✚ *E4.*

FOUNTAIN HILLS

$$$$ ⛐ **CopperWynd Resort and Club.** Nestled high on a mountain ridge above Scottsdale and Fountain Hills, this secluded resort offers breathtaking views of mountains and the Sonoran Desert. Luxurious guest rooms have imported handmade furniture, granite counters, fireplaces, custom linens, and a private terrace overlooking serene desert vistas. The expansive two- and three-bedroom villas are equipped with kitchens, washers and dryers, and private garages. The Spa at CopperWynd is one of the top spas in the area, and Alchemy, the resort's restaurant, is perfect for a romantic evening. **Pros:** gorgeous views; comfortable and quiet desert getaway; blissful spa; plenty of package deals. **Cons:** for the price, in-room televisions and other amenities should be upgraded. ⊠ *13225 N. Eagle Ridge Dr., Fountain Hills* ☎ *480/333–1900 or 877/707–7760* ⊕ *www.copperwynd.com* ⬎ *32 rooms, 8 villas* ⬧ *In-room: Internet, Wi-Fi. In-hotel: 2 restaurants, bar, tennis courts, pools, gym, spa, public Wi-Fi, no-smoking rooms* ☰ *AE, D, DC, MC, V* ✚ *H2.*

LITCHFIELD PARK

$$$ ⛐ **Wigwam Resort.** Built in 1918 as a retreat for executives of the Goodyear Company, the Wigwam has a long and storied history. After significant renovations, the resort maintains its historical character while delivering a modern-day, first-class luxury experience. The property, which can be accessed by chauffeured golf carts, is stunning, and features great golf and a true Old West experience that puts less of an emphasis on "old." **Pros:** as part of Starwood's Luxury Collection, the Wigwam's standards are higher than they've ever been. **Cons:** no matter how extreme the renovation, historical properties will always have antiquated elements that don't meet every expectation. ⊠ *300 Wigwam Blvd., Litchfield Park* ☎ *623/935–3811 or 800/327–0396* ⊕ *www.wigwamresort.com* ⬎ *259 rooms, 72 suites* ⬧ *In-room: safe, Internet, refrigerator (some). In-hotel: 3 restaurants, bars, golf courses, tennis courts, pools, gym, spa, children's programs (ages 6–12), parking (free)* ☰ *AE, D, DC, MC, V* ✚ *A4.*

NORTH CENTRAL PHOENIX

$ ☎ **Best Western Inn Suites.** Just north of the Pointe Hilton, this affordable all-suites hotel is often overlooked as an option in the neighborhood, but it has the same proximity to everything as the Hilton, including great recreation areas (Piestewa Peak Mountain Preserve); great dining options (Via Delosantos, Basis, Ticoz, and Lola Tapas are all nearby); and it's less than 1 mi from AZ 51, which offers quick and easy access to major freeways, Valley shopping, and Sky Harbor Airport. Pillow-top mattresses and upgraded furnishings are recent additions. **Pros:** the price is right, especially for the area. **Cons:** underwhelming staff etiquette. ✉ *1615 E. Northern Ave., North Central Phoenix* ☎ *602/997–6285* ⊕ *www. bwsuite.com* ↪ *77 rooms, 32 2-room suites* ♿ *In-room: Internet, Wi-Fi. In-hotel: pool, gym, laundry service, public Wi-Fi, parking (free), some pets allowed, no-smoking rooms* ⊟ *AE, D, DC, MC, V ✛C3*

$$$$ ☎ **JW Marriott Desert Ridge Resort & Spa.** Arizona's largest resort has an immense entryway with floor-to-ceiling windows that allow the sandstone lobby, the Sonoran Desert, and the resort's amazing water features to meld together in a single prospect. This sprawling and busy property includes four acres of water fun with a popular "lazy river," where you can flop on an inner tube and float the day away. Young 'uns love the Kokopelli Kids program, while adults can rejuvenate at Revive Spa or tee off at the on-site golf courses. Each elegantly decorated room has a balcony or patio. **Pros:** perfect for luxuriating with family and/or groups of friends. **Cons:** a bit impersonal for the price tag; not ideal for cozy getaways. ✉ *5350 E. Marriott Dr., North Central Phoenix* ☎ *480/293–5000 or 800/835–6206* ⊕ *www.jwdesertridgeresort.com* ↪ *869 rooms, 81 suites* ♿ *In-room: safe, refrigerator (some), Internet. In-hotel: 9 restaurants, room service, bars, golf courses, tennis courts, pools, spa, bicycles, children's programs (ages 4–12), public Wi-Fi, no-smoking rooms* ⊟ *AE, D, DC, MC, V ✛F1.*

Ⓒ Fodor's Choice ★

$$$ ☎ **Pointe Hilton at Piestewa Peak.** The highlight of this family-oriented Hilton is the 9-acre recreation area Hole-in-the-Wall River Ranch. It has swimming pools with waterfalls, a 130-foot waterslide, and a 1,000-foot "river" that winds past a miniature golf course, tennis courts, and artificial buttes. Accommodations in the newly updated stucco buildings vary from standard two-room suites to a grand three-bedroom house; all have balconies. It is also adjacent to the very busy AZ 51, though it manages to filter out most freeway noise. Kids can enjoy the "Coyote Camp" youth programs while adults take in area golf and the Tocasierra Spa. **Pros:** adjacent to the Phoenix Mountain Preserve, making it an ideal base for hiking and biking trips; great summer deals. **Cons:** often seems to be operating at half staff. ✉ *7677 N. 16th St., North Central Phoenix* ☎ *602/997–2626 or 800/876–4683* ⊕ *www.pointehilton. com* ↪ *431 suites, 130 casitas, 1 house* ♿ *In-room: kitchen (some), refrigerator (some), Wi-Fi. In-hotel: 3 restaurants, bars, tennis courts, pools, gym, spa, bicycles, children's programs (ages 6–12), parking (free), no-smoking rooms* ⊟ *AE, D, DC, MC, V ✛C3.*

Ⓒ

PARADISE VALLEY

$$$ ⌂ **Hermosa Inn.** This boutique hotel's ranch-style lodge was the home and studio of cowboy artist Lon Megargee in the 1930s; today the adobe structure houses Lon's at the Hermosa, justly popular for its New American cuisine. Villas as big as private homes and individually decorated casitas hold an enviable collection of art. The Hermosa, on 6 acres of lushly landscaped desert, is a blessedly peaceful alternative to some of the larger resorts. **Pros:** luxurious but cozy; flat-screen TVs. **Cons:** inconsistent housekeeping service. ✉ *5532 N. Palo Cristi Rd., Paradise Valley* ☎ *602/955–8614 or 800/241–1210* ⊕ *www.hermosainn.com* ⇨ *4 villas, 3 haciendas, 11 casitas, 17 ranchos* ☖ *In-room: kitchen (some), refrigerator (some), Wi-Fi. In-hotel: restaurant, bar, pool, parking (free), no-smoking rooms, public Wi-Fi, some pets allowed* ☰ *AE, D, DC, MC, V* ⌾ *CP* ✛ *C4.*

$$$$ ⌂ **Intercontinental Montelucia Resort & Spa.** New to the luxury resort scene, this hotel brings a touch of the Mediterranean to Paradise Valley with its exquisite dark furnishings and light stone work, its impeccable Joya Spa, its pool pavilion and a Spanish-inspired wedding chapel. Spacious rooms feature sunken tubs, large balconies, featherbeds and handmade Moroccan light fixtures. The hotel's restaurant, Prado, brings a superb mix of Spanish and Mediterranean cuisine to the table, while the Kasbah patio is another heavenly place to watch the Pardise Valley sunsets. **Pros:** inner-city getaway with stellar sunset views and a new approach to luxury. **Cons:** while the grounds are beautiful, the layout is boxy, awkward, and confusing; fee to rent cabanas ✉ *4949 E. Lincoln Dr., Paradise Valley, Phoenix* ☎ *480/627–3200 or 800/245–2051* ⊕ *www.icmontelucia.com* ⇨ *252 guest rooms, 41 suites* ☖ *In-room: kitchen (some), refrigerator (some), Internet, Wi-Fi. In-hotel: 5 restaurants, room service, bar, concierge, tennis court, pools, gym, spa, public Wi-Fi, parking (free), some pets allowed, no-smoking rooms* ☰ *AE, D, DC, MC, V* ✛ *D4.*

$$$$ ⌂ **JW Marriott Camelback Inn Resort, Golf Club & Spa.** A gorgeous renovation in 2008 had many locals fearing that some of the Valley's last threads of true cowboy character were being sacrificed for a competitive edge. While some of the old-fashioned elements rode off into the sunset, the inn's true Western integrity lives on in noteworthy harmony with haute contemporary style. Built on 125 acres in the mid-1930s, the hacienda-style resort remains top-notch, and the grounds are still gloriously adorned with stunning cacti and desert flowers. Rooms are spacious and elegant, with luxury amenities, and seven suites have private swimming pools. **Pros:** a specialty restaurant (BLT Steak), a world-class spa and golf course; upscale retail space; stunning place to catch a sunset. **Cons:** a bit formal and stuffy. ✉ *5402 E. Lincoln Dr., Paradise Valley* ☎ *480/948–1700 or 800/242–2635* ⊕ *www.camelbackinn.com* ⇨ *453 rooms, 18 suites* ☖ *In-room: kitchen (some), Internet, Wi-Fi. In-hotel: 6 restaurants, bar, golf courses, tennis courts, pools, spa, children's programs (ages 5–12), public Wi-Fi, parking (free), no-smoking rooms* ☰ *AE, D, DC, MC, V* ✛ *D3.*

$$$$ ⌂ **Sanctuary on Camelback Mountain.** This luxurious boutique hotel is
Fodor's Choice the only resort on the north slope of Camelback Mountain. Secluded
★ mountain casitas are painted in desert hues and feature breathtaking

views of Paradise Valley. Chic spa casitas surround the pool and are outfitted with contemporary furnishings and private patios. Bathrooms are travertine marble with elegant sinks and roomy tubs. For those who enjoy going *eau* and even *au naturel,* some suites have outdoor tubs. An infinity-edge pool, Zen meditation garden, and Asian-inspired Sanctuary Spa make this a haven for relaxation. The hotel's restaurant, elements, is the hot spot for cocktails at sunset and award-winning cuisine. **Pros:** inner-city getaway with mountain seclusion; unparalleled views of Camelback's Praying Monk Rock. **Cons:** it can be hard to find your room on the sprawling property; walking between buildings can mean conquering slopes or flights of stairs. ⊠ *5700 E. McDonald Dr., Paradise Valley, Phoenix* ☎ *480/948–2100 or 800/245–2051* ⊕ *www. sanctuaryaz.com* ⟿ *98 casitas* & *In-room: kitchen (some), refrigerator (some), Internet, Wi-Fi. In-hotel: restaurant, room service, bar, tennis courts, pools, gym, spa, public Wi-Fi, parking (free), no-smoking rooms* ⊟ *AE, D, DC, MC, V* ✛ *D4.*

SOUTH PHOENIX

$$$$
☾
Fodor'sChoice
★

🏨 **Arizona Grand Resort.** This beautifully renovated, all-suites resort next to South Mountain Park is home to Oasis, one of the largest water parks in the country, and one of the Valley's more challenging golf courses. Years of construction yielded bright, stunning results that are modern but warm, fitting to a place called the Valley of the Sun. Fitting for families, this massive property feels like a true getaway, even though it sits just off I–10. Enjoy a four-story sports center, a spa, multiple restaurants, tennis, horseback riding, and mountain biking. **Pros:** great family or large-group location, nicely upgraded rooms. **Cons:** huge property can overwhelm. ⊠ *8000 S. Arizona Grand Pkwy., South Phoenix* ☎ *602/438–9000 or 877/800–4888* ⊕ *www.arizonagrandresort. com* ⟿ *640 suites* & *In-room: Wi-Fi, refrigerator. In-hotel: 6 restaurants, bars, room service, golf course, tennis courts, pools, gym, spa, bicycles, laundry facilities, public Wi-Fi, parking (free)* ⊟ *AE, D, DC, MC, V* ✛ *D6.*

SCOTTSDALE

CENTRAL SCOTTSDALE

$$$$
☾
Fodor'sChoice
★

🏨 **FireSky Resort & Spa.** FireSky was built on the belief that a hotel should "relieve travelers of their insecurity and loneliness." This boutique resort achieves that by providing an elegant, intimate, eco- and family-friendly environment. Attentive staff focus on even the smallest details—personal and professional—to anticipate and alleviate worries. Rooms are done in pleasing contemporary Western decor, and have crisp linens, cozy bathrobes, and brand-name bath amenities. Jurlique, the full-service European spa, offers massages and treatments that the muscles will remember fondly. A hosted wine reception is offered to guests nightly. Soothe your soul and your *soles* in the luxurious sand-bottom pool. Kids are welcomed with special "KimptonKids" guest kits. **Pros:** the lavish pool and lounge area are considered among the area's nicest; organic food offerings; designer in-room recycling bins; pet-friendly; special rooms for tall people. **Cons:** rooms with parking-lot view are disappointing for the price tag. Ask for a pool room. ✉4925 N. Scottsdale Rd., Central Scottsdale ☎480/945–7666 or 800/528–7867 ⊕www.fireskyresort.com ⤶196 rooms, 8 suites ⚡In-room: refrigerator (some), Wi-Fi. In-hotel: restaurant, bars, pools, public Internet, public Wi-Fi, all pets allowed, no-smoking rooms ═AE, D, DC, MC, V ✢E4.

$$$ ⟐**Hotel Indigo.** This Scottsdale spot is perfect for what it is: simple, modern, and, most of all, centrally located. Eclectic rooms are colorfully accented with clean lines, with plasma-screen TVs, and exceptionally comfy beds. Suites feature entire walls covered with images of Arizona's spectacular slot canyons. Large, natural-stone showers feature Aveda products. The Golden Bean café serves Starbucks coffee, and the Phi Bar offers a nice selection of wine and beer. **Pros:** great value; ideal Scottsdale location; pet-friendly. **Cons:** walls aren't thick enough to block out the Top 40 music piped through the entryway. ✉4415 N. Civic Center Plaza, Central Scottsdale ☎480/941–9400 ⊕www.ichotelsgroup.com ⤶117 rooms, 9 suites ⚡In-room: safe, refrigerator (some), Internet, Wi-Fi. In-hotel: restaurant, bar, pool, gym, laundry service, parking (free), no-smoking rooms═AE, D, DC, MC, V ✢F4

$$$$ ⟐**Mondrian Hotel Scottsdale.** Like its Los Angeles predecessor, this urban
Fodor's Choice resort is a museum of modern art. Surrounded by lush landscaping, the
★ property features two oasis-worthy pools. Outfitted with fireplaces, sofas, and televisions, the poolside cabanas could tempt travelers to shed their sightseeing ambitions. Modern-style rooms include 42-inch plasma TVs, entertainment centers with iPod connections, and comfy beds with down comforters and pillows. Indulge in a sinful bite at Asia de Cuba restaurant, then redeem yourself with the fitness center or on-site Agua Spa. **Pros:** great location for shopping, entertainment, and Valley activities; modern property in every way. **Cons:** decor is not for everyone, check pictures online before booking. ✉7353 E. Indian School Rd., Central Scottsdale ☎480/308–1100 or 800/697–1791 ⊕www.mondrianscottsdale.com ⤶177 rooms, 15 suites, 2 apartments ⚡In-room: safe, refrigerator, Internet, Wi-Fi. In-hotel: restaurant, room service, bar, pool, gym, spa, laundry service, parking (free), no-smoking rooms ═AE, D, DC, MC, V ✢F4.

$$$$ ⟐**The Phoenician.** In a town where luxurious, expensive resorts are the
☺ rule, the Phoenician still stands apart, primarily in the realm of service. The gilded, marbled lobby with towering fountains is the backdrop for a $25 million fine-art collection. Large rooms in the main building and outlying casitas are decorated with elegant 1960s furniture and have private patios and oversize marble bathrooms. There's a secluded tennis garden and 27 holes of premier golf. The Centre for Well Being Spa has a meditation atrium and a pool lined with mother-of-pearl tiles, where you can drift off to another world. Afterward, you can take in a sophisticated afternoon tea or dinner at J&G Steakhouse. **Pros:** you get what you pay for in terms of luxury; highest industry standards. **Cons:** high prices, even in the off-season; not a laid-back resort experience. ✉6000 E. Camelback Rd., Central Scottsdale ☎480/941–8200 or 800/888–8234 ⊕www.the phoenician.com ⤶647 rooms, 108 suites ⚡In-room: safe, refrigerator (some), Internet, Wi-Fi. In-hotel: 7 restaurants, bars, room service,

2

golf courses, tennis courts, pools, gym, children's programs (ages 5–12), public Wi-Fi, parking (free), no-smoking rooms ▭AE, D, DC, MC, V ✢E4.

NORTH SCOTTSDALE

$ ☶**Comfort Inn.** This may be one of the nicest Comfort Inns you'll ever lay eyes on, and it's in a quiet, upscale North Scottsdale neighborhood along the Scottsdale Road corridor. The three-story glass entryway is bright and welcoming.

Rooms are utilitarian but moderately updated, clean, and have free HBO. There are trendy restaurants and shopping opportunities within easy walking distance, making this a comfortable, affordable, and family-friendly alternative. **Pros:** quiet; perfect for the price in this area. **Cons:** while rooms are predictable for a Comfort Inn, the service can vary greatly. ⊠*7350 E. Gold Dust Rd., at Scottsdale Rd., North Scottsdale* ☎*480/596–6559 or 888/296–9776* ⊕*www.comfortinnscottsdale.com* ⇆*123 rooms, 1 suite* ⌂*In-room: refrigerator, Wi-Fi. In-hotel: pool, gym, public Wi-Fi, parking (free), no-smoking rooms* ▭*AE, D, DC, MC, V* ⋈*CP* ✢*E2.*

$$$$ ☶**Fairmont Scottsdale Princess.** Home of the Tournament Players Club
☾ Stadium golf course and the FBR Phoenix Open, this resort covers 450 breathtakingly landscaped acres of desert. Willow Stream Spa, one of the top spa spots in the country, has a dramatic rooftop pool, and kids love the fishing pond and waterslides. Renovated rooms are done in a chic blend of contemporary styles, as are the new Fairmont Gold hotel-within-a-hotel boutique rooms. Service is what you'd expect at a resort of this caliber: excellent and unobtrusive. Home to the acclaimed Bourbon Steak restaurant. **Pros:** upscale favorite, especially with families; extras like in-room espresso machines; close to shopping. **Cons:** mission-meets-modern decor doesn't work with the exterior of the resort. ⊠*7575 E. Princess Dr., North Scottsdale* ☎*480/585–4848 or 800/344–4758* ⊕*www.fairmont.com/Scottsdale/* ⇆*513 rooms, 119 casitas, 72 villas, 2 suites* ⌂*In-room: safe, Wi-Fi. In-hotel: 5 restaurants, bars, golf courses, tennis courts, pools, gym, spa, children's programs (ages 6–16), parking (free), some pets allowed, no-smoking rooms* ▭*AE, D, DC, MC, V* ✢*E1.*

$$$$ ☶**Four Seasons Scottsdale at Troon North.** This is a logical choice for seri-
☾ ous golfers, as it's adjacent to two Troon North premier courses, where
Fodor'sChoice guests receive preferential tee times and free shuttle service. The resort
★ is tucked in the shadows of Pinnacle Peak, near the popular hiking trail. Large, casita-style rooms have separate sitting and sleeping areas as well as outdoor garden showers, fireplaces, and balconies or patios. Suites come with telescopes and star charts. Talavera, the hotel's main restaurant, is elegant and accommodating. **Pros:** while developments are breathing down its neck, this resort remains a true, remote desert oasis. **Cons:** far from everything. ⊠*10600 E. Crescent Moon Dr., North*

Scottsdale ☎*480/515–5700 or 888/207–9696* 🌐*www.fourseasons.com/scottsdale* *210 rooms, 22 suites* *In-room: safe, refrigerator (some), Internet, Wi-Fi. In-hotel: 3 restaurants, bar, tennis courts, pools, gym, golf course, spa, children's programs (ages 5–12), laundry service, parking (free), no-smoking rooms* *AE, D, DC, MC, V* *F1.*

$$$ **Gainey Suites Hotel.** This independently owned and completely remodeled boutique hotel is a rare find for both amenities and price. Floor plans vary from studios to two-bedroom suites that sleep eight, all with fully equipped kitchens and flat-panel wide-screen TVs. Cozy conversation areas in the lobby and an evening hors-d'oeuvres reception create a warm atmosphere. The hotel is directly adjacent to the Gainey Village development, with boutique shopping and upscale dining, as well as a spa. **Pros:** the hotel layout, price, and inclusive breakfast buffet are ideal for families and groups. **Cons:** comfortable but fairly generic decor, not ideal for a romantic getaway. ✉*7300 E. Gainey Suites Dr., North Scottsdale* ☎*480/922–6969 or 800/970–4666* 🌐*www.gaineysuiteshotel.com* *162 suites* *In-room: kitchen, refrigerator, Internet, Wi-Fi. In-hotel: pool, gym, laundry facilities, public Wi-Fi, no-smoking rooms* *AE, D, MC, V* *CP* *E3.*

$$$$ **Hyatt Regency Scottsdale at Gainey Ranch.** When you stay here, it's easy to imagine that you're relaxing at an ocean-side resort instead of in the desert. Shaded by towering palms and with manicured gardens and paths, the property has water everywhere—a large pool area has a beach, a three-story waterslide, waterfalls, and a lagoon. The two-story lobby, filled with Native American art, opens to outdoor conversation areas where fires burn in stone fireplaces on cool nights. Large, updated rooms have balconies or patios and 37-inch LCD TVs. Three golf courses at nearby Gainey Ranch Golf Club will suit any duffer's fancy. Spa Avania aims to soothe the soul, while kids get their kicks at Camp Hyatt. **Pros:** lots of pools for all; oasis atmosphere. **Cons:** if you're early to bed, avoid a room near the lobby. ✉*7500 E. Doubletree Ranch Rd., North Scottsdale* ☎*480/444–1234 or 800/233–1234* 🌐*www.scottsdale.hyatt.com* *461 rooms, 7 casitas, 22 suites* *In-room: Internet, Wi-Fi. In-hotel: 4 restaurants, bars, golf courses, tennis courts, pools, gym, spa, bicycles, children's programs (ages 3–12), executive floor, parking (free), no-smoking rooms* *AE, D, DC, MC, V* *F2.*

$$$$ Fodor's Choice ★ **Westin Kierland Resort & Spa.** Original artwork by Arizona artists is displayed throughout the Westin Kierland, and the spacious rooms all have balconies or patios with views of the mountains or the resort's water park and tubing river, where kids can enjoy programs like "Club Teen." Kierland Commons, within walking distance, is a planned village of upscale specialty boutiques and restaurants. A new leisure center specifically accommodates nonbusiness travelers. Of the eight restaurants, Deseo is the star, presided over by well-known chef Douglas Rodriguez, regarded as the inventor of Nuevo Latino cuisine. **Pros:** bagpipers stroll around the courtyard at sunset; amazing beds and bedding; organic superfood menu; programs for kids' photography and scuba certification. **Cons:** bagpipers, both Internet access and customer service can be unreliable. ✉*6902 E. Greenway Pkwy., North Scottsdale* ☎*480/624–1000* 🌐*www.kierlandresort.com* *732*

2

rooms, 63 suites, 32 casitas ⟨&⟩ In-room: refrigerator (some), Internet, Wi-Fi. In-hotel: 8 restaurants, bars, golf courses, tennis courts, pools, gym, spa, children's programs (ages 4–17), public Wi-Fi, parking (free), no-smoking rooms ⊟AE, D, DC, MC, V ✛E1.

$$ ⚏**Wingate Inn & Suites–Scottsdale.** Located right off the 101, in the Scottsdale Airpark, this affordable hotel is an ideal base of operations. Cool and modern throughout, it has clean, simply decorated rooms.

WORD OF MOUTH

"Try The Wingate Inn and Suites in Scottsdale. We use them for our corporate guests all the time and it's always been very good, and not too expensive. Just off the 101, one exit south of where you need to get off to go to Taliesin. The standard rooms are perfect for one night. I would recommend it without hesitation." —jkgourmet

A beautiful pool and waterfall are great for escaping the summer heat. Fill up on the complimentary breakfast before strolling around Taliesin West. **Pros:** clean and spacious rooms; comfortable beds; good price for location. **Cons:** convenient Airpark and freeway location; more practical than perfect. ⊠14255 N. 87th St., North Scottsdale ☎480/922–6500 or 877/570–6500 ⊕www.scottsdalewingate.com ⟿82 rooms, 35 suites ⟨&⟩In-room: refrigerator, Internet, Wi-Fi. In-hotel: pool, gym, laundry service, parking (free) ⊟AE, D, DC, MC, V ✛F2.

OLD TOWN

$$$ ⚏**Hotel Valley Ho.** One of Scottsdale's newer hotels is actually one of its oldest. Originally opened in 1956, it was a hangout for celebrities, including Natalie Wood, Robert Wagner, and Tony Curtis. In 2001 the hotel was restored to its former '50s fabulousness—complete with Trader Vic's, the hotel's original restaurant and lounge with legendary cocktails. A large pool is at the heart of this Frank Lloyd Wright–inspired hotel surrounded by lush landscaping and an outdoor grill and dining area. A 6,000-square-foot spa, a fitness center, and 10,000 square feet of meeting space have been added as well as the Tower, which houses 35 residential suites. **Pros:** retro decor; great history; hip, youthful style. **Cons:** the busy location and retro-hip decor are not for everyone; check pictures online before booking. ⊠6850 E. Main St., Old Town ☎480/248–2000 ⊕www.hotelvalleyho.com ⟿190 rooms, 35 condo (tower) suites, 4 terrace suites, 2 executive suites ⟨&⟩In-room: Internet, Wi-Fi. In-hotel: 3 restaurants, bars, pool, gym, spa, public Wi-Fi, no-smoking rooms ⊟AE, D, DC, MC, V ✛E4.

$$ ⚏**Ramada Limited Scottsdale.** There are two attractive things about this exterior-corridor, three-story motel: the location, which is within walking distance of Scottsdale's Old Town, and the price, which includes complimentary Continental breakfast. The simple but clean rooms have standard, serviceable furnishings. **Pros:** great price, great location in the heart of Scottsdale. **Cons:** rooms are dated; pool noise and busy street noise can be heard in rooms. ⊠6935 E. 5th Ave., Old Town ☎480/994–9461 or 800/528–7396 ⊕www.RamadaScottsdale.com ⟿92 rooms ⟨&⟩In-room: refrigerator, Wi-Fi. In-hotel: pool, gym, laundry facilities, parking (free), some pets allowed, no-smoking rooms ⊟AE, D, DC, MC, V ⦿CP ✛E4.

Royal Palms Resort & Spa

Arizona Grand Resort

Sanctuary on Camelback Mountain

The Westin Kierland Resort & Spa

JW Marriott Desert Ridge Resort & Spa   Four Seasons Scottsdale at Troon North

TEMPE AND AROUND

CHANDLER

$$ ⊞**Crowne Plaza San Marcos Golf Resort.** When it opened in 1912 the
☾ San Marcos was the first golf resort in Arizona, and it's still one of the
state's most treasured landmarks. The palm-studded, mission-style San
Marcos has undergone luxury upgrades, while maintaining its historic
beauty and charm: the Images day spa and restyled rooms with pillow-
top mattresses, high-thread-count sheets, and down-filled duvets. Each
room and suite has either a balcony or patio, and the quiet, single-level
golf-course casitas offer patios with *"Fore!-star"* views. **Pros:** a diamond
in the Valley's remote rough. **Cons:** far from the central Valley; despite
its name, it is less a resort and more a conference-oriented hotel. ⊠ *One
San Marcos Pl., Chandler* ☏*480/812–0900* ⊕*www.sanmarcosresort.
com* ⥂*238 rooms, 45 casitas, 12 suites* ⟨⟩*In-room: Internet, Wi-Fi
(some). In-hotel: 2 restaurants, room service, bars, golf course, pools,
spa, parking (free), no-smoking rooms* ⊟*AE, D, DC, MC, V* ⊹*H6.*

$$$$ ⊞**Sheraton Wild Horse Pass Resort & Spa.** On the grounds of the Gila River
☾ Indian community, 11 mi south of Sky Harbor Airport, the culture and
heritage of the Pima and Maricopa tribes are reflected in every aspect of
this property. Guest rooms are detailed with Native American art and
textiles (but also have flat-screen TVs), and Kai Restaurant combines
Southwestern and Native American culinary traditions. Families enjoy
the Koli Center for on-site equestrian activities and the kids-oriented
activity pool. A 2½-mi replica of the Gila River meanders through the
property; you can take a boat to the Whirlwind Golf Clubhouse, the
nearby Wild Horse Pass Casino, or Rawhide Western Town. Keep your
eyes open for the wild horses for which the resort is named—or keep
them comfortably closed at the Aji Spa. **Pros:** great views and service;
ideal for families and older travelers looking to escape urban chaos.
Cons: conferences can sometimes overrun the place; so spread out it
requires a lot of walking. ⊠*5594 W. Wild Horse Pass Blvd., Chandler*
☏*602/225–0100 or 800/325–3535* ⊕*www.wildhorsepassresort.com*
⥂*474 rooms, 26 suites* ⟨⟩*In-room: safe, Internet, refrigerator (some).
In-hotel: 4 restaurants, bars, golf courses, tennis courts, pools, gym,
spa, laundry service, public Wi-Fi, parking (free), no-smoking rooms*
⊟*AE, D, DC, MC, V* ⊹*C6.*

TEMPE

$$$ ⊞**aloft Tempe.** True to its name, this hip hotel, located right on Tempe's
☾ Rio Salado waterfront, features loft-inspired design, with modern, mini-
malist decor. Bright, flashy, and fun, aloft is unlike anything the Valley
has seen. It seeks to create a social experience for travelers, pulling them
out into community areas where "energy flows" instead of encouraging
them to hole up in their rooms. Built with the intention of getting guests
to socialize, the modern European-style rooms are small, affording views
of Tempe Town Lake on the south side. Bathrooms are also stylish but
utilitarian. **Pros:** 42-inch LCD TVs, eco-friendly, highly social; adjacent
to Town Lake and ASU action. **Cons:** adjacent to Town Lake and ASU
action; social lodging experience not for everyone. ⊠*951 E. Playa
Del Norte Drive, Tempe* ☏*480/621–3300 or 888/867–7492* ⊕*www.*

starwoodhotels.com/alofthotels ↄ*136 rooms* ⌂ *In-room: refrigerator, Ethernet, Wi-Fi. In-hotel: 2 restaurants, bar, pool, gym, public Wi-Fi, parking (free), no-smoking rooms* ⊟*AE, D, DC, MC, V* ⊕*E6.*

$$$ 🖼 **The Buttes Marriott Resort.** Two miles east of Sky Harbor Airport, nes-
☾ tled in among desert buttes at Interstate 10 and AZ 60, this hotel joins
dramatic architecture (the lobby's back wall is the volcanic rock itself)
and classic Southwest design (pine and saguaro-rib furniture, works by
major regional artists) with stunning Valley views. Purchased and com-
pletely renovated by Marriott, the Buttes has reemerged as a beacon on
the hill, and now includes the Naranda "Revive" spa facility. "Radial"
rooms are the largest; inside rooms face the huge free-form pools with
waterfall, hot tubs, and a poolside cantina. The Top of the Rock restau-
rant is elegant. Kids can enjoy the new water slide and summer activi-
ties. **Pros:** beautiful, centrally located Tempe property; great beds; sand
volleyball; friendly service. **Cons:** "city views" also include freeway and
parking-lot views. ✉*2000 Westcourt Way, Tempe* ☎*602/225-9000
or 888/867–7492* ⊕*www.marriott.com* ↄ*345 rooms, 9 suites* ⌂*In-
room: refrigerator (some), Wi-Fi. In-hotel: 4 restaurants, bars, tennis
courts, pool, gym, spa, laundry service, executive floor, public Wi-Fi,
parking (free), no-smoking rooms* ⊟*AE, D, DC, MC, V* ⊕*D6.*

$$ 🖼 **Tempe Mission Palms Hotel.** A handsome, casual lobby and an energetic
young staff set the tone at this three-story courtyard hotel. Rooms are
Southwestern in style and quite comfortable. Between the Arizona State
University campus and Old Town Tempe, this is a convenient place to
stay if you're attending ASU sports events, and Harry's Place becomes a
lively sports lounge at game time. **Pros:** nice hotel with friendly service
and a rooftop pool, right at the center of ASU and Mill Avenue activity. **Cons:** all that activity can be bad for light sleepers. ✉*60 E. 5th
St., Tempe* ☎*480/894–1400 or 800/547–8705* ⊕*www.missionpalms.
com* ↄ*297 rooms, 6 suites* ⌂*In-room: refrigerator (some), Internet,
Wi-Fi. In-hotel: restaurant, room service, bar, tennis courts, basketball,
pool, gym, public Wi-Fi, parking (free), no-smoking rooms* ⊟*AE, D,
DC, MC, V* ⊕*E6.*

NIGHTLIFE AND THE ARTS

Updated by
Cara LaBrie

Over the past decade the Valley of the Sun has gone from a "cow town"
to "now town," and the nightlife and culture options are no exception.
Downtown Phoenix and Scottsdale are especially packed with entertainment choices.

THE ARTS

For weekly listings of theater, arts, and music, check out Thursday's
Arizona Republic, pick up a free issue of the independent weekly *New
Times*, or check out *Where Phoenix/Scottsdale Magazine*, available free
in most hotels. Good online sources of information on events in the
Valley are the *Arizona Republic* Web site (⊕*www.azcentral.com*) and
⊕*www.showup.com*. Both have extensive nightlife and arts listings;
ShowUp has some good last-minute deals on performances.

TICKETS **Arizona State University Public Events Box Office** (☎*480/965–6447* ⊕*www. herbergercollege.asu.edu/calendar*) sells tickets for ASU events. **Tickets. com** (⊕*www.tickets.com*) sells tickets for ASU Public Events at ASU Gammage Auditorium, Kerr Theatre, and the Maricopa County Events Center. **Ticketmaster** (☎*480/784–4444* ⊕*www.ticketmaster.com*) sells tickets for nearly every event in the Valley and has outlets at Fry's and Macy's stores.

MAJOR PERFORMANCE VENUES

To feed its growing tourism industry Phoenix has cooked up enticing entertainment venues that attract everything from major-league sporting events to the hottest music acts and the most raved-about theater productions.

PHOENIX The **Celebrity Theatre** (✉*440 N. 32nd St., Airport* ☎*602/267–1600* ⊕*www.celebritytheatre.com*) is a 2,600-seat theater-in-the-round hosting concerts and other live performances.

Cricket Pavilion (✉*2121 N. 83rd Ave., West Phoenix* ☎*602/254–7200* ⊕*www.cricket-pavilion.com*) is an outdoor amphitheater that books major live concerts.

The **Dodge Theatre** (✉*400 W. Washington St., Downtown Phoenix* ☎*602/379–2800* ⊕*www.dodgetheatre.com*) is Phoenix's high-tech, state-of-the-art entertainment venue. The space morphs from an intimate Broadway stage setup to a concert hall seating 5,000. There are great views from almost every seat.

Herberger Theater Center (✉*222 E. Monroe St., Downtown Phoenix* ☎*602/254–7399* ⊕*www.herbergertheater.org*) is the permanent home of the Arizona Theatre Company and Actors Theatre of Phoenix; it also hosts performances of visiting dance troupes, orchestras, and Broadway shows.

Mesa Arts Center (✉*1 E. Main St., Mesa* ☎*480/644–6500* ⊕*www. mesaartscenter.com*) has risen to the demand for culture and creative art and is fast becoming one of the Valley's top destinations for exhibits, visual-art performances, and A-list concerts.

The **Orpheum Theatre** (✉*203 W. Adams St., Downtown Phoenix* ☎*602/534–5600, 602/262–7272 box office*), built in 1927 and renovated throughout the '90s, is a glamorous theater showcasing the Arizona Ballet, children's theater, and film festivals.

Facing the Herberger Theater is **Symphony Hall** (✉*225 E. Adams St., Downtown Phoenix* ☎*602/495–1999 or 800/776–9080* ⊕*www.phoenix symphony.org*), home of the Phoenix Symphony and Arizona Opera.

SCOTTSDALE **Kerr Cultural Center** (✉*6110 N. Scottsdale Rd., Central Scottsdale* ☎*480/ 596–2660* ⊕*www.asukerr.com*) showcases smaller theater and dance performances.

Scottsdale Center for the Arts (✉*7380 E. 2nd St., Old Town* ☎*480/994–2787* ⊕*www.scottsdalearts.org*) hosts cultural events on the Scottsdale Mall as well as year-round performances in two intimate theater settings.

TEMPE Frank Lloyd Wright designed the **ASU Gammage Auditorium** (✉*Arizona State University, Mill Ave. at Apache Blvd., Tempe* ☎*480/965–3434*

Frank Lloyd Wright's architectural legacy in the Valley of the Sun includes ASU Gammage Auditorium in Tempe.

⊕*www.asugammage.com*), which presents more Broadway shows outside of the Big Apple than any other venue in the nation.

Herberger College of Fine Arts at Arizona State University (✉*Arizona State University, Mill Ave. at Apache Blvd., Tempe* ☎480/965–6447 ⊕*www. herbergercollege.asu.edu*) includes Katzin Concert Hall, Lyceum Theatre, Galvin Playhouse, and the Evelyn Smith Music Theatre and Organ Hall, which houses an 1,800-pipe Fritts Organ. Numerous performances are offered during the school year, from September through April, and many are free.

The **Maricopa County Events Center** (✉*19403 R. H. Johnson Blvd., Sun City West* ☎623/544–2888 ⊕*www.maricopacountyeventscenter.com*) attracts national tours of comedians and musicians.

The Chandler Center for the Arts(✉*250 N. Arizona Ave., Chandler West* ☎480/782–2680 ⊕*www.chandlercenter.org*), features some of the nation's most popular touring performances for families and children.

CLASSICAL MUSIC

Arizona Opera (✉*4600 N. 12th St., Downtown Phoenix* ☎602/266–7464 ⊕*www.azopera.com*) stages an opera season in both Tucson and Phoenix. The Phoenix season runs from October to March at Symphony Hall.

Phoenix Symphony Orchestra (✉*1 N. 1st St., Downtown Phoenix* ☎602/ 495–1999 or 800/776–9080 ⊕*www.phoenixsymphony.org*) is the resident company at Symphony Hall. Its season, which runs September through May, includes orchestral works from classical and contemporary composers, a chamber series, composer festivals, and outdoor pops concerts.

CLOSE UP

Spas in the Valley of the Sun

There's no better place for relaxation than at one of Phoenix's rejuvenating resort spas. Many feature Native American–inspired treatments and use indigenous ingredients such as agave and desert clay. Enjoy not only the treatments but the spa amenities, including pools, steam rooms, and relaxation areas. *For contact information, see Where to Stay.* Prices are subject to change.

★ **Fodor's Choice** | **Aji Spa at the Sheraton Wild Horse Pass Resort & Spa.** A gem on the grounds of the Gila River Indian community, Aji incorporates its Native American surroundings into every aspect of the spa, from the name ("Aji" is Pima for sanctuary) to its Sonoran design and treatments. The Bahn or Blue Coyote Wrap ($195–$215 for 80 minutes) begins with a dry-brush exfoliation and an application of Azulene mud, and culminates with a cedar-sage oil massage. For the true local feel, try the Pima Medicine massage, which includes ancient Indian healing techniques. ($145–$165). Massages start at 50 minutes for $125.

Alvadora at the Royal Palms Resort & Spa. Romance is not limited to the restaurant and rooms here. Alvadora offers treatments that incorporate herbs, flowers, oils, and minerals indigenous to the Mediterranean, like the Royal Body Polish which sloughs off the old and enhances new, soft skin ($135). The massage menu ranges from a 60-minute classic ($145) to couples' massage sessions ($280–$400) and the controversial watsu (aqua shiatsu) ($145 for 60 minutes). Spa use for nonresort guests is only Sunday through Thursday, and requires purchase of a spa package.

Four Seasons Troon North. The elegant Spa at Four Seasons Troon North is a moderate little bit of heaven hidden in the serene foothills of the Sonoran desert. The list of massages seems endless, and includes a 50-minute Head Over Heals rub with two therapists at once ($310), or an 80-minute moonlight balcony massage ($220–$370). Body treatments range from $95 to $310. Try the the Golfers' Massage in which muscles are kneaded with warmed golf balls ($155–$210).

Golden Door Spa at the Boulders Resort. If you're seeking the serenity of the desert, this is the place. Influenced by Asian and Native American cultures, the soothing Southwestern spa is divided into two wings—east for relaxation and west for activity, which includes a movement studio for Pilates, tai chi, and yoga. Try a Native American–inspired treatment like the Turquoise Wrap ($215), which includes a Hopi blue-cornmeal body scrub and a turquoise clay wrap, or surrender to an Asian-inspired 50-minute Shiatsu massage ($225), or take a walk through the Hopi-inspired path-to-tranquillity labyrinth.

★ **Fodor's Choice** | **Joya Spa at Montelucia Resort.** This new, two-story spa offers up a stairway to heaven and the heavens, literally. Everything here is meticulously handcrafted, handpicked, or hand-placed to summon the healing spirits. Enjoy the Eastern body hammam experience with any treatment ($45) or the signature 90-minute Joyambrosia using organic moon-kissed oils, citrus, spices, and mint ($165–$245). The amazing Couples' Romance Journey is a four-hour session that will feel like twenty-four ($995–$1,195).

2

Jurlique Spa at FireSky Resort and Spa. With its unforgettably elegant and relaxing interior, Jurlique focuses on repairing and restoring from within by relying on plant science and a combination of Eastern and Western spa philosophies. Try a 90-minute Zen Harmony facial or any 90-minute massage for $170–$190. One-and-a-half- to 6½-hour spa packages range from $175 to $620. The herbal water therapies are heaven "scent," as are the all-natural Jurlique products.

Revive Spa at JW Marriott Desert Ridge Resort. A huge, two-story temple devoted to the health and healing of the human body, Revive at Desert Ridge features 41 luxury treatment rooms, an Olympic-size swimming pool, private balconies for outdoor massages, indoor relaxation rooms with fireplaces, outdoor celestial showers, a healthful bistro, a fitness center, and a full salon. A pumpkin-enzyme peeling mask is just $20; a caviar facial is $195. Massages range from $125 to $190 and body treatments from $130 to $225.

Sanctuary Spa at Sanctuary on Camelback Mountain. This sleek Zen-like spa has 11 Asian-inspired indoor-outdoor treatment rooms nestled against Camelback Mountain. Try a watsu in-water body massage ($150–$210), a transporting 30-minute Thai Foot Reflexology massage ($95–$170), or a Bamboo Lemongrass Scrub ($90–$210). A 60-minute massage starts at $150.

The Spa at JW Marriott's Camelback Inn. One of the Valley's most popular spas blends Mediterranean and desert themes. Aches and pains will melt away with the 60-minute Native Hot Stone Massage (starts at

$125); the Sonoran Rose Facial is two treatments in one, and incorporates the hands and arms ($135). The new Thai Table Massage incorporates yoga and compressions to increase energy flow ($130).

Spa Avania at the Hyatt Regency Scottsdale at Gainey Ranch. Spa Avania's claim to fame is that it's "the first complete spa experience choreographed to your body's perfect timing." The gorgeous stone-tiled spa seeks to cleanse the body of unnatural stimuli and give equilibrium through the senses, the way nature intended. Specialty treatments include a 30-minute blackberry-balm hand massage ($80), golfer massage ($165), and couples' massage ($405–$525). Two- to four-hour spa packages range from $289 to $555.

VH Spa at the Hotel Valley Ho. After seeing the rebirth of the Hotel Valley Ho, guests should feel comfortable entrusting renovation of the body and soul to the hip, colored-glass VH (Vitality Health) Spa. Get a popular 60-minute poolside cabana massage ($155), or go full spa with the unique Red Flower Hammam Full-Body Treatment Massage, a Turkish-inspired detoxification that scrubs the skin with coffee, olive stones, and fresh lemon ($185), or consult for a better body through Tibetan technique ($250).

Willow Stream Spa at the Fairmont Scottsdale Princess. This is one of the Valley's most elaborate spas. Inspired by Havasu Canyon, a hidden oasis in the Grand Canyon, there's water everywhere. A 60-minute massage starts at about $160 or you can splurge for the two-hour Havasupai Body Treatment ($319), under waterfalls of varying pressure.

Rawhide Western Town, or another wild west show with dinner, is a great recipe for family fun.

DANCE

Ballet Arizona (☎ *602/381–1096* ⊕ *www.balletaz.org*), the state's professional ballet company, presents a full season of classical and contemporary works (including pieces commissioned for the company) in Tucson and Phoenix, where it performs at the Orpheum Theater, downtown. The season runs from October through May.

THEATER

Actors Theatre of Phoenix (☎ *602/253–6701* ⊕ *www.atphx.org*) is the resident theater troupe at the Herberger Theater Center. It presents a full season of drama, comedy, and musical productions from September through May.

Arizona Theatre Company (☎ *602/256–6995* ⊕ *www.aztheatreco.org*) is based in Tuscon but also performs at the Herberger Theater Center. Productions, held from September through June, range from classic dramas to musicals and new works by emerging playwrights.

Black Theater Troupe (☎ *602/258–8128* ⊕ *www.blacktheatretroupe.org*) presents original and contemporary dramas and musical revues, as well as adventurous adaptations, between September and May.

☺ **Childsplay** (✉ *900 S. Mitchell Dr., Tempe* ☎ *480/921–5700* ⊕ *www.childsplayaz.org*) is the state's theater company for young audiences and families, which runs during the school year. Rotating through many a venue, these players deliver high-energy performances.

☺ **Great Arizona Puppet Theatre** (✉ *302 W. Latham St., Downtown Phoenix* ☎ *602/262–2050* ⊕ *www.azpuppets.org*), which performs in a historic building featuring lots of theater and exhibit space, mounts a yearlong cycle of inventive puppet productions that change frequently.

Phoenix Theatre (✉*100 E. McDowell Rd., Downtown Phoenix* ☎*602/254–2151* ⊕*www.phxtheatre.org*), across the courtyard from the Phoenix Art Museum, stages musical and dramatic performances as well as productions for children by the Cookie Company.

WILD WEST SHOWS

☺ **Rawhide Western Town and Steakhouse**
Fodor'sChoice **at Wild Horse Pass** (✉*5700 W. North*
★ *Loop Rd., Gila River Indian Community, Chandler* ☎*480/502–5600 or 800/527–1880* ⊕*www.rawhide.com*), a Valley favorite for more than four decades, calls the 2,400-acre master-planned Wild Horse Pass Development in the Gila River Indian Community home. Featuring its legendary steak house and saloon, Main Street and all of its retail shops, and the Six Gun Theater, Rawhide is the kitschiest place in town to experience the Old West. Enjoy canal rides along the Gila River Riverwalk, train rides, and a Native American village honoring the history and culture of the Akimel O'othom and Pee Posh Tribes. Transform yourself into the Wild West, where you can watch a stunt show featuring gunslingers, have a fellow guest arrested and tossed in jail, or watch trick roping performed by the pros.

☺ **Rockin' R Ranch** (✉*6136 E. Baseline Rd., Mesa* ☎*480/832–1539* ⊕*www.rockinr.net*) includes a petting zoo, a reenactment of a Wild West shoot out, and—the main attraction—a nightly cookout with a Western stage show. Pan for gold or take a wagon ride until the "vittles" are served, followed by music and entertainment.

EXPERIENCE THE WILD WEST

In addition to the state and county fairs, and some seasonal shows, there are several places in and around Phoenix to get a taste of what the West was like way back when. Rawhide and the Rockin' R Ranch, closer to town, are the more kid-friendly, while Pioneer Living History Village and Goldfield Ghost Town (*see Side Trips*) are more sedate, with a stronger emphasis on authentic historic buildings.

NIGHTLIFE

From brewpubs, sports bars, and coffeehouses to dance clubs, megaconcerts, and country venues, the Valley of the Sun offers nightlife of all types. Nightclubs, comedy clubs, upscale lounges, and wine bars abound in downtown Phoenix, along Camelback Road in North Central Phoenix, and in Scottsdale and Tempe, as well as the other suburbs.

Among music and dancing styles, country-and-western has the longest tradition here. Jazz venues, rock clubs, and hotel lounges are also numerous and varied. Phoenix continues to get hipper and more cosmopolitan, so cigar lovers and martini sippers will find plenty of places to indulge. There are also more than 30 gay and lesbian bars, primarily on 7th Avenue, 7th Street, and the stretch of Camelback Road between the two.

You can find listings and reviews in the *New Times* free weekly newspaper, distributed Wednesday, "The Rep Entertainment Guide" of the

Arizona Republic, or online at ⊕*www.azcentral.com,* the paper's Web site. *PHX Downtown,* a free monthly available in downtown establishments, has an extensive calendar of events from art exhibits and poetry readings to professional sports. The local gay scene is covered in *Echo Magazine,* which you can pick up all over town.

BARS AND LOUNGES

PHOENIX **Bomberos Café & Wine Bar** (✉*8801 N. Central Ave., North Central Phoenix, Phoenix* ☏*602/687–8466* ⊕*www.bomberoswinebar.com*) occupies a former firehouse. This little neighborhood ember burns bright with its pleasant outdoor patio, delectable paninis and bruschetta, rich desserts, Illy coffees, and a rich selection of unique and flavorful world wines.

Fez On Central (✉*3815 N. Central Ave., Central Phoenix* ☏*602/287–8700* ⊕*www.fezoncentral.com*) is a stylish restaurant by day and a gay-friendly, hip hot spot by night. The sleek interior and fancy drinks make you feel uptown, while the happy-hour prices and location keep this place grounded.

★ **Jade Bar** (✉*5700 E. McDonald Dr., Sanctuary on Camelback Resort, Paradise Valley* ☏*480/948–2100*) has spectacular views of Paradise Valley and Camelback Mountain, an upscale, modern bar lined with windows, and a relaxing fireplace-lit patio.

Lisa G Café Wine Bar (✉*2337 N. 7th St., Central Phoenix* ☏*602/253–9201* ⊕*www.lisagwinebar.com*) has a clean, homey, hip atmosphere with superb wine and eats (try Lisa's famous meatballs). It's a great happy-hour stop before having dinner at neighboring restaurants.

Majerle's Sports Grill (⊕*www.majerles.com*) (✉*24 N. 2nd St., Downtown Phoenix* ☏*602/253–9004*) (✉*3095 W. Chandler Blvd., Chandler* ☏*480/899–7999*), operated by former Suns basketball player Dan Majerle, offers a comprehensive menu for pre- and postgame celebrations as well as some of the best people-watching potential in town.

Postino Winebar (✉*3939 E. Campbell Ave., Camelback Corridor, Phoenix* ☏*602/852–3939* ⊕*www.postinowinecafe.com*) occupies a former post office in the Arcadia neighborhood. More than 40 wines are poured by the glass. Order a few grazing items off the appetizer menu (the bruschetta is unmatched by any in the Valley) and settle in, or carry out a bottle of wine, hunk of cheese, and loaf of bread for a twilight picnic.

Seamus McCaffrey's Irish Pub (✉*18 W. Monroe St., Downtown Phoenix* ☏*602/253–6081* ⊕*www.seamusmccaffreys.com*) is a fun and friendly place to enjoy one of the dozen European brews on draft. A small kitchen turns out traditional Irish fare.

SCOTTSDALE **AZ88** (✉*7353 Scottsdale Mall, Scottsdale Civic Center, Old Town, Scottsdale* ☏*480/994–5576*) is great for feasting on huge portions of great food and lavish quantities of liquor, but also for feasting your eyes on the fabulous people who flock here on weekend nights to see and be seen.

Fox Sports Grill (✉*16203 N. Scottsdale Rd., North Scottsdale, Scottsdale* ☏*480/368–0369* ⊕*www.foxsportsgrill.com*) is where trendy, stylish sports fans gather to watch live Fox Sports broadcasts on flat-screen TVs, play pool, and socialize in the sleek VIP room.

Kazimierz World Wine Bar (✉ *7137 E. Stetson Dr., Old Town, Scottsdale* ☎ *480/946–3004* ⊕ *www.kazbar.net*) is entered through a door marked THE TRUTH IS INSIDE, beyond which lies a dark, cave-like wine bar with comfy chairs and good music.

The Salty Senorita (✉ *336 N. Scottsdale Rd., Old Town, Scottsdale* ☎ *480/946–7258* ⊕ *www.saltyseniorita.com*) is known more for its extensive margarita selection and lively patio crowd than for its food. The restaurant–bar touts 51 different margaritas—with some recipes so secret they won't tell you what goes in them—try the El Presidente or the Chupacabra.

Six Lounge and Restaurant (✉ *7316 E. Stetson Dr., Old Town, Scottsdale* ☎ *480/663–6620* ⊕ *www.6az.com*) is a crowded see-and-be-seen hot spot attracting the Valley's designer-clad jet-setters who groove to the tunes of a DJ.

TEMPE AND AROUND

Casey Moore's Oyster House (✉ *850 S. Ash Ave., Tempe* ☎ *480/968–9935* ⊕ *www.caseymoores.com*) is a laid-back institution where rockers, hippies, and families come together in a 1910 house rumored to be haunted by ghosts. Enjoy 28 beers on tap and fresh oysters at this Irish pub–style favorite.

Dos Gringos Trailer Park (✉ *1001 E. 8th St., Tempe* ☎ *480/968–7879* ✉ *4209 N. Craftsman Ct., Old Town, Scottsdale* ☎ *480/423–3800*) is a kitschy indoor–outdoor cantina that will remind you of trips over the Mexican border, or at least spring break. Crowds (mostly college students and twentysomethings) swig margaritas and beer in a multilevel courtyard surrounded by TVs and limestone fountains.

The Monastery Too (✉ *4810 E. McKellips, Mesa* ☎ *480/474–4477*) is a casual beer and wine pub where you grill your own burgers and nosh on picnic food. You can play horseshoes, chess, or volleyball.

BLUES, JAZZ, AND ROCK

Fodor'sChoice
★ **Char's Has the Blues** (✉ *4631 N. 7th Ave., Central Phoenix* ☎ *602/230–0205* ⊕ *www.charshastheblues.com*) is one of the Valley's top blues clubs, with nightly bands.

Marquee Theatre (✉ *730 N. Mill Ave., Tempe* ☎ *480/829–0607*) hosts mainly headlining rock-and-roll entertainers.

★ **Rhythm Room** (✉ *1019 E. Indian School Rd., Central Phoenix* ☎ *602/265–4842* ⊕ *www.rhythmroom.com*) attracts excellent local and national rock artists, as well as blues, seven nights a week. The perfect sidekick, Rack Shack Blues BBQ, in the parking lot, cooks up good barbecue Wednesday through Saturday evenings.

Sugar Daddy's Blues (✉ *3102 N. Scottsdale Rd., North Scottsdale* ☎ *480/970–6556* ⊕ *www.sugardaddysaz.com*) serves rhythm, blues, and eclectic Cajun-meets-Southwestern food nightly until 2 AM. A gratis graffiti-clad limo will pick you up anywhere within a 7-mi radius of the bar.

CASINOS

There are six casinos on Indian reservations around the Valley of the Sun (three with hotels). Compared with Las Vegas, they offer smaller venues and a low-key atmosphere. The casinos follow Arizona gaming law, such as no betting cash—chips only.

Casino Arizona at Indian Bend (✉ *9700 E. Indian Bend Rd., North Scottsdale* ☎ *480/850–7777* ⊕ *www.casinoaz.com*) draws locals for blackjack, poker, keno, more than 200 slot machines, and an off-track-betting room that has wide-screen TVs.

Casino Arizona at Salt River (✉ *524 N. 92nd St., South Scottsdale* ☎ *480/850–7777, 480/850–7790 for free transportation* ⊕ *www.casinoaz.com*) is the largest casino in the area, with five restaurants, four lounges, a sports bar, a 250-seat theater featuring live performances, two large blackjack rooms, and a keno parlor. There's live music and dancing most nights.

Fort McDowell Casino (✉ *AZ 87 at Fort McDowell Rd., Fountain Hills* ☎ *800/843–3678* ⊕ *www.fortmcdowellcasino.com*) is popular with the resort crowd. In addition to the cards, slot machines, bingo hall, and keno games, off-track greyhound wagering takes place in a classy mahogany room with 18 giant video screens. Take advantage of the free Valley-wide shuttle.

Gila River Casino Wild Horse Pass (✉ *5550 W. Wild Horse Pass, Chandler* ☎ *800/946–4452* ⊕ *www.wingilariver.com*) as part of the Wild Horse Pass Resort & Spa, includes 500 slots, live poker, blackjack, keno, and complimentary soft drinks.

COFFEEHOUSES

Gold Bar Espresso (✉ *3141 S. McClintock Dr., Suite 6, Tempe* ☎ *480/839–3082* ⊕ *www.goldbarespresso.org*) is an inviting coffeehouse decorated with funky antiques. The coffee is first-rate, and there's live jazz on weekends.

★ **Lux Coffee Bar** (✉ *4404 N. Central, Downtown Phoenix* ☎ *602/696–9976* ⊕ *www.luxcoffee.com*), with local art and retro furniture, is an eclectic gathering place where artists, architects, and downtown businesspeople enjoy excellent classic European espresso drinks.

Paisley Violin European Cafe (✉ *1030 N.W. Grand Ave., Downtown Phoenix* ☎ *602/254–7843* ⊕ *www.thepaisley.com*) is an offbeat, beatnik coffeehouse–café with live local music Wednesday through Saturday nights. Nosh on Mediterranean food and sip a cappuccino amid local art and mismatched furniture. This is a good place to start and finish after visiting art galleries on First Fridays.

Drip Coffee Lounge (✉ *2325 N. 7th St., Central Phoenix* ☎ *602/795-9905* ⊕ *www.dripcoffeelounge.com.com*) is emerging as a favorite for Central Phoenix's hip, young urban community for a morning cuppa Joe or a quick lunch.

COMEDY

The Comedy Spot (✉ *7117 E. 3rd Ave., Old Town, Scottsdale* ☎ *480/945–4422* ⊕ *www.thecomedyspot.net*) features local and national stand-up talent. They also offer classes for wannabe comedians on Sunday.

The Tempe Improv (⊠*930 E. University Dr., Tempe* ☎*480/921–9877* ⊕*www. tempeimprov.com*), part of a national chain, showcases better-known headliners from Thursday to Sunday. Get there early for good seats.

Theater 168 (⊠*7117 E. McDowell Rd., Scottsdale* ☎*480/423–0120* ⊕*www.theater168.com*) has clean, family-friendly comedy shows performed by Jester'Z Improvisational Troupe on Thursday, Friday, and Saturday nights at 8 PM.

COUNTRY AND WESTERN

★ **Greasewood Flat** (⊠*27535 N. Alma School Pkwy., North Scottsdale* ☎*480/585–9430* ⊕*www.greasewoodflat.net*) isn't fancy; in fact, it's downright ramshackle, but the burgers are delicious and the crowds friendly. There's a dance floor with live music Thursday through Sunday. In winter, wear jeans and a jacket, since everything is outside; to keep warm, folks congregate around fires burning in halved oil drums.

Handlebar-J (⊠*7116 E. Becker La., Central Scottsdale* ☎*480/948–0110* ⊕*www.handlebarj.com*) is a lively restaurant and bar with a Western line-dancing, 10-gallon-hat–wearing crowd.

DANCE CLUBS

★ **Axis/Radius** (⊠*7340 E. Indian Plaza Rd., Central Scottsdale* ☎*480/970–1112* ⊕*www.axis-radius.com*) is the dress-to-impress locale where you can party at side-by-side clubs connected by a glass catwalk.

Cherry Lounge & Pit (⊠*411 S. Mill Ave., Tempe* ☎*480/966–3573* ⊕*www. thecherryloungeaz.com*) is considered by locals to be the best dance club in the Valley. The fact that it is equipped with plenty of patron-accessible dance poles and that free pole-dancing lessons are offered during nonpeak hours probably gave it a leg up.

Myst (⊠*7340 E. Shoeman La., Old Town, Scottsdale* ☎*480/970–5000* ⊕*www.mystaz.com*) is an ultraswanky dance club where you can sip cocktails in a sunken lounge or hang out at the white-hot Milk Bar adorned with white-leather seating and an all-white bar. Upstairs is the private VIP lounge, complete with skyboxes overlooking the dance floor.

GAY AND LESBIAN BARS

Ain't Nobody's Bizness (⊠*3031 E. Indian School Rd., Central Phoenix* ☎*602/224–9977*) is the most popular lesbian bar in town; you'll also find a few gay men at this male-friendly establishment, well known as one of the most fun in town.

★ **Amsterdam** (⊠*718 N. Central Ave., Downtown Phoenix* ☎*602/258–6122* ⊕*www.amsterdambar.com*) attracts a young crowd that wants to see and be seen; it's where Phoenix's beautiful gay people hang out.

B.S. West (⊠*7125 E. 5th Ave., Old Town, Scottsdale* ☎*480/945–9028* ⊕*www.bswest.com*) is tucked behind a shopping center on Scottsdale's main shopping drag and draws a stylish, well-heeled crowd.

Charlie's (⊠*727 W. Camelback Rd., Central Phoenix* ☎*602/265–0224* ⊕*www.charliesphoenix.com*), a longtime favorite of local gay men, has a country-western look (cowboy hats are the accessory of choice) and friendly staff.

CashInnCarry (⊠ *2140 E. McDowell Rd., Downtown Phoenix* ☎ *602/244–9943* ⊕ *www.cashinncountry.net* has an eclectic clientele of women and features music just as diverse, from Latin to country.

MICROBREWERIES

★ **Four Peaks Brewing Company** (⊠ *1340 E. 8th St., Tempe* ☎ *480/303–9967* ⊕ *www.fourpeaks.com*) is the former redbrick home of Bordens Creamery. Ten different brews are on tap, and pub grub, pizza, and burgers fill the menu.

Rock Bottom Brewery (⊠ *8668 E. Shea Blvd., North Scottsdale* ☎ *480/998–7777* ⊠ *21001 N. Tatum Blvd., Desert Ridge Mall, North Central Phoenix* ☎ *480/513–9125* ⊠ *14205 S. 50th St., Ahwatukee, Phoenix* ☎ *480/598–1300* ⊕ *www.rockbottom.com*) has tasty pub grub (start with the giant soft pretzels served with spicy spinach dip) and beer brewed on the premises. Watch out: the bill tends to rack up quickly.

San Tan Brewing Company (⊠ *8 San Marcos Pl., Old Town, Chandler* ☎ *480/917–8700* ⊕ *www.santanbrewing.com*) combines good food with great beer and an energetic pub atmosphere without the tired, hole-in-the-wall or overly commercial feel. Wash down some raspberry mushrooms and a stuffed burger with a San Tan IPA.

Sonora Brewhouse (⊠ *322 E. Camelback Rd., Central Phoenix, Phoenix* ☎ *602/279–8909* ⊕ *www.sonorabrewhouse.com*) is a great hangout with mediocre pub grub and outstanding locally crafted brews like Light Cream Ale, Trooper IPA, and Brewer's Den Hefeweizen, one of the Valley's best.

SHOPPING

Since its resorts began multiplying in the 1930s and '40s, Phoenix has acquired many high-fashion clothiers and leisure-wear boutiques, but you can still find the Western clothes that in many parts of town still dominate the fashion. Jeans and boots, cotton shirts and dresses, 10-gallon hats, and bola ties (the state's official neckwear) are still the staples. On the scene as well are the arts of the Southwest's true natives—Navajo weavers, sand painters, and silversmiths; Hopi weavers and kachina-doll carvers; Pima and Tohono O'odham (Papago) basket makers and potters; and many more. Inspired by the region's rich cultural traditions, contemporary artists have flourished here, making Phoenix—particularly Scottsdale, a city with more art galleries than gas stations—one of the Southwest's largest art centers (alongside Santa Fe, New Mexico).

Today's shoppers find the best of the old and the new—all presented with Southwestern style. Upscale stores, one-of-a-kind shops, and outlet malls sell the latest fashions, cowboy collectibles, handwoven rugs, traditional Mexican folk art, and contemporary turquoise jewelry.

Most of the Valley's power shopping is concentrated in Central Phoenix, downtown Scottsdale, and the Kierland area in North Scottsdale, but auctions and antiques shops cluster in odd places—and as treasure hunters know, you've always got to keep your eyes open.

SHOPPING CENTERS

Although some of Phoenix's malls are gorgeously landscaped outdoor areas, most, like Scottsdale Fashion Square are indoor complexes. Cool stores with icy air-conditioning can be just the ticket for relief from the midday desert heat.

Arizona Mills (✉ *5000 Arizona Mills Circle, I–10 and Baseline Rd., Tempe* ☎ *480/491–7300* ⊕ *www.arizonamills.com*), a mammoth "value-oriented retail and entertainment mega mall," features more than 175 outlet stores and sideshows, including Off 5th–Saks Fifth Avenue, Kenneth Cole, and Last Call from Neiman Marcus. When you tire of bargain hunting, relax in the food court, cinemas, or faux rain forest.

★ **Biltmore Fashion Park** (✉ *24th St. and Camelback Rd., Camelback Corridor, Phoenix* ☎ *602/955–8400* ⊕ *www.shopbiltmore.com*) has a posh, parklike setting. Macy's, Saks Fifth Avenue, and Borders are the anchors for more than 70 stores and upscale boutiques such as Cornelia Park. It's accessible from the Camelback Esplanade and the Ritz Carlton by a pedestrian tunnel that runs beneath Camelback Road.

The Borgata (✉ *6166 N. Scottsdale Rd., Paradise Valley* ☎ *602/953–6311* ⊕ *www.borgata.com*), an outdoor re-creation of the Italian village of San Gimignano, with courtyards, stone walls, turrets, and fountains, is a lovely setting for browsing upscale boutiques or just sitting at an outdoor café.

Chandler Fashion Center (✉ *3111 W. Chandler Blvd., Chandler* ☎ *480/812–8488* ⊕ *www.chandlermall.com*) features anchor stores Nordstrom, Dillard's, Macy's, and Sears, along with more than 180 other national retail chains such as Coach, Pottery Barn, and Cheesecake Factory.

Cofco Chinese Cultural Center (✉ *668 N. 44th St., South Phoenix* ☎ *602/273–7268* ⊕ *www.phxchinatown.com*) is adorned with replicas of pagodas, statues, and traditional Chinese gardens. It's the place to find Asian restaurants, gift shops, and the Super L, a huge Asian grocery store. Take a stroll through the market's fish department—you'll forget you're in the desert.

Kierland Commons (✉ *Greenway Pkwy. at Scottsdale Rd., North Scottsdale, Scottsdale* ☎ *480/348–1577* ⊕ *www.kierlandcommons.com*), next to the Westin Kierland Resort, is one of the city's newest shopping areas. "Urban village" is the catchphrase for this outdoor pedestrian mall with restaurants and upscale chain retailers, among them J. Crew and Tommy Bahama.

★ **Mill Avenue Shops** (✉ *Mill Ave., between Rio Salado Pkwy. and University Dr., Downtown, Tempe* ☎ *480/921–2300* ⊕ *www.millavenue.com*), named for the landmark Hayden Flour Mill, is an increasingly commercial and construction-laden area, but it's still a fun-filled walk-and-shop experience. Directly west of the Arizona State University campus, Mill Avenue is an active melting pot of students, artists, residents, and tourists. Shops include Borders, Urban Outfitters, a few remaining locally owned stores, and countless bars and restaurants. The Valley Art Theater is a Mill Avenue institution and Tempe's home of indie cinema. Twice a year (in early December and March/April), the Mill Avenue area is the place to find indie arts and crafts when it hosts the Tempe Festival of the Arts.

Fodor'sChoice ★ **Old Town Scottsdale** (⊠ *Between Goldwater Blvd., Brown Ave., 5th Ave. and 3rd St., Old Town, Scottsdale*) is the place to go for authentic Southwest-inspired gifts, clothing, art, and artifacts. Despite its massive modern neighbors, this area and its merchants have long respected and maintained the single-level brick storefronts that embody Scottsdale's upscale cow-town charm. More than 100 businesses meet just about any aesthetic want or need, including Gilbert Ortega, one of the premier places for fine Native American jewelry and art. Some of Scottsdale's best restaurants are also found in this pleasing maze of merchandizing.

★ **Scottsdale Fashion Square** (⊠ *Scottsdale and Camelback Rds., Camelback Corridor, Scottsdale* ☎ *480/941–2140* ⊕ *www.fashionsquare.com*) has a retractable roof and many specialty shops unique to Arizona. There are also Nordstrom, Dillard's, Neiman Marcus, Macy's, Juicy Couture, Louis Vuitton, Tiffany, Cartier, and Arizona's only Gucci store. A huge food court, restaurants, and a cineplex complete the picture.

★ **The Shops Gainey Village** (⊠ *8787 N. Scottsdale Rd., North Scottsdale* ☎ *480/458–8064* ⊕ *www.theshopsgaineyvillage*), near historic Gainey Ranch, makes for stiff shopping competition in the area. Composed primarily of upscale boutiques, this stylish strip mall also features fine dining at hot spots like Bloom and Thai Foon and nosh spots like Paradise Bakery, the Coffee Bean, and Pei Wei Asian Café.

OPEN-AIR MARKETS

It can be a real treat to visit a farmers' market even if you're not a local doing grocery shopping. Phoenix markets often feature funky tortillas and Mexican wares, so you can sample some goodies and maybe find some presents to take home. Two of metropolitan Phoenix's best markets are in the tiny town of Guadalupe, which centers around Interstate 10, Baseline Road, and Warner Road. Take Interstate 10 south to Baseline Road, go east ½ mi, and turn south on Avenida del Yaqui to find open-air vegetable stalls, roadside fruit stands, and tidy houses covered in flowering vines. A conversational knowledge of Spanish will aid you in shopping. To find the fresh wares of a Valley farmers' market, visit ⊕ *www.arizonafarmersmarkets.com*, a comprehensive calendar listing started and maintained by longtime market coordinators Dee and John Logan.

Guadalupe Farmer's Market (⊠ *9210 S. Ave. del Yaqui, Guadalupe* ☎ *480/730–1945*) has all the fresh ingredients you'd find in a rural Mexican market—tomatillos, varieties of chile peppers (fresh and dried), fresh-ground *masa* (cornmeal) for tortillas, spices like cumin and cilantro, and on and on. It's open every day year-round: from 9 AM to 6 PM in fall, winter, and spring; to 7 PM in summer; and to 5 PM Sunday. **Mercado Mexico** (⊠ *8212 S. Ave. del Yaqui, Guadalupe* ☎ *480/831–5925*) carries ceramics, paper-, tin-, and lacquerware, all at unbeatable prices. Stock up from 10 AM to 6 PM daily, year-round.

The Southwest continues to inspire contemporary artists. You can see some locally crafted pieces yourself at the Wilde Meyer Galleries.

SPECIALTY SHOPS

ANTIQUES AND COLLECTIBLES

The Central Phoenix corridor, between 7th Street and 7th Avenue, has many antiques stores. Most shops sit north of Thomas and south of Camelback. Prices, though reasonable, are firm at most shops. A surprise to many visitors is the Old Town district of suburban Glendale, with more than 80 antiques and collectibles shops nestled around Historic Old Towne and Catlin Court, which are listed on the National Register of Historic Places.

Antique Centre (⊠2012 N. Scottsdale Rd., Central Scottsdale ☎480/ 675–9500 ⊕www.antiquecenteraz.com) has a hodgepodge of collectibles and trinkets. **Glendale Old Towne & Catlin Court** (⊠59th and Glendale Aves., Glendale) antiques district has a plethora of shops and restaurants in colorful, century-old bungalows. Stop in at antiques-filled Aunt Pittypat's Kitchen for breakfast or lunch, or have a cup of tea at the Spicery, which is in an 1895 Victorian home.

ARTS AND CRAFTS

Art One (⊠4120 N. Marshall Way, Old Town, Scottsdale ☎480/946– 5076 ⊕www.artonegalleryinc.com) carries works by students as well as local and emerging artists.

Fodor's Choice **Cosanti Originals** (⊠6433 Doubletree Ranch Rd., Paradise Valley ☎800/ ★ 752–3187 ⊕www.cosanti.com) is the studio where architect Paolo Soleri's famous bronze and ceramic wind chimes are made and sold. You can watch the craftspeople at work, then pick out your own—prices are surprisingly reasonable.

Drumbeat Indian Arts (✉ *4143 N. 16th St.*, *Central Phoenix* ☎ *602/266–4823* ⊕ *www.drumbeatindianarts.com*) is a small, interesting shop specializing in Native American music, movies, books, drums, and crafts supplies. If you're lucky, you might find authentic fry bread and Navajo tacos being cooked in the parking lot on weekends.

★ **The Heard Museum Shop** (✉ *2301 N. Central Ave.*, *Downtown Phoenix* ☎ *602/252–8344* ⊕ *www.heard.org*) is hands-down the best place in town for Southwestern Native American and other crafts, both traditional and modern. Prices tend to be high, but quality is assured, with many one-of-a-kind items among the collection of rugs, kachina dolls, pottery, and other crafts; there's also a wide selection of lower-priced gifts.

Trailside Galleries (✉ *7330 Scottsdale Mall, Old Town, Scottsdale* ☎ *480/945–7751* ⊕ *www.trailsidegalleries.com*) has been showcasing works by members of the Cowboy Artists of America for more than 40 years, and specializes in traditional American paintings and sculptures.

Fodor'sChoice **Wilde Meyer Galleries** ⊕ (✉ *4142 N. Marshall Way, Old Town, Scotts-*
★ *dale* ☎ *480/945–2323* ✉ *Colores by Wilde Meyer, 7100 E. Main St.*, *Old Town, Scottsdale* ☎ *480/947–1489* ⊕ *www.wildemeyer.com*) has two locations around the Valley of the Sun and another in Tucson; it's the place to go for the true colors of the Southwest. In addition to one-of-a-kind paintings, the galleries also feature rustic, fine-art imports from around the state and the world, including furniture, sculptures, and jewelry. Look for Linda Carter Holman's "Latin Ladies" paintings and works by Scottsdale's own Sherri Belassen, whose unique cowboys and cattle will leave you with a colorful new Western perspective.

FOOD AND WINE SHOPS

★ **AJ's Fine Foods** (✉ *5017 N. Central Ave.*, *Phoenix* ☎ *602/230–7015* ✉ *7141 E. Lincoln Dr.*, *Scottsdale* ☎ *480/998–0052* ✉ *7131 W. Ray Rd.*, *Chandler* ☎ *480/705–0011* ✉ *20050 N. 67th Ave.*, *Glendale* ☎ *623/537–2310* ✉ *15031 Thompson Peak Pkwy.*, *North Scottsdale* ☎ *480/314–6500* ⊕ *www.ajsfinefoods.com*) is the Valley's grandest upscale grocery store and a great place to fill your basket with exclusive local creations ranging from Goldwater's salsas and sauces—created by the daughters of the late senator Barry Goldwater—to Sada's Pepper Melody and Rene's Desert Rub spice mixes. It's possible to spend hours at any of the 13 identical Valley locations, and it's also possible to spend far more money than you would at an average grocery store, but the vast inventory of unusual products not found together anywhere else and the first-class, one-stop shopping experience make it all worthwhile. The wine selection is among the best in town, and the sommelier-quality staff will gladly offer suggestions. Be sure to partake of the fresh, chef-prepared food offerings, like homemade soups, salad, pizza, specialty sandwiches, and gourmet take-out entrées from the bistro.

★ **Sportsman's Fine Wine & Spirits** (✉ *3205 E. Camelback Rd.*, *Phoenix* ☎ *602/955–9463* ✉ *10893 N. Scottsdale Rd.*, *Scottsdale* ☎ *480/948–0520* ✉ *6685 W. Beardsley Rd.*, *Glendale* ☎ *623/572–9463* ✉ *15955 N. Dial Blvd.*, *North Scottsdale* ☎ *480/348–9040* ⊕ *www.sportsmans4wine.com*) is the place to go to "lift your spirits." Sportsman's stocks fine wines and rare beverage finds from both local and international sources. They also sell cheeses and other delicious wine accompaniments including *panini* sandwiches, roasted garlic, hummus, bruschetta, baked feta, and warm pretzels.

VINTAGE CLOTHING AND FURNITURE

In certain parts of the Valley "old" is the new "new." The Melrose District, on 7th Avenue between Indian School and Camelback roads in Central Phoenix, is banking on its Old Phoenix charm in a slow but steady race to become the next hip historic neighborhood. New faces on old buildings are the perfect welcome mat for progress with forthcoming lofts, condos, eateries, and big plans for public art, but the overall charm is anchored by its variety of vintage stores. Open hours are generally 11 to 6, and many stores are closed Monday and Tuesday.

Home Again (⊠ *4302 N. 7th Ave., North Central Phoenix* ☎ *602/424–0488*) is a down-home store that buys and sells vintage and modern home furnishings and antiques. A registered antiques dealer, Home Again welcomes dealers.

Melrose Vintage (⊠ *4238 N. 7th Ave., North Central Phoenix* ☎ *602/636–0300*) has a cheerful, dollhouse-like yellow exterior, and that's not the only thing that makes it memorable. The no-nonsense staff knows its stuff, which includes tasteful and fun low- to high-end shabby-chic furnishings—everything from ribbon to armoires.

Phoenix Metro Retro (⊠ *5102 N. Central Ave., North Central Phoenix* ☎ *602/279–0702* ⊕ *www.phoenixmetroretro.com*) is it a hip New York loft? No, it's a vintage, midcentury, and modern furniture store. Cool and inviting, Metro Retro aptly exhibits the talent and time it takes for people like owner Carl Reese to find those "perfect" pieces for your purchasing pleasure.

Retro Redux (⊠ *4303 N. 7th Ave., North Central Phoenix* ☎ *602/234–0120*) has a selection of vintage clothing, costume jewelry, period pictures, furnishings, and accessories that's as fun and funky as its name.

Vintage Solutions (⊠ *3604 N. 16th St., North Central Phoenix* ☎ *602/604–1831*) is the place for sweet deals on deco and midcentury furniture, collectibles, and accessories that stand the test of time. A local newspaper recently called the owners and operators of Vintage Solutions "eagle-eye tchotchke aficionados who know a good deal when they see one, and aren't above passing their savings on to you."

SIDE TRIPS NEAR PHOENIX

The following sights are within a 1- to 1½-hour drive of Phoenix. To the north, the thriving artist communities of Carefree and Cave Creek are popular Western attractions. Arcosanti and Wickenburg are half- or full-day trips from Phoenix. Stop along the way to visit the petroglyphs of Deer Valley Rock Art Center and the reenactments of Arizona territorial life at the Pioneer Living History Village. You also might consider Lake Pleasant, Arcosanti, and Wickenburg as stopovers on the way to or from Flagstaff, Prescott, or Sedona.

South of Phoenix, an hour's drive takes you back to prehistoric times and the site of Arizona's first known civilization at Casa Grande Ruins National Monument, a vivid reminder of the Hohokam who began farming this area more than 1,500 years ago.

DEER VALLEY ROCK ART CENTER

15 mi north of downtown Phoenix.

GETTING HERE AND AROUND
Take I–17 north from Phoenix for 15 mi, exit at W. Deer Valley Rd., and drive 2 mi west.

EXPLORING
Deer Valley Rock Art Center has the largest concentration of ancient petroglyphs in the metropolitan Phoenix area. Some 1,500 of the cryptic symbols are here, left behind by Native American cultures that lived in the Valley (or passed through) during the last 1,000 years. After watching a video about the petroglyphs, pick up a pair of binoculars ($1) and an informative trail map and set out on the ¼-mi path. Telescopes point to some of the most skillful petroglyphs; they range from human and animal forms to more abstract figures. *Also see Petroglyphs CloseUp box in Eastern Arizona.* ⊠3711 W. Deer Valley Rd., North Phoenix ☎623/582–8007 ⊕www.asu.edu/clas/shesc/dvrac ⊠$7 ⊙May–Sept., Tues.–Sun. 8–2; Oct.–Apr., Tues.–Sat. 9–5, Sun. noon–5.

PIONEER LIVING HISTORY VILLAGE

25 mi north of downtown Phoenix.

GETTING HERE AND AROUND
Take I–17 north from downtown Phoenix 25 mi. Just north of Carefree Hwy. (AZ 74), take Exit 225, turn left on Pioneer Rd. to entrance.

EXPLORING
ⓒ The **Pioneer Living History Museum** contains 28 original and reconstructed buildings from throughout territorial Arizona. Costumed guides filter through the bank, schoolhouse, and print shop, as well as the Pioneer Opera House, where classic melodramas are performed daily. It's popular with the grade-school field-trip set, and it's your lucky day if you can tag along for their tour of the site—particularly when John the Blacksmith forges, smelts, and answers sixth-graders' questions that adults are too know-it-all to ask. ⊠3901 W. Pioneer Rd., Pioneer ☎623/465–1052 ⊕www.pioneer-arizona.com ⊠$7 ⊙Oct.–May, Wed.–Sun. 9–5; June–Sept., Wed.–Sun. 8–2.

CAVE CREEK AND CAREFREE

30 mi north of downtown Phoenix.

Some 30 mi north of Phoenix, resting high in the Sonoran Desert at an elevation of 2,500 feet, the towns of Cave Creek and Carefree look back to a lifestyle far different from that of their more populous neighbors to the south.

Side Trips Near Phoenix

Globe

FORT APACHE RESERVATION
SAN CARLOS RESERVATION

Miami
Claypool
Inspiration
Hayden
PINAL MTS
Superior

Apache Trail

Theodore Roosevelt Lake
Upper Ruins
Roosevelt
Tonto National Monument
Four Peaks
Theodore Roosevelt Lake Dam

SIERRA ANCHA

TONTO BASIN

Fish Creek Canyon
Tortilla Flat
SUPERSTITION MTS
Superstition Mountains
Peralta Trail
Peralta Rd.

Boyce Thompson Arboretum

MAZATZAL MOUNTAINS

Payson

Tonto National Forest

Sunflower
Bartlett Res.
Saguaro Lake

SALT RIVER RES.

Goldfield
Apache Junction

Florence Junction

Florence

Casa Grande Ruins National Monument

TO TUCSON

FORT McDOWELL RES.
McDowell MTS

Scottsdale
Mesa
Guadalupe
Chandler

Hohokam Pima Nat'l Mon

Cave Creek
Carefree

Paradise Valley
Camelback Mountain

Tempe

Huhugam Heritage Center

GILA RIVER RESERVATION

MARICOPA RES.

Deer Valley Rock Art Center

Carefree Hwy
Pima Rd

New River

PHOENIX
Glendale
Peoria
Sun City

Avondale

SOUTH MTS
Montezuma Peak

SIERRA ESTRELLA

Arcosanti
Cordes Junction

Black Canyon City
Bumble Bee

TO FLAGSTAFF

Pioneer Arizona Living History Museum

Sun City West

Buckeye

GILA BEND MOUNTAINS
GILA BEND RES.

BRADSHAW MOUNTAINS

Lake Pleasant

Wickenburg
Morristown

Peeples Valley
Yarnell
Congress

Aguila

15 mi
15 km

Cave Creek got its start with the discovery of gold in the region. When the mines and claims "played out," the cattlemen arrived, and the sounds of horse hooves and lowing cattle replaced those of miners' picks. The area grew slowly and independently from Phoenix to the south, until a paved road connected the two in 1952. Today the mile-long main stretch of town on Cave Creek Road is a great spot to have some hot chili and cold beer, try on Western duds, or learn the two-step in a "cowboy" bar. You're likely to run into folks dressed in cowboy hats, boots, and bold belt buckles. Horseback riders and horse-drawn wagons have the right of way here, and the 25-MPH speed limit is strictly enforced by county deputies. You can amble up the hill and rent a horse for a trip into the Tonto National Forest in search of some long-forgotten native petroglyphs or take a jeep tour out to the forest.

Just about the time the dirt-road era ended in Cave Creek, planners were sketching out a new community, which became neighboring Carefree. The world's largest sundial, at the town's center, is surrounded by crafts shops, galleries, artists' workshops, and cafés. Today Cave Creek and Carefree sit cheek by jowl—but the one has beans, beef, biscuits, and beer, while the other discreetly orders up a notch or two.

GETTING HERE AND AROUND

Follow I–17 north of downtown Phoenix for 15 mi. Exit at Carefree Hwy. (AZ 74) and turn right, then go 12 mi. Turn left onto Cave Creek Rd. and go 3 mi to downtown Cave Creek, then another 4 mi on Cave Creek Rd. to Carefree. Pick up maps and information about the area at the Chamber of Commerce.

ESSENTIALS

Visitor Info Carefree–Cave Creek Chamber of Commerce. ⊠ *748 Easy St., No. 9, Carefree* ☎ *480/488–3381* ⊕ *www.carefreecavecreek.org* ⊗ *Weekdays 8–4.*

EXPLORING

Exhibits at the **Cave Creek Museum** depict pioneer living, mining, and ranching. See the last original 1920s tuberculosis cabin and a collection of Indian artifacts from the Hohokam and Yavapai tribes. ⊠ *6140 E. Skyline Dr., Cave Creek* ☎ *480/488–2764* ⊕ *www.cavecreekmuseum. org* ⌂ *$3* ⊗ *Oct.–May, Wed. and Thurs., Sat. and Sun. 1–4:30, Fri. 10–4:30. Closed Mon., Tues.*

↻ Pseudo-Western **Frontier Town** (⊠ *6245 E. Cave Creek Rd., Cave Creek*) has wooden sidewalks, ramshackle buildings, and souvenir shops. Grab a sandwich and a bottle of Cave Creek Chili Beer—with a real chile pepper in each bottle—at **Silver Spur** (⊠ *6245 E. Cave Creek Rd., Cave Creek* ☎ *480/488–3317* ⊕ *www.silverspoonsaloon.com*).

The **Heard Museum North,** a satellite of the big Heard in Downtown Phoenix, has one gallery with its own small, permanent collection of Native American art. It also hosts two rotating exhibits during the year. The gift shop is well stocked with expensive, high-quality items. ⊠ *32633 N. Scottsdale Rd., at Carefree Hwy., Scottsdale* ☎ *480/488–9817* ⊕ *www. heard.org* ⌂ *$5* ⊗ *Mon.–Sat. 10–5, Sun. 11–5.*

2

Bakery Café at el Pedregal Marketplace (✉ *34505 N. Scottsdale Rd., at Carefree Hwy., Carefree* ☎ *480/488–4100*). Adjacent to the Boulders Resort and not far from the Heard Museum North, this is a good place to pick up a breakfast or lunch of fresh-baked goods or to take a shopping break with a sandwich and a cool drink.

SPORTS AND THE OUTDOORS

HORSEBACK RIDING

Spur Cross Stable (✉ *44029 Spur Cross Rd., Cave Creek* ☎ *480/488–9117 or 800/758–9530* ⊕ *www.horsebackarizona.com*) has well-cared-for horses that will take you on 1- to 7-hour rides to the high Sonoran Desert of the Spur Cross Preserve and the Tonto National Forest. Some rides include visits to petroglyph sites and a saddlebag lunch.

TENNIS AND GOLF

The **Boulders Resort Golf Club** (✉ *The Boulders, 34631 N. Tom Darlington Dr., Carefree* ☎ *480/488–9028 or 866/397–6520* ⊕ *www.theboulders.com* ⚐ *North Course: 18 holes. Par 71. South Course: 18 holes. Par 72* ⚐ *Facilities: Driving range, putting green, golf carts, rental clubs, pro shop, lessons, restaurant, bar*) has two championship 18-hole, par-72 courses, and eight tennis courts.

WHERE TO EAT

$$$$
AMERICAN

✗**Binkley's Restaurant.** This upscale, casual restaurant is a diamond in the Valley's last bit of rough. In a town of cowboy bars and gut bombs, chef Kevin Binkley makes a world-class impression with tasting menus featuring delicate portions of such dishes as black-truffle whipped potatoes, loupe de mer with coconut quinoa and grapefruit hollandaise, and red-wine-poached filet mignon. (For something a little more casual and inexpensive, try his newly opened Café Bink at 36899 North Tom Darlington Drive in Carefree). ✉ *6920 E. Cave Creek Rd., Cave Creek* ☎ *480/437–1072* ⊕ *www.binkleysrestaurant.com* ⊟ *AE, D, DC, MC, V*

$
CAFÉ

✗**Cave Creek Coffee Company & Wine Bar.** The eating, drinking, and live entertainment are so great here that even Phoenician homebodies have been known to make the out-of-the-way journey. Some of acoustic music's finest artists perform at this peaceful, first-rate venue, which claims to be Arizona's version of Austin City Limits. The eclectic menu offers breakfast burritos, artisanal sandwiches, salads, pizzas, antipasti, and sweets. ✉ *6033 E. Cave Creek Rd., Cave Creek* ☎ *480/488–0603* ⊕ *www.cavecreekcoffee.com* ⊟ *AE, D, DC, MC, V.*

$$–$$$
AMERICAN

✗**Horny Toad Restaurant.** The Horny Toad is a rustic spot for barbecued pork ribs and steak, but the real star is the fried chicken. The quirky menu features a range of fare from soup "de joor" to Icelandic cod and carne asada. ✉ *6738 E. Cave Creek Rd., Cave Creek* ☎ *480/488–9542* ⊕ *www.thehornytoad.com* ⊟ *AE, D, DC, MC, V.*

$$
AMERICAN

✗**Tonto Bar & Grill at Rancho Manana.** Old West ambience oozes from every corner of the Tonto Bar & Grill, from the hand-carved ceiling beams to the *latilla* (stick)-covered patios with views of the pristine Sonoran Desert. Try the cowboy Cobb salad or the Tonto burger piled with fried onions and Tillamook cheddar for lunch; lamb chops with leek fondue or grilled grouper with orange-tomato salsa are good choices at dinner. ⊠*5736 E. Rancho Manana Blvd., Cave Creek* ☎*480/488–0698* ⊕*www.tontobarandgrill.com* ☰*AE, D, DC, MC, V.*

WHERE TO STAY

$$$–$$$$
Fodor'sChoice
★

▣ **The Boulders Resort and Golden Door Spa.** One of the country's top resorts (and one of the only ones with an all-organic approach) hides amid hill-size, 12-million-year-old granite boulders and the lush Sonoran Desert. Casitas snuggled against the rocks have exposed log-beam ceilings and curved, pueblo-style half-walls. Each has a patio with a view, a wood-burning fireplace, and a spacious bathroom with deep soaking tub. An upscale mall, el Pedregal Marketplace, adjoins the resort, and there are two golf courses. The Golden Door spa is one of the best in the state. **Pros:** remote desert getaway; also in the center of Cave Creek and Carefree shopping, events, and activities. **Cons:** on-site dining is priced above average; minimum 45-minute drive to Phoenix attractions. ⊠*34631 N. Tom Darlington Dr., Carefree* ☎*480/488–9009 or 800/553–1717* ⊕*www.theboulders.com* ⤳*160 casitas, 60 villas and haciendas* ♿*In-room: safe, kitchen (some), refrigerator, Wi-Fi, Ethernet. In-hotel: 5 restaurants, room service, golf courses, tennis courts, pools, gym, spa, concierge, parking (no fee), no elevator* ☰*AE, D, DC, MC, V.*

$ ▣ **Cave Creek Tumbleweed Hotel.** Innkeepers Gary and Jeri Rust have kept the 1950s flavor of this Western hotel intact. There's a fireplace in the lobby and a quiet pool outside. Red-and-tan rooms have Southwestern and cowboy accents. The hotel is a short walk from restaurants and shops in town. **Pros:** a true Old West experience; quite affordable for the area. **Cons:** sparse accommodations. ⊠*6333 E. Cave Creek Rd., Cave Creek* ☎*480/488–3668* ⊕*www.tumbleweedhotel.com* ⤳*32 rooms, 8 casitas* ♿*In-room: kitchen (some). In-hotel: pool, no-smoking rooms, no elevator* ☰*AE, MC, V.*

NIGHTLIFE

Watch real cowboys and cowgirls two-step to live music at **Buffalo Chip Saloon** (⊠*6811 E. Cave Creek Rd., Cave Creek* ☎*480/488–9118* ⊕*www.buffalochipsaloon.com*), where you can also gorge on mesquite-grilled chicken and buffalo chips—hot, homemade potato chips. Reservations are suggested for the all-you-can-eat Friday-night fish fry that draws crowds. There's live music and dancing Thursday through Saturday. At **Silver Spur Saloon** (⊠*6245 E. Cave Creek Rd., Cave Creek* ☎*480/488–3317*) you can enjoy live music on weekends. **Harold's Cave Creek Corral** (⊠*6895 E. Cave Creek Rd., Cave Creek* ☎*480/488–1906* ⊕*www.haroldscorral.com*) is just across the dirt parking lot from the Buffalo Chip Saloon. Harold's has two full bars, a huge dance floor with live bands on weekends, a game room, 15 TVs, and a restaurant—serving some of the best ribs in the Valley.

SHOPPING

Cave Creek and Carefree have a thriving arts community, with hundreds of artists and dozens of galleries. **El Pedregal** (⊠*34505 N. Scottsdale Rd., at Carefree Hwy., Carefree* ☎*480/488–1072*) is a two-tier shopping plaza at the foot of a 250-foot boulder formation. In spring and summer there are open-air Thursday-night concerts in the courtyard amphitheater. In addition to its posh boutiques and specialty stores, el Pedregal is home to some of the finest art galleries in the area. **Spanish Village** (✉ *7208 E. Ho Rd., Ho and Hum Rds., Carefree* ☎ *480/488–0350*), an outdoor shopping area complete with bell tower, fountains, courtyards, and winding alleyways. You can while away an afternoon browsing 30 shops, then contemplate dinner at one of several casual restaurants.

2

WICKENBURG

70 mi northwest of downtown Phoenix.

This town, land of guest ranches and tall tales, is named for Henry Wickenburg, whose nearby Vulture Mine was the richest gold strike in the Arizona Territory. In the late 1800s Wickenburg was a booming mining town on the banks of the Hassayampa River, with a seemingly endless supply of gold, copper, and silver. Nowadays Wickenburg's Old West history attracts visitors to its sleepy downtown and Western museum. There's a group of good antiques shops, most of which are on Tegner and Frontier streets.

GETTING HERE AND AROUND

Follow I–17 north from Phoenix for about 25 mins to Carefree Hwy. (AZ 74) junction. About 30 mi west on AZ 74, take U.S. 89/93 north and go another 10 mi to Wickenburg.

Maps for self-guided walking tours of the town's historic buildings are available at the Wickenburg Chamber of Commerce, in the town's old Santa Fe Depot.

ESSENTIALS

Visitor Info Wickenburg Chamber of Commerce (✉ *216 N. Frontier St.* ☎ *928/684–5479 or 800/942–5242* ⊕ *www.wickenburgchamber.com*).

EXPLORING

On the northeast corner of Wickenburg Way and Tegner Street, check out the **Jail Tree,** to which prisoners were chained, the desert heat sometimes finishing them off before their sentences were served.

☺ The **Desert Caballeros Western Museum** has one of the best collections of Western art in the nation, with paintings and sculpture by Remington, Bierstadt, Joe Beeler (founder of the Cowboy Artists of America), and others. Kids enjoy the re-creation of a turn-of-the-20th-century Main Street that includes a general store, period clothing, and a large collection of cowboy gear. ✉ *21 N. Frontier St.* ☎ *928/684–2272* ⊕ *www. westernmuseum.org* ✆ *$7.50* ◔ *Mon.–Sat. 10–5, Sun. noon–4.*

The self-guided trails of **Hassayampa River Preserve** wind through lush cottonwood-willow forests, mesquite trees, and around a 4-acre, spring-fed pond and marsh habitat. Waterfowl, herons, and Arizona's rarest raptors shelter here. ✉ *3 mi southeast of Wickenburg on U.S. 60* ☎ *928/684–2772* ✆ *$5* ◔ *Mid-Sept.–mid-May, Wed.–Sun. 8–5; summer hrs vary depending on fire danger and weather. Call to confirm.*

☺ **Robson's Mining World** is a replica of a 19th-century mining town that has the world's largest collection of antique mining equipment, the Nellie Meda gold mine, more than 30 buildings, a restaurant, a saloon, and

The Boulders Resort and Golden Door Spa

Rancho de los Caballeros

2

a general store. Visitors can stay at the old mining hotel, which has 26 simple rooms. Attractions include hanging out in town, panning for gold, or hiking in the desert or the nearby Harcuvar Mountains. The restaurant serves juicy prime rib and a miners' pie filled with meat, potatoes, and vegetables and baked in pastry. ⊠ *Milepost 90, 29 mi west of Wickenburg on U.S. 60 to AZ 71, Box 3465, Wickenburg* ☎*928/415–0983* ⊕*www.robsonsminingworld.com* ☾*Call for reservations.*

The **Vulture Mine** was once the largest producing gold mine in Arizona, though its vein has long since run out. A small town originally grew up around the mine, but the only things left today are a few storage buildings and a home where caretakers live. The self-guided tour through this "ghost town" wanders past mining memorabilia; old buildings including bunkhouses, the jail, and a blacksmith shop; the mine shaft itself; and the infamous hanging tree, where more than a dozen ore thieves (high graders) were hanged. ■**TIP**➔Vulture Mine offers no protective safeguards for its aged buildings, shafts, and equipment. Wander at your own risk and keep an eye on children. Head west from Wickenburg on U.S. 60 for about 6 mi, then turn left onto Vulture Mine Road and travel 12 mi to the mine at the end of the pavement. ⊠*Vulture Mine Rd., Vulture Mine* ☎*602/859–2743* ⊠*$10* ☾*Sept.–Apr., daily 8–4.*

WHERE TO EAT AND STAY

¢–$ ✕**Anita's Cocina.** Reliable Tex-Mex fare is served at Anita's. The fresh
MEXICAN tamales are tasty for lunch or dinner. And if you're not in the mood for Mexican, fret not; Anita's also has pizza. Try a fruit burrito for dessert. ⊠*57 N. Valentine St.* ☎*928/684–5777* ⊕*www.anitascorp. com* ⊟*MC, V.*

$$$–$$$$ ⊞ **Kay El Bar Ranch.** On the National Register of Historic Places, this remote guest ranch is personable and low-key. Some of the biggest mesquite trees in Arizona shade the lodge, a family cottage with private patio (built in 1914), two separate casitas, and a charming adobe cookhouse. In the evening everyone gathers in the living room by the stone fireplace for cocktails and homemade hors d'oeuvres. **Pros:** one of the few remaining true Arizona dude ranch experiences. **Cons:** only open six months out of the year. ⊠*37500 S. Rincon Rd.* ⊙*Box 2480, 85358* ☎*928/684–7593 or 800/684–7583* ⊕*www.kayelbar.com* ⇨*8 rooms, 1 house, 2 casitas* ⚒*In-room: no phone, no TV. In-hotel: restaurant, pool, no elevator* ⊟*MC, V* ☾*Closed May–mid-Oct.* ⊚*FAP.*

$$$$ ⊞**Rancho de los Caballeros.** This 20,000-acre property combines the
☾ guest-ranch experience with first-class amenities. Meals are served in the
Fodor'sChoice lodge's bright, festive dining room, and everyone is asked to dress for
★ each night's sit-down dinner. Rooms are spacious and done in low-key Southwestern style. Some contain two queen-size beds and can be creatively configured through a system of adjoining doors to annex separate living rooms or sleeping quarters for children. Activities ranging from skeet shooting to horseback riding are available. The Los Caballeros Golf Club course is considered one of the country's top resort courses. **Pros:** large rooms, casitas, and suites; abundant activity roster; a great place for family gatherings. **Cons:** remote location; long hikes to rooms. ⊠*1551 S. Vulture Mine Rd.* ☎*928/684–5484 or 800/684–5030* ⊕*www.sunc.com* ⇨*79 rooms* ⚒*In-room: Internet. In-hotel: Wi-Fi,*

restaurant, bar, golf course, spa, tennis courts, pool, bicycles, children's programs (ages 5–12), no elevator ⊟MC, V ⊘*Closed mid-May–early Oct.* ⏋⃝|BP

NIGHTLIFE

The **Rancher Bar** (⊠910 W. Wickenburg Way ☎928/684–5957) is a modern-day saloon where real live wranglers and cowboys meet up to shoot some pool, and the breeze, after a hard day's work.

ARCOSANTI

65 mi north of downtown Phoenix.

GETTING HERE AND AROUND

From Phoenix, take I–17 north 65 mi to exit 262 (Condes Junction). Follow the partly paved road 2.5 mi northeast to the community.

EXPLORING

The evolving complex and community of **Arcosanti** was masterminded by Italian architect Paolo Soleri to be a self-sustaining habitat in which architecture and ecology function in symbiosis. Building began in 1970, but Arcosanti is a bit tired-looking these days and hasn't quite achieved Soleri's original vision. It's still worth a stop to take a tour, have a bite at the café, and purchase one of the hand-cast bronze wind-bells made at the site. ☎928/632–7135 ⊕*www.arcosanti.org* ⌦*Tour $10* ⊘*Daily 9–5; tours hourly 10–4.*

CASA GRANDE RUINS NATIONAL MONUMENT

36 mi southeast of downtown Phoenix.

GETTING HERE AND AROUND

Take U.S. 60 east (Superstition Freeway) to Florence Junction (U.S. 60 and AZ 89), and head south 16 mi on AZ 89 to Florence. Casa Grande is 9 mi west of Florence on AZ 287 or, from I–10, 16 mi east on AZ 387 and AZ 87. Note: follow signs to ruins, not to town of Casa Grande. When leaving the ruins, take AZ 87 north 35 mi back to U.S. 60.

EXPLORING

The **Casa Grande Ruins National Monument,** whose original purpose still eludes archaeologists, was unknown to European explorers until Father Kino, a Jesuit missionary, first recorded the site's existence in 1694. The area was set aside as federal land in 1892 and named a national monument in 1918. Although only a few prehistoric sites can be viewed, more than 60 are in the monument area, including the 35-foot-tall—that's four stories—Casa Grande (Big House). The tallest Hohokam building known, Casa Grande was built in the early 14th century and is believed by some to have been an ancient astronomical observatory or a center of government, religion, trade, or education. Allow an hour to explore the site, longer if park rangers are giving a talk or leading a tour. ■TIP➔On your way out, cross the parking lot by the covered picnic grounds and climb the platform for a view of a ball court and two platform mounds, said to date from the 1100s. *1100 W. Ruins Dr., Coolidge* ☎520/723–3172 ⊕*www. nps.gov/cagr* ⌦*$5* ⊘*Daily 8–5.*

THE APACHE TRAIL

Fodor'sChoice
★

President Roosevelt called this 150-mi drive "the most awe-inspiring and most sublimely beautiful panorama nature ever created." A stretch of winding highway, the AZ 188 portion of the Apache Trail closely follows the route forged through wilderness in 1906 to move construction supplies for building the Roosevelt Dam, which lies at the northernmost part of the loop.

PLANNING YOUR TIME

Although the drive itself can be completed in one day, it's advisable to spend a night in Globe, continuing the loop back to Phoenix the following day.

GETTING HERE AND AROUND

From the town of Apache Junction you can choose to drive the trail in either direction; there are advantages to both. If you begin the loop going clockwise—heading eastward on AZ 188 to the Superstition Mountains, the Peralta Trail, Boyce Thompson Arboretum, Globe, Tonto National Monument, Theodore Roosevelt Lake Reservoir & Dam, and Tortilla Flat—your drive may be more relaxing; you'll be on the farthest side of this narrow dirt road some refer to as the "white-knuckle route," with its switchbacks and drop-offs straight down into spectacular Fish Creek Canyon. ■TIP➜This 42-mi-long drive is not for anyone afraid of heights. But if you follow the route counterclockwise—continuing on U.S. 60 past the town of Apache Junction—you'll be able to appreciate each attraction better.

SUPERSTITION MOUNTAINS

30 mi east of downtown Phoenix.

GETTING HERE AND AROUND

From Phoenix, take I–10 and then U.S. 60 (the Superstition Freeway) east through suburbs of Tempe, Mesa, and Apache Junction.

EXPLORING

As the Phoenix metro area gives way to cactus- and creosote-dotted desert, the massive escarpment of the **Superstition Mountains** heaves into view and slides by to the north. The Superstitions are supposedly where the legendary Lost Dutchman Mine is, the location—not to mention the existence—of which has been hotly debated since pioneer days.

The best place to learn about the "Dutchman" Jacob Waltz and the Lost Dutchman Mine is at **Superstition Mountain Museum** (⊠ *4087 N. Apache*

WORD OF MOUTH

"The Best Unexpected Day: . . . we got in the car and headed to the Apache Trail. . . . On the drive we stopped at Goldfield, an old ghost town and then at the Lost Dutchman Mine and Superstition Mountain looming in the background . . . There was something so simplistic about it all—the views, dust, cacti, and company made the ride so enjoyable . . . We didn't make it to the top of the Apache Trail—I am afraid of heights! I couldn't believe the number of SUVs hauling huge boats and campers . . . winding . . . winding . . . winding down the steep, and did I mention winding, mountain?" —seetheworld

Trail, AZ 188, Apache Junction ☎*480/983–4888* ⊕*www.superstition mountainmuseum.org* ⊟*$5* ⊙*Daily 9–4).* The museum exhibits include a collection of mining tools, historical maps, and artifacts relating to the "gold" age of the Superstition Mountains.

Goldfield became an instant city of about 4,000 residents after a gold strike in 1892; the town dried up five years later when the gold mine flooded. Today the **Goldfield Ghost Town** (⊠*4650 N. Mammoth Mine Rd., 4 mi northeast of Apache Junction on AZ 188, Goldfield* ☎*480/983–0333* ⊕*www.goldfieldghosttown.com*) is an interesting place to grab a cool drink, pan for gold, go for a mine tour, or take a desert jeep ride or horseback tour of the area. The ghost town's shops are open daily 10 to 5, the saloon daily 10 to 8, and gunfights are held hourly from noon to 4.

PERALTA TRAIL

25 mi east of downtown Phoenix.

GETTING HERE AND AROUND
About 11½ mi southeast of Apache Junction, off U.S. 60, take Peralta Trail Rd., just past King's Ranch Rd., an 8-mi, rough gravel road that leads to the start of the Peralta Trail.

EXPLORING
The 4-mi round-trip **Peralta Trail** winds 1,400 feet up a small valley for a spectacular view of **Weaver's Needle,** a monolithic rock formation that is one of Arizona's more famous sights. Allow a few hours for this rugged and challenging hike, bring plenty of water, sunscreen, a hat, and a snack or lunch, and don't hike it in the middle of the day in summer.

BOYCE THOMPSON ARBORETUM

12 mi east of Florence Junction.

GETTING HERE AND AROUND
From Florence Junction, take U.S. 60 east for 12 mi.

EXPLORING
★ At the foot of Picketpost Mountain in Superior, the **Boyce Thompson Arboretum** is often called an oasis in the desert: the arid rocky expanse gives way to lush riparian glades home to 3,200 different desert plants and more than 230 bird and 72 terrestrial species. The arboretum offers a living album of the world's desert and semiarid region plants, including exotic species such as Canary Islands date palms and Australian eucalyptus. Trails offer breathtaking scenery in the gardens and the exhibits, especially during the spring wildflower season. A variety of tours are offered year-round. Benches with built-in misters offer relief from the heat. Bring along a picnic and enjoy the beauty. ⊠*37615 U.S. 60, Superior* ☎*520/689–2811* ⊕*www.ag.arizona.edu/bta* ⊟*$7.50* ⊙*May–Aug., daily 6–3; Sept.–Apr., daily 8–4.*

EN ROUTE A few miles past the arboretum, **Superior** is the first of several modest mining towns and the launching point for a dramatic winding ascent through the Mescals to a 4,195-foot pass that affords panoramic views

The Lost Dutchman Mine

Not much is known about Jacob "the Dutchman" Waltz, except that he was born around 1808 in Germany (he was "Deutsch," not "Dutch") and emigrated to the United States, where he spent several years at mining camps in the Southeast, in the West, and finally in Arizona. There's documentation that he did indeed have access to a large quantity of gold, though he never registered a claim for the mine that was attributed to him.

GOLDEN RUMORS

In 1868 Waltz appeared in the newly developing community of Pumpkinville, soon to become Phoenix. He kept to himself on his 160-acre homestead on the bank of the Salt River. From time to time he would disappear for a few weeks and return with enough high-quality ore to keep him in a wonderful fashion. Soon word was out that "Crazy Jake" had a vast gold mine in the Superstition Mountains, east of the city near the Apache Trail.

At the same time, stories about a wealthy gold mine discovered by the Peralta family of Mexico were circulating. Local Apaches raided the mine, which was near their sacred Thunder Mountain. In what became known as the Peralta Massacre, the Peraltas and more than 100 people working for them at the mine were killed. Rumors soon spread that Waltz had saved the life of a young Mexican who was part of Peralta's group—one of few who had escaped—and was shown the Peralta's mine as a reward.

SEARCHING THE SUPERSTITIONS

As the legend of the Dutchman's mine grew, many opportunists attempted to follow Waltz into the Superstition Mountains. A crack marksman, Waltz quickly discouraged several who tried to track him. The flow of gold continued for several years.

In 1891 the Salt River flooded, badly damaging Waltz's home. When the floodwaters receded, neighbors found Waltz there in a weakened condition. He was taken to the nearby home and boardinghouse of Julia Thomas, who nursed the Dutchman for months. When his death was imminent, he reportedly gave Julia the directions to his mine.

Julia and another boarder searched for the mine fruitlessly. In her later years she sold maps to the treasure, based upon her recollections of Waltz's description. Thousands have searched for the lost mine, many losing their lives in the process—either to the brutality of fellow searchers or that of the rugged desert—and more than a century later gold seekers are still trying to connect the pieces of the puzzle.

THE LEGEND TODAY

There's no doubt that the Dutchman had a source of extremely rich gold ore. But was it in the Superstition Mountains, nearby Goldfields, or maybe even in the Four Peaks region? Wherever it was, it's still hidden. Perhaps the best-researched books on the subject are T. E. Glover's *The Lost Dutchman Mine of Jacob Waltz* and the companion book *The Holmes Manuscript*. Ron Feldman of OK Corral (☎ 480/982–4040 ⊕ *www.okcorrals. com*) in Apache Junction has become an expert on the subject during his 30-plus years in the region. He leads adventurers on pack trips into the mysterious mountains to relive the lore and legends.

of this copper-rich range and its huge, dormant, open-pit mines. Collectors will want to watch for antiques shops through these hills, but be forewarned that quality varies considerably. A gradual descent will take you into **Miami** and **Claypool**, once-thriving boomtowns that have carried on quietly since major-corporation mining ground to a halt in the 1970s. Working-class buildings are dwarfed by the mountainous piles of copper tailings to the north. At a stoplight in Claypool AZ 188 splits off northward to the Apache Trail, but continue on U.S. 60 another 3 mi to make the stop in the city of Globe.

2

GLOBE

51 mi east of Apache Junction, 25 mi east of Superior, and 3 mi east of Claypool's AZ 188 turnoff.

In the southern reaches of Tonto National Forest, Globe is the most cosmopolitan of the area's mining towns. Initially, it was gold and silver that brought miners here—the city allegedly got its name from a large, circular boulder of silver, with lines like continents, found by prospectors—although the region is now known for North America's richest copper deposits. ■**TIP→**If you're driving the Apache Trail loop, stop in Globe to fill up the tank; it's the last chance to gas up until looping all the way back to U.S. 60 at Apache Junction. Globe is worth more than a quick pit stop, though; its charm is its lack of prestige—and, in some cases, modernity.

GETTING HERE AND AROUND

Globe is at the intersection of AZ 60 and 188. At the Globe Chamber of Commerce, open weekdays 8–5, Saturday 10–2, Sunday 11–2, you can pick up brochures detailing the self-guided Historic Downtown Walking Tour.

ESSENTIALS

Visitor Info Globe Chamber of Commerce (⊠ *1360 N. Broad St., Globe, 1¼ mi north of downtown on U.S. 60* ☎ *928/425–4495 or 800/804–5623* ⊕ *www. globemiamichamber.com*).

EXPLORING

A good place to begin a visit to Globe is the **Gila County Historical Museum** (⊠ *1330 N. Broad St.* ☎ *928/425–7385*), where you can see the collection of memorabilia from the area's mining days. The museum, which is free, is open Monday to Saturday, 9 to 4.

The restored late-19th-century Gila County Courthouse houses the free **Cobre Valley Center for the Arts** (⊠ *101 N. Broad St.* ☎ *928/425–0884* ⊕ *www.cvarts.org*) and showcases works by local artists. It's open Monday to Saturday, 10 to 4.

For a step 800 years back in time, tour the 2 acres of the excavated Salado Indian site at the **Besh-Ba-Gowah Archaeological Park** on the southeastern side of town. After a trip through the small museum and a video introduction, enter the area full of remnants of more than 200 rooms occupied here by the Salado during the 13th and 14th centuries. Public areas include the central plaza (also the principal burial ground), roasting pits, and open patios. Besh-Ba-Gowah is a name given by the Apaches, who, arriving in the 17th century, found the pueblo abandoned and moved in—loosely translated, the name means "metal camp," and remains left on the site point to it as part of an extensive commerce and trading network. ⊠*150 N. Pine St.* ☎*928/425–0320 or 800/804–5623* ⊴*$3* ⊘*Daily 9–5.*

WHERE TO EAT AND STAY

¢–$ ✕**Chalo's.** This roadside spot offers top-notch Mexican and Tex-Mex
MEXICAN food for a slightly different flavor than your average Mexican plate. Chalo's specialty is using green chiles. Fortunately, you can request mild or spicy versions of green-chile enchiladas, burros, and practically anything else on the menu. Be sure to ask for water. Try the savory stuffed sopapillas, filled with pork and beef, beans, and red or green chiles. It's a favorite among locals, so plan for an early lunch or dinner to avoid a wait. ⊠*902 E. Ash St.* ☎*928/425–0515* ⊕*www.chalos.com* ⊟*AE, D, MC, V.*

¢–$ ⊡**Noftsger Hill Inn.** Built in 1907, this B&B was originally the North Globe Schoolhouse; now classrooms serve as guest rooms, filled with mining-era antiques and affording fantastic views of the Pinal Mountains and historic Old Dominion Mine. All rooms have private baths; one has air-conditioning, and the rest have evaporative coolers, which work well at this higher elevation. You can walk off "miner-size" breakfasts on the enjoyable hike through the scenic Copper Hills behind the old school. **Pros:** giant windows offer pleasant natural light, and many rooms have original classroom chalkboards devoted to guest comments. **Cons:** the spacious, former-schoolhouse rooms aren't exactly cozy. ⊠*425 North St.* ☎*928/425–2260 or 877/780–2479* ⊕*www.noftsger hillinn.com* ⌂*6 rooms* ⌂*In-room: no a/c (some), VCR (some), no TV (some). In-hotel: no-smoking rooms, no elevator* ⊟*MC, V* ⊺◯*BP.*

NIGHTLIFE

Run by the San Carlos Apache tribe, **Apache Gold** (⊠*U.S. 70, 5 mi east of Globe* ☎*800/272–2438* ⊕*www.apachegoldcasinoresort.com*) has more than 500 slots, blackjack, keno, bingo, and video and live poker. Call about the free shuttle from most of Globe's hotels and motels. The Apache Grill Restaurant offers gourmet dishes, and the Wickiup Buffet serves authentic Apache and Southwestern cuisine.

SHOPPING

Broad Street, Globe's main drag, is lined with antiques and gift shops. On Ash, between Hill and South East streets, **Copper City Rock Shop** (⊠*566 Ash St.* ☎*928/425–7885*) specializes in mineral products, many from Arizona. **Past Times** (⊠*150 W. Mesquite* ☎*928/425–2220*) carries antique furniture and accessories, including vintage glassware and kitchen items. **True Blue Jewelry** (⊠*200 N. Willow St.* ☎*928/425–8361* ⊕*www.truebluejewelry.com*) carries high-quality jewelry made with turquoise supplied by Globe's Sleeping Beauty Mine. Ask to watch the five-minute video about turquoise mining and preparing it for use. Try **Turquoise Ladies** (⊠*996 N. Broad St.* ☎*928/425–6288*) for owner June Stratton's collection of uniquely Globe souvenirs and stories.

Hikers in the Superstition mountains—perhaps searching for the riches of the Lost Dutchman Mine.

EN ROUTE At the stoplight 3 mi south of Globe on U.S. 60, AZ 188 splits off to the northwest. About 25 mi later on AZ 188, heading toward the Tonto National Monument, you'll see towering quartzite cliffs about 2 mi in the distance—look up and to the left for glimpses of the 40-room **Upper Ruins,** 14th-century condos left behind by the Salado people. They can't be seen from within the national monument, so make sure you've got binoculars.

TONTO NATIONAL MONUMENT

30 mi northeast of the intersection of U.S. 60 and AZ 188.

Tonto National Monument has a well-preserved complex of 13th-century Salado cliff dwellings. There's a self-guided walking tour of the Lower Cliff Dwellings, but if you can, take a ranger-led tour of the 40-room Upper Cliff Dwellings, offered on selected mornings from November to April. Tour reservations are required and should be made as far as a month in advance. ⊠*AZ 188, Roosevelt* ✉*HC 02, Box 4602 85545* ☎*928/467–2241* ⊕*www.nps.gov/tont* ⊠*$3* ☉*Daily 8–5.*

THEODORE ROOSEVELT LAKE RESERVOIR AND DAM

5 mi northwest of Tonto National Monument on AZ 188.

Flanked by the desolate Mazatzal and Sierra Anchas mountain ranges, **Theodore Roosevelt Lake Reservoir & Dam** is an aquatic recreational area—a favorite with bass anglers, water-skiers, and boaters. This is the largest masonry dam on the planet, and the massive bridge is the longest two-lane, single-span, steel-arch bridge in the nation.

EN
ROUTE

Past the reservoir, AZ 188 turns west and becomes a meandering dirt road, eventually winding its way back to Apache Junction via the magnificent, bronze-hue volcanic cliff walls of **Fish Creek Canyon,** with views of the sparkling lakes, towering saguaros, and, in the springtime, vast fields of wildflowers.

TORTILLA FLAT

18 mi southwest of Roosevelt Dam; 18 mi northeast of Apache Junction.

Close to the end of the Apache Trail, this old-time restaurant and country store are what is left of an authentic stagecoach stop at **Tortilla Flat.** This is a fun place to stop for a well-earned rest and refreshment—miner- and cowboy-style grub, of course—before heading back the last 18 mi to civilization. Enjoy a hearty bowl of killer chili and some prickly-pear-cactus ice cream while sitting at the counter on a saddle barstool.

Grand Canyon National Park

WORD OF MOUTH

"We viewed the sunset from the main area outside Bright Angel lodge—beautiful! We caught the sunrise from the South Kaibab trailhead—beautiful! Next day, cloudy, misty, light rain, sun peeking though clouds—beautiful! Don't get too hung up on being at the right spot for the sunrise/sunset, it's all spectacular!"

—BlackandGold

WELCOME TO
GRAND CANYON NATIONAL PARK

TOP REASONS TO GO

★ **Its status:** This is one of those places where you really want to say, "Been there, done that!"

★ **Awesome vistas:** Painted desert, sandstone canyon walls, pine and fir forests, mesas, plateaus, volcanic features, the Colorado River, streams, and waterfalls make for some jaw-dropping moments.

★ **Year-round adventure:** Outdoor junkies can bike, boat, camp, fish, hike, ride mules, white-water raft, watch birds and wildlife, cross-country ski, and snowshoe.

★ **Continuing education:** Adults and kids can get schooled, thanks to free park-sponsored nature walks and interpretive programs.

★ **Sky-high and river-low experiences:** Experience the canyon via plane, train, and automobile, as well as helicopter, boat, bike, mule, or on foot.

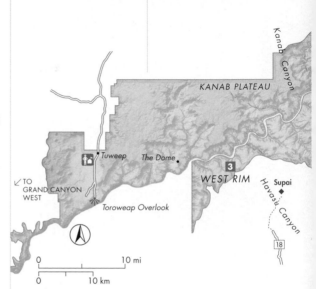

1 South Rim. The South Rim is where the action is: Grand Canyon Village's lodging, camping, eateries, stores, and museums, plus plenty of trailheads into the canyon. Visitor services and facilities are open and available every day of the year, including holidays. Three free shuttle routes cover 30-some stops, and visitors who'd rather relax than rough it can treat themselves to comfy hotel rooms and elegant restaurant meals (lodging and camping reservations are essential).

2 North Rim. Of the nearly 5 million people who visit the park annually, 90% enter at the South Rim, but many believe the North Rim is even more gorgeous—and worth the extra effort. Accessible only from mid-May to mid-October (or the first good snowfall), the North Rim has legitimate bragging rights: at more than 8,000 feet above sea level (and 1,000 feet higher than the South Rim), it offers precious solitude and seven developed viewpoints. Rather than staring into the canyon's depths, you get a true sense of its expanse.

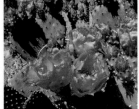
Beavertail cactus in bloom.

3

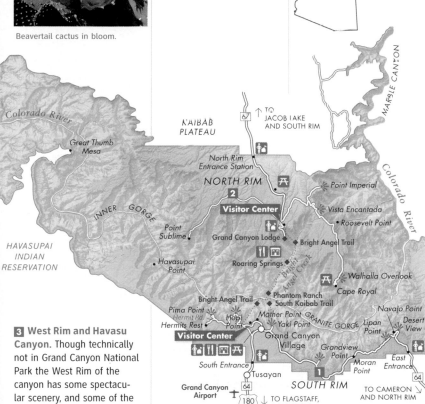

3 **West Rim and Havasu Canyon.** Though technically not in Grand Canyon National Park the West Rim of the canyon has some spectacular scenery, and some of the most gorgeous waterfalls in the United States. The Skywalk, part of the Hualapai Tribe's efforts to expand its tourism offerings on the West Rim, is a U-shaped glass bridge suspended above the Colorado River—not for the faint of heart.

Desert view watchtower was designed by Mary Colter in 1932.

GETTING ORIENTED

Grand Canyon National Park is a superstar—biologically, historically, and recreationally. One of the world's best examples of arid-land erosion, the canyon provides a record of three of the four eras of geological time. Almost two billion years worth of the Earth's history is written in the colored layers of sedimentary rock stacked from the river bottom to the top of the plateau. In addition to its diverse fossil record, the park reveals prehistoric traces of human adaptation to an unforgiving environment. It's also home to several major ecosystems, five of the world's seven life zones, three of North America's four desert types, and all kinds of rare, endemic, and protected plant and animal species.

GRAND CANYON NATIONAL PARK PLANNER

When to Go

There's no bad time to visit the canyon, though the busiest times of year are summer and spring break. Visiting during these peak seasons, as well as holidays, requires patience and a tolerance for crowds. Note that weather changes on a whim in this exposed high-desert region. *You cannot visit the North Rim in the winter due to weather conditions and related road closures.*

AVG. HIGH/LOW TEMPS.

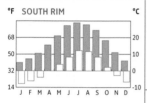

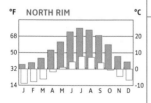

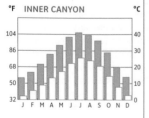

Planning Your Trip

Plan ahead: mule rides require at least a six-month advance reservation, and longer for the busy season (they can be reserved up to 13 months in advance). For lodgings in the park, reservations are also essential; they're taken up to 13 months in advance. **Grand Canyon National Park Lodges** (☎ 888/297–2757 ⊕ www.grandcanyonlodges. com) runs the South Rim park lodging. For North Rim reservations, contact **Grand Canyon Lodge** (☎ 877/386–4383 ⊕ www.grandcanyonlodgenorth.com).

Before you go, get the complimentary *Trip Planner,* updated regularly, from the **Grand Canyon National Park** (⊕ www. nps.gov/grca) Web site. Visit **Grand Canyon Chamber of Commerce** (☎ 928/638–2901 or 888/472–2696 ⊕ www.grandcanyonchamber.com) or ⊕ www.thecanyon. com, a commercial site with general information. Once you arrive, pick up the free detailed map and *The Guide,* a newspaper with a schedule of free programs.

The park is most crowded near the east and south entrances and in Grand Canyon Village, as well as on the scenic drives, especially the 23-mi Desert View Drive. ⇨ See "Tips for Avoiding Grand Canyon Crowds."

Admission Fees and Permits

A fee of $25 per vehicle or $12 per person for pedestrians and cyclists is good for one week's access at both rims.

The $50 Grand Canyon Pass gives unlimited access to the park for 12 months. The annual National Parks and Recreational Land Pass (☎ 888/275–8747 ⊕ store.usgs. gov/pass ≣ $80) provides unlimited access to all national parks and federal recreation areas for 12 months.

No permits are needed for day hikers; but backcounty permits are necessary for overnight hikers. Permits are limited, so make your reservation as far in advance as possible—they're taken up to four months ahead of arrival. (☎ 928/638–7875 ☐ 928/638–2125 ≣ $10, plus $5 per person per night ⊕ www.nps.gov/grc). Camping in the park is restricted to designated campgrounds (☎ 877/444–6777 ⊕ www.recreation.gov).

Getting Here and Around

The best route into the park from the east or south is from Flagstaff. Take U.S. 180 northwest to the park's southern entrance and Grand Canyon Village. To go on to the North Rim, go north from Flagstaff on U.S. 89 to Bitter Springs, then take U.S. 89A to the junction of Highway 67 and travel south on the highway for about 40 mi. From the west on Interstate 40, the most direct route to the South Rim is on U.S. 180 and Highway 64.

The more remote North Rim is off-limits during winter. From mid-October (or the first heavy snowfall) through mid-May, there are no services, and Highway 67 south of Jacob Lake is closed.

The South Rim is open to car traffic year-round, though access to Hermits Rest is limited to shuttle buses part of the year. There are three free shuttle routes: The Hermits Rest Route operates March through November, between Grand Canyon Village and Hermits Rest. The Village Route operates year-round in the village area; it provides the easiest access to the Canyon View Information Center. The Kaibab Trail Route goes from Canyon View Information Center to Yaki Point, including a stop at the South Kaibab Trailhead.

■TIP➔In summer, South Rim roads are congested, and it's easier, and sometimes required, to park your car and take the free shuttle. Running from one hour before sunrise until one hour after sunset, shuttles arrive every 15 to 30 minutes at 30 clearly marked stops.

North Las Vegas Airport in Las Vegas is the primary air hub for flights to **Grand Canyon National Parks Airport (GCN)** (☏928/638–2446). You can also make connections into the Grand Canyon from **Phoenix Sky Harbor International Airport (PHX)** (☏602/273–3300 ⊕www.phxskyharbor. com). The nearest airport is to the North Rim is **St. George Municipal Airport** (☏435/634–5822 ⊕www.sgcity.org/ airport) in Utah, 164 mi north.

Xanterra South Rim (☏928/638–2822) offers 24-hour taxi service in Tusayan and the South Rim. **Flagstaff Express Shuttle** (☏928/225–2290 or 800/563–1980 ⊕flagstaffexpress.com) offers service from Phoenix to Flagstaff and Grand Canyon Village. **Open Road Tours** (☏928/226–8060 or 877/226–8060 ⊕www.openroad-tours.com) offers shuttle service from Flagstaff and Williams to Tusayan and Grand Canyon Village. From mid-May to mid-October, the **Trans Canyon Shuttle** (☏928/638–2820 ⊕www.trans-canyonshuttle.com) travels daily between the South and North rims. One-way fare is $80, round-trip $150. Reservations are required.

What Time is it?

The park is in the Mountain Standard time zone year-round. Daylight Savings Time is not observed.

Festivals and Events

May Williams Rendezvous Days. A black powder shooting competition, 1800s-era crafts, and a parade fire up Memorial Day weekend in honor of Bill Williams, the town's namesake mountain man. ☏928/635–4061 ⊕www. williamschamber.com.

Sept. Grand Canyon Music Festival. Three weekends when mostly chamber music fills the Shrine of Ages amphitheater at Grand Canyon Village. In the early 1980s, music aficionados Robert Bonfiglio and Clare Hoffman hiked through the Grand Canyon and decided the stunning spectacle should be accompanied by the strains of a symphony. One of the park rangers agreed, and the wandering musicians performed an impromptu concert. Encouraged by the experience, Bonfiglio and Hoffman started the festival. ☏928/638–9215 or 800/997–8285 ⊕www. grandcanyonmusicfest.org.

Dec. Mountain Village Holiday. Williams hails the holidays with a parade of lights, ice-skating rink, and live entertainment. ☏928/635–4061 ⊕www.williamschamber.com.

3

Updated by
Carrie Frasure

When it comes to the Grand Canyon, there are statistics, and there are sensations. While the former are impressive—the canyon measures in at an average width of 10 mi, length of 277 mi, and depth of a mile—they don't truly prepare you for that first impression. Seeing the canyon for the first time is an astounding experience—one that's hard to wrap your head around. In fact, it's more than an experience, it's an emotion, one that is only just beginning to be captured with the superlative "Grand."

Nearly 5 million visitors come to the park each year. They can access the canyon via two main points: the South Rim and the North Rim. The width from the North Rim to the South Rim varies from 600 feet to 18 mi, but traveling between rims by road requires a 215-mi drive. Hiking arduous trails from rim to rim is a steep and strenuous trek of at least 21 mi, but it's well worth the effort. You'll travel through five of North America's seven life zones. (To do this any other way, you'd have to travel from the Mexican desert to the Canadian woods.) In total, 630 mi of trails traverse the canyon, 51 of those miles maintained. West of Grand Canyon National Park, the tribal lands of the Hualapai and the Havasupai lie on the West Rim of the canyon.

GRAND CANYON SOUTH RIM

Visitors to the canyon converge mostly on the South Rim, and mostly during the summer. Grand Canyon Village is here, with most of the park's lodging and camping, trailheads, restaurants, stores, and museums, along with a nearby airport and railroad depot. Believe it or not, the average stay in the park is a mere four hours; this is not advised! You need to spend several days to truly appreciate this marvelous place, but at the very least, give it a full day. Hike down into the canyon, or along the rim, to get away from the crowds and experience nature at its finest.

SCENIC DRIVES

Desert View Drive. This heavily traveled 23-mi stretch of road follows the rim from the East entrance to the Grand Canyon Village. Starting from the less congested entry near Desert View, road warriors can get their first glimpse of the canyon from the 70-foot-tall Watchtower, the top of which provides the highest viewpoint on the South Rim. Eight overlooks, the remains of an ancestral Puebloan dwelling at the Tusayan Ruin and Museum, and the secluded and lovely Buggeln picnic area make for great stops along the South Rim. The Kaibab Trail Route shuttle bus travels Desert View Drive and takes 30 minutes to ride round-trip without getting off at any of the three stops: South Kaibab Trailhead, Yaki Point, and Pipe Creek Vista.

WORD OF MOUTH

"We saw mule deer and elk from the bus just west of the village. Even more exciting was the condor (#23) we found sitting in a tree just past Kolb Studio. Surprisingly, real condors often attend the late afternoon ranger talk on condors given daily in this location . . ."   —sms73

Hermit Road. The Santa Fe Company built Hermit Road, formerly known as West Rim Drive, in 1912 as a scenic tour route. Nine overlooks dot this 7-mi stretch, each worth a visit. The road is filled with hairpin turns, so make sure you adhere to posted speed limits. The historic roadway reopened after an extensive rehabilitation in 2008. As part of the project, a 3-mi Greenway trail now offers easy access to cyclists looking to enjoy the original 1913 Hermit Rim Road. From March through November, the improved Hermit Road is closed to private auto traffic because of congestion; during this period, a free shuttle bus will carry you to all the overlooks. Riding the bus round-trip without getting off at any of the viewpoints takes 75 minutes; the return trip stops only at Mohave and Hopi points.

EXPLORING

HISTORIC SITES

Kolb Studio. Built in 1904 by the Kolb brothers as a photographic workshop and residence, this building provides a view of Indian Gardens, where, in the days before a pipeline was installed, Emery Kolb descended 3,000 feet each day to get the water he needed to develop his prints. Kolb was doing something right; he operated the studio until he died in 1976 at age 95. The gallery here has changing exhibitions of paintings, photography, and crafts. There's also a bookstore. During the winter months, a ranger-led tour of the studio illustrates the role the Kolb brothers had on the development of the Grand Canyon. Call ahead to sign up for the tour. ⊠ *Grand Canyon Village, near Bright Angel Lodge* ☎ *928/638–2771* ⊠ *Free* ☉ *Mid-May–mid-Oct., daily 8–5; mid-Oct.– mid-May, daily 8–6.*

Lookout Studio. Built in 1914 to compete with the Kolbs' photographic studio, the building was designed by architect Mary Jane Colter. The combination lookout point and gift shop has a collection of fossils and geologic samples from around the world. An upstairs loft provides another excellent overlook into the gorge below. ⊠ *About 0.25 mi west of Hermit Road Junction on Hermit Rd.* 🎟*Free* ⊙ *Daily 9–5.*

Powell Memorial. A granite statue honors the memory of John Wesley Powell, who measured, charted, and named many of the canyons and creeks of the Colorado River. It was here that the dedication ceremony for Grand Canyon National Park took place on April 3, 1920. ⊠ *About 3 mi west of Hermit Road Junction on Hermit Rd.*

Tusayan Ruin and Museum. Completed in 1932, the museum offers a quick orientation to the lifestyles of the prehistoric and modern Indian populations associated with the Grand Canyon and the Colorado Plateau. Adjacent, an excavation of an 800-year-old dwelling gives a glimpse at the lives of some of the area's earliest residents. ⊠ *About 20 mi east of Grand Canyon Village on Desert View Dr.* ☎*928/638–7968* 🎟*Free* ⊙ *Daily 9–5.*

SCENIC STOPS

The Abyss. At an elevation of 6,720 feet, the Abyss is one of the most awesome stops on Hermit Road, revealing a sheer drop of 3,000 feet to the Tonto Platform, a wide terrace of Tapeats sandstone layers about two-thirds of the way down the canyon. From the Abyss you'll also see several isolated sandstone columns, the largest of which is called the Monument. ⊠ *About 5 mi west of Hermit Road Junction on Hermit Rd.*

★ **Desert View and Watchtower.** From the top of the 70-foot stone-and-mortar watchtower, even the muted hues of the distant Painted Desert to the east and the Vermilion Cliffs rising from a high plateau near the Utah border are visible. In the chasm below, angling to the north toward Marble Canyon, an imposing stretch of the Colorado River reveals itself. Up several flights of stairs, the Watchtower houses a glass-enclosed observatory with powerful telescopes. ⊠ *About 23 mi east of Grand Canyon Village on Desert View Dr.* ☎*928/638–2736* ⊙ *Daily 8–8, hrs vary in winter.*

Grandview Point. At an elevation of 7,496 feet, the view from here is one of the finest in the canyon. To the northeast is a group of dominant buttes, including Krishna Shrine, Vishnu Temple, Rama Shrine, and Shiva Temple. A short stretch of the Colorado River is also visible. Directly below the point, and accessible by the steep and rugged Grandview Trail, is Horseshoe Mesa, where you can see remnants of Last Chance Copper Mine. ⊠ *About 12 mi east of Grand Canyon Village on Desert View Dr.*

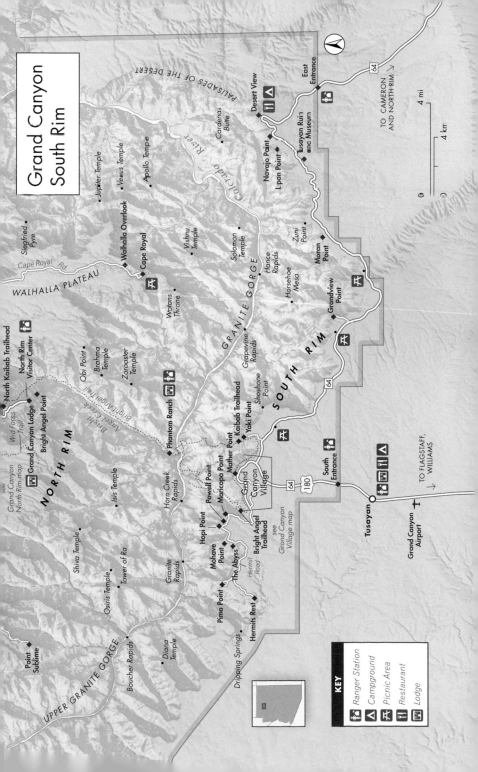

Grand Canyon South Rim

PALISADES OF THE DESERT

Colorado River

GRANITE GORGE

SOUTH RIM

NORTH RIM

WALHALLA PLATEAU

UPPER GRANITE GORGE

Temples and Points:
Point Sublime
Shiva Temple
Osiris Temple
Tower of Ra
Isis Temple
Diana Temple
Boucher Rapids
Granite Rapids
Dripping Springs
Siegfried Pyre
Jupiter Temple
Venus Temple
Apollo Temple
Obi Point
Brahma Temple
Zoroaster Temple
Wotans Throne
Vishnu Temple
Solomon Temple
Hance Rapids
Cardenas Butte
Horseshoe Mesa
Zuni Point
Moran Point
Grapevine Rapids
Shoshone Point
Horn Creek Rapids
Hermits Rest
Pima Point
The Abyss
Mohave Point
Hopi Point
Maricopa Point
Powell Point
Mather Point
Yaki Point

North Kaibab Trailhead
North Rim Visitor Center
Grand Canyon Lodge
Bright Angel Point
Bright Angel Trail
Bright Angel Creek
Phantom Ranch
Kaibab Trailhead
Grand Canyon Village
Bright Angel Trailhead
Hermit Road

Walhalla Overlook
Cape Royal
Cape Royal Rd.

Desert View
East Entrance
Tusayan Ruin and Museum
Navajo Point
Lipan Point
Grandview Point
South Entrance
Tusayan
Grand Canyon Airport
Wid Forks Trail

see Grand Canyon North Rim map
see Grand Canyon Village map

TO CAMERON AND NORTH RIM

TO FLAGSTAFF, WILLIAMS

64
180

0   4 mi
0   4 km

KEY

- Ranger Station
- Campground
- Picnic Area
- Restaurant
- Lodge

BEST GRAND CANYON VIEWS

The best time of day to see the canyon is before 10 AM and after 2 PM, when the angle of the sun brings out the colors of the rock, and clouds and shadows add dimension. Colors deepen dramatically among the contrasting layers of the canyon walls just before and during sunrise and sunset.

Hopi Point is the top spot on the South Rim to watch the sun set; Yaki and Pima points also offer vivid views. For a grand sunrise, try Mather or Yaki points.

Arrive at least 30 minutes early for sunrise views and as much as 90 minutes for sunset views. For another point of view, take a leisurely stroll along the Rim Trail and watch the color change along with the views. Timetables are listed in *The Guide* and are posted at park visitor centers.

★ **Hermits Rest.** This westernmost viewpoint and Hermit Trail, which descends from it, were named for "hermit" Louis Boucher, a 19th-century French-Canadian prospector who had a number of mining claims and a roughly built home down in the canyon. Views from here include Hermit Rapids and the towering cliffs of the Supai and Redwall formations. The stone building at Hermits Rest sells curios and refreshments. ⊠*About 8 mi west of Hermit Road Junction on Hermit Rd.*

★ **Hopi Point.** From this elevation of 7,071 feet, you can see a large section of the Colorado River; although it appears as a thin line, the river is nearly 350 feet wide below this overlook. The overlook extends farther into the canyon than any other point on Hermit Road. The unobstructed views make this a popular place to watch the sunset. Across the canyon to the north is Shiva Temple, which remained an isolated section of the Kaibab Plateau until 1937. That year, Harold Anthony of the American Museum of Natural History led an expedition to the rock formation in the belief that it supported life that had been cut off from the rest of the canyon. Imagine the expedition members' surprise when they found an empty Kodak film box on top of the temple. Directly below Hopi Point lies Dana Butte, named for a prominent 19th-century geologist. In 1919, an entrepreneur proposed connecting Hopi Point, Dana Butte, and the Tower of Set across the river with an aerial tramway, a technically feasible plan that fortunately has not been realized. ⊠*About 4 mi west of Hermit Road Junction on Hermit Rd.*

Lipan Point. Here, at the canyon's widest point, you can get an astonishing visual profile of the gorge's geologic history, with a view of every eroded layer of the canyon. The spacious panorama stretches to the Vermilion Cliffs on the northeastern horizon and features a multitude of imaginatively named spires, buttes, and temples—intriguing rock formations named after their resemblance to ancient pyramids. You can also see Unkar Delta, where a creek joins the Colorado to form powerful rapids and a broad beach. Ancestral Puebloan farmers worked the

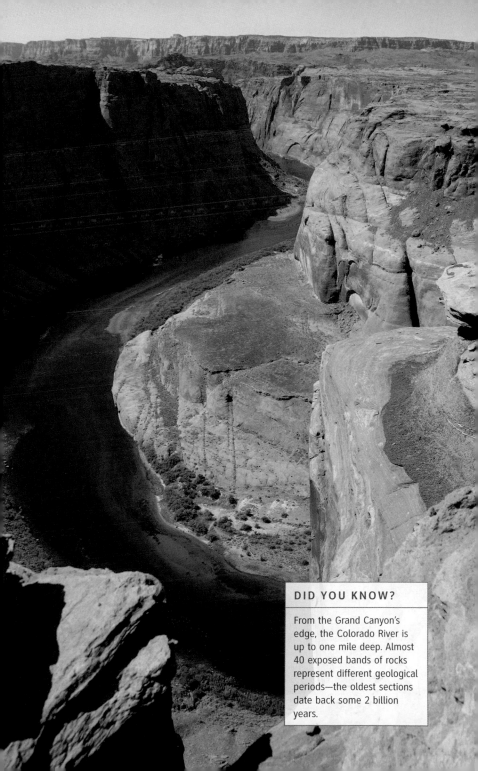

DID YOU KNOW?

From the Grand Canyon's edge, the Colorado River is up to one mile deep. Almost 40 exposed bands of rocks represent different geological periods—the oldest sections date back some 2 billion years.

GRAND CANYON, GREAT ITINERARIES

GRAND CANYON IN 1 DAY

Start early, pack a picnic lunch, and take the shuttle to **Canyon View Information Plaza** just north of the south entrance, to pick up information and see your first incredible view at **Mather Point**. Continue east along **Desert View Drive** for about 2 mi to **Yaki Point**, your first stop. Next, hop back on the shuttle to head 7 mi east to **Grandview Point**, for a good view of the buttes Krishna Shrine and Vishnu Temple. Go 4 mi east and catch the view at **Moran Point**, then 3 mi to the **Tusayan Ruin and Museum**, where a small display is devoted to the history of the ancestral Puebloans. Continue another mile east to **Lipan Point** to view the Colorado River. In less than a mile, you'll arrive at **Navajo Point**, the highest elevation on the South Rim. **Desert View and Watchtower** is the final stop along the shuttle route.

On the return shuttle, hop off at any of the picnic areas for lunch. Once back at Grand Canyon Village, walk the paved **Rim Trail** to **Maricopa Point**. Along the way, pick up souvenirs in the village and stop at the historic **El Tovar Hotel** for dinner (be sure to make reservations well in advance). If you have time, take the shuttle on **Hermit Road** to **Hermits Rest**, 7 mi away. It's a good place to watch the sunset.

GRAND CANYON IN 3 DAYS

On Day 1, follow the one-day itinerary for the morning, but spend more time exploring Desert View Drive and enjoy a leisurely picnic or lunch in Grand Canyon Village. Travel Hermit Road on your second morning, and drive to Grand Canyon Airport for a late-morning small plane or helicopter tour of the area. Have lunch in **Tusayan** and cool off during the IMAX film *Grand Canyon: Discovery & Adventure*. Back in the Village, take in a free ranger-led program. On your third day, take a hike partway down the canyon on **Bright Angel Trail**. It takes twice as long to hike back up, so plan accordingly. Pick up trail maps at **Canyon View Information Plaza**, and bring plenty of water.

Alternatively, spend days 2 and 3 exploring **Grand Canyon West**. Fill the first day with a Hummer tour along the rim, a helicopter ride into the canyon, or a pontoon boat ride on the Colorado River. The next day, raft the Class V and VI rapids or hike 8 mi into **Havasu Canyon** to the small village of Supai and the Havasupai Lodge. You'll need a Havasupai tribal permit to hike here.

GRAND CANYON IN 5 DAYS

Between May and October, you can visit the North Rim as well as the South. Follow the three-day South Rim itinerary and, early on your fourth day, start the long but rewarding drive to the North Rim, where you can spend the last couple of days of your trip. The most popular trails here are **Transept Trail**, which starts near the Grand Canyon Lodge, and **Cliff Springs Trail**, which starts near **Cape Royal**. Before leaving the area, drive Cape Royal Road 11 mi to **Point Imperial**—at 8,803 feet, it's the highest vista on either rim.

Unkar Delta for hundreds of years, growing corn, beans, and melons. ⊠*About 25 mi east of Grand Canyon Village on Desert View Dr.*

Maricopa Point. This site merits a stop not only for the arresting scenery, which includes the Colorado River below, but also for its view of a defunct mine. On your left, as you face the canyon, are the Orphan Mine, a mine shaft, and cable lines leading up to the rim. The mine, which started operations in 1893, was worked first for copper and then for uranium until the venture came to a halt in 1969. The Battleship, the red butte directly ahead of you in the canyon, was named during the Spanish-American War, when warships were in the news. ⊠*About 2 mi west of Hermit Road Junction on Hermit Rd.*

★ **Mather Point.** You'll likely get your first glimpse of the canyon from this viewpoint, one of the most impressive and accessible (and most crowded) on the South Rim. Named for the National Park Service's first director, Stephen Mather, this spot yields extraordinary views of the Grand Canyon, including deep into the Inner Gorge and numerous buttes: Wotan's Throne, Brahma Temple, and Zoroaster Temple, among others. The Grand Canyon Lodge, on the North Rim, is almost directly north from Mather Point and only 10 mi away—yet you have to drive 215 mi to get from one spot to the other. ⊠*Near Canyon View Information Plaza.*

Mohave Point. Some of the canyon's most magnificent stone spires and buttes visible from this lesser-known overlook include the Tower of Set; the Tower of Ra; and Isis, Osiris, and Horus Temples. From here you can view the 5,401-foot Cheops Pyramid, a grayish rock formation behind Dana Butte, plus some of the strongest rapids on the Colorado River. The Granite and Salt Creek rapids are navigable, but not without plenty of effort. ⊠*About 5 mi west of Hermit Road Junction on Hermit Rd.*

Moran Point. This point was named for American landscape artist Thomas Moran, who was especially fond of the play of light and shadows from this location. He first visited the canyon with John Wesley Powell in 1873. "Thomas Moran's name, more than any other, with the possible exception of Major Powell's, is to be associated with the Grand Canyon," wrote noted canyon photographer Ellsworth Kolb. It's fitting that Moran Point is a favorite spot of photographers and painters. ⊠*About 17 mi east of Grand Canyon Village on Desert View Dr.*

Navajo Point. A possible site of the first Spanish view into the Canyon in 1540, this peak is also at the highest natural elevation (7,498 feet) on the South Rim. ⊠*About 21 mi east of Grand Canyon Village on Desert View Dr.*

Pima Point. Enjoy a bird's-eye view of Tonto Platform and Tonto Trail, which winds its way through the canyon for more than 70 mi. Also to the west, two dark, cone-shaped mountains—Mt. Trumbull and Mt. Logan—are visible on the North Rim on clear days. They rise in stark contrast to the surrounding flat-top mesas and buttes. ⊠*About 7 mi west of Hermit Road Junction on Hermit Rd.*

Trailview Overlook. Look down on a dramatic view of the Bright Angel and Plateau Point trails as they zigzag down the canyon. In the deep

Tips for Avoiding Grand Canyon Crowds

It's hard to commune with nature while you're searching for a parking place, dodging video cameras, and stepping away from strollers. However, this scenario is likely only during the peak months of mid-May through mid-October. One option is to bypass Grand Canyon National Park altogether and head to the West Rim of the canyon, tribal land of the Hualapai and Havasupai. If only the park itself will do, the following tips will help you to keep your distance and your cool.

TAKE ANOTHER ROUTE

Avoid road rage by choosing a different route to the South Rim, foregoing the traditional highways 64 and U.S. 180 from Flagstaff. Take U.S. 89 north from Flagstaff instead, passing near Sunset Crater and Wupatki national monuments. When you reach the Cameron Trading Post at the junction with Highway 64, take a break—or stay overnight. This is a good place to shop for Native American artifacts, souvenirs, and the usual postcards, dream-catchers, recordings, and T-shirts. There are also high-quality Navajo rugs, jewelry, and other authentic handicrafts, and you can sample Navajo tacos. U.S. 64 to the west takes you directly to the park's east entrance; the scenery along the Little Colorado River Gorge en route is eye-popping. It's 23 mi from the east entrance to the visitor center at Canyon View Information Plaza.

BYPASS THE SOUTH RIM

Although the North Rim is just 10 mi across from the South Rim, the trip to get there by car is a five-hour drive of 215 mi. At first it might not sound like the trip would be worth it, but the payoff is huge. Along the way, you will travel through some of the prettiest parts of the state and be granted even more stunning views than those on the more easily accessible South Rim. Those who make the North Rim trip often insist it offers the canyon's most beautiful views and best hiking. To get to the North Rim from Flagstaff, take U.S. 89 north past Cameron, turning left onto U.S. 89A at Bitter Springs. En route you'll pass the area known as Vermilion Cliffs. At Jacob Lake, take Highway 67 directly to the Grand Canyon North Rim. The road to the North Rim closes from around mid-October through mid-May because of heavy snow, but in summer months and early fall, it's a wonderful way to beat the crowds at the South Rim.

RIDE THE RAILS

There is no need to deal with all of the other drivers racing to the South Rim. Forget the hassle of the twisting rim roads, jaywalking pedestrians, and jammed parking lots, and sit back and relax in the comfy train cars of the **Grand Canyon Railway**. Live music and storytelling enliven the trip as you journey past the landscape through prairie, ranch, and national park land to the log-cabin train station in Grand Canyon Village. You won't see the Grand Canyon from the train, but you can walk or catch the shuttle at the restored, historic Grand Canyon Railway Station. The vintage train departs from the Williams Depot every morning, and makes the 65-mi journey in 2¼ hours. You can do the round-trip in a single day; however, you may choose to stay overnight at the South Rim and return to Williams the following afternoon. ⇨ *See Grand Canyon Railway Hotel in Where to Stay.* ☎ *800/843-8724* ⊕ *www.thetrain.com* ✉ *$70–$190 round-trip.*

gorge to the north flows Bright Angel Creek, one of the region's few permanent tributary streams of the Colorado River. Toward the south is an unobstructed view of the distant San Francisco Peaks, as well as Bill Williams Mountain (on the horizon) and Red Butte (about 15 mi south of the canyon rim). ⊠*About 2 mi west of Hermit Road Junction on Hermit Rd.*

Yaki Point. Stop here for an exceptional view of Wotan's Throne, a flattop butte named by François Matthes, a U.S. Geological Survey scientist who developed the first topographical map of the Grand Canyon. The overlook juts out over the canyon, providing unobstructed views of inner canyon rock formations, South Rim cliffs, and Clear Creek Canyon. This point marks the beginning of the South Kaibab Trail and is one of the best places on the south rim to watch the sunset. ⊠*2 mi east of Grand Canyon Village on Desert View Dr.*

Fodor's Choice **Yavapai Point.** The word Yavapai means "sun people" in Paiute, a group
★ of nomadic Indians associated with the Grand Canyon. Appropriately, this is one of the best locations on the South Rim to watch the sunset. Dominated by the Yavapai Observation Station, this point offers panoramic views of the mighty gorge through a wall of windows. Exhibits showcased here include videos of the canyon floor and the Colorado River, a scaled diorama of the canyon with national park boundaries, fossils and rock fragments used to re-create the complex layers of the canyon walls, and a display on the natural forces used to carve the chasm. Rangers dig even deeper into Grand Canyon geology with the free ranger program Geo-Glimpse, offered twice daily. A guided afternoon nature walk completes the offerings. Check ahead for special event and walk schedules. ⊠*Adjacent to Grand Canyon Village* Free ⊗ *Daily 8–8, hrs vary in winter.*

VISITOR CENTERS

Canyon View Information Plaza. The park's main orientation center near Mather Point provides pamphlets and resources to help plan your sightseeing. Park rangers are on hand to answer questions and aid in planning canyon excursions. A bookstore is stocked with books covering all topics on the Grand Canyon, and a daily schedule of ranger-led hikes and evening lectures is posted on a bulletin board inside. The information center can be reached by a short walk from Mather Point, by a short ride on the shuttle bus Village Route, or by a leisurely 1-mi walk on the Greenway Trail—a paved pathway that meanders through the forest. ⊠*East side of Grand Canyon Village* 928/638–7888 ⊗ *Daily 8–5, outdoor exhibits may be viewed anytime.*

Desert View Information Center. Near the Watchtower, at Desert View Point, the Grand Canyon Association offers a nice selection of books, park pamphlets, and educational materials. ⊠*East entrance* 800/858–2808 or 928/638–7893 ⊗ *Daily 9–5; hrs vary in winter.*

Verkamp's Visitor Center. After 102 years of selling memorabilia and knickknacks on the South Rim, Verkamp's Curios closed in 2008 only to reopen a couple of months later as the park's newest visitor center. The building now serves as a bookstore, ranger station, and museum with exhibits on the pioneer history of the region. ⊠*Desert View Dr.,*

Switchbacks on the canyon's trails make the steep grade level enough for hikers (and mules).

across from El Tovar Hotel, Grand Canyon Village ☎928/638–7146 ⊙*Daily 8–5.*

Yavapai Observation Station. Shop in the bookstore, catch the park shuttle bus, or pick up information for the Rim Trail here. ⊠*1 mi east of Market Plaza, Grand Canyon* ☎928/638–7890 ⊙*Daily 8–8; hrs vary in winter.*

SPORTS AND THE OUTDOORS

AIR TOURS

★ Flights by plane and helicopter over the canyon are offered by a number of companies, departing for the Grand Canyon Airport at the south end of Tusayan. You'll have more visibility from a helicopter but they are louder and more expensive than the fixed-wing planes. Prices and lengths of tours vary, but you can expect to pay about $109–$120 per adult for short plane trips and approximately $145–$235 for brief helicopter tours.

OUTFITTERS AND EXPEDITIONS **Air Grand Canyon** (⊠*Grand Canyon Airport, Grand Canyon* ☎928/638–2686 *or* 800/247–4726 ⊕*www.airgrandcanyon.com*) offers 40- to 50-minute fixed-wing air tours over the North Rim, the Kaibab Plateau, and the Dragon Corridor, one of the cross canyons. Tours start at 9 AM and run every hour on the hour. **Grand Canyon Airlines** (⊠*Grand Canyon Airport* ☎928/638–2359 *or* 866/235–9422 ⊕*www.grandcanyonair lines.com*) flies a fixed-wing on a 50-minute tour of the eastern edge of the Grand Canyon, the North Rim, and the Kaibab Plateau. All-day combination tours combine flightseeing with jeep tours and float trips on the Colorado River. Get an up-close view of Grand Canyon geology and the Colorado River on 30- and 50-minute tours with **Grand Canyon Helicopters** (✉ *Grand Canyon Airport* ☎ *928/638–2764 or 800/541–4537* ⊕ *www.grandcanyonhelicoptersaz.com/gch*). **Maverick Helicopters** (✉ *Grand Canyon Airport* ☎ *928/638–2622 or 800/962–3869* ⊕ *www.maverickhelicopters.com*) offers 25- and 45-minute tours of the eastern Grand Canyon, the North Rim, and the Dragon Corridor. A landing tour option sets you down in the canyon for a short snack below the rim. **Papillon Grand Canyon Helicopters** (✉ *Grand Canyon Airport* ☎ *928/638–2419 or 800/528–2418* ⊕ *www.papillon.com*) offers both fixed-wing and helicopter tours of the canyon and combination tours with off-road jeep tours and smooth-water rafting trips.

BICYCLING

The South Rim's limited opportunities for off-road biking, narrow shoulders on park roads, and heavy traffic may disappoint hard-core cyclists. Bicycles are permitted on all park roads and on the multi-use Greenway System. Bikes are prohibited on all other trails, including the Rim Trail. Mountain bikers visiting the South Rim may be better off meandering through the ponderosa pine forest on the Tusayan Bike Trail. No rentals are available at the South Rim. Bicycle camping sites are available at Mather Campground for $6 per person.

HIKING

Although permits are not required for day hikes, you must have a backcountry permit for longer trips *(Admission Fees and Permits at the start of this chapter)* ⇨ *See*. Some of the more popular trails are listed in this chapter; more detailed information and maps can be obtained from the Backcountry Information Center. Also, rangers can help design a trip to suit your abilities.

Remember that the canyon has significant elevation changes and, in summer, extreme temperature ranges, which can pose problems for people who aren't in good shape or who have heart or respiratory problems. ■TIP➔ **Carry plenty of water and energy foods.** The majority of each year's 400 search-and-rescue incidents result from hikers underestimating the size of the canyon, hiking beyond their abilities, or not packing sufficient food and water.

⚠ **Under no circumstances should you attempt a day hike from the rim to the river and back.** Remember that when it's 80°F on the South Rim, it's 110°F on the canyon floor. Allow two to four days if you want to hike rim to rim (it's easier to descend from the North Rim, as it is more than 1,000 feet higher than the South Rim). Hiking steep trails from rim to rim is a strenuous trek of at least 21 mi and should only be attempted by experienced canyon hikers.

Fodor'sChoice
★
EASY
Rim Trail. The South Rim's most popular walking path is the 9-mi (one way) Rim Trail, which runs along the edge of the canyon from Mather Point (the first overlook on Desert View Drive) to Hermits Rest. This walk, which is paved to Maricopa Point, visits several of the South Rim's historic landmarks. Allow anywhere from 15 minutes to a full day; the Rim Trail is an ideal day hike, as it varies only a few hundred feet in elevation from Mather Point (7,120 feet) to the trailhead at

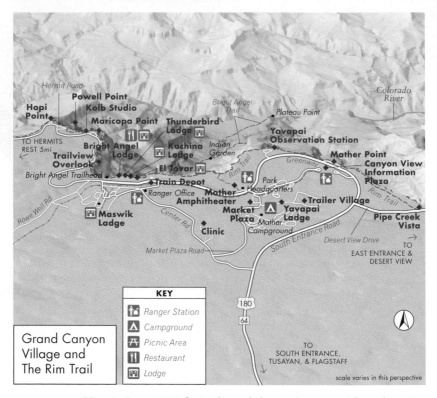

Grand Canyon Village and The Rim Trail

KEY

- 🚹 Ranger Station
- ⛺ Campground
- 🎪 Picnic Area
- 🍴 Restaurant
- 🏠 Lodge

Hermits Rest (6,640 feet). The trail also can be accessed from the major viewpoints along Hermit Road, which are serviced by shuttle buses during the busy summer months. ■TIP→ On the Rim Trail, water is only available in the Grand Canyon Village area and at Hermits Rest.

NEED A BREAK? If you've been driving too long and want some exercise, along with great views of the canyon, it's an easy 1.25-mi-long hike from the **Information Plaza** to El Tovar Hotel. The Greenway path runs through a quiet wooded area for about 0.5 mi, and then along the rim for another 0.75 mi.

MODERATE ★ **Bright Angel Trail.** Well-maintained, this is one of the most scenic hiking paths from the South Rim to the bottom of the canyon (9.6 mi each way). Rest houses are equipped with water at the 1.5- and 3-mi points from May through September and at Indian Garden (4 mi) year-round. Water is also available at Bright Angel Campground, 9.25 mi below the trailhead. Plateau Point, about 1.5 mi below Indian Garden, is as far as you should attempt to go on a day hike; plan on spending six to nine hours. Bright Angel Trail is the easiest of all the footpaths into the canyon, but because the climb out from the bottom is an ascent of 5,510 feet, the trip should be attempted only by those in good physical condition and should be avoided in midsummer due to extreme heat. The top of the trail, a tight set of switchbacks called Jacob's Ladder can be icy in winter. Originally a bighorn sheep path and later

3

used by the Havasupai, the trail was widened late in the 19th century for prospectors and is now used for both mule and foot traffic. ■TIP→Hikers going downhill should yield to those going uphill. Also note that mule trains have the right-of-way—and sometimes leave unpleasant surprises in your path.

DIFFICULT **Clear Creek Trail.** Make this 9-mi hike only if you are prepared for a multiday trip. The trail departs from Phantom Ranch at the bottom of the canyon and leads across the Tonto Platform to Clear Creek, where drinking water is usually available, but should be treated.

Grandview Trail. Accessible from the parking area at Grandview Point, the trailhead is at 7,400 feet. The path heads down into the canyon for 4.8 mi to the junction and campsite at East Horseshoe Mesa Trail. Classified as a wilderness trail, the route is aggressive and not as heavily traveled as some of the more well-known trails, such as Bright Angel and Hermit; allow six to nine hours, round-trip. There is no water available along the trail, which follows a steep descent to 4,800 feet at Horseshoe Mesa, where Hopi Indians once collected mineral paints.

Hermit Trail. Beginning on the South Rim just west of Hermits Rest (and 8 mi west of Grand Canyon Village), this steep, 9.7-mi (one way) trail drops more than 5,000 feet to Hermit Creek, which usually flows year-round. It's a strenuous hike back up and is recommended for experienced long-distance hikers only; plan for six to nine hours. There's an abundance of lush growth and wildlife, including desert bighorn sheep, along this trail. The trail descends from the trailhead at 6,640 feet to the Colorado River at 2,300 feet. Day hikers should not go past Santa Maria Spring at 5,000 feet. For much of the year, no water is available along the way; ask a park ranger about the availability of water at Santa Maria Spring and Hermit Creek before you set out. All water from these sources should be treated before drinking. The route leads down to the Colorado River and has inspiring views of Hermit Gorge and the Redwall and Supai formations. Six miles from the trailhead are the ruins of Hermit Camp, which the Santa Fe Railroad ran as a tourist camp from 1911 until 1930.

★ **South Kaibab Trail.** This trail starts at Yaki Point on Desert View Drive, 4 mi east of Grand Canyon Village. Because the route is so steep—descending from the trailhead at 7,260 feet down to 2,480 feet at the Colorado River—and has no water, many hikers return via the less-demanding Bright Angel Trail; allow four to six hours. During this 6.4-mi trek to the Colorado River, you're likely to encounter mule trains and riders. At the river, the trail crosses a suspension bridge and

WORD OF MOUTH

"Taking the first step into the canyon was just amazing. We started down the series of switch-backs … We took the obligatory pictures at Ooh-Ahh Point and continued on to Cedar Ridge . The views were magnificent. This highlights the reason to hike into the canyon. You get such a different perspective with all of the rock formations right around you. I can't really find the words to express what it is like to travel down into the canyon and be surrounded by so many ancient rocks and buttes."

—caligirl56

runs on to Phantom Ranch. Along the trail there is no water and very little shade. There are no campgrounds, though there are portable toilets at Cedar Ridge (6,320 feet), 1.5 mi from the trailhead. Toilets and an emergency phone are also available at the Tipoff, 4.6 mi down the trail (3 mi past Cedar Ridge). The trail corkscrews down through some spectacular geology. Look for (but don't remove) fossils in the limestone when taking water breaks. ■TIP→ Even though an immense network of trails winds through the Grand Canyon, the popular corridor trails (Bright Angel and South Kaibab) are recommended for hikers new to the region.

JEEP TOURS

Jeep rides can be rough; if you have had back injuries, check with your doctor before taking a 4X4 tour.

OUTFITTERS AND EXPEDITIONS

Grand Canyon Jeep Tours & Safaris. If you'd like to get off the pavement and see parts of the park that are accessible only by dirt road, a Jeep tour can be just the ticket. From March through October, this tour operator leads daily, 1½- to 4½-hour, off-road tours within the park, as well as in Kaibab National Forest. Combo tours adding helicopter and airplane rides are also available. ⊠ *Box 1772, 86023* ☎ *928/638–5337 or 800/320–5337* ⊕ *www.grandcanyonjeeptours.com* ⊠ *$45–$209* ☐ *AE, MC, V* ⚲ *Reservations essential.*

Grand Canyon Old West Jeep Tours. This tour company offers off-road jeep adventures and backcountry ATV adventures. From March through November, there are two- and three-hour, off-road and helicopter-jeep combo tours of the South Rim. The all-day trip to the inner canyon on the Hualapai Indian reservation is offered year-round. ⊠ *Grand Canyon* ☎ *928/638–2000 or 866/638–4386* ⊕ *www.grandcanyonjeeps. com* ⊠ *$63–$256* ☐ *AE, D, MC, V* ⚲ *Reservations essential.*

Marvelous Marv's Grand Canyon Tours. For a personalized experience, take this private tour of the Grand Canyon and surrounding sights any time of year. Tours include round-trip transportation from your hotel or campground in Williams, Tusayan, or Grand Canyon, admission to the park, scenic viewpoint stops, a short hike, and personal narration of the geology and history of the area. ⊡ *Box 544, Williams 86046* ☎ *928/707–0291* ⊕ *www.marvelousmarv.com* ⊠ *$85* ☐ *No credit cards* ⚲ *Reservations essential.*

MULE RIDES

★ Mule rides provide an intimate glimpse into the canyon for those who have the time, but not the stamina to see the canyon on foot. ■TIP→ Reservations are essential and are accepted up to 13 months in advance.

These trips have been conducted since the early 1900s. A comforting fact as you ride the narrow trail: no one's ever been killed while riding a mule that fell off a cliff. (Nevertheless, the treks are not for the faint of heart or people in questionable health.)

OUTFITTERS

Grand Canyon National Park Lodges Mule Rides. These trips delve into the canyon from the South Rim. Riders must be at least 55 inches tall, weigh less than 200 pounds, and understand English. Children under 15 must be accompanied by an adult. Riders must be in fairly good physical condition, and pregnant women are advised not to take these trips. The all-day ride to Plateau Point costs $153.95 (box lunch included). An overnight with a stay at Phantom Ranch at the bottom of the canyon is $420.09 ($743.03 for two riders). Two nights at Phantom Ranch, an option available from November through March, will set you back $592.83 ($991.38 for two). Meals are included. Reservations, especially during the busy summer months, are a must, but you can check at the Bright Angel Transportation Desk to be placed on the waiting list. ⌖6312 S. Fiddlers Green Circle, Suite 600, N. Greenwood Village, CO 80111 ☏303/297–2757 or 888/297–2757 ⊕www.grandcan yonlodges.com ⊙May–Sept., daily ⚒Reservations essential.

> ## ARRANGING TOURS
>
> Transportation-services desks are maintained at El Tovar, Bright Angel, Maswik Lodge, and Yavapai Lodge (closed in winter) in Grand Canyon Village. The desks provide information and handle bookings for sightseeing tours, taxi and bus services, mule and horseback rides, and accommodations at Phantom Ranch (at the bottom of the Grand Canyon). The concierge at El Tovar can also arrange most tours, with the exception of mule rides and lodging at Phantom Ranch. On the North Rim, Grand Canyon Lodge has general information about local services.

3

SKIING

Although you can't schuss down into the Grand Canyon, you can cross-country ski in the woods near the rim when there's enough snow, usually mid-December though early March. Trails, suitable for beginner and intermediate skiers, begin 0.3 mi north of the Grandview Lookout and travel through the Kaibab National Forest. Contact the **Tusayan Ranger District** (⌖Box 3088, Grand Canyon 86023 ☏928/638–2443 ⊕www. fs.fed.us/r3/kai) for details.

EDUCATIONAL OFFERINGS

Grand Canyon Field Institute. Instructors lead guided educational tours, hikes around the canyon, and weekend programs at the South Rim. With more than 100 classes a year, tour topics include everything from archaeology and backcountry medicine to photography and natural history. Contact GCFI for a schedule and price list. Discounted classes are available for members. Dues for an individual membership is $35 a year. ⌖Box 399, Grand Canyon ☏928/638–2485 or 866/471–4435 ⊕www.grandcanyon.org/fieldinstitute ⚏$105–$695 ▤AE, D, MC, V ⚒Reservations essential.

Interpretive Ranger Programs. The National Park Service sponsors all sorts of orientation activities, such as daily guided hikes and talks. The focus may be on any aspect of the canyon—from geology and flora and fauna to history and early inhabitants. For schedules on the South Rim, go to Canyon View Information Plaza, pick up a free copy of *The Guide*, or check online. ☏928/638–7888 ⊕www.nps.gov/grca ⚏Free.

☾ **Junior Ranger Program for Families.** The Junior Ranger Program provides a free, fun way to look at the cultural and natural history of this sublime destination. These hands-on educational programs for children ages 4

GRAND CANYON NATIONAL PARK: TOP PICKS HIKING TRAILS

	Grade	Miles (One Way)	Beginning Elevation	Ending Elevation	Mules	Campground	Open Info*	Water	Shuttle Access	Ranger Station	Toilet/Restroom	Emergency	Hiking Level	Trail Conditions
SOUTH RIM														
Bright Angel Trail South	Steep	9.6 mi	6860 ft	2480 ft (Colorado River)	Y	Y	Y/R	Seasonal	Y	Y	Y	Y	Moderate-Difficult	Maintained
Grandview Trail	Very Steep	3.2 mi	7400 ft	4800 ft (Horseshoe Mesa)		Y	Y/R	Untreated	Y		Y		Difficult	Maintained
Hermit Trail	Steep	9.7 mi	6640 ft	2300 ft (Colorado River)			Y/R	Untreated	Y		Y**	Y**	Difficult	Unmaintained
Rim Trail	Level	9 mi	6640 ft	7120 ft (Mather Point)			Y/R	Y**	Y		Y	Y	Easy-Difficult	Maintained
South Kaibab Trail	Steep	6.4 mi	7260 ft	2400 ft (Colorado River)	Y		Y/R	Y**	Y	Y	Y	Y	Difficult	Unmaintained
NORTH RIM														
Cape Final Trail	Level/Incline	2.0 mi	7840 ft	7916 ft (Cape Final)			mid-May –mid-Oct.						Easy-Moderate	Maintained
Ken Patrick Trail	Level/Incline	10 mi	8250 ft	8803 ft (Point Imperial)			mid-May –mid-Oct.						Easy-Difficult	Unmaintained
North Kaibab Trail	Steep	7.1 mi	8241 ft	2400 ft (Colorado River)	Y	Y	mid-May –mid-Oct.	Y	Y	Y	Y		Moderate	Maintained
Transept Trail	Level	1.5 mi	8255 ft	8200 ft (Campground)			mid-May –mid-Oct.				Y	Y	Easy	Maintained
Uncle Jim Trail	Level	2.5 mi	8300 ft	8244 ft (Uncle Jim Point)	Y		mid-May –mid-Oct.						Easy-Difficult	Maintained
Widforss Trail	Level/Incline	4.9 mi	8080 ft	7900 ft (Widforss Point)			mid-May –mid-Oct.						Easy-Difficult	Unmaintained

*(South Rim trails occasionally close due to weather or trail conditions) **(Trailhead) Y/R = year-round

to 14 include guided adventure hikes, ranger-led "discovery" programs, and book readings. ☎*928/638–7888* ⊕*www.nps.gov/grca* ✉*Free.*

Xanterra Motorcoach Tours. Narrated by knowledgeable guides, tours include the Hermits Rest Tour, which travels along the old wagon road built by the Santa Fe Railway; the Desert View Tour, which glimpses the Colorado River's rapids and stops at Lipan Point; Sunrise and Sunset Tours; and Combination Tours. Children 16 and younger are free when accompanied by a paying adult. ⌖*6312 S. Fiddlers Green Circle, Suite 600, N. Greenwood Village, CO 80111* ☎*303/297–2757 or 888/297–2757* ⊕*www.grandcanyonlodges.com* ✉*$18–$50.*

SHOPPING

Nearly every lodging facility and retail store at the South Rim stocks Native American arts and crafts and Grand Canyon books and souvenirs. Prices are comparable to other souvenir outlets, though you may find some better deals in Williams. However, a portion of the proceeds from items purchased at Hopi House, Desert Watchtower, and the visitor center go to the Grand Canyon Association.

Desert View Trading Post (✉*Desert View Dr., near the Watchtower at Desert View* ☎*928/638–3150*) sells a mix of traditional Southwestern souvenirs and authentic Native American arts and crafts.

★ **Hopi House** (✉*Desert View Dr., east of El Tovar Hotel, Grand Canyon Village* ☎*928/638–2631*) has the widest selection of Native American handicrafts in the vicinity.

GRAND CANYON NORTH RIM

The North Rim stands 1,000 feet higher than the South Rim and has a more alpine climate, with twice as much annual precipitation. Here, in the deep forests of the Kaibab Plateau, the crowds are thinner, the facilities fewer, and the views even more spectacular. Due to snow, the North Rim is off-limits in the winter. The park buildings are closed mid-October through mid-May. The road closes when the snow makes it impassable—usually by the end of November.

Lodgings are available but limited; the North Rim only offers one historic lodge and restaurant and a single campground. Dining options have opened up a little with the addition of the Grand Cookout, offered nightly with live entertainment under the stars. Your best bet may be to pack your camping gear and hiking boots and take several days to explore the lush Kaibab Forest. The canyon's highest, most dramatic rim views also can be enjoyed on two wheels (via primitive dirt access roads) and on four legs (courtesy of a trusty mule).

SCENIC DRIVE

★ **Highway 67.** Open mid-May to mid-October (and often until Thanksgiving), the two-lane paved road climbs 1,400 feet in elevation as it passes through the Kaibab National Forest. Also called the "North

Freebies at the Grand Canyon

While you're here, be sure to take advantage of the many freebies offered at Grand Canyon National Park. The most useful of these services is the system of free shuttle buses at the South Rim; it caters to the road-weary, with three routes winding through the park—Hermits Rest Route, Village Route, and Kaibab Trail Route. Of the bus routes, the Hermits Rest Route runs only from March through November; the other two run year-round, and the Kaibab Trail Route provides the only access to Yaki Point. Hikers coming or going from the Kaibab Trailhead can catch the Hikers Express, which departs three times each morning from the Bright Angel Lodge, makes a quick stop at the Backcountry Office, and then heads out to the South Kaibab Trailhead.

Ranger-led programs are always free and offered year-round, though more are scheduled during the busy spring and summer seasons. These programs might include activities such as stargazing and topics such as geology and the cultural history of prehistoric peoples. Some of the more in-depth programs may include a fossil walk or a condor talk. Check with the visitor center for seasonal programs including wildflower walks and fire ecology.

Kids ages 4 to 14 can get involved with the park's Junior Ranger program, with ever-changing activities including hikes and hands-on experiments.

Despite all of these options, rangers will tell you that the best free activity in the canyon is watching the magnificent splashes of color on the canyon walls during sunrise and sunset.

Rim Parkway," this scenic route crosses the limestone-capped Kaibab Plateau—passing broad meadows, sun-dappled forests, and small lakes and springs—before abruptly falling away at the abyss of the Grand Canyon. Wildlife abounds in the thick ponderosa pine forests and lush mountain meadows. It's common to see deer, turkeys, and coyotes as you drive through this remote region. Point Imperial and Cape Royal can be reached by spurs off this scenic drive running from Jacob Lake to Bright Angel Point.

EXPLORING

HISTORIC SITE

Grand Canyon Lodge. Built in 1928 by the Union Pacific Railroad, the massive stone structure is listed on the National Register of Historic Places. Its huge sunroom has hardwood floors, high-beam ceilings, and a marvelous view of the canyon through plate-glass windows. On warm days, visitors sit in the sun and drink in the surrounding beauty on an outdoor viewing deck, where National Park Service employees deliver free lectures on geology and history. ⊠ *Off Hwy. 67, near Bright Angel Point, North Rim.*

Grand Canyon
North Rim

KEY
- Ranger Station
- Campground
- Picnic Area
- Restaurant
- Lodge

TO JACOB LAKE, MARBLE CANYON AND SOUTH RIM

North Rim Entrance Station

TO POINT SUBLIME

KAIBAB PLATEAU

NORTH RIM

Wildforss Trail

Ken Patrick Trail

Point Imperial Road

Point Imperial

Bourke Point

Vista Encantada

Tritle Peak

Roosevelt Point

Aloko Point

Siegfried Pyre

North Rim Visitor Center

Grand Canyon Lodge
Bright Angel Point

WALHALLA PLATEAU

Cape Royal Road

Obi Point

Cape Final Trail

Jupiter Temple

Chuar Butte

Temple Butte

Cottonwood Campground

Shiva Temple

Osiris Temple

Isis Temple

Bright Angel Creek

North Kaibab Trail

Brahma Temple

Walhalla Ruins

Venus Temple

Zoroaster Temple

Cliff Springs Trail

Cape Royal

Apollo Temple

Granite Rapids

Horn Creek Rapids

Phantom Ranch

Cape Royal Trail

Wotans Throne

Vishnu Temple

Cardenas Butte

Bright Angel Trail

SOUTH RIM

GRANITE GORGE

Hopi Point

The Abyss

Mather Point

South Kaibab Trail

Grapevine Rapids

Solomon Temple

Hermit Road

Yaki Point

Grand Canyon Village

Hance Rapids

Desert View

Navajo Point

TO FLAGSTAFF, WILLIAMS

Lipan Point

SOUTH CANYON

MARBLE CANYON

Tatahatso Point

Point Hansbrough

PAINTED DESERT

NAVAJO INDIAN RESERVATION

Nankoweap Rapids

Nankoweap Mesa

Kwagunt Butte

Colorado River

PALISADES OF THE DESERT

445

67

64

5 mi
5 km

SCENIC STOPS

★ **Bright Angel Point.** The trail, which leads to one of the most awe-inspiring overlooks on either rim, starts on the grounds of the Grand Canyon Lodge and runs along the crest of a point of rocks that juts into the canyon for several hundred yards. The walk is only 0.5 mi round-trip, but it's an exciting trek accented by sheer drops on each side of the trail. In a few spots where the route is extremely narrow, metal railings ensure visitors' safety. The temptation to clamber out to precarious perches to have your picture taken could get you killed—every year several people die from falls at the Grand Canyon. ⊠*North Rim Dr.*

Cape Royal. A popular sunset destination, Cape Royal showcases the canyon's jagged landscape; you'll also get a glimpse of the Colorado River, framed by a natural stone arch called Angels Window. In autumn, the aspens turn a beautiful gold, adding even more color to an already magnificent scene of the forested surroundings. At Angels Window Overlook, **Cliff Springs Trail** starts its 1-mi route (round-trip) through a forested ravine. The trail terminates at Cliff Springs, where the forest opens to another impressive view of the canyon walls. ⊠*Cape Royal Scenic Dr., 23 mi southeast of Grand Canyon Lodge.*

⚠ Practice basic safety precautions to reduce the risks of summer-storm-related dangers. The safest place to be during a thunderstorm is in a building or in a vehicle with the windows closed.

Point Imperial. At 8,803 feet, Point Imperial has the highest vista point at either rim; it offers magnificent views of both the canyon and the distant country: the Vermilion Cliffs to the north, the 10,000-foot Navajo Mountain to the northeast in Utah, the Painted Desert to the east, and the Little Colorado River Canyon to the southeast. ⊠*2.7 mi left off Cape Royal Scenic Dr. on Point Imperial Rd., 11 mi northeast of Grand Canyon Lodge.*

Fodor'sChoice **Point Sublime.** Talk about solitude. Here you can camp within feet of the
★ canyon's edge. Sunrises and sunsets are spectacular. The winding road, through gorgeous high country, is only 17 mi, but it will take you at least two hours, one way. The road is intended only for vehicles with high-road clearance (pickups and four-wheel-drive vehicles). It is also necessary to be properly equipped for wilderness road travel. Check with a park ranger or at the information desk at Grand Canyon Lodge before taking this journey. You may camp here only with a permit from the Backcountry Office. ⊠*North Rim Dr., Grand Canyon; about 20 mi west of North Rim Visitor Center.*

Roosevelt Point. Named after the president who gave the Grand Canyon its national park status in 1919, this is the best place to see the confluence of the Little Colorado River and the Grand Canyon. The cliffs above the Colorado River south of the junction are known as the Palisades of the Desert. A short woodland loop trail leads to this eastern viewpoint. ⊠*Cape Royal Rd., 18 mi east of Grand Canyon Lodge.*

Flora and Fauna of the Grand Canyon

Eighty-nine mammal species inhabit Grand Canyon National Park, as well as 355 species of birds and 56 kinds of reptiles and amphibians, and 17 kinds of fish. The rare Kaibab squirrel is found only on the North Rim—you can recognize them by their all-white tails and the long tufts of white hair on their ears. The pink Grand Canyon rattlesnake lives at lower elevations within the canyon. Hawks and ravens are visible year-round. The endangered California condor has been reintroduced to the canyon. Park rangers give daily talks on the magnificent birds, whose wingspan measures 9 feet. In spring, summer, and fall, mule deer, recognizable by their large antlers, are abundant at the South Rim. Don't be fooled by gentle appearances; these guys can be aggressive. It's illegal to feed them, as it will disrupt their natural habitats, and increase your risk of getting bitten.

The best times to see wildlife are early in the morning and late in the afternoon. Look for out-of-place shapes and motions, keeping in mind that animals occupy all layers in a natural habitat and not just at your eye level. Use binoculars for close-up views. While out and about try to fade into the woodwork by keeping your movements limited and noise at a minimum.

More than 1,700 species of plants color the park. The South Rim's Coconino Plateau is fairly flat, at an elevation of about 7,000 feet, and covered with stands of piñon and ponderosa pines, junipers, and Gambel's oak trees. On the Kaibab Plateau on the North Rim, Douglas fir, spruce, quaking aspen, and more ponderosas prevail. In spring you're likely to see asters, sunflowers, and lupine in bloom at both rims.

Vista Encantada. This point on the Walhalla Plateau offers views of the upper drainage of Nankoweap Creek, a rock pinnacle known as Brady Peak, and the Painted Desert to the east. This is an enchanting place for a picnic lunch. ⊠ *Cape Royal Rd., 16 mi southeast of Grand Canyon Lodge.*

Walhalla Overlook. One of the lowest elevations on the North Rim, this overlook has views of the Unkar Delta, a fertile region used by ancestral Puebloans as farmland. These ancient people also gathered food and hunted game on the North Rim. A flat path leads to the remains of the Walhalla Glades Pueblo, which was inhabited from 1050 to 1150. ⊠ *Cape Royal Rd., 22.5 mi southeast of Grand Canyon Lodge.*

VISITOR CENTER

North Rim Visitor Center. View exhibits, peruse the bookstore, and pick up useful maps and brochures. Interpretive programs are often scheduled in the summer. If you're craving coffee, it's a short walk from here to the Roughrider Saloon at the Grand Canyon Lodge. ⊠ *Near the parking lot on Bright Angel Peninsula* ☎ *928/638–7864* ⊙ *Mid-May–mid-Oct., daily 8–6.*

SPORTS AND THE OUTDOORS

BICYCLING

Mountain bikers can test the many dirt access roads found in this remote area, including the 17-mi trek to Point Sublime. It's rare to spot other people on these primitive roads. **The Outfitters Station,** offers Schwinn bicycles on a hourly, half-day, or full-day basis. Be sure to take a cruise on the tandem bicycle or the retro Surrey for a leisurely ride in a place you won't soon forget. Children's bike are available. ✉ *Grand Canyon Lodge, North Rim* ☎ *928/638–2611* ⊕ *www.grandcanyonforever.com.*

Bicycles and leashed pets are allowed on the 1.2 mi (one way) **Bridle Trail,** which follows the road from Grand Canyon Lodge to the North Kaibab Trailhead. Bikes are prohibited on all other national park trails.

HIKING

EASY **Cape Final Trail.** This 2-mi hike follows an old jeep trail through a ponderosa pine forest to the canyon overlook at Cape Final with panoramic views of the northern canyon, the Palisades of the Desert, and the impressive spectacle of Juno Temple. To access the trailhead, park at the dirt parking lot 5 mi south of Roosevelt Point on Cape Royal Road.

☾ **Cape Royal Trail.** Informative signs on natural history add to this popular
★ 0.6-mi, round-trip, paved path to Cape Royal; allow 30 minutes round-trip. At an elevation of 7,685 feet on the southern edge of the Walhalla Plateau, this popular viewpoint offers expansive views of Wotans Throne, Vishnu Temple, Freya Castle, Horseshoe Mesa, and the Colorado River. The trail also offers several nice views of Angels Window.

☾ **Cliff Springs Trail.** An easy 1-mi (round-trip), one-hour walk near Cape Royal, Cliff Springs Trail leads through a forested ravine to an excellent view of the canyon. The trailhead begins across from Angels Window Overlook. Narrow and precarious in spots, it passes ancient dwellings, winds beneath a limestone overhang, and ends at Cliff Springs.

☾ **Roosevelt Point Trail.** On Cape Royal Road, this easy 0.2-mi round-trip
★ trail loops through the forest to the scenic viewpoint. Allow 20 minutes for this short, secluded hike.

☾ **Transept Trail.** This 3-mi (round-trip), 1½-hour trail begins at 8,255 feet near the Grand Canyon Lodge's east patio. Well-maintained and -marked, it has little elevation change, sticking near the rim before reaching a dramatic view of a large stream through Bright Angel Canyon. The route leads to a side canyon called Transept Canyon, which geologist Clarence Dutton named in 1882, declaring it "far grander than Yosemite." Check the posted schedule to find a ranger talk along this trail; it's also a great place to view fall foliage.

MODERATE **Ken Patrick Trail.** This primitive trail begins at a trailhead on the east side of the North Kaibab trailhead parking lot. It travels 10 mi one way (allow 6 hours) from the trailhead at 8,250 feet to Point Imperial at 8,803 feet. It crosses drainages and occasionally detours around fallen trees. The end of the road brings the highest views from either rim. Note that there is no water along this trail. ⚠ Flash floods can occur any time of the year, especially from June through September when thunderstorms

DID YOU KNOW?

Mule trips take riders on the Bright Angel and South Kaibab trails. Day trips go partway down the canyon and two-day trips include an overnight stay at Phantom Ranch on the canyon floor.

develop rapidly. Check forecasts before heading into the canyon and use caution when hiking in narrow canyons and drainage systems.

Uncle Jim Trail. This 5-mi, three-hour loop trail starts at the North Kaibab Trail parking lot at 8,300 feet and winds south through the forest, past Roaring Springs Canyon and Bright Angel Canyon. The highlight of this rim hike is Uncle Jim Point, which, at 8,244 feet, overlooks the upper sections of the North Kaibab Trail.

★ **Widforss Trail.** Round-trip, Widforss Trail is 9.8 mi, with an elevation change of 200 feet. The trailhead, at 8,080 feet, is across from the North Kaibab Trail parking lot. Allow six hours for the hike, which passes through shady forests of pine, spruce, fir, and aspen on its way to Widforss Point, at 7,900 feet. Here you'll have good views of five temples: Zoroaster, Brahma, and Deva to the southeast and Buddha and Manu to the southwest. You are likely to see wildflowers in summer, and this is a good trail for viewing fall foliage. It's named in honor of artist Gunnar M. Widforss, renowned for his paintings of national park landscapes.

DIFFICULT **North Kaibab Trail.** At 8,241 feet, the trailhead to North Kaibab Trail is about 2 mi north of the Grand Canyon Lodge and is open only from May through October. It is recommended for experienced hikers only, who should allow four days for the full hike. The long, steep path drops 5,840 feet over a distance of 14.5 mi to Phantom Ranch and the Colorado River, so the National Park Service suggests that day hikers not go farther than Roaring Springs (5,020 feet) before turning to hike back up out of the canyon. After about 7 mi, Cottonwood Campground (4,080 feet) has drinking water in summer, restrooms, shade trees, and a ranger.
■ TIP→ For a fee, a shuttle takes hikers to the North Kaibab trailhead twice daily from Grand Canyon Lodge.

MULE RIDES

☺ **Canyon Trail Rides.** This company leads mule rides on the easier trails of the North Rim. A one-hour ride (minimum age 7) runs $40. Half-day trips on the rim or into the canyon (minimum age 10) cost $75; full-day trips (minimum age 12) go for $165. Full-day trips into the canyon follow the North Kaibab Trail to Roaring Springs where you'll have time to explore and eat a sack lunch. Weight limits vary from 200 to 220 pounds. Available daily from May 15 to October 15, these excursions are popular, so make reservations in advance. ⌖ *Box 128, Tropic, UT 84776* ☎ *435/679–8665* ⊕ *www.canyonrides.com.*

EDUCATIONAL OFFERINGS

☺ **Discovery Pack Junior Ranger Program.** Children ages 9 to 14 can take part in these hands-on educational programs and earn a Junior Ranger certificate and badge. ☎ *928/638–7967* ⊕ *www.nps.gov/grca* ✉ *Free.*

Interpretive Ranger Programs. Daily guided hikes and talks may focus on any aspect of the canyon—from geology and flora and fauna to history and the canyon's early inhabitants. For schedules, go to the Grand Canyon Lodge or pick up a free copy of *The Guide* to the North Rim. ☎ *928/638–7967* ⊕ *www.nps.gov/grca* ✉ *Free.*

THE WEST RIM AND HAVASU CANYON

Known as "The People" of the Grand Canyon, the Pai Indians—the Hualapai and Havasupai—have lived along the Colorado River and the vast Colorado Plateau for more than 1,000 years. Both tribes traditionally moved seasonally between the plateau and the canyon, alternately hunting game and planting crops. Today, they rely on their tourism offerings outside the natioanl park as an economic base.

GRAND CANYON WEST AND THE HUALAPAI TRIBE

70 mi north of Kingman, 186 mi northwest of Williams.

The plateau-dwelling Hualapai ("people of the tall pines") acquired a larger chunk of traditional Pai lands with the creation of their reservation in 1883. Hualapai tribal lands include diverse habitats ranging from rolling grasslands to rugged canyons, and travel from elevations of 1,500 feet at the Colorado River to more than 7,300 feet at Aubrey Cliffs. In recent years, the Hualapai have been attempting to foster tourism on the West Rim—most notably with the spectacular Skywalk, a glass walkway suspended 70 feet over the edge of the canyon rim. Not hampered by the regulations in place at Grand Canyon National Park, Grand Canyon West offers helicopter flights down into the bottom of the canyon, horseback rides to rim viewpoints, and boat trips on the Colorado River.

The Hualapai Reservation encompasses a million acres along 108 mi of the Colorado River in the Grand Canyon. Peach Springs, on historic Route 66, is the tribal capital and the location of the Hualapai Lodge. The increasingly popular West Rim is more than 120 mi away on freeway roads.

GETTING HERE AND AROUND

The West Rim is a five-hour drive from the South Rim of Grand Canyon National Park or a 2½-hour drive from Las Vegas. From Kingman, drive north 42 mi on Stockton Hill Rd. Turn right (north) on to Pierce Ferry Rd. and follow for 7 mi. Turn right (east) on to Diamond Bar Rd. and follow for 21 mi to Grand Canyon West entrance.

The dusty, 14-mi stretch of unpaved road leading to Grand Canyon West can be off-putting to some. For a different approach along Diamond Bar Road, visitors can schedule Park & Ride services from the Grand Canyon West Welcome Center on Pierce Ferry Road for a nominal fee; reservations are required (☎702/260–6506, 702/878–9378 *reservations*).

EXPLORING INDIAN COUNTRY

When visiting Indian reservations, respect tribal laws and customs. Remember you are a guest in a sovereign nation. Do not wander into residential areas or take photographs of residents without first asking permission. Possessing or consuming alcohol is illegal on tribal lands. In general, the Hualapai and Havasupai are quiet, private people. Offer respect and do not pursue conversations or personal interactions unless invited to do so.

Visitors aren't allowed to travel in their own vehicles to the viewpoints once they reach the West Rim, but must purchase a tour package from **Destination Grand Canyon West**. The Hualapai Tribe offers the basic Hualapai Legacy tour package ($29.95 per person plus tax), which includes a Hualapai visitation permit and shuttle transportation. A free shuttle will take you to Eagle Point, where the Indian Village walking tour visits authentic dwellings; Hualapai Ranch, site of Western performances, cookouts, and horseback and wagon rides;

> ## CANYON TOURS FROM VEGAS
>
> Perhaps the easiest way to visit the West Rim from Vegas is with a tour. **Bighorn Wild West Tours** will pick you up in a Hummer at your Vegas hotel for an all-day trip that includes the shuttle-bus package and lunch, for $219. The 14-mi, dirt access road is rough, and high-clearance vehicles are a necessity. ☎ *702/385–4676 or 888/385–4676.*

and Guano Point, where the "High Point Hike" offers panoramic views of the Colorado River. For an extra cost you can add a helicopter trip into the canyon, a boat trip on the Colorado, an off-road Hummer adventure, a horseback or wagon ride to the canyon rim, or a walk on the Skywalk. Local Hualapai guides add a Native American perspective to a canyon trip that you won't find on North and South Rim tours.

The **Skywalk** is a cantilevered glass bridge suspended nearly 4,000 feet above the Colorado River and extending 70 feet from the edge of the Grand Canyon that opened in 2007. Approximately 10 feet wide, the bridge's deck, made of tempered glass several inches thick, has 5-foot glass railings on each side making an unobstructed open-air platform. Visitors must store all personal effects, including cameras, cell phones, and video cameras, in lockers before entering the Skywalk. A professional photographer takes personal photographs on the walkway, which can be purchased from the gift shop. At this writing, a three-level, 6,000-square-foot visitor center was under construction at the site. Slated to be completed in 2009, it will include a museum, movie theater, VIP lounge, gift shop, and multiple restaurants. A short walk takes visitors to the Indian Village, where educational displays uncover the culture of five different Native American tribes (Havasupai, Plains, Hopi, Hualapai, and Navajo). Intertribal, powwow-style dance performances entertain visitors at the nearby amphitheater. ✉ *Grand Canyon West* ☎ *702/878–9378 or 877/716–9378* ⊕ *www.destinationgrandcanyon.com* 💲 *$29.95 entrance fee; $8 impact fee; Skywalk $29.95* ☉ *Daily.*

SPORTS AND THE OUTDOORS

RAFTING One-day river trips are offered by the Hualapai tribe through the **Hualapai River Runners** (✉ *887 Rte. 66, Peach Springs* ☎ *928/769–2219 or 888/255–9550* ⊕ *www.destinationgrandcanyon.com*) from March through October. The trips, which cost $328, leave from the Hualapai Lodge at 8 AM and return between 6:30 and 8:30 PM. Lunch, snacks, and beverages are provided. Children must be eight or older to take the trip, which runs several rapids with the most difficult rated as Class V or VI, depending on the river flow.

HAVASU CANYON AND THE HAVASUPAI TRIBE

141 mi northwest from Williams to the head of Hualapai Hilltop.

Major flooding in 2008 altered Havasu Canyon's famous landscape and it was closed to visitors for almost ten months. Supai re-opened in June 2009 but water and mud damage have changed some of the beautiful waterfalls, their streams and pools, and the amount of blue-green travertine. ■TIP→Be sure to call the Havasupai Tourist Enterprise (☎928/448–2121) before visiting for more information.

With the establishment of Grand Canyon National Park in 1919, the Havasupai ("people of the blue green water") were confined to their summer village of Supai and the surrounding 518 acres in the 5-mi-wide and 12-mi-long Havasu Canyon. In 1975, the reservation was substantially enlarged, but is still completely surrounded by national park lands on all but its southern border. Each year, about 25,000 tourists fly, hike, or ride into Havasu Canyon to visit the Havasupai. Despite their economic reliance on tourism, the Havasupai take their guardianship of the Grand Canyon seriously, and severely limit visitation in order to protect the fragile canyon habitats. Dubbed the "Shangri-la of the Grand Canyon," the waterfalls have drawn visitors to this remote, inaccessible Indian reservation.

GETTING HERE AND AROUND

From Williams, drive west on I–40 for 43 mi. Take the Seligman exit and continue west on AZ 66 for 30 mi. The last gas station is at the junction of AZ 66 and Indian Hwy. 18. Follow Indian Hwy. 18 north for 63 miles to Hulapai Hilltop and the parking area.

The Havasupai restrict the number of visitors to the canyon; you must have reservations. They ask that hikers call ahead before taking the trek into the canyon. Hualapai Trail leaves from Hualapai Hilltop. From an elevation of 5,200 feet, the trail travels down a moderate grade to Supai village at 3,200 feet. Bring plenty of water and avoid hiking during the middle of the day, when canyon temperatures can reach into the 100s. If you'd rather ride, you can rent a horse for the trip down for $150 round-trip, or $75 one way. Riders must be able to mount and dismount by themselves; be at least 4 feet, 7 inches; and weigh less than 250 pounds. Reservations must be made at least six weeks in advance with Havasupai Tourist Enterprise, which requires a 50% deposit. You'll need to spend the night if you're hiking or riding.

Another option is a helicopter ride into the canyon with **Air West Helicopters** (☎623/516–2790 ☉Mid-Mar.–mid-Oct., Thurs., Fri., Sun., and Mon. 10–1; mid-Oct.–mid-Mar., Fri. and Sun. 10–1). Flights leave from Hualapai Hilltop and cost $85 per person each way. Reservations are not accepted and visitors are transported on a first-come, first-served basis. Tribal members are boarded prior to tourists.

EXPLORING

Havasu Canyon, south of the middle part of Grand Canyon National Park's South Rim and away from the crowds, is the home of the Havasupai, a tribe that has lived in this isolated area for centuries. You'll discover why they are known as the "people of the blue green waters," when you see the canyon's waterfalls. Accumulated travertine formations in some of the most popular pools were washed out in massive flooding decades ago and again in 2008, destroying some of the otherworldly scenes pictured in older photos, but the place is still magical.

The 600 tribal members now live in the village of Supai, accessible only down the 8-mi-long **Hualapai Trail,** which drops 2,000 feet from the canyon rim to the tiny town. The quiet and private Havasupai mostly remain apart from the modest flow of tourists, which nevertheless plays a vital role in the tribal economy.

MAIL BY MULE

Arguably, the most remote mail route in the United States follows a steep 8-mi trail to the tiny town of Supai in Havasu Canyon. Havasupai tribal members living deep within the confines of the Grand Canyon rely on this route for the delivery of everything from food to furniture. During a typical week, more than a ton of mail is sent into the canyon by mule, with each animal carrying a cargo of about 130 pounds.

To reach Havasu's waterfalls, you must hike downstream from the village of Supai. Both **Havasu Falls** and **Mooney Falls** are still flowing but the recent flooding changed the falls and their pools; well-known Navajo Falls was washed out completely.

Pack adequate food and supplies. Prices for food and sundries in Supai are more than double what they would be outside the reservation. The tribe does not allow alcohol, drugs, pets, or weapons. ⊠*Havasupai Tourist Enterprise, Supai* ☎*928/448–2141, 928/448–2121 general information, 928/448–2111, or 928/448–2201 lodging reservations* ⊕*www.havasupaitribe.com* ✉*$35 entrance fee; $5 impact fee*

WHAT'S NEAR THE GRAND CANYON?

The northwest section of Arizona is geographically fascinating. In addition to the Grand Canyon, it's home to national forests, national monuments, and national recreation areas. Towns, however, are small and scattered. Many of them cater to visiting adventurers, and Native American reservations dot the map.

NEARBY TOWNS AND ATTRACTIONS

NEARBY TOWNS

Towns near the canyon's South Rim include the tiny town of Tusayan, just 1 mi south of the entrance station, and Williams, the "Gateway to the Grand Canyon," 58 mi south.

Tusayan has the basic amenities and an airport that serves as a starting point for airplane and helicopter tours of the canyon. The cozy mountain town of **Williams,** founded in 1882 when the railroad passed through, was once a rough-and-tumble joint, replete with saloons and bordellos. Today it reflects a much milder side of the Wild West, with 3,000 residents and 1,512 motel rooms. Wander along main street— part of historic Route 66, but locally named, like the town, after trapper

Bill Williams—and indulge in Route 66 nostalgia inside antiques shops or souvenir and T-shirt stores.

The communities closest to the North Rim include Fredonia, 76 mi north; Marble Canyon, 80 mi northeast; Lees Ferry, 85 mi east; and Jacob Lake, 45 mi north.

Fredonia, a small community of about 1,200, approximately an hour's drive north of the Grand Canyon, is often referred to as the gateway to the North Rim; it's also relatively close to Zion and Bryce Canyon national parks. **Marble Canyon** marks the geographical beginning of the Grand Canyon at its northeastern tip. It's a good stopping point if you are driving U.S. 89 to the North Rim. En route from the South Rim to the North Rim is **Lees Ferry,** where most of the area's river rafts start their journey. The tiny town of **Jacob Lake,** nestled high in pine country at an elevation of 7,925 feet, was named after Mormon explorer Jacob Hamblin, also known as the "Buckskin Missionary." It has a hotel, café, campground, and lush mountain countryside.

ESSENTIALS

Contact Information Kaibab National Forest, North District (⊠ 430 S. Main St., Box 248, Fredonia 86022 ☎ 928/643-7395 ⊕ www.fs.fed.us/r3/ kai). **Kaibab National Forest, Tusayan Ranger District** (⊠ Hwy. 64, Box 3088, Grand Canyon 86023 ☎ 928/638-2443 ⊕ www.fs.fed.us/r3/kai). **Kaibab National Forest, Williams Ranger District** (⊠ 742 S. Clover Rd., Williams 86046 ☎ 928/635-5600 ⊕ www.fs.fed.us/r3/kai). **Kaibab Plateau Visitor Center** (⊠ Hwy. 89A/AZ 67, HC 64, Jacob Lake 86022 ☎ 928/643-7298 ⊕ www. fs.fed.us/r3/kai). **Williams Visitor Center** (⊠ 200 W. Railroad Ave., at Grand Canyon Blvd., Williams ☎ 928/635-1418 or 800/863-0546 ⊕ www.williams chamber.com ⊙ Spring, fall, and winter, daily 8–5; summer, daily 8–6:30).

NEARBY ATTRACTIONS

Glen Canyon National Recreation Area. This huge preserve covers more than 1,500 square mi in northeastern Arizona and southern Utah, including Lake Powell, which has more than 1,900 mi of shoreline. You can swim, water-ski, fish, boat, hike, and camp. South of Lake Powell, the landscape gives way to the Echo Cliffs, orange sandstone formations rising up to 1,000 feet above the surrounding desert. At Bitter Springs, U.S. 89 ascends the cliffs and provides a spectacular view of the Kaibab Plateau and Vermilion Cliffs. The Carl Hayden Visitor Center at Glen Canyon Dam has a three-dimensional map of the area. Dam tours originate out of the visitor center and are offered on a first-come, first-served basis for a $5 fee. ⊠ Visitor center, U.S. 89 and Scenic View Dr., 2 mi west of Page ⬚ Box 1507, Page 86040 ⊕ www. nps.gov/glca ☎ 928/608–6404, 928/608-6072 for dam tours ☎ $15 per vehicle for 7 days ⊙ Visitor center: daily 8–4:30, with extended summer hours.

At **National Geographic Visitor Center Grand Canyon** (⊠ Hwy. 64/U.S. 180, 2 mi south of the Grand Canyon's south entrance, Box 3309, Tusayan ☎ 928/638–2203 or 928/638-2468 ⊕ www.explorethecanyon.com ☎ $12.81 ⊙ Mar.–Oct., daily 8:30–8:30; Nov.–Feb., daily 10:30–6:30) you can schedule and purchase tickets for air tours and daily Colorado River trips; buy a national park pass, and access the park by special

Lava Falls is the largest and most well-known of the rapids in the Grand Canyon.

entry lanes. However, the biggest draw at the visitor center is the six-story IMAX screen which features the 34-minute movie *Grand Canyon: Discovery & Adventure*. You can learn about the geologic and natural history of the canyon, soar above stunning rock formations, and ride the rapids through the rocky gorge.

🕲 **Planes of Fame Museum.** A good stop 30 mi north of Williams, at the junction of U.S.180 and State Route 64 in Valle, this satellite of the Air Museum Planes of Fame in Chino, California, chronicles the history of aviation with an array of historic and modern aircraft. One of the featured pieces is a C-121A Constellation "Bataan," the personal aircraft General MacArthur used during the Korean War. Guided tours of this historic plane are offered for $3. Visitors are not allowed inside the cockpits. ✉ *755 Mustang Way, Valle* ☎ *928/635–1000* ⊕ *www.planesoffame.org* 🎟 *$5.95* ⊗ *Daily 9–5, extended summer hrs.*

★ **Vermilion Cliffs.** West from the town of Marble Canyon are these spectacular cliffs, more than 3,000 feet high in many places. Keep an eye out for condors; the giant endangered birds were reintroduced into the area in 1996. Reports suggest that the birds, once in captivity, are surviving well in the wilderness.

SCENIC DRIVES AND VISTAS

U.S. 89. The route north from Cameron Trading Post (Cameron, Arizona) on U.S. 89 offers a stunning view of the **Painted Desert** to the right. The desert, which covers thousands of square miles stretching to the south and east, is a vision of subtle, almost harsh beauty, with windswept plains and mesas, isolated buttes, and barren valleys in pastel patterns. About 30 mi north of Cameron Trading Post, the Painted Desert country gives way to sandstone cliffs that run for miles. Brilliantly hued and ranging in color from light pink to deep orange, the **Echo Cliffs** rise to more than 1,000 feet in many places. They are essentially devoid of vegetation, but in a few high places, thick patches of tall cottonwood and poplar trees, nurtured by springs and water seepage from the rock escarpment, manage to thrive.

U.S. 89A. At Bitter Springs, 60 mi north of Cameron, U.S. 89A branches off from U.S. 89, running north and providing views of **Marble Canyon,** the geographical beginning of the Grand Canyon. Like the Grand Canyon, Marble Canyon was formed by the Colorado River. Traversing a gorge nearly 500 feet deep is **Navajo Bridge,** a narrow steel span built in 1929 and listed on the National Register of Historic Places. Formerly used for car traffic, it now functions only as a pedestrian overpass.

AREA ACTIVITIES

SPORTS AND THE OUTDOORS

Pedal the depths of the Kaibab National Forest on the **Tusayan Bike Trail** (⊠*Tusayan Ranger Distric,* ⊠*Hwy. 64, Box 3088,Tusayan* ☎*928/638–2443* ⊕*www.fs.fed.us/r3/kai).* Following linked loop trails at an elevation of 6,750 feet, you can bike as few as 3 mi or as many as 32 mi round-trip along old logging roads through ponderosa pine forest. Keep an eye out for elk, mule deer, hawks, eagles, pronghorn antelope, turkeys, coyote, and porcupines. Open for biking year-round (but most feasible March through October), the trail is accessed on the west side of Highway 64, a half-mile north of Tusayan.

Cyclists also can enjoy the scenery along abandoned sections of Route 66 on the **Historic Route 66 Mountain Bike Tour.** Maps of the tour, which include the 6-mi **Ash Fork Hill Trail** and the 5-mi **Devil Dog Trail,** are available at the Williams Visitor Center.

FISHING Fish for trout, crappie, catfish, and smallmouth bass at a number of lakes surrounding Williams. To fish on public land, anglers ages 14 and older are required to obtain a fishing license from the **Arizona Game and Fish Department** (⌂*3500 S. Lake Mary Rd., Flagstaff 86001* ☎*928/774–5045* ⊕*www.gf.state.az.us*).

The stretch of ice-cold, crystal-clear water at Lees Ferry off the North Rim provides arguably the best trout fishing in the Southwest. Many rafters and anglers stay the night in a campground near the river or in nearby Marble Canyon before hitting the river at dawn. **Marble Canyon Outfitters** (⌂*Box 6032, Marble Canyon 86036* ☎*928/355–2225 or 800/726–1789* ⊕*www.leesferryflyfishing.com*), at Marble Canyon Lodge, sells Arizona fishing licenses and offers guided fishing trips. **Lees Ferry Anglers** (⊠*Milepost 547, N. U.S. 89A, HC 67 Box 30, Marble Canyon 86036* ☎*928/355–2261, 800/962–9755 outside Arizona* ⊕*www.leesferry.com*) has guides and state fishing licenses and gear for sale.

HORSEBACK **Apache Stables.** There's nothing like a horseback ride to immerse you in the
RIDING Western experience. From stables behind the Moqui Lodge near Tusayan,

White-Water Rafting at the Grand Canyon

So you're ready to tackle the churning white water of the Colorado River as it rumbles and hisses its way through the Grand Canyon? Well, you're in good company: the crafty, one-armed Civil War veteran John Wesley Powell first charted these dangerous rapids during the summer of 1869. It wasn't until 1938, though, that the first commercial river trip made its way down this fearsome corridor. Running the river has come a long way since then—and since Norman Neville made the first trip by kayak, in 1941, in a craft he built out of scrap lumber, partly salvaged from an outhouse.

BEFORE YOU GO

Keep in mind that seats fill up fast due to the restricted number of visitors allowed on the river each season by the National Park Service. ■TIP→Due to the limited availability, reservations for multiday trips should be made a year or two in advance. Once you've secured your seat, all that's left to do is pack your bags and get geared up for an experience of a lifetime. Lots of people book trips for summer's peak period: June through August. If you're flexible, take advantage of the Arizona weather; May to early June and September are ideal rafting times in the Grand Canyon. *For outfitters, see Rafting under Area Activities.*

WHAT TO EXPECT

White-water rafting still offers all the excitement of those early days—without the danger and discomfort. Most trips begin at Lees Ferry, a few miles below the Glen Canyon Dam near Page. There are tranquil half- and full-day float trips from the Glen Canyon Dam to Lees Ferry, as well as raft trips that run from three to 18

days. The shorter three- and four-day voyages either begin or end at Phantom Ranch at the bottom of the Grand Canyon at river mile 87. On the longer trips, you'll encounter the best of the canyon's white water along the way, including Lava Falls, listed in the *Guinness Book of World Records* as "the fastest navigable white water stretch in North America."

Life jackets, beverages, tents, sheets, tarps, sleeping bags, dry bags, first aid, and food are provided—but you'll still need to plan ahead by packing clothing, a rain suit, hats, sunscreen, toiletries, and other sundries. Commercial outfitters allow each river runner two waterproof bags to store items during the day. Just keep in mind that one of the bags will be filled up with the provided sleeping bag and tarp, which only leaves one for your personal belongings.

While most people band together as a group, there is still plenty of open space for solitude. After the first night, most rafters give up on pitching tents and spread their sleeping bags under the stars.

WORD OF MOUTH

Travelers at Fodors.com agree that this is well worth the advance planning:

"If you are the slightest bit adventurous . a rafting trip in the Grand Canyon is the TRIP OF A LIFETIME!" —canyonwren

"Basically there are three things going on down there—a great geology lesson with incredible scenery, daily side-hikes up beautiful side-canyons that are each unique, and some of the most thrilling and exciting white-water in the USA with numerous big rapids and five real thumpers." —Bill_H

these folks offer gentle horses and a ride that will meet most budgets. Choose from one- and two-hour trail rides or the popular campfire rides and horse-drawn wagon excursions. ⊠*Forest Service Road 328, 1 mi north of Tusayan* ⌑*Box 158, Grand Canyon 86023* ☎*928/638–2891* ✑*$25.50–$85.50* ⊕*www.apachestables.com* ☾*Mar.–Nov., daily.*

RAFTING **Arizona Raft Adventures** (⊠*4050 E. Huntington Rd., Flagstaff* ☎*928/526– 8200 or 800/786–7238* ⊕*www.azraft.com*) organizes 6- to 16-day paddle and/or motor trips for all skill levels. Trips, which run $1,920 to $3,900, depart April through October.

With a reputation for high quality and a roster of 3- to 13-day trips, **Canyoneers** (⌑*Box 2997, Flagstaff 86003* ☎*928/526–0924 or 800/525– 0924* ⊕*www.canyoneers.com*) is popular with those who want to do some hiking as well. The five-day trip "Best of the Grand" trip includes a hike down to Phantom Ranch. Three- to 14-day motorized and oar trips, available April through September, cost between $995 and $3,595.

You can count on **Grand Canyon Expeditions** (⌑*Box O, Kanab, UT 84741* ☎*435/644–2691 or 800/544–2691* ⊕*www.gcex.com*) to take you down the Colorado River safely and in style: it limits the number of people on each boat to 14, and evening meals might include filet mignon, pork chops, or shrimp. The April through mid-September trips cost $2,400 to $3,600 for 8 to 16 days.

SKIING **Elk Ridge Ski and Outdoor Recreation** (⊠*Off I–40* ⌑*2467 S. Perkins-* ☾ *ville Rd., Williams 86046* ☎*928/814–5038* ⊕*www.elkridgeski.com*) is usually open from mid-December through much of March, weather permitting. There are four groomed runs (including one for beginners), areas suitable for cross-country skiing, and a hill set aside for tubing. The lodge rents skis, snowboards, and inner tubes. From Williams, take South 4th Street/Perkinsville Road for 2½ mi, and then turn right at Ski Run Road/Forest Road 106 and go another 1½ mi. During heavy snows, four-wheel drive or chains may be necessary.

WHERE TO EAT AND STAY

ABOUT THE RESTAURANTS

Inside the park, you can find everything from cafeteria food to casual café fare to elegant evening specials. There's a coffeehouse with organic joe. Reservations are accepted (and recommended) only at El Tovar Dining Room; they can be made up to six months in advance with El Tovar room reservations, 30 days in advance without. The dress code is casual across the board, but El Tovar is your best option if you're looking to dress up a bit and thumb through an extensive wine list. On the North Rim there is one restaurant, a cafeteria, and the Grand Cookout experience. Drinking water and restrooms are not available at most picnic spots. Options outside the park, in Tusayan and Williams to the south and Jacob Lake to the north, range from fast food to nice sit-down restaurants. Near the park, even the priciest places allow casual dress. On the Hualapai and Havasupai reservations in Havasu Canyon and on the West Rim, dining is limited.

ABOUT THE HOTELS

The park's accommodations include three "historic rustic" facilities and four motel-style lodges. Of the 922 rooms, cabins, and suites, only 203, all at the Grand Canyon Lodge, are at the North Rim. Outside El Tovar Hotel, the canyon's architectural crown jewel, frills are hard to find. Rooms are basic but comfortable, and most guests would agree that the best in-room amenity is a view of the canyon. Though rates vary widely, most rooms fall in the $125 to $175 range.

■ TIP→Reservations are a must, especially during the busy summer season. If you want to get your first choice (especially Bright Angel Lodge or El Tovar), make reservations as far in advance as possible; they're taken up to 13 months ahead. You might find a last-minute cancellation, but you shouldn't count on it. Although lodging at the South Rim will keep you close to the action, the frenetic activity and crowded facilities are off-putting to some. With short notice, the best time to find a room on the South Rim is during winter. And though the North Rim is less crowded than the South Rim, lodging (remember that rooms are limited) is available only from mid-May through mid-October.

Outside the park, Tusayan's hotels offer a convenient location but no bargains, while Williams can provide price breaks on food and lodging, as well as a respite from the crowds. Extra amenities (e.g., swimming pools and Internet access) are also more abundant. Reservations are always a good idea. Lodging options are even more limited on the West Rim.

ABOUT THE CAMPGROUNDS

Inside the park, camping is permitted only in designated campsites. Some campgrounds charge nightly camping fees in addition to entrance fees, and some accept reservations up to five months in advance through ⊕*www.recreation.gov*. Others are first-come, first-served. The South Rim has three campgrounds, one with RV hookups. The North Rim's single in-park campground does not offer hookups. All four campgrounds are near the rims and easily accessible. In-park camping in a spot other than a developed rim campground requires a permit from the Backcountry Information Center, which also serves as your reservation. Permits can be requested by mail or fax; applying well in advance is recommended. Call ☎*928/638–7875* between 1 and 5 Monday through Friday for information. Numerous backcountry campsites dot the canyon—be prepared for a considerable hike. The three established backcountry campgrounds require a trek of 4.6 to 16.6 mi.Outside the park, two campgrounds, one with hookups, are within 7 mi of the South Rim, and two are within about 45 mi of the North Rim. Developed and undeveloped campsites are available, first-come, first-served, in the Kaibab National Forest. There is no camping on the West Rim, but you can pitch a tent on the beach near the Colorado River at the primitive campground on Diamond Creek Road. Hikers heading to the falls in Havasu Canyon can stay at the primitive campground in Supai.

WHAT IT COSTS					
	¢	$	$$	$$$	$$$$
Restaurant	under $8	$8–$12	$13–$20	$21–$30	over $30
Hotel	under $70	$70–$120	$121–$175	$176–$250	over $250

Restaurant prices are per person for a main course at dinner. Hotel prices are for a standard double in high season, excluding taxes and service charges.

3

WHERE TO EAT

IN THE PARK: SOUTH RIM

$$$
STEAK
✗**Arizona Room.** The canyon views from this casual Southwestern-style steak house are the best of any restaurant at the South Rim. The menu includes such delicacies as chile-crusted pan-seared wild salmon, chipotle barbecue baby back ribs, roasted vegetable and black bean enchiladas, and blackened prime rib. For dessert, try the cheesecake with prickly-pear syrup paired with one of the house's specialty coffee drinks. Seating is first-come, first served, so arrive early to avoid the crowds. ⊠*Bright Angel Lodge, Desert View Dr., Grand Canyon Village* ☎*928/638–2631* ⊕*www.grandcanyonlodges.com* ⚒*Reservations not accepted* ☐*AE, D, DC, MC, V* ⊗*Closed Jan.–mid-Feb. No lunch Nov.–Feb.*

$$
SOUTHWESTERN
✗**Bright Angel Restaurant.** The draw here is casual, affordable dining. No-surprises dishes will fill your belly at breakfast, lunch, or dinner. Entrées include such basics as salads, steaks, pasta, fajitas, and fish. Or you can step it up a notch and order some of the same selections straight from the Arizona Room menu including prime rib, baby back ribs, and wild salmon. For dessert try the warm apple grunt cake topped with vanilla ice cream. Be prepared to wait for a table: the dining room bustles all day long. The plain decor is broken up with large-pane windows and original artwork. Don't wait until the last minute to use the restroom: you have to leave the restaurant, walk through the lobby, and down a flight of stairs to get there—where you'll most likely need to wait in line with all of the other canyon visitors. ⊠*Bright Angel Lodge, Desert View Dr., Grand Canyon Village* ☎*928/638–2631* ⊕*www.grandcanyon lodges.com* ⚒*Reservations not accepted* ☐*AE, D, DC, MC, V.*

¢
AMERICAN
✗**Canyon Café.** Fast-food favorites here include pastries, burgers, and pizza. Open for breakfast, lunch, and dinner, the cafeteria also serves specials, chicken potpie, fried catfish, and fried chicken. There isn't a fancy bar here, but you can order beer and wine with your meal. Resembling an old-fashioned diner, this cafeteria seats 345 guests at a time and has easy-to-read signs that point the way to your favorite foods. ⊠*Yavapai Lodge, Desert View Dr., Grand Canyon Village* ☎*928/638–2631* ⊕*www.grandcanyonlodges.com* ⚒*Reservations not accepted* ☐*AE, D, DC, MC, V* ⊗*Closed mid-Dec.–Feb.*

$$$
SOUTHWESTERN
Fodor's Choice
★
✗**El Tovar Dining Room.** No doubt about it—this is the best restaurant for miles. Modeled after a European hunting lodge, this rustic 19th-century dining room built of hand-hewn logs is worth a visit. Breakfast, lunch, and dinner are served beneath the beamed ceiling.

The cuisine is modern Southwestern with an exotic flair. Start with the buffalo carpaccio on roasted poblano crostini or the mozzarella roulades of prosciutto and basil pesto. The dinner menu includes such dishes as citrus-marmalade-glazed duck with roasted poblano black bean rice, grilled New York strip steak with buttermilk-cornmeal onion rings, and a salmon tostada topped with organic greens and tequila vinaigrette. The dining room also offers an extensive wine list. ■TIP→Dinner reservations can be made up to six months in advance with room reservations and 30 days in advance for all other visitors. ⊠*El Tovar Hotel, Desert View Dr., 10 Albright Ave., Grand Canyon Village 86023* ☎*303/297–2757 or 888/297–2757 (reservations only), 928/638–2631 Ext. 6432* ⊕*www.grandcanyonlodges.com* ⚍*Reservations essential* ⊟*AE, D, DC, MC, V.*

> **WORD OF MOUTH**
>
> "My experience dining in National Parks is that you are paying for location, atmosphere and not food. We had a truly memorable dinner at El Tovar 2 years ago—during a sunset thunderstorm where the lights kept flickering, the room shook with thunder. One could just imagine being there 100 years ago. I have no memory of what we ate or how it was."
>
> —gail

¢ ✕**Maswik Cafeteria.** You can get a burger, hot sandwich, pasta, or Mexican fare at this food court. This casual eatery is ¼ mi from the rim. Lines will be long during high season lunch and dinner, but everything moves fairly quickly. ⊠*Maswik Lodge, Desert View Dr., Grand Canyon Village* ☎*928/638–2631* ⊕*www.grandcanyonlodges.com* ⚍*Reservations not accepted* ⊟*AE, D, DC, MC, V.*

AMERICAN

IN THE PARK: NORTH RIM

¢ ✕**Deli in the Pines.** Dining choices are very limited on the North Rim, but this is your best bet for a meal on a budget. Selections include pizza, salads, deli sandwiches, hot dogs, homemade breakfast pastries, and soft-serve ice cream. Best of all, there is an outdoor seating area for dining alfresco. It's open for breakfast, lunch, and dinner. ⊠*Grand Canyon Lodge, Bright Angel Point, North Rim* ☎*928/638–2611 Ext. 766* ⚍*Reservations not accepted* ⊟*AE, D, DC, MC, V* ⊗*Closed mid-Oct.–mid-May.*

AMERICAN

$$$ ✕**Grand Canyon Lodge Dining Room.** The historic lodge has a huge, high-ceilinged dining room with spectacular views and very good food; you might find pork medallions, roast chicken, and salmon steaks on the dinner menu. Food here takes a flavorful turn with Southwestern spices and organic selections. It's also open for breakfast and lunch. A full-service bar and an impressive wine list add to the relaxed atmosphere of the only full-service, sit-down restaurant on the North Rim. ⊠*Grand Canyon Lodge, Bright Angel Point, North Rim* ☎*928/638–2611 Ext. 760* ⊟*AE, D, DC, MC, V* ⊗*Closed mid-Oct.–mid-May.*

AMERICAN ★

$$$$ ✕**Grand Cookout.** Dine under the stars and enjoy live entertainment at this chuckwagon-style dining experience—the newest addition to the North Rim's limited dining options. Fill up on Western favorites including barbecue beef brisket, roasted chicken, baked beans, and cowboy biscuits. The food is basic and tasty, but the real draw is the nightly performance

AMERICAN ☾

TOP PICNIC SPOTS

Bring your picnic basket and enjoy dining alfresco surrounded by some of the most beautiful backdrops in the country. Be sure to bring water, as it's unavailable at many of these spots, as are restrooms.

■ **Buggeln**, 15 mi east of Grand Canyon Village on Desert View Drive, has some secluded, shady spots.

■ **Cape Royal**, 23 mi south of the North Rim Visitor Center, is the most popular designated picnic area on the North Rim due to its panoramic views.

■ **Grandview Point** has, as the name implies, grand views; it is 12 mi east of the Village on Desert View Drive.

■ **Point Imperial**, 11 mi northeast of the North Rim Visitor Center, has shade and some privacy.

3

of Western music and tall tales. Transportation from the Grand Canyon Lodge to the cookout is included in the price. Be sure to call before 4 PM for dinner reservations. Advance reservations are taken up to seven days in advance at the Grand Canyon Lodge registration desk. ⊠ *Grand Canyon Lodge, North Rim* ☎ *928/638–2611* ⚲ *Reservations essential* ☐ *AE, D, DC, MC, V* ⊙ *Closed mid-Oct.–mid-May.*

OUTSIDE THE PARK

$ ✕ **Café Tusayan.** This cozy café might not look like much, but it serves up
STEAK some of the most filling and wholesome food in Tusayan. You won't find fancy entrées with special French sauces. What you will find is a large menu of omelets, salads, burgers, salmon, pasta, and steaks. Breakfast is served all day long and the homemade pies are worth a stop all on their own. ⊠ *Hwy. 64/U.S. 180, Tusayan* ☎ *928/638–2151* ☐ *MC, V.*

$$ ✕ **Canyon Star Restaurant and Saloon.** Relax in the rustic dining room
AMERICAN at the Grand Hotel for breakfast, lunch, or dinner. The dinner menu
☺ includes steak, grilled chicken, barbecue ribs, enchiladas, and salmon. Most nights there's entertainment: live music, karaoke, or Native American dance performances—all great for families. There's even a kids' menu. In the summer, be sure to reserve a table. ⊠ *Hwy. 64/U.S. 180, Tusayan* ☎ *928/638–3333* ☐ *AE, DC, MC, V.*

$$ ✕ **The Coronado Room.** When pizza and burgers just won't do, the restau-
CONTINENTAL rant at the Best Western Grand Canyon Squire Inn is the best upscale choice in Tusayan. The menu has everything from escargot to elk steak. Even though the Coronado Room takes pride in its fine-dining atmosphere, dress is casual and comfortable. Reservations are a good idea, particularly in the busy season. ⊠ *Hwy. 64/U.S. 180, Tusayan* ☎ *928/638–2681* ☐ *AE, D, DC, MC, V* ⊙ *No lunch.*

$ ✕ **Cruisers Café 66.** Talk about nostalgia. Imagine your favorite '50s-style,
AMERICAN high school hangout—with cocktail service. Good burgers, salads, and
☺ malts are family-priced, but a choice steak is available, too, for $25.
Fodor's Choice The Grand Canyon Brewery, accessed by a side entrance, adds to the
★ casual fun—just saddle up to a hand-carved log barstool and order one

of five microbrews on tap. A large mural of the town's heyday along the "Mother Road" and historic cars out front make this a Route 66 favorite. Kids enjoy the relaxed atmosphere and jukebox tunes. ⊠*233 W. Rte. 66, Williams* ☎*928/635–2445* ▭*AE, D, MC, V.*

$ ✕**Pancho McGillicuddy's.** Established in 1893 as the Cabinet Saloon, this
MEXICAN   restaurant is on the National Register of Historic Places. Gone are the
★   spittoons and pipes—the smoke-free dining area now has Mexican-inspired decor and such specialties as "armadillo eggs," the local name for deep-fried jalapeños stuffed with cheese. Other favorites include fish tacos, buzzard wings—better known as hot wings—and pollo verde (chicken breasts smothered in a sauce of cheese, sour cream, and green chiles). The bar has TVs tuned to sporting events and pours more than 30 tequilas. ⊠*141 Railroad Ave., Williams* ☎*928/635–4150* ▭*AE, D, MC, V.*

¢   ✕**Twisters.** Kick up some Route 66 nostalgia at this old-fashioned soda
AMERICAN   fountain and gift shop. Dine on hamburgers and hot dogs, a famous
☺   Twisters sundae, Route 66 Beer Float, or cherry phosphate—all to the sounds of '50s tunes. The kids' menu features cartoon characters and a selection of corn dogs, hot dogs, hamburgers, chicken strips, and peanut butter and jelly sandwiches. The adjoining gift shop is a blast from the past, with Route 66 merchandise, classic Coca-Cola memorabilia, and fanciful items celebrating the careers of such characters as Betty Boop, James Dean, Elvis, and Marilyn Monroe. ⊠*417 E. Rte. 66, Williams* ☎*928/635–0266* ▭*AE, D, MC, V.*

WHERE TO STAY

IN THE PARK: SOUTH RIM
$–$$ 🖼 **Bright Angel Lodge.** Famed architect Mary Jane Colter designed this
☺   1935 log-and-stone structure, which sits within a few yards of the canyon rim and blends superbly with the canyon walls. It offers a similar location to El Tovar for about half the price. Accommodations are in motel-style rooms or cabins. Lodge rooms don't have TVs, and some rooms do not have private bathrooms. Scattered among the pines are 50 cabins, which do have TVs and private baths; some have fireplaces. Expect historic charm but not luxury. The Bright Angel Dining Room serves family-style meals all day and a warm apple grunt dessert large enough to share. The Arizona Room serves dinner only. Adding to the experience are an ice-cream parlor, gift shop, and small history museum. **Pros:** some rooms have canyon views; all are steps away from the rim; Internet kiosks and transportation desk for the mule ride check-in are in the lobby. **Cons:** the popular lobby is always packed; parking here is problematic; stairs throughout the building and lack of elevators make accessibility an issue. ⊠*Desert View Dr., Grand Canyon Village* ✑*Box 699, Grand Canyon 86023* ☎*888/297–2757 reservations only, 928/638–2631* ⊕*www.grandcanyonlodges.com* ⤴*37 rooms, 6 with shared toilet and shower, 13 with shared shower; 49 cabins* ♿*In-room: no a/c (some), safe (some), refrigerator (some), no TV (some). In-hotel: 2 restaurants, bar, no-smoking rooms* ▭*AE, D, DC, MC, V.*

$$ **El Tovar Hotel.** A registered National Historic Landmark, the "archi-
Fodor's Choice tectural crown jewel of the Grand Canyon" was built in 1905 of Oregon
★ pine logs and native stone. The hotel's proximity to all of the canyon's
facilities, its European hunting-lodge atmosphere, and its renowned
dining room make it the best place to stay on the South Rim. It's usu-
ally booked well in advance (up to 13 months ahead), though it's eas-
ier to get a room during winter months. Three suites (El Tovar, Fred
Harvey, and Mary Jane Colter) and several rooms have canyon views
(these are booked early), but you can enjoy the view anytime from the
cocktail-lounge back porch. **Pros:** historic lodging just steps from the
South Rim; fabulous lounge with outdoor seating and canyon views;
best in-park dining on-site. **Cons:** books up quickly, no Internet access.
✉ *Desert View Dr., Grand Canyon Village* ⌂ *Box 699, Grand Can-
yon 86023* 🖀 *888/297–2757 reservations only, 928/638–2631* ⊕ *www.
grandcanyonlodges.com* ⮫ *66 rooms, 12 suites* ♿ *In-room: refrigera-
tor. In-hotel: restaurant, room service, bar, no-smoking rooms* ▭ *AE,
D, DC, MC, V.*

$$ **Kachina Lodge.** On the rim halfway between El Tovar and Bright
Angel Lodge, this motel-style lodge has many rooms with partial can-
yon views ($10 extra). Although lacking the historical charm of the
neighboring lodges, these rooms are a good bet for families and are
within easy walking distance of dining facilities at El Tovar and Bright
Angel Lodge. There are also several rooms for people with physical dis-
abilities. There's no air-conditioning, but evaporative coolers keep the
heat at bay. Check in at El Tovar Hotel to the east. **Pros:** partial canyon
views in half the rooms; family-friendly; accessible rooms. **Cons:** no
Internet access; check-in takes place at El Tovar Hotel; limited parking.
✉ *Desert View Dr., Grand Canyon Village* ⌂ *Box 699, Grand Canyon 86023* 🖀 *888/297–2757 reservations only, 928/638–2631* ⊕ *www.
grandcanyonlodges.com* ⮫ *49 rooms* ♿ *In-room: safe, refrigerator. In-
hotel: no-smoking rooms* ▭ *AE, D, DC, MC, V.*

$ **Maswik Lodge.** The lodge, named for a Hopi kachina who is said
☺ to guard the canyon, is ¼ mi from the rim. Accommodations, nestled in the ponderosa pine forest, range from rustic cabins to more
modern rooms. The cabins are the cheapest option but are available
only spring through fall. Some rooms have air-conditioning, and the
rest have ceiling fans. Teenagers like the lounge, where they can shoot
pool, throw darts, or watch the big-screen TV. There is also an Internet
room. Kids under 16 stay free. **Pros:** larger rooms here than in historic
lodgings; good for families; Internet access; affordable dining options.
Cons: plain rooms lack historic charm; tucked away from the rim in
the forest. ✉ *Grand Canyon Village* ⌂ *Box 699, Grand Canyon 86023*
🖀 *888/297–2757 reservations only, 928/638–2631* ⊕ *www.grandcanyon
lodges.com* ⮫ *250 rooms, 28 cabins* ♿ *In-room: no a/c (some), safe
(some), refrigerator (some). In-hotel: restaurant, bar, public Internet,
no-smoking rooms* ▭ *AE, D, DC, MC, V.*

¢ **Phantom Ranch.** In a grove of cottonwood trees on the canyon floor,
Phantom Ranch is accessible only to hikers and mule trekkers. The
wood-and-stone buildings originally made up a hunting camp built
in 1922. There are 40 dormitory beds and 14 beds in cabins, all with

3

Perched on the North Rim's edge—1,000 feet higher than the South Rim—is the Grand Canyon Lodge.

shared baths. Seven additional cabins are reserved for mule riders, who buy their trips as a package. The mess hall–style restaurant, one of the most remote eating establishments in the United States, serves family-style meals, with breakfast, dinner, and box lunches available. Reservations, taken up to 13 months in advance, are a must for services and lodging. **Pros:** only inner-canyon lodging option; fabulous canyon views; remote access limits crowds. **Cons:** accessible only by foot or mule; few amenities. ⊠ *On canyon floor, at intersection of Bright Angel and Kaibab trails* ✆ *Box 699, Grand Canyon 86023* ☎ *303/297–2757 or 888/297–2757* ⊕ *www.grandcanyonlodges.com* ⟳ *4 dormitories and 2 cabins for hikers, 7 cabins with outside showers for mule riders* ♿ *In-room: no a/c, no phone, no TV. In-hotel: restaurant, no-smoking rooms* ⊟ *AE, D, DC, MC, V.*

$$ 🛏 **Thunderbird Lodge.** This motel with comfortable, no-nonsense rooms is next to Bright Angel Lodge in Grand Canyon Village. For $10 more, you can get a room with a partial view of the canyon. Rooms have either two queen beds or one king. Check in at Bright Angel Lodge, the next hotel to the west. Some rooms do not have air-conditioning, but instead have evaporative coolers. **Pros:** partial canyon views in some rooms; family-friendly; accessible rooms. **Cons:** no Internet access; check-in takes place at Bright Angel Lodge; limited parking. ⊠ *Desert View Dr., Grand Canyon Village* ✆ *Box 699, Grand Canyon 86023* ☎ *888/297–2757 reservations only, 928/638–2631* ⊕ *www.grandcanyon lodges.com* ⟳ *55 rooms* ♿ *In-room: safe, refrigerator. In-hotel: no-smoking rooms* ⊟ *AE, D, DC, MC, V.*

$ 🛏 **Yavapai Lodge.** The largest motel-style lodge in the park is tucked in a piñon and juniper forest at the eastern end of Grand Canyon

Village, near the RV park. The basic rooms are near the park's general store, the visitor center (½ mi), and the rim (¼ mi). The cafeteria, open for breakfast, lunch, and dinner, serves standard park-service food. An Internet room is available to guests. **Pros:** transportation-activities desk on-site in the lobby; near Market Plaza in Grand Canyon Village; forested grounds. **Cons:** no Internet access in rooms; farthest in-park lodging from the rim. ⊠ *Grand Canyon Village* ⌂ *Box 699, Grand Canyon 86023* ☎ *888/297–2757 reservations only, 928/638–2961* ⊕ *www.grandcanyon lodges.com* ⤳ *358 rooms* ⌂ *In-room: no a/c (some), refrigerator (some). In-hotel: restaurant, public Internet, no-smoking rooms* ☰ *AE, D, DC, MC, V* ☼ *Closed Jan. and Feb.*

> ## DUFFEL SERVICE: LIGHTEN YOUR LOAD
>
> Hikers staying at either Phantom Ranch or Bright Angel campground can also take advantage of the ranch's duffel service: bags or packs weighing 30 pounds or less can be transported to the ranch by mule for a fee of $62.43 each way. As is true for many desirable things at the Canyon, reservations are a must.

CAMPGROUNDS AND RV PARKS

¢ ⚠ **Bright Angel Campground.** This campground is near Phantom Ranch on the South and North Kaibab trails, at the bottom of the canyon. There are toilet facilities and running water, but no showers. If you plan to eat at the Phantom Ranch Canteen, book your meals ahead of time. Reservations for all services, taken up to four months in advance, are a must. A backcountry permit, which serves as your reservation, is required to stay here. ⊠ *Intersection of South and North Kaibab trails, Grand Canyon* ⌂ *Backcountry Office, Box 129, Grand Canyon 86023* ☎ *928/638–7875* 🖷 *928/638–2125 www.nps.gov* ⤳ *30 tent sites, 2 group sites* ⌂ *Flush toilets, drinking water, picnic tables* ⚠ *Backcountry permit required* ☼ *Open year-round.*

¢ ⚠ **Desert View Campground.** Popular for spectacular views of the canyon from the nearby Watchtower, this campground fills up fast in summer. Fifty RV (without hookups) and tent sites are available on a first-come, first-served basis. ⊠ *Desert View Dr., 23 mi east of Grand Canyon Village off Hwy. 64* ⌂ *Backcountry Office, Box 129, Grand Canyon 86023* ☎ *928/638–7875* 🖷 *928/638–2125* ⌂ *Grills, flush toilets, drinking water, picnic tables* ⤳ *50 campsites* ⚠ *Reservations not accepted* ☼ *Mid-May–mid-Oct.*

¢ ⚠ **Indian Garden.** Halfway down the canyon is this campground, en route to Phantom Ranch on the Bright Angel Trail. Running water and toilet facilities are available, but not showers. A backcountry permit, which serves as a reservation, is required. You can book up to four months in advance. ⊠ *Bright Angel Trail, Grand Canyon* ⌂ *Backcountry Office, Box 129, Grand Canyon 86023* ☎ *928/638–7875* 🖷 *928/638–2125* ⌂ *Pit toilets, drinking water, picnic tables* ⤳ *15 tent sites, 1 large site* ⚠ *Reservations essential* ☼ *Open year-round.*

¢ ⚠ **Mather Campground.** Mather has RV and tent sites but no hookups.
★ No reservations are accepted from December to March, but the rest of the year, especially during the busy spring and summer seasons, they are a good idea, and can be made up to five months in advance. Ask at

the campground entrance for same-day availability. ✉ *Off Village Loop Dr., Grand Canyon Village 86023* ☎*877/444–6777* ⊕*www.recreation. gov* ⟋*308 sites for RVs and tents* ⟋*Flush toilets, public telephone, drinking water, guest laundry, showers, fire grates, picnic tables, dump station* ⊙*Open year-round.*

IN THE PARK: NORTH RIM

$$
Fodor's Choice
★

Grand Canyon Lodge. This historic property, constructed mainly in the 1920s and '30s, is the premier lodging facility in the North Rim area. The main building has locally quarried limestone walls and timbered ceilings. Lodging options include small, rustic cabins; larger cabins (some with a canyon view and some with two bedrooms); and slightly more modern motel rooms. The two-bedroom Pioneer cabins got a face-lift in 2008 and now sleep up to six people. The hand-carved Aspen lodge furniture adds to the rustic atmosphere. However, the best of the bunch are the Rim View Western, especially log cabins 301 and 306, which have private porches perched on the lip of the canyon. Other cabins with fabulous canyon views include 305, 309, and 310. Because of their premier location, these cabins are snapped up fast and need to be reserved a year in advance. **Pros:** steps away from gorgeous North Rim views; close to several easy hiking trails. **Cons:** as the only in-park North Rim lodging option, this lodge fills up fast; few amenities. ✉*Grand Canyon National Park, Hwy. 67, North Rim* ☎*877/386–4383, 928/638–2611 May–Oct., 928/645–6865 Nov.– Apr.* ⊕*www.grandcanyonforever.com* ⟋*40 rooms, 178 cabins* ⟋*In-room: no a/c, refrigerator (some), no TV. In-hotel: 3 restaurants, bar, bicycles, laundry facilities at the campground, public Internet at the General Store, no-smoking rooms* ▭*AE, D, MC, V* ⊙*Closed mid-Oct.–mid-May.*

CAMPGROUNDS
¢

North Rim Campground. The only designated campground at the North Rim of Grand Canyon National Park sits 3 mi north of the rim, and has 83 RV and tent sites (no hookups). You can reserve a site up to five months in advance. Leashed pets are allowed at the campground. ✉*Hwy. 67, North Rim86052* ☎*877/444–6777* ⊕*www.recreation.gov* ⟋*83 campsites* ⟋*Flush toilets, dump station, drinking water, guest laundry, showers, fire grates, picnic tables, general store* ⟋*Reservations essential* ⊙*Mid-May–mid-Oct., possibly later, weather permitting.*

OUTSIDE THE PARK

$$$
☾
★

Best Western Grand Canyon Squire Inn. About 1 mi south of the park's south entrance, this motel lacks the historic charm of the older lodges at the canyon rim, but has more amenities, including a small cowboy museum in the lobby and an upscale gift shop. Children enjoy the bowling alley, arcade, and outdoor swimming pool. Updated rooms with flat-screen TVs are spacious and furnished in Southwestern style. Those in the rear have a view of the woods. Kiosks in the lobby provide Internet access to registered guests. **Pros:** a cool pool in the summer and a steamy sauna for cold winter nights; children's activities at the Family Fun Center; high-speed Internet. **Cons:** hall noise can be an issue with all of the in-hotel activities. ✉*100 Hwy. 64, Grand Canyon* ☎*928/638–2681 or 800/622–6966* ⊕*www.grandcanyonsquire.com*

🛏250 rooms, 4 suites & In-room: refrigerator (some), Wi-Fi. In-hotel: restaurant, bar, pool, gym, laundry facilities, Wi-Fi, no-smoking rooms ▤AE, D, DC, MC, V.

$ 🎯 **Canyon Motel and RV Park.** Rail cars, cabooses, and cottages make up this 13-acre property on the outskirts of Williams. The best room is the 1929 Santa Fe red caboose: It's family-friendly, with two sides separated by a bathroom, giving parents a little privacy. The original wooden floor and tool equipment add to the authenticity. Another caboose looks much like a standard hotel room inside, as do the flagstone cottage rooms built from the local sandstone known for its variegated colors. A Pullman passenger car holds three rooms (rail-car suites), each with its own bathroom. The motel also has a few dry campsites (no water available) and a 47-space RV park with full hookups. **Pros:** family-friendly property with hiking, horseshoes, and playground; general store and recreation room; owners are friendly and helpful. **Cons:** a few miles from Williams dining options; RV park traffic. ⊠1900 E. Rodeo Rd., Williams ☎928/635–9371 or 800/482–3955 ⊕www.thecanyonmotel. com 🛏18 rooms, 5 rail-car suites & In-room: no a/c (some), no phone, refrigerator. In-hotel: pool, no elevator, laundry facilities, Wi-Fi, no-smoking rooms ▤D, MC, V �ⓘCP.

$$$ 🎯 **Grand Canyon Railway Hotel and Resort.** This hotel was designed to ★ resemble the train depot's original Fray Marcos lodge. Neoclassical Greek columns flank the grand entrance, which leads to a lobby with maple-wood balustrades, an enormous flagstone fireplace, and oil paintings of the Grand Canyon by local artist Kenneth McKenna. Original bronzes by Frederic Remington also adorn the lobby. The pleasant Southwestern-style accommodations have large bathrooms. Adjacent to the lobby is Spenser's, a pub with an ornate 19th-century hand-carved bar. Riding the train to the canyon in railcars that date from the 1920s can be a relaxing alternative to the long drive. **Pros:** Grand Canyon Railway package options; pet resort; game room and outdoor playground for family fun. **Cons:** noisy location; high traffic volume; limited food options. ⊠235 N. Grand Canyon Blvd., Williams ☎928/635–4010 or 800/843–8724 ⊕www.thetrain.com 🛏288 rooms, 10 suites & In-room: refrigerator (some), Internet. In-hotel: restaurant, bar, pool, gym, laundry facilities, Wi-Fi, no-smoking rooms ▤AE, D, MC, V.

$$$ 🎯 **The Grand Hotel.** At the south end of Tusayan, this popular hotel has ★ bright, clean rooms decorated in Southwestern colors. The lobby has a stone-and-timber design, cozy seating areas, and Wi-Fi access. Live Native American dancing and cowboy singers lead the entertainment in the Canyon Star Wild West Saloon during evenings in the peak season. At the bar, you can sit on a saddle that was once used for canyon mule trips. **Pros:** coffee stand for a quick morning pick-me-up; gift shop stocked with outdoor gear and regional books. **Cons:** no in-room Internet access; restaurant and lounge hours are not reliable; facilities often closed during off-season. ⊠Hwy. 64/U.S. 180, Grand Canyon ☎928/638–3333 or 888/634–7263 ⊕www.grandcanyongrandhotel. com 🛏120 rooms,12 suites & In-hotel: restaurant, bar, pool, gym, laundry facilities, Wi-Fi, no-smoking rooms ▤AE, D, DC, MC, V.

$$ ⌂**Havasupai Lodge.** At this writing, Supai and the Havasu Lodge are closed to visitors due to flooding in August 2008. They are expected to reopen in summer 2009; call ☎928/448–2121 for more information. These are fairly spartan accommodations, but you won't mind much when you see the natural beauty surrounding you. The lodge and restaurant are at the bottom of Havasu Canyon and are operated by the Havasupai tribe. In addition to the room rate, there is a $35 per-person tribal entry fee and a $5 environmental-care fee. Reservations are essential and can be made up to a year in advance. **Pros:** near the famous waterfalls; Havasupai staff offers Native American perspective on the natural and cultural history of the Grand Canyon. **Cons:** accessible only by foot, horseback, or helicopter; rooms are plain and worn; no phones or TVs. ✉*Supai* ☎*928/448–2111 or 928/448–2201* ⊕*www.havasupaitribe.com* ⊃24 *rooms* ♿*In-room: no phone, no TV. In-hotel: no-smoking rooms* ▤*MC, V.*

$ ⌂**Hualapai Lodge.** At Peach Springs, the hotel has a comfortable lobby with a large fireplace that is welcoming on chilly nights near the West Rim. The rooms are clean but basic. **Pros:** concierge desk arranges river trips with the Hualapai River Runners; on-site restaurant mixes things up with Native American dishes; Hualapai locals add a different perspective to the canyon experience. **Cons:** basic rooms lack historic charm; location is off the beaten path. ✉*900 Rte. 66, Peach Springs* ☎*928/769–2230 or 888/255–9550* ⊕*www.destinationgrandcanyon. com* ⊃57 *rooms* ♿*In-hotel: restaurant, pool, gym, laundry facilities, Wi-Fi, no-smoking rooms* ▤*AE, D, MC, V.*

$$ ⌂**Hualapai Ranch.** Cabins are clean and neat, but also very small and unassuming. The front porches make for a good place to sit and unwind after a hectic day exploring the sights at the West Rim. The cabins are adjacent to a small "Western" town, where visitors can pose for snapshots, sign up for guided horseback tours and wagon rides, watch gunfight re-enactments in the dusty streets, and visit a petting zoo. Accommodations include two meals, a Hualapai visitation permit, and motor-coach transfers to the rim overlooks at Guano Point and Eagle Point. **Pros:** front porches offer relaxed desert views; rustlers tell tall tales and strike up a tune at campfire programs; dining room serves meals all day long. **Cons:** no phones or TVs. ☏*6206 W. Desert Inn, Suite B, Las Vegas, NV* ☎*702/878–9378 or 889/878–9378* ⊕*www. destinationgrandcanyon.com* ⊃20 *cabins* ♿*In-room: no phone, no TV, Wi-Fi. In-hotel: restaurant, no-smoking rooms* ▤*AE, MC, V.*

$ ⌂**Jacob Lake Inn.** The bustling lodge at Jacob Lake Inn is a popular stop for those heading to the North Rim. This 5-acre complex in Kaibab National Forest has basic cabins and standard motel rooms that overlook the highways. Avoid the older facilities by asking for one of the new rooms. They aren't as nostalgic and private as the cabins, but they do offer fresher surroundings. **Pros:** grocery store, coffee shop and restaurant; quiet rooms. **Cons:** small bathroom in cabins; worn furnishings; old-fashioned key locks. ✉*Hwy. 67/U.S. 89A, Fredonia* ☎*928/643–7232* ⊕*www.jacoblake.com* ⊃32 *rooms, 26 cabins* ♿*In-room: no a/c (some), no phone (some), no TV (some), Internet (some),*

Wi-Fi (some). In-hotel: restaurant, some pets allowed, no-smoking rooms ⊟*AE, D, MC, V.*

$ ⚏**Marble Canyon Lodge.** This Arizona Strip lodge opened in 1929 on
★ the same day the Navajo Bridge was dedicated. Three types of accommodations are available: rooms in the original building, standard motel rooms in the newer building, and two-bedroom apartments. You can play the 1920s piano or sit on the porch swing of the native-rock lodge and look out on Vermilion Cliffs and the desert. Zane Grey and Gary Cooper are among well-known past guests. **Pros:** convenience store and trading post; great fishing on the Colorado River. **Cons:** no-frills rustic lodging; more than 70 mi to the Grand Canyon North Rim. ⊠*¼ mi west of Navajo Bridge on U.S. 89A* ☐*Box 6001, Marble Canyon 86036* ☎*928/355–2225 or 800/726–1789* ⟿*46 rooms, 8 apartments* ⚅*In-room: no a/c (some), no phone, Wi-Fi. In-hotel: restaurant, bar, laundry facilities, some pets allowed, no-smoking rooms* ⊟*AE, D, MC, V.*

$$–$$$ ⚏**Red Feather Lodge.** This motel and adjacent hotel are a good value about 6 mi from the canyon. A Southwestern theme dominates the large rooms. The motel portion of the lodge is closed January through March, except to guests with pets and smokers. Rooms have cable TV with movies and video games, and there is Internet access in the rooms and lobby for a fee. An outdoor pool and hot tub are open seasonally. **Pros:** good price for being so close to park; complimentary Continental breakfast. **Cons:** this older hotel shows more wear and tear than other nearby lodging facilities. ⊠*Hwy. 64/U.S. 180, Tusayan 86023* ☎*928/638–2414 or 866/561–2425* ⊕*www.redfeatherlodge. com* ⟿*212 rooms, 1 suite* ⚅*In-room: refrigerator (some), Wi-Fi. In-hotel: restaurant, pool, gym, some pets allowed, no-smoking rooms* ⊟*AE, D, DC, MC, V* ⚏*CP.*

$$ ⚏**Red Garter B&B.** This restored saloon and bordello from 1897 now houses a small, antique-filled B&B. Guest rooms are on the second floor; ask for the "Best Gal's Room," which has its own sitting room overlooking the train tracks. All four rooms (two are interior, with skylights) are very quiet, as the only train traffic is the Grand Canyon Railway. Even if you don't stay here, the fresh pastries served in the first-floor coffee shop are worth a stop. **Pros:** on-site coffee shop and bakery; decorated in antiques and period pieces; centrally located. **Cons:** all rooms are only accessible by stairs; parking is across the street; over an hour drive to canyon. ⊠*137 W. Railroad Ave., Williams* ☎*928/635–1484 or 800/328–1484* ⊕*www.redgarter.com* ⟿*4 rooms* ⚅*In-room: no phone, Wi-Fi. In-hotel: no kids under 8, no-smoking rooms* ⊟*D, MC, V* ⚏*CP* ⊗*Closed Dec.–mid-Feb.*

$$ ⚏**Sheridan House Inn.** Nestled among 2 acres of pine trees near Route
★ 66, this B&B has decks looking to the tall ponderosa pines and a flagstone patio with a hot tub. Average-size bedrooms all have king beds and marble bathrooms. Hearty breakfasts—scrambled eggs, fruit plates, bacon, sausage, potatoes, eggs Benedict, and buttermilk pancakes—will ready you for the hour-long drive to the canyon. K.C. and Mary Seidner are gracious hosts who will gladly help guests plan itineraries. **Pros:** quiet location; game room has puzzles and board games; the entertainment room has a pool table and piano. **Cons:** a long drive to the

canyon and a short drive from downtown Williams; parking is at the bottom of the hill. ⊠*460 E. Sheridan Ave., Williams* ☎*928/635–9441 or 888/635–9345* ⇝*6 rooms, 2 suites* ♿*In-room: no a/c, DVD (some), Wi-Fi. In-hotel: no-smoking rooms* ⊟*AE, D, MC, V* ⑩|*BP.*

¢ ⛺**Diamond Creek.** The Hualapai permit camping on their tribal lands
CAMP-   here, with an overnight camping permit of $25 per person per night,
GROUNDS which can be purchased at the Hualapai Lodge. You can camp on the beach of the Colorado River, but this smooth beach is a popular with river runners as a launch point and a pullout as the only place on the river accessed by road other than Lees Ferry. The camping area is primitive, with only a picnic table and pit toilets. No fires are allowed, but grills may be used, and rock pit barbecues are available. The campground is accessed by a 22-mi drive down the gravel Diamond Creek Road. The road can be braved by high-clearance passenger vehicles, but your best bet is one with four-wheel-drive capabilities, especially in the summer when storms are commonplace. ⌂*900 Rte. 66, Peach Springs 86434* ☎*928/769–2230 or 888/255–9550* ⊕*www.destinationgrandcanyon. com* ⇝*Open camping* ♿*Pit toilets, picnic tables* ☉*Mid-Mar.–Oct.*

¢ ⛺**Havasu Canyon.** At this writing, Supai and the Havasu Canyon campground are closed to visitors due to flooding in August 2008. It is expected to reopen in summer 2009; call ☎*928/448–2121* for more information. You can stay in the primitive campgrounds in Havasu Canyon for $17 per person per night, in addition to the $35-per-person entry fee plus a $5 environmental-care fee. The extensive campground has 100 sites and is 2 mi from the Supai village. Cottonwood trees provide plenty of shade and picnic tables can be found near many of the campsites. You can pack in a stove, but no campfires are allowed. ⌂*Havasupai Tourist Enterprises, Box 160, Supai 86435* ☎*928/448–2121, 928/448–2174, 928/448–2180, or 928/448–2141* ⊕*www.havasupaitribe.com* ⇝*100 campsites* ♿*Food service, general store, pit toilets, drinking water, picnic tables* ♿*Reservations essential.*

¢ ⛺**Kaibab National Forest.** Both developed and undeveloped campsites are available on a first-come, first-served basis at this forest that surrounds Williams and extends to the Grand Canyon, encompassing Cataract Lake, Kaibab Lake, Dogtown Lake, and White Horse Lake. Campgrounds are open May through September and range in rates from $14 to $18 per night. Developed campgrounds have pit toilets, fire rings, and picnic tables. There is a dump station, but no hookups at Kaibab, Dogtown, and White Horse Lake. ☎*928/699–1239 or 877/444–6777* ⊕*www.fs.fed.us/r3/kai.*

North-Central Arizona

WORD OF MOUTH

"We are so glad we [visited the Chapel of the Holy Cross]. The chapel looks as though it is somehow growing out of the red rock. And the views from the chapel itself are amazing . . . It's a very peaceful and beautiful place, a lovely way to end our trip . . . our only regret was that our vacation couldn't have lasted longer!"
—caligirl56

WELCOME TO NORTH-CENTRAL ARIZONA

TOP REASONS TO GO

★ **Mother Nature:** Stunning red rocks, snowcapped mountains, and crisp country air rejuvenate the most cynical city dwellers.

★ **Father Time:** Ancient Native American sites, such as Walnut Canyon and Montezuma's Castle, show life before Columbus "discovered" America. You can learn their history in the excellent national monument visitor centers.

★ **Main Street charm:** Jerome and Prescott exude small-town hospitality with turn-of-the-20th-century architecture and charming bed-and-breakfasts.

★ **Beat the heat:** It's the high desert, but a very cool place; temperatures throughout north-central Arizona are typically 20 degrees cooler than in the Phoenix area.

★ **Let your aura out:** The free spirit and energy of Sedona is delightfully infectious, even for skeptics.

1 Flagstaff. College-town enthusiasm and high-country charm combine to make this one of Arizona's most outdoors-friendly towns. Hiking, biking, skiing, and climbing are local passions, and there are state and national parks to explore.

2 Sedona. Surrounded by the Coconino National Forest, Sedona's residents call their home a museum without walls. The town's red rocks lure visitors from around the world. You'll enjoy breathtaking views, fantastic cuisine, and a dash of New Age whimsy.

3 The Verde Valley, Jerome, and Prescott. Remote but still accessible, the towns of the Verde Valley embrace the life of yesteryear. You can take the Verde Canyon Railroad or visit Montezuma's Castle and see nature's untouched beauty and history. Whiskey Row in Prescott still exudes turn-of-the-20th-century charm, and Jerome, less commercial than Sedona, is emerging as a new hub for artisans.

GETTING ORIENTED

4

Nestled between the Grand Canyon and Phoenix, north-central Arizona has enough natural beauty and sophisticated attractions to compete with its neighbors to the north and south. Most visitors flock to Sedona, world-renowned for red rocks, pink jeeps, and New Age energy. The surrounding area of Verde Valley may not attract the same hordes, but this means some welcome peace and quiet. Flagstaff is surrounded by the Coconino National Forest and wrapped around the base of the tallest mountains in the state (the San Francisco Peaks). Phoenicians flee the summertime heat to cool off in the mountains and explore Prescott and Jerome.

Old Flagstaff sandstone courthouse from 1894.

Map labels

Colorado

CANYON

Grand Canyon National Park

PLATEAU

NAVAJO RESERVATION

Wupatki National Monument

PAINTED DESERT

180

89

SAN FRANCISCO PEAKS

Sunset Crater Volcano National Monument

Humphreys Peak 12,633 ft

Winona

40

Flagstaff

1

89A

Walnut Canyon National Monument

Two Guns

Oak Creek Canyon

17

Meteor Crater

Slide Rock State Park

MOGOLLON PLATEAU

2

Sedona

Mormon Lake

Red Rock State Park

179

Cottonwood

Bridgeport

87

VERDE VALLEY

260

Montezuma Castle National Monument

0   40 miles

Fort Verde State Historic Park

0   60 km

Camp Verde

17

260

NORTH-CENTRAL ARIZONA PLANNER

When to Go

Autumn, when the wet season ends, the stifling desert temperatures moderate (it's 20 degrees cooler than Phoenix), and the mountain aspens reach their full golden splendor, is a great time to visit this part of Arizona. During the summer months many Phoenix residents travel north to escape the 100-degree temperatures, meaning excessive traffic along Interstate 17 just north of Phoenix on Friday and Sunday evenings. Hotels are less expensive in winter, but mountain temperatures dip below zero, and snowstorms can occur weekly, especially near Flagstaff.

Sedona has springlike temperatures even in January, when it's snowing in Flagstaff, but summer temperatures above 90°F are common.

Getting Here and Around

Don't plan on flying into Flagstaff, Sedona, or Prescott: commercial flights are limited, and besides, getting here is half the fun; the scenery is gorgeous. You'll definitely want a car, and north-central Arizona is only a two-hour drive from Phoenix.

Avoid interstates when possible; the back ways can be more direct and have the best views of the stunning landscape. Instead of Route 17, take 89A through Verde Valley and Oak Creek Canyon.

It makes sense to rent a car in this region, since trails and monuments stretch miles past city limits and many area towns cannot be reached by the major bus companies. The major rental agencies have offices in Flagstaff, Prescott, and Sedona.

Weekend traffic around Sedona can be heavy, so leave early and allow for extra time.

Making the Most of Your Time

Sedona will probably occupy most of your time, so plan to spend at least two days there, hiking or shopping. Oak Creek Canyon and Chapel of the Holy Cross are must-sees. Then, depending on your preferences, spend your time looking (window-shopping or stargazing) or doing (hiking, exploring). If you can, plan to be in Sedona midweek, when the weekend crowds aren't around.

Outdoors enthusiasts should head to Flagstaff for a day to enjoy the Mount Elden Trail System or hit the slopes at Arizona Snowbowl. Flagstaff also has the Lowell Observatory.

Prescott and Jerome can be combined for a day or less. You can check out the pulse of downtown Prescott's museum and famous Whiskey Row, then spend a night in a historic hotel; Jerome has several quaint B&Bs, as well as a shopping district that may offer more affordable treasures than Sedona.

For scenic views, nothing beats the Verde Canyon Railroad. Native American historic sites such as Montezuma's Castle and Tuzigoot National Monument offer perspective on native life centuries ago.

Sample Itineraries

Have an extra half-day? Here are some ideas about how to spend it:

■ Nature lovers should visit either the Coconino or Prescott national forest. Stop in at a local coffeehouse and get sandwiches for a picnic, then head out on a scenic trail to enjoy some solitude.

■ History buffs have a host of choices, whether it's Walnut Canyon, the Mine Museum in Jerome, Meteor Crater, or Fort Verde State Historic Park.

■ Bargain hunters might not fare so well in the luxury boutiques of Sedona, but artisans and antiques dealers have enclaves in Jerome, Prescott, and Flagstaff.

Local Food and Lodging

You'll find lots of American comfort food in this part of the country: barbecue restaurants, steak houses, and burger joints predominate. If you're looking for something different, Sedona and Flagstaff have the majority of good, multiethnic restaurants in the area, and if you're craving Mexican, you're sure to find something authentic and delicious (note that burritos are often called "burros" around here). Sedona is the best place in the area for fine dining. Some area restaurants close in January and February—the slower months in the area—so call ahead. Reservations are suggested from April through October.

Flagstaff and Prescott have the more affordable lodging options, with lots of comfortable motels and B&Bs, but no real luxury. The opposite is true in Sedona, which is filled with opulent resorts and hideaways, most offering solitude and spa services—just don't expect a bargain. Reservations are essential for Sedona and suggested for Flagstaff and Prescott. Little Jerome has a few B&Bs, but call ahead if you think you might want to spend the night. If you're in for a thrill, many of the historic hotels have haunted rooms.

WHAT IT COSTS

	¢	$	$$	$$$	$$$$
Restaurant	under $8	$8–$12	$13–$20	$21–$30	over $30
Hotel	under $70	$70–$120	$121–$175	$176–$250	over $250

Restaurant prices are per person for a main course at dinner. Hotel prices are for a standard double in high season, excluding taxes and service charges.

Into Thin Air

It's wise, especially if you're an outdoors enthusiast, to start in the relatively lowland areas of Prescott and the Verde Valley, climbing gradually to Sedona and Flagstaff—it can take several days to grow accustomed to the high elevation in Flagstaff.

Festivals and Events

Sept. Sedona Jazz on the Rocks Festival. Top jazz musicians attract a sellout crowd that fills the town to capacity for five days. ☎ *928/282–1985* ⊕ *www.sedonajazz.com.*

Route 66 Days. Classic and muscle cars roar into Flagstaff the second weekend in September for this fun auto show with live music and a host of vendors. ☎ *928/779–0898* ⊕ *www.flagstaffroute66days.com.*

Festival of Science. This 10-day series of exhibits and guest speakers in Flagstaff is made stellar by its observatories. ☎ *800/842-7293* ⊕ *www.scifest.org.*

Updated by
Mara Levin

Red-rock buttes ablaze in the slanting light of late afternoon, the San Francisco Peaks tipped white from a fresh snowfall, pine forests clad in dark green needles—north-central Arizona is rich in natural attractions, a landscape of vast plateaus punctuated by steep ridges and canyons.

To the north of Flagstaff the San Francisco Peaks, a string of tall volcanic mountains, rise over 12,000 feet, tapering to the 9,000-foot Mount Elden and a scattering of diminutive cinder cones. To the south, a seemingly endless stand of ponderosa pines covers this part of the Colorado Plateau before the terrain plunges dramatically into Oak Creek Canyon. The canyon then opens to reveal red buttes and mesas in the high-desert areas surrounding Sedona. The desert gradually descends to the Verde Valley, crossing the Verde River before reaching the 7,000-foot Black Range, over which lies the Prescott Valley.

Flagstaff, the hub of this part of Arizona, was historically a way station en route to southern California. First the railroads, then Route 66 carried westbound traffic right through the center of town. Many of those who were "just passing through" stayed and built a community, revitalizing downtown with cafés, an activity-filled square, eclectic shops, and festivals. The town's large network of bike paths and parks abuts hundreds of miles of trails and forest roads, an irresistible lure for outdoors enthusiasts. Not surprisingly, the typical resident of Flagstaff is outdoorsy, young, and has a large, friendly dog in tow.

Down AZ 89A in Sedona, the average age and income rises considerably. This was once a hidden hamlet used by Western filmmakers, but New Age enthusiasts flocked to the region in the 1980s believing it was the center of spiritual powers. Well-off executives and retirees followed soon after, building clusters of McMansions throughout the area. Sophisticated restaurants, upscale shops, luxe accommodations, and New Age entrepreneurs cater to both these populations, and to the tourist trade which brings close to 5 million visitors a year. It can be difficult, though not impossible, to find a moment of serenity, even in wilderness areas. A hike into apparently remote territory is often disturbed by a tour plane buzzing above or a gonzo mountain biker who brakes for no one. Despite these quibbles, the beauty here is unsurpassed.

Pioneers and miners are now part of north-central Arizona's past, but the wild and woolly days of the Old West are not forgotten. The preserved fort at Camp Verde recalls frontier life, and the decrepit facades of the funky former mining town of Jerome have an infectious charm. The many Victorian houses in temperate Prescott attest to the attempt to bring "civilization" to Arizona's territorial capital.

North-central Arizona is also rich in artifacts from its earliest inhabitants: several national and state parks—among them Walnut Canyon, Wupatki, Montezuma Castle, and Tuzigoot national monuments—hold well-preserved evidence of the architectural accomplishments of Native American Sinagua and other Ancestral Puebloans who made their homes in the Verde Valley and the region near the San Francisco Peaks.

FLAGSTAFF

146 mi northwest of Phoenix, 27 mi north of Sedona via Oak Creek Canyon.

Few travelers slow down long enough to explore Flagstaff, a town of 54,000 known locally as "Flag"; most stop only to spend the night at one of the town's many motels before making the last leg of the trip to the Grand Canyon, 80 mi north. Flag makes a good base for day trips to ancient Native American sites and the Navajo and Hopi reservations, as well as to the Petrified Forest National Park and the Painted Desert, but the city is a worthwhile destination in its own right. Set against a lovely backdrop of pine forests and the snowcapped San Francisco Peaks, downtown Flagstaff retains a frontier flavor.

In summer Phoenix residents head here seeking relief from the desert heat, since at any time of the year temperatures in Flagstaff are about 25°F cooler than in Phoenix. They also come to Flagstaff in winter to ski at the small Arizona Snowbowl, about 15 mi northeast of town among the San Francisco Peaks.

GETTING HERE AND AROUND

Flagstaff lies at the intersection of Interstate 40 (east–west) and Interstate 17 (running south from Flagstaff), 134 mi north of Phoenix via Interstate 17. If you're driving from Sedona to Flagstaff or the Grand Canyon, head north through the wooded Oak Creek Canyon: it's the most scenic route.

Flagstaff Pulliam Airport is 3 mi south of town off Interstate 17 at Exit 337. Horizon Air flies from Los Angeles to Flagstaff and US Airways Express flies from Phoenix to Flagstaff.Amtrak comes into the downtown Flagstaff station twice daily. There's no rail service into Prescott or Sedona.

Flagstaff Express provides transportation via shuttle van or private car between Phoenix, Flagstaff, and the Grand Canyon.

A walking-tour map of the area is available at the visitor center in the Tudor Revival–style Santa Fe Depot, an excellent place to begin sightseeing.

PLANNING YOUR TIME

You can see most of Flagstaff's attractions in a day—especially if you visit the Lowell Observatory or the Northern Arizona University Observatory in the evening, which is also when the Museum Club is best experienced.

Consult the schedule of tour times if you want to visit the Riordan State Historic Park. Devote at least an hour to the excellent Museum of Northern Arizona. The Historic Railroad District downtown is a good place for lunch. If you're a skier, spend part of a winter's day at Arizona Snowbowl; in summer you can spend a couple of hours on the skyride and scenic trails at the top. Take your time enjoying the trails on Mount Elden, and remember to pace yourself in the higher elevations; allow a full day for hiking. The Lava River Cave is an easy—if dark—hike that can be comfortably done in an hour.

ESSENTIALS

Transportation Contacts Flagstaff Express (☎ 800/563–1980 ⊕ www.flag staffexpress.com). **Flagstaff Pulliam Airport** (☎ 928/556–1234). **A Friendly Cab** (☎ 928/774–4444).**Sun Taxi** (☎ 928/774–7400).

Visitor Info Flagstaff Visitor Center (⊠ Santa Fe Depot, 1 E. Rte. 66, Downtown ☎ 928/774–9541 or 800/842–7293 ⊕ www.flagstaffarizona.org).

EXPLORING

❼ Arizona Snowbowl. Although still one of Flagstaff's largest attractions, droughts can make snowy slopes a luxury. Fortunately, visitors can enjoy the beauty of the area year-round. The Agassiz ski lift climbs to a height of 11,500 feet in 25 minutes, and doubles as a skyride through the Coconino National Forest in summer. From this vantage point you can see up to 70 mi; views may even include the North Rim of the Grand Canyon. There's a lodge at the base with a restaurant, bar, and ski school. To reach the ski area, take U.S. 180 north from Flagstaff; it's 7 mi from the Snowbowl exit to the skyride entrance. ⊠ *Snowbowl Rd., North Flagstaff* ☎ *928/779–1951* ⊕ *www.arizonasnowbowl.com* ⟟ *Skyride $10* ⊗ *Skyride: Memorial Day–early Sept., daily 10–4; early Sept.–mid-Oct., Fri.–Sun. 10–4, weather permitting.*

❶ Historic Downtown District. Storied Route 66 runs right through the heart of downtown Flagstaff. The late-Victorian, Tudor Revival, and early–art deco architecture in this district recalls the town's heyday as a logging and railroad center. The **Santa Fe Depot** (⊠ *1 E. Rte. 66, Downtown*) now houses the visitor center. Highlights include the 1927 **Hotel Monte Vista** (⊠ *100 N. San Francisco St., Downtown* ⊕ *www. hotelmontevista.com*), built after a community drive raised $200,000 in 60 days. The construction was promoted as a way to bolster the burgeoning tourism in the region, and the hotel was held publicly until the early 1960s. The 1888 **Babbitt Brothers Building** (⊠ *12 E. Aspen Ave., Downtown*) was constructed as a building-supply store and then turned

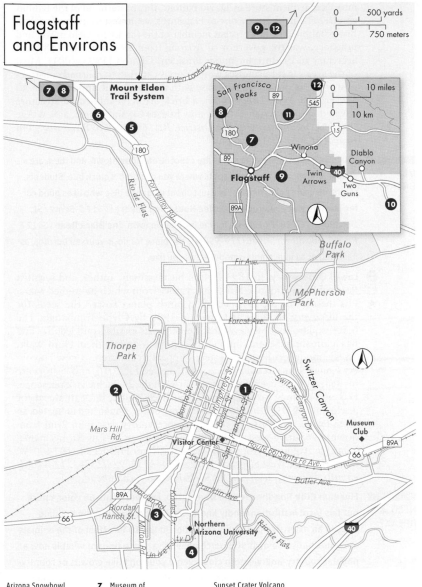

Flagstaff
and Environs

Mount Elden
Trail System

San Francisco Peaks

Winona

Diablo
Canyon

Flagstaff

Twin
Arrows

Two
Guns

Buffalo
Park

Fir Ave.

McPherson
Park

Cedar Ave.

Forest Ave.

Thorpe
Park

Switzer Canyon

Mars Hill
Rd.

Museum
Club

Visitor Center

Route 66/Santa Fe Ave.

Clay Ave.

Butler Ave.

Franklin Ave.

Riordan
Ranch St.

**Northern
Arizona University**

into a department store by David Babbitt, the mastermind of the Babbitt empire. The Babbitts are one of Flagstaff's wealthiest founding families. Bruce Babbitt, the most recent member of the family to wield power and influence, was the governor of Arizona from 1978 through 1987 and Secretary of the Interior under President Clinton (1993–2001). Most of the area's first businesses were saloons catering to railroad construction workers, which was the case with the 1888 **Vail Building** (⊠*5 N. San Francisco St., Downtown*), a brick art deco–influenced structure covered with stucco in 1939. It now houses Crystal Magic, a New Age shop. ⊠*Downtown Historic District, Rte. 66 north to Birch Ave., and Beaver St. east to Agassiz St.*

NEED A BREAK?

The town's most interesting shops are concentrated downtown, and there are a couple of brewpubs and some spots where you can grab a quick bite. Students, skiers, new and aging hippies, and just about everyone else who likes good coffee jam into **Macy's European Coffee House and Bakery** (⊠*14 S. Beaver St., Downtown* ☎*928/774–2243*) for the best cup in town. The **Black Bean** (⊠*12 E. Rte. 66, Downtown* ☎*928/779–9905*) is the place for do-it-yourself burritos, as healthful or as guacamole-smothered as you like.

② **Lowell Observatory.** In 1894 Boston businessman, author, and scientist ☪ Percival Lowell founded this observatory from which he studied Mars. ★ His theories of the existence of a ninth planet sowed the seeds for the discovery of Pluto at Lowell in 1930 by Clyde Tombaugh. The 6,500-square-foot Steele Visitor Center hosts exhibits and lectures and has a gift shop. Several interactive exhibits—among them Pluto Walk, a scale model of the solar system—appeal to children. A new Discovery Channel research telescope is anticipated for 2010, and visitors are invited, on some evenings, to peer through the 24-inch Clark telescope. Day and evening viewings are offered year-round, but call ahead for a schedule. ■TIP➔The Clark observatory dome is open and unheated, so dress for the outdoors. To reach the observatory, less than 2 mi from downtown, drive west on Route 66, which resumes its former name, Santa Fe Avenue, before it merges into Mars Hill Road. ⊠*1400 W. Mars Hill Rd., West Flagstaff* ☎*928/774–3358, 928/233–3211 recorded info* ⊕*www.lowell.edu* ⊠*$6* ☽*Hrs vary; call ahead.*

NEED A BREAK?

Museum Club Roadhouse and Danceclub. For real Route 66 color, check out this local institution fondly known as the Zoo, because the building housed an extensive taxidermy collection in the 1930s. Most of the animals are gone, but some owls still perch above the dance floor of what is now a popular country-and-western club. Even if you don't like crowds or country music, it's worth stopping in for a drink and to see this gigantic log cabin constructed around five trees; the entryway is a huge wishbone-shaped pine. ⊠*3404 E. Rte. 66, Downtown* ☎*928/526–9434* ⊕*www.museumclub. com* ⊠*Free* ☽*Daily 11 AM–2 AM.*

❻ **Museum of Northern Arizona.** This institution, founded in 1928, is respect- ☪ ed worldwide for its research and its collections centering on the natural ★ and cultural history of the Colorado Plateau. Among the permanent exhibitions are an extensive collection of Navajo rugs and a Hopi kiva (men's ceremonial chamber). A gallery devoted to area geology is usually a hit with children: it includes a life-size model dilophosaurus, a carnivorous dinosaur that once roamed northern Arizona. Outdoors, a life-zone exhibit shows the changing vegetation from the bottom of the Grand Canyon to the highest peak in Flagstaff. A nature trail, open only in summer, heads down across a small stream into a canyon and up into an aspen grove. Also in summer, the museum hosts exhibits and the works of Native American artists, whose wares are sold in the museum gift shop. ⊠*3101 N. Fort Valley Rd., North Flagstaff* ☎*928/774–5213* ⊕*www.musnaz.org* ☞*$7* ⊙*Daily 9–5.*

WORTH NOTING

8 Lava River Cave. Subterranean lava flow formed this mile-long cave roughly 700,000 years ago. Once you descend into its boulder-strewn maw, the cave is spacious, with 40-foot ceilings, but claustrophobes take heed: about halfway through the cave tapers to a 4-foot-high squeeze that can be a bit unnerving. A 40°F chill pervades the cave throughout the year so take warm clothing. To reach the turnoff for the cave, go approximately 9 mi north of Flagstaff on U.S. 180, then turn west onto FR 245. Turn left at the intersection of FR 171 and look for the sign to the cave. The trip is approximately 45 minutes from Flagstaff. Although the cave is on Coconino National Forest Service property, the only thing here is an interpretive sign, so it's definitely something you tackle at your own risk. ■TIP→Pack a flashlight (or two). ⊠*FR 171B*

4 Northern Arizona University Observatory. The observatory, with its 24-inch telescope, was built in 1952 by Dr. Arthur Adel, a scientist at Lowell Observatory whose study of infrared astronomy pioneered research into molecules that absorb light passing through the Earth's atmosphere. Today's studies of Earth's shrinking ozone layer rely on some of Dr. Adel's early work. Visitors to the observatory—which houses one of the largest telescopes that the public is allowed to move and manipulate—are usually hosted by friendly students and faculty members of the university's Department of Physics and Astronomy. ⊠*Bldg. 47, Northern Arizona Campus Observatory, Dept. of Physics and Astronomy, S. San Francisco St., just north of Walkup Skydome, University* ☎*928/523–7170* ☞*Free* ⊙*Viewings Fri. 7:30–10 PM, weather permitting.*

5 Pioneer Museum. The Arizona Historical Society operates this museum in a volcanic-rock building constructed in 1908. The structure was Coconino County's first hospital for the poor, and the current displays include one of the depressingly small nurses' rooms, an old iron lung, and a reconstructed doctor's office. Most of the exhibits, however, touch on more cheerful aspects of Flagstaff history—like road signs and children's toys. The museum holds a folk-crafts festival on July 4, with blacksmiths, weavers, spinners, quilters, and candle makers. Their crafts, and those of other local artisans, are sold in the museum's gift shop. The museum is part of the Fort Valley Park complex, in a wooded residential section at the northwest end of town. ⊠*2340 N. Fort Valley Rd., North Flagstaff* ☎*928/774–6272* ⊕*www.arizonahistoricalsociety. org* ☞*$3* ⊙*Mon.–Sat. 9–5.*

3 **Riordan State Historic Park.** This artifact of Flagstaff's logging heyday is near Northern Arizona University. The centerpiece is a mansion built in 1904 for Michael and Timothy Riordan, lumber-baron brothers who married two sisters. The 13,300-square-foot, 40-room log-and-stone structure—designed by Charles Whittlesley, who was also responsible for El Tovar Hotel at the Grand Canyon—contains furniture by Gustav Stickley, father of the American Arts and Crafts design movement. One room holds "Paul Bunyan's shoes," a 2-foot-long pair of boots made by Timothy in his workshop. Everything on display is original to the house. The mansion may be explored on a guided tour only; reservations are suggested. ⌂ *409 W. Riordan Rd., University* ☎ *928/779–4395* ⊕ *www.azstateparks.com* ⌨ *$6* ☉ *May–Oct., daily 8:30–5, with tours on the hr 9–4; Nov.–Apr., daily 10:30–5, with tours on the hr 11–4.*

SPORTS AND THE OUTDOORS

HIKING

You can explore Arizona's alpine tundra in the San Francisco Peaks, part of the Coconino National Forest, where more than 80 species of plants grow on the upper elevations. The habitat is fragile, so hikers are asked to stay on established trails (there are lots of them). ■**TIP→**Flat-landers should give themselves a day or two to adjust to the altitude before lengthy or strenuous hiking. The altitude here will make even the hardiest hikers breathe a little harder, so anyone with cardiac or respiratory problems should be cautious about overexertion.

The rangers of the **Coconino National Forest** (⌂ *1824 S. Thompson St., North Flagstaff* ☎ *928/527–3600* ⊕ *www.fs.fed.us/r3/coconino*) maintain many of the region's trails, and can provide you with details on hiking in the area; the forest's main office is open weekdays 8 to 4:30.

Mount Elden Trail System. Most trails in the 35-mi-long Mount Elden Trail System lead to views from the dormant volcanic field, across the vast ponderosa pine forest, all the way to Sedona. The most challenging trail in the Mount Elden system, which happens to be the route with the most rewarding views, is along the steep switchbacks of the **Elden Lookout Trail** (⌂ *Off U.S. 89, 3 mi east of downtown Flagstaff*). If you traverse the full 3 mi to the top, keep your focus on the landscape rather than the tangle of antennae and satellite dishes that greets you at the top. The 4-mi-long **Sunset Trail** (⌂ *Off U.S. 180, 3 mi north of downtown Flagstaff, then 6 mi east on FR 420/Schultz Pass Rd.*) proceeds with a gradual pitch through the pine forest, emerging onto a narrow ridge nicknamed the Catwalk. By all means take pictures of the stunning valley views, but make sure your feet are well placed. The access road to this trail is closed in winter.

Flagstaff is in the **Peaks District** (⌂ *Peaks Ranger Station, 5075 N. U.S. 89, East Flagstaff* ☎ *928/526–0866*) of the Coconino National Forest, and there are many trails to explore. The **Humphreys Peak Trail** (⌂ *Trailhead: Snowbowl Rd., 7 mi north of U.S. 180*) is 9 mi round-trip, with a vertical climb of 3,843 feet to the summit of Arizona's highest mountain (12,643 feet). Those who don't want a long hike can do just the first mile of the adjacent, 5-mi-long **Kachina Trail**

(⊠*Trailhead: Snowbowl Rd., 7 mi north of U.S. 180*); gently rolling, this route is surrounded by huge stands of aspen and offers fantastic vistas. In fall, changing leaves paint the landscape shades of yellow, russet, and amber.

HORSEBACK RIDING

The wranglers at **Hitchin' Post Stables** (⊠*4848 Lake Mary Rd., South Flagstaff* ☎928/774–1719) lead rides into Walnut Canyon and operate horseback or horse-drawn wagon rides with sunset barbecues. In winter they'll take you through Coconino National Forest on a sleigh.

MOUNTAIN BIKING

With more than 30 mi of challenging trails a short ride from town, it was inevitable that one of Flagstaff's best-kept secrets would leak out. The mountain biking on Mount Elden is on par with that of more celebrated trails in Colorado and Utah.

The **Coconino National Forest** has some of the best trails in the region. A good place to start is the **Lower Oldham Trail** (⊠*Trailhead: Cedar St.*), which originates on the north end of Buffalo Park in Flagstaff; there's a large meadow with picnic areas and an exercise path. The terrain rolls, climbing about 800 feet in 3 mi, and the trail is technical in spots but easy enough to test your tolerance of the elevation. Many fun trails spur off this one. They're all hemmed in by roads and cabins so it's difficult to get too lost.

The very popular **Schultz Creek Trail** (⊠*Trailhead: Schultz Pass Rd., near intersection with U.S. 180*) is fun and suitable for strong beginners, although seasoned experts will be thrilled as well. Most opt to start at the top of the 600-foot-high hill and swoop down the smooth, twisting path through groves of wildflowers and stands of ponderosa pines and aspens, ending at the trailhead four giddy miles later.

Sunset Trail (⊠*Trailhead: Elden Lookout Rd., 7 mi from intersection with Schultz Pass Rd.*), near the summit of Mount Elden, affords amazing views off the ridge rendered barren by a 1977 fire. The trail narrows into the aptly nicknamed Catwalk, with precipitous drops a few feet on either side. Fear, either from the 9,000-foot elevation or the sheer exposure, is not an option. You need to be at least a moderately experienced mountain biker to attempt this trail. When combined with Elden Lookout Road and Schultz Creek Trail, the usual loop, the trail totals 15 mi and climbs almost 2,000 feet. You can avoid the slog up Mount Elden by parking one vehicle at the top of Elden Lookout Road, at the trailhead, and a friend's vehicle at the bottom.

You can rent mountain bikes, get good advice, and purchase trail maps at **Absolute Bikes** (⊠*200 E. Rte. 66, Downtown* ☎928/779–5969). From mid-June through mid-October, the **Flagstaff Nordic Center** (⊠*U.S. 180, 16 mi north of Flagstaff, North Flagstaff* ☎928/220–0550 ⊕*www.flag staffnordiccenter.com*) opens its cross-country trails to mountain bikers. A map of the **Urban Trails System,** available at the Flagstaff Visitor Center (⊠*1 E. Rte. 66, Downtown* ☎928/774–9541 *or* 800/842–7293), details biking options in town.

ROCK CLIMBING

Vertical Relief Rock Gym (⊠*205 S. San Francisco St., Downtown* ☎*928/556–9909*) has the tallest indoor climbing walls in the Southwest, as well as climbing excursions throughout the Flagstaff area.

SKIING AND SNOWBOARDING

The ski season usually starts in mid-December and ends in mid-April. The **Arizona Snowbowl** (⊠*Snowbowl Rd., North Flagstaff* ☎*928/779–1951, 928/779–4577 snow report* ⊕*www.arizonasnowbowl.com*), 7 mi north of Flagstaff off U.S. 180, has 32 downhill runs (37% beginner, 42% intermediate, and 21% advanced), four chairlifts, and a vertical drop of 2,300 feet. There are a couple of good bump runs, but it's better for beginners or those with moderate skill; serious area skiers take a road trip to Telluride. Still, it's a fun place to ski or snowboard. The Hart Prairie Lodge has an equipment-rental shop and a SKIwee center for ages 4 to 7. All-day adult lift tickets are $49. Half-day discounts are available, and group-lesson packages (including two hours of instruction, an all-day lift ticket, and equipment rental) are a good buy at $74. A children's program (which includes progress card and full supervision 9–3:30) runs $70. Many Flagstaff motels offer ski packages, including transportation to Snowbowl.

The **Flagstaff Nordic Center** (⊠*U.S. 180, 16 mi north of Flagstaff, North Flagstaff* ☎*928/220–0550* ⊕*www.flagstaffnordiccenter.com*) is 9 mi north of Snowbowl Road. There are 25 mi of well-groomed cross-country trails here that are open from 8 to 4 daily, with longer hours on Friday (6 to 9). Coffee, hot chocolate, and snacks are served at the lodge. You can also buy sleds for a nearby run called Crowley Pit. A day pass for skiing costs $12 on weekdays and $15 on weekends. Friday evening trail passes cost $10. An instruction package costs $45, including equipment. Renting equipment by itself is $15.

TOURS

The **Ventures** program, run by the education department of the Museum of Northern Arizona (☎*928/774–5213* ⊕*www.musnaz.org*), offers tours of the area led by local scientists, artists, and historians. Trips might include rafting excursions down the San Juan River, treks into the Grand Canyon or Colorado Plateau backcountry, or bus tours into the Navajo reservation to visit with Native American artists. Prices start at about $160 for cultural tours and go up to $1,250 for outdoor adventures, with most tours in the $750 to $850 range.

WHERE TO EAT

$
AMERICAN

✕**Beaver Street Brewery and Whistle Stop Cafe.** Popular among the wood-fired pizzas is the Enchanted Forest, with Brie, portobello mushrooms, roasted red peppers, spinach, and artichoke pesto. Whichever pie you order, expect serious amounts of garlic. Sandwiches, such as the Southwestern chicken with three types of cheese, come with a hefty portion of tasty fries. You won't regret ordering one of the down-home desserts, like the super-gooey chocolate bread pudding. Among the excellent microbrews usually on tap, the raspberry ale is a local favorite. ⊠*11 S.*

Beaver St., Downtown ☎*928/779–0079* ⊕*www.beaverstreetbrewery. com* ▭*AE, D, DC, MC, V.*

$$$ ✕ **Black Bart's Steakhouse Saloon.** The Wild West decor at this rollick-
AMERICAN   ing, brightly lit barn of a restaurant is a bit cornball, but the barbe-
cued chicken is tender and flavorful; just don't expect to see vegetables
on your plate unless they're deep-fried. Northern Arizona University
music students entertain while they wait on tables, so don't be sur-
prised if your server suddenly jumps onstage to belt out a couple of
show tunes. ✉*2760 E. Butler Ave., Downtown* ☎*928/779–3142 or
800/574–4718* ⊕*www.blackbartssteakhouse.com* ▭*AE, D, DC, MC,
V* ⊙*No lunch.*

¢–$ ✕ **Bun Huggers.** Since 1979 the best burger in town has been flipped
AMERICAN   over a mesquite-fired grill at this no-frills joint. Also try the tasty, if
decadent, deep-fried zucchini served with shredded cheddar cheese and
ranch dressing. There's a small salad bar here, but it seems like an after-
thought, existing only to appease guilty consciences. ✉*901 S. Milton
Rd., University* ☎*928/779–3743* ▭*AE, D, MC, V.*

$$ ✕ **Buster's Restaurant.** At lunchtime, families and students from nearby
AMERICAN   Northern Arizona University settle into comfy booths to enjoy fresh sea-
food, homemade soups, salads, giant burgers, and steaks. What better
environment in which to ask Mom or Dad for some extra money, or to
discuss those first-semester grades? Try the *lahvosh* appetizer—a huge
cracker heaped with toppings ranging from smoked salmon to mushrooms—or the Caesar salad with grilled Cajun chicken. At night single
professionals and skiers crowd the bar and work through its impressive beer selection. ✉*1800 S. Milton Rd., University* ☎*928/774–5155*
⊕*www.busters-restaurant.com* ▭*AE, D, DC, MC, V.*

¢–$ ✕ **Café Espress.** The menu is largely vegetarian at this natural-foods
CAFÉ   restaurant. Stir-fried vegetables, pasta, Mediterranean salads, tempeh
burgers, pita pizzas, fish or chicken specials for lunch, and wonderful
baked goods made on the premises all come at prices that will make you
feel good, too. This hip and friendly place opens for breakfast every day
at 7. ✉*16 N. San Francisco St., Downtown* ☎*928/774–0541* ▭*AE,
MC, V* ⊙*No dinner.*

$$$ ✕ **Cottage Place.** Regarded by locals as one of the best fine-dining ven-
CONTINENTAL   ues in the area, this restaurant in a cottage built in 1909 has intimate
★   dining rooms and an extensive wine list. The menu strays slightly from
Continental to include some classic American dishes, such as char-
broiled lamb chops. The grilled herb salmon and the chateaubriand
for two are recommended. Dinner includes soup and salad, but save
room for chocolate decadence. ✉*126 W. Cottage Ave., Downtown*
☎*928/774–8431* ⊕*www.cottageplace.com* ▭*AE, MC, V* ⊙*Closed
Mon. and Tues. No lunch.*

¢   ✕ **La Bellavia.** At this favorite bohemian breakfast and lunch nook the
CAFÉ   trout and eggs platter is the standard—two eggs served with Idaho trout
★   flavored with a hint of lemon, rounded off by a buttermilk pancake.
Other options include Swedish oat pancakes, seven-grain French toast,
and 10 varieties of eggs Benedict. A palette of creative sandwiches and
familiar salads makes this a worthwhile lunch stop as well. The café
doubles as a gallery for local artists, whose work hangs on the walls.

✉*18 S. Beaver St., Downtown* ☎*928/774–8301* ⊕*www.labellavia restaurant.com* ☐*MC, V* ⊗*No dinner.*

$$–$$$
ITALIAN

✗**Pasto.** This downtown Italian restaurant—two intimate dining rooms in adjacent historic buildings—is popular for good food at reasonable prices. Southern Italian standards like lasagna and spaghetti with meatballs are on the menu along with more innovative fare, such as artichoke orzo. A courtyard in the back, tucked among higher buildings, has a romantic urban feel. ✉*19 E. Aspen St., Downtown* ☎*928/779–1937* ⊕*www.pastorestaurant.com* ☐*D, MC, V* ⊗*Closed Tues.*

$
MEXICAN

✗**Salsa Brava.** This cheerful Mexican restaurant, with light-wood booths and colorful designs, eschews heavy Sonoran-style fare in favor of the grilled dishes found in Guadalajara. It's considered the best Mexican food in town—but there's not much competition. The fish tacos are particularly good. Or wake up your taste buds with a breakfast of huevos rancheros. ✉*2220 E. Rte. 66, East* ☎*928/779–5293* ⊕*www. salsabravaflagstaff.com* ☐*AE, D, MC, V.*

WHERE TO STAY

Trains pass through the downtown area along Route 66 (also called Santa Fe Avenue) about every 15 minutes throughout the day and night. Light sleepers may prefer to stay in the south or east sections of town to avoid hearing trains rumbling through; at least the whistles are no longer blown within the downtown district.

$$
⌂**Abineau Lodge.** This contemporary mountain inn with a rustic feel is on 4 acres bordering the immense Coconino National Forest. Two separate living rooms, one on each level, and a deck for stargazing make for a comfortable retreat. A big draw here for dog-lovers is playing with the pack of retired sled dogs, the owners' well-loved Siberian huskies. **Pros:** pleasant common areas; hot tub and sauna. **Cons:** seven miles south of town; huskies howl "The Siberian Serenade" in early morning. ✉*10155 Mountainaire Rd., South Flagstaff* ☎*928/525–6212 or 888/715–6386* ⊕*www.abineaulodge.com* ☞*8 rooms, 2 suites* ☖*In-room: no TV. In-hotel: no kids under 8, no-smoking rooms, Wi-Fi* ☐*AE, D, MC, V* ⊠*BP.*

¢–$
⌂**Hotel Weatherford.** With a columned veranda, this hotel, built in 1897, is a dramatic presence at the hub of town. Imbued with a creaky charm, some rooms are spartan and a bit worn around the edges but comfortable. Three rooms with a shared bath are an especially good value. Forgo TV, telephones, and reliable hot water for a taste of the Old West. The two clubs downstairs have a bustling nightlife scene. **Pros:** historical charm mixes with a cool music scene. **Cons:** guests will hear noise from bars until the wee hours; dated plumbing; no elevator (all rooms require climbing one or two flights of stairs). ✉*23 N. Leroux St., Downtown* ☎*928/779–1919* ⊕*www.weatherfordhotel.com* ☞*10 rooms, 7 with bath* ☖*In-room: no a/c, no phone, no TV. In-hotel: restaurant, bars* ☐*AE, D, DC, MC, V.*

$$–$$$
⌂**Inn at 410.** This downtown B&B is an inviting alternative to Flag's chain motels. All the accommodations in the beautifully restored 1907 residence are suites with private baths and fireplaces. Pancakes with

A visit to Meteor Crater complements Arizona's many observatories for a different look at the impact of the heavens.

blue cornmeal and piñon nuts, and curried cornbread pudding with pumpkin sauce highlight a tantalizing breakfast menu. No kids under 10 allowed in some rooms. **Pros:** convenient downtown location, complimentary cookies and cocktails every afternoon. **Cons:** noise from next-door restaurant and train in some rooms, inconsistent hospitality. ✉ *410 N. Leroux St., Downtown* ☎ *928/774–0088 or 800/774–2008* ⊕ *www.inn410.com* ᴖ *9 suites* ⚬ *In-room: no phone, refrigerator, DVD. In-hotel: no-smoking rooms* ▤ *MC, V* ⑴ *BP.*

$$ 🔲 **Little America of Flagstaff.** The biggest hotel in town is deservedly popu-
★ lar. It's a little distance from the roar of the trains, the grounds are surrounded by evergreen forests, and it's one of the few places in Flagstaff with room service. Plush rooms have comfortable sitting areas with French provincial–style furniture. Other pluses are an above-average in-house restaurant, courtesy van service to the airport and the Amtrak station, and a gift shop with great Southwestern stuff. **Pros:** large, very clean rooms; many amenities including walking trails. **Cons:** large-scale property can feel impersonal. ✉ *2515 E. Butler Ave., Downtown* ☎ *928/779–2741 or 800/352–4386* ⊕ *www.littleamerica.com/flagstaff* ᴖ *247 rooms* ⚬ *In-room: kitchen (some), refrigerator, safe, Wi-Fi. In-hotel: restaurant, room service, bar, pool, gym, laundry facilities, laundry service* ▤ *AE, D, DC, MC, V.*

$$ 🔲 **Starlight Pines Bed and Breakfast.** If you prefer the clean lines of 1920s design to Victorian froufrou, consider staying at this stylish B&B on the city's east side. Guest rooms are lovely, with art deco pieces including Tiffany lamps and other antiques. Enjoy a soak in your claw-foot tub after a day's hike. **Pros:** pretty, immaculate rooms; very hospitable hosts. **Cons:** a short drive from downtown; train whistles can still be heard. ⊠*3380 E. Lockett Rd., East Flagstaff* ☎*928/527–1912 or 800/752–1912* ⊕*www.starlightpinesbb.com* ☞*4 rooms* ♿*In-room: no TV, Wi-Fi. In-hotel: no kids under 10, no-smoking rooms* ▭*D, MC, V* |◎|*BP.*

NIGHTLIFE AND THE ARTS

THE ARTS

There is no shortage of cultural entertainment in Flagstaff, including several summer festivals.

Flagstaff Cultural Partners/Coconino Center for the Arts (⊠*2300 N. Fort Valley Rd., North Flagstaff* ☎*928/779–2300* ⊕*www.culturalpartners.org*) has gallery space for exhibitions, a theater, and performance space. The **Flagstaff Symphony Orchestra** (☎*928/774–5107* ⊕*www.flagstaffsymphony. org*) has year-round musical events. The 1917 **Orpheum Theater** (⊠*15 W. Aspen St., Downtown* ☎*928/556–1580* ⊕*www.orpheumpresents. com*) features music acts, films, lectures, and plays. **Theatrikos Theatre Company** (⊠*11 W. Cherry Ave., Downtown* ☎*928/774–1662* ⊕*www. theatrikos.com*) is a highly regarded performance-art group.

A Celebration of Native American Art (⊠*3101 N. Fort Valley Rd., North Flagstaff* ☎*928/774–5211*), featuring exhibits of work by Zuni, Hopi, and Navajo artists, is held at the Museum of Northern Arizona from late May through September.

NIGHTLIFE

Flagstaff's large college contingent has plenty of places to gather after dark; most are in historic downtown and most charge little or no cover. It's easy to walk from one rowdy spot to the next. For information on what's going on, pick up the free *Flagstaff Live*.

The **Hotel Weatherford** (⊠*23 N. Leroux St., Downtown* ☎*928/779–1919*) has a double bill: Charly's hosts late-night jazz and blues bands; the Exchange Pub tends to attract folksy ensembles. **Flagstaff's Green Room** (⊠*15 N. Agassiz St., Downtown* ☎*928/226–8669*), an environmentally conscious bar, rolls out an eclectic mix of live music and hardy stout nightly until 2 AM. The **Monte Vista Lounge** (⊠*100 N. San Francisco St., Downtown* ☎*928/774–2403*) packs 'em in with nightly live blues, jazz, classic rock, and punk. **San Felipe's Coastal Cantina** (⊠*103 N. Leroux, Downtown* ☎*928/779–6000*) is the place for tequila, fish tacos, dancing, and a raucous spring-break atmosphere.

SHOPPING

For fine arts and crafts—everything from ceramics and stained glass to weaving and painting—visit the **Artists Gallery** (⊠*17 N. San Francisco St., Downtown* ☎*928/773–0958*), a local artists' cooperative. **Babbitt's Backcountry Outfitters** (⊠*12 E. Aspen Ave., Downtown* ☎*928/774–4775*) is the place to pick up any sporting-goods needs. The **Black Hound Gallerie** (⊠*120 N. Leroux St., Downtown* ☎*928/774–2323*) specializes in posters, prints, and funky kitsch of all kinds. **Bookman's** (⊠*1520 S. Riordan Ranch Rd., University* ☎*928/774–0005*) is packed solid with used books on every topic; a cybercafé and live folk music occupy a corner of the store. **Carriage House Antique & Gift Mall** (⊠*413 N. San*

4

Francisco St., Downtown ☎928/774–1337) has 20-odd vendors selling vintage clothing and jewelry, furniture, fine china, and other collectibles. The **Museum of Northern Arizona Gift Shop** (⊠3101 N. Fort Valley Rd., University ☎928/774–5213) carries high-quality jewelry and crafts. **Winter Sun Trading Company** (⊠107 N. San Francisco St., Downtown ☎928/774–2884) sells medicinal herbs, unique fragrances, jewelry, and crafts. **Zani** (⊠9 N. Leroux St., Downtown ☎928/774–9409) stocks hip home furnishings, handmade paper, and greeting cards.

SIDE TRIPS NEAR FLAGSTAFF

Travelers heading straight through town bound for the Grand Canyon often neglect the area north and east of Flagstaff, but a detour has its rewards. If you don't have time to do everything, take a quick drive to Walnut Canyon—it's only about 15 minutes out of town.

EAST OF FLAGSTAFF

⑨ Walnut Canyon National Monument
★ consists of a group of cliff dwellings constructed by the Sinagua people, who lived and farmed in and around the canyon starting around AD 700. The more than 300 dwellings here were built between 1080 and 1250, and abandoned, like those at so many other settlements in Arizona and New Mexico, around 1300. The Sinagua traded far and wide with other Native Americans, including people at Wupatki. Even macaw feathers, which would have come from tribes in what is now Mexico, have been excavated in the canyon. Early Flagstaff settlers looted the site for pots and "treasure"; Woodrow Wilson declared this a national monument in 1915, which began a 30-year process of stabilizing the site.

> **WORD OF MOUTH**
>
> "Walnut Canyon was amazing—the cliffs are very protected so the cliff dwellings have been well preserved as compared to some of the sites we have visited which were just out on the open mesa. It is a reasonable hike to the bottom of the canyon, but very worthwhile."   —mykidssherpa

Part of the fascination of Walnut Canyon is the opportunity to enter the dwellings, stepping back in time to an ancient way of life. Some of the Sinagua homes are in near-perfect condition in spite of all the looting, because of the dry, hot climate and the protection of overhanging cliffs. You can reach them by descending 185 feet on the 1-mi stepped **Island Trail,** which starts at the visitor center. As you follow the trail, look across the canyon for other dwellings not accessible on the path. Island Trail takes about an hour to complete at a normal pace. Those with health concerns should opt for the easier ½-mi **Rim Trail,** which has overlooks from which dwellings, as well as an excavated, reconstructed pit house, can be viewed. Picnic areas dot the grounds and line the roads leading to the park. ■**TIP➔**Wear layers, as the climate can change quickly. Guides conduct tours on Wednesday, Saturday, and Sunday from late May through early September. ⊠ *Walnut Canyon Rd.,*

3 mi south of I–40, Exit 204, Winona ☎928/526–3367 ⊕www.nps.gov/waca ☜$5 ⊙Nov.–Apr., daily 9–5; May–Oct., daily 8–5.

❿ Meteor Crater, a natural phenomenon in a privately owned park 43 mi east of Flagstaff, is impressive if for no other reason than its sheer size. A hole in the ground 600 feet deep, nearly 1 mi across, and more than 3 mi in circumference, Meteor Crater is large enough to accommodate the Washington Monument or 20 football fields. It was created by a meteorite crash 49,000 years ago. The area looks so much like the surface of the moon that NASA made it one of the official training sites for the Project Apollo astronauts. You can't descend into the crater because of the efforts of its owners to maintain its condition—

THE SINAGUA PEOPLE

The achievements of the Sinagua people, who lived in north-central Arizona from the 8th through the 15th centuries, reached their height in the 12th and 13th centuries, when related groups occupied most of the San Francisco Volcanic Field and a large portion of the upper and middle Verde Valley. The Sinagua sites around modern-day Camp Verde, Clarkdale, and Flagstaff provide a window onto this remarkable culture. Some of the best examples of surviving Sinagua architecture can be found at Walnut Canyon and Wupatki National Monument, northeast of Flagstaff.

scientists consider this to be the best-preserved crater on Earth—but guided rim tours, given every hour on the hour from 9 to 3, give useful background information. There's a small snack bar, and the Rock Shop sells specimens from the area and jewelry made from native stones. Take Interstate 40 east of Flagstaff to Exit 233, then drive 6 mi south on Meteor Crater Road. ⊠*Meteor Crater Rd. (43 mi east of Flagstaff), Winslow* ☎*928/289–5898 or 800/289–5898* ⊕*www.meteorcrater.com* ☜*$15* ⊙*June–Aug., daily 7–7; Sept.–May, daily 8–5.*

SAN FRANCISCO VOLCANIC FIELD

The San Francisco Volcanic Field north of Flagstaff encompasses 2,000 square mi of fascinating geological phenomena, including ancient volcanoes, cinder cones, valleys carved by water and ice, and the San Francisco Peaks themselves, some of which soar to almost 13,000 feet. There are also some of the most extensive Native American dwellings in the Southwest: don't miss Sunset Crater and Wupatki. These national monuments can be explored in relative solitude during much of the year. ■TIP➔The area is short on services, so fill up on gas and consider taking a picnic.

⓫ Sunset Crater Volcano National Monument lies 14 mi northeast of Flagstaff ★ off U.S. 89. Sunset Crater, a cinder cone that rises 1,000 feet, was an active volcano 900 years ago. Its final eruption contained iron and sulfur, which give the rim of the crater its glow and thus its name. You can walk around the base, but you can't descend into the huge, fragile cone. The **Lava Flow Trail,** a half-hour, mile-long, self-guided walk, provides a good view of the evidence of the volcano's fiery power: lava formations and holes in the rock where volcanic gases vented to the surface.

If you're interested in hiking a volcano, head to **Lenox Crater,** about 1 mi east of the visitor center, and climb the 280 feet to the top of the cinder cone. The cinder is soft and crumbly, so wear closed, sturdy shoes. From **O'Leary Peak,** 5 mi from the visitor center on Forest Route 545A, enjoy great views of the San Francisco Peaks, the Painted Desert, and beyond. The road is unpaved and rutted, though, so it's advisable to take only high-clearance vehicles, especially in winter. In addition, there's a gate, about halfway along the route, which is usually closed, and when it is it means a steep 2½-mi hike to the top on foot. To get to the area from Flagstaff, take Santa Fe Avenue east to U.S. 89, and head north for 12 mi; turn right onto the road marked Sunset Crater and go another 2 mi to the visitor center. ⊠*Sunset Crater–Wupatki Loop Rd., 14 mi northeast of Flagstaff* ☎*928/556–0502* ⊕*www.nps.gov/sucr* ⊠*$5, including Wupatki National Monument and Doney Mountain* ☉*Nov.–Apr., daily 9–5; May–Oct., daily 8–5.*

⓬ ★ Families from the Sinagua and other Ancestral Puebloans are believed to have lived together in harmony on the site that is now **Wupatki National Monument,** farming and trading with one another and with those who passed through. The eruption of Sunset Crater may have influenced migration to this area a century after the event, as freshly laid volcanic cinders held in moisture needed for crops. Although there's evidence of earlier habitation, most of the settlers moved here around 1100 and left the pueblo by about 1250. The 2,700 identified sites contain archaeological evidence of a Native American settlement.

The national monument was named for the Wupatki (meaning "tall house" in Hopi) site, which was originally three stories high, built above an unexplored system of underground fissures. The structure had almost 100 rooms and an open ball court—evidence of Southwestern trade with Mesoamerican tribes for whom ball games were a central ritual. Next to the ball court is a blowhole, a geologic phenomenon in which air is forced upward by underground pressure.

Other sites to visit are Wukoki, Lomaki, and the Citadel, a pueblo on a knoll above a limestone sink. Although the largest remnants of Native American settlements at Wupatki National Monument are open to the public, other sites are off-limits. If you're interested in an in-depth tour, consider a ranger-led overnight hike to the **Crack-in-Rock Ruin.** The 14-mi (round-trip) trek covers areas marked by ancient petroglyphs and dotted with well-preserved sites. The trips are only conducted in April and October; call by February or August if you'd like to take part in the lottery for one of the 100 available places on these $50 hikes. Between the Wupatki and Citadel ruins, the **Doney Mountain** affords 360-degree

Sedona Vortex Tour

CLOSE UP

What is a vortex? The word "vortex" comes from the Latin *vertere*, which means "to turn or whirl." In Sedona, a vortex is a funnel created by the motion of spiraling energy. Sedona has long been believed to be a center for spiritual power because of the vortexes of subtle energy in the area. This energy isn't described as electricity or magnetism, though it's said to leave a slight residual magnetism in the places where it's strongest.

New Agers believe there are four major vortexes in Sedona: Airport, Cathedral Rock, Boynton Canyon, and Bell Rock. Each manifests a different kind of energy, and this energy interacts with the individual in its presence. People come from all over the world to experience these energy forms, hoping for guidance in spiritual matters, health, and relationships.

Juniper trees, which are all over the Sedona area, are said to respond to vortex energy in a way that reveals where this energy is strongest. The stronger the energy, the more axial twist the junipers bear in their branches.

Airport Vortex is said to strengthen one's "masculine" side, aiding in self-confidence and focus. **Cathedral Rock Vortex** nurtures one's "feminine" aspects, such as patience and kindness. You'll be directed to **Boynton Canyon Vortex** if you're seeking balance between the masculine and feminine. And finally **Bell Rock Vortex**, the most powerful of all, strengthens all three aspects: masculine, feminine, and balance.

These energy centers are easily accessed, and vortex maps are available at crystal shops all over Sedona.

views of the Painted Desert and the San Francisco Volcanic Field. It's a perfect spot for a sunset picnic. In summer, rangers give lectures. ⊠ *Sunset Crater–Wupatki Loop Rd., 19 mi north of Sunset Crater visitor center* ☎ *928/679–2365* ⊕ *www.nps.gov/wupa* ⊠ *$5, including Sunset Crater National Monument and Doney Mountain* ⊙ *Daily 9–5.*

SEDONA AND OAK CREEK CANYON

119 mi north of Phoenix, I–17 to AZ 179 to AZ 89A; 60 mi northeast of Prescott, U.S. 89 to AZ 89A; 27 mi south of Flagstaff on AZ 89A.

It's easy to see what draws so many people to Sedona. Red-rock buttes—Cathedral Rock, Bear Mountain, Courthouse Rock, and Bell Rock, among others—reach up into an almost always blue sky, and both colors are intensified by dark-green pine forests. Surrealist Max Ernst, writer Zane Grey, and many filmmakers drew inspiration from these vistas—more than 80 Westerns were shot in the area in the 1940s and '50s alone.

These days, Sedona lures enterprising restaurateurs and gallery owners from the East and West coasts. New Age followers, who believe that the area contains some of the Earth's more important vortexes (energy centers), also come in great numbers believing that the "vibe" here confers a sense of balance and well-being, and enhances creativity.

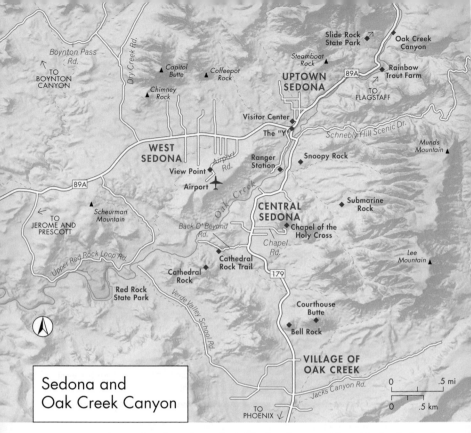

Sedona and
Oak Creek Canyon

Expansion since the early 1980s has been rapid, and lack of planning has taken its toll in unattractive developments and increased traffic. The town has been chosen to take part in the federally sponsored Main Street program, which means, among other things, that a number of Red Rock Territorial–style buildings in the Uptown section will be preserved and that a separate parking district will be built.

The town itself is young, and there are few historic sites; the main downtown activity is shopping, mostly for Southwestern-style paintings, clothing, rugs, jewelry, and Native American artifacts. Just beyond the shops and restaurants, however, canyons, creeks, ancient dwellings, and the red rocks beckon. The area is easy to hike or bike, or you can take a jeep tour.

GETTING HERE AND AROUND

Sedona stretches along AZ 89A, its main thoroughfare, which runs roughly east–west through town. To reach Sedona more directly from Phoenix, take Interstate 17 north for 113 mi until you come to AZ 179; it's another 15 mi on that road into town. The trip should take about 2½ hours. The 27-mi drive from Sedona to Flagstaff on AZ 89A, which winds its way through Oak Creek Canyon, is breathtaking.

Sedona Airport, in West Sedona, is a base for several air tours but has no regularly scheduled flights.

The Sedona–Phoenix Shuttle makes eight trips daily between those cities; the fare is $45 one-way, $85 round-trip. You can also get on or off at Camp Verde, Cottonwood, or the Village of Oak Creek. Reservations are required.

Weekend traffic near Sedona, especially during the high season, can approach gridlock on the narrow highways. Leave for your destination at first light to bypass the day-trippers, late risers, and midday heat.

Sedona is roughly divided into three neighborhoods: Uptown, which is a walkable shopping district; West Sedona, which is a 4-mi-long commercial strip; and Central Sedona, which encompasses everything south of the "Y" where AZ 179 and AZ 89A intersect.

Sedona Trolley offers two types of daily orientation tours, both departing from the main bus stop in Uptown and lasting less than an hour. One goes along AZ 179 to the Chapel of the Holy Cross, with stops at Tlaquepaque and some galleries; the other passes through West Sedona to Boynton Canyon (Enchantment Resort). Rates are $12 for one or $21 for both.

If you want to explore the red rocks of Sedona, you can rent a four-wheel drive from one of the local agencies such as Farabee's Jeep Rentals.

PLANNING YOUR TIME

In warmer months visit air-conditioned shops at midday and do hiking and jeep tours in the early morning or late afternoon, when the light is softer and the heat less oppressive. Many of the most memorable spots in Sedona are considered energy centers; vortex maps of the area are available at most of Sedona's New Age stores.

The vistas of Sedona from Airport Mesa at sunset can't be beat. The Upper Red Rock Loop has great photo opportunities.

You might want to drive out to Boynton Canyon, sacred to the Yavapai Apache, who believe it was their ancient birthplace. This is also the site of the Enchantment Resort, where all are welcome to hike the canyon and stop in for lunch or a late-afternoon drink on the terrace.

ESSENTIALS

Transportation Contacts Farabee's Jeep Rentals (☎ *928/282–8700* ⊕ *www. sedonajeeprentals.com).* **Sedona Airport** (☎ *928/282–4487).* **Sedona– Phoenix Shuttle Service** (☎ *928/282–2066, 800/448–7988 in Arizona* ⊕ *www. sedona-phoenix-shuttle.com).* **Sedona Taxi** (☎ *928/204–9111).* **Sedona Trolley** (☎ *928/282–4211* ⊕ *www.sedonatrolley.com)*

Visitor Info Sedona Visitor Center (✉ *331 Forest Rd., just off AZ89A* ☎ *928/282–7722 or 800/288–7336* ⊕ *www.visitsedona.com)*.

EXPLORING

TOP ATTRACTIONS

Bell Rock. With its distinctive shape right out of your favorite Western film and its proximity to the main drag ensuring a steady flow of admirers, you may want to arrive early to see this popular butte. The parking lot next to the Bell Rock Pathway often fills by mid-morning even midweek. The views from here are good, but an easy and fairly accessible path follows mostly gentle terrain for 1 mi to the base of the butte. Mountain bikers, parents with all-terrain baby strollers, and not-so-avid hikers should have little problem getting there. No official paths climb the rock itself, but many forge their own routes (at their own risk). ⊠ *AZ 179, several hundred yards north of Bell Rock Blvd., Village of Oak Creek.*

Cathedral Rock. It's almost impossible not to be drawn to this butte's towering, variegated spires. The approximately 1,200-foot-high Cathedral Rock looms dramatically over town. When you emerge from the narrow gorge of Oak Creek Canyon, this is the first recognizable formation you'll spot. ■TIP➔The butte is best seen toward dusk from a distance. Hikers may want to drive to the Airport Mesa and then hike the rugged but generally flat path that loops around the airfield. The trail is ½ mi up Airport Road off AZ 89A in West Sedona; the reward is a panoramic view of Cathedral Rock without the crowds. Those not hiking should drive through the Village of Oak Creek, and 5 mi west on Verde Valley School Road to its end, where you can view the butte from a beautiful streamside vantage point and take a dip in Oak Creek if you wish. ⊠ *5 mi to end of Verde Valley School Rd., west off AZ 179, Village of Oak Creek.*

FLAGSTAFF AND SEDONA
There might only be 30 mi separating Flagstaff and Sedona, but they're very different places. Flagstaff's natural terrain and earthiness lend a "granola-y" feel to the city, and the Northern Arizona University students here enhance it. Meanwhile, Sedona's beauty is no secret, and residents (full- and part-time) pay a premium to enjoy it.

Cathedral Rock Trail. A vigorous but nontechnical 1½-mi scramble up the slickrock (smooth, rather than slippery, sandstone), this path leads to a nearly 360-degree view of red-rock country. Follow the cairns (rock piles marking the trail) and look for the footholds in the rock. Carry plenty of water: though short, the trail offers little shade and the pitch is steep. You can see the Verde Valley and Mingus Mountain in the distance. Look for the barely discernible "J" etched on the hillside marking the former ghost town of Jerome 30 mi distant. ⊠ *Trailhead: About ½ mi down Back O' Beyond Rd. off AZ 179, 3 mi south of Sedona.*

Chapel of the Holy Cross. You needn't be religious to be inspired by the setting and the architecture here. Built in 1956 by Marguerite Brunwige Staude, a student of Frank Lloyd Wright, this modern landmark, with a huge cross on the facade, rises between two red-rock peaks. Vistas of the town and the surrounding area are spectacular. Though there is only one regular service—Monday at 5 PM—all are welcome for quiet meditation. A small gift shop sells religious artifacts and books. A trail east of the chapel leads you—after a 20-minute walk over occasional loose-rock surfaces—to a seat surrounded by voluptuous red-limestone walls, worlds away from the bustle and commerce around the chapel. ⊠ *Chapel Rd., off AZ 179, Village of Oak Creek* ☎ *928/282–4069* ⊕ *www.chapeloftheholycross.com* ⊠ *Free* ⊙ *Daily 9–5.*

DID YOU KNOW?

Between Flagstaff and Sedona, route 89A runs through Oak Creek Canyon. Over time, softer rock has eroded to carve out the canyon and create the dramatic rock formations you see today.

★ **Oak Creek Canyon.** Whether you want to swim, hike, picnic, or enjoy beautiful scenery framed through a car window, head north through the wooded Oak Creek Canyon. It's the most scenic route to Flagstaff and the Grand Canyon, and worth a drive-through even if you're not heading north. The road winds through a steep-walled canyon, where you crane your neck for views of the dramatic rock formations above. Although the forest is primarily evergreen, the fall foliage is glorious. Oak Creek, which runs along the bottom, is lined with tent campgrounds, fishing camps, cabins, motels, and restaurants. ⊠ *AZ 89A, beginning 1 mi north of Sedona, Oak Creek Canyon.*

ⓒ **Slide Rock State Park.** A good place for a picnic, Slide Rock is 7 mi north of Sedona. On a hot day you can plunge down a natural rock slide into a swimming hole (bring an extra pair of jeans or a sturdy bathing suit and river shoes to wear on the slide). The site started as an early-20th-century apple orchard, and the natural beauty attracted Hollywood—a number of John Wayne and Jimmy Stewart movies were filmed here. A few easy hikes run along the rim of the gorge. Fly-fishing for trout is possible when it's too cold for swimming. One downside is the traffic, particularly on summer weekends; you might have to wait to get into the park after mid-morning. Unfortunately, the popularity of the stream has led to the occasional midsummer closing due to E. coli–bacteria infestations; the water is tested daily and there is a water-quality hotline at 602/542–0202. ⊠ *6871 N. AZ 89A, Oak Creek Canyon* ☎ *928/282–3034* ⊕ *www.azstateparks.com* ⊠ *$10 per vehicle for up to 4 persons* ☉ *Labor Day–Memorial Day, daily 8–5; Memorial Day–Labor Day, daily 8–7.*

ⓒ **Snoopy Rock.** Kids love this: when you look almost directly to the east, this butte really does look like the famed Peanuts beagle lying atop red rock instead of his doghouse. You can distinguish the formation from several places around town, including the mall in Uptown Sedona, but to get a clear view, venture up Schnebly Hill Road. Park by the trailhead on the left immediately before the paved road deteriorates to dirt. Marg's Draw, one of several trails originating here, is worthwhile, gently meandering 100 feet down-canyon, through the tortured desert flora to Morgan Road. Backtrack to the parking lot for close to a 3-mi hike. ■ TIP➔ Always carry plenty of water, no matter how easy the hike appears. ⊠ *Schnebly Hill Rd., off AZ 179, Central.*

WORTH NOTING

Courthouse Butte. The red sandstone seems to catch on fire toward sunset, when this monolith is free of shadow. From the highway, Courthouse Butte sits in back of Bell Rock and can be viewed without any additional hiking or driving. ⊠ *AZ 179, Village of Oak Creek.*

Rainbow Trout Farm. North-central Arizona may not be the most obvious fishing destination, but this stocked farm is a fun way to spend a few hours if you're so inclined. Anglers young and old almost always enjoy a sure catch, and you can rent a cane pole here with a hook and bait for $1. There's no charge if your catch is under 8 inches; above that it's $8 to $12, depending on the length. The real bargain is that the staff will

Red Rock Geology

It's hard to imagine that the land-locked desert surrounding Sedona was, for much of prehistoric time, an area of dunes and swamps on the shore of an ancient sea. The ebb and flow of this sea shaped the land. When the sea rose, it planed the dunes before dropping more sediment on top. The process continued for a few hundred million years. Eventually the sediment hardened into gray layers of limestone on top of the red sandstone. When North America collided with another continental plate, the land buckled and lifted, forming the Rocky Mountains and raising northern Arizona thousands of feet. Volcanoes erupted in the area, capping some of the rock with erosion-resistant basalt.

Oak Creek started flowing at this time, eroding through the layers of

sandstone and limestone. Along with other forces of erosion, the creek carved out the canyons and shaped the buttes. Sedona's buttes stayed intact because a resilient layer of lava had hardened on top and slowed the erosion process considerably. As iron minerals in the sandstone were gradually exposed to the elements, they turned red in a process similar to rusting. The iron minerals, in turn, stained the surrounding colorless quartz and grains of sand—it only takes 2% red-iron material to give the sandstone its red color.

Like the rings of a tree, the striations in the rock document the passage of time and the events, limestone marking the rise of the sea, sandstone when the region was coastline.

4

clean and pack your fish for 50¢ each. ⊠ *3500 N. AZ 89A, 3 mi north of Sedona, Oak Creek Canyon* ☎ *928/282–5799* ⊙ *Daily 9–5.*

Red Rock State Park. Two miles west of Sedona via AZ 89A is the turnoff for this 286-acre state park, a less crowded alternative to Slide Rock State Park, though without the possibility for swimming. The 5 mi of interconnected park trails are well marked, and provide beautiful vistas. There are daily ranger-guided nature walks, bird-watching excursions on Wednesday and Saturday, and a guided hike to Eagle's Nest scenic overlook—the highest point in the park—every Saturday. Call ahead for times, which change with the season. ⊠ *4050 Red Rock Loop Rd., West* ☎ *928/282–6907* ⊕ *www.azstateparks.com* ⊠ *$6 per car* ⊙ *Oct.–Mar., daily 8–5; Apr. and Sept., daily 8–6; May–Aug., daily 8–8.*

SPORTS AND THE OUTDOORS

The Brins Fire consumed 4,500 acres in Sedona in 2006. Although no people or structures were harmed, the human-ignited fire threatened the Oak Creek Canyon area and serves as a reminder for fire safety. Take precautions and use common sense. Extinguish all fires with water. Never toss a cigarette butt. And don't hesitate to ask questions of local park rangers.

■TIP➜A Red Rock Pass is required to park in the Coconino National Forest from Oak Creek Canyon through Sedona and the Village of Oak Creek.

Passes cost $5 for the day, $15 for the week, or $20 for an entire year, and can be purchased at four visitor centers surrounding and within Sedona. Passes are also available from vending machines at popular trailheads—including Boynton Canyon, Bell Rock, and Huckaby—and at many Sedona hotels. Locals widely resent the pass, feeling that free access to national forests is a right. The Forest Service counters that it doesn't receive enough federal funds to maintain the land surrounding Sedona, trampled by 5 million visitors each year, and that a parking fee is the best way to raise revenue. ☎928/282–4119 *information only* ⊕*www.redrockcountry.org.*

BALLOONING

Northern Light Balloon Expeditions (☎928/282–2274 *or* 800/230–6222 ⊕*www.northernlightballoon.com*) is one of the only two companies with permits to fly over Sedona. **Red Rock Balloon Adventures** (☎928/284–0040 *or* 800/258–3754 ⊕*www.redrockballoons.com*) prices generally start at $195 per person for one to two hours.

GOLF

The **Oak Creek Country Club** (⊠*690 Bell Rock Blvd., Village of Oak Creek* ☎928/284–1660 ⊕*www.oakcreekcountryclub.com*) is a good semiprivate 18-hole, par 72 course designed by Robert Trent Jones. Green fees are $115 in high season and $69 during the summer months. Lessons and rental clubs are available.

FodorsChoice **Sedona Golf Resort** (⊠*35 Ridge Trail Dr., Village of Oak Creek* ☎928/284–
  ★ *9355 or* 877/733–6630 ⊕*www.sedonagolfresort.com*), a gorgeous par-71 course, was designed by Gary Panks to take advantage of the many changes in elevation and scenery. Golf courses are a dime a dozen in Arizona, but this one is regarded as one of the best in the state. The restaurant—with panoramic red rock vistas—serves breakfast and lunch daily.

HIKING AND BACKPACKING

For free detailed maps, hiking advice, and information on campgrounds, contact the rangers of the **Coconino National Forest** (⊠*Sedona Ranger District, 250 Brewer Rd., West* ☎928/282–4119 ⊕*www.fs.fed.us/r3/ coconino* ☉ *Weekdays 8–4:30*). Ask here or at your hotel for directions to trailheads for Doe's Mountain (an easy ascent, with many switchbacks), Loy Canyon, Devil's Kitchen, and Long Canyon.

Among the paths in Coconino National Forest, the popular **West Fork Trail** (⊠*Trailhead: AZ 89A, 9½ mi north of Sedona*) traverses the Oak Creek Canyon for a 3-mi hike. A walk through the woods between sheer red-rock walls and a dip in the stream make a great summer combo. The trailhead is about 3 mi north of Slide Rock State Park.

Any backpacking trip in the **Secret Mountain Wilderness** near Sedona guarantees stunning vistas, otherworldly rock formations, and Zen-like serenity, but little water, so pack a good supply. ▪TIP➔Plan your trip for the spring or fall: summer brings 100°F heat and sudden thunderstorms that flood canyons without warning. Most individual trails in the wilderness are too short for anything longer than an overnighter, but several trails can be linked up to form a memorable multiday trip. Contact the Sedona Ranger District for full details.

HORSEBACK RIDING

Among the tour options at **Trail Horse Adventures** (✉ *Dead Horse Ranch State Park, Cottonwood* ☎*866/958–7245* ⊕*www.trailhorseadventures.com*) are a midday ride with picnic, a ride along the Verde River to Native American cliff dwellings, and a full-moon ride with a campfire cookout. Rides range from about $60 for an hour to about $125 for an entire day.

JEEP TOURS

Several jeep-tour operators headquartered along Sedona's main Uptown drag conduct excursions, some focusing on geology, some on astronomy, some on vortexes, some

WORD OF MOUTH

"My husband and I were in Sedona last June and I would definitely recommend the Pink Jeep tour. It takes you on 'roads' that no car can travel on and you see some wonderful scenery. You also make a couple of stops to walk around and see breathtaking views. Plus the ride itself is great! It was a lot of fun and one of our best memories of that trip. I highly recommend it."

—teddysmom

on all three. You can even find a combination jeep tour and horseback ride. Prices start at about $55 per person for two hours and go upward of $100 per person for four hours. Although all the excursions are safe, many are not for those who dislike heights or bumps.

A Day in the West (☎*928/282–4320 or 800/973–3662* ⊕*www.adayin thewest.com*) can take you to all the prime spots and combine a jeep tour with a horseback ride or local wine tasting. The ubiquitous **Pink Jeep Tours** (✉*204 N. AZ 89A, Sedona* ☎*928/282–5000 or 800/873–3662* ⊕*www.pinkjeep.com*) are a popular choice. **Sedona Red Rock Jeep Tours** (✉*270 N. AZ 89A, Sedona* ☎*928/282–6826 or 800/848–7728* ⊕*www.redrockjeep.com*) is a reliable operator that spins some good cowboy tales on its jeep tours.

MOUNTAIN BIKING

Given the red-rock splendor, challenging terrain, miles of single track, and mild weather, you might think Sedona would be a mountain-biking destination on the order of Moab or Durango. Inexplicably, you won't find the Lycra-clad throngs patronizing pasta bars or throwing back microbrews on the Uptown mall, but all the better for you: the mountain-biking culture remains fervent but low-key. A few strategically located, excellent bike shops can outfit you and give advice.

As a general rule, mountain bikes are allowed on all trails and jeep paths unless designated as wilderness or private property. The rolling terrain, which switches between serpentine trails of buff red clay and mounds of slickrock, has few sustained climbs but ∎**TIP➜**be careful of blind drop-offs that often step down several feet in unexpected places. The thorny trailside flora makes carrying extra inner tubes a must, and an inner tube sealant is a good idea, too. If you plan to ride for several hours, pack a gallon of water and start early in the morning on hot days. Shade is rare, and with the exception of (nonpotable) Oak Creek, water is nonexistent.

For the casual rider, **Bell Rock Pathway** (✉*Trailhead: 5 mi south of Sedona on AZ 179*) is a scenic and easy ride traveling 3 mi through some of the most breathtaking scenery in red rock country. Several single-track trails spur off this one making it a good starting point for many other rides in Sedona. **Submarine Rock Loop** is perhaps the most popular single-track loop in the area, and for good reason. The 10-mi trail is a heady mixture of prime terrain and scenery following slickrock and twisty trails up to Chicken Point, a sandstone terrace overlooking colorful buttes. The trail continues as a bumpy romp through washes almost all downhill. Be wary of blind drop-offs in this section. It wouldn't be overly cautious to scout any parts of the trail that look sketchy.

A few hundred yards south of Bell Rock Pathway, **Bike and Bean** (⊠*6020 AZ 179, Village of Oak Creek* ☎*928/284–0210* ⊕*www.bike-bean. com*) offers rentals, tours, trail maps, their own blend of coffee, and advice on trails and conditions.

WHERE TO EAT

Some Sedona restaurants close in January and February, so call before you go; if you're planning a visit in high season (April to October), make reservations.

¢ ✕**Coffee Pot Restaurant.** Locals and tourists alike swarm to this spacious
AMERICAN diner for scrumptious breakfast and brunch food served by a friendly waitstaff. One hundred and one omelet options are the stars of the show, and include such concoctions as the quirky peanut butter and jelly or the basic ham and cheese. Warm homemade biscuits always hit the spot. An extensive lunch menu that includes everything from Mexican dishes to a Greek salad rounds out the offerings. ⊠*2050 W. 89A, West* ☎*928/282–6626* ▭*D, MC, V* ⊘*No dinner.*

$$$ ✕**Cowboy Club.** At this upscale restaurant you can hang out in the casual
STEAK Cowboy Club or dine in the more formal Silver Saddle Room, where suede booths are surrounded by cowboy art and a pair of large cattle horns. High-quality cuts of beef are the specialty, but the fried chicken served with cumin mashed potatoes is delicious, too. ⊠*241 AZ 89A, Uptown* ☎*928/282–4200* ⊕*www.cowboyclub.com* ▭*AE, D, DC, MC, V.*

$$ ✕**Dahl & DiLuca.** Andrea DiLuca and Lisa Dahl have created one of the
ITALIAN most popular Italian restaurants in town: Andrea runs the kitchen, and
★ Lisa meets and greets diners when she's not making delicious homemade soups like white bean with ham and hearty minestrone. Specialties here include tortellini with a portobello mushroom sauce and pollo piccata (chicken in a lemon, capers, and chardonnay sauce). Renaissance reproductions and café seating give the impression of a Roman piazza. Make reservations or you may be seated at the bar—good food but far less romantic. ⊠*2321 W. AZ 89A, West* ☎*928/282–5219* ⊕*www. dahlanddiluca.com* ▭*AE, D, MC, V* ⊘*No lunch.*

$$$ ✕**Heartline Café.** Fresh flowers and innovative cuisine that even the staff
CONTINENTAL struggles to characterize are this attractive café's hallmarks. Local ingre-
★ dients pepper the menu, giving a Sedona twist to continental fare, and favorites include pecan-crusted trout with Dijon sauce and oak-grilled salmon marinated in tequila and lime. Appealing vegetarian plates are also available. Desserts include a phenomenal crème brûlée, as well as

Jeep Tours get you close to Sedona's red rocks while someone else does the driving.

homemade truffles at the chef's whim. ■TIP➔The owners also do gourmet takeout next door 7 days a week—perfect prep for picnics under the red rocks. ⊠*1610 W. AZ 89A, West* ☎*928/282–0785* ⊕*www.heart linecafe.com* ⊟*AE, D, MC, V* ☽*No lunch Mon.–Thurs.*

$$$$
FRENCH
★
✕**L'Auberge.** The most formal dining room in Sedona, on the L'Auberge de Sedona resort property, promises a quiet, civilized evening of indulgence. Chef Jonathan Agelman offers a fusion of American cuisine with French influences, and among the house favorites is the venison accompanied by wild game cassoulet and broccolini. You can make the most of L'Auberge's 1,200-bottle wine cellar by enjoying the five-course wine-paired meal for $140. The lavish Sunday brunch is well worth the splurge. ⊠*L'Auberge de Sedona, 241 AZ 89A, Uptown* ☎*928/282–1667* ⊕*www.lauberge.com* ⊟*AE, D, DC, MC, V.*

¢
CAFÉ
✕**New Frontiers Natural Marketplace.** Healthy fare at this mostly organic grocery and deli runs the gamut from grab-and-go sandwiches to the well-stocked salad bar to hot items like honey-glazed salmon, cheese or chicken enchiladas, and turkey meat loaf. Get supplies for your red-rock picnic or relax at the indoor-outdoor dining area. ⊠ *1420 W. AZ 89A, West* ☎*928/282–6311* ⊟*AE, D, MC, V.*

$$
MEXICAN
✕**Oaxaca Restaurant.** Tasty standards complement some of the best uptown canyon vistas at this modern Mexican restaurant with a lovely balcony. The smoky kick of the salsa, along with the sun-kissed scenery, may transport you south of the border, but dishes are prepared under the auspices of owner Carla Butler, a dietitian who shuns the traditional use of lard and cholesterol-containing oils in favor of healthier options—with delicious results. ⊠*321 N. AZ 89A, Uptown* ☎*928/282–4179* ⊕*www.oaxacarestaurant.com* ⊟*AE, DC, MC, V.*

$$$ ✕**René at Tlaquepaque.** Ease into the plush banquettes at this lace-cur-
CONTINENTAL tained restaurant for classic French and Continental dishes. Recom-
mended starters include French onion soup and the spinach and wild
mushroom salad in a hazelnut vinaigrette. Rack of lamb is the house spe-
cialty, and the Dover sole is a real find, far from the white cliffs. Crêpes
Suzettes for two, prepared table-side, is an impressive dessert. There's a
well-selected wine list, too. Service is formal, but resort-casual attire is
acceptable. ⊠*Tlaquepaque Arts & Crafts Village, Unit B–117, AZ 179,
Central* ☎*928/282–9225* ⊕*www.rene-sedona.com* ☰*AE, MC, V.*

¢ ✕**Sally's Mesquite Grill and BBQ.** Although it offers limited indoor seat-
SOUTHERN ing, this Uptown hideaway behind a long row of tourist shops is worth
★ a visit. It's super casual, with just an ordering window where you can
select pulled pork sandwiches and homemade comfort food such as
beans or coleslaw. The barbecue sauce has a bit of a kick, and the french
fries (also made from scratch) are fabulous. Hours vary with the season,
so call ahead. ⊠*250 Jordan Rd., No. 9, Uptown* ☎*928/282–6533*
⊕*www.sallysbbq.com* ☰*MC, V.*

$$$ ✕**Shugrue's Hillside.** Almost everything is good here—including the red-
AMERICAN rock views from every seat—which has made this one of the most pop-
ular restaurants in Sedona, but the salads and meats are particularly
noteworthy. The Caesar salad is refreshingly traditional, and the inventive ginger-walnut chicken salad is large enough to share. Rack of lamb
and filet mignon are prepared and presented simply, and there's a small,
well-priced wine list. Service is friendly rather than formal, and dining
views don't get much better than the upstairs deck. ⊠*671 AZ 179,
Central* ☎*928/282–5300* ⊕*www.shugrues.com* ☰*AE, DC, MC, V.*

$$–$$$ ✕**Takashi.** Anyone seeking serenity and a respite from heavy meals will
JAPANESE enjoy this Japanese restaurant, which provides aesthetic pleasure in
everything from tea (with little bits of floating popcorn and brown
rice) to dessert (sweet ginger or red-bean ice cream). Salads include
spicy sushi-quality tuna with Japanese mayonnaise on a bed of cabbage and fresh vegetables. Combination dinners such as sashimi with
tempura or teriyaki let you sample a bit of everything. ⊠*465 Jordan
Rd., Uptown* ☎*928/282–2334* ⊕*www.takashisedona.com* ☰*AE, DC,
MC, V* ☺*Closed Mon. No lunch weekends.*

$ ✕**Thai Spices.** This small, no-frills restaurant has a loyal following of
THAI vegetarians and health-food enthusiasts, though not everything is meatless. The curries, especially red curry with tempeh, are delicious, and can
be prepared at the spice level of your choice. Traditional pad thai with
chicken is satisfyingly homey, and the spicy beef salad, a house specialty
only for the brave, will make your hair stand on end. ⊠*2986 W. AZ
89A, West* ☎*928/282–0599* ⊕*www.thaispices.com* ☰*MC, V.*

WHERE TO STAY

$$$–$$$$ 🏠**Adobe Village and Graham Inn.** Some of the rooms at this inn south of
★ Sedona have Jacuzzi tubs and balconies that look out onto the red rocks.
Each of the four individually decorated casitas on the lot next door has a
gas fireplace that opens into both the sitting area and the bathroom area,
which is outfitted with a two-person Jacuzzi tub. What makes this place
really special, though, is the impeccable yet casual service. **Pros:** way-

above-average hospitality; extras like complimentary trail mix to go and hearty afternoon snacks; walk to hiking trails. **Cons:** some road noise; drive to town. ⊠ *150 Canyon Circle Dr., Village of Oak Creek* ☎ *928/284–1425 or 800/228–1425* ⊕ *www.adobevillagegrahaminn.com* ➪ *6 rooms, 1 suite, 4 private villas* ⚐ *In-room: kitchen (some), refrigerator (some), Wi-Fi, DVD. In-hotel: pool, no-smoking rooms* ☰ *AE, D, MC, V* ⊠ *BP.*

$$$–$$$$ ⊡ **Alma de Sedona.** The Alma de Sedona continues to be an enchanting B&B, with spectacular views and ultracomfortable beds. The inn was built well off the main drag and in the shadow of the buttes for views and privacy. Understated, elegant, and inviting rooms all have private entrances and patios. Bath salts and candles await in the bathrooms, most of which have 2-person Jacuzzi tubs. **Pros:** central location; excellent views. **Cons:** overpriced for a B&B; decor could use updating; no elevator (some rooms require climbing stairs). ⊠ *50 Hozoni Dr., West* ☎ *928/282–2737 or 800/923–2282* ⊕ *www.almadesedona.com* ➪ *12 rooms* ⚐ *In-room: refrigerator, Wi-Fi. In-hotel: pool, no-smoking rooms* ☰ *MC, V* ⊠ *BP.*

$$$ ⊡ **Amara Resort.** You might not expect to find a boutique hotel in small, outdoorsy Sedona, but here is the Amara next to gurgling Oak Creek. Sleek rooms deviate from the usual Sedona look, with low-slung beds and work desks with ergonomic seating. Other cushy extras include in-room DVD players and Aveda bath products. Step out onto your room's private balcony or terrace to take in expansive red-rock views. **Pros:** good spa and restaurant; walk to uptown. **Cons:** pricey city-chic in a somewhat generic hotel feels incongruous with setting. ⊠ *310 N. AZ 89, Uptown* ☎ *928/282–4828 or 866/455–6610* ⊕ *www.amararesort.com* ➪ *92 rooms, 8 suites* ⚐ *In-room: Wi-Fi, DVD. In-hotel: 1 restaurant, bar, concierge, no-smoking rooms, public Internet, gym* ☰ *AE, D, DC, MC, V.*

$$–$$$ ⊡ **Boots & Saddles.** Irith and Sam are the worldly and consummate hosts at this quiet inn tucked behind the main street in West Sedona. The romantic rooms are decorated in an upscale Western motif, complete with genuine cowboy artifacts, and most have decks with hot tubs and telescopes for stargazing. **Pros:** hosts go the extra mile to pamper and advise; private decks. **Cons:** first-floor rooms get noise from upstairs guests. ⊠ *2900 Hopi Dr., West* ☎ *928/282–1944 or 800/201–1944* ⊕ *www.oldwestbb.com* ➪ *6 rooms* ⚐ *In-room: refrigerator, Wi-Fi, DVD. In-hotel: no-smoking rooms* ☰ *AE, D, MC, V* ⊠ *BP.*

$$$–$$$$ ⊡ **Briar Patch Inn.** This B&B in verdant Oak Creek Canyon has Southwestern-themed rooms in wooden cabins, many with decks overlooking the creek. On summer mornings you can sit outside and enjoy home-baked breads and fresh egg dishes while listening to live classical music. Yoga classes are also held on the premises. **Pros:** tranquil creek-side setting with beautiful gardens. **Cons:** somewhat rustic; cabins can be dark. ⊠ *3190 N. AZ 89A, Oak Creek Canyon* ☎ *928/282–2342 or*

Local arts and crafts often represent the Native American heritage in Arizona.

888/809–3030 ⊕*www.briarpatchinn.com* ↬*18 cottages* ⌂*In-room: refrigerator, kitchen (some), no TV (some). In-hotel: Wi-Fi, no-smoking rooms* ⊟*AE, MC, V* ⓧⓘ*BP.*

$$ ⊡**The Canyon Wren.** The best value in the Oak Creek Canyon area, this
★ small B&B has freestanding cabins with views of the canyon walls, and hosts Milena and Mike regard guests' privacy first and foremost. It's likely that their two lovable dogs, Zoey and Wookiee, will greet you on arrival. Cabins have private decks and fireplaces. **Pros:** romantic yet homey, wonderful hosts and breakfast. **Cons:** may be too rustic for some, 6 mi to town. ⊠*6425 N. AZ 89A, Oak Creek Canyon* ☎*928/282–6900 or 800/437–9736* ⊕*www.canyonwrencabins.com* ↬*4 cabins* ⌂*In-room: no phone, kitchen, no TV. In-hotel: no-smoking rooms* ⊟*AE, D, MC, V* ⓧⓘ*CP.*

$–$$ ⊡**Desert Quail Inn.** Close to a lion's share of the trailheads, this is a good base for outdoor adventures, and the front desk has plenty of maps and advice on offer. Rooms, though dated (circa 1980), are spacious and bright, and the in-room refrigerators are stocked with fresh fruit—a nice touch. **Pros:** large, clean rooms. **Cons:** two-story roadside motel; outdated decor. ⊠*6626 AZ 179, Village of Oak Creek* ☎*928/284–1433 or 800/385–0927* ⊕*www.desertquailinn.com* ↬*41 rooms* ⌂*In-room: refrigerator. In-hotel: pool, laundry facilities* ⊟*AE, D, DC, MC, V.*

$$$$ ⊡**El Portal Sedona.** This stunning hacienda is one of the most beautifully designed boutique hotels in the Southwest. Decor accents include authentic Tiffany and Roycroft pieces, French doors leading to balconies or a grassy central courtyard, stained-glass windows and ceiling panels, river-rock or tile fireplaces, and huge custom-designed beds. Wine and hors d'oeuvres are served in the afternoon, and the inn also serves dinner Wednesday through Saturday evenings. **Pros:** very attractive building, central location next to Tlaquepaque shops and restaurants. **Cons:** even breakfast is expensive, gym and pool (privileges) next door at the Los Abrigos Resort are substandard. ⊠ *95 Portal La., Central* ☎*928/203–9405 or 800/313–0017* ⊕*www.elportalsedona.com* ↩*11 rooms, 1 suite* ♿*In-room: refrigerator, DVD, Wi-Fi. In-hotel: some pets allowed, no-smoking rooms* ⊟*AE, D, MC, V* ⦿❘*BP.*

$$$$ ⊞**Enchantment Resort.** The rooms and suites at this resort are tucked
★ into small, pueblo-style buildings in serene Boynton Canyon. Accommodations come in many configurations, and multiple bedrooms can be joined to create large, elaborate suites. All have beehive gas fireplaces, private decks, and superb views. The resort's world-class spa, Mii Amo, offers all-inclusive packages, along with myriad treatments and innovative spa cuisine. **Pros:** gorgeous setting, state-of-the-art spa, numerous on-site activities. **Cons:** twenty-minute drive into town. ⊠ *525 Boynton Canyon Rd., West* ☎*928/282–2900 or 800/826–4180* ⊕*www. enchantmentresort.com* ↩*107 rooms, 115 suites* ♿*In-room: Wi-Fi, safe, kitchen (some). In-hotel: 3 restaurants, bar, tennis courts, pools, gym, spa, bicycles, children's programs (ages 4–12)* ⊟*AE, D, MC, V.*

$$$–$$$$ ⊞**Junipine Resort.** These one- and two-bedroom cabins nestled in a juniper and pine forest (hence the name) are spacious and airy, with vaulted ceilings and fireplaces. An excellent value for groups of four or more, some of the cabins are more than 1,400 square feet and sleep up to eight people. Junipine's most enchanting feature might be the sound of Oak Creek roaring below, though, lulling you to sleep by the fire. **Pros:** huge, well-equipped cabins; trailheads on-site. **Cons:** individually owned condo units have been individually decorated in styles that may not appeal to everyone; the group appeal can mean some partying neighbors. ⊠ *8351 N. AZ 89A, Oak Creek Canyon* ☎*928/282–3375 or 800/742–7463* ⊕*www.junipine.com* ↩*50 suites* ♿*In-room: kitchen, no TV (some), DVD (some). In-hotel: restaurant, no-smoking rooms* ⊟*AE, D, MC, V.*

$$$–$$$$ ⊞**L'Auberge de Sedona.** This hillside resort consists of a central lodge
★ building; creek-side rooms; and—the major attraction—cabins in the woods along Oak Creek. Rooms in the lodge are decorated in lush country-European style, and the cabins have wood-burning fireplaces. Phoenix couples flock to this hideaway and dine in the hotel's French restaurant, one of the most romantic eateries in Arizona. **Pros:** luxurious rooms and cabins; secluded setting yet close to town. **Cons:** exclusive feel; in-house restaurant very pricey. ⊠ *301 L'Auberge La., Uptown* ⦿*Box B, 86336* ☎*928/282–1661 or 800/905–5745* ⊕*www.lauberge. com* ↩*21 rooms, 31 cottages* ♿*In-room: refrigerator, safe. In-hotel: 2 restaurants, pool, public Wi-Fi, spa* ⊟*AE, D, DC, MC, V.*

$$–$$ ⊞**Lodge at Sedona.** Rooms in this rambling wood-and-stone Craftsman house have a refined rustic style; some have fireplaces, redwood decks, or hot tubs. For solitude, walk the seven-path classic labyrinth (made of local rock) and through the gardens. A chef prepares a five-course breakfast each morning. **Pros:** tranquil setting yet short walk from West Sedona, friendly staff. **Cons:** limited views. ⊠ *125 Kallof Pl., West* ☎*928/204–1942 or 800/619–4467* ⊕*www.lodgeatsedona.com*

SPAS IN SEDONA

While some prefer to harness Sedona's rejuvenating energy at a vortex site, others seek renewal at one of the many spas in town. From all-inclusive spa retreats nestled in Red Rock canyons to inexpensive bodywork performed by healing arts students, Sedona has relaxing options for every budget and preference.

With its history of Native American traditions, Sedona is thought of as one of the most sacred healing spots on earth. Spas incorporate indigenous materials, like red-rock clay, into their spa services—and choosing your treatments is part of the pleasure. Some of Sedona's spas are destinations in themselves, offering all-inclusive experiences tailored to individual needs and desires.

If you're staying at the Enchantment Resort, you can enjoy the revered ★ **Mii Amo Spa** (☎ 928/203–8500 ⊕ www.miiamo.com). Set in spectacular Boynton Canyon, Mii Amo is a state-of-the-art facility with indoor and outdoor pools and treatment rooms. Meditate in the sand-floor crystal grotto before your Watsu water therapy or deep tissue massage. Afterward, dine in the spa's healthy and tasty café (no egg yolks in these omelettes), wearing only your spa robe if you like.

The **Sedona Rouge Hotel and Spa** (☎ 866/312–4111 ⊕ www.

sedonarouge.com) is a more understated healing environment, open to the public as well as to its boutique hotel guests. Deepak Chopra chooses this simple and tranquil setting for his weeklong "SynchroDestiny" workshops each year. Skilled therapists meet with clients first to discuss individual goals before embarking on treatments like the Seven Sacred Pools Massage (which brings balance to the body's seven energy centers or chakras).

Sedona's upscale resorts also offer an array of spa amenities for their guests. At the luxurious **L'Auberge** (☎ 800/905–5745 ⊕ www.lauberge. com) you can indulge in an outdoor massage on the bank of gurgling Oak Creek, or restore balance to your skin with a grapeseed antioxidant scrub. Better yet, select four treatments and lunch for a custom spa package here.

Students at The Northern Arizona Massage Therapy Institute, **NAMTI** (☎ 928/282–7737 ⊕ www.namti. com), offer quality one-hour massage, craniosacral, and reflexology treatments for the bargain price of $30.

The popular **Sedona New Day Spa** (☎ 928/282–7502 ⊕ www. sedonanewdayspa.com) uses local ingredients for clay masks, body wraps, and crystal therapy. They also have a separate spa for men.

🛏 5 rooms, 9 suites △ In-room: Wi-Fi, no phone, TV (some), DVD (some). In-hotel: restaurant, pool, gym, concierge, some pets allowed, no-smoking rooms ▤ D, MC, V ◎ BP.

$ 🏨 **Sedona Motel.** Built on a terrace removed from the highway in order to afford it the same expansive views as the pricier resorts, this motel is pretty typical in all other respects. It's within easy reach of most of Sedona's attractions, and the rooms are well kept. **Pros:** good value, convenient walk to shops and restaurants, red-rock views. **Cons:** some road noise. ⊠*218 AZ 179, Central* ☎*928/282–7187 or 877/828–7187* ⊕*www.thesedonamotel.com* ⌂*16 rooms* ♿*In-room: refrigerator* ▭*D, MC, V.*

$$ ⛰**Sky Ranch Lodge.** There may be no better vantage point in town from which to view Sedona's red-rock canyons than the private patios and balconies at Sky Ranch Lodge, near the top of Airport Mesa. Some rooms have stone fireplaces and some have kitchenettes. Paths on the grounds wind around fountains and, in summer, through colorful flower gardens. **Pros:** good value, great views. **Cons:** less expensive rooms have few amenities. ⊠*Top of Airport Rd., West* ☎*928/282–6400* ⊕*www. skyranchlodge.com* ⌂*92 rooms, 2 cottages* ♿*In-room: kitchen (some), refrigerator (some). In-hotel: pool, some pets allowed, no-smoking rooms* ▭*AE, MC, V.*

¢ ⛰**Sugar Loaf Lodge.** Though it may be hard to believe, there are still bargains in Sedona, and this one-story, family-run motel delivers. All rooms have refrigerators and microwaves, and the pool and hot-tub area serves as a gathering spot for swapping tales with fellow travelers—many from Europe—at the end of the day. **Pros:** it's cheap, it's clean. **Cons:** older furnishings, part of the driveway is unpaved. ⊠*1870 W. AZ 89A, West* ☎*928/282–9451 or 877/282–0632* ⊕*www.sedonasugar loaf.com* ⌂*16 rooms* ♿*In-room: refrigerator, Wi-Fi. In-hotel: pool, no-smoking rooms* ▭*AE, MC, V* ⧓*CP.*

NIGHTLIFE AND THE ARTS

Nightlife in Sedona tends to be sedate, although on high-season weekends there's usually live music at the Enchantment Resort. Shugrue's Hillside also regularly presents local musicians. Offerings vary from jazz to rock and pop; in all cases, call ahead. The weeklong Sedona **Jazz on the Rocks Festival** (☎928/282–1985 ⊕*www.sedonajazz.com*), held every September, attracts a sellout crowd and culminates with a huge outdoor concert. **Chamber Music Sedona** (☎928/204–2415 ⊕*www.chambermusic sedona.org*) hosts a concert series from October through May.

The **Sedona Arts Center** (⊠N. *AZ 89A and Art Barn Rd., Uptown* ☎928/282–3809 ⊕*www.sedonaartscenter.com*) offers classes in all mediums and hosts the innovative and growing Sedona International Film Festival every March.

The closest thing to a rollicking cowboy bar in Sedona is **Relics Restaurant & Nightclub at Rainbow's End** (⊠3235 *W. AZ 89A, West* ☎928/282–1593), a steak house with a dance floor and live rock or country-and-Western music most nights.

SHOPPING

With a few exceptions, most of the stores in what is known as the Uptown area (north of the "Y," running along AZ 89A to the east of its intersection with AZ 179) cater to the tour-bus trade with Native American jewelry and New Age souvenirs. If this isn't your style, the largest concentration of stores and galleries is in Central Sedona, along AZ 179, south of the "Y," with plenty of offerings for serious shoppers.

There are three main art-gallery complexes in Sedona—Hozho and Tlaquepaque are the best of the three, though Hillside is very close to Hozho. Each has smaller galleries within the larger complex; several are listed below. The **Hillside Courtyard & Marketplace** (⊠671 AZ 179, Central ☎928/282–4500) has several galleries. The **Hozho Center** (⊠431 AZ 179, Central ☎928/204–2257), a minute or two north of Hillside on AZ 179, is a small, upscale complex in a beige Santa Fe–style building, with galleries and fine-art souvenirs. **Tlaquepaque Arts & Crafts Village** (⊠AZ 179, just south of "Y," Central ☎928/282–4838) is home to more than 100 shops and galleries and several restaurants, and remains one of the best places for travelers to find mementos from their trip to Sedona. The complex of clay-tile-roofed buildings arranged around a series of courtyards shares its name and architectural style with a crafts village just outside Guadalajara. It's a lovely place to browse, but beware: prices tend to be high, and locals joke that it's pronounced "to-lock-your-pocket."

STORES AND GALLERIES

Souvenirs in Sedona run the gamut, from authentic Southwestern art to jewelry, and more than enough crystals to bring you inner harmony. **Canyon Outfitters** (⊠2701 W. AZ 89A, West ☎928/282–5293) is good for gearing up with maps, clothing, and camping equipment before your outdoor adventures. **Crystal Magic** (⊠2978 W. 89A, West ☎928/282–1622 ⊕www.crystalmagicsedona.com) dabbles in the metaphysical, with crystals, jewelry, and books for the new age. **El Prado Galleries** (⊠Tlaquepaque, AZ 179, No. 101, Bldg. E, Central ☎928/282–7390 ⊕www.elpradogalleries.com) is a good bet for Southwestern art. **Esteban's** (⊠Tlaquepaque, AZ 179, No. 103, Bldg. B, Central ☎928/282–4686) focuses on ceramics and Native American crafts. **Garland's Navajo Rugs** (⊠411 AZ 179, Central ☎928/282–4070 ⊕www.garlandsrugs.com) has a collection of new and antique rugs, as well as Native American kachina dolls, pottery, and baskets. **Isadora** (⊠Tlaquepaque, AZ 179, No. 120, Bldg. A, Central ☎928/282–6232) has beautiful handwoven jackets and shawls. **James Ratliff Gallery** (⊠Hozho Center,431 AZ 179, Central ☎928/282–1404 ⊕www.jamesratliffgallery.com) has fun and functional pieces by not-yet-established artists. **Kuivato Glass Gallery** (⊠Tlaquepaque, AZ 179, No. 125, Bldg. B, Central ☎928/282–1212) carries gorgeous glassware. **Lanning Gallery** (⊠Hozho Center, 431 AZ 179, Central ☎928/282–6865 ⊕www.lanninggallery.com) sells Southwestern art and jewelry. **Looking West** (⊠242 N. AZ 89A, Uptown ☎928/282–4877) sells the spiffiest cowgirl-style getups in town. **Sedona Pottery** (⊠411 AZ 179, Central ☎928/282–1192) sells unusual pieces, including flower-arranging bowls, egg separators, and life-size ceramic statues by shop owner Mary Margaret Sather.

THE VERDE VALLEY, JEROME, AND PRESCOTT

About 90 mi north of Phoenix, as you round a curve approaching Exit 285 off Interstate 17, the valley of the Verde River suddenly unfolds in a panorama of grayish-white cliffs, tinted red in the distance and dotted with desert scrub, cottonwood, and pine. For hundreds of years many Native American communities, especially those of the southern Sinagua

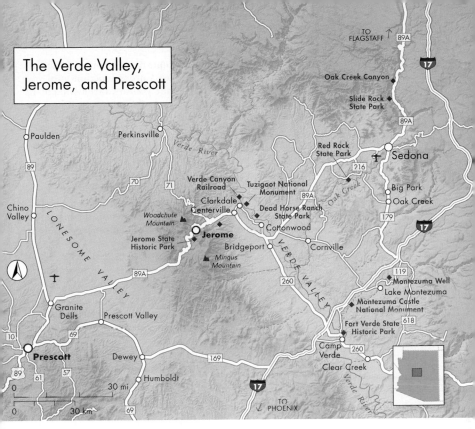

The Verde Valley, Jerome, and Prescott

people, lined the Verde River. Rumors of great mineral deposits brought Europeans to the Verde Valley as early as 1583, when Hopi Indians guided Antonio de Espejo here, but it wasn't until the second half of the 19th century that this wealth was commercially exploited. The discovery of silver and gold in the Black Hills, which border the valley on the southwest, gave rise to boomtowns like Jerome—and to military installations such as Fort Verde, set up to protect the white settlers and wealth seekers from the Native American tribes they displaced. Mineral wealth was also the impetus behind the establishment of Prescott as a territorial capital by President Lincoln and other Unionists who wanted to keep the riches out of Confederate hands.

VERDE VALLEY

94 mi north of Phoenix on I–17.

Often overlooked by travelers on trips to Prescott or Flagstaff, the Verde Valley offers several enjoyable diversions, including the historical wonders at Montezuma Castle and Tuzigoot. And if you're tired of the car, the Verde Canyon Railroad in Clarkdale is a great way to get off road without doing the driving.

GETTING HERE AND AROUND

From Phoenix, it's a leisurely and picturesque route through Verde Valley. Follow Interstate 17 north 25 mi past Cordes Junction until you see the turnoff for AZ 260, which will take you to Cottonwood in 12 mi. Here you can pick up AZ 89A, which leads southwest to Prescott (41 mi) or northeast to Sedona (19 mi).

EXPLORING

The military post for which **Fort Verde State Historic Park** is named was built between 1871 and 1873 as the third of three fortifications in this part of the Arizona Territory. To protect the Verde Valley's farmers and miners from Tonto Apache and Yavapai raids, the fort's administrators oversaw the movement of nearly 1,500 Native Americans to the San Carlos and Fort Apache reservations. A museum details the history of the area's military installations, and three furnished officers' quarters show the day-to-day living conditions of the top brass—it's a good break from the interstate if you've been driving for too long. Signs from any of Interstate 17's three Camp Verde exits will direct you to the 10-acre park. ⊠ *125 E. Hollomon St.* ☎ *928/567–3275* ⊕ *www. azstateparks.com* 🖾 *$3* ⊗ *Thurs.–Mon. 9–5.*

The five-story, 20-room cliff dwelling at **Montezuma Castle National Monument** was named by explorers who believed it had been erected by the Aztecs. Southern Sinagua Native Americans actually built the roughly 600-year-old structure, which is one of the best-preserved prehistoric dwellings in North America—and one of the most accessible. An easy paved trail (1/3 mi round-trip) leads to the dwelling and to adjacent Castle A, a badly deteriorated six-story living space with about 45 rooms. No one is permitted to enter the site, but the viewing area is close by. From Camp Verde, take Main Street to Montezuma Castle Road.

Somewhat less accessible than Montezuma Castle—but equally striking—is the **Montezuma Well** (☎ *928/567–4521*), a unit of the national monument. Although there are some Sinagua and Hohokam sites here, the limestone sinkhole with a limpid blue-green pool lying in the middle of the desert is the park's main attraction. This cavity—55 feet deep and 365 feet across—is all that's left of an ancient subterranean cavern; the water remains at a constant 76°F year-round. It's a short hike up here, but the peace, quiet, and the views of the Verde Valley reward the effort. To reach Montezuma Well from Montezuma Castle, return to Interstate 17 and go north to Exit 293; signs direct you to the well, which is 4 mi east of the freeway. The drive includes a short section of dirt road. ⊠ *Montezuma Castle Rd., 7 mi northeast of Camp Verde* ☎ *928/567–3322* ⊕ *www.nps.gov/moca* 🖾 *$5* ⊗ *Labor Day–Memorial Day, daily 8–5; Memorial Day–Labor Day, daily 8–6.*

The 423-acre spread of **Dead Horse Ranch State Park,** which combines high-desert and wetlands habitats, is a pleasant place to while away the day. You can fish in the Verde River or the well-stocked Park Lagoon, or hike on some 6 mi of trails that begin in a shaded picnic area and wind along the river; adjoining forest service pathways are available for those who enjoy longer treks. Birders can check off more than 100 species from the Arizona Audubon Society lists provided by the rangers. Bald eagles perch along the Verde River in winter, and the common black hawks—a misnomer for these threatened birds—nest here in summer. It's 1 mi north of Cottonwood, off Main Street. ⊠*675 Dead Horse Ranch Rd., Cottonwood* ☎*928/634–5283* ⊕*www.azstateparks.com* ⊡ *$6 per car* ⊙*Daily 8–5.*

The high-desert soil of the Verde Valley is working for the winemakers at **Page Springs Cellars** (⊠*1500 N. Page Springs Rd., Cornville* ☎*928/639–3004* ⊕*www.pagespringscellars.com* ⊙*Daily 11–6*), which focus on grapes popular in the Rhône wine region of France.

Tuzigoot National Monument isn't as well preserved as Montezuma Castle, but it's more impressive in scope. Tuzigoot is another complex of the Sinagua people, who lived on this land overlooking the Verde Valley from about AD 1000 to 1400. The pueblo, constructed of limestone and sandstone blocks, once rose three stories and incorporated 110 rooms. Inhabitants were skilled dry farmers and traded with peoples hundreds of miles away. Implements used for food preparation, as well as jewelry, weapons, and farming tools excavated from the site, are displayed in the visitor center. Within the site, you can step into a reconstructed room. ⊠*3 mi north of Cottonwood on Broadway Rd., between Cottonwood's Old Town and Clarkdale, Clarkdale* ☎*928/634–5564* ⊕*www.nps.gov/tuzi* ⊡*$5* ⊙*Sept.–May, daily 8–5; June–Aug., daily 8–6.*

★ Train buffs come to the Verde Valley to catch the 22-mi **Verde Canyon Railroad**, which follows a dramatic route through the Verde Canyon, the remains of a copper smelter, and much unspoiled desert that is inaccessible by car. The destination—the city of Clarkdale—might not be that impressive, but the ride is undeniably scenic. Knowledgeable announcers regale riders with the area's colorful history and point out natural attractions along the way—in winter you're likely to see bald eagles. This four-hour trip is especially popular in fall-foliage season and in spring, when the desert wildflowers bloom; book well in advance. Round-trip rides cost $54.95. For $79.95 you can ride the much more comfortable living-room-like first-class cars, where hot hors d'oeuvres, coffee, and a cocktail are included in the price. ■TIP→Reservations are required. ⊠*Arizona Central Railroad, 300 N. Broadway, Clarkdale* ☎*800/320–0718* ⊕*www.verdecanyonrr.com.*

SPORTS AND THE OUTDOORS

The **Verde Ranger District** office of the **Prescott National Forest** (⊠*300 E. AZ 260, Camp Verde* ☎*928/567–4121* ⊕*www.fs.fed.us/r3/prescott*) is a good resource for places to hike, fish, and boat along the Verde River.

The **Black Canyon Trail** (⊠ *AZ 260, 4 mi south of Cottonwood, west on FR 359 4½ mi*) is a bit of a slog, rising more than 2,200 feet in 6 mi, but the reward is grand views from the gray cliffs of Verde Valley to the red buttes of Sedona to the blue range of the San Francisco Peaks.

WHERE TO EAT

¢   ✕ **Casa Antigua.** On the main drag in Camp Verde, this tiny eatery serves

MEXICAN   traditional Mexican food. Try the *carne asada* (marinated, grilled beef) tacos and the chicken *burros* (as burritos are often called in this part of Arizona). ⊠ *396 S. Main St., Camp Verde* ☎ *928/567–6300* ⊟ *AE, D, MC, V* ⊘ *Closed Sun.*

$$ ✕ **Manzanita Restaurant.** You might not expect to find sophisticated cook-

CONTINENTAL   ing in Cornville, 6 mi east of Cottonwood, but a European-born chef prepares Continental fare here, using organic produce and locally raised meat whenever possible. Roast duckling à l'orange and rack of lamb are beautifully presented; try the mushroom soup if it's available. ⊠ *11425 E. Cornville Rd., Cornville* ☎ *928/634–8851* ⊕ *www.themanzanita restaurant.com* ⊟ *AE, D, MC, V* ⊘ *No lunch Mon.–Tues.*

JEROME

★   *3½ mi southwest of Clarkdale, 20 mi northwest of Camp Verde, 33 mi northeast of Prescott, 25 mi southwest of Sedona on AZ 89A.*

Jerome was once known as the Billion Dollar Copper Camp, but after the last mines closed in 1953 the booming population of 15,000 dwindled to 50 determined souls. Although its population has risen back to almost 500, Jerome still holds on to its "ghost town" designation, and several B&Bs and eateries regularly report spirit sightings. It's hard to imagine that this town was once the location of Arizona's largest JCPenney store and one of the state's first Safeway supermarkets! Jerome saw its first revival during the mid-1960s, when hippies arrived and turned it into an arts colony of sorts, and it has since become a tourist attraction. In addition to its shops and historic sites, Jerome is worth visiting for its scenery: it's built into the side of Cleopatra Hill, and from here you can see Sedona's red rocks, Flagstaff's San Francisco Peaks, and even eastern Arizona's Mogollon Rim country.

Jerome is about a mile above sea level, but structures within town sit at elevations that vary by as much as 1,500 feet, depending on whether they're on Cleopatra Hill or at its foot. Blasting at the United Verde (later Phelps Dodge) mine regularly shook buildings off their foundations—the town's jail slid across a road and down a hillside, where it sits today. And that's not all that was unsteady about Jerome. In 1903 a reporter from a New York newspaper called Jerome "the wickedest town in America," due to its abundance of drinking and gambling establishments; town records from 1880 list 24 saloons. Whether by divine retribution or drunken accidents, the town burned down several times.

GETTING HERE AND AROUND

You can get a map of the town's shops and its attractions at the visitor-information trailer on AZ 89A. The three streets in the main shopping area—Hull, Main, and Hill—run parallel to each other on the hillside.

Getting there is half the fun with a classic train ride on the Verde Canyon Railroad.

Street parking is easy to come but be prepared for some steep climbing up and down Cleopatra Hill when you're exploring by foot.

PLANNING YOUR TIME
The town can easily be explored in an afternoon with a stop for lunch, but the historic charm and shopping opportunities entice some visitors to stay overnight. Jerome currently has around 50 retail establishments (that's more than one for every 10 residents). Except for the state-run historic park, attractions and businesses don't always stay open as long as their stated hours if things are slow.

ESSENTIALS
Visitor Info Jerome Chamber of Commerce (☎ *928/634-2900* ⊕ *www. jeromechamber.com*).

EXPLORING
Of the three mining museums in town, the most inclusive is part of **Jerome State Historic Park.** Just outside town, signs on AZ 89A will direct you to the turnoff for the park, reached by a short, precipitous road. The museum occupies the 1917 mansion of Jerome's mining king, Dr. James "Rawhide Jimmy" Douglas Jr., who purchased Little Daisy Mine in 1912. You can see some of the tools and heavy equipment used to grind ore, but accounts of the town's wilder elements—such as the House of Joy brothel—are not so prominently displayed. ⊠*State Park Rd.* ☎*928/634-5381* ⊕*www.azstateparks.com* ⤉*$3* ⊙*Daily 8–5.*

The **Mine Museum** in downtown Jerome is staffed by the Jerome Historical Society. The museum's collection of mining stock certificates alone is worth the (small) price of admission—the amount of money that

Cliff dwellings of the Sinagua people have been preserved for about 600 years at Montezuma Castle.

changed hands in this town 100 years ago boggles the mind. ✉ *200 Main St.* ☎ *928/634–5477* 🎟 *$2* ⏱ *Daily 9–5.*

WHERE TO EAT

$$–$$$
AMERICAN

✗ **The Asylum.** Don't be put off by the name, a tribute to its past identity—this charming restaurant inside the Jerome Grand Hotel is the standout choice in town for fine dining, good wines, and wonderful vistas. Interior burgundy walls hung with local artists' work create a warm and romantic setting. Signature dishes include achiote-rubbed pork tenderloin and sea bass with a poblano chile-chardonnay lemon sauce. Don't miss the butternut squash soup, with just the right blend of sweetness and spice. ✉ *200 Hill St.* ☎ *928/639–3197* ⊕ *www.the asylum.biz* ✍ *Reservations recommended* ▭ *AE, D, MC, V.*

¢
AMERICAN

✗ **Flatiron Cafe.** Ask where to have lunch or a late-afternoon snack, and nearly every Main Street shop owner will direct you to a tiny eatery at the fork in the road. The menu includes healthful sandwiches, such as black-bean hummus with feta cheese, and many coffee drinks. Breakfast is also served. ✉ *416 Main St.* ☎ *928/634–2733* ⊕ *www.flatironcafe jerome.com* ▭ *MC, V* ⏱ *Closed Tues. No dinner.*

$
AMERICAN

✗ **Haunted Hamburger/Jerome Palace.** After the climb up the stairs from Main Street to this former boardinghouse, you'll be ready for the hearty burgers, chili, cheese steaks, and ribs that dominate the menu. Lighter fare, including such meatless selections as the guacamole quesadilla, is also available. Eat on the outside deck overlooking Verde Valley or in the upstairs dining room, where "Claire," the resident ghost, purportedly hangs out. ✉ *410 Clark St.* ☎ *928/634–0554* ▭ *MC, V.*

¢ ✗**Red Rooster Café.** The old Safeway
AMERICAN is now a café with tin ceilings and
country accents, yet the delicious
meat-loaf sandwich is nontradition-
al, served on whole-wheat bread
with Dijon mustard *sans* mashed
potatoes. An eclectic menu includes
green-chile quiche and a turkey pita
topped with bacon, avocado, and
chipotle mayonnaise. Leave room
for the delicate bread pudding made
from croissants. ⊠*363 S. Main St.*
☎*928/634–7087* ⊕*www.redrooster
cafe.com* ⊟*MC, V* ⊘*Closed Mon.*

WORD OF MOUTH

"I would drive to Jerome on the
way [to Sedona] and walk and
have lunch at the Asylum at the
Jerome Grand Hotel . . . great
food and it's haunted. Jerome is a
lovely old mining town and they
have lots of artists and great for
shopping for an hour or two."
—TahitiTams

4

WHERE TO STAY

$–$$ 🏨**Ghost City Inn.** The outdoor veranda at this 1898 B&B affords sweep-
ing views of the Verde Valley and Sedona. Most rooms are decorated
in Victorian style and all have private entrances and baths. Afternoon
tea with cookies is an unexpected luxury for this formerly rough-and-
ready town. **Pros:** authentic historic charm; fabulous views. **Cons:** some
smaller rooms; many stairs. ⊠*541 N. Main St.* ☎*928/634–4678 or
888/634–4678* ⊕*www.ghostcityinn.com* ✍*6 rooms* ⅊*In-room: Wi-
Fi. In-hotel: no kids under 10, some pets allowed, no-smoking rooms*
⊟*AE, D, MC, V* ⎹⎥*BP.*

$–$$ 🏨**Jerome Grand Hotel.** This full-service hotel is housed in the town's for-
mer hospital, built in 1927. Rooms are comfy, with homey furnishings
that part with the institutional past, and many have splendid views. The
hotel's restaurant, The Asylum, is superb. **Pros:** great restaurant; historic
property; great ghost-hunting. **Cons:** creaky; sharing your room with
ghosts. ⊠*200 Hill St.* ☎*928/634–8200 or 888/817–6788* ⊕*www.
jeromegrandhotel.net* ✍*22 rooms, 1 suite* ⅊*In-room: Wi-Fi. In-hotel:
restaurant, bar* ⊟*D, MC, V* ⎹⎥*CP.*

$–$$ 🏨**Surgeon's House.** Plants, knickknacks, bright colors, and plenty of
★ sunlight make this Mediterranean-style home a welcoming place to stay.
Multicourse breakfasts might include overstuffed burritos or a marinated fruit compote. There are two suites and two rooms, including a
former chauffeur's quarters that has a skylight and private patio. **Pros:**
friendly host; knockout vistas; unique gardens. **Cons:** rigid breakfast
time; some rooms have tiny bathrooms; climbing some stairs is required.
⊠*101 Hill St.* ☎*928/639–1452 or 800/639–1452* ⊕*www.surgeons
house.com* ✍*2 rooms, 2 suites* ⅊*In-room: kitchen (some), no TV,
Wi-Fi. In-hotel: some pets allowed* ⊟*MC, V* ⎹⎥*BP.*

NIGHTLIFE

Jerome's a ghost town, so don't expect a hopping nightlife, although
there are some places to have fun. **Paul & Jerry's Saloon** (⊠*Main St.*
☎*928/634–2603*) attracts a (relative) crowd to its two pool tables and
old wooden bar. On weekends there's live music and a lively scene at
the **Spirit Room** (⊠*Main St. and AZ 89A* ☎*928/634–8809*); the mural
over the bar harks back to the days when it was a dining spot for the
prostitutes of the red-light district.

SHOPPING

Jerome has its share of art galleries (some perched precariously on Cleopatra Hill), along with boutiques, and they're funkier than those in Sedona. Main Street and, just around the bend, Hull Avenue are Jerome's two primary shopping streets. Your eyes may begin to glaze over after browsing through one boutique after another, most offering tasteful Southwestern paraphernalia.

Aurum (⊠*369 Main St.* ☎*928/634–3330*) focuses on contemporary art jewelry in silver and gold; about 30 artists are represented. **Designs on You** (⊠*233 Main St.* ☎*928/634–7879*) carries attractively styled women's clothing. **Jerome Artists Cooperative Gallery** (⊠*502 Main St.* ☎*928/639–4276*) specializes in jewelry, sculpture, painting, and pottery by local artists. **Nellie Bly** (⊠*136 Main St.* ☎*928/634–0255*), specializing in art glass, stocks perfume bottles and outstanding kaleidoscopes. **Raku Gallery** (⊠*250 Hull Ave.* ☎*928/639–0239*) stocks the work of 300 artists; you'll find wrought-iron furniture, free-blown glass, and fountains. **Sky Fire** (⊠*140 Main St.* ☎*928/634–8081*) has two floors of items to adorn your person and your house, from Southwestern-pattern dishes to handcrafted Mission-style hutches.

EN ROUTE The drive down a mountainous section of AZ 89A from Jerome to Prescott is gorgeous (if somewhat harrowing in bad weather), filled with twists and turns through **Prescott National Forest**. A scenic turnoff near Jerome provides one last vista and a place to apply chains during surprise snowstorms. There's camping, picnicking, and hiking at the crest of Mingus Mountain. If you're coming to Prescott from Phoenix, the route that crosses the Mogollon Rim, overlooking the Verde Valley, has nice views of rolling hills and is less precipitous.

PRESCOTT

33 mi southwest of Jerome on AZ 89A to U.S. 89, 100 mi northwest of Phoenix via I–17 to AZ 69.

In a forested bowl 5,300 feet above sea level, Prescott is a prime summer refuge for Phoenix-area dwellers. It was proclaimed the first capital of the Arizona Territory in 1864 and settled by Yankees to ensure that gold-rich northern Arizona would remain a Union resource. (Tucson and southern Arizona were strongly pro-Confederacy.) Although early territorial settlers thought that the area's original inhabitants were of Aztec origin, today it's believed that they were ancestors of the Yavapai, whose reservation is on the outskirts of town. The Aztec theory—inspired by *The History and Conquest of Mexico,* a popular book by historian William Hickling Prescott, for whom the town was named—has left its mark on such street names as Montezuma, Cortez, and Alarcon.

Despite a devastating downtown fire in 1900, Prescott remains the "West's most Eastern town" with a rich trove of late-19th-century New England–style architecture. With two institutions of higher education, Yavapai College and Prescott College, Prescott could be called a college town, but it doesn't really feel like one, perhaps because so many retirees also reside here, drawn by the temperate climate and low cost of living.

The 1916 Yavapai County Courthouse stands in the heart of Prescott, bounded by Gurley, Goodwin, Cortez, and Montezuma streets, and guarded by an equestrian bronze of turn-of-the-20th-century journalist and lawmaker Bucky O'Neill, who died while charging San Juan Hill in Cuba with Teddy Roosevelt during the Spanish-American War. Those interested in architecture will enjoy the Victorian neighborhoods. Many Queen Annes have been beautifully restored, and a number are now B&Bs.

GETTING HERE AND AROUND

The most direct route to Prescott from Phoenix is to take Interstate 17 north for 60 mi to Cordes Junction and then drive northwest on AZ 69 for 36 mi into town. Interstate 17, a four-lane divided highway, has several steep inclines and descents (complete with a number of runaway-truck ramps), but it's generally an easy and scenic thoroughfare.

The city's main drag is Gurley Street, which AZ 69 merges into from the east. Most of the town's Victorian neighborhoods, shops and restaurants are within walking distance of the Courthouse Plaza, sitting just off Gurley Street on Montezuma. Art galleries and saloons line Cortez and Montezuma streets to the north and west of the courthouse.

Prescott Municipal Airport is 8 mi north of town on U.S. 89. United Airlines and Frontier Airlines offer connecting service to Prescott Municipal Airport from Phoenix.

PLANNING YOUR TIME

Tourism in Prescott can be bustling but is rarely overwhelming. Any day will do to tour the Victorian homes and antiques shops, but if you enjoy museums, note that museum hours are stunted on Sundays, and you won't want to rush through the extensive grounds of the Sharlot Hall Museum. Devoting a full day to tour Prescott is ample, and an overnight allows for hearing plenty of live music on Whiskey Row.

ESSENTIALS

Transportation Contacts Prescott Municipal Airport (☎ *928/445-7860*).

Visitor Info Prescott Area Coalition for Tourism (☎ *928/708-9336* ⊕ *www. visit-prescott.com*).

EXPLORING

❶ Phippen Museum of Western Art. The paintings and bronze sculptures of George Phippen, along with works by other artists of the West, form the permanent collection of this museum about 5 mi north of downtown. Phippen met with a group of prominent cowboy artists in 1965 to form the Cowboy Artists of America, a group dedicated to preserving the Old West as they saw it. He became the president but died the next year. A memorial foundation set up in his name opened the doors of this museum in 1984. ⊠ *4701 U.S. 89N86303* ☎ *928/778-1385* ⊕ *www. phippenartmuseum.org* ⊠ *$5* ◷ *Tues.–Sat. 10–4, Sun. 1–4.*

❹ Sharlot Hall Museum. Local history is documented at this remarkable museum. Along with the original ponderosa-pine log cabin, which housed the territorial governor, and the museum, named for historian and poet Sharlot Hall, the parklike setting contains three fully restored period homes and a transportation museum. Territorial times are the

Prescott

EAGLE RIDGE

0 _____ 1/2 mile

0 _____ 1/2 km

Yavapol Loop

W. *Wipple St.*

A St.

B St.

C St.

Ruth St.

Damerson St.

W. *Merrit Ave*

Hillside Ave.

Campbell

Navajo Dr.

Lincoln St.

1st St.

2nd St.

5th St.

6th St.

Granite

Creek

Atchison Topeka Santa Fe Railroad

TO
MUNICIPAL
AIRPORT

89

TO YAVAPAI
RESERVATION

MILLER VALLEY

Madison St.

Montezuma

St.

Sonora

GRANITE
CREEK
PARK

Churchill St.

Rush St.

*ROUGHRIDER
PARK* ◆ Yavapai
College

Marston
Ave.

69

*Miller
Valley
Rd.*

Sheldon

Grove Ave.

Sheldon St.

Bradshaw Dr.

Overland Tr.

Cortez St.

Willis St.

McCormick St.

Marina St.

Alarcon St.

Virginia St.

❷

Ken
Linndley
Field

**Courthouse
Plaza** ◆

Summit Ave.

Park Ave.

Gurley St.

❹

Montezuma St.

❸

Carlton St.

Mount Vernon Ave.

Pleasant St.

Goodwin St.

Washington St.

Arizona St.

Rush St.

❶

focus, but natural history and artifacts of the area's prehistoric peoples are also on display. Kids under 18 get in free. ⊠*415 W. Gurley St., 2 blocks west of Courthouse Plaza, Downtown* ☎*928/445–3122* ⊕*www.sharlot.org* ⊠*$5* ⊘*Mon.–Sat. 10–4, Sun. 12–4.*

❷ **Smoki Museum.** The 1935 stone-and-log building, which resembles an Indian pueblo, is almost as interesting as the Native American artifacts inside. Baskets, kachinas, pottery, rugs, and beadwork make up the collection, which represents Native American culture from the pre-Columbian period to the present. ⊠*147 N. Arizona St., Downtown* ☎*928/445–1230* ⊕*www.smokimuseum.org* ⊠*$5* ⊘*Tues.–Sat. 10–4, Sun. 1–4.*

❸ **Whiskey Row.** Twenty saloons and houses of pleasure once lined this stretch of Montezuma Street, along the west side of Courthouse Plaza. Social activity is more subdued these days, and the historic bars provide an escape from the street's many boutiques. ⊠*Downtown.*

**NEED A
BREAK?**

Bistro St. Michael is a great place to relax over a coffee or grab a bowl of black-bean chili and watch the people on Whiskey Row. The café and bar has been restored to its original 1901 style. The service at the counter is brisk, and will leave you plenty of time for antiquing or museum

browsing for the remainder of the day. ✉ *205 W. Gurley St., Downtown* ☎ *928/778–2500.*

SPORTS AND THE OUTDOORS

HIKING AND
CAMPING

More than a million acres of national forest land surround Prescott. Thumb Butte is a popular hiking spot, but there are lots of other trekking and overnighting options. Contact the **Bradshaw Ranger District** (✉ *2230 E. AZ 69, Hwy. 69* ☎ *928/443–8000* ⊕ *www.fs.fed.us/r3/prescott*) for information about hiking trails and campgrounds in the Prescott National Forest south of town down to Horse Thief Basin. Campgrounds near Prescott are generally not crowded.

The **Thumb Butte Loop Trail** (✉ *Thumb Butte Rd., 3 mi west of Prescott following Gurley St., which turns into Thumb Butte*), a 2-mi trek on a paved yet steep loop, takes you 600 feet up near the crest of its namesake. The vistas are large, but you won't be alone on this popular trail.

HORSEBACK
RIDING

Granite Mountain Stables (✉ *2400 W. Shane Dr., 7 mi northeast of Prescott* ☎ *928/771–9551* ⊕ *www.granitemountainstables.com*) has daily guided trail rides and lessons costing about $35.

WHERE TO EAT

$
ITALIAN

✗ **Genovese's.** Reasonably priced, classic southern Italian fare makes this restaurant near Courthouse Plaza a local favorite. The decor is right out of 1975, but the family recipes, like chicken marsala, make up for the lack of ambience. Try the cannelloni stuffed with shrimp, crab, ricotta cheese, and spinach. Save room for spumoni ice cream or a cannoli. ✉ *217 W. Gurley St., Downtown* ☎ *928/541–9089* ⊕ *www.genovesesrestaurant.net* ▭ *AE, MC, V.*

¢
AMERICAN

✗ **Kendall's Famous Burgers and Ice Cream.** A classic diner, replete with booths and a 1950s-style soda fountain, Kendall's serves hamburgers cooked to order with your choice of 14 condiments. If you've seen the movie *Billy Jack*, you'll probably recognize this place from the scene where the Native Americans and the townies get into a big fight in an ice-cream shop. Make sure to try the homemade french fries. ✉ *113 S. Cortez St., Downtown* ☎ *928/778–3658* ▭ *D, MC, V.*

$$–$$$
AMERICAN

✗ **Murphy's.** Mesquite-grilled meats and beer brewed exclusively for the restaurant are the specialties at this classy bar and grill, a sort of local institution set in a restored, polished-up 1890 mercantile building. The baby back ribs, fresh steamed clams, and fresh fried catfish are standouts. Businessfolk do their moving and shaking at lunchtime here, and the spirited bar stays open until 1 AM. ✉ *201 N. Cortez St., Downtown* ☎ *928/445–4044* ⊕ *www.murphysrestaurants.com* ▭ *AE, D, MC, V.*

$$
AMERICAN

✗ **The Palace.** Legend has it that the patrons who saved the Palace's ornately carved 1880s Brunswick bar from a Whiskey Row fire in 1900 continued drinking at it while the row burned across the street. Whatever the case, the bar remains the centerpiece of the beautifully restored turn-of-the-20th-century structure, with a high, pressed-tin ceiling. Steaks and chops are the stars here, but the grilled fish and hearty corn chowder are fine, too. ✉ *120 S. Montezuma St., Downtown* ☎ *928/541–1996* ⊕ *www.historicpalace.com* ▭ *AE, MC, V.*

4

$ ✕**Prescott Brewing Company.** Good beer, good food, good service, and
AMERICAN good prices—for a casual meal, it's hard to beat this cheerful restaurant on the town square. In addition to chili, fish-and-chips, and Brit-
ish-style bangers and mash, vegetarian enchiladas made with tofu and
pasta salad are on the menu. Fresh-baked beer bread comes with many
entrées. ✉*130 W. Gurley St., Downtown* ☎*928/771–2795* ⊕*www.
prescottbrewingcompany.com* ▭*AE, D, DC, MC, V.*

$$$ ✕**The Rose Restaurant.** In a well-maintained Victorian home, the Rose
AMERICAN serves inspired dishes that straddle nouvelle and Continental fare.
Choose from entrées like braised lamb shank, duck breast with sweet-
potato cake and raspberry sauce, or almond-crusted halibut as Sina-
tra music plays softly in the background. Desserts, especially the
apple-caramel tart, are equally stellar. ✉*234 S. Cortez St., Down-
town* ☎*928/777–8308* ⊕*www.theroserestaurant.com* ▭*AE, MC, V*
⊘*Closed Mon. and Tues. No lunch.*

WHERE TO STAY

$$ 🛏**Hassayampa Inn.** Built in 1927 for early automobile travelers, the
Hassayampa Inn oozes character. The ceiling in the lobby is hand-
painted, and some rooms still have the original furnishings. Don't get
a room by the old-fashioned elevator or you'll be jarred by the clanging
metal gate every time it opens and closes. The Peacock Room, the hotel's
pretty—if overly formal—dining room, has tapestried booths and bet-
ter-than-average continental food. In the cocktail lounge, listen to live
jazz while you sip on a martini. **Pros:** cental location; historic charm.
Cons: thin walls and small bathrooms. ✉*122 E. Gurley St., Downtown*
☎*928/778–9434 or 800/322–1927* ⊕*www.hassayampainn.com* ⌨*58
rooms, 10 suites* ♿*In-room: Wi-Fi. In-hotel: restaurant, bar* ▭*AE, D,
DC, MC, V* ⊺⊙*BP.*

¢–$ 🛏**Hotel St. Michael.** Don't expect serenity on the busiest corner of Court-
house Plaza, but for low rates and historic charm it's hard to beat this
hotel in operation since 1900. Rooms have 1920s–'40s-era antiques;
some face the plaza and others look out on Thumb Butte. The first-
floor Bisto St. Michael, where a full breakfast is included with your
stay, serves great coffee and croissants. **Pros:** excellent breakfast; has
character. **Cons:** noise from bars until the wee hours; some rooms are
very worn. ✉*205 W. Gurley St., Downtown* ☎*928/776–1999 or
800/678–3757* ⊕*www.stmichaelhotel.com* ⌨*71 rooms* ♿*In-hotel:
restaurant* ▭*AE, D, DC, MC, V* ⊺⊙*BP.*

$–$$ 🛏**Hotel Vendome.** This World War I–era hostelry has seen miners, health
seekers, and such celebrities as cowboy star Tom Mix walk through its
doors. Old-fashioned touches, including the original claw-foot tubs,
remain, and like many other historic hotels the Vendome has its obligatory resident ghost (her room costs slightly more). **Pros:** central location;
good value. **Cons:** creaky floors raise noise factor. ✉*230 Cortez St.,
Downtown* ☎*928/776–0900 or 888/468–3583* ⊕*www.vendomehotel.
com* ⌨*16 rooms, 4 suites* ♿*In-hotel: bar, no-smoking rooms* ▭*AE,
D, DC, MC, V* ⊺⊙*CP.*

$$–$$$ 🛏**Prescott Resort Conference Center and Casino.** On a hill on the outskirts
of town, this upscale property run by the Yavapai Tribe has views of the
mountain ranges surrounding Prescott and the Valley, although many

guests hardly notice, so riveted are they by the poker machines and slots in Arizona's only hotel casino. There are plenty of recreational facilities to occupy those able to resist the one-armed bandits. **Pros:** nicely updated in 2008, comfortable rooms. **Cons:** large-scale property feels impersonal; drive to town center. ⊠*1500 AZ 69* ☎*928/776–1666 or 800/967–4637* ⊕*www.prescottresort.com* ↶*161 rooms* ⌂*In-room: refrigerator, Wi-Fi. In-hotel: restaurant, bar, tennis courts, pool, gym, public Wi-Fi, no-smoking rooms* ⊟*AE, D, DC, MC, V.*

NIGHTLIFE AND THE ARTS

Prescott's popular **Bluegrass Festival on the Square** (⊕*www.prescottblue grassfestival.com*) takes place in June. The town had its first organized cowboy competition in 1888, and lays claim to having the world's oldest rodeo: the annual **Frontier Days** (⊕*www.worldsoldestrodeo.com*) roundup, held on July 4 weekend at the Yavapai County Fairgrounds. In August the **Cowboy Poets Gathering** (⊕*www.azcowboypoets.org*) brings together campfire bards from around the country.

The **Prescott Fine Arts Association** (⊠*208 N. Marina St., Downtown* ☎*928/445–3286* ⊕*www.pfaa.net*) sponsors musicals and dramas, plays for children, and a concert series. The association's gallery also presents rotating exhibits by local, regional, and national artists. The **Prescott Jazz Society** (⊠*129½ N. Cortez St., Downtown* ☎*928/237–7908* ⊕*www.pjazz.org*) has an intimate storefront lounge. The **Yavapai Symphony Association** (⊠*228 N. Alarcon St., Suite B, Downtown* ☎*928/776–4255* ⊕*www.yavapaisymphony.org*) hosts performances by the Phoenix and Flagstaff symphonies; call ahead for schedules and venues.

Montezuma Street's Whiskey Row, off Courthouse Plaza, is nowhere near as wild as it was in its historic heyday, but most bars have live music—with no cover charge—on weekends. The **Hassayampa Inn** (⊠*122 E. Gurley St., Downtown* ☎*928/778–9434*) is an upscale, art nouveau piano bar. **Jersey Lilly Saloon** (⊠*116 Montezuma St., Downtown* ☎*928/771–0997*), above Matt's Saloon, is a former brothel with live entertainment, a great patio, and a large dance floor. The Brunswick bar at **Lyzzard's Lounge** (⊠*120 N. Cortez St., Downtown* ☎*928/778–2244*) was shipped from England via the Colorado River. **Raven Cafe** (⊠*142 N. Cortez St., Downtown* ☎*928/717–0009*) is a contemporary, attractive coffeehouse and bar that doubles as a live-music venue in the evening.

SHOPPING

Shops selling antiques and collectibles line Cortez Street, just north of Courthouse Plaza. You'll find fun stuff—especially Western kitsch—as well as some good buys on valuable pieces. Courthouse Plaza, especially along Montezuma Street, is lined with specialty and gift shops. Many match those in Sedona for quality. Be sure to check out **Arts Prescott** (⊠*134 S. Montezuma St., Downtown* ☎*928/776–7717* ⊕*www.artsprescott. com*), a cooperative gallery of talented local artisans. **Bella Home Furnishings** (⊠*115 W. Willis St., Downtown* ☎*928/445–0208*) has vintage home furnishings and artwork. At 14,000 square feet, the **Merchandise Mart Antique Mall** (⊠*205 N. Cortez St., Downtown* ☎*928/776–1728*) is the largest of the town's collections of collectors. **Sun West Gallery** (⊠*152 S. Montezuma St., Downtown* ☎*928/778–1204*) has artwork, furnishings, and Native American Zapotec rugs. Don't miss the back room's selection of beads from around the world. Exquisite work of local and national artists is beautifully displayed at **Van Gogh's Ear** (⊠*156 S. Montezuma St., Downtown* ☎*928/776–1080*).

Northeast Arizona

WORD OF MOUTH

"I went to the Upper [Antelope] Canyon and the sun shining down in the canyon was spectacular. The hardest part was bouncing in the truck on the way to and from the entrance. Make sure you take a tripod and a plastic bag for your camera during the truck ride. Dust."

—Myer

WELCOME TO NORTHEAST ARIZONA

TOP REASONS TO GO

★ **Drive the Rim Roads at Canyon de Chelly:** Visit one of the most spectacular natural wonders in the Southwest—it rivals the Grand Canyon for beauty. It's a must for photography buffs.

★ **Go boating at Glen Canyon:** Get to know this stunning, mammoth reservoir by taking a boat out on Lake Powell amid the towering cliffs.

★ **Explore Hubbell Trading Post:** Take the self-guided tour to experience the relationship between the traders and the Navajo.

★ **Shop for handmade crafts on the Hopi Mesas:** Pick up crafts by some of Arizona's leading Hopi artisans, who sustain their culture through continuous occupation of the ancient villages on these mesas.

★ **Take a jeep tour through Monument Valley:** On an excursion through this 92,000-acre area, see firsthand the landscape depicted in such iconic Western films as *Stagecoach* and *The Searchers*.

Antelope Canyon

1 Navajo Nation East. Vastly underrated Canyon de Chelly National Monument offers some of the most spectacular panoramas in the world, and Window Rock is the governmental and cultural hub of the Navajo people.

2 The Hopi Mesas. An artistically rich and dramatically situated tribal land entirely surrounded by Navajo Nation, the Hopi Mesas rise above the high-desert floor, rife with trading posts and art galleries selling fine weavings, jewelry, and crafts.

3 Navajo Nation West. Just 80 mi east of the Grand Canyon's South Rim, the bustling community of Tuba City anchors the western portion of Navajo Nation—it's an excellent base for checking out the region's painted-desert landscapes and Navajo trading posts.

4 Monument Valley. You've probably seen images of this Ancestral Puebloan stomping ground in everything from classic Western movies to Ansel Adams photos; you can explore this sweeping valley on a variety of Navajo-led tours.

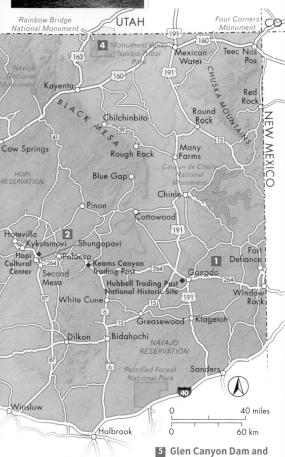

Rainbow Bridge
National Monument

UTAH

Four Corners
Monument

4 Monument Valley
(Navajo Tribal
Park)

Mexican
Water

Teec Nos
Pos

Navajo
National
Monument

Kayenta

Red
Rock

BLACK MESA

Chilchinbito

Round
Rock

CHUSKA MOUNTAINS

NEW MEXICO

Cow Springs

Rough Rock

Many
Farms

HOPI
RESERVATION

Blue Gap

Canyon de Chelly
National
Monument

Chinle

Pinon

Cottowood

Hotevilla
Kykotsmovi
Hopi
Cultural
Center

Polacca

Shungopavi

Keams Canyon
Trading Post

Second
Mesa

Garado

Fort
Defiance

Hubbell Trading Post
National Historic Site

Window
Rock

White Cone

Greasewood

Klagetoh

NAVAJO
RESERVATION

Dilkon

Bidahochi

Petrified Forest
National Park

Sanders

Winslow

Holbrook

Lake Powell Resort

0   40 miles

0   60 km

GETTING ORIENTED

Relatively few visitors experience the vast, sweeping northeast quadrant of Arizona, which comprises the Navajo and Hopi reservations, but efforts to spend a few days here are rewarded with stunning scenery and the chance to learn about some of the world's most vibrant indigenous communities. This is part of the West's great Four Corners Region, home to the underrated and spectacular Canyon de Chelly National Monument as well as the dramatic buttes and canyons of Monument Valley. The one portion of the area outside tribal lands is Page, the base for exploration of crystalline Lake Powell's 200 mi of shoreline.

5 **Glen Canyon Dam and Lake Powell.** The one section of northeastern Arizona not set on tribal lands is dominated by the nation's second-largest man-made body of water, Lake Powell, and 710-foot-tall Glen Canyon Dam; it's a boating paradise, and the town of Page has the greatest number of hotels and restaurants in the region.

5

NORTHEAST ARIZONA PLANNER

Making the Most of Your Time

Northeastern Arizona encompasses an enormous area but relatively few key attractions, so it's best to use one or two primary communities (Page or Tuba City on the west side, Kayenta on the north, and Chinle or Window Rock on the east) as bases for day trips to outlying attractions.

If your time is limited, put Canyon de Chelly and Monument Valley at the top of your list—if you're ambitious, you could explore these two sites on consecutive days, spending the night in either Chinle, Kayenta, or in Monument Valley itself. Focus on the South Rim Drive at Canyon de Chelly, and in Monument Valley book a jeep tour with the highly respected Sacred Monument Tours. On travel days from one base community to another, plan a scenic drive, such as AZ 264 from Tuba City to Window Rock (don't miss the great crafts shopping at Second Mesa) or AZ 98 to U.S. 160 to U.S. 191 from Page to Chinle. Give yourself at least two days to get to know any one part of the region, and as much as a week to 10 days to fully explore all of it.

Getting Here and Around

It's virtually impossible to see much of northeastern Arizona without a car—this is your best bet not only for getting here, but also for visiting attractions and communities throughout the region.

Many visitors see northeastern Arizona as part of a road-tripping adventure through the Four Corners Region, perhaps combining a visit here with trips to the national parks of southern Utah and southwestern Colorado. This "en route" road-tripping strategy makes the most sense for most travelers, especially given the region's stunningly scenic drives.

Most of the 25,000 square mi of the Navajo Reservation and other areas of northeastern Arizona are off the beaten track. It's prudent to stay on the well-maintained paved thoroughfares. If you don't have the equipment for wilderness travel—including a four-wheel-drive vehicle and provisions—and do not have backcountry experience, stay off the dirt roads unless they are signed and graded and the skies are clear. Be on the lookout for ominous rain clouds in summer or signs of snow in winter. Never drive into dips or low-lying areas during a heavy rainstorm. If you heed these simple precautions, car travel through the region will be as safe as anywhere else. While driving around the Navajo Nation, tune in to 660 AM (KTNN) for local news and weather.

A tour of Navajo-Hopi country can involve driving significant distances between widely scattered communities, so a detailed, up-to-date road map is essential. Road service, auto repairs, and other automotive services are few and far between, so service your vehicle before venturing into the Navajo and Hopi reservations (or do so in the larger communities, such as Tuba City, Kayenta, and Window Rock), and carry emergency equipment and supplies.

If You Like Hiking

Some of the best hikes in this region are in Canyon de Chelly, up the streambed between the soaring vermilion, orange, and white sandstone cliffs, with the remains of the ancient Ancestral Puebloan communities frequently in view. The Navajo National Monument offers impressive hikes to Beta-Takin, a settlement dating back to AD 1250, and Keet Seel, which dates back as far as AD 950. Both are in alcoves at the base of gigantic overhanging cliffs. Remember, you cannot hike or camp on private property or tribal land without a backcountry permit.

Local Food and Lodging

Northeastern Arizona is a vast area with small hamlets and towns scattered miles apart, and there are few stores or restaurants along the highway. With the exception of Page, which has slightly more culinary variety, the region's towns mostly offer restaurants serving basic but tasty Native American and Southwestern cuisine. Navajo and Hopi favorites include mutton stew, Hopi *piki* (paper-thin, blue-corn bread), and Navajo fry bread. Navajo tacos are fry bread piled with refried beans, ground beef, lettuce, tomato, scallions, cheese, avocado, sour cream, and salsa. Top the fry bread with butter, honey, and sugar for dessert.

Page also has the area's greatest concentration of lodgings, most of them fairly standard chain motels and hotels, but this base camp for exploring Lake Powell also has a few bed-and-breakfasts as well as houseboat rentals. You'll find a handful of well-maintained chains in the Navajo Nation, mostly in Kayenta, Chinle, Tuba City, and Window Rock. Additionally, in 2008 the Navajo Nation opened the upscale View Hotel right in the heart of Monument Valley, next to the park visitor center. This is also a popular area for both tent and RV camping—you can obtain a list of campgrounds from the Page/Lake Powell Chamber of Commerce and the Navajo Nation Visitor Center.

WHAT IT COSTS

	¢	$	$$	$$$	$$$$
Restaurant	under $8	$8–$12	$13–$20	$21–$30	over $30
Hotel		under $70	$70–$120	$121–$175	$176–$250	over $250

Restaurant prices are per person for a main course at dinner. Hotel prices are for a standard double in high season, excluding taxes and service charges.

Festivals and Events

A number of festivals and events take place among the Navajo and Hopi communities.

Aug. Central Navajo Fair. Several horse races, an arts and crafts market, the Miss Central Navajo Pageant, and several live-music performances are part of this celebration in Chinle. ☎ 928/674-9448.

Aug.–Sept. Hopi Harvest Festival. A celebration featuring Harvest and Butterfly social dances. ☎ 928/737-2754

Sept. Navajo Nation Annual Tribal Fair. The world's largest Native American fair includes a rodeo, traditional Navajo music and dances, food booths, and an intertribal powwow over the first weekend of September after Labor Day, at Window Rock. ☎ 928/871-6647 ⊕ www.navajonationfair.com.

What Time Is It?

Unlike the rest of Arizona (including the Hopi Reservation), the Navajo Reservation observes daylight saving time. Thus for half the year–April to October–it's an hour later on the Navajo Reservation than everywhere else in the state.

5

Updated
by Andrew
Collins

Northeast Arizona is a vast and magnificent land of lofty buttes, towering cliffs, and turquoise skies so clear that horizons appear endless. Most of the land in the area belongs to the Navajo and Hopi peoples, who adhere to ancient traditions based on spiritual values, kinship, and an affinity for nature. In many respects life on the Hopi Mesas has changed little during the last two centuries, and visiting this land can feel like traveling to a foreign country or going back in time.

In such towns as Tuba City and Window Rock it's not uncommon to hear the gliding vowels and soft consonants of the Navajo language, a tongue as different from Hopi as English is from Chinese. As you drive in the vicinity, tune your radio to AM 660 KTNN (⊕ *www.ktnnonline. com*), the Voice of the Navajo Nation since 1985. You'll quickly understand why the U.S. Marine Navajo "code talkers" communicating in their native tongue were able to devise a code within their language that was never broken by the Japanese.

In the Navajo Nation's approximate center sits the nearly 3,000-square-mi Hopi Reservation, a series of adobe villages built on high mesas overlooking the cultivated land. On Arizona's northern and eastern borders, where the Navajo Nation continues into Utah and New Mexico, the Navajo and Canyon de Chelly national monuments contain haunting cliff dwellings of ancient people who lived in the area some 1,500 years ago. Glen Canyon Dam, which abuts the far northwestern corner of the reservation on U.S. 89, holds back more than 200 mi of emerald waters known as Lake Powell.

Most of northeast Arizona is desert country, but it's far from boring: eerie and spectacular rock formations as colorful as desert sunsets highlight immense mesas, canyons, and cliffs; towering stands of ponderosa pine cover the Chuska Mountains to the north and east of Canyon de Chelly. Navajo Mountain to the north and west in Utah soars more than 10,000 feet, and the San Francisco Peaks climb to similar heights to the south and west by Flagstaff. According to the Navajo creation myth, these are two of the four mountainous boundaries of the sacred land where the Navajo first emerged from Earth's interior.

NAVAJO NATION EAST

Land has always been central to the history of the Navajo people: it's embedded in their very name. The Tewa were the first to call them *Navahu*—which means "large area of cultivated land." But according to the Navajo creation myth, they were given the name *ni'hookaa diyan diné*—"holy earth people"—by their creators. Today tribal members call themselves the Diné. The eastern portion of the Arizona Navajo Nation (in Navajo, *diné bikéyah*) is a dry but often surprisingly green land, especially in the vicinity of the aptly named Beautiful Valley, south of Canyon de Chelly along U.S. 191. A landscape of rolling hills, wide arroyos, and small canyons, the area is dotted with traditional Navajo hogans, sheepfolds, cattle tanks, and wood racks. The region's eastern-most portion is marked by tall mountains and towering sandstone cliffs cut by primitive roads that are generally accessible only on horseback or with four-wheel-drive vehicles.

ESSENTIALS

Visitor Info Navajo Nation Tourism Office (☎ *928/810–8501* ⊕ *www. discovernavajo.com*).

WINDOW ROCK

192 mi from Flagstaff; 26 mi from Gallup, New Mexico.

Named for the immense arch-shaped "window" in a massive sandstone ridge above the city, Window Rock is the capital of the Navajo Nation and the center of its tribal government. With a population of around 3,000, this community serves as the business and social center for Navajo families throughout the reservation. Window Rock is a good place to stop for food, supplies, and gas.

GETTING HERE AND AROUND

From Flagstaff follow I–40 east for 160 mi, then Hwy. 12 north. From Gallup, New Mexico follow U.S. 491 north and then NM 264 west (which becomes AZ 264).

EXPLORING

The **Navajo Nation Council Chambers** is a handsome structure that resembles a large ceremonial hogan. The murals on the walls depict scenes from the history of the tribe, and the bell beside the entrance was a gift to the tribe by the Santa Fe Railroad to commemorate the thousands of Navajos who worked to build the railroad. Visitors can observe sessions of the council, where 88 delegates representing 110 reservation chapters meet on the third Monday of January, April, July, and October. Turn east off Indian Highway 12, about ½ mi north of AZ 264, to reach the Council Chambers. **Window Rock Navajo Tribal Park & Veteran's Memorial,** near the Council Chambers, is a memorial park

Navajo Nation and Hopi Reservation Rules

CLOSE UP

Visitors to the Navajo Nation and Hopi Reservation should observe several rules, as follows:

Alcohol and Drugs: The possession and consumption of alcoholic beverages or illicit drugs is illegal on Hopi and Navajo land. You can't purchase alcohol legally while you are on the reservations, and you shouldn't bring any with you.

Camping: No open fires are allowed in reservation campgrounds; you must use grills or fireplaces. You may not gather firewood on the reservation—bring your own. Camping areas have quiet hours from 11 PM to 6 AM. Pets must be kept on a leash or confined. Don't litter.

Hopi Shrines: Hopi spirituality is intertwined with daily life, and objects that seem ordinary to you may have deeper significance. If you come upon a collection of objects at or near the Hopi Mesas do not disturb them.

Permits and Permissions: No off-trail hiking, rock climbing, or other off-road travel is allowed unless you are accompanied by a local guide. A

tribal permit is required for fishing. Violations of fish and game laws are punishable by heavy fines, imprisonment, or both.

Photography: Always ask permission before taking photos of locals. Even if no money is requested, consider offering a dollar or two to the person whose photo you have taken. The Navajo are very open about photographs; the Hopi do not allow photographs at all, including videos, tape recordings, notes, or even sketches.

Religious Ceremonies: Should you see a ceremony in progress, look for posted signs indicating who is welcome. If there are no signs, check with local shops or the village community to see if the ceremony is open to the public. Unless you're specifically invited, stay out of kivas (ceremonial rooms) and stay on the periphery of dances or processions.

Respect for the Land: Do not wander through residential areas or disturb property. Do not disturb or remove animals, plants, rocks, petrified wood, or artifacts. They are protected by Tribal Antiquity and federal laws.

---

honoring Navajo veterans, including the famous World War II code talkers. ⊠ *AZ 264* ☎ *928/871–6647, 928/871–6417 for guided tours* ⊕ *www.navajonationparks.org.* ⊙ *Daily 8–5.*

The **Navajo Nation Museum,** on the grounds of the former Tse Bonito Park off AZ 264, is devoted to the art, culture, and history of the Navajo people and has an excellent library on the Navajo Nation. The museum hosts exhibitions of Native artists each season; call for a list of shows. In the same building as the Navajo Nation Museum is the Navajo Nation Visitor Center, a great resource for all sorts of information on reservation activities. ⊠ *AZ 264, next to Quality Inn Navajo Nation* ☎ *928/871–7941* ⊕ *www.navajonationmuseum.org* ⊠ *Free* ⊙ *Mon. and Sat. 8–5, Tues.–Fri. 8–8.*

Within walking distance of the Navajo Museum, the **Navajo Arts and Crafts Enterprises** (☎ *866/871–4090* ⊕ *www.gonavajo.com/navajoart*) sells local artwork, including pottery, jewelry, and blankets.

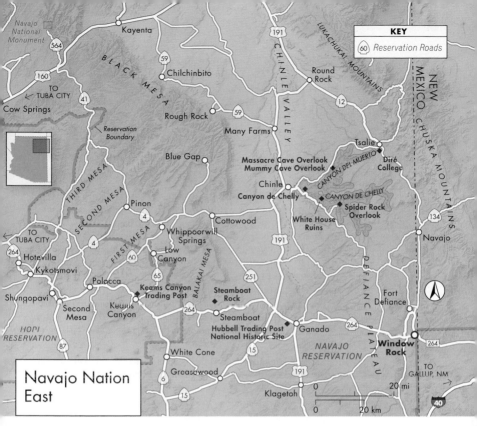

Navajo Nation
East

Amid the sandstone monoliths on the border between Arizona and New Mexico, the **Navajo Nation Botanical and Zoological Park** displays about 30 species of domestic and wild animals, birds, and amphibians that figure in Navajo legends, as well as examples of plants used by traditional people. Most of the animals here were brought in as orphans or after sustaining injuries—they include black bears, mountain lions, golden eagles, gila monsters, and western rattlesnakes. It's the only Native American–owned-and-operated zoo in the United States. ⊠ *AZ 264, northeast of Navajo Nation Museum* ☏ *928/871–6574* ⊕ *www. discovernavajo.com/zbp.html* 🎫 *Free* ⊙ *Mon.–Sat. 10–5.*

Many all-Indian rodeos are held near the center of downtown at the **Navajo Tribal Fairgrounds.** The community hosts the annual multiday Fourth of July celebration, with a major rodeo, ceremonial dances, and a parade. The Navajo Nation Tribal Fair, much like a traditional state fair, is held in early September. It offers standard county-fair rides, midway booths, contests, powwow competitions, and an all-Indian rodeo. ⊠ *AZ 264* ☏ *928/871–6647 or 928/871–6478 Navajo Nation Fair Office* ⊕ *www.navajonationfair.com.*

WHERE TO STAY

¢–$ 🖬 **Navajoland Inn and Suites.** This well-kept, affordable property in St. Michaels, formerly a Days Inn, is 3 mi west of Window Rock, and has standard rooms decorated in contemporary Southwestern style with 25-inch TVs, irons and boards, and free local phone calls. Guests appreciate the indoor pool and hot tub. **Pros:** friendly staff, closest reliable accommodation to Hubbell Trading Post, very well maintained. **Cons:** basic rooms, not much curb appeal. ✉ *392 W. AZ 264, St. Michaels* ☎ *928/871–5690* ⊕ *www.navajoland-innsuites.com* ⌁ *65 rooms, 8 suites* ♿ *In-room: refrigerator, Wi-Fi. In-hotel: restaurant, pool, gym, some pets allowed* ⊟ *AE, D, MC, V.*

¢–$ 🖬 **Quality Inn Navajo Nation Capital.** Rooms in this two-story beam-and-stucco hotel are decorated with a Navajo-style palette of tan, orange, and yellow that complements the basic pine furniture. The Diné Restaurant serves Navajo and Southwestern fare (you can build your own Navajo tacos) plus a handful of American standards, and the gift shop sells authentic Navajo jewelry. **Pros:** within walking distance of Navajo Museum, decent restaurant, convenient location. **Cons:** on busy road with dull settings, cookie-cutter decor. ✉ *48 W. AZ 264, at Hwy. 12,* ☎ *928/871–4108 or 800/662–6189* ⊕ *www.qualityinnwindowrock. com* ⌁ *56 rooms* ♿ *In-room: refrigerator, Ethernet. In-hotel: restaurant, public Internet, some pets allowed* ⊟ *AE, D, MC, V* ⍟ *CP.*

SHOPPING

★ An outlet of the **Navajo Arts and Crafts Enterprises** (✉ *AZ 264 at Hwy. 12, next to Quality Inn Navajo Nation Capital* ☎ *928/871–4090 or 866/871–4095* ⊕ *www.gonavajo.com/navajoart*) stocks tribal art purchased from craftspeople across the reservation, including stunning silverwork, traditional Navajo dolls, pottery, and rugs. Local artisans are occasionally at work here. Major credit cards are accepted.

CANYON DE CHELLY

30 mi west of Window Rock on AZ 264, then north 25 mi on U.S. 191.

GETTING HERE AND AROUND

U.S. 191 runs North-South through the town of Chinle, the closest town to the Canyon de Chelly entrance.

Guided tours allow visits directly into the canyons, not just the park drives high above them; jeep tours even have the option of camping overnight. Each kind of tour has its pros and cons: you'll cover the most ground in a jeep; horseback trips get you close to one of the park's most notable geological formations, Spider Rock; and guided walks provide the most leisurely pace and an excellent opportunity to interact with your guide and ask questions. You can also plan a custom treks lasting up to a week.

PLANNING YOUR TIME

To get even a basic sense of the park's scope and history, plan to spend at least a full day here. If time is short, the best strategy is to spend some time at the visitor center and then drive the most magnificent of the two park roads, South Rim Drive. You could, theoretically, drive both park roads in one day, but it's better to set aside a second day for North Rim Drive, or take the North Rim Drive as an alternative route to Kayenta, by way of Tsaile. From the different overlooks along the park roads you'll be treated to amazing photo ops of the valley floors below, and you can also access certain dwellings. For a more in-depth look at Canyon de Chelly, consider one of the guided hiking, jeep, or horseback tours into the canyon.

Both Canyon de Chelly and Canyon del Muerto have a paved rim drive with turnoffs and parking areas. Each drive takes a minimum of two hours—allow more if you plan to hike to White House Rim, picnic, or spend time photographing the sites. Overlooks along the rim drives provide incredible views of the canyon; be sure to stay on trails and away from the canyon edge, and to control children and pets at all times.

The visitor center has exhibits on the history of the cliff dwellers and provides information on scheduled hikes, tours, and National Park Service programs offered throughout the summer months.

EXPLORING

Fodor's Choice
★

Home to Ancestral Puebloans from AD 350 to 1300, the nearly 84,000-acre **Canyon de Chelly** (pronounced d'*shay*) is one of the most spectacular natural wonders in the Southwest. On a smaller scale, it rivals the Grand Canyon for beauty. Its main gorges—the 26-mi-long Canyon de Chelly ("canyon in the rock") and the adjoining 35-mi Canyon del Muerto ("canyon of the dead")—comprise sheer, heavily eroded sandstone walls that rise to 1,100 feet over dramatic valleys. Ancient pictographs and petroglyphs decorate some of the cliffs, and within the canyon complex there are more than 7,000 archaeological sites. Stone walls rise hundreds of feet above streams, hogans, tilled fields, and sheep-grazing lands.

You can view prehistoric sites near the base of cliffs and perched on high, sheltering ledges, some of which you can access from the park's two main drives along the canyon rims. The dwellings and cultivated fields of the present-day Navajo lie in the flatlands between the cliffs, and those who inhabit the canyon today farm much the way their ancestors did. Most residents leave the canyon in winter but return in early spring to farm.

★ Canyon de Chelly's **South Rim Drive** (36 mi round-trip with seven overlooks) starts at the visitor center and ends at **Spider Rock Overlook,** where cliffs plunge 1,000 feet to the canyon floor. The view here is of two pinnacles, Speaking Rock and Spider Rock. Other highlights on the South Rim Drive are Junction Overlook, where Canyon del Muerto joins Canyon de Chelly; White House Overlook, from which a 2½-mi round-trip trail leads to the **White House Ruin,** with remains of nearly 60 rooms and several kivas; and Sliding House Overlook, where you can see dwellings on a narrow, sloped ledge across the canyon. The carved and sometimes narrow trail down the canyon side to White House Ruin is the only access into Canyon de Chelly without a guide—but if you have a fear of heights, this may not be the hike for you.

The only slightly less breathtaking **North Rim Drive** (34 mi round-trip with four overlooks) of Canyon del Muerto also begins at the

DID YOU KNOW?

Spider rock rises 800 feet from the canyon floor and is considered a sacred place. Tours of Canyon de Chelly take you into the canyon and not just along the park roads above.

WALKING
TOURS

Footpath Journey Tours (☎928/724–3366 ⊕*www.footpathjourneys.com*) offers custom four- to seven-day treks into the canyon starting at $800 per person, not including food.

WHERE TO EAT

Chinle is the closest town to Canyon de Chelly. There are good lodgings with restaurants, as well as a supermarket and a campground. Be aware that you may be approached by panhandlers in the grocery store parking lot. In late August each year, Chinle is host to the Central Navajo Fair, a public celebration complete with a rodeo, carnival, and traditional dances.

$–$$ ✕**Garcia's Restaurant.** The lobby restaurant at Chinle's Holiday Inn is
AMERICAN   low-key but a bit lacking in natural light and rather ordinary by most standards, but it is one of the area's more reliable dining options, especially for dinner. You can count on well-prepared specialties such as mutton stew with fry bread and honey. They also sell a box picnic for guests. ⊠*Indian Hwy. 7* ☎*928/674–5000* ⊕*www.holidayinn.com* ▤*AE, D, DC, MC, V* ⊘*No lunch mid-Nov.–Mar.*

$ ✕**The Junction.** Across the parking lot from the Best Western Canyon
AMERICAN   de Chelly Inn, this sun-filled, airy dining room with cream-color walls, large windows, a long granite counter, and a mix of attractive booths and tables has a cheerier feel than any other restaurant in town, and the kitchen turns out pretty tasty American, Southwestern, and Chinese food, too. Specialties include posole stew, pizzas, and sheepherder's sandwiches (their vision consists of a tortilla or fry bread stuffed with steak, Swiss cheese, grilled onions, chiles, and tomatoes). A small kiosk by the front door sells gifts and jewelry. ⊠*100 Main St.* ⊕*Box 295, Chinle 86503* ☎*928/674–5875 or 800/327–0354* ⊕*www.canyon dechelly.com* ▤*AE, D, DC, MC, V.*

WHERE TO STAY

$ ⛫**Best Western Canyon de Chelly Inn.** This two-story motel about 3 mi from Canyon de Chelly but close to the junction with U.S. 191 has cheerful rooms with modern, no-frills oak furnishings. All rooms have coffeemakers. The on-site Junction restaurant is one of the only spots in town to serve three meals a day, year-round, and there's a very good gift shop off the lobby. **Pros:** usually slightly less expensive than the Holiday Inn, fun retro-motel exterior, indoor pool with hot tub and sauna is open 24 hours. **Cons:** not within walking distance of the park. ⊠*100 Main St.* ⊕*Box 295, Chinle 86503* ☎*928/674–5875 or 800/327–0354* ⊕ *www.canyondechelly.com* ⊷*102 rooms* ⚬*In-room: Wi-Fi. In-hotel: restaurant, room service, pool, no elevator* ▤*AE, D, DC, MC, V.*

$–$$ ⛫**Holiday Inn Canyon de Chelly.** Once Garcia's Trading Post, this hotel near Canyon de Chelly is less generic than you might expect: the exterior is territorial fort in style, although the rooms are predictably pastel and contemporary. Off the lobby there's a gift shop stocked with local Native American arts and crafts, plus a decent restaurant. **Pros:** attractive adobe-style building, nice pool and gym, a short drive from park entrance. **Cons:** not especially memorable decor, dull roadside setting. ⊠ *Indian Hwy. 7* ⬧*Box 1889, Chinle 86503* ☏*928/674–5000 or 888/465–4329* ⊕*www.holidayinn.com* ⬩*108 rooms* ♿*In-room: refrigerator, Wi-Fi. In-hotel: restaurant, gym, pool* ▭*AE, D, DC, MC, V.*

¢ 🏨**Many Farms Inn.** Many Farms High School runs this no-frills, clean facility, which is staffed by Navajo students of hotel management. It's not fancy, but rooms are pleasant and contain two single beds, which means single or double occupancy only. Bathrooms are shared, and you have to go to the first floor to use pay phones or watch TV. **Pros:** super-cheap, great opportunity to interact with local students, nice views of area rock formations. **Cons:** rooms lack amenities, no Internet, 20-minute drive north of Canyon de Chelly. ⊠ *U.S. 191 and Indian Hwy. 59* ⬧*Box 307, Many Farms 86538* ☏*928/781–6362* ⊕*www.manyfarms.bia.edu* ⬩*30 rooms* ♿*In-room: no phone, refrigerator, no TV. In-hotel: gym, no elevator* ▭*No credit cards* ⊙*Closed weekends Aug.–May.*

$ 🏨**Thunderbird Lodge.** In an ideal location within the national monu-
★ ment's borders, this pleasant establishment has stone-and-adobe units that match the site's original 1896 trading post. The cafeteria is in the original trading post and serves reasonably priced soups, salads, sandwiches, and entrées, including charbroiled steaks. The lodge also offers jeep tours of Canyon de Chelly and Canyon del Muerto. **Pros:** inside the actual park borders, steeped in history, tours offered right from hotel. **Cons:** rustic decor, no high-speed Internet. ⊠ *Indian Hwy. 7* ⬧*Box 548, Chinle 86503* ☏*928/674–5841 or 800/679–2473* ⊕*www.tbirdlodge.com* ⬩*73 rooms* ♿*In-room: Wi-Fi. In-hotel: restaurant, no elevator* ▭*AE, D, DC, V.*

HUBBELL TRADING POST NATIONAL HISTORIC SITE

40 mi south of Canyon de Chelly, off AZ 264; 30 mi west of Window Rock.

GETTING HERE AND AROUND

The National Park Service visitor center exhibits illustrate the post's history, and you can take a self-guided tour of the grounds and Hubbell home and visit the Hubbell Trading Post, which contains a fine display of Native American artistry. The visitor center has a fairly comprehensive bookstore specializing in Navajo history, art, and culture; local weavers often demonstrate their craft on-site.

EXPLORING

John Lorenzo Hubbell, a merchant and friend of the Navajo, established this trading post in 1876. Hubbell taught, translated letters, settled family quarrels, and explained government policy to the Navajo, and during an 1886 smallpox epidemic he turned his home into a hospital and ministered to the sick and dying. He died in 1930, and is buried near the trading post.

The Navajo and the Hopi

Both the Navajo and Hopi base their culture on the land around them, but they are very different from one another. The Navajo refer to themselves as the Diné (pronounced din-*eh*)—"the people"—and live on 17 million acres in Arizona, New Mexico, Utah, and Colorado. The Hopi trace their roots back to the original settlers of the area, whom they call the *Hisatsinom,* or "people of long ago"—they are also known as Anasazi, meaning both "ancient ones" and "ancient enemies." Hopi culture is more formal and structured than that of the Navajo, and their religion has remained stronger and purer. For both tribes unemployment is high on the reservation, and poverty a constant presence.

NAVAJO

The Navajos use few words and have a subtle sense of humor that can pass you by quickly if you're not a good listener. From childhood they are taught not to talk too much, be loud, or show off. Eye contact is considered impolite. If you're conversing with Navajos, some may look down or away even though they are paying attention to you. Likewise, touching is seen differently; handshaking may be the only physical contact that you see. When shaking hands, a light touch is preferred to a firm grip, which is considered overbearing.

"CODE TALKERS"

Although most Navajos speak English with varying degrees of mastery, listen closely to the language of the Diné. Stemming from the Athabascan family of languages, it is difficult for outsiders to learn because of subtle accentuation. The famous Marine Corps Navajo "code talkers" of World War II saved thousands of lives in the South Pacific by creating a code within their native Navajo language. Their unbreakable radio messages mystified the Japanese, and got through safely and accurately to American troops. These Native Americans are true patriots, who today speak humbly of their accomplishments. Many "code talkers" still alive today reside in the area around Tuba City.

HOPI

Hopi mythology holds that a white-skinned people will save the tribe from its difficult life. Long ago, however, in the face of brutal treatment by whites, most Hopi became convinced that salvation would originate elsewhere. (Some Hopi now look to the Dalai Lama for redemption.)

CEREMONIAL DANCES

Most Hopi ceremonies take place in village plazas and kivas (underground ceremonial chambers) and last two days or longer; outsiders are sometimes permitted to watch segments of some ceremonies but are never allowed into kivas unless invited.

RESERVATION REALITIES

Although not easy to witness, the disappointment of the Hopi and the despair of the Navajo are easy to understand after a visit to the reservation. Most Navajo and Hopi disapprove of the practice, but some panhandlers cluster at shopping centers and view sites, hoping to glean a few tourist dollars. Visitors should respond to panhandlers with a polite but firm "no." If you wish to help, make a donation to a legitimate organization that raises funds at reservation grocery stores.

The **Hubbell Trading Post National Historic Site** is famous for "Ganado red" Navajo rugs, which are sold at the store here. The quality is outstanding, and prices are high but fair—rugs can cost anywhere from $100 to more than $30,000. Considering the time that goes into weaving each one, the prices are quite reasonable. It's hard to resist the beautiful designs and colors, and it's a pleasure just to browse around this rustic spot, where Navajo artists frequently show their work. Documents of authenticity are provided for all works. Note: when photographing weavers, ask permission first. They expect a few dollars in return. ⊠ *AZ 264, 1 mi west of town, Ganado* ☎ *928/755–3475 park office, 928/755–3254 store* ⊕ *www.nps.gov/hutr* ⊡ *Free; $2 to tour Hubbell home* ⊙ *May–early Sept., daily 8–6; mid-Sept.–Apr., daily 8–5.*

EN ROUTE About 20 mi west of Hubbell Trading Post on AZ 264 is **Steamboat Rock,** an immense, jutting peninsula of stone that resembles an early steamboat, complete with a geologically formed waterline. At Steamboat Rock you are only 5 mi from the eastern boundary of the Hopi Reservation.

5

THE HOPI MESAS

The Hopi occupy 12 villages in regions referred to as First Mesa, Second Mesa, and Third Mesa. Although these areas have similar languages and traditions, each has its own individual features. Generations of Hopitu, "the peaceful people," much like their Puebloan ancestors, have lived in these largely agrarian settlements of stone-and-adobe houses, which blend in with the earth so well that they appear to be natural formations. Television antennae, satellite dishes, and automobiles notwithstanding, these Hopi villages still exude the air of another time.

Descendants of the ancient Hisatsinom, the Hopi number about 12,000 people today. Their culture can be traced back more than 2,000 years, making them one of the oldest known tribes in North America. They successfully developed "dry farming," and grow many kinds of vegetables and corn (called maize) as their basic food—in fact the Hopi are often called the "corn people." They incorporate nature's cycles into most of their religious rituals. In the celebrated Snake Dance ceremony, dancers carry venomous snakes in their mouths to appease the gods and to bring rain. In addition to farming the land, the Hopi create fine pottery and basketwork and excel in wood carving of kachina dolls.

ESSENTIALS

Vistor Info Inter Tribal Council of Arizona: Hopi Tribe (☎ *928/734–3000* ⊕ *www.itcaonline.com/tribes_hopi.html).*

KEAMS CANYON TRADING POST

43 mi west of Hubbell Trading Post on AZ 264.

The trading post established by Thomas Keam in 1875 to do business with local tribes is now the area's main tourist attraction, offering a primitive campground, restaurant, service station, and shopping center, all set in a dramatic rocky canyon. An administrative center for the

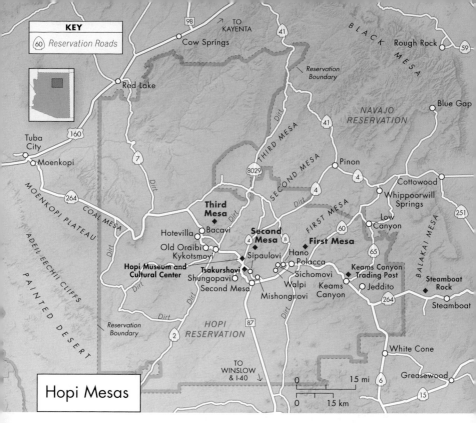

Hopi Mesas

Bureau of Indian Affairs, Keams Canyon also has a number of government buildings. A road, accessible by passenger car, winds northeast 3 mi into the 8-mi wooded canyon. At **Inscription Rock,** about 2 mi down the road, frontiersman Kit Carson engraved his name in stone. There are several picnic spots in the canyon.

WHERE TO EAT

¢–$ ✕**Keams Canyon Restaurant.** A typical no-frills roadside diner with Formi-
AMERICAN   ca tabletops, Keams offers both American and Native American dishes, including Navajo tacos heaped with ground beef, chili, beans, lettuce, and grated cheese. Daily specials, offered at $1 to $2 off the regular price, may include anything from barbecued ribs to lamb chops to crab legs. There's also an ice-cream stand in the same building. ⊠*Keams Canyon Shopping Center, AZ 264, Keams Canyon* ☎*928/738–2296* ▭*D, MC, V* ☾*No dinner weekends.*

SHOPPING

Keams Canyon Arts and Crafts and McGee's Art Gallery (⊠*AZ 264, Keams Canyon* ☎*928/738–2295* ⊕*www.hopiart.com*), upstairs from the Keams Canyon Restaurant, sells first-rate, high-quality Hopi crafts such as handcrafted jewelry, pottery, beautiful carvings, basketry, and artwork.

FIRST MESA

★ *11 mi west of Keams Canyon, on AZ 264.*

First Mesa villages are renowned for their polychrome pottery and kachina-doll carvings. The first village that you approach is Polacca; the older and more impressive villages of Hano, Sichomovi, and Walpi are at the top of the sweeping mesa. From Polacca a paved road (off AZ 264) angles up to a parking lot near the village of Sichomovi, and to the Punsi Hall Visitor Center. ■**TIP**→You must get permission at Punsi Hall to take the guided walking tour of Hano, Sichomovi, and Walpi. Admission is by tour only, so call ahead to find out when they're offered.

The older Hopi villages have structures built of rock and adobe mortar in simple architectural style. **Hano** actually belongs to the Tewa, a New Mexico Pueblo tribe. In 1696 the Tewa Indians sought refuge with the Hopi on First Mesa after an unsuccessful rebellion against the Spanish in the Rio Grande Valley. Today the Tewa live close to the Hopi but maintain their own language and ceremonies. **Sichomovi** is built so close to Hano that only the residents can tell where one ends and the other begins. Constructed in the mid-1600s, this village is believed to have been built to ease overcrowding at Walpi, the highest point on the mesa. **Walpi** (☎928/737–9556), built on solid rock and surrounded by steep cliffs, frequently hosts ceremonial dances. It's the most pristine of the Hopi villages, with cliff-edge houses and vast scenic vistas. Inhabited for more than 1,100 years (dating back to 900 AD), Walpi's cliff-edge houses seem to grow out of the nearby terrain. Today only about 10 residents occupy this settlement, which has neither electricity nor running water; one-hour guided tours of the village are available. Note that Walpi's steep terrain makes it a less than ideal destination for acrophobes. ⌂*Punsi Hall Visitor Center, First Mesa* ☎*928/737–2262* 🎫*Guided First Mesa tours $8, Walpi tours $5* ☉*First Mesa tours Nov.–mid-Mar., daily 9:30–4; mid-Mar.–Oct., daily 9–5, except when ceremonies are being held; Walpi tours by appointment.*

SECOND MESA

8 mi southwest of First Mesa, on AZ 264.

The Mesas are the Hopi universe, and Second Mesa is the "Center of the Universe." **Shungopavi,** the largest and oldest village on Second Mesa, which was founded by the Bear Clan, is reached by a paved road angling south off AZ 264, between the junction of AZ 87 and the Hopi Cultural Center. The villagers here make silver overlay jewelry and coil plaques. Coil plaques are woven from galleta grass and yucca and are adorned with designs of kachinas, animals, and corn. The art of making the plaques has been passed from mother to daughter for generations, and fine coil plaques have become highly sought-after collector's items. The famous Hopi snake dances (closed to the public) are held here in August during even-numbered years. Two smaller villages are off a paved road that runs north from AZ 264, about ⅕ mi east of the Hopi Cultural Center. **Mishongnovi,** the easternmost settlement, was established in the late 1600s. For permission to visit **Sipaulovi,** which was originally at the

base of the mesa before being moved to its present site in 1680, call the Sipaulovi Village Community Center (☎928/737–2570).

At the **Hopi Museum and Cultural Center,** you can stop for the night, learn about the people and their reservation, and eat authentic Hopi cuisine. The museum here is dedicated to preserving Hopi traditions and to presenting those traditions to non-Hopi visitors. A gift shop sells works by local Hopi artisans at reasonable prices, and a modest picnic area on the west side of the building is a pleasant spot for lunch with a view of the San Francisco Peaks. ⊠*AZ 264, Second Mesa* ☎*928/734–2401* ⊕*www.hopiculturalcenter.com* ⊠*Museum $4* ⊙*Mid-Mar.–Oct., weekdays 8–4:30, weekends 9–3; Nov.–mid-Mar., weekdays 8–4:30.*

WHERE TO EAT AND STAY

$ ✕**Hopi Cultural Center Restaurant.** The restaurant at the Hopi Cultural
SOUTHWESTERN Center is an attractive, light-filled room where you can sample tradi-
★ tional tribal fare. Authentic dishes include Indian tacos, Hopi blue-corn pancakes, piki (paper-thin blue-corn bread), fry bread (delicious with honey or salsa), and *nok qui vi* (a tasty stew made with tender bits of lamb, hominy, and mild green chiles). Breakfast is served starting at 6 in summer, an hour later in winter. ⊠*5 mi west of AZ 87 on AZ 264, Second Mesa* ☎*928/734–2401* ⊕*www.hopiculturalcenter.com* ▤*DC, MC, V.*

$ ▤**Hopi Cultural Center Motel.** This Hopi-run establishment is the only place to eat or sleep in the immediate area, but because of its remote location it almost always has vacant rooms. The attractive adobe building with a tan and reddish-brown exterior contains clean, quiet, moderately priced rooms with coffeemakers. **Pros:** adjacent to cultural center, only place to stay for miles in either direction, peaceful setting. **Cons:** remote unless you are here to explore Hopi culture, fairly basic rooms, no high-speed Internet. ⊠*5 mi west of AZ 87 on AZ 264, Second Mesa* ☎*928/734–2401* ⊕*www.hopiculturalcenter.com* ⇌*30 rooms* ⌂*In-hotel: no elevator* ▤*DC, MC, V.*

SHOPPING

The venerable **Hopi Arts and Crafts/Silvercrafts Cooperative Guild** (⊠*383 AZ 264, Second Mesa* ☎*928/734–2463 or 866/718–8476*), west of the Hopi Cultural Center and in existence since the 1940s, hosts craftspeople selling their wares; you might even see silversmiths at work here. Shops at the **Hopi Cultural Center** (⊠*AZ 264, Second Mesa* ☎*928/734–2401*) carry the works of local artists and artisans. At **Hopi Fine Arts** (⊠*AZ 264 at AZ 87, Second Mesa* ☎*928/737–2222*), proprietor and musician Alph Secakuku is a native of the Hopi Pueblo and an authority on all arts and crafts of the Hopi people. He represents about 75 active artisans in his user-friendly gallery. **Tsu-Kurs-Ovi** (⊠*AZ 264, Second Mesa* ☎*928/734–2478*), 1½ mi east of the Hopi Cultural Center, is a small shop where Hopi come to buy bundles of sweet grass and sage, deer hooves with which to make rattles, and ceremonial belts adorned with seashells. The proprietor's wife, Janice Day, is a renowned Hopi basket maker. The shop has one of the largest collections of Hopi baskets in the Southwest.

5

THIRD MESA

12 mi northwest of Second Mesa, on AZ 264.

Third Mesa villages are known for their agricultural accomplishments, textile weaving, wicker baskets, silver overlay, and plaques. You'll find crafts shops and art galleries, as well as occasional roadside vendors, along AZ 264. ■TIP➔The Hopi Tribal Headquarters and Office of Public Relations in Kykotsmovi should be visited first for necessary permissions to visit the villages of Third Mesa.

Kykotsmovi, at the eastern base of Third Mesa, is literally translated as "ruins on the hills" for the many sites on the valley floor and in the surrounding hills. Present-day Kykotsmovi was established by Hopi people from Oraibi—a few miles west—who either converted to Christianity or who wished to attend school and be educated. Kykotsmovi is the seat of the Hopi Tribal Government.

Old Oraibi, a few miles west and on top of Third Mesa at about 7,200 feet in elevation, is believed to be the oldest continuously inhabited community in the United States, dating from around AD 1150. It was also the site of a rare, bloodless conflict between two groups of the Hopi people; in 1906, a dispute, settled uniquely by a "push of war" (a pushing contest), sent the losers off to establish the town of Hotevilla. Oraibi is a dusty spot, and, as a courtesy tourists are asked to park their cars outside and approach the village on foot.

Hotevilla and **Bacavi** are about 4 mi west of Oraibi, and their inhabitants are descended from the former residents of that village. The men of Hotevilla continue to plant crops and beautiful gardens along the mesa slopes. ⊠*Cultural Preservation Office, AZ 264* ⌂*Box 123, Kykotsmovi 86039* ☎*928/734–3000 or 928/734–3612* ⊕*www.nau. edu/~hcpo-p* ⊙ *Weekdays 8:30–5.*

EN ROUTE

Beyond Hotevilla, AZ 264 descends from Third Mesa, exits the Hopi Reservation, and crosses into Navajo territory, past **Coal Canyon,** where Native Americans have long mined coal from the dark seam just below the rim. The colorful mudstone, dark lines of coal, and bleached white rock have an eerie appearance, especially by the light of the moon. Twenty miles west of Coal Canyon, at the junction of AZ 264 and U.S. 160, is the town of Moenkopi, the last Hopi outpost. Established as a farming community, it was settled by the descendants of former Oraibi residents.

NAVAJO NATION WEST

The Hopi Reservation is like a doughnut hole surrounded by the Navajo Nation. If you approach the Grand Canyon from U.S. 89, via Flagstaff, north of the Wupatki National Monument, you'll find two significant sites in the western portions of the Navajo Reservation, the Cameron Trading Post and Tuba City. Situated 45 mi west of the Hopi town of Hotevilla, Tuba City is a good stopover if you're traveling east to the Hopi Mesas or northeast to Page.

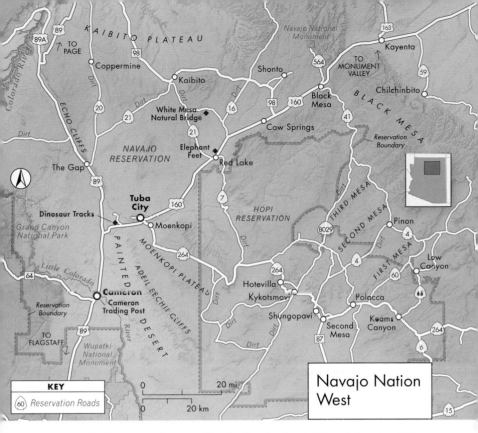

At Cameron, the turnoff point for the South Rim of the Grand Canyon, the Cameron Trading Post was built in 1916 and commemorates Ralph Cameron, a pre-statehood territorial-legislative delegate. The sheer walls of the Little Colorado River Canyon about 10 mi west of U.S. 89 along AZ 64 are quite impressive, and also worth a stop.

TUBA CITY

52 mi northwest of Third Mesa on AZ 264.

Tuba City, believed to be named after a Hopi chief "Tsuve," has about 8,200 permanent residents and is the administrative center for the western portion of the Navajo Nation. In addition to a hotel, hostel, and a few restaurants, this small town has a hospital, a bank, a trading post, and a movie theater. In late October Tuba City hosts the Western Navajo Fair, a celebration combining traditional Navajo song and dance with a parade, pageant, and countless arts-and-crafts exhibits.

EXPLORING

The octagonal **Tuba City Trading Post** (⊠ *Main St. at Moenave Rd.* ☎ *928/283–5441*), founded in the early 1870s, sells groceries and authentic, reasonably priced Navajo rugs, pottery, baskets, and jewelry—it's adjacent to the Quality Inn Navajo Nation.

★ In 2007 the tribe opened the dramatic 7,000-square-foot **Explore Navajo Interactive Museum,** which is set inside a geodesic dome–shaped structure, meant to recall a traditional Navajo hogan, and contains a vast trove of artifacts, photos, artwork, and memorabilia. One of the more poignant exhibits tells of the infamous "Long Walk" of 1864, when the U.S. military forced the Navajo to leave their native lands and march to an encampment at Fort Sumner, New Mexico, where they were confined for more than four years. The museum also operates the small **Navajo Code Talkers Memorial Museum** in the back of the Tuba City Trading Post next door. Both facilities are adjacent to the Quality Inn Navajo Nation. ✉ *Main St.* ☎ *800/644–8383* ⊕ *www.explorenavajo. com* ☜ *$9* ⊙ *Mon.–Sat. 8–6, Sun. noon–6.*

About 5½ mi west of Tuba City, between mileposts 316 and 317 on U.S. 160, is a small sign for the **Dinosaur Tracks.** More than 200 million years ago a dilophosaurus—a carnivorous bipedal reptile over 10 feet tall—left tracks in mud that turned to sandstone. There's no charge for a look. Ask the locals about guiding you to the nearby petroglyphs and freshwater springs.

Four miles west of the dinosaur tracks on U.S. 160 is the junction with U.S. 89. This is one of the most colorful regions of the **Painted Desert,** with amphitheaters of maroon, orange, and red rocks facing west; it's especially glorious at sunset.

WHERE TO EAT

$–$$
SOUTHWESTERN
✕ **Hogan Restaurant.** The fare at this spot adjacent to the Quality Inn Navajo Nation is mostly Southwestern and Mexican, but the menu also lists basic American and Navajo dishes, including tasty barbecue ribs, honey-glazed ham, and herb-roasted chicken. The chicken enchiladas and beef tamales are also quite good. Breakfast is served, too. ✉ *Main St. (AZ 264)* ☎ *928/283–5260* ⊕ *www.qualityinntubacity.com* ☰ *AE, D, DC, MC, V.*

¢–$
AMERICAN
✕ **Kate's Cafe.** A favorite of locals, this all-American café serves breakfast—try the vegetarian omelet—lunch, and dinner. At lunch choose from hearty Baja burgers (topped with tomato, avocado, bacon, and Monterey Jack), Kate's club sandwich, grilled chicken, or salads. Dinner selections include several pasta specials and a charbroiled New York strip steak. There may be a wait, but for local color and fine food at reasonable prices, this is the place to go. Espresso and designer-coffee drinks are also served. ✉ *Main St. (AZ 264)* ☎ *928/283–6773* ⊕ *www. javansuch.com* ☰ *No credit cards.*

WHERE TO STAY

¢
🛏 **Grey Hills Inn.** Hotel management students at Grey Hills High School run this unusual lodging, a former dormitory with large, clean rooms and comfortable beds. Warm service, paintings, and other touches add character to otherwise plain rooms and the rather drab, institutional setting. Bathrooms and showers are down the hall, but the rates are reasonable. A share of the inn's profits helps support the students' class. **Pros:** chance to interact with local students, extremely affordable. **Cons:** no-frills decor, no high-speed Internet, shared bathrooms. ✉ *Grey Hills High School, U.S. 160, ½ mi north of AZ 264* ☐ *Box 160, Tuba City 86045* ☎ *928/283–4450* ↳ *32 rooms with shared bath* ☰ *MC, V.*

SHOPPING

The **Native American swap meet** (✉ *Main St.*), behind the community center and next to the baseball field, held every Friday from 8 AM on, has great deals on jewelry, jewelry-making supplies, semiprecious stones, rugs, pottery, and other arts and crafts; there are also food concessions and booths selling herbs.

CAMERON TRADING POST

25 mi southwest of Tuba City on U.S. 89.

Cameron Trading Post and Motel, established in 1916 overlooking a spectacular gorge and vintage suspension bridge, is one of the few remaining authentic trading posts in the Southwest. A convenient stop if you're driving from the Hopi Mesas to the Grand Canyon, it has reasonably priced dining, lodging, camping, and shopping.

WHERE TO STAY

$ **Cameron Trading Post.** At the turnoff for the Western entrance to
Fodor's Choice the Grand Canyon's South Rim, this trading post dates back to 1916.
★ Southwestern-style rooms have carved-oak furniture, tile baths, and balconies overlooking the Colorado River. Native-stone landscaping— including fossilized dinosaur tracks—and a small, well-kept garden are pleasant. Make your reservations far in advance for high season. **Pros:** impressive collection of Southwestern art in the trading post gallery and gift shop; restaurant serves up Native American specialties and American favorites; historic lodging. **Cons:** high traffic volume, highway noise, basic rooms. ✉ *U.S. 89, milepost 466* ⌂ *Box 339, Cameron, AZ 86020* ☎ *928/679–2231 or 800/338–7385 Ext. 414 (for hotel)* ⊕ *www. camerontradingpost.com* ✎ *62 rooms, 4 suites* ⌂ *In-room: Wi-Fi. In-hotel: restaurant, no elevator, some pets allowed, no-smoking rooms* ⊟ *AE, D, DC, MC, V.*

SHOPPING

EN ROUTE

As you proceed toward Kayenta, 22 mi northeast of Tuba City on U.S. 160, you'll come to the tiny community of Red Lake. Off to the left of the highway is a geologic phenomenon known as **Elephant Feet.** These massive eroded-sandstone buttes offer a great family photo opportunity: pose under the enormous columns. Northwest of here at the end of a graded dirt road in Navajo backcountry is **White Mesa Natural Bridge,** a massive arch of white sandstone that extends from the edge of White Mesa. The long **Black Mesa** plateau runs for about 15 mi along U.S. 160. Above the prominent escarpments of this land formation, mining operations—a major source of revenue for the Navajo Nation—delve into the more than 20 billion tons of coal deposited there.

MONUMENT VALLEY

The magnificent Monument Valley stretches to the northeast of Kayenta into Utah. At a base altitude of about 5,500 feet, the sprawling, arid expanse was once populated by Ancestral Puebloan people (more popularly known by the Navajo word *Anasazi,* which means both "ancient ones" and "enemy ancestors") and in the last few centuries has been

5

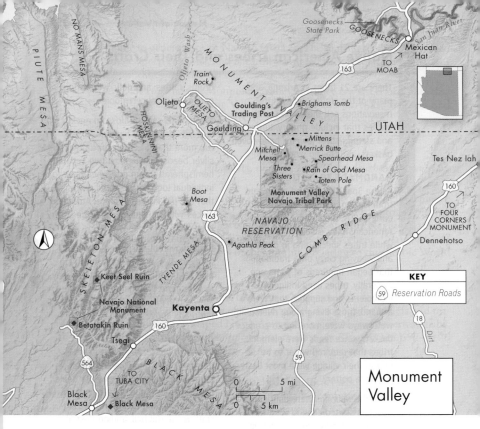

or 800/528–1234 ⊕*www.bestwestern.com* ⌐54 rooms ⅍In-room:
Wi-Fi (some). In-hotel: pool, no elevator, public Wi-Fi ▭AE, D, DC,
MC, V.

$$ 🏨**Hampton Inn of Kayenta.** This warm and inviting hotel is the best
accommodation in the area, and it's little different from any other
in the chain, even given its excellent restaurant and Navajo-inspired
design. The contemporary, comfortable rooms and lobby are tastefully
decorated with Southwest textures, and the restaurant is staffed by
Native Americans wearing traditional Navajo garb. There's a free Con-
tinental-breakfast bar, a patio with a beehive fireplace, and a notably
impressive gift shop with top-quality Native American art and unique
gifts. Packages are available that include discounted guided tours of
Monument Valley. **Pros:** clean and updated rooms, welcoming staff,
excellent restaurant. **Cons:** on busy and unattractive road. ⊠*U.S. 160*
⌂*Box 1219, Kayenta 86033* ☎*928/697–3170* ⊕*www.hamptoninn.*
com ⌐*73 rooms* ⅍*In-room: Wi-Fi. In-hotel: restaurant, pool, some*
pets allowed ▭*AE, D, DC, MC, V* ⧓CP.

$$ 🏨**Holiday Inn Monument Valley.** This '70s-style, bland-looking cluster of
buildings overlooking a bland highway lined with gas stations doesn't
offer much curb appeal. But a welcoming staff, prosaic but clean rooms,
and a commendable on-site restaurant make it a worthwhile option,
especially if the nearby Hampton Inn is already booked. The gift shop

offers traditional local arts and crafts. **Pros:** nice restaurant, friendly staff. **Cons:** on unappealing stretch of road, a bit dated. ⊠*U.S. 160 just south of junction with U.S. 163* ☏*Box 307, Kayenta 86033* ☎*928/697–3221 or 888/465–4329* ⊕*www.holidayinn.com* ⤤*162 rooms* ♿*In-room: Wi-Fi. In-hotel: restaurant, pool, gym, laundry facilities* ⊟*AE, D, DC, MC, V.*

MONUMENT VALLEY NAVAJO TRIBAL PARK

24 mi northeast of Kayenta, off U.S. 163.

GETTING HERE AND AROUND

It's impossible not to drive slowly on this park's bumpy roads, which are best conquered with an SUV or all-wheel-drive vehicle (especially during rainy times of year), but if you take your time and exercise caution, you can make the entire drive in a conventional car. If in doubt, inquire at the drive's entrance gate. Call ahead for road conditions in winter.

> ### WORD OF MOUTH
>
> "We did our Monument Valley tour with Simpson's Trailhandler Tours, and I can't recommend them highly enough. They were great. We did a photo tour, just the two of us and our Navajo guide. He took us all sorts of great places, and at one point, played his flute and sang Navajo songs for us."
>
> —Floridafran

EXPLORING

For generations, the Navajo have grown crops and herded sheep in Monument Valley, considered to be one of the most scenic and mesmerizing destinations in the Navajo Nation. Within Monument Valley lies the 30,000-acre **Monument Valley Navajo Tribal Park**, where eons of wind and rain have carved the mammoth red-sandstone monoliths into memorable formations. The monoliths, which jut hundreds of feet above the desert floor, stand on the horizon like sentinels, frozen in time and unencumbered by electric wires, telephone poles, or fences—a scene virtually unchanged for centuries. These are the very same nostalgic images so familiar to movie buffs who recall the early Western films of John Wayne. A 17-mi self-guided driving tour on an extremely rough dirt road (there's only one road, so you can't get lost) passes the memorable **Mittens** and **Totem Pole** formations, among others. Also be sure to walk (15 minutes round-trip) from North Window around the end of Cly Butte for the views.

FodorśChoice ★

The **Monument Valley Visitor Center** has an extensive crafts shop and exhibits devoted to ancient and modern Native American history. Most of the independent guided tours here use enclosed vans and charge about $20 to $25 for 2½ hours. You can generally find Navajo guides—who will escort you to places that you are not allowed to visit on your own—in the center or through the booths in the parking lot. In the fall of 2008 the tribe opened the handsome View Hotel just in time to celebrate the park's 50th anniversary. A full renovation and expasion of the visitor center is slated to open again by the end of 2009. Both the hotel and visitor center sit on a gradual rise overlooking the valley, with big-sky views in every direction. The park also has a 99-site campground, which closes from early October through April. ⊠ *Visitor center, off U.S. 163, 24 mi north of Kayenta, Monument Valley* ☏*Box 2520, Window*

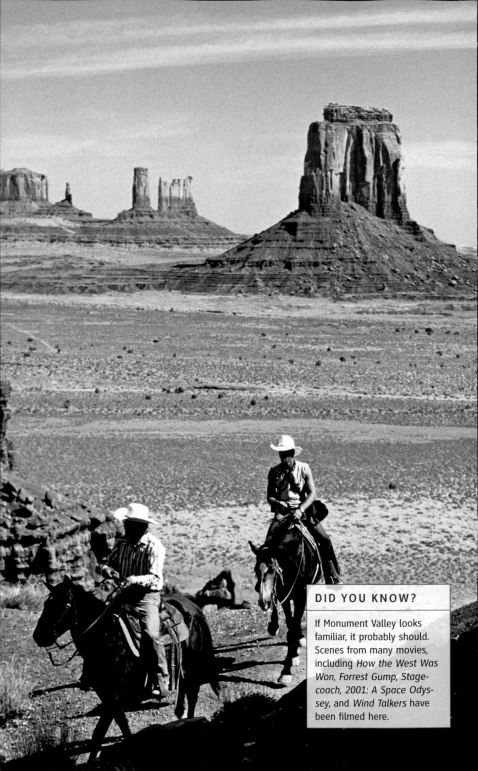

DID YOU KNOW?

If Monument Valley looks familiar, it probably should. Scenes from many movies, including *How the West Was Won, Forrest Gump, Stagecoach, 2001: A Space Odyssey,* and *Wind Talkers* have been filmed here.

Rock 86515 ☎435/727–5874 park visitor center, 928/871–6647 Navajo Parks & Recreation Dept. ⊕www. navajonationparks.org ☑$5 ⊙Visitor center May–Sept., daily 6 AM–8 PM; Mar. and Apr., daily 7–7; Oct.–Feb., daily 8–5.

SPORTS AND THE OUTDOORS

HIKING, HORSEBACK RIDING, AND JEEP TOURS

Jeep tours of the valley, from hour-long to overnight, can be arranged through Roland Cody Dixon at **Roland's Navajoland Tours** (☎520/697–3524 or 800/368–2785); he offers cultural tours with crafts demonstrations, camping, and photography. **Sacred Monument Tours** (☎435/727–3218 or 928/380–4527 ⊕www.monumentvalley.net) has hiking, jeep, photography, and horseback-riding tours into Monument Valley. **Simpson's Trailhandler Tours** (☎435/727–3362 ⊕www.trailhandlertours.com) offers four-wheel-drive jeep tours as well as photography and hiking tours. **Totem Pole Tours** (☎435/727–3313 or 866/422–8687 ⊕www.moab-utah.com/totempole) offers jeep tours, some including entertainment and outdoor barbecues.

WHERE TO EAT

¢–$
SOUTHWESTERN
★

✕**View Restaurant.** Connected to the View Hotel through a second-floor breezeway, this airy space comprises a few high-ceilinged rooms with massive plate-glass windows framing mesmerizing views of the valley—in warm weather you can dine outside on a terrace, awed by the same panorama. Navajo rugs and local art hang on the walls above the light-wood tables and chairs, and the tribal visitors center's extensive curio shop is attached. The food is well prepared if fairly typical of the region: green chile stew, Navajo tacos, steaks, and the like. There's also a smaller self-serve section where you can grab sandwiches and light snacks. ⊠Off U.S. 163, 24 mi north of Kayenta ☎435/727–5555 ⊕www.monumentvalleyview.com ⊟AE, MC, V.

WHERE TO STAY

$$–$$$
Fodor'sChoice
★

⌂ **View Hotel.** The Navajo tribe opened this sleek, three-story, red-stucco hotel on a bluff beside the visitor center in fall 2008. It's the first lodging ever to open inside the Monument Valley Navajo Tribal Park, and the astounding vistas from every room in the hotel—even the elevators, which have windows—live up to the name. Nearly all the rooms face east toward the iconic Mittens and Totem Pole formations (a few look west and still enjoy terrific views). All have private balconies, flat-screen TVs, tile floors, and brightly hued Navajo bedspreads. You can read or relax in a cavernous lobby with tall windows, leather chairs, and hand-carved furnishings, or work out in a small gym looking out toward Mitchell Butte. More rooms and a full-service spa are planned with a further expansion in the next year or two. **Pros:** unbelievable panoramas from every room; stylish furnishings; eco-conscious bath products, appliances, and buildings standards. **Cons:** priciest lodging in the region; very remote. ⊠Off U.S. 163, 24 mi north of Kayenta ⌂Box 360289,

5

Monument Valley, UT 84536 ☎*435/727–5555* ⊕*www.monument valleyview.com* ↩*96 rooms* ⏆*In-room: refrigerator, Wi-Fi. In-hotel: restaurant, gym* ☰*AE, D, DC, MC, V.*

▌OFF THE
BEATEN
PATH

Four Corners Monument. An inlaid brass plaque marks the only point in the United States where four states meet: Arizona, New Mexico, Colorado, and Utah. Despite the Indian wares and booths selling greasy food, there's not much else to do here but pay a fee and stay long enough to snap a photo; you'll see many a twisted tourist trying to get an arm or a leg in each state. The monument is a 75-mi drive from Kayenta and is administered by the Navajo Nation Parks & Recreation Department. ✉*7 mi northwest of the U.S. 160 and U.S. 64 junction, Teec Nos Pos* ☎*928/871–6647 Navajo Parks & Recreation Dept.* ⊕*www. navajonationparks.org* ✍*$3* ⊙*Oct.–May, daily 8–5; June–Sept., daily 7*AM*–8* PM.

GOOSENECKS REGION, UTAH

Fodor's Choice
★

33 mi north of Monument Valley Navajo Tribal Park, on UT 316.

Monument Valley's scenic route, U.S. 163, continues from Arizona into Utah, where the land is crossed, east to west, by a stretch of the San Juan River known as the Goosenecks—named for the myriad twists and curves it takes. This barren, erosion-blasted gorge has a stark beauty. This spot is a well-known take-out point for white-water runners on the San Juan, a river that vacationing sleuths will recognize as the setting of many of Tony Hillerman's Jim Chee mystery novels.

GETTING HERE AND AROUND

The scenic overlook for the Goosenecks is reached by turning west from U.S. 163 onto UT 261, 4 mi north of the small community of **Mexican Hat,** then proceeding on UT 261 for 1 mi to a directional sign at the road's junction with UT 316. Turn left onto UT 316 and proceed 4 mi to the vista-point parking lot.

WHERE TO STAY

$
★

▥ **San Juan Inn & Trading Post.** The inn's Southwestern-style, rustic rooms overlooking the river at Mexican Hat are clean and well maintained, and the setting against the red rocks is quite inspiring. Diners can watch the river at the Old Bridge Grille, which serves great grilled steak and juicy hamburgers, fresh trout, and inexpensive Navajo dishes—it's also the only place for 100 mi in any direction with a liquor license. **Pros:** magnificent setting, affordable rooms, parking is right outside your room. **Cons:** very basic room decor, no high-speed Internet. ✉*U.S. 163* ⌂*Box 310276, Mexican Hat, UT 84531* ☎*435/683–2220 or 800/447–2022* ⊕*www.sanjuaninn.net* ↩*36 rooms* ⏆*In-room: dial-up. In-hotel: restaurant, no elevator, gym, laundry facilities, some pets allowed* ☰*AE, D, DC, MC, V.*

GOULDING'S TRADING POST

2 mi west of entrance road to Monument Valley Navajo Tribal Park, off U.S. 163 on Indian Hwy. 42.

Established in 1924 by Harry Goulding and his wife "Mike," this trading post provided a place where Navajos could exchange livestock and handmade goods for necessities. Goulding's is probably best known, though, for being used as a headquarters by director John Ford when he filmed the Western classic *Stagecoach*. Today the compound has a lodge, restaurant, museum, gift shop, grocery store, and campground. The Goulding Museum displays Native American artifacts and Goulding family memorabilia, as well as an excellent multimedia show about Monument Valley.

WHERE TO STAY

$$–$$$ 🖼 **Goulding's Lodge.** Nestled beneath a massive red-rock monolith, this two-level property affords spectacular views of Monument Valley from each room's private balcony. Before the View Hotel opened nearby with even more impressive views, this was the only lodging in the region offering truly knockout views. It has more history than its new competitor, but it's not nearly as plush. The on-premises Stagecoach restaurant, serving American fare, is decorated with Western movie memorabilia. Goulding's also conducts custom guided tours and provides Navajo guides into the backcountry. **Pros:** right in heart of Monument Valley, incredibly peaceful, indoor pool open all year. **Cons:** remote location, simple rooms, not cheap. ✉ *Off U.S. 163, 24 mi north of Kayenta* ✆*Box 360001, Monument Valley, UT 84536* 🖷*435/727–3231* ⊕*www.gouldings.com* 🛏*62 rooms* ♿*In-room: refrigerator, VCR, DVD, dial-up. In-hotel: restaurant, pool, no elevator, laundry facilities* ▭*AE, D, DC, MC, V.*

CAMPING ¢ 🏕 **Goulding's Good Sam Campground.** Views of Monument Valley are the draw at this clean, modern campground. Check in at Goulding's grocery store (in Goulding's Trading Post). Campers have access—at no additional charge—to the 17-mi-loop drive around Monument Valley. Shuttle vans provide free transportation to Goulding's restaurant and museum. ✉ *Off U.S. 163, 24 mi north of Kayenta* ✆*Box 360001, Monument Valley, UT 84536* 🖷*435/727–3235* 🛏*66 RV sites, 50 tent sites* ♿*Flush toilets, full hookups, guest laundry, showers, grills, general store, play area, swimming (indoor pool)* ▭*AE, D, DC, MC, V* ☉*Open year-round; limited service Nov.–Mar. 15.*

NAVAJO NATIONAL MONUMENT

53 mi southwest of Goulding's Trading Post, 21 mi west of Kayenta.

GETTING HERE AND AROUND

From Kayenta, take U.S. 160 southwest to AZ 564 and follow signs 9 mi north to monument.

AZ 564 turns north off U.S. 160 at the Black Mesa gas station and convenience store, and leads to the visitor center. No food, gasoline, or hotel lodging is available at the monument.

The visitor center houses a small museum, exhibits of prehistoric pottery, and a good crafts shop. Free campground and picnic areas are nearby, and rangers sometimes present campfire programs in summer.

EXPLORING

Fodor'sChoice
★

At the **Navajo National Monument** two unoccupied 13th-century cliff pueblos, Betatakin and Keet Seel, stand under the overhanging cliffs of Tsegi Canyon. The largest ancient dwellings in Arizona, these stone-and-mortar complexes were built by Ancestral Puebloans, obviously for permanent occupancy, but abandoned after less than half a century.

The well-preserved, 135-room **Betatakin** (Navajo for "ledge house") is a cluster of cliff dwellings that seem to hang in midair before a sheer sandstone wall. When discovered in 1907 by a passing American rancher, the apartments were full of baskets, pottery, and preserved grains and ears of corn—as if the occupants had been chased away in the middle of a meal. For an impressive view of Betatakin, walk to the rim overlook about ½ mi from the visitor center. Ranger-led tours (a 5-mi, four-hour, strenuous round-trip hike including a 700-foot descent into the canyon) leave once a day from late May to early September at 8 AM and return between noon and 1 PM. No reservations are accepted; groups of no more than 25 form on a first-come, first-served basis.

Keet Seel (Navajo for "broken pottery") is also in good condition in a serene location, with 160 rooms and five kivas. Explorations of Keet Seel, which lies at an elevation of 7,000 feet and is 8½ mi from the visitor center on foot, are restricted: only 20 people are allowed to visit per day, and only between late May and early September, when a ranger is present at the site. A permit—which also allows campers to stay overnight nearby—is required. ■TIP➜Trips to Keet Seel are very popular, so reservations are taken up to two months in advance. Anyone who suffers from vertigo might want to avoid this trip: the trail leads down a 1,100-foot near-vertical rock face. ⊠*AZ 564, Black Mesa* ⌕*HC 71, Box 3, Tonalea 86044* ☎*928/672–2700* ⊕*www.nps.gov/nava* ⊠*Free* ⊙*Mid-May.–mid-Sept., weekdays 8–5, weekends 8–7; Mid-Sept.–mid-May., daily 9–5; tours late May–early Sept.*

SPORTS AND THE OUTDOORS

HIKING Hiking is the best way for adventurous souls to see Keet Seel at the Navajo National Monument. It's a fairly strenuous hike to the sites, but if you're fit and leave early enough, it's well worth it to visit some of the best-preserved ancient dwellings in the Southwest. It's free, but the trail is open only from late May through early September, and you need to call ahead to make a reservation, usually at least two months in advance. ⌕*Navajo National Monument, HC 71, Box 3, Tonalea 86044* ☎*928/672–2366* ⊠*Free* ⊙*Apr.–Oct., weekdays 8–5, weekends 8–7; tours late May–early Sept.*

WHERE TO STAY

$ **Anasazi Inn–Tsegi Canyon.** On U.S. 160, 10 mi east of Black Mesa and 9
AMERICAN mi west of Kayenta, this is the closest lodging to Navajo National Monument. The one-story property with a bright turquoise roof offers basic, clean accommodations with exterior entrances and commanding views

Ancestral Puebloans, construction methods, and their mysterious fate are worth pondering during a visit to Navajo National Monument.

of Tsegi Canyon. There's also a well-stocked gift shop and a restaurant that serves sandwiches, burgers, and basic Navajo fare—it's decent if nothing special, but it's also the only dining option for miles around. **Pros:** close to Navajo National Monument, affordable. **Cons:** dated furnishings, remote location, no high-speed Internet. ⊠ *Off U.S. 160, 9 mi west of Kayenta* ⬠ *Box 1543, Kayenta, AZ 86033* ☎ *928/697–3793* ⊕ *www.anasaziinn.com/tsegicanyon* ⬡ *57 rooms* ⬡ *In-room: dial-up. In-hotel: restaurant, no elevator* ⊟ *AE, D, MC, V.*

GLEN CANYON DAM AND LAKE POWELL

Lake Powell is the heart of the huge 1.25-million-acre Glen Canyon National Recreation Area. Created by the barrier of Glen Canyon Dam in the Colorado River, Lake Powell is ringed by red cliffs that twist off into 96 major canyons and countless inlets (most accessible only by boat) with huge, red-sandstone buttes randomly jutting from the sapphire waters. It extends through terrain so rugged it was the last major area of the United States to be mapped. You could spend 30 years exploring the lake and still not experience everything there is to see. The Sierra Club has started a movement to drain the lake to restore water-filled Glen Canyon, which some believe was more spectacular than the Grand Canyon, but the lake is likely to be around for years to come.

South of Lake Powell the landscape gives way to **Echo Cliffs,** orange-sandstone formations rising 1,000 feet and more above the highway in places. At **Bitter Springs** the road ascends the cliffs and provides a

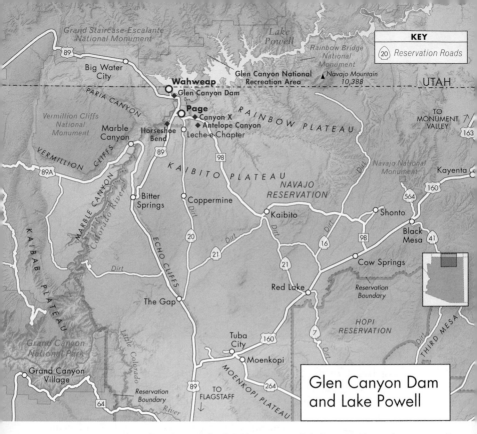

spectacular view of the 9,000-square-mi Arizona Strip to the west and the 3,000-foot Vermilion Cliffs to the northwest.

PAGE

90 mi west of the Navajo National Monument, 136 mi north of Flagstaff on U.S. 89.

Built in 1957 as a Glen Canyon Dam construction camp, Page is now a tourist spot and a popular base for day trips to Lake Powell; it has also become a major point of entry to the Navajo Nation. The nearby Vermilion Cliffs are where the California condor, an endangered species, has been successfully reintroduced into the wild. The town's human population of nearly 7,100 makes it the largest community in far-northern Arizona, and each year more than 3 million people come to play at Lake Powell.

GETTING HERE AND AROUND

Most of the motels, restaurants, and shopping centers are concentrated along **Lake Powell Boulevard**, the name given to U.S. 89 as it loops through the business district.

The only airline that offers service directly to northeastern Arizona is Great Lakes Aviation, which flies into Page Municipal Airport from

Phoenix as well as from Denver (with a stop in Farmington, New Mexico).

ESSENTIALS

Transportation Contacts Great Lakes Aviation (☎ *800/554–5111* ⊕ *www. greatlakesav.com*). **Page Municipal Airport** (☎ *928/645–4337* ⊕ *www.cityof page.org/airport.htm*).

Visitor Info Page/Lake Powell Chamber of Commerce (☎ *928/645–2741 or 888/261–7243* ⊕ *www.pagelakepowelltourism.com*).

EXPLORING

At the corner of North Navajo Drive and Lake Powell Boulevard is the **John Wesley Powell Memorial Museum,** whose namesake led the first known expeditions down the Green River and the rapids-choked Colorado through the Grand Canyon between 1869 and 1872. Powell mapped and kept detailed records of his trips, naming the Grand Canyon and many other geographic points of interest in northern Arizona. Artifacts from his expeditions are displayed in the museum. The museum also doubles as the town's visitor information center. A travel desk dispenses information and allows you to book boating tours, raft trips, scenic flights, accommodations in Page, or Antelope Canyon tours. When you sign up for tours here, concessionaires give a donation to the nonprofit museum with no extra charge to you. ⊠ *6 N. Lake Powell Blvd.* ☎ *928/645–9496 or 888/597–6873* ⊕ *www.powellmuseum.org* 🖭 *$5* ⊙ *Weekdays 9–5; Memorial Day–Labor Day also open Sat., call for hrs.*

The **Navajo Village Heritage Center** imparts an understanding of life on the reservation. You can take a guided tour of a traditional Navajo hogan and bread oven. For $50 per person (or $130 per family) the village hosts a 2½-hour "Evening with the Navajo–Grand Tour," which includes an hour of cultural entertainment and a Navajo taco dinner around a campfire. Less extensive (and expensive) versions of the tour are also available. ⊠ *531 Haul Rd. 86040* ☎ *928/660–0304* ⊕ *www. navajo-village.com* 🖭 *$5* ⊙ *Apr.–Oct., daily 10–3.*

SPORTS AND THE OUTDOORS

For water sports on Lake Powell, see Wahweap below. **Glen Canyon Recreation Area** (☎ *928/608–6200* ⊕ *www.nps.gov/glca*) has a helpful Web site.

AIR TOURS Page-based **American Aviation** (☎ *928/608–1060 or 866/525–3247* ⊕ *www.americanaviationwest.com*) offers flightseeing tours of Monument Valley, Lake Powell and Rainbow Bridge, and Bryce.

FLOAT TRIPS **Colorado River Discovery** (☎ *888/522–6644* ⊕ *www.raftthecanyon.com*) offers waterborne tours, including a 5½-hour guided rafting excursion down a calm portion of the Colorado River on comfortable, motor-ized pontoon boats ($74). The scenery—multicolor-sandstone cliffs adorned with Native American petroglyphs—is spectacular. The trips are offered twice daily from April through September, and once a day March and October (no tours in winter). The company also offers full-day rowing trips along the river, using smaller boats maneuvered by well-trained guides ($155). These trips—offered Sunday, Monday, and

Wednesday—are quieter and more low-key, and provide a more intimate brush with this magnificent body of water.

GOLF   **Lake Powell National Golf Course** (✉ *400 Clubhouse Dr., off U.S. 89* ☎ *928/645–2023* ⊕ *www.golf lakepowell.com* 🏌 *18 holes. Par 72. Green Fees: $69* 🏌 *9 holes. Par 36.* ☞ *Facilities: golf carts*) has wide fairways, tiered greens with some of the steepest holes in the Southwest, and a generous lack of hazards. From the fairways you can enjoy spectacular vistas of Glen Canyon Dam and Lake Powell.

HIKING   The **Glen Canyon Hike** (✉ *Off U.S. 89*), a short walk from the parking lot down a flight of uneven rock steps, takes you to a viewpoint on the canyon rim high above the Colorado River, and provides fantastic views of the Colorado as it flows through Glen Canyon. To reach the parking lot, turn west on Scenic View Drive, 1½ mi south of Carl Hayden Visitor Center.

The **Horse Shoe Bend Trail** (✉ *Off U.S. 89*) has some steep up and down paths and a bit of deep sand to maneuver; however, the views are well worth the hike. The trail leads up to a bird's-eye view of Glen Canyon and the Colorado River downstream from Glen Canyon Dam. There are some sheer drop-offs here, so watch children. To reach the trail, drive 4 mi south of Page on U.S. 89 and turn west onto a blacktop road 1/5 mi south of mile marker 545. It's a ¾-mi hike from the parking area to the top of the canyon.

WHERE TO EAT

★   ✕ **Dam Bar and Grille.** The Grille's vaguely industrial-looking decor is
AMERICAN   quite urbane for this part of the world, and the kitchen turns out filling,
$–$$ well-prepared food. Consider the 8-ounce cowboy steak topped with sautéed mushrooms and Swiss cheese, the smoked baby back ribs, the lobster salad, or the burger topped with bacon and cheddar. The Dam comprises a whole complex of establishments that also includes a sushi bar, coffeehouse, and nightclub. ✉ *644 N. Navajo Dr.* ☎ *928/645–2161* ⊕ *www.damplaza.com* ⊟ *AE, MC, V.*

$–$$ ✕ **Fiesta Mexicana.** From the faux village-plaza decor, carved-wood
MEXICAN   booths, and piped-in mariachi music, this festive downtown eatery feels entirely predictable but quite pleasant. Part of a regional chain of Four Corners Mexican restaurants, Fiesta Mexicana prepares a nice range of traditional favorites, including particularly good chicken fajitas and massive margaritas. Dine on the covered patio for the best people-watching. ✉ *125 S. Lake Powell Blvd.* ☎ *928/645–4082* ⊟ *AE, D, MC, V.*

WHERE TO STAY

$ ☷ **Best Western Arizonainn.** On a bluff at the northern end of Page, this modern, well-run motel has large rooms with queen-size beds and Southwestern-print bedspreads, and has fantastic views of Lake Powell, just 2 mi away. Butterfield Steakhouse serves Southwestern and standard American fare. **Pros:** panoramic views, close to downtown shopping and dining, nice gym and pool. Cons: run-of-the-mill decor. ⊠*716 Rim View Dr.* ⚐*Box 250, Page 86040* ☏*928/645–2466 or 800/826–2718* ⊕*www.bestwestern. com/arizonainn* ⟵*103 rooms* ⚷*In-room: Ethernet. In-hotel: restaurant, bar, pool, gym, laundry facilities, some pets allowed* ⊟*AE, D, DC, MC, V* ⏹*CP.*

$$ ⊡**Best Western at Lake Powell.** The newer of the two Best Westerns in town is a modern, three-story motel on a high bluff overlooking Glen Canyon Dam with dazzling views of the Vermilion Cliffs. The large rooms are functional but with tasteful, Southwestern-inspired color schemes and designs, and the beds are quite plush. Pros: attractive room interiors, excellent views, close to downtown shopping and dining. Cons: pricier than the other Best Western. ⊠*208 N. Lake Powell Blvd.* ☏*928/645-5988 or 888/794–2888* ⊕*www.bestwestern.com/ atlakepowell* ⟵*132 rooms* ⚷*In-room: Wi-Fi. In-hotel: pool, gym, laundry facilities* ⊟*AE, D, DC, MC, V* ⏹*CP.*

$ ⊡**Canyon Colors B&B.** Run by personable New England transplants Bev
★ and Rich Jones, this desert-country B&B occupies a simple, modern house in a quiet residential neighborhood near downtown. The Sunflower and Paisley rooms, which can accommodate three and two, respectively, have queen beds and wood-burning stoves. The B&B also has an extensive video library, including many videos of Lake Powell and the Navajo Nation. Pros: personal attention, peaceful setting, central location. Cons: very small, need to book well ahead in summer. ⊠*225 S. Navajo Dr.* ⚐*Box 3657, 86040* ☏*928/645–5979 or 800/536–2530* ⊕*www.canyoncolors. com* ⟵*2 rooms* ⚷*In-room: Wi-Fi, refrigerator, VCR. In-hotel: public Internet, pool, no elevator* ⊟*AE, MC, V* ⏹*BP.*

$$ ⊡**Courtyard by Marriott.** Page's top hotel lies just below the stunning grounds of Lake Powell National Golf Course, and has airy rooms decorated in a Southwestern motif with plush bedding and large TVs, health and fitness facilities, and dining at Peppers, which serves predictable but reliable American and Mexican standards. Pros: lovely setting by golf course; good restaurant; the best and most modern room amenities in town. Cons: pricey by Page standards; uphill walk to downtown restaurants and shopping. ⊠*600 Clubhouse Dr.* ⚐*Box 4150, Page 86040* ☏*928/645–5000 or 888/236–2427* ⊕*www.courtyard.com* ⟵*153 rooms* ⚷*In-room: Wi-Fi. In-hotel: restaurant, bar, pool, gym, laundry facilities* ⊟*AE, D, DC, MC, V.*

$ ⊡**Days Inn & Suites.** Although part of an uneven chain of low-frills
★ motels, the Page Days Inn is first-rate among budget-friendly properties in the region. The attractive Southwest-style building sits atop a plateau with expansive views of the region, although it doesn't directly view Lake Powell. Rooms are plainly furnished, but have large windows or doors opening to small balconies. Pros: many rooms have balconies, super-

5

Houseboats are a unique lodging option; they're also great for exploring Lake Powell's almost 4,000 miles of shoreline.

friendly staff, panoramic views. **Cons:** need a car to get to downtown shopping and restaurants, rooms look rather ordinary, on a busy road at edge of town. ✉ *961 N. U.S. 89* ☎ *928/645–2800 or 877/525–3769* ⊕ *www.daysinn.net* ☞ *82 rooms* ⌂ *In-room: refrigerator, Wi-Fi. In-hotel: pool, some pets allowed* ☰ *AE, D, MC, V* ⦿ *CP.*

CAMPING
⌂
☾ **Page–Lake Powell Campground.** Lake Powell is a popular destination and very busy in summer months, so make reservations if you're planning to stay at this in-town campground. The Antelope Point launch ramp on Lake Powell is 7 mi away. ✉ *849 S. Coppermine Rd.,* ☎ *928/645–3374 www.pagecampground.com* ☞ *85 RV sites, 20 tent sites* ⌂ *Flush toilets, full hookups, partial hookups (electric and water), dump station, guest laundry, showers, picnic tables, general store, swimming (indoor pool)* ☰ *MC, V* ⦿ *Open year-round.*

SHOPPING

There are numerous gift shops and clothing stores in the downtown area along Lake Powell Boulevard. There's lots of junk, but you can find authentic Native American arts and crafts, too. **Big Lake Trading Post** (✉ *1501 AZ 98* ☎ *928/645–2404* ⊕ *www.biglaketradingpost.com*)
★ has a gas station, convenience store, car wash, and coin laundry. **Blair's Dinnebito Trading Post** (✉ *626 Navajo Dr.* ☎ *928/645–3008* ⊕ *www. blairstradingpost.com*) has been around for more than half a century. Authentic Native American arts and crafts are only a small part of what this store sells. Need tack equipment, rodeo ropes, rugs, saddlery, pottery? It's all here and reasonably priced. Wander upstairs and visit the Elijah Blair collection and memorabilia rooms. The gift shop at **Lake Powell Resort** (✉ *100 Lake Shore Dr., Wahweap* ☎ *928/645–2433*

⊕*www.lakepowell.com*) carries authentic Native American rugs, pottery, jewelry, and baskets, as well as tourist T-shirts and postcards.

ANTELOPE CANYON

4 mi east of Page on the Navajo Reservation, on AZ 98.

GETTING HERE AND AROUND

Access to Antelope Canyon is restricted by the Navajo Tribe to licensed tour operators. The tribe charges a $6 per-person fee, included in the price of tours offered by the licensed concessionaires in Page. The easiest way to book a tour is in town at the John Wesley Powell Memorial Museum Visitor Center; you pay nothing extra for the museum's service. If you'd like to go directly to the tour operators, you can do that, too; visit ⊕*www.navajonationparks.org/htm/antelopecanyon.htm* for a list of approved companies. Most companies offer 1- to 1½-hour sightseeing tours for about $25 to $30, or longer photography tours for $40 to $50. ■TIP➔The best time to see the canyon is between 8 AM and 2 PM.

EXPLORING

★ You've probably seen dozens of photographs of **Antelope Canyon,** a narrow, red-sandstone slot canyon with convoluted corkscrew formations, dramatically illuminated by light streaming down from above. And you're likely to see assorted shutterbugs waiting patiently for just the right shot of these colorful, photogenic rocks, which are actually petrified sand dunes of a prehistoric ocean that once filled this portion of North America. The best photos are taken at high noon, when light filters through the slot in the canyon surface. This is one place where you'll need to protect your camera equipment against blowing dust. Access to the canyon is limited to those on licensed tours. ⊠*AZ 98, Page* ⌂*Box 2520, Window Rock 86515* ☎*928/871–6647 Navajo Parks & Recreation Dept.* ⊕*www.navajonationparks.org* ⊟*$6, included in tour cost.*

ANTELOPE CANYON TOURS

Antelope Canyon Navajo Tours (☎*928/698–3384* ⊕*www.navajotours. com*) offers 1-hour sightseeing tours and 2-hour photography tours.

Antelope Canyon Tours (☎*928/645–9102 or 866/645–9102* ⊕*www. antelopecanyon.com*) offers several tours daily from 8 AM to 3 PM for sightseers and photographers. The photo tour gives serious and amateur photographers the opportunity to wait for the right light to photograph the canyon and get basic information on equipment setup.

John Wesley Powell Memorial Museum Visitor Center (☎*928/645–9496* ⊕*www.powellmuseum.org*) arranges and books 1½-hour tours and 2-hour photography tours. Photo tours leave from Page at 8 and 9:30 AM and return about 2 PM. The shorter sightseeing tours leave frequently between 8 AM and 4 PM.

Overland Canyon Tours (☎*928/608–4072* ⊕*www.overlandcanyontours. com*) is one of only a few Native American–operated tour companies in Page. Tours include a narrative explaining the canyon's history and geology. On private property, the isolated slot canyon known as **Canyon**

5

X can be toured only by Navajo guide Harley Klemm and his company, Overland Canyon Tours, which also operates popular tours to Antelope Canyon. Only one tour is given per day—departure times vary—and tours are offered by advance reservation only, with a limit of six participants. Because the area is rugged, children are not allowed, and participants should have good physical mobility to climb crevasses and some rough terrain.

GLEN CANYON NATIONAL RECREATION AREA

GETTING HERE AND AROUND

Just off the highway at the north end of the bridge is the **Carl Hayden Visitor Center,** where you can learn about the controversial creation of Glen Canyon Dam and Lake Powell and enjoy panoramic views of both. To enter the visitor center you must go through a metal detector. Absolutely no bags are allowed inside.

EXPLORING

Once you leave the Page business district heading northwest, the **Glen Canyon Dam National Recreation Area** and Lake Powell behind it immediately become visible. This concrete-arch dam—all 5 million cubic feet of it—was completed in September 1963, its power plant an engineering feat that rivaled the Hoover Dam. The dam's crest is 1,560 feet across and rises 710 feet from bedrock and 583 feet above the waters of the Colorado River. When Lake Powell is full, it's 560 feet deep at the dam. The plant generates some 1.3 million kilowatts of electricity when each generator's 40-ton shaft is producing nearly 200,000 horsepower. Power from the dam serves a five-state grid consisting of Colorado, Arizona, Utah, California, and New Mexico, and provides energy for some 1.5 million users.

With only 8 inches of annual rainfall, the Lake Powell area enjoys blue skies nearly year-round. Summer temperatures range from the 60s to the 90s. Fall and spring are usually balmy, with daytime temperatures often in the 70s and 80s, but chilly weather can set in. Nights are cool even in summer, and in winter the risk of a cold spell increases, but all-weather houseboats and tour boats make for year-round cruising.

Boaters and campers should note that regulations require the use of portable toilets on the lake and lakeshore to prevent water pollution.

⊠*U.S. 89, 2 mi west of town, Page* ☎*928/608–6404* ⊕*www. nps.gov/glca* ⊠*$15 per vehicle or $7 per person (entering on foot or*

SLOT CANYONS

Slot canyons are unique to the Southwest. Carved through sandstone by wind and water, they are narrow at the top—some are only a foot wide on the surface—and wider at the bottom, which can be more than 100 feet below ground level. The play of light as it filters down through the slot onto the sandstone walls makes them remarkable subjects for photographs, but they are dangerous, particularly during the summer rainy season when flash floods can rush through them and sweep away an unwary hiker. Before hiking into a slot canyon, consult with locals and pay attention to weather forecasts.

by bicycle), good for up to 7 days, $16 per week boating fee ☉ *Visitor center June–Aug., daily 8–6; Sept.–Nov. and Mar.–May, daily 8–5; Dec.–Feb., daily 8–4.*

WAHWEAP

5 mi north of Glen Canyon Dam on U.S. 89.

Most waterborne-recreational activity on the Arizona side of the lake is centered on this vacation village, where everything needed for a lakeside holiday is available: tour boats, fishing, boat rentals, dinner cruises, and more. The Lake Powell Resort has excellent views of the lake area, and you can take a boat tour from the Wahweap Marina. Keep in mind that you must pay the Glen Canyon National Recreation Area entry fee upon entering Wahweap—this is true even if you're just passing through or having a meal at Lake Powell Resort.

EXPLORING

★ A boat tour to **Rainbow Bridge National Monument** is a great way to see the enormity of the lake and its incredible, rugged beauty. This 290-foot red-sandstone arch is the world's largest natural bridge, and can be reached by boat or strenuous hike *(⇨ See Hiking).* The lake level is down due to the prolonged drought throughout the region, so expect a 1½-mi hike from the boat dock to the monument. The bridge can also be viewed by air. To the Navajos this is a sacred area with deep religious and spiritual significance, so outsiders are asked not to hike underneath the arch itself. ☎ *928/608–6200* ⊕ *www.nps.gov/rabr.*

SPORTS AND THE OUTDOORS

BOAT TOURS Excursions on double-decker scenic cruisers piloted by experienced guides leave from the dock of **Lake Powell Resort** (⊠ *100 Lake Shore Dr., Wahweap* ☎ *928/645–2433 or 800/528–6154).* The most popular tour is the full-day trip to Rainbow Bridge National Monument for $144 (a box lunch is included); a half-day version is available, too. There's also a 2½-hour sunset dinner cruise ($99) featuring a prime-rib dinner—vegetarian lasagna meals are available if ordered in advance. It's served on the fully enclosed decks of the 95-foot *Canyon King* paddle wheeler, a reproduction of a 19th-century bay boat. Two-hour Antelope Canyon cruises are another favorite, costing about $38.

BOATING One of the most scenic lakes of the American West, Lake Powell has 186 mi of clear sapphire waters edged with vast canyons of red and orange rock. Ninety-six major side canyons intricately twist and turn into the main channel of Lake Powell, into what was once the main artery of the Colorado River through Glen Canyon. In some places the lake is 500 feet deep, and by June the lake's waters begin to warm and stay that way well into October.

An $80 million project begun in 2003 and under construction in four phases, **Antelope Point Marina** (⊡ *BIA Hwy. N22B, Mile Marker 4, Navajo Nation 86040* ☎ *602/952–0114* ⊕ *www.antelopepointlake powell.com*) will include a Navajo Cultural Center, artist studios, more than 300 wet slips for houseboats and watercraft, a floating marina village and restaurant, and 225 luxury casitas. As of this writing, the first

Midday light on Antelope Canyon's sandstone walls is a favorite shot for many photographers.

two phases (infrastructure and the marina village) had been completed; the luxury casitas and cultural center are slated to open in 2010. At **Aramark's Lake Powell Resorts & Marinas** (☎ *928/645–1004 or 800/528–6154 ⊕www.visitlakepowell.com*) houseboat rentals range widely in size, amenities, and price, depending upon season. *For more information on houseboats, see Houseboating in Where to Stay, below.*

You may want to rent a powerboat or personal watercraft along with a houseboat to explore the many narrow canyons and waterways on the lake. A 19-foot powerboat for eight passengers runs approximately $400 and up per day. **Stateline Marina** (✉ *U.S. 89, State Line, UT* ☎928/645–1111), 1½ mi north of Lake Powell Resort, is part of Aramark's Lake Powell Resorts & Marinas and site of the boat-rental office. It's here that you pick up rental houseboats, powerboats, kayaks, Jet Skis, and personal watercraft. There's also a public launch ramp if you're towing your own boat. **Wahweap Marina** (✉*100 Lake Shore Dr., Wahweap* ☎928/645–2433) is the largest of the four full-service Lake Powell marinas run by Aramark's Lake Powell Resorts & Marinas. There are 850 slips and the most facilities, including a decent diner, public launch ramp, fishing dock, and a marina store where you can buy fishing licenses and other necessities. It's the only full-service marina on the Arizona side of the lake (the other three—Hite, Bullfrog, and Halls Crossing—are in Utah).

FISHING   Anglers delight in the world-class bass fishing on Lake Powell. You'll hear over and over how the big fish are "biting in the canyons," so you'll need a small vessel if you plan on fishing for the big one. Landing a 20-pound striper isn't unusual (the locals' secret is to use anchovies for bait). Fishing licenses for both Arizona and Utah are available at the **Marina Store at Wahweap Marina** (✉ *100 Lake Shore Dr., Wahweap* ☎ *928/645–1136*). **Stix Bait & Tackle** (✉ *5 S. Lake Powell Blvd., Page* ☎ *928/645–2891 www.stixbaitandtackle.com*) can recommend local fishing guides.

HIKING   Bring plenty of water when hiking and drink often. It's important to remember when hiking at Lake Powell to watch the sky for storms: it may not be raining where you are, but flooding can occur in downstream canyons—particularly slot canyons—from a storm miles away.

Only seasoned hikers in good physical condition will want to try either of the trails leading to **Rainbow Bridge**; both are about 26 to 28 mi round-trip through challenging and rugged terrain. This site is considered sacred by the Navajo, and it's requested that visitors show respect by not walking under the bridge. Take Indian Highway 16 north toward the Utah state border. At the fork in the road, take either direction for about 5 mi to the trailhead leading to Rainbow Bridge. Excursion boats pull in at the dock at the arch, but no supplies are sold there. **Navajo Nation Parks and Recreation Department** (✉ *Bldg. 36A, E. AZ 264* 🏠 *Box 2520, Window Rock 86515* ☎ *928/871–6647* ⊕ *www.navajonation parks.org*) provides backcountry permits (a small fee is charged), which must be obtained before hiking to Rainbow Bridge. Write to the office, and allow about a month to process the paperwork.

WHERE TO EAT AND STAY

$$–$$$ ✕ **Rainbow Room.** The bi-level signature restaurant at the Lake Powell
AMERICAN   Resort occupies a cavernous round room affording 270-degree views of
Fodor's Choice   the lake, surrounding vermilion cliffs, and massive Navajo Mountain
★   in the distance. Serving the best food in the region, the kitchen focuses on organic, healthful ingredients in producing such toothsome dishes as a Southwestern Cobb salad with crispy chicken, fire-roasted chiles, and smoked jalapeño-buttermilk dressing, and wild-mushroom-stuffed quail with roast-shallot-mashed potatoes, roasted organic veggies, and a bourbon-molasses glaze. ✉ *100 Lake Shore Dr., 7 mi north of Page off U.S. 89, Wahweap* ☎ *928/645–2433* ⊕ *www.lakepowell.com* ☐ *AE, D, DC, MC, V.*

$$–$$$ ▦ **Lake Powell Resort.** This sprawling property consisting of several one-
Fodor's Choice   and two-story buildings, run by Aramark, sits on a promontory above
★   Lake Powell and serves as the center for recreational activities in the area. The brightly colored Southwestern-style suites in the newest building are particularly attractive, and most have wonderful lake view. Restaurants include the airy Rainbow Room, a coffeehouse, and a seasonal pizza parlor. **Pros:** stunning lake setting, couldn't be closer to the water, nice range of restaurants. **Cons:** rooms aren't especially fancy, it can be a long way from your room to the restaurant and lobby; confusing and cumbersome online reservations system. ✉ *100 Lake Shore Dr., 7 mi north of Page off U.S. 89, Wahweap* 🏠 *Box 1597, Page 86040* ☎ *928/645–2433 or 800/528–6154* ⊕ *www.lakepowell.com* ⇆ *350 rooms* ⚭ *In-room: refrigerator. In-hotel: 3 restaurants, bar, pools, some pets allowed* ☐ *AE, D, DC, MC, V.*

5

CAMPING
Beautiful campsites are abundant on Lake Powell, from large beaches to secluded coves, with the most desirable areas accessible only by boat. You're allowed to camp anywhere along the shores of the lake unless it's restricted by the National Park Service; however, camping within ¼ mi of the shoreline requires a portable toilet or bathroom facilities on your boat. Campfires are allowed on the shoreline, but since there's little firewood available around the lake you'll need to bring your own.

¢ **Wahweap Campground.** This campground in the Wahweap Marina complex, which is run by the National Park Service concessionaire, has views of the lake and serves both RVers and tent campers. There are showers and coin-laundry services at the nearby grocery store. *U.S. 89, 5 mi north of Page near shore of Lake Powell, Wahweap* *928/645–1059* *112 tent sites, 94 full hookups* *Flush toilets, full hookups, dump station, drinking water, fire pits, grills, picnic tables* *AE, D, DC, MC, V* *Open year-round.*

HOUSEBOATS
Without a doubt, the most popular and fun way to vacation on Lake Powell is to rent a houseboat. Houseboats, ranging in size from 36 to 59 feet and sleeping 6 to 12 people, come complete with marine radios, fully equipped kitchens, and bathrooms with hot showers; you need only bring sheets and towels. The larger, deluxe boats are a good choice in hot summer months, since they have air-conditioning. **Aramark's Lake Powell Resorts & Marinas** (*800/528–6154* *www.lakepowell.com*) is the only concessionaire that rents boats on Lake Powell. There are many vacation packages available. One houseboat that sleeps 10 runs from $1,000 for three nights in winter to about $3,400 for seven nights during the summer peak. At the other end of the spectrum, 75-foot luxury houseboats, which sleep 12, cost as much as $12,485 for seven nights. You receive hands-on instruction before you leave the marina.

Eastern Arizona

WORD OF MOUTH

"I would head up over the White Mountains. It will (literally!) be like a breath of fresh air after Phoenix and Tucson, a very different Arizona. Reminded me of the Black Forest! From there you could go to the Petrified Forest ."

—wildblueyonder

WELCOME TO EASTERN ARIZONA

TOP REASONS TO GO

★ **View nature's handiwork at Salt River Canyon:** Watch the desert cacti disappear as the country's pine delights your senses.

★ **Get outside:** No place for couch potatoes, eastern Arizona is home to some of the state's best recreation areas for skiing, fishing, golfing, camping, and exploring. If you love the outdoor life, you may fall in love with this place.

★ **Be petrified:** Marvel at huge petrified logs and the dazzling colors of nature at Petrified Forest National Park.

★ **Hit the road:** Whether you're traveling the Colorado Trail National Scenic Byway or getting your kicks on Route 66, these roads were made for travelers.

★ **Discover native traditions:** The rich culture and heritage of Native American tribes permeates this area.

Salt River Canyon

1 The White Mountains. In a state known for its extreme temperatures, residents of the White Mountains are proud of their home's relatively staid climate. The comfortable conditions and panoramic mountain views draw thousands here in the summer, making the region a playground for golfers, hikers, and fishermen. But there's plenty to do if you don't want to get your hands dirty.

2 The Petrified Forest and the Painted Desert. Forget about a Hollywood sci-fi thriller—the Petrified Forest actually takes you back in time. One of Arizona's most unusual sites, the park has yielded fossils dating back 225 million years. A visit to the forest is like exploring an outdoor museum. It's worth the trip, especially if you catch the brilliant colors of the Painted Desert at midday.

Holbrook

PAINTED DESERT

NAVAJO
RESERVATION

Petrified
Forest
National Park

2

Sanders

40

191

61

191

NEW MEXICO

Hunt

St. Johns

Snowflake
Taylor

Concho

180

77

61

Lyman Lake
State Park

Springerville
Volcanic Field

Show Low

Vernon

60

Pintop-Lakeside

260

Hon-Dah

McNary

260

Greer

Springerville

Eagar

60

Escudilla
Mtn.

191

Nutrioso

WHITE MOUNTAIN
APACHE
RESERVATION

73

Sunrise Park
Resort

Mt.
Baldy

1

Williams Valley

Alpine

WHITE   MOUNTAINS

Blue Range
Primitive Area

Fort
Apache

Salt River

Coronado Trail

Hannagan
Meadow

191

Rose Peak

GETTING ORIENTED

Eastern Arizona is a large, somewhat loosely defined series of small towns and historic sites. Visitors searching for an escape from the desert heat head for the White Mountains and its majestic vistas of ponderosa pines. Others seek history and head northeast to the 186,000-acre Petrified Forest National Park. No matter the destination, don't forget to stop and experience the area's local flavor, whether it's a museum of Native American crafts or a drive through a town whose name was derived from a losing hand of cards.

6

Petroglyph

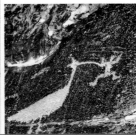

EASTERN ARIZONA PLANNER

When to Go

If you're a skier, winter is the time to tour the White Mountains. Sunrise Park Resort has 10 lifts and 65 trails, and a private snowboarders' park.

If you're not a winter-sports enthusiast, it's probably best to plan your trip to eastern Arizona for the high season (May through October). Residents of Phoenix and Tucson flock here to escape unbearably hot temperatures, but you can still find some solitude if you rent a cabin or choose a smaller, more remote resort or bed-and-breakfast.

Eastern Arizona is enjoyable year-round, but many lodging facilities, restaurants, and tourist attractions are closed in autumn and winter, so call ahead. The opening and closing dates of many seasonal properties are dependent on when the snow starts (and when it melts).

Getting Here and Around

There isn't much choice: you'll be driving to and around eastern Arizona. Amtrak offers limited service, but it isn't that helpful for travelers. Part of the experience in eastern Arizona is the drive. Rent a car in Phoenix or Tucson, or even Flagstaff, and enjoy the open road.

If you're arriving from points west via Flagstaff, Interstate 40 leads directly to Holbrook, where drivers can take AZ 77 south into Show Low or U.S. 180 southeast to Springerville-Eagar. Visitors departing from the Phoenix area should take the scenic drive northeast on U.S. 60, or the only slightly faster AZ 87 north to AZ 260 east, both of which lead to Show Low. From Tucson, AZ 77 north connects with U.S. 60 at Globe, and continues through Show Low up to Holbrook. From New Mexico, drivers can enter the state on Interstate 40 and take U.S. 191 south into Springerville-Eagar, or continue on to Holbrook and reach the White Mountains via AZ 77. For those who want to drive the Coronado Trail south-to-north, U.S. 70 and AZ 78 link up with U.S. 191 from Globe to the west and New Mexico to the east, respectively.

Weather conditions change rapidly in eastern Arizona. Before heading out on a daylong excursion—particularly during the winter—be sure to call the Arizona Department of Transportation's Traveler Information Service (☎511).

Making the Most of Your Time

The Petrified Forest is the main attraction for most of eastern Arizona's visitors. Plan to reserve a day for the forest and the Painted Desert, with one or two additional days for exploring. Depending on your preferences, you can add day trips and excursions. Fans of the great outdoors have their choice of activities in the White Mountains. Those who like a little less sweat in their vacations can hit the open road and explore historic Route 66 or the Colorado Trail.

Pinetop-Lakeside offers the best base for your trip, with a wide range of lodging facilities and amenities. Neighboring area towns, such as Snowflake-Taylor or Holbrook, have storied motels and B&Bs. If solitude is your goal, consider staying at a lodge surrounded by private forest.

Paradise for Outdoors Enthusiasts

Like hiking? Hikers and mountain bikers of all abilities enjoy the White Mountains' 225 mi of interconnecting loop trails, open to visitors on foot or on nonmotorized wheels. Ranger stations have maps. Allow an hour for each 2 mi of trail, plus an additional hour for every 1,000 feet gained in altitude. Carry water and watch out for poison ivy.

Like fishing? Anglers flock to the more than 65 lakes, streams, and reservoirs in the White Mountains. In winter only artificial lures and flies are permitted. An Arizona fishing license is required; on tribal land you'll also need a White Mountain Apache fishing license. Want an easier catch? Some lodges have private lakes stocked with trout.

Like golfing? The High Country's links draw golfers from all over, and these mountain fairways angle through lush forests and past lakes and springs.

Like skiing? The 11,000-foot White Mountains offer hilly, wooded landscapes that invite downhill and cross-country skiing adventurers. Greer's nearby Pole Knoll Trail System and surrounding Forest Service roads make for 33 mi of cross-country trails. No matter where you stay in the White Mountains, Sunrise Park Resort is never more than an hour's drive away.

Local Food and Lodging

Luxury travel this is not. Some local lodges, such as the Greer Lodge Resort, are expanding and offering more luxury services such as massages. Most places, however, offer clean rooms without many frills. Fine dining is difficult to find; home-style cooking, steak houses, and the occasional authentic Mexican joint pepper most towns. Reservations are suggested during the busy summer months, and remember that some places are closed in winter.

WHAT IT COSTS

	¢	$	$$	$$$	$$$$
Restaurant	under $8	$8–$12	$13–$20	$21–$30	over $30
Hotel	under $70	$70–$120	$121–$175	$176–$250	over $250

Restaurant prices are per person for a main course at dinner. Hotel prices are for a standard double in high season, excluding taxes and service charges.

Native American Sites

North of Springerville-Eagar, Casa Malpais Archaeological Park is a prehistoric pueblo site with construction characteristics of both the Ancient Puebloan and Mogollon peoples. Nearby Lyman Lake State Park has petroglyph trails with some of the region's more accessible rock art. West of Holbrook, Homolovi Ruins State Park is home to a large complex of Hopi ancestral pueblos. Petroglyphs and pueblos dating back more than 600 years can be found at stops along the 28-mi park road in Petrified Forest National Park.

Camping

Apache-Sitgreaves National Forest (☎ *928/333–4301* ⊕ *www.fs.fed.us/r3/asnf*) has a listing of all public camping facilities in the region, most of which operate from April to November. To ensure a site at a fee campground, use the **National Recreation Reservation Service** (☎ *877/444–6777* ⊕ *www.recreation.gov*)., which charges a reservation fee of $10 per transaction. Book your campground site well in advance with the Game and Fish Division of the **White Mountain Apache Tribe** (☎ *928/338–4385* ⊕ *www. wmat.nsn.us*).

6

Updated by
Cara LaBrie

In a state of dramatic natural wonders, eastern Arizona is often overlooked—truly a tragedy, as it's one of Arizona's great outdoor playgrounds. In the White Mountains, northeast of Phoenix, you can hike, fish, swim, and, at night, gaze upward at millions of twinkling stars. The region's winter sports are just as varied: you can ski downhill or cross-country, snowboard, snowshoe, and snowmobile on hundreds of miles of designated trails.

The White Mountains are unspoiled high country at its best. Certain areas have been designated as primitive wilderness, and remain preserved. In these vast tracts the air is rent with piercing cries of hawks and eagles, and majestic herds of elk graze in verdant, wildflower-laden meadows. Past volcanic activity has left the land strewn with cinder cones, and the whole region is bounded by the Mogollon Rim (pronounced *muh*-gee-on)—a 200-mi geologic upthrust that splits the state—made famous as the "Tonto Rim" in Zane Grey's books. Much of the plant life is unique to this region; this is one of the few places in the country where such desert plants as juniper and manzanita grow intermixed with mountain pines and aspen.

The human aspects of the landscape are equally appealing. Historic Western towns are friendly outposts of down-home hospitality, and the many prehistoric sites are reminders of the native cultures that once flourished here and are still a vital presence. The Fort Apache Reservation, home to the White Mountain Apache Tribe, is north of the Salt River, and the San Carlos Apache Tribal Reservation is south of the river. Visitors are welcome to explore most reservation lands. All that's required is a permit, easily obtained from tribal offices.

Historic sites and natural wonders also attract visitors to eastern Arizona. To the north, along historic Route 66, are the Painted Desert and Petrified Forest National Park, and Homolovi Ruins State Park. The austere mesas of the Painted Desert are famous for their multihued sedimentary layers. Nature also has worked wonders on the great fallen logs

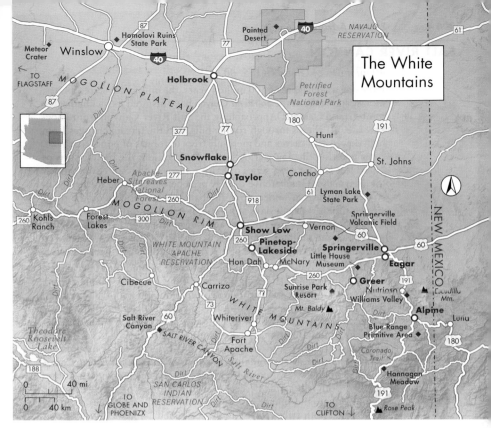

of the Petrified Forest National Park. In Triassic times the park was a
great, steamy swampland; some 225 million years ago, seismic activity
forced the swamp's decaying plant matter (and a number of deceased
dinosaurs) deep underground, where it eventually turned to stone. Fifty
miles west of these unusual geologic remains, Homolovi Ruins State
Park marks the site of four major ancestral Hopi pueblos, two of which
contain more than 1,000 rooms.

THE WHITE MOUNTAINS

With elevations climbing to more than 11,000 feet, the White Mountains area of east-central Arizona is a winter wonderland and a summer haven from the desert heat. In the 1870s, U.S. soldier and diarist
John Gregory Bourke labeled the White Mountains region "a strange
upheaval, a freak of nature, a mountain canted up on one side; one rides
along the edge and looks down two or three thousand feet into . . . a
weird scene of grandeur and rugged beauty." The area, although much
less remote than in Bourke's time is still grand and rugged, carved by
deep river canyons and tall cliffs covered with ponderosa pine.

geography. The 8-mi **Panorama Trail,** rated moderate, affords astonishing views from the top of extinct double volcanoes known as the Twin Knolls, and passes though a designated wildlife habitat area; the trailhead is 6 mi east on Porter Mountain Road, off AZ 260.

You can get trail brochures or other information from the **Apache-Sitgreaves National Forests** (⊠ *Lakeside Ranger Station, 2022 W. White Mountain Blvd., Lakeside* ☎ *928/368–2100* ⊕ *www.fs.fed.us/r3/asnf*), including a $2 booklet on the White Mountains Trail System.

FISHING   East of Pinetop-Lakeside and 9 mi south of AZ 260, 260-acre **Hawley Lake** (⊠ *AZ 473, Hawley Lake* ☎ *928/338–4385*) sits on Apache territory and yields mostly rainbow trout; rental boats are available in the marina. Tribal permits are required for all recreational activities: contact **White Mountain Apache Fish & Game Department** (☎ *928/338–4385*) for details. **Paradise Creek Anglers** (⊠ *560 W. White Mountain Blvd., Lakeside* ☎ *928/367–6200 or 800/231–3831* ⊕ *www.paradisecreek anglers.com*) offers fishing advice, lessons, and equipment rentals.

GOLF   **Pinetop Lakes Golf & Country Club** (⊠ *4643 Buck Springs Rd., Pinetop* ☎ *928/369–4531* ⊕ *www.pinetoplakesgolf.com* ⚑ *18 holes. Green Fees: $30–47* ⌘ *Facilities: Driving range, putting green, golf carts, rental clubs, lessons, restaurant, bar*) has fewer trees than other area courses, but it offers several water hazards to compensate. The shorter course is wonderful for public play. The club also has a driving range, putting greens, and tennis courts, not to mention a restaurant and lounge. It's open April to October.

HORSEBACK   **Porter Mountain Stables** (⊠ *4048 Porter Mountain Rd., Lakeside* ☎ *928/368–*
RIDING   *5306*) offers one-hour to all-day horseback trips in the summer; they are open from Memorial Day to Labor Day.

SKIING AND   The **Skier's Edge** (⊠ *560 W. White Mountain Blvd., Pinetop* ☎ *928/367–*
SNOW SPORTS   *6200 or 800/231–3831* ⊕ *www.skiersedgepinetop.com*) has crosscountry and downhill skis as well as snowboards and boots. **Snowriders** (⊠ *857 E. White Mountain Blvd., Pinetop* ☎ *928/367–5638 or 800/762–0256* ⊕ *www.azsnowriders.com*) sells and rents skis and snowboards and gear from December through March 15, weather permitting.

WHERE TO EAT

$$$$ ✕ **Charlie Clark's Steak House.** From golfers relishing a successful day on
AMERICAN   the links to locals in search of good food, Charlie Clark's has been the meeting place of the White Mountains since it opened in 1938. Prime rib is the house specialty—a delicate "ladies cut" is available for those with smaller appetites. Minnesota walleye pike adds a Midwestern spin to the menu. ⊠ *1701 E. White Mountain Blvd., Pinetop* ☎ *928/367–4900* ⊕ *www.charlieclarks.com* ⊟ *AE, D, MC, V.*

$ ✕ **Los Corrales.** Bright yellows and oranges make for a cheerful family-
MEXICAN   style eatery, which attracts locals with Mexican seafood dishes such as *camarones a la crema* (shrimp and mushrooms in cream sauce) and luncheon specials. Dessert specialties include fried ice cream and apple chimichanga. A small bar serves drinks. ⊠ *845 E. White Mountain Blvd., Lakeside* ☎ *928/367–5585* ⊟ *AE, D, DC, MC, V.*

Mt. Baldy rises above the pine treeline at 11,403 feet—it's the tallest peak in the White Mountains.

WHERE TO STAY

$ **Hon-Dah Resort Casino and Conference Center.** Stuffed high-country animals atop a mountain of boulders welcome you to Apache Tribe–operated Hon-Dah. The main draw is the casino, with hundreds of slot machines, live poker and blackjack, and weekend entertainment. Large guest rooms all have coffeemakers and wet bars. A high-roof atrium holds the pool and hot tub. The Indian Pine Restaurant serves three daily meals, and a small gift shop sells local Apache crafts. **Pros:** best destination for travelers who aren't interested in roughing it; very big draw for the casino crowd. **Cons:** the resort can get noisy in the evening. ⊠777 AZ 260, Pinetop ☎928/369–0299 or 800/929–8744 ⊕www.hon-dah.com ⌖126 rooms, 2 suites ⌂In-room: refrigerator, Wi-Fi. In-hotel: restaurant, bars, pool, no-smoking rooms ☐AE, D, DC, MC, V.

$$ **Lake of the Woods Resort.** Janet Pierson was so taken with Lakeside after her first visit that she and two friends decided to buy Lake of the Woods Resort. Housed next to the resort's private lake, guests can fish for trout, hike, rent a boat, and enjoy the natural surroundings of the area. Novice fishermen take note: Pierson and crew stock the lake a half-dozen times a year with trout. It's almost as easy as shooting fish in a barrel. **Pros:** on Lakeside's main street, with a rural, but not removed, atmosphere; stocked private lake. **Cons:** only phone on-site for guests is a pay phone in the main building. ⊠2244 W. White Mountain Blvd., Lakeside ☎928/368–5353 ⊕www.lakeofthewoodsaz.com ⌖26 cabins, 7 houses ⌂In-room: kitchen, no phone In-hotel: some pets allowed ☐MC, V.

Eastern Arizona attracts outdoor lovers for horseback riding, hiking, fishing, golfing, and skiing.

and then closes again in fall from mid-October until the first heavy snowfall. **Pros:** comfortable accommodations; best access to ski amenities. **Cons:** not the best winter destination for those who don't want to hit the slopes; closed between seasons. ⊠ *AZ 273, 7 mi south of AZ 260* ☖ *Box 117, Greer 85927* 🕾 *928/735–7669 or 800/772–7669* ⊕ *www. sunriseskipark.com* 🛏 *100 rooms, 1 suite* ☖ *In-room: no a/c, refrigerator (some). In-hotel: 2 restaurants, bar, pool, Wi-Fi, no-smoking rooms, no elevator* ⊟ *AE, D, DC, MC, V.*

GREER

★ *35 mi southeast of Pinetop-Lakeside and 15 mi southwest of Eagar on AZ 260.*

The charming community of Greer sits just south of AZ 260 among pine, spruce, willow, and aspen on the banks of the Little Colorado River. At an elevation of 8,500 feet, this portion of gently sloping National Forest land is covered with meadows and reservoirs and is dominated by 11,590-foot Baldy Peak. Much of the surrounding area remains under the control of the Apache tribe, so visitors must take care to respect Apache law and land.

GETTING HERE AND AROUND

Take AZ 373 south from AZ 260. AZ 373 is also Greer's main street, which winds through the village and crosses the Little Colorado River, eventually coming to a dead end. It's affectionately called the Road to Nowhere.

EXPLORING

Listed on the National Register of Historic Places, the **Butterfly Lodge Museum** was built as a hunting lodge in 1914 by John Butler, the husband of "Aunt Molly" (of Molly Butler Lodge fame), for author James Willard Schultz and his artist son, Lone Wolf, a prolific painter of Indian and Western scenes. There's a small gift shop. Take time to watch the surrounding meadow come to life with beautiful butterflies, from which the lodge got its name. ⊠ *AZ 373 at CR 1126* ☎ *928/735–7514* ⊕ *www.wmonline. com/butterflylodge.htm* ⊠ *$2* ⊙ *June–Aug., Thurs.–Sun. 10–5.*

SPORTS AND THE OUTDOORS

The **Tin Star Trading Post** (⊠ *38940 AZ 373* ☎ *928/735–7540*) sells sleds in winter and tackle the rest of the year. Fishing licenses, groceries, and camping supplies are also for sale. You can grab a cup of joe at the Post's coffee shop. Buy supplies for an afternoon picnic and feel free to use their wireless Internet service for a quick e-mail check.

FISHING The three Greer Lakes are actually the Bunch, River, and Tunnel reservoirs. Bait and fly-fishing options are scenic and plentiful, and there are several places to launch a boat. Winding through Greer, the Little Colorado River's West Fork is well stocked with brookies and rainbows, and has 23 mi of fishable waters.

HIKING The difficult but accessible **Mount Baldy Trail** begins at **Sheeps Crossing,** southwest of Greer on AZ 273. In just under 8 mi (one way) the trail climbs the northern flank of 11,590-foot Mount Baldy, the second-highest peak in Arizona. Note that the summit of Baldy is on the White Mountain Apache Reservation. Considered sacred land, this final ¼ mi is off-limits to non-Apaches. The boundary is clearly marked; please respect it, no matter how much you wish to continue to the peak.

SKIING Cross-country skiers find Greer an ideally situated hub for some of the mountain's best trails. About 2½ mi west of AZ 373 on AZ 260, a trailhead marks the starting point for the **Pole Knoll Trail System,** nearly 30 mi of well-marked, groomed cross-country trails interlacing through the Apache-Sitgreaves National Forest and color-coded by experience level. Trail maps are available from the **Apache-Sitgreaves National Forest** (⊠ *Springerville Ranger District, 165 S. Mountain Ave., Springerville* ☎ *928/333–4372* ⊕ *www.fs.fed.us/r3/asnf*).

WHERE TO EAT

$ ✕ **Greer Mountain Resort Country Cafe.** This plant-hung diner-café is open
AMERICAN from 7 AM to 3 PM. Grab a seat by the fireplace and sample the homemade ranch beans, a signature grilled-cheese sandwich with green chiles and tomato—because every dish in Arizona tastes better with green chiles—or fresh-baked cobbler. On those cooler days, the homemade

6

site itself may only be visited on a tour; these leave from the museum at 9, 11, and 2. ✉*318 E. Main St., Springerville* ☎*928/333–5375* ✆*$8* ⊙*Museum daily 8–4.*

The **Little House Museum** has a collection of local pioneer and ranching memorabilia, but it's the mesmerizing tones from a rare collection of automatic musical instruments that you remember—as well as the museum's colorful curator, Wink Crigler, with her tales of this region's lively past. Tours to archaeological digs and petroglyphs are available by appointment. To reach the ranch, go 10 mi southwest of Eagar on AZ 260, turn south onto South Fork Road, and go 3 mi. ✉*X Diamond Ranch, S. Fork Rd., 10 mi southwest of Eagar* ☎*928/333–2286* ⊕*www.xdiamondranch.com* ✆*$12* ⊙*By reservation only.*

The **Renée Cushman Art Collection Museum** is open to the public only by special appointment, but a visit is worth the effort. Renée Cushman's extensive collection of objets d'art—some acquired on her travels, some collected with the accumulated resources of three wealthy husbands, and some willed to her by her artistic father—is administered by the Church of Latter-day Saints. Her treasure includes a Rembrandt engraving, Tiepolo pen-and-inks, and an impressive collection of European antiques, some dating back to the 15th century. Call the **Springerville-Eagar Regional Chamber of Commerce** (☎*928/333–2123*) to arrange your visit.

SPORTS AND THE OUTDOORS

For your mountain-sports needs the **Sweat Shop** (✉*42 N. Main St., Eagar* ☎*928/333–2950*) rents skis, snowboards, and mountain bikes.

FISHING **Becker Lake** (✉*U.S. 60, 2 mi northwest of Springerville* ☎*928/367–4281*) is a specialty lake for trout fishing; call for seasonal bait requirements. **Big Lake** (✉*AZ 273, 24 mi south of AZ 260* ☎*928/735–7313*), known to many as the "queen of all trout lakes," is stocked each spring and fall with rainbow, brook, and cutthroat trout. **Nelson Reservoir** (✉*U.S. 191, Nutrioso*), between Springerville-Eagar and Alpine, is well stocked with rainbow, brown, and brook trout. The **Speckled Trout** (✉*224 E. Main St., Springerville* ☎*928/333–0852*) offers fishing-guide services and sells Orvis-licensed fly-fishing equipment. A small gift shop features books, linens, and wind chimes, along with nonalcoholic drinks like espresso and fruit smoothies. **Troutback** (✉*450 S. Clark Rd., Show Low* ☎*928/532–3474 or 800/403–4092* ⊕*www.troutback.com*) is a fly-fishing guide service that will create half- or full-day fishing trips for novices and seasoned anglers alike throughout the White Mountains. Equipment, including boats, waders, fly rods and reels, and float tubes, is available for rent. **Western United Drug** (✉*105 E. Main St., Springerville* ☎*928/333–4321*) stays open 365 days a year, and has a well-stocked sporting-goods and outdoor-equipment section.

WHERE TO EAT

$ ✗**Booga Reds.** The delicious home-style cooking, such as fish-and-chips
AMERICAN   and roast-beef dinner, is worth a stop. Should your palate demand something spicier, try one of the many Mexican dishes—the enchiladas are wonderful. Save room for the daily fruit or cream pie. Booga Reds opens at 6 AM for an early breakfast but closes relatively early—

The White Mountains elevation makes the area a great place to stay cool in the summer.

at 9 PM—so make your dinner an early one, too. ⊠*521 E. Main St., Springerville* ☎*928/333–2640* ▭*MC, V.*

$$ ✕**Java Blues.** Not your typical mountain eatery, Java Blues oozes a cof-
AMERICAN feehouse vibe with its overstuffed couches and stained-glass windows.
Salads, soups, sandwiches, and a Greek Board—a variety of Greek
meats and cheeses served with toasted baguette—are on the lunch menu.
A separate dinner menu and a full bar make it a favorite evening spot,
too, featuring the only fettuccine Alfredo in town and chicken-fried
steak. The restaurant opens early and serves dinner six nights a week.
⊠*341 E. Main St., Springerville* ☎*928/333–5282* ▭*MC, V.*

WHERE TO STAY

$ ⚏**Reed's Lodge.** It's an older motel, but a town favorite. The rooms of
this mostly single-story motel have Western accents such as knotty-
pine paneling and Navajo-print bedspreads. Perks include a recreation
room with pool table, video games, and a pinball machine; a gift shop;
and complimentary bicycles. Enjoy coffee, tea, cocoa, or cider every
morning. Proprietor Roxanne Knight will arrange visits for guests on a
working cowboy-style (not dude) ranch, cattle drives, horseback adven-
tures, four-wheel-drive tours, wildlife- and petroglyph-viewing trips, or
fossil-hunting expeditions. **Pros:** well priced. **Cons:** modest accommoda-
tions, few frills. ⊠*514 E. Main St., Springerville* ☎*928/333–4323 or
800/814–6451* ⊕*www.k5reeds.com* ⮡*45 rooms, 5 suites* ⌂*In-room:
Wi-Fi, refrigerator (some). In hotel: no-smoking rooms, no elevator,
some pets allowed* ▭*AE, D, DC, MC, V.*

$ ⚏**Rode Inn.** Don't let the John Wayne motif scare you away—two card-
board figures of "The Duke" in full cowboy regalia are perched on a

Flyfishing (☎928/339–4829 ⊕*www.azmtflyfishing.com*) guides anglers to top fishing streams and teaches novices.

GOLF **Alpine Country Club** (⊠*58 County Rd. 2122, Alpine* ☎928/339–4944) is off U.S. 180, 3 mi east of U.S. 191. At 8,500 feet above sea level, it's one of the highest golf courses in the Southwest. Even if you don't play golf, stop in for New Mexican–style food—enchiladas here are stacked, not rolled—and breathtaking scenery at the club's Aspen Room Restaurant. It's 1 mi south of Alpine on Blue River Road. The course is closed from November to April, and the restaurant is closed Monday.

HIKING The **Escudilla National Recreation Trail** (⊠*U.S. 191, Hulsey Lake*) is more idyllic than arduous; the 3-mi trail wends through the Escudilla Wilderness to the summit of towering, 10,912-foot **Escudilla Mountain,** Arizona's third-tallest peak. The trail climbs 1,300 feet to a fire tower ¼ mi from the summit. From Alpine, take U.S. 191 north and follow the signs to Hulsey Lake (about 5 mi).

SNOW SPORTS **Williams Valley Winter Sports Area** (⊠*FSR 249, Alpine* ☎928/339–4384 *for Alpine Ranger District information*), 2½ mi west of town, has 12½ mi of cross-country and snowshoe trails of varying difficulty maintained by the Alpine Ranger District. Toboggan Hill is a favorite for families, with sleds, toboggans, and tubes. Shelters, picnic facilities, and toilets are available. Pick up an Apache-Sitgreaves National Forest map and "Winter Sports" brochure from the Alpine Ranger District, and call for conditions prior to heading out.

WHERE TO EAT AND STAY

$ 🏨**Downs' Ranch Hide-Away.** Looking for a vacation that is really back-of-beyond? For stress relief, do as the locals do and go "down on the Blue." Blue, Arizona, on the Blue River in the Blue Range Primitive Area, along the Arizona–New Mexico border, is one of the most remote sections of the state and a sure cure for the city-life blues. Try hiking or horseback riding to explore Blue River, pine forests, canyons, Native American dwellings, wildlife—or just sit on the porch and enjoy a hefty helping of serenity. Cabins have complete kitchens, and owners Bill and Mona Bunnell suggest you bring food. Let them know in advance if you need meals arranged. The ranch accepts only cash, checks, traveler's checks, or money orders. **Pros:** a truly one-of-a-kind way to commune with Mother Nature; open year-round. **Cons:** zero amenities. ⌂*Box 77, Blue 85922* ☎928/339–4952 ⊕*www.dcoutfitters. com/downsRanch.php* ✎*downsranchhideaway@frontiernet.net* ⌨4 *cabins* ⊟*No credit cards.*

$–$$ 🏨**Tal-Wi-Wi Lodge.** This lodge draws many repeat visitors—particularly
★ car and motorcycle enthusiasts—to its lush meadows, a favorite for bird-watchers. Motel-style rooms are simple and clean, with three of the most popular rooms offering wood-burning fireplace-stoves, indoor hot tubs, or both. In the evening stroll the grounds and gaze at the Milky Way in the brilliant night sky. With satellite TV and live country music on weekends, the lodge saloon draws a loyal local following. The cozy, casual restaurant is open May through November and serves breakfast on weekends and dinner Thursday through Saturday. Prime rib is the house specialty, but they also serve pizza and homemade pies. **Pros:** best

place to stay in Alpine, with absolutely majestic views of the area. **Cons:** very bare-bones and rustic. ⌧ *U.S. 191* ⌂ *Box 169, Alpine 85920* ☎ *928/339–4319* ⊕ *www.talwiwilodge.com* ⌖ *20 rooms* ⌂ *In-room: no a/c, no TV. In-hotel: restaurant, bar, some pets allowed, public Wi-Fi, no-smoking rooms* ☰ *MC, V.*

OFF THE
BEATEN
PATH

Blue Range Primitive Area. Directly east of Hannagan Meadow, these unspoiled 170,000 acres, lovingly referred to by locals as "the Blue," comprise the last designated primitive area in the United States. The diverse terrain surrounds the Blue River and is crossed by the Mogollon Rim from east to west. No motorized or mechanized equipment is allowed—including mountain bikes; passage is restricted to foot or horseback. Many trails interlace the Blue: prehistoric paths of the ancient native peoples, cowboy trails to move livestock between pastures and water sources, access routes to lookout towers and fire trails. Avid backpackers and campers may want to spend a few days exploring the dozens of hiking trails. Even though trail access is fairly good, hikers need to remember that this is primitive, rough country, and it's essential to carry adequate water supplies.

HANNAGAN MEADOW

6

50 mi south of Springerville-Eagar, 23 mi south of Alpine.

GETTING HERE AND AROUND

The Coronado Trail stretch of U.S. 191 passes through this remote part of the state.

EXPLORING

★ **Hannagan Meadow** is a pastorally mesmerizing location. Lush and isolated at a 9,500-foot-plus elevation, the meadow is home to elk, deer, and range cattle, as well as blue grouse, wild turkeys, and the occasional eagle. Adjacent to the meadow, the Blue Range Primitive Area provides access to miles of untouched wilderness and some beautiful rugged terrain, and it's a designated recovery area for the endangered Mexican gray wolf. It's believed that Francisco Vásquez de Coronado and his party came through the meadow on their famed expedition in 1540 to find the Seven Cities of Cibola.

SPORTS AND THE OUTDOORS

Want to get away from it all? The **Apache Ranger District** of the Apache-Sitgreaves National Forest offers secluded spaces for outdoors adventures year-round. Hikers and anglers can check out the 11,000-acre **Bear Wallow Wilderness Area** (west of U.S. 191 and bordered by FSR 25 and 54), which has cool, flowing streams stocked with native Apache trout. The **Rose Spring Trail** is a pleasant 5½-mi hike with a moderate gradient and magnificent views from the Mogollon Rim's edge; the trailhead is at the end of Forest Service Road 54. **Reno Trail** and **Gobbler Trail** both drop into the main canyon from well-marked trailheads off Forest Service Road 25. Reno Trail meanders 2 mi through conifer forest and aspen, while Gobbler Trail is 2½-mi long with views overlooking the Black River and Fort Apache Indian Reservation. This designated wilderness (and some of its trails) borders the San Carlos

Apache Indian Reservation, where an advance permit is required for entry. In the winter, try the 8½ mi of groomed cross-country trails of the **Hannagan Meadow Winter Recreation Area** (⊠ *U.S. 191, Hannagan Meadow*), which also is part of the Apache-Sitgreaves forest. The 4½-mi **Clell Lee Loop** is an easy route; the advanced-level, ungroomed **KP Rim Loop** traverses upper elevations of the Blue Primitive Range and provides some of the most varied (and tranquil) remote skiing in the state. The area just northeast of U.S. 191 is a snowmobiling playground. Trailheads are at U.S. 191 and Forest Service Road 576. There are no rental shops nearby, so bring your own equipment.

Contact **Apache-Sitgreaves National Forest** (⊠ *Alpine Ranger District, U.S. 191* ⏚ *Box 469, Alpine 85920* ☏ *928/339–4384* ⊕ *www.fs.fed. us/r3/asnf*) for trail maps and information.

WHERE TO STAY

$$ 🏨 **Hannagan Meadow Lodge.** Antiques and floral prints impart a genteel,
★   Victorian feel to this lodge. The dining room has hewn-log beams and a glass wall that overlooks a pristine meadow. Log cabins are more rustic; some have full kitchens and fireplaces, whereas others are equipped with microwaves, stove tops, and wood-burning stoves. The solitude of the area is enhanced by the absence of phones and TVs in rooms and cabins. The general store sells sundries as well as fishing supplies, and rents snowshoes, cross-country skis, and mountain bikes. Continental breakfast is provided in the summer. **Pros:** gorgeous setting. **Cons:** guests should not rely on daily room cleaning; much more lodge than hotel. ⊠ *U.S. 191, 22 mi south of Alpine, Hannagan Meadow* ⏚ *HC 61, Box 335, Alpine 85920* ☏ *928/339–4370* ⊕ *www.hannaganmeadow. com* ⌘ *7 rooms, 10 cabins* ⚷ *In-room: no a/c, no phone, kitchen (some), no TV. In-hotel: restaurant, bicycles, public Wi-Fi, some pets allowed, no elevator* ⊟ *MC, V.*

THE PETRIFIED FOREST AND THE PAINTED DESERT

Only about 1½ hours from Show Low and the lush, verdant forests of the White Mountains, Arizona's diverse and dramatic landscape changes from pine-crested mountains to the sun-baked terrain of the Petrified Forest and lunarlike landscape of the Painted Desert.

PETRIFIED FOREST NATIONAL PARK

Northern Entrance: 54 mi east of Homolovi Ruins State Park and 27 mi east of Holbrook on I–40; Southern Entrance: 18 mi east of Holbrook on U.S. 180.

Updated by
Cara LaBrie

Though named for its famous fossilized trees, Petrified Forest National Park has something to see for history buffs of all stripes, from a segment of Route 66 to ancient dwellings to even more ancient fossils. And the good thing is that most of Petrified Forest's treasures can easily be viewed without a great amount of athletic conditioning. Much can be seen by driving along the main road, from which historic sites are

readily accessible. By combining a drive along the park road with a short hike here and there and a visit to one of the park's landmarks, you can see most of the sights in as little as half a day.

GETTING HERE AND AROUND

Holbrook, the nearest larger town, is roughly 20 mi from either of the park's two entrances on U.S. 40.

Parking is free, and there's ample space at all trailheads, as well as at the visitor center and the museum. The main park road extends 28 mi from the Painted Desert Visitor Center (north entrance) to the Rainbow Forest Museum (south entrance). For park road conditions, call ☎928/524–6228.

TIMING

The park is rarely crowded. Weath-

> ## LOOK AND TOUCH—BUT DON'T TAKE
>
> One of the most commonly asked questions about the Petrified Forest is, "Can I touch the wood?" Fortunately, yes! Park rangers encourage visitors to use their sense that's often ignored at museums and historical sites: touch. Feel comfortable to touch anything, pick it up, inspect it . . . just make sure you put it back exactly where you found it. Some of the park's visitor centers also have "touching tables" where you can more comfortably interact with objects. Feel free to ask questions and feel your way through the experience!

er-wise, the best time to visit is in the autumn, when nights are chilly but daytime temperatures hover near 70°F. Half of all yearly rain falls between June and August, so it's a good time to spot blooming wildflowers. The park is least crowded in winter, because of cold winds and occasional snow, though daytime temperatures are in the 50s and 60s.

ESSENTIALS

Accessibility The visitor center, museum, and overlooks on the scenic drive are wheelchair accessible. All trails are paved, and all are accessible except Blue Mesa, which is very steep.

Admission Fees Entrance fees are $10 per car for seven consecutive days or $5 per person on foot, bicycle, motorcycle, or bus.

Admission Hours The park is open daily 8 AM–5 PM from Labor Day through Memorial Day, and daily 7 AM–7 PM Memorial Day through Labor Day. The park is in the mountain time zone.

Permits Permits are required for backcountry hiking and camping, and are free (limit of 15 days) at Painted Desert Visitor Center or the Rainbow Forest Museum before 4 PM.

Visitor Information Petrified Forest National Park (✉ *1 Park Rd., Petrified Forest, AZ* ☎ *928/524–6228* ⊕ *www.nps.gov/pefo*).

EXPLORING

There are few places where the span of geologic and human history is as wide or apparent as it is at **Petrified Forest National Park**. Fossilized trees and countless other fossils date back to the Triassic Period, while a stretch of the famed Route 66 of more modern lore is protected within park boundaries. Ancestors of the Hopi, Zuni, and Navajo left petroglyphs, pottery, and even structures built of petrified wood. Nine park sites are on the National Register of Historic Places; one, the Painted

Petrified Forest National Park

CHINDE MESA

Pilot Rock

PAINTED DESERT

Digger Wash

Wash

Lithodendron Wash

Wilderness Area
(Camping permit required)

BLACK FOREST

Chinde Point

Painted Desert Inn
National Historic
Landmark

Pintado Point

Nizhoni Point

Whipple Point

Lacey Point

Wildhorse Wash

Visitor Center

Exit 311

No access
to I-40

TO
ALBUQUERQUE,
NM

TO
FLAGSTAFF
AND HOLBROOK

40

PAINTED

Puerco Pueblo

Newspaper Rock

The Tepees

Blue Mesa

DESERT

Twin Buttes

Park Boundary

Agate Bridge

Jasper Forest

Crystal Forest

Wilderness Area

TO
HOLBROOK

PUERCO RIDGE

THE FLATTOPS

180

Rainbow Forest Museum

Giant Logs

Long Logs

Agate House

Entrance Station

TO
ST. JOHNS

180

0   2 mi

0   2 km

KEY	
👫	*Ranger Station/Information*
🚻	*Restrooms*
⛱	*Picnic Area*
⛺	*Wilderness Camping*

Walking Petrified Forest's short trails can be a nice break from driving along I-40, which crosses the park.

Desert Inn, is one of only 3% of such sites that are further listed as National Historic Landmarks.

SCENIC DRIVE

Painted Desert Scenic Drive. A 28-mi scenic drive takes you through the park from one entrance to the other. If you begin from the north, the first 5 mi of the drive takes you along the edge of a high mesa, with spectacular views of Painted Desert. Beyond lies the desolate Painted Desert Wilderness Area. After the 5 mi point, the road crosses Interstate 40, then swings south toward the Puerco River across a landscape covered with sagebrush, saltbrush, sunflowers, and Apache plume. Past the river, the road climbs onto a narrow mesa leading to Newspaper Rock, a panel of Pueblo Indian rock art. Then the road bends southeast, enters a barren stretch, and passes tepee-shaped buttes in the distance. Next you come to Blue Mesa, roughly the park's midpoint and a good place to stop for views of petrified logs. The next stop on the drive is Agate Bridge, really a 100-foot log over a wide wash. The remaining overlooks are Jasper Forest and Crystal Forest, where you can get a further glimpse of the accumulated petrified wood. On your way out of the park, stop at the Rainbow Forest Museum for a rest and to shop for a memento. ⊠ *Begins at Painted Desert Visitor Center.*

HISTORIC SITES

Agate House. This eight-room pueblo is thought to have been built entirely of petrified wood 700 years ago. Researchers believe it might have been used as a temporary dwelling by seasonal farmers or traders from one of the area tribes. ⊠ *Rainbow Forest Museum parking area.*

PETRIFIED FOREST IN ONE DAY

A nonstop drive through the park (*28 mi*) takes only 45 minutes, but you can spend most of a day exploring if you stop along the way. From almost any vantage point you can see the multicolored rocks and hills that were home to prehistoric humans and ancient dinosaurs.

Entering the park from the north, stop at **Painted Desert Visitor Center** and see a 20-minute introductory film. **Painted Desert Inn visitor center**, 2 mi south of the north entrance, provides further orientation in the form of guided ranger tours. Drive south 8 mi to reach **Puerco Pueblo**, a 100-room pueblo built before 1400. Continuing south, you'll find Puebloan petroglyphs at **Newspaper Rock** and, just beyond, the **Teepees**, cone-shaped rock

formations covered with manganese and other minerals.

Blue Mesa is roughly the midpoint of the drive, and the start of a 1-mi, moderately steep loop hike that leads you around badland hills made of bentonite clay. Drive on for 5 mi until you come to **Jasper Forest**, just past **Agate Bridge**, with views of the landscape strewn with petrified logs. **Crystal Forest**, 18 mi south of the north entrance, is named for the smoky quartz, amethyst, and citrine along the 0.8-mi loop trail. **Rainbow Forest Museum**, at the park's south entrance, has restrooms, a bookstore, and exhibits. Just behind Rainbow Forest Museum is **Giant Logs**, a 0.4-mi loop that takes you to "Old Faithful," the largest log in the park, estimated to weigh 44 tons.

6

Newspaper Rock. See huge boulders covered with petroglyphs believed to have been carved by the Pueblo Indians more than 500 years ago. ⌧*6 mi south of Painted Desert Visitor Center on the main park road.*

Painted Desert Inn National Historic Site. You'll find cultural-history exhibits, as well as the murals of Fred Kabotic, a popular 1940s artist whose work was commissioned by Mary Jane Colter. American Indian crafts are displayed in this museum and mini visitor center. Check the schedule for daily events. ⌧*2 mi north of Painted Desert Visitor Center on the main park road* ☎*928/524–6228* ⊕*www.nps.gov/pefo* ⌦*Free* ⊙*Daily 8–5 Labor Day–Memorial Day, Daily 7–7 Memorial Day– Labor Day.*

Puerco Pueblo. This is a 100-room pueblo, built before 1400 and said to have housed Ancestral Puebloan people. Many visitors come to see petroglyphs, as well as a solar calendar. ⌧*10 mi south of the Painted Desert Visitor Center on the main park road.*

SCENIC STOPS

★ **Agate Bridge.** Here you'll see a 100-foot log spanning a 40-foot-wide wash. ⌧*19 mi south of Painted Desert Visitor Center on the main park road.*

Crystal Forest. The fragments of petrified wood strewn here once held clear quartz and amethyst crystals. ⌧*20 mi south of Painted Desert Visitor Center on the main park road.*

★ **Giant Logs.** A short walk leads you past the park's largest log, known as "Old Faithful." It's considered the largest because of its diameter (9 feet, 9 inches), as well as how tall it once was. ✉*28 mi south of Painted Desert Visitor Center on the main park road.*

Jasper Forest. More of an overlook than a forest, this spot has a large concentration of petrified trees in jasper or red. ✉*17 mi south of Painted Desert Visitor Center on the main park road.*

The Tepees. Witness the effects of time on these cone-shaped rock formations colored by iron, manganese, and other minerals. ✉*8 mi south of Painted Desert Visitor Center on the main park road.*

VISITOR CENTERS

Painted Desert Visitor Center. This is the place to go for general park information and an informative 20-minute film on the park. Proceeds from books purchased here will fund continued research and interpretive activities for the park. ✉*North entrance, off I–40, 27 mi east of Holbrook* ☎*928/524–6228* ☾ *Labor Day–Memorial Day, daily 8–5; Memorial Day–Labor Day, daily 7–7. Post office open weekdays 11–1.*

Rainbow Forest Museum and Visitor Center. The museum houses artifacts of early reptiles, dinosaurs, and petrified wood. Be sure to see Gurtie, a skeleton of a phytosaur, a crocodile-like carnivore. ✉*South entrance, off U.S. 180, 18 mi southeast of Holbrook* ☎*928/524–6228* ☾*Labor Day–Memorial Day, daily 8–5; Labor Day–Memorial Day, daily 7–7.*

Painted Desert Inn National Historic Site. This third visitor center at the park isn't as large, but here you can get information as well as view cultural history exhibits. ✉*2 mi north of Painted Desert Visitor Center on the main park road* ☎*928/524–6228* ☾ *Labor Day–Memorial Day, daily 8–5; Memorial Day–Labor Day, daily 7–7.*

SPORTS AND THE OUTDOORS

As with visits to all national parks, you don't get the full experience unless you take time to smell the roses—or in this case, get close enough to see the multihued lines streaking a petrified log. However, because the park goes to great pains to maintain the integrity of the fossil- and artifact-strewn landscape, sports and outdoor options in the park are limited. Off-highway activity is restricted to on-trail hiking and horseback riding.

HIKING

All trails begin off the main road, with restrooms at or near the trailheads. Most maintained trails are relatively short, paved, clearly marked, and, with a few exceptions, easy to moderate in difficulty. Hikers with greater stamina can make their own trails in the wilderness area, located just north of the Painted Desert Visitor Center. Watch your step for rattlesnakes, which are common in the park—if left alone and given a wide berth, they are passed easily enough.

EASY **Crystal Forest.** The easy 0.8-mi loop leads you past petrified wood that once held quartz crystals and amethyst chips. ⊠*20 mi south of the Painted Desert Visitor Center.*

Giant Logs. At 0.4 mi, Giant Logs is the park's shortest trail. The loop leads you to "Old Faithful," the park's largest log—it's 9 feet, 9 inches at its base, weighing 44 tons. ⊠*Directly behind Rainbow Forest Museum, 28 mi south of Painted Desert Visitor Center.*

Long Logs. While barren, the easy 0.6-mi loop passes the largest concentration of wood in the park. ⊠*26 mi south of Painted Desert Visitor Center.*

☾ **Puerco Pueblo.** A relatively flat and interesting 0.3-mi trail takes you past remains of a home of the Ancestral Puebloan people, built before 1400. The trail is paved and handicapped accessible. ⊠*10 mi south of Painted Desert Visitor Center.*

MODERATE **Agate House.** A fairly flat 1-mi trip takes you to an eight-room pueblo
Fodor'sChoice sitting high on a knoll *See Historic Sites, What to See.* ⊠*26 mi south*
★ *of Painted Desert Visitor Center.*

Blue Mesa. Although it's only 1 mi long and it's significantly steeper than the rest, this trail at the park's midway point is one of the most popular. ⊠*14 mi south of Painted Desert Visitor Center.*

Painted Desert Rim. The 1-mi trail is at its best in early morning or late afternoon, when the sun accentuates the brilliant red, blue, purple, and other hues of the desert and petrified forest landscape. ⊠*Tawa Point and Kachina Point, 1 mi north of Painted Desert Visitor Center.*

DIFFICULT **Kachina Point.** This is the trailhead for wilderness hiking. A 1-mi trail leads to the Wilderness Area, but from there you're on your own. With no developed trails, hiking here is cross-country style, but expect to see strange formations, beautifully colored landscape, and maybe, just maybe, a pronghorn antelope. ⊠*On the northwest side of the Painted Desert Inn Museum.*

HORSEBACK RIDING

Horseback riding in Petrified Forest is limited mostly to the wilderness area (paved roads and trails are off-limits), but that doesn't mean it's a limiting experience. There are no outfitters in the park who provide horses or guides, but you can load/unload and park your trailer on the northwest side of Painted Desert Inn, 2 mi north of the Painted Desert Visitor Center.

There are no maintained trails in this section of the park, but riders are advised to stick to dry washes as much as possible so as to minimize impact to the fragile desert ecosystem. The first switchback into the Wilderness Area is steep, sometimes unstable, and often exposed; so some riders lead their horses down on foot. But once you reach the desert floor, the grade is relatively flat and easy to ride. If you decide to camp overnight, there is no fee, but a free permit is required and available at either visitor center. A designated zone north of Lithodendron Wash

6

Different minerals in different concentrations cause the rich colors in petrified wood, and in the painted desert.

is set aside for camping, though no campsites are maintained. Group camping is limited to eight people and four horses.

EDUCATIONAL OFFERINGS

Children 12 and younger can learn more about the park's extensive human, animal, and geologic history as they train to become a Junior Ranger.

Park Rangers lead regular programs along the Great Logs Trail, inside the Painted Desert Inn Museum, and to the Puerco Pueblo. Ask at either visitor center for the availability of special tours, such as the after-hours lantern tour of the Painted Desert Inn Museum. You can view which ranger programs are currently being offered at ⊕ *www.nps.gov/pefo*.

WHERE TO EAT AND STAY

There is no lodging or campgrounds within the Petrified Forest. Backcountry camping is allowed if you obtain a free permit at the visitor center or museum; the only camping allowed is minimal-impact camping in a designated zone north of Lithodendron Wash in the Wilderness Area. Group size is limited to 8. RVs are not allowed. There are no fire pits or designated sites, nor is any shade available. Also note that if it rains, that pretty Painted Desert formation turns to sticky clay.

Dining in the park is limited to a cafeteria in the Painted Desert Visitor Center and snacks in the Rainbow Forest Museum. You may want to pack a lunch and eat at one of the park's picnic areas.

HOLBROOK

35 mi east of Homolovi State Park via I–40.

Downtown Holbrook is a monument to Route 66 kitsch. The famous "Mother Road" traveled through the center of Holbrook before Interstate 40 replaced it as the area's major east–west artery, and remnants of the "good ole days" can be found all over town. Route 66 itself still runs through Holbrook, following Navajo Boulevard and Hopi Drive. It makes a sharp corner at the intersection of these two roads, and used to cause traffic jams. The Downtowner, a popular coffee shop on this corner, served simple meals and coffee to sleepy truck drivers. As if traffic weren't already scrambled enough, crowds from the movie theater at what is today East Hopi Drive brought Route 66 to a standstill. Moviegoers, who filled the streets at the end of the show, considered it their right to block traffic; after all, many had traveled over 100 mi to see the movie.

DINO-MITE

Holbrook's affinity for dinosaurs is almost as legendary as its Route 66 identity. After all, dinosaurs called this area home long before travelers were cruising the open road. Some fossils are on display at the Petrified Forest National Park, but for a more amusing peek, take a drive down Navajo Boulevard, Holbrook's main thoroughfare, to see the kitschy display firsthand. Models of brightly colored dinosaurs stare down as the traffic passes, making for a perfect photo opportunity. Also, Interstate 40 east of Holbrook has roadside pseudo-museums with gift shops that sell T-shirts, stuffed dinosaurs, or petrified wood.

Before Route 66 rolled into Holbrook, the town was a notorious hangout for cowboys from the vast Aztec Land and Cattle Company, better known as the Hashknife Outfit for the shape of their brand. For a walking-tour map, call the and see the sites, including the infamous Bucket of Blood Saloon.

ESSENTIALS

Visitor Info Holbrook Chamber of Commerce (⊠ *100 E. Arizona St., Holbrook* ☎ *928/524–6558 or 800/524–2459* ⊕ *www.ci.holbrook.az.us*).

EXPLORING

★ The **Old Courthouse Museum** (☎ *800/524–2459* ⊠ *100 E. Arizona St., Holbrook* ⊕ *www.ci.holbrook.az.us* ⊠ *Free* ☉ *Daily 8–5*), at the corner of Arizona Street and Navajo Boulevard, holds memorabilia from the Route 66 heyday along with Old West and railroad records.

WHERE TO EAT AND STAY

$$
ITALIAN

✕**Mesa Italiana Restaurant.** While getting your kicks on Route 66, stop by to enjoy a hearty meal at one of Holbrook's most popular restaurants, where the chef prepares authentic-tasting traditional Italian dishes. Locals recommend the fresh pasta, including the spaghetti with Italian mushrooms. Don't forget the spumoni for dessert. For a more low-key environment, check out its adjoining grill that serves up burgers and steak. ⊠*2318 E. Navajo Blvd.* ☏*928/524–6696* ▤*AE, D, MC, V* ⊗*No lunch.*

$ 🖵**Holbrook Days Inn.** This clean, simple hotel has free Continental breakfast and local phone calls; it's a pleasant, convenient choice for a good price. Rooms have coffeemakers, hair dryers, and cable TV. **Pros:** heated indoor pool and hot tub; close to local restaurants. **Cons:** lacks the historic charm of

WORD OF MOUTH

"Headed into Holbrook. Found the Wigwam. It was as kitschy-wonderful as I had hoped. It was also the best mattresses we had slept on so far. Just cute as a button . . . a concrete wigwam is great sound insulation when the train went by. I didn't hear a thing." —starrsville

most of its lodging neighbors. ⊠*2601 Navajo Blvd.* ☏*928/524–6949* ⊕*www.daysinn.com* ⌕*52 rooms, 3 suites* ⌂*In-room: Wi-Fi, refrigerator (some). In-hotel: pool, laundry facilities* ▤*AE, D, MC, V* ⏻*CP.*

¢–$ 🖵**Wigwam Motel.** One of the iconic images of Route 66 and listed on
★ the National Register of Historic Places, the Wigwam consists of 15 bright-white concrete tepees where you can sleep inexpensively in a quirky environment. As you might expect, wigwams are phoneless, but—here's to Mother Progress—these have cable TV. A small lobby museum exhibits Mexican, Native American, and military relics collected by the owner's family. The 180-pound, polished, petrified-wood sphere is one of the largest in the Southwest. All the classic cars parked by the tepees also belong to the owners. **Pros:** impeccably kitschy, one of the signature spots along Route 66. **Cons:** very sparse accommodations. ⊠*711 W. Hopi Dr.* ☏*928/524–3048* ⊕*www.galerie-kokopelli.com/wigwam* ⌕*15 rooms* ⌂*In-room: no phone* ▤*MC, V.*

SHOPPING

McGees Beyond Native Tradition (⊠*2114 E. Navajo Blvd.* ☏*928/524–1977 or 800/524–9183* ⊕*www.hopiart.com*) is the area's premier source of high-quality Native American jewelry, rugs, Hopi baskets, and kachina dolls. The owners have longstanding relationships with reservation artisans and a knowledgeable staff that adroitly assists first-time buyers and seasoned collectors.

HOMOLOVI RUINS STATE PARK

53 mi east of Flagstaff, 33 mi west of Holbrook.

GETTING HERE AND AROUND

Located off AZ 87 just 5 miles northeast of Winslow, Homolovi Ruins State Park is sacred to the Hopi people.

Amtrak trains depart daily from Flagstaff to Winslow. There's no train service to Phoenix; visitors traveling from Phoenix will need to take the Amtrak shuttle—which departs from Phoenix-area bus stations four times daily bound for Flagstaff—and stay overnight in Flagstaff to catch the early-morning train to Winslow. From Albuquerque, Winslow is only a four-hour ride, with trains leaving daily.

EXPLORING

★ Homolovi is a Hopi word meaning "place of the little hills." The pueblo sites here at **Homolovi Ruins State Park** are thought to have been occupied between AD 1200 and 1425, and include 40 ceremonial kivas and two pueblos containing more than 1,000 rooms each. The Hopi believe their immediate ancestors inhabited this place and still hold the site to be sacred. Many rooms have been excavated and recovered for protection. Weekdays in June and July you can see archaeologists working the site. Mobility-impaired persons should check with the ranger station for alternate access information; rangers conduct guided tours. The Homolovi Visitor Center has a small museum with Hopi pottery and Ancestral Puebloan artifacts; it also hosts workshops on native art, ethnobotany, and traditional foods. ⊠ *AZ 87, 5 mi northeast of Winslow* ☝ *HCR 63, Box 5, Winslow 86047* ☎ *928/289–4106* ⊕ *www. azstateparks.com* 🎫 *$5* ⊙ *Visitor Center, daily 8–5.*

The Ancestral Puebloan petroglyphs of **Rock Art Ranch,** in Chevelon Canyon, are startlingly vivid after more than 1,000 years. Brantly Baird, owner of this working cattle ranch, will guide you along the ¼-mi trail, explaining Western and archaeological history. It's mostly easy walking, except for the climb in and out of Chevelon Canyon, where there are handrails. Baird houses his Native American artifacts and pioneer farming implements in his own private museum. It's out of the way and on a dirt road, but you'll see some of the best rock art in northern Arizona. Reservations are required. ⊠ *Off AZ 87, 13 mi southeast of Winslow* ☝ *Box 224, Joseph City 85032* ☎ *928/386–5047* 🎫 *Fee varies* ⊙ *May–Oct. by appointment only.*

WHERE TO STAY

Homolovi Ruins State Park is 5 mi northeast of the town of Winslow. Frequent flooding on the Little Colorado River frustrated the attempts of Mormon pioneers to settle here, but with the coming of the railroad the town roared into life. Later, Route 66 sustained the community until Interstate 40 passed north of town. New motels and restaurants sprouted near the interstate exits, and downtown was all but abandoned. Downtown Winslow is now revitalizing, with La Posada Hotel as its showpiece, but dining options are still scarce.

$$-$$$ 🏨 **La Posada Winslow.** One of the great railroad hotels, La Posada ("resting place") exudes the charm of an 18th-century Spanish hacienda. Architect Mary Colter, famous for her work at the Grand Canyon, designed and decorated the 68,000-square-foot hotel. Spanish and Native American furniture, antiques, and art permeate her designs. The lobby is a gallery for paintings by Tina Mion, one of the owners. Individually decorated

6

rooms are restored to 1930s style, and the lush gardens are a swath of green in the red-rock Colorado Plateau. Ongoing renovations will open La Posada's East Wing for the first time in 2010, and add 14 rooms to the property. If you can't stay for the night, take a self-guided tour of the hotel ($3 donation). **Pros:** historic charm; unique architecture. **Cons:** dated rooms, ongoing renovations. ⊠*303 E. 2nd St., Winslow* ☎*928/289–4366* ⊕*www.laposada.org* ₹*37 rooms* ♿*In-room: no phone. In-hotel: restaurant, bar, no-smoking rooms, no elevator* ⊟*AE, D, MC, V.*

CAMPING   ♨**Homolovi Ruins State Park Campground.** At an elevation of 4,900 feet, ¢   this campsite for tents and RVs is a short walk from Homolovi I pueblo and the Little Colorado River, and close to several other archaeological sites and trails leading to petroglyphs and evidence of prehistoric habitations. Bring a sun umbrella, as there are no shade trees. ⊠*AZ 87, 5 mi northeast of Winslow* ☎*928/289–4106* ♿*Flush toilets, partial hookups (electric and water), dump station, drinking water, showers, fire pits, grills, picnic tables* ₹*53 campsites.*

Tucson

WORD OF MOUTH

"If you want nightlife and shopping, go to Phoenix. If you want quiet, laid-back, beautiful surroundings with fabulous hiking opportunities, try Tucson."

—tucsonartist

WELCOME TO TUCSON

TOP REASONS TO GO

★ **Get close to the cacti:** Unique to this region, the saguaro is the quintessential symbol of the Southwest. See them at Sabino Canyon and Saguaro National Park.

★ **Eat Mexican food:** Tucson boasts that it's the "Mexican Food Capital," and you won't be disappointed at any of the authentic restaurants listed in this chapter.

★ **Explore the Arizona-Sonora Desert Museum:** Anyone who thinks that museums are boring hasn't been here, where you can learn about the region in a gorgeous, mostly outdoor, setting.

★ **Tour Mission San Xavier del Bac:** The "White Dove of the Desert" is the oldest building in Tucson. Ornate carvings and frescoes inside add to the mystical quality of this active parish on the Tohono O'odham reservation.

★ **Stroll the U of A campus:** Stop in at one of the five museums, then walk University Boulevard and 4th Avenue for a taste of Tucson's hipper element.

1 Downtown. Three historic districts here—Barrio Historico, El Presidio, and Armory Park—encompass the downtown area.

2 The University of Arizona. The 353-acre campus, classified as an arboretum, has several top-rated museums. At the west entrance, University Boulevard is lined with boutiques, cafés, and bookstores.

3 Central and East Tucson. This mostly residential area is home to Tucson's zoo, its largest indoor shopping mall (Park Place), and its best municipal golf course (Randolph Park).

CATALINA MOUNTAINS

Sabino Canyon
Visitor Center

Sunrise Dr.

4

CATALINA FOOTHILLS

Rillito River

Fort Lowell Rd.

Ft. Lowell
Park

**Fort Lowell
Historic Site**

Cloud Rd.

TO
SANTA CATALINA
MOUNTAINS

E. Grant Rd.

Tucson
Botanical
Gardens

Pima St.

E. Tanque Verde Rd.

Pima St.

Morris K. Udall
Park

Speedway Blvd.

**UNIVERSITY OF
ARIZONA**

5th St.

CENTRAL TUCSON

E. Broadway Blvd.

Reid
Park
Zoo

Randolph
Park

16th St.

22nd St.

3

TO
SAGUARO
NATIONAL
PARK EAST

Broadway Blvd.

Palo Verde
Park

Jesse Owens
District Park

22nd St.

EAST TUCSON

32nd St.

Freedom
Park

Golf Links Rd.

Escalante Rd.

210

**DAVIS-MONTHAN
AIR FORCE BASE**

**GETTING
ORIENTED**

The metropolitan Tucson area covers more than 500 square mi in a valley ringed by mountains—the Santa Catalinas to the north, the Santa Ritas to the south, the Rincons to the east, and the Tucson Mountains to the west. Saguaro National Park bookends Tucson, with one section on the far east side and the other out west near the world-class Arizona-Sonora Desert Museum. The central portion of the city has most of the shops, restaurants, and businesses, but not many tourist sights. Downtown's historic district and the neighboring University area are much smaller and easily navigated on foot. Up north in the Catalina Foothills, you'll find first-class resorts, restaurants, and hiking trails, most with spectacular views of the entire valley.

Agave plant

4 The Catalina Foothills. North of River Road the land becomes hilly and streets wind up to beautiful homes and resorts. At the east end, Sabino Canyon offers prime hiking.

5 Northwest. Suburban sprawl at it finest, this part of town just keeps grow-

ing. Two dude ranches are holdouts from a quieter era.

6 Westside. The untamed Tucson Mountain region embraces miles of saguaro forests, the Arizona-Sonora Desert Museum, and Mission San Xavier del Bac on the Tohono O'odham reservation.

7

TUCSON PLANNER

When to Go

Summer lodging rates (late May–September) are hugely discounted, even at many of the resorts, but there's a good reason: summer in Tucson is hot! Swimming and indoor activities like visiting museums (and spa treatments) are doable; but only the hardiest hikers and golfers stay out past noon in summer.

Tucson averages only 12 inches of rain a year. Winter temperatures hover around 65°F during the day and 38°F at night. Summers are unquestionably hot—July averages 104°F during the day and 75°F at night—but, as Tucsonans are fond of saying, "it's a dry heat."

The International Gem and Mineral Show descends on Tucson in February; book your hotel in advance or you'll be hard-pressed to find a room.

Visitor Information

The **Metropolitan Tucson Convention and Visitors Bureau** (⊠ *100 S. Church Ave., Suite 7199, Downtown* 🕾 *520/624–1817 or 800/638–8350* ⊕ *www.visittucson.org*) in La Placita Village is open from 9 to 5 weekdays and 9 to 4 on weekends.

Getting Here and Around

You can fly to Tucson International Airport, but cheaper, nonstop flights into Phoenix—a two-hour drive away down Interstate 10—are often easier to find. Once in town, a car is essential to get to the outlying tourist sights.

Tucson International Airport (TUS) (🕾 *520/573–8000* ⊕ *www.tucsonairport.org*) is 8½ mi south of downtown, off the Valencia exit of Interstate 10. Many hotels have a courtesy airport shuttle; inquire when making reservations.

Arizona Stagecoach (🕾 *520/889–1000* ⊕ *www.azstagecoach.com*) will carry you between the airport and all parts of Tucson and Green Valley for $9 to $38, depending on the location. Within the city limits, public transportation, which is geared primarily to commuters, is available through **Sun Tran** (🕾 *520/792–9222* ⊕ *www.suntran.com*), Tucson's bus system.

Taxi rates vary widely since they're unregulated in Arizona, but the taxi companies listed below charge $2 per mile plus an initial pickup fee ($4.50 from the airport, $2 from elsewhere in town). It's always wise to inquire about the cost of a trip before getting into a cab. It should be about $24 from the airport to central Tucson. One of the more reliable cab companies is **Allstate Taxi** (🕾 *520/798–1111*). **Yellow Cab** (🕾 *520/624–6611* ⊕ *www.yellowcabtucson.com*) also operates **Fiesta Taxi** (🕾 *520/622–7777*), whose drivers speak English and Spanish.

Amtrak (⊠ *400 E. Toole Ave., Downtown* 🕾 *520/623–4442 or 800/872–7245* ⊕ *www.amtrak.com*) serves the city with westbound and eastbound trains six times a week.

You'll need a car to get around Tucson and the surrounding area, and it makes sense to rent at the airport; all the major car-rental agencies are represented. **Carefree Rent-a-Car** (🕾 *520/790–2655*), a local company, rents reliable used cars at good rates. Driving time from the airport to the center of town varies, but it's usually less than a half hour; add 15 minutes to any destination during rush hours (7:30 AM–9 AM and 4:30 PM–6 PM). Parking is not a problem in most parts of town, except near the university, where there are several pay lots.

What to Do and Where to Do It

Fall, winter, and spring in Tucson are mild with little rainfall, making the Tucson area wonderful for outdoor sports. The city has miles of bike paths (shared by joggers and walkers) and plenty of open spaces with memorable desert views, and some of the best golf courses in the country. Hikers enjoy the desert trails in Saguaro National Park, Sabino Canyon, and Catalina State Park—all within 20 minutes of central Tucson; in summer there are cooler treks in nearby mountain ranges—Mount Lemmon to the north and Madera Canyon to the south. Equestrians can find scenic trails at one of the many area stables or dude ranches.

Making the Most of Your Time

Even if you have only one day, you can experience both the wild and developed parts of Tucson. You can visit the Arizona-Sonora Desert Museum in the morning and combine it with a stop at Mission San Xavier del Bac or Old Tucson Studios. On the way back to town, stop in Downtown's Barrio Historico and El Presidio neighborhoods to meander the adobe-lined streets, then have dinner at one of the outstanding Mexican restaurants in Downtown or South Tucson.

Another option is spending a half-day in Saguaro National Park. Set out in the early morning when it's cooler and the liveliest time for wildlife. If you're based in the Foothills, you can choose Sabino Canyon instead; the saguaros are almost as plentiful and the vistas are equally rewarding. Nature in the morning can be combined with an afternoon in the University area: visit any of the five campus museums, then stroll University Boulevard and 4th Avenue for ethnic eats and vintage boutiques.

If you have another day for exploring and like to shop, head south to the Mexican border. If you haven't seen Mission San Xavier yet, it's directly en route to Tubac, an artists' colony with historic sights as well as galleries. You can then head back toward Tucson, stopping at the Titan Missile Museum or at one of the casinos.

Native Cultures

Mexican Americans make up about 30% of Tucson's population, and play a major role in all aspects of daily life. The city's south-of-the-border soul is visible in its tile-roof architecture, mariachi festivals, and abundance of Mexican restaurants. Native Americans have a strong presence as well, especially the Tohono O'odham and the Pascua Yaqui. Mission San Xavier del Bac, a thriving reservation parish, is a good spot to experience religious festivals around Christmas and Easter, and to sample fry bread, a favorite Indian snack.

Festivals and Events

Feb. Tucson Gem and Mineral Show. This huge trade show is the largest of its kind in the world. ☎ *800/638-8350* ⊕ *www.tgms.org.*

Feb. La Fiesta de los Vaqueros. America's largest outdoor midwinter rodeo is at the Tucson Rodeo Grounds. ☎ *520/741-2233* ⊕ *www.tucsonrodeo.com.*

Apr. Fiesta de Saguaro. Hispanic culture and heritage are celebrated at Saguaro National Park. ☎ *520/733-5153* ⊕ *www.nps.gov/sagu.*

July Saguaro Harvest. The majestic saguaro's fruit is harvested at Colossal Cave Mountain Park. ☎ *520/647-7121* ⊕ *www.colossalcave.com.*

Updated by
Mara Levin

The Old Pueblo, as Tucson is affectionately known, is built upon a deep Native American, Spanish, Mexican, and Old West foundation. Arizona's second-largest city is both a bustling center of business and a relaxed university and resort town. Metropolitan Tucson has more than 850,000 residents, including thousands of snowbirds, who flee colder climes to enjoy the sun that shines on the city more than 340 days out of 365.

The city has a tri-cultural (Hispanic, Anglo, Native American) population, and the chance to see how these cultures interact—and to sample their cuisines—is one of the pleasures of a visit. The city is particularly popular among golfers, but the area's many hiking trails will keep non-duffers busy, too. If the weather is too hot to stay outdoors comfortably, museums like the Arizona State Museum and the Center for Creative Photography offer a cooler alternative.

This college town has Mexican and Native American cultural influences, a striking landscape, and all the amenities of a resort town, as well as its fair share of ubiquitous strip malls and tract-home developments. High-tech industries have moved into the area, but the economy still relies heavily on tourism and the university—although, come summer, you'd never guess; when the snowbirds and students depart, Tucson can be a sleepy place.

EXPLORING TUCSON

Central Tucson—which has most of the shops, restaurants, and businesses—is roughly bounded by Craycroft Road to the east, Oracle Road to the west, River Road to the north, and 22nd Street to the south. The older Downtown section, east of Interstate 10 off the Broadway-Congress exit, is smaller and easy to navigate on foot. Downtown streets don't run on any sort of grid, however, and many are one-way, so it's best to get a good, detailed map. The city's Westside area is the vast region west of Interstate 10 and Interstate 19, which includes the western section of Saguaro National Park and the San Xavier Indian Reservation.

DOWNTOWN

The area bordered by Franklin Street on the north, Cushing Street on the south, Church Avenue on the east, and Main Avenue on the west contains more than two centuries of Tucson's history, dating from the original walled fortress, El Presidio de Tucson, built by the Spanish in 1776, when Arizona was still part of New Spain. A good deal of the city's history was destroyed in the 1960s, when large sections of Downtown's barrio were bulldozed to make way for the Tucson Convention Center, high-rises, and parking lots. However, within the area's three small historic districts it's still possible to explore Tucson's architectural and cultural past.

Numbers in the text correspond to numbers in the margin and on the Downtown Tucson map.

TOP ATTRACTIONS

❶ **"A" Mountain.** The original name of this mountain, Sentinel Peak, west of Downtown, came from its function as a lookout point for the Spanish, though the Pima village and cultivated fields that once lay at the base of the peak are long gone. In 1915 fans of the University of Arizona football team whitewashed a large "A" on its side to celebrate a victory, and the tradition has been kept up ever since—the permanent "A" is now red, white, and blue. During the day the peak's a great place to get an overview of the town's layout; at night the city lights below form a dazzling carpet, but the teenage hangout–make-out scene may make some uncomfortable. ⊠ *Congress St. on Sentinel Peak Rd., Downtown.*

Downtown Historic Districts. **El Presidio Historic District,** north of the Convention Center and the government buildings that dominate downtown, is an architectural thumbnail of the city's former self. The north–south streets Court, Meyer, and Main are sprinkled with traditional Mexican adobe houses sitting cheek by jowl with territorial-style houses, with wide attics and porches. Paseo Redondo, once called Snob Hollow, is the wide road along which wealthy merchants built their homes. The area most closely resembling 19th-century Tucson is the **Barrio Historico,** also known as Barrio Viejo. The narrow streets of this neighborhood, including Convent Avenue, have a good sampling of thick-wall adobe houses. The houses are close to the street, hiding the yards and gardens within. To the east of the Barrio Historico, across Stone Avenue, is the **Armory Park** neighborhood, mostly constructed by and for the railroad workers who settled here after the 1880s. The brick or wood territorial-style homes here were the Victorian era's adaptation to the desert climate.

❹ **El Tiradito (*The Castaway*).** No one seems to know the details of the story behind this little shrine, but everyone agrees a tragic love triangle was involved. A bronze plaque indicates only that it's dedicated to a sinner who is buried here on unconsecrated ground. The candles that line the cactus-shrouded spot attest to its continuing importance in local Catholic lore. People light candles and leave *milagros* (miracles; little icons

7

in a lot behind the museum at Washington and Meyer streets. ⊠*140 N. Main Ave., Downtown* ☎*520/624–2333* ⊕*www.TucsonMuseumof Art.org* ⊠*$8* ☉*Tues.–Sat. 10–4, Sun. noon–4. Guided tours Oct.– May, Tues.–Sun.*

NEED A BREAK? On the patio of the Stevens Home, part of the Tucson Museum of Art and Historic Block, Cafe A La C'Arte (⊠*150 N. Main Ave., Downtown* ☎*520/628–8533*) serves fanciful salads, soups, and sandwiches on week-days from 11 to 3.

WORTH NOTING

② **Santa Cruz River & River Park.** When Europeans arrived in what is now Arizona, the Santa Cruz River had wide banks suitable for irrigation; over time its banks have been narrowed and contained and are now lined by River Park. These days it's a dry wash, or arroyo, most of the year, but sudden summer thunderstorms and rainwater from upper ele-vations can turn it into a raging river in a matter of hours. It's a favorite spot for walkers, joggers, bicyclists, and horseback riders. The park has a bike path, restrooms, drinking fountains, and sculptures created by local artists. ⊠*West Congress St., at Bonita Ave., Downtown.*

③ **Sosa-Carillo-Fremont House.** One of Tucson's oldest adobe residences, this was the only building spared when the surrounding barrio was torn down to build the Tucson Convention Center. The restored house, now a branch of the Arizona Historical Society, is furnished in 1880s fashion and has changing displays of territorial life. The house is in the Convention Center complex. The friendly, knowledgeable docents of the historical society conduct walking tours of the downtown his-toric districts (departing from here) every Saturday at 10 from Novem-ber through mid-April for $10. ⊠*151 S. Granada Ave., Downtown* ☎*520/622–0956* ⊕*www.arizonahistoricalsociety.org* ⊠*$3* ☉*Wed.– Sat. 10–4; walking tours Nov.–Apr., Sat. at 10.*

⑤ **St. Augustine Cathedral.** Although the imposing white-and-beige, late-19th-century, Spanish-style building was modeled after the Cathedral of Queretaro in Mexico, a number of its details reflect the desert set-ting: above the entryway, next to a bronze statue of St. Augustine, are carvings of local desert scenes with saguaro cacti, yucca, and prickly pears—look closely and you'll find the horned toad. Compared with the magnificent facade, the modernized interior is a bit disappoint-ing. ■TIP➔For a distinctly Southwestern experience, attend the maria-chi mass celebrated Sunday at 8 AM. ⊠*192 S. Stone Ave., Downtown* ☎*520/623–6351* ⊠*Free* ☉*Daily 7–6.*

THE UNIVERSITY OF ARIZONA

The U of A (as opposed to rival ASU, in Tempe) is a major economic influence in Tucson, with a student population of more than 34,000. The land for the university was "donated" by a couple of gamblers and a saloon owner in 1891—their benevolence reputedly inspired by a bad hand of cards—and $25,000 of territorial (Arizona was still a territory back then) money was used to build Old Main, the original building,

Colorful adobe buildings come in many shades beyond the natural clay color.

and hire six faculty members. Money ran out before Old Main's roof was placed, but a few enlightened citizens pitched in funds to finish it. Most of the city's populace was less than enthusiastic about the institution: they were disgruntled when the 13th Territorial Legislature granted the University of Arizona to Tucson and awarded Phoenix what was considered the real prize—an insane asylum and a prison.

The university's flora is impressive—it represents a collection of plants from arid and semiarid regions around the world. An extremely rare mutated, or "crested," saguaro grows at the northeast corner of the Old Main building. The long, grassy Mall in the heart of campus—itself once a vast cactus garden—sits atop a huge underground student activity center, and makes for a pleasant stroll on a balmy evening.

Numbers in the text correspond to numbers in the margin and on the University of Arizona map.

TOP ATTRACTIONS

❷ Arizona Historical Society's Museum. Flanking the entrance to the museum are statues of two men: Father Kino, the Jesuit who established San Xavier del Bac and a string of other missions, and John Greenaway, indelibly linked to Phelps Dodge, the copper-mining company that helped Arizona earn statehood in 1912. The museum houses the headquarters of the state Historical Society and has exhibits exploring the history of southern Arizona, the Southwest United States, and northern Mexico, starting with the Hohokam Indians and Spanish explorers. The harrowing "Life on the Edge: A History of Medicine in Arizona" exhibit promotes a new appreciation of modern drugstores in present-day Tucson. Children enjoy the exhibit on copper mining (complete with an

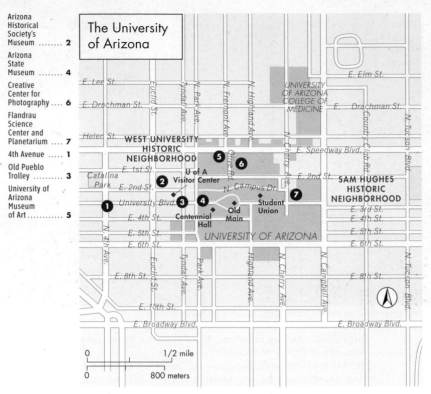

The University of Arizona

atmospheric replica of a mine shaft and camp) and the stagecoaches in the transportation area. The library has an extensive collection of historic Arizona photographs and sells inexpensive reprints. Admission is free on the first Saturday of every month. Park in the garage at the corner of 2nd and Euclid streets and get a free parking pass in the museum. ✉*949 E. 2nd St., University* ☎*520/628–5774* ⊕*www. arizonahistoricalsociety.org* 🖾*$5* ☉*Mon.–Sat. 10–4; library weekdays 10–2, Sat. 10–1.*

❹ Arizona State Museum. Inside the main gate of the university is Arizona's oldest museum, dating from territorial days (1893) and recognized as one of the world's most important resources for the study of Southwestern cultures. Exhibits in the original (south) building focus on the state's ancient history, including fossils and a fascinating sample of tree-ring dating. "Paths of Life: American Indians of the Southwest" is a permanent exhibit that explores the cultural traditions, origins, and contemporary lives of 10 native tribes of Arizona and Sonora, Mexico. ✉*Park Ave. at University Blvd., University* ☎*520/621–6302* ⊕*www. statemuseum.arizona.edu* 🖾*Free* ☉*Mon.–Sat. 10–5, Sun. noon–5.*

❻ Center for Creative Photography. Ansel Adams conceived the idea of a
★ photographer's archive and donated the majority of his negatives to this museum. In addition to its superb collection of his work, the center has

works by other major photographers, including Paul Strand, W. Eugene Smith, Edward Weston, and Louise Dahl-Wolfe. Changing exhibits in the main gallery display selected pieces from the collection, but if you'd like to see the work of a particular photographer in the archives, call to arrange an appointment. ✉ *1030 N. Olive Rd., north of 2nd St., University* ☎ *520/621–7968* ⊕ *www.creativephotography.org* ▧ *Free* ☉ *Weekdays 9–5, weekends 1–4.*

❼ **Flandrau Science Center and Planetarium.** Attractions include a 16-inch
♺ public telescope; the impressive Star Theatre, where a multimedia show brings astronomy to life; an interactive meteor exhibit; and a Mineral Museum, which displays more than 2,000 rocks and gems, some quite rare. Admission includes all exhibits and one planetarium show. ✉ *1601 E. University Blvd., at Cherry Ave., University* ☎ *520/621–4515, 520/621–7827 recorded message* ⊕ *www.gotuasciencecenter.org* ▧ *$7.50* ☉ *Exhibits Thurs. 9–3, Fri. 9–3 and 6 PM–9 PM, Sat. noon–9, Sun. noon–5. Planetarium show times vary. Observatory Wed.–Sat. 7 PM–10 PM.*

❶ **4th Avenue.** Students and counterculturists favor this ½-mi strip of 4th Avenue, where vintage-clothing stores rub shoulders with ethnic eateries from Guatemalan to Greek. After dark, 4th Avenue bars pulse with live and recorded music. ✉ *Between University Blvd. and 9th Ave.*

**NEED A
BREAK?**

Just outside the west campus gate, University Boulevard is lined with student-oriented eateries. Sinbad's (✉ *810 E. University Blvd., University* ☎ *520/623–4010*), nestled in the verdant Geronimo Plaza, serves falafel and other Middle Eastern fare, and has a great patio. The Chinese and Thai fast food at Pei Wei (✉ *845 E. University Blvd., University* ☎ *520/884–7413*) is flavorful, healthy, and affordable. Beer lovers should head to Gentle Ben's (✉ *865 E. University Blvd., University* ☎ *520/624–4177*), a burger-and-brew pub that also makes a scrumptious veggie burger. The deck upstairs has a good view of the sunset.

WORTH NOTING

❸ **Old Pueblo Trolley.** You can ride historic electric trolleys through the streets of Tucson along University Boulevard and 4th Avenue past shops and restaurants on Friday through Sunday. The route passes restored historic buildings on part of the original 1898 streetcar track and terminates near the west gate of the university campus. ✉ *360 E. 8th St., University* ☎ *520/792–1802* ⊕ *www.oldpueblotrolley.org* ▧ *Fri. and Sat. $1, Sun. 25¢* ☉ *Fri. 6 PM–10 PM, Sat. noon–midnight, Sun. noon–6.*

❺ **University of Arizona Museum of Art.** This small museum houses a collection of European paintings from the Renaissance through the 17th century, along with modern works by Georgia O'Keeffe and Jackson Pollock. A highlight is the Kress Collection's *retablo* from Ciudad Rodrigo: 26 panels of an altarpiece made in 1488 by Fernando Gallego. ✉ *Fine Arts Complex, Bldg. 2, southeast corner of Speedway Blvd. and Park Ave., University* ☎ *520/621–7567* ⊕ *www.artmuseum.arizona.edu* ▧ *Free* ☉ *Tues.–Fri. 9–5, weekends noon–4.*

CENTRAL AND EAST TUCSON

Tucson expanded north and east from the university during the 1950s and '60s, and currently continues to spread southeast. The sights worth seeing in this mostly residential area include the Tucson Botanical Gardens, the small Reid Park Zoo, and the Fort Lowell Park and Museum. Colossal Cave Mountain Park and Pima Air and Space Museum are on the southeast outskirts. Saguaro National Park East is also on this far side of town.

TIMING   If it's warm, visit outdoor attractions such as the zoo or Tucson Botanical Gardens in the morning; note that Colossal Cave stays at a constant, cool temperature, so it's a good option on a hot day.

Numbers in the text correspond to numbers in the margin and on the Central and East Tucson and Catalina Foothills maps.

EXPLORING

⑤ **Colossal Cave Mountain Park.** This limestone grotto 20 mi east of Tucson is the largest dry cavern in the world. Guides discuss the fascinating crystal formations and relate the many romantic tales surrounding the cave, including the legend that an enormous sum of money stolen in a stagecoach robbery is hidden here. Forty-five-minute cave tours begin every 30 minutes and require a ½-mi walk and climbing 363 steps. The park includes a ranch area with trail rides ($27 per hour), a gemstone-sluicing area, a small museum, nature trails, a butterfly garden, a snack bar, and a gift shop. Parking is $5 per vehicle. ⊕ *Take Broadway Blvd. or 22nd St. East, to Colossal Cave Rd.* ✉ *16721 E. Old Spanish Trail, Eastside* ☎ *520/647–7275* ⊕ *www.colossalcave.com* ☜ *$8.50* ☉ *Oct.– mid-Mar., daily 9–5; mid-Mar.–Sept., daily 8–6.*

③ **Fort Lowell Park and Museum.** Fertile soil and proximity to the Rillito River once enticed the Hohokam to construct a village on this site. Centuries later, a fort (in operation from 1873–91) was built here to protect the fledgling city of Tucson against the Apaches. The former commanding officer's quarters at this tiny museum has artifacts from military life in territorial days. Admission to the museum is free on the first Saturday of every month. The park has a playground, ball fields, tennis courts, and a duck pond. ✉ *2900 N. Craycroft Rd., Central* ☎ *520/885–3832* ☜ *Museum $3* ☉ *Wed.–Sat. 10–4.*

④ **Pima Air and Space Museum.** This huge facility ranks among the largest private collections of aircraft in the world. More than 200 airplanes are on display in hangars and outside, including a presidential plane used by both John F. Kennedy and Lyndon B. Johnson, a full-scale replica of the Wright brothers' 1903 Wright Flyer; the SR-71 reconnaissance jet; and a mock-up of the X-15, the world's fastest aircraft. World War II planes are particularly wellrepresented. Meander on your own or take a free walking tour of the hangars led by volunteer docents every day at 10:15. The open-air tram tour (an additional $6 fee) narrates all outside aircraft. Hour-long van tours of Aerospace Maintenance and Regeneration Center (AMARC)—affectionately called "The Boneyard"—at Davis-Monthan Air Force Base provide an eerie glimpse of hundreds of mothballed aircraft lined up in rows on a vast tract of

Central and
East Tucson

desert. You must reserve in advance for the $7 AMARC tour, which is available only on weekdays. ✉ *6000 E. Valencia Rd., I–10, Exit 267, South* ☎ *520/574–0462* ⊕ *www.pimaair.org* ☛ *$15.50* ☾ *Daily 9–5, last admission at 4.*

2 **Reid Park Zoo.** This small but well-designed zoo won't tax the children's—or your—patience. There are plenty of shady places to sit, a wonderful gift shop, and a snack bar to rev you up when your energy flags. The zoo's adorable newborns and the South American enclosure with its rain forest and exotic birds are popular. ■ **TIP→** If you're visiting in summer, go early in the day when the animals are active. The park surrounding the zoo has multiple and imaginative playground structures and a lake where you can feed ducks and rent paddleboats. ✉ *Reid Park, 1100 S. Randolph Way (off 22nd St.), Central* ☎ *520/791–3204* ⊕ *www.tucsonzoo.org* ☛ *$6* ☾ *Daily 9–4.*

1 **Tucson Botanical Gardens.** The 5 acres are home to a variety of experiences: a tropical greenhouse; a sensory garden, where you can touch and smell the plants and listen to the abundant bird life; historical gardens that display the Mediterranean landscaping the property's original owners planted in the 1930s; a garden designed to attract birds; and a cactus garden. Other special gardens showcase wildflowers, Australian plants, and Native American crops and herbs. Call ahead to find out what's blooming. A delightful café is open daily October–May. All paths are wheelchair accessible. ⊠ *2150 N. Alvernon Way, Central* ☎ *520/326–9686* ⊕ *www.tucsonbotanical.org* ⊠ *$7* ⊙ *Daily 8:30–4:30.*

CATALINA FOOTHILLS (NORTH)

Considered by some to be the "Beverly Hills of Tucson," the Catalina Foothills area is home to posh resorts and upscale shopping. Because the neighborhood backs on the beautiful Santa Catalina mountains, it also has an abundance of hiking trails.

TIMING If you want to venture farther into the mountains, head up to Mount Lemmon: it's time-consuming (a one-hour drive each way), but the higher elevation and cooler temperatures make it an excellent midday destination in summer.

TOP ATTRACTIONS

❶ Sabino Canyon. Year-round, but especially in summer, locals flock to
★ Coronado National Forest to hike, picnic, and enjoy the waterfalls, streams, swimming holes, and shade trees. No cars are allowed, but a narrated tram ride (about 45 minutes round-trip) takes you up a WPA-built road to the top of the canyon; you can hop off and on at any of the nine stops or hike any of the numerous trails. There's also a shorter tram ride to adjacent Bear Canyon, where a much more rigorous but rewarding hike leads to the popular Seven Falls (it'll take about 1½ hours each way from the drop-off point, so carry plenty of water). If you're in Tucson near a full moon, take the special night tram and watch the desert come alive with nocturnal critters. ⊠ *Sabino Canyon Rd. at Sunrise Dr., Foothills* ☎ *520/749–2861 recorded tram information, 520/749–8700 visitor center* ⊕ *www.fs.fed.us/r3/coronado* ⊠ *$5 per vehicle; tram $3–$8* ⊙ *Visitor center weekdays 8–4:30, weekends 8:30–4:30; call for tram schedules.*

WORTH NOTING

❷ De Grazia's Gallery in the Sun. Arizonan artist Ted De Grazia, who depicted Southwest Native American and Mexican life in a manner some find kitschy and others adore, built this sprawling, spacious, single-story museum with the assistance of Native American friends, using only natural material from the surrounding desert. You can visit De Grazia's workshop, former home, and grave. Although the original works are not for sale, the museum's gift shop has a wide selection of prints, ceramics, and books by and about the colorful artist. ⊠ *6300 N. Swan Rd., Foothills* ☎ *520/299–9191* ⊕ *www.degrazia.org* ⊠ *Free* ⊙ *Daily 10–4.*

❸ Mount Lemmon. Part of the Santa Catalina range, Mount Lemmon—named for Sara Lemmon, the first woman to reach the peak of this mountain, in 1881—is the southernmost ski slope in the continental United States, but you don't have to be a skier to enjoy it: it's a popular place for picnicking, and there are 150 mi of marked and well-maintained trails for hiking. The mountain's 9,157-foot elevation brings relief from summer heat.

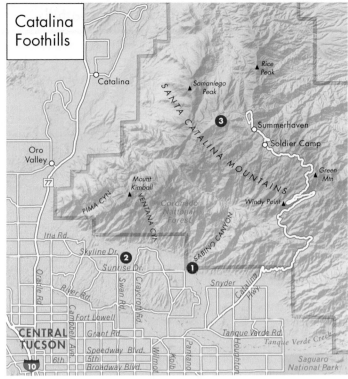

Mount Lemmon Highway twists its way for 28 mi up the mountainside. Every 1,000-foot climb in elevation is equivalent, in terms of climate, to traveling 300 mi north: you'll move from typical Sonoran Desert plants in the foothills to vegetation similar to that found in southern Canada at the top. Rock formations along the way look as though they were carefully balanced against each other by sculptors from another planet.

At milepost 18 of your ascent, on the left-hand side of the road, is the Palisades Ranger Station of **Coronado National Forest** (☎520/749–8700 ⊙8–4:30). Rangers have information on the mountain's campgrounds, hiking trails, and picnic spots. Even if you don't make it to the top of the mountain, you'll find stunning views of Tucson at Windy Point, about halfway up. Look for a road on your left between the Windy Point and San Pedro lookouts; it leads to Rose Canyon Lake, a lovely reservoir.

Just before you reach the ski area, you'll pass through the tiny alpine-style village of **Summerhaven,** which has some casual restaurants, gift shops, and pleasant lodges. An excursion up the mountain can be capped off with breakfast, lunch, or a slice of homemade pie at **Mount Lemmon Café** (☎520/576–1234), the first building on the left as you enter the village.

Mount Lemmon Highway ends at **Mount Lemmon Ski Valley** (☎520/576–1321). Skiing depends on natural conditions—there's no artificial

Tucson History: City in the Foothills

Native Americans have lived along the waterways in this valley for thousands of years. During the 1500s Spanish explorers arrived to find Pima Indians growing crops in the area. Father Eusebio Francisco Kino, a Jesuit missionary whose influence is still strongly felt throughout the region, first visited the area in 1687, and returned a few years later to build missions.

The name Tucson came from the Native American word *stjukshon* (pronounced *stook*-shahn), meaning "spring at the foot of a black mountain." The springs at the foot of Sentinel Peak, made of black volcanic rock, are now dry. The name was pronounced *tuk*-son by the Spanish explorers who built a wall around the city in 1776 to keep Native Americans from reclaiming it. At the time, this *presidio* (fortified city), called San Augustin del Tuguison, was the northernmost Spanish settlement in the area, and present-day Main Avenue is a quiet reminder of the former Camino Real ("royal road") that stretched from this tiny walled fort all the way to Mexico City.

Four flags have flown over Tucson—Spanish, Mexican, Confederate, and, finally, the Stars and Stripes. Tucson's allegiance changed in 1820 when Mexico declared independence from Spain, and again in 1853 when the Gadsden purchase made it part of the United States, though Arizona didn't become a state until 1912. In the 1850s the Butterfield stage line was extended to Tucson, bringing adventurers, a few settlers, and more than a handful of outlaws. The arrival of the railroad in 1880 marked another spurt of growth, as did the opening of the University of Arizona in 1891.

Tucson's 20th-century growth occurred after World War I, when veterans with damaged lungs sought the dry air and healing power of the sun, and again during World War II with the opening of Davis-Monthan Air Force Base and the rise of local aeronautical industries. It was also around this time that air-conditioning made the desert climate hospitable year-round.

snow, so call ahead. There are 16 runs, open daily in winter, ranging from beginner to advanced. Lift tickets cost $35 for an all-day pass and $30 for a half-day pass (starting at 1 PM). Equipment rentals and instruction are available. Off-season you can take a ride ($9) on the chairlift, which whisks you to the top of the slope—some 9,100 feet above sea level. Many ride the lift, then hike on one of several trails that crisscross the summit. There are some concessions at the ski lift.

■TIP→There are no gas stations on Mount Lemmon Highway, so gas up before you leave town and check the road conditions in winter. To reach the highway, take Tanque Verde Road to Catalina Highway, which becomes Mount Lemmon Highway as you head north. ⊠ *Mount Lemmon Hwy., Northeast* ☎ *520/576–1400 recorded snow report, 520/547–7510 winter road conditions* ⊜ *$5 per vehicle* ☉ *Daily, depending on snow in ski season.*

NORTHWEST TUCSON, THE WESTSIDE, AND THE SONORAN DESERT

Once a vast, open space dotted with horse ranches, Northwest Tucson is now a rapidly growing residential area encompassing the townships of Oro Valley and Marana. Families and retirees are moving here in droves, and the traffic congestion proves the point, but you'll also find first-rate golf resorts and restaurants here, as well as the oases of Tohono Chul Park and Catalina State Park, which calm the senses.

WORD OF MOUTH

"Get to the Arizona–Sonora Desert Museum as soon as they open or you will miss the animals' activity. It is definitely worth it. Getting there early can leave you with a good portion of your day left to do other things." —slknova

The Westside is far less developed, and beautiful vistas of saguaro-studded hills are around every bend. Saguaro National Park West, the Desert Museum, Old Tucson Studios, and the San Xavier Mission are all in this section of town. If you're interested in the flora and fauna of the Sonoran Desert—as well as some of its appearances in the cinema—heed the same advice given the pioneers: go west.

TIMING A good idea is to start the morning at Saguaro National Park and then head over to the Arizona–Sonora Desert Museum, where you can lunch at the Ironwood Terrace or the more upscale Ocotillo Café. How long you spend at Saguaro National Park depends on whether you choose a short walk to see petroglyphs at Signal Hill on the Loop Drive (an hour should suffice) or hike a longer mountain trail, but leave yourself at least two hours for your visit at the Desert Museum. The hottest part of an afternoon can be spent ducking in and out of attractions at Old Tucson Studios or enjoying the indoor sanctuary of San Xavier mission, although the mission is also a good stop if you're heading out of town to Tubac or Tumacácori.

TOP ATTRACTIONS

❶ Arizona–Sonora Desert Museum. The name "museum" is a bit misleading, since this delightful site is actually a beautifully planned zoo and botanical garden featuring the animals and plants of the Sonoran Desert. Hummingbirds, cactus wrens, rattlesnakes, scorpions, bighorn sheep, and prairie dogs all busy themselves in ingeniously designed habitats. An Earth Sciences Center has an artificial limestone cave and a hands-on meteor and mineral display. The coyote and javelina (wild, pig-like mammals with oddly oversized heads) exhibits have "invisible" fencing that separates humans from animals, and the Riparian Corridor section affords great underwater views of otters and beavers. The restaurants and gift shop, which carries books, jewelry and crafts, are outstanding. ✉ *2021 N. Kinney Rd., Westside* ☎ *520/883–2702* ⊕ *www.desertmuseum.org* ✍ *$13* ☉ *Mar.–Sept., daily 7:30–5; Oct.–Feb., daily 8:30–5.*

FodorsChoice

★

❹ Mission San Xavier del Bac. The oldest Catholic church in the United States still serving the community for which it was built, San Xavier was founded in 1692 by Father Eusebio Francisco Kino, who established

FodorsChoice

★

SPORTS AND THE OUTDOORS

Tucson's urban status doesn't prevent visitors from enjoying outdoor activites within the city and in the nearby area. Though summer heat can limit your options, golf and hiking are popular year-round.

ADVENTURE AND ECOTOURS

Baja's Frontier Tours (☎520/887–2340 or 800/726–7231 ⊕www.bajas frontiertours.com) explores the natural and cultural history of Tucson and the greater Southwest by van and motorcoach. **Southwest Trekking** (✉ Box 57714, Tucson ☎520/296–9661 ⊕www.swtrekking.com) arranges top-notch guided mountain biking, hiking, and camping outings. **Sunshine Jeep Tours** (☎520/742–1943 ⊕www.sunshinejeeptours. com) arranges trips into the Sonoran Desert outside Tucson in four-wheel-drive vehicles. **Trail Dust Adventures** (☎520/747–0323 ⊕www. traildustadventures.com) offers open-air Jeep tours that explore the desert and mountains outside the city. Cookouts and cattle drives are added options.

BALLOONING

Balloon America flies passengers above the Santa Catalinas on hot-air balloon tours (✑Box 31255, Tucson 85751 ☎520/299–7744 ⊕www. balloonrideusa.com) departing the east side of Tucson from October through May. **Fleur de Tucson Balloon Tours** (✑4635 N. Caida Pl., Tucson 85718 ☎520/529–1025 ⊕www.fleurdetucson.net), operates out of Northwest and has two flight options: over the Tucson Mountains and Saguaro National Park West, or over the Avra Valley.

BASEBALL

It doesn't have as many teams as Phoenix, but Tucson does have its share of baseball spring training action: the Arizona Diamondbacks and the Colorado Rockies are in the Tucson area from mid-February until the end of March. The Diamondbacks play at Tucson Electric Park, south of town near the airport. The Rockies play at Hi Corbett Field, which is adjacent to Reid Park. Not surprisingly, some people plan vacations around scheduled training dates; there are plenty of local fans, too.

Arizona Diamondbacks (✉Tucson Electric Park, 2400 E. Ajo Way, South ☎520/434–1367 or 866/672–1343 ⊕www.dbacks.com). **Colorado Rockies** (✉Hi Corbett Field, 3400 E. Camino Campestre, Central ☎520/327–9467 or 800/388–7625 ⊕www.coloradorockies.com).

BICYCLING

Tucson, ranked among America's top five bicycling cities by *Bicycling* magazine, has well-maintained bikeways, routes, lanes, and paths all over the city. Scenic-loop roads in both sections of Saguaro National Park offer rewarding rides for all levels of cyclists. Most bike stores in Tucson carry the monthly newsletter of the Tucson chapter of **GABA** (*Greater Arizona Bicycling Association* ✑Box 43273, Tucson 85733 ⊕www.bikegaba.org), which lists rated group rides, local bike rentals, and more. You can pick up a map of Tucson-area bike routes at the **Pima Association of Governments** (✉177 N. Church Ave., Suite 405, Downtown 85701 ☎520/792–1093 ⊕www. pagnet.org).

Don't let the name fool you: the Arizona Sonora Desert Museum is also a zoo and botanical garden.

Mountain bikes, comfort bikes, and road bikes can be rented by the day or week at **Fair Wheel Bikes** (✉ *1110 E. 6th St., University* ☎ *520/884–9018*). **Tucson Bicycles** (✉ *4743 E. Sunrise Dr., Foothills* ☎ *520/577–7374*) rents a selection of road and mountain bikes and organizes group rides of varying difficulty.

BIRD-WATCHING

The naturalist and illustrator Roger Tory Peterson (1908–96) considered Tucson one of the country's top birding spots, and avid "life listers"—birders who keep a list of all the birds they've sighted and identified—soon see why. In the early morning and early evening Sabino Canyon is alive with cactus and canyon wrens, hawks, and quail. Spring and summer, when species of migrants come in from Mexico, are great hummingbird seasons. In the nearby Santa Rita Mountains and Madera Canyon you can see elegant trogons nesting in early spring. The area also supports species usually found only in higher elevations. You can get the latest word on the bird on the 24-hour line at the **Tucson Audubon Society** (☎ *520/798–1005* ⊕ *www.tucsonaudubon.org*); sightings of rare or interesting birds in the area are recorded regularly.

The society's **Audubon Nature Shop** (✉ *300 E. University Blvd., Suite 120, University* ☎ *520/629–0510*) carries field guides, bird feeders, binoculars, and natural-history books. The **Wild Bird Store** (✉ *3526 E. Grant Rd., Central* ☎ *520/322–9466*) is an excellent resource for bird-watching information, books, and trail guides.

Several companies offer birding tours in the Tucson area. **Borderland Tours** (✉ *2550 W. Calle Padilla, Northwest* ☎ *520/882–7650 or 800/525–7753* ⊕ *www.borderland-tours.com*) leads bird-watching

CLOSE UP

Rodeo Lesson: Basics of the Sport

Cowboys vied for the unofficial titles of best roper and rider at the end of the big cattle drives of the late 19th century. As their day jobs were curtailed in scope by the spread of railroads and the fencing-in of the West, they made the contests more formalized and the sport of rodeo was born.

The five standard events in contemporary rodeo are calf roping, bull riding, steer wrestling, saddle bronc-riding, and bareback bronc-riding. ("Bronc" is short for bronco, an unbroken range horse with a tendency to buck, or throw, a rider.) Two other events are recognized in championship competitions: single-steer roping and team roping. The barrel race, a saddle-horse race around a series of barrels, is a popular contest for women.

Participants pay entry fees, and the prize money won is their only compensation. More than half of all rodeos are independent of state and county fairs, livestock shows, or other attractions, and many are held in arenas devoted to the purpose. The equipment, however, is simple and may be improvised.

In 1929 the Rodeo Association of America was formed to regulate the sport. The contestants themselves took a hand in 1936 after a strike in Boston Garden and organized the Cowboy Turtles Association—"turtles" because they had been slow to act. This group was renamed the Rodeo Cowboys Association (RCA) in 1945, and became the Professional Rodeo Cowboys Association (PRCA) in 1975. Its rules became accepted by most rodeos.

Catalina State Park (⊠ *11570 N. Oracle Rd., Northwest* ☎ *520/628–5798* ⊕ *www.pr.state.az.us*) is crisscrossed by hiking trails. One of them, the relatively easy, two-hour (5.5-mi round-trip) Romero Canyon Trail, leads to Romero Pools, a series of natural *tinajas*, or stone "jars," filled with water much of the year. The trailhead is on the park's entrance road, past the restrooms on the right side.

★ The Bear Canyon Trail in **Sabino Canyon** (⊠ *Sabino Canyon Rd. at Sunrise Dr., Foothills* ☎ *520/749–8700* ⊕ *www.fs.fed.us/r3/coronado*), also known as Seven Falls Trail, is a three-hour, 7.8-mi round-trip that is moderately easy and fun, crossing the stream several times on the way up the canyon. Kids enjoy the boulder-hopping, and all are rewarded with pools and waterfalls as well as views at the top. The trailhead can be reached from the parking area by either taking a five-minute Bear Canyon Tram ride or walking the 1.8-mi tram route.

The local chapter of the **Sierra Club** (⊠ *738 N. 5th Ave., University* ☎ *520/620–6401*) welcomes out-of-towners on weekend hikes. The **Southern Arizona Hiking Club** (☎ *520/751–4513* ⊕ *www.sahcinfo.org*) leads weekend hikes of varying difficulty. For hiking on your own, a good source is **Summit Hut** (⊠ *5045 E. Speedway Blvd., Central* ☎ *520/ 325–1554*), which has a collection of hiking reference materials and a friendly staff who will help you plan your trip. Packs, tents, bags, and climbing shoes can be rented and purchased here.

HORSEBACK RIDING

Colossal Cave Stables (⊠*16600 Colossal Cave Rd., Eastside* ☎*520/647–3450*) takes riders into Saguaro National Park East on one-hour, two-hour, all-day or sunset rides. Wranglers at **Cocoraque Ranch** (⊠*6255 N. Diamond Hills Ln, Westside* ☎*520/682–8594*) lead riders on real cattle drives through their working cattle ranch and along trails into Saguaro National Park West. **Pantano Riding Stables** (⊠*4450 S. Houghton Rd., Eastside* ☎*520/298–8980* ⊕*www.*

horsingaroundarizona.com) is a reliable operator offering one- and two-hour rides. **Pusch Ridge Stables** (⊠*13700 N. Oracle Rd., Northwest* ☎*520/825–1664*), adjacent to Catalina State Park, can serve up a cowboy-style breakfast on your trail ride; one-hour, sunset, and overnight rides are available.

RODEO

In the last week of February, Tucson hosts **Fiesta de Los Vaqueros,** the largest annual winter rodeo in the United States, a five-day extravaganza with more than 600 events and a crowd of more than 44,000 spectators a day at the **Tucson Rodeo Grounds** (⊠*4823 S. 6th Ave., South* ☎*520/294–8896* ⊕*www.tucsonrodeo.com*). The rodeo kicks off with a 2-mi parade of horseback riders (Western and fancy-dress Mexican *charro*), wagons, stagecoaches, and horse-drawn floats; it's touted as the largest nonmotorized parade in the world. Local schoolkids especially love the celebration—they get a two-day holiday from school. Daily seats at the rodeo vary from $12 to $25.

WHERE TO EAT

Tucson boldly proclaims itself to be the "Mexican Food Capital of the United States" and most of the Mexican food in town is Sonoran style. This means prolific use of cheese, mild peppers, corn tortillas, pinto beans, and beef or chicken. The majority of the best Mexican restaurants are concentrated in South Tucson and downtown, though some favorites have additional locations around town. If Mexican's not your thing, there are plenty of other options: you won't have any trouble finding excellent sushi, Thai, Italian, and Ethiopian food at reasonable prices.

For sampling local cuisine, there are several Southwestern restaurants in town. Up in the Foothills, upscale Southwestern cuisine flourishes at such restaurants as Janos at the Westin La Paloma, the Grill at Hacienda del Sol Resort, and the Ventana Room at Loews Ventana Canyon. A recent trend in Tucson dining is combining hip restaurants with chic shopping. Choose from sushi, steak, Italian, or tapas at La Encantada in the Foothills. Casa Adobes Plaza, in the Northwest, offers Wildflower

Grill, Bluefin Seafood, or trendy, thin-crust pizza at Sauce—and the gelato shop here is handy for dessert. St. Philip's Plaza, in the lower Foothills, has Acacia and Vivace, both with lovely patio dining.

Cheaper but no less tasty fare as varied as Chinese, Guatemalan, and Middle-Eastern can be enjoyed on the west side of U of A's campus, along University Boulevard and 4th Avenue, a great area for people-watching and barhopping as well as quelling hunger pangs.

PLANNING INFORMATION

Although the city's selection of restaurants is impressive, Tucson doesn't offer much in the way of late-night dining. Most restaurants in town are shuttered by 10 PM; some spots that keep later hours are noted below.

WHAT IT COSTS					
	¢	$	$$	$$$	$$$$
AT DINNER	under $8	$8–$12	$13–$20	$21–$30	over $30

Prices are per person for a main course.

DOWNTOWN TUCSON

$$
SOUTHWESTERN

✗**Barrio.** Lively at lunchtime, this trendy grill serves the most innovative cuisine in the downtown area. Try a "little plate" of black tiger shrimp rubbed with tamarind paste, or stuffed Anaheim chile in red bell-pepper cream. Entrées are as varied as the simple but delicious fish tacos and the linguine with chicken, dried papaya, and mango in a chipotle-chardonnay cream sauce. Save room for an elegant dessert of fresh berries drenched in crème anglaise or a chilled chocolate custard topped with caramel. ⊠*135 S. 6th Ave., Downtown* ☎*520/629–0191* ⊕*barriofoodanddrink.com* ▬*AE, D, DC, MC, V* ☉*Closed Mon. No lunch weekends* ⊹*B5.*

$$
MEXICAN
Fodor's Choice
★

✗**Café Poca Cosa.** In what is arguably Tucson's most creative Mexican restaurant, the chef prepares recipes inspired by different regions of her native country. The menu, which changes daily, might include chicken mole or pork *pibil* (made with a tangy Yucatecan barbecue seasoning). Servings are plentiful, and each table gets a stack of warm corn tortillas and a bowl of beans to share. Order the daily Plato Poca Cosa, and the chef will select one beef, one chicken, and one vegetarian entrée for you to sample. The bold-color walls are hung with Latin American art. ⊠*110 E. Pennington St., Downtown* ☎*520/622–6400* ⊕*cafepocacosa inc.com* ▬*MC, V* ☉*Closed Sun. and Mon.* ⊹*B5.*

$
AMERICAN

✗**Cup Café.** This charming spot off the lobby of Hotel Congress is at the epicenter of Tucson's hippest downtown scene, but it's also a down-home, friendly place. Try the eggs, potatoes, chorizo, and cheese for breakfast or a veggie burger for lunch. The Brie melted over artichoke hearts and apple slices on a baguette appetizer complements such entrées as chicken satay or "Tornados" of beef. Open until 10 PM weeknights and 1 AM weekends, it becomes interestingly crowded in the evening with patrons from Club Congress, the hotel nightclub.

BEST BETS FOR TUCSON DINING

Fodor's offers a listing of quality dining experiences at every price range, from the city's best cheap eateries to its most upscale restaurants. Here, we've compiled our top picks by price and experience. The best properties—in other words, those that provide a remarkable experience in their price range—are designated in the listings with the Fodor's Choice logo.

Fodor's Choice ★

Beyond Bread, p. 373
Café Poca Cosa, p. 368
El Minuto, p. 372
Grill at Hacienda del Sol, p. 376
Janos, p. 376

Best by Price

¢

Beyond Bread, p. 373

$

Bangkok Cafe, p. 373
Micha's, p. 378
Sauce, p. 378
Zemam, p. 374
Zinburger, p. 377

$$

Café Poca Cosa, p. 368
Feast, p. 373
North, p. 376

$$$

Acacia, p. 376
Grill at Hacienda del Sol, p. 376
Wildflower Grill, p. 378

$$$$

Janos, p. 376

Best by Cuisine

BEST MEXICAN

Café Poca Cosa, p. 368
El Minuto, p. 372
Mi Nidito, p. 378

SOUTHWESTERN

Grill at Hacienda del Sol, p. 376
Janos, p. 376

Best by Experience

BEST BREAKFAST

Arizona Inn, p. 372
Hungry Fox, p. 373
Tohono Chul Tea Room, p. 378

BEST HOTEL DINING

Arizona Inn Restaurant, p. 372
Gold at Westward Look Resort, p. 377
The Grill at Hacienda del Sol, p. 376
Ventana Room at Loews Ventana Canyon Resort, p. 376

BEST PATIO DINING

Acacia, p. 376
J Bar, p. 376
Tohono Chul Tea Room, p. 378
Vivace, p. 377

BEST VIEW

Arizona Inn Restaurant, p. 372
Gold, p. 377
Ventana Room, p. 376

CHILD-FRIENDLY

Beyond Bread, p. 373
Pinnacle Peak Steakhouse, p. 375
Sauce, p. 378

GOOD FOR GROUPS

Bluefin Seafood Bistro, p. 377
Montana Avenue, p. 375
North, p. 376

HOT SPOTS

Café Poca Cosa, p. 368
North, p. 376
Barrio, p. 368
Zinburger, p. 377

SPECIAL OCCASION

Grill at Hacienda del Sol, p. 376
Janos, p. 376
Wildflower Grill, p. 378

7

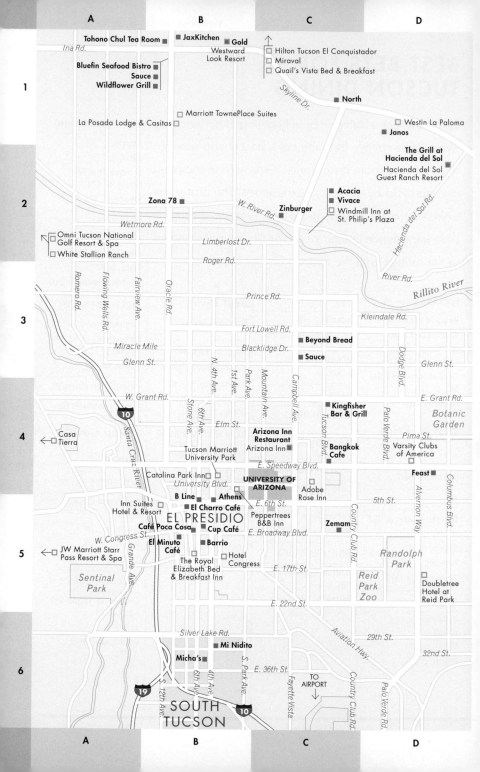

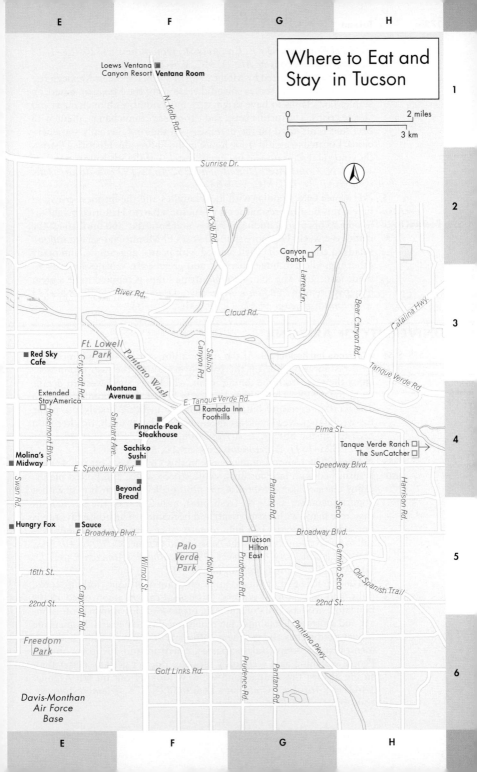

Where to Eat and Stay in Tucson

E   F   G   H

Loews Ventana Canyon Resort **Ventana Room**

N. Kolb Rd.

Sunrise Dr.

N. Kolb Rd.

Canyon Ranch

Larrea Ln.

River Rd.

Cloud Rd.

Bear Canyon Rd.

Catalina Hwy.

Sabino Canyon Rd.

Tanque Verde Rd.

Red Sky Cafe

Ft. Lowell Park

Pantano Wash

Creycroft Rd.

Montana Avenue

E. Tanque Verde Rd.

Ramada Inn Foothills

Pima St.

Extended StayAmerica

Rosemont Blvd.

Sahuara Ave.

Pinnacle Peak Steakhouse

Tanque Verde Ranch
The SunCatcher

Harrison Rd.

Molina's Midway

Sachiko Sushi

E. Speedway Blvd.

Speedway Blvd.

Swan Rd.

Beyond Bread

Pantano Rd.

Seco

Camino Seco

Hungry Fox

Sauce

E. Broadway Blvd.

Palo Verde Park

Kolb Rd.

Prudence Rd.

Tucson Hilton East

Broadway Blvd.

Old Spanish Trail

16th St.

Craycroft Rd.

Willmot St.

22nd St.

22nd St.

Freedom Park

Pantano Pkwy.

Davis-Monthan Air Force Base

Golf Links Rd.

Prudence Rd.

Pantano Rd.

0   2 miles
0   3 km

E   F   G   H

1   2   3   4   5   6

⊠*Hotel Congress, 311 E. Congress St., Downtown* ☎*520/798–1618* ⊕*hotelcongress.com* ▭*AE, D, MC, V* ✛*B5.*

$
MEXICAN

✕**El Charro Café.** Started by Monica Flin in 1922, the oldest Mexican restaurant in town still serves splendid versions of the Mexican-American staples Flin claims to have originated, most notably chimichangas and cheese crisps. The tortilla soup and *carne seca* chimichanga, made with beef that is air-dried on the premises—on the roof, actually—are delicious. Located in an old stone house in the El Presidio Historic District, the colorful restaurant and bar exude festive—if slightly touristy—vibes. ⊠*311 N. Court Ave., Downtown* ☎*520/622–1922* ⊕*elcharrocafe. com* ▭*AE, D, DC, MC, V* ✛*B5.*

$
MEXICAN
Fodor's Choice
★

✕**El Minuto Café.** Popular with local families and the business crowd at lunch, this bustling restaurant is in Tucson's Barrio Historico neighborhood and open until midnight Friday and Saturday and until 10 PM the rest of the week. For more than 50 years El Minuto has served *topopo* salads (a crispy tortilla shell heaped with beans, guacamole, and many other ingredients), huge burritos, and green-corn tamales (in season) made just right. The spicy *menudo* (tripe soup) is reputed to be a great hangover remedy. ⊠*354 S. Main Ave., Downtown* ☎*520/882–4145* ⊕*elminutocafe.com* ▭*AE, D, DC, MC, V* ✛*B5.*

UNIVERSITY OF ARIZONA

$$$–$$$$
CONTINENTAL

✕**Arizona Inn Restaurant.** At the Arizona Inn, one of Tucson's most elegant restaurants, dine on the patio overlooking the lush grounds or enjoy the view from the dining room, which has Southwestern details from the 1930s. The culinary range is broad, from bouillabaisse to a vegetarian corn and butternut squash cannelloni. Locals also come for weekday power-breakfast meetings, Sunday brunch, or afternoon high tea in the library. ⊠*Arizona Inn, 2200 E. Elm St., University* ☎*520/325–1541* ⊕*arizonainn.com* ▭*AE, MC, V* ✛*C4.*

$$
GREEK

✕**Athens.** The tranquil dining room in this Greek spot off 4th Avenue is furnished with lace curtains, white stucco walls, and potted plants. Enjoy classics like *kotopoulo stin pita* (grilled chicken breast with a yogurt-cucumber sauce on fresh pita), moussaka, or the *pastitsio* (a casserole made with pasta, meat, and béchamel). The house favorite is braised lamb shoulder in a light tomato sauce over pasta or potatoes— call to reserve your order of the lamb ahead of time. ⊠*500 N. 4th Ave., at 6th St., University* ☎*520/624–6886* ⊕*athenson4th.com* ▭*AE, D, DC, MC, V* ☾*Closed Sun. No lunch* ✛*B5.*

¢
AMERICAN

✕**B Line.** In the heart of 4th Avenue's amalgam of antique clothing stores, pubs, and natural-food grocers, this casual café in a converted 1920s bungalow attracts a mix of students, professors, downtown professionals, and artists with its simple but refined meals and desserts. Homemade biscuit sandwiches and excellent coffee start the day; the lunch–dinner menu features soups, salads, pastas, burritos, and 13 brews on tap. People-watching as a secondary pleasure doesn't get any better than sitting against the wraparound window looking out on 4th Avenue. ⊠*621 N. 4th Ave., University* ☎*520/882–7575* ⊕*blinerestaurant. com* ▭*MC, V* ✛*B5.*

CENTRAL TUCSON

$ **✕Bangkok Cafe.** This is not only the best Thai food in town, it is top-
THAI notch for Thai-food fans. You'll find all your favorite dishes in this bright, spacious café, along with exceptionally pleasant service and reasonable prices. Thoong-Tong appetizers, fried veggie-filled pouches, are blissfully good. The spice-heat level of any dish can be adjusted at your request, from 1 through 5 (just keep in mind that a 5 might cause steam to blow out the top of your head). There are plenty of options for vegetarians, and tofu is available to add to any dish. Try to avoid the dinner rush (6:30 to 8:30) on weekends, or you'll wait a while to be seated. ⌂2511 E. Speedway Blvd., Central ☎520/323–6555 ▭AE, MC, V ⊗Closed Sun. ✛C4.

¢ **✕Beyond Bread.** Twenty-seven varieties of bread are made at this bus-
CAFÉ tling bakery with Central and Eastside locations, and highlights from
⟳ the huge sandwich menu include Annie's Addiction (hummus, tomato,
Fodor's Choice sprouts, red onion, and cucumber) and Brad's Beef (roast beef, provo-
★ lone, onion, green chiles, and Russian dressing); soups and salads are equally scrumptious. Eat inside or on the patio, or order takeout, but be sure to splurge on one of the incredible desserts. The second location is at 6260 East Speedway Boulevard. ⌂3026 N. Campbell Ave., Central ☎520/322–9965 ⊕beyondbread.com ▭AE, D, MC, V ⊗No dinner Sun. ✛C3. F4.

$–$$ **✕Feast.** At this unassuming, informal bistro you order at the counter—
AMERICAN after marveling at the display case filled with choices like potato gnocchi with sausage and spinach, sautéed sea bass with fingerling potatoes, and a beet with tarragon-cultured-mascarpone salad—then choose a table; and the friendly staff will bring you each dish as it's ready. Locals might just call in their order (after checking the daily specials online) and zip in to pick up tasty, gourmet takeout. Though the eclectic cuisine is hard to categorize, it is always yummy—including the homemade desserts. ⌂4122 E. Speedway, Central ☎520/326–9363 ⊕eatatfeast. com ▭AE, D, MC, V ⊗ Closed Mon. ✛D4.

$$$ **✕Kingfisher Bar and Grill.** Kingfisher is a standout for American cuisine.
AMERICAN The emphasis is on fresh seafood, especially oysters and mussels, but the kitchen does baby back ribs and steak with equal success. Try the delicately battered fish-and-chips or the clam chowder on the late-night menu, served from 10 PM to midnight. Bright panels of turquoise and terra-cotta, black banquettes, and neon lighting make for a chic space in the main dining room, or sit in the cozy bar area with locals who appreciate a good meal with their cocktails. ⌂2564 E. Grant Rd., Central ☎520/323–7739 ⊕kingfishertucson.com ▭AE, D, DC, MC, V ⊗No lunch weekends ✛C4.

¢ **✕Hungry Fox.** Hungry customers have been coming here for good ol'
AMERICAN fashioned breakfasts, served until 2 PM, since 1962. It's the home of the double yolk, meaning when you order one egg, you'll get two (and so on). You'll also get a real slice of Tucson life at this cheerful, unpretentious place decorated with cow and farm photos, and a spoon collection that lines the walls. Hearty country dinners, such as meatloaf and lasagna, are now served Friday through Sunday at the same bargain prices.

7

Work up your appetite hiking through the desert before you tuck into some of the best Mexican food north of the border.

☒ *4637 E. Broadway Blvd., Central* ☎ *520/326–2835* ⊕ *hungryfox. com* ▭ *AE, D, MC, V* ☺ *No dinner Mon.–Thurs.* ✛ *E5.*

$
MEXICAN

✕ **Molina's Midway.** Tucked into a side street just north of Speedway, this unassuming and charming Mexican restaurant holds its own against any in South Tucson. Specialties include Sinchiladas (chicken or beef with chiles, cheese, and a cream sauce) and *carne asada* (chunks of mildly spiced steak) wrapped in soft corn or flour tortillas. Seating is plentiful and the service is friendly; several smaller rooms keep the noise level down. ☒ *1138 N. Belvedere, Central* ☎ *520/325–9957* ▭ *AE, D, MC, V* ☺ *Closed Mon.* ✛ *E4.*

$$
SOUTHWESTERN

✕ **Red Sky Cafe.** Trained in Paris, chef-owner Steve Schultz returned to Tucson to create his own contemporary cuisine, a fusion of French, Californian, and Southwestern flavors; the result is well-prepared, exquisitely presented meals. For a starter, try the foie gras with a potato pancake. Main courses, generously portioned, include soup or salad made with fresh (and often exotic) produce from the U of A's greenhouses and other local farms. ☒ *Plaza Palomino, 2900 N. Swan Rd., Central* ☎ *520/326–5454* ⊕ *redskycafeandcatering.com* ▭ *AE, MC, V* ✛ *E3.*

¢–$
ETHIOPIAN

✕ **Zemam.** It can be hard to get a table in this small eatery—except in summer, when the lack of air-conditioning presents a challenge. The sampler plate of any three items allows you to try dishes like *yesimir wat* (a spicy lentil dish) and *lega tibs* (a milder beef dish with a tomato sauce). Most of the food has a stewlike consistency, so don't come if you feel the need to crunch. Everything is served on a communal platter with *injera*, a spongy bread, and eaten with the hands. ☒ *2731 E. Broadway*

Blvd., Central ☎520/323–9928 ⚑*Reservations not accepted* ▭*MC,*
V 🍸*BYOB* ⊘*Closed Mon.* ✛*C5.*

$ ✗**Zona 78.** Fresh food takes on a whole new meaning at this contempo-
ITALIAN rary bistro emphasizing inventive pizzas, pastas, and salads. The casual
interior's focal point is a huge stone oven, where the pies are fired with
toppings like Australian blue cheese, kalamata olives, sausage, and even
chicken with peanut sauce. Whole-wheat crust is an option, and there
are also baked salmon and chicken entrées. The house-made mozzarella is delectable, either on top of a pizza or in a salad with organic
tomatoes. The newer eastside location at *7301 E. Tanque Verde Road*
has the same low-key, neighborhood feel. ⊠*78 W. River Rd., Central*
☎*520/888–7878* ⊕*zona78.com* ▭*AE, D, MC, V* ✛*B2.*

EASTSIDE

$$ ✗**Montana Avenue.** The more sedate but equally charming sister restau-
AMERICAN rant to Zinburger, North, and Wildflower, Montana Avenue satisfies
with upscale comfort food in a sophisticated setting, this one named
for the chic dining district in L.A.'s Santa Monica. There's no view
here, but floor-to-ceiling windows create a bright backdrop for nou-
velle dishes like shrimp risotto with shiitake mushrooms and buttermilk
chicken with chayote squash. Just for fun, indulge in their sumptuous
macaroni and cheese, grown-up style. ⊠*6390 E. Grant Rd., East-
side* ☎*520/298–2020* ⊕*foxrestaurantconcepts.com* ▭*AE, D, MC,
V* ✛*F4.*

$ ✗**Pinnacle Peak Steakhouse.** Anybody caught eating newfangled foods
STEAK like fish tacos here would probably be hanged from the rafters—along
☺ with the ties snipped from city slickers who overdressed. This cow-
boy steak house serves basic, not stellar, cowboy fare: mesquite-broiled
steak, chicken, and grilled fish with salad and pinto beans. The restau-
rant is part of the somewhat kitschy Trail Dust Town, a re-creation of
a turn-of-the-20th-century town, complete with a working antique car-
ousel and a narrow-gauge train. Gunfights are staged outside nightly at
7, 8, and 9. Expect a long wait on weekends. ⊠*6541 E. Tanque Verde
Rd., Eastside* ☎*520/296–0911* ⊕*pinnaclepeaktucson.com* ⚑*Reserva-
tions not accepted* ▭*AE, D, DC, MC, V* ⊘*No lunch* ✛*F4.*

$$ ✗**Sachiko Sushi.** Don't let the bland interior or the strip-mall setting
JAPANESE dissuade you; many locals consider this the best Japanese restaurant in
Tucson. Inside, you'll find perfectly prepared sushi and sashimi, generous combinations of tempura and teriyaki, and friendly service. The
owner's wife is Korean, so you'll also find quite a few Korean classics,
like beef and pork *bulgogi* (barbecued with vegetables) and tofu kimchi,
on the menu. Try a bowl of udon noodles, served in broth with assorted
meat, seafood, or vegetables; it's a satisfying meal in itself. ⊠*1101
Wilmot Rd., Eastside* ☎*520/886–7000* ⊕*www.sachikorestaurant.com*
▭*AE, DC, MC, V* ⊘*No lunch Sun.* ✛*F4.*

7

CATALINA FOOTHILLS (NORTH)

$$$ ✕**Acacia.** One of Tucson's premier chefs, Albert Hall, opened his own
SOUTHWESTERN restaurant in 2006 in one of the area's most artistic settings. A glass
waterfall sculpture by local artist Tom Philabaum graces one wall, and
bold red-and-blue glass plates and stemware seem to float atop the
tables. Roasted plum tomato–and–basil soup, a recipe from Albert's
mom, is a favorite starter. Creative dishes like wild salmon with a pecan
honey-mustard glaze and wood-roasted quail filled with pancetta, moz-
zarella, roasted tomatoes, and Oaxacan risotto are among the many
tempting entrées. Weekend evenings bring live jazz to the patio, which
overlooks pretty, flower-filled St. Philip's Plaza. ⊠*4340 N. Campbell
Ave., St. Philip's Plaza, Foothills* ☎*520/232–0101* ⊕*acaciatucson.com*
▭*AE, D, MC, V* ⊹*C2.*

$$$ ✕**The Grill at Hacienda del Sol.** Tucked into the foothills and surrounded
SOUTHWESTERN by flowering gardens, this special-occasion restaurant, a favorite among
Fodor'sChoice locals hosting out-of-town visitors, provides an alternative to the chile-
★ laden dishes of most Southwestern nouvelle cuisine. Wild-mushroom
bisque, pecan-grilled buffalo, and pan-seared sea bass are among the
menu choices. Tapas (and most items on the full menu) can be enjoyed
on the more casual outdoor patio, accented by live flamenco guitar
music. The lavish Sunday brunch buffet is worth a splurge. ⊠*Hacienda
del Sol Guest Ranch Resort, 5601 N. Hacienda del Sol Rd., Foothills*
☎*520/529–3500* ⊕*haciendadelsol.com* ▭*AE, DC, MC, V* ⊹*2D.*

$$$$ ✕**Janos.** Chef Janos Wilder was one of the first to reinvent Southwestern
SOUTHWESTERN cuisine, and the menu, wine list, and service place this restaurant among
Fodor'sChoice the finest in the West. The hillside location on the grounds of the Westin
★ La Paloma is a stunning backdrop for such dishes as sweet and spicy
glazed quail with butternut-squash cannelloni, salmon with a scallop
mousse served on polenta, and venison loin with chile-lime paste and
pecans. Have a drink or a more casual meal of Caribbean fare next door
at J Bar, a lively and lower-priced venue for sampling Janos's innovative
cuisine. Twinkling city lights make patio seating a romantic choice here.
⊠ *Westin La Paloma, 3770 E. Sunrise Dr., Foothills* ☎*520/615–6100*
⊕*janos.com* ▭*AE, DC, MC, V* ☉*Closed Sun. No lunch* ⊹*D1.*

$$ ✕**North.** This trendy eatery in the upscale La Encantada Shopping Cen-
ITALIAN ter boasts an urban-loft look with exposed-pipe ceiling, white leather
booths, dark concrete floors, and an open kitchen—and it draws crowds
for its excellent thin-crust pizzas, pasta, fish, and steak. Alfresco dining
on plush lounge furniture affords views of the city and quieter con-
versation; on most evenings the expansive bar area inside buzzes with
Tucson's young professionals. ⊠*2995 E. Skyline Dr., La Encantada,
Foothills* ☎*520/299–1600* ⊕*foxrestaurantconcepts.com* ▭*AE, D,
MC, V* ⊹*C1.*

$$$$ ✕**Ventana Room.** This formal (jacket required) restaurant is a triumph of
CONTINENTAL dining elegance: muted colors, a fireplace, grand views of the city lights,
and waiters who attend to every detail. A classical guitarist strums
romantic melodies on weekends. The contemporary Continental menu
contains such entrées as a mixed grill of game (venison, quail, and buf-
falo) with black barley and huckleberries, and potato-wrapped striped
sea bass with spinach, tomato, and sweet-basil wine sauce. There's

also a spa tasting menu for a lighter meal. ✉*Loews Ventana Canyon Resort, 7000 N. Resort Dr., Foothills* ☎*520/299–2020 Ext. 5194* ⊕*ventanaroom.com* ✑*Jacket required* ▭*AE, D, DC, MC, V* ⊘*No lunch* ✛*E1.*

$$–$$$
ITALIAN
✕**Vivace.** A nouvelle Italian bistro in the lovely St. Philip's Plaza, Vivace has long been a favorite with Tucsonans. Wild mushrooms and goat cheese in puff pastry is hard to resist as a starter. The fettuccine with grilled salmon is a nice lighter alternative to such entrées as a rich osso buco. For dessert, the molten chocolate cake with spumoni is worth the 20 minutes it takes to create. Patio seating is especially inviting on warm evenings. ✉*4310 N. Campbell Ave., Foothills* ☎*520/795–7221* ▭*AE, D, MC, V* ⊘*Closed Sun.* ✛*C2.*

$
AMERICAN
✕**Zinburger.** Have a glass of wine or a cocktail with your gourmet burger and fries at this high-energy, somewhat noisy, and unquestionably hip new burger joint. Open until 11 PM on Friday and Saturday, late by Tucson standards, Zinburger delivers tempting burgers—try the Kobe beef with cheddar and wild mushrooms—and decadent milk shakes made of exotic combinations like dates and honey or melted chocolate with praline flakes. A few creative salads, including one with ahi tuna, round out the menu. ✉*1865 E. River Rd., Foothills* ☎*520/299–7799* ⊕*foxrestaurantconcepts.com* ▭*AE, D, DC, MC, V* ✛*C2.*

NORTHWEST TUCSON

7

$$
SEAFOOD
✕**Bluefin Seafood Bistro.** What's a nice little fish restaurant doing in the middle of the desert? Consistently turning out well-prepared, fresh seafood like cashew-crusted mahi-mahi; Scottish salmon; and a mixed grill of lobster, shrimp, and scallops in a classy setting. Tucked into the courtyard of Casas Adobes Plaza, the two-story bistro has three comfortable seating areas—in the brick-walled bar listening to live jazz, upstairs in the mellow dining room, or outside on the patio. The late-night menu, which includes New England and Manhattan clam chowder, is served until midnight on Friday and Saturday, providing a less expensive, lighter option in this part of town. ✉*7053 N. Oracle Rd., Northwest* ☎*520/531–8500* ⊕*bluefintucson.com* ▭*AE, D, MC, V* ✛*B1.*

$$$
SOUTHWESTERN
✕**Gold.** Every seat in this casually elegant and quiet dining room at the Westward Look Resort, high in the Catalina Foothills, has a spectacular view of the city below. The fare includes classics like sautéed halibut and roasted rack of lamb in truffle port sauce, as well as regional specialties such as mesquite-grilled buffalo sirloin and pinenut-crusted chicken. All are served with organically grown vegetables picked from the chef's on-site garden. ✉*Westward Look Resort, 245 E. Ina Rd., Northwest* ☎*520/297–1151* ⊕*westwardlook.com* ▭*AE, DC, MC, V* ✛*B1.*

$$
AMERICAN
✕**JaxKitchen.** A recent entry to the Tucson dining scene, Jax serves up modern comfort food in a cozy, sophisticated setting more reminiscent of Chicago or Boston than the Sonoran Desert. Their unique versions of "shrimp and grits" (sautéed shrimp atop creamy polenta) and tomato soup with grilled Brie and Gruyère cheeses are heavenly, and the daily fish entrée is served with Meyer lemon–infused risotto. The dining room is cleverly divided by a half-wall, so conversation still feels intimate even when the place is bustling. Save room for milk and cookies like

your mother never served—a plate of assorted warm cookies surrounding a cup of bourbon-spiked milk to dip them in. ✉ *7286 N. Oracle Rd., Northwest* 📷 *520/219–1235* ⊕ *jaxkitchen.com* ▤ *AE, MC, V* ⊗ *Closed Mon. No lunch Sun.* ⊕ *B1.*

$
ITALIAN
☾
✕ **Sauce.** Modern Italian fuses with fast food here at North Restaurant's casual little sister in Casa Adobes Plaza. Delicious thin-crust pizzas, chopped salads, pastas, and panini are ordered at the counter in this lively, family-friendly spot decorated in a contemporary twist on the colors of Italy's flag—green, white, and tomato-red. The food is fast, fresh, and affordable, without sacrificing sophisticated taste. Two additional locations, on East Broadway in Eastside and North Campbell in Central, are identical in both decor and menu. ✉ *7117 N. Oracle Rd., Northwest* 📷 *520/297–8575* ⊕ *foxrestaurantconcepts.com* ▤ *AE, D, MC, V* ⊕ *B1, C3, E5.*

$
SOUTHWESTERN
✕ **Tohono Chul Tea Room.** The food is fine, but what stands out here is the location—inside a wildlife sanctuary, surrounded by flowering desert gardens. The Southwestern interior has Mexican tile, light wood, and a cobblestone courtyard. Dine outside on the back patio to watch hummingbirds and butterflies. House favorites include tortilla soup with avocado, breads and scones baked on the premises, and grilled raspberry-chipotle chicken. Open daily from 8 to 5, the Tea Room is popular for Sunday brunch. ✉ *Tohono Chul Park, 7366 N. Paseo del Norte, Northwest* 📷 *520/797–1222* ⊕ *tohonochulpark.org* ▤ *AE, MC, V* ⊗ *No dinner* ⊕ *B1.*

$$$
AMERICAN
✕ **Wildflower Grill.** A glass wall separates the bar from the dining area, where an open kitchen, high ceiling with painted clouds, and rose-color banquettes complete the light and airy effect. Wildflower Grill is well known for its creative American fare and stunning presentation, and the menu has compelling choices like warm Maine lobster salad; bow-tie pasta with grilled chicken, tomatoes, spinach, and pine nuts; and rack of lamb with a Dijon crust. The decadently huge desserts are equally top-notch. Request a banquette in the evening if you want quiet conversation, as the room can be noisy. ✉ *7037 N. Oracle Rd., Northwest* 📷 *520/219–4230* ⊕ *foxrestaurantconcepts.com* ▤ *AE, D, DC, MC, V* ⊗ *No lunch Sun.* ⊕ *B1.*

SOUTH TUCSON

$
MEXICAN
✕ **Micha's.** Family-owned for 24 years, this local institution is a nondescript Mexican diner serving some of the best Sonoran classics this side of the border. House specialties include *machaca* (shredded beef) enchiladas and chimichangas, and *cocido,* a hearty vegetable-beef soup. Homemade chorizo spices up breakfast, which is served daily. ✉ *2908 S. 4th Ave., South* 📷 *520/623–5307* ⊕ *michascatering.com* ▤ *AE, DC, MC, V* ⊗ *No dinner Mon.* ⊕ *B6.*

$
MEXICAN
✕ **Mi Nidito.** A perennial favorite among locals (the wait is worthwhile), Mi Nidito—"my little nest"—has also hosted its share of visiting celebrities. Following President Clinton's lunch here, the rather hefty Presidential Plate (bean tostada, taco with barbecued meat, chiles rellenos, chicken enchilada, and beef tamale with rice and beans) was added to the menu. Top that off with the mango chimichangas for dessert,

and you're talkin' executive privilege. ⊠*1813 S. 4th Ave., South* ☎*520/622–5081* ⊕*minidito.net* ⊟*AE, DC, MC, V* ⊘*Closed Mon. and Tues.* ✛*B6.*

WHERE TO STAY

When it comes to places to spend the night, the options in Tucson run the gamut: there are luxurious desert resorts, bed-and-breakfasts ranging from bedrooms in modest homes to private cottages nestled on wildlife preserves, as well as small to medium-size hotels and motels.

If you like being able to walk to sights, shops, and restaurants, plan on staying in the Downtown or University neighborhoods. You won't find a hotter scene than Downtown's Hotel Congress, with nightly music pulsing at Club Congress or the Rialto Theatre across the street. For a quieter but equally convenient base, opt for one of the charming B&Bs near the U of A campus. The posh resorts, primarily situated in the Catalina Foothills and Northwest areas, although farther away from town, have many activities on-site, as well as some of Tucson's top-rated restaurants, golf courses and spas, and can arrange transportation to shopping and sights. Tucson's JW Marriott Starr Pass is the only one southwest of town; seemingly isolated, it is actually closer to Downtown and the Westside sights. For a unique experience, you can check into a Southwestern-style dude ranch—one of them a former cattle ranch from the 1800s—on the outskirts of town (unless otherwise indicated, price categories for guest ranches include all meals and most activities). If you are seeking accommodations that can change your life, book a stay at one of Tucson's world-class health spas, Canyon Ranch or Miraval. Both provide pampering, serenity, and guidance for attaining an improved sense of well-being.

PLANNING INFORMATION

Summer rates (late May through September) are up to 60% lower than those in the winter. Note that unless you book months in advance, you'll be hard pressed to find a Tucson hotel room at any price the week before and during the huge gem and mineral show, which is held the first two weeks in February. Also, resorts typically charge an additional daily fee for "use of facilities," such as pools, tennis courts, and exercise classes and equipment, so be sure to ask what is included when you book a room.

WHAT IT COSTS				
¢	$	$$	$$$	$$$$
FOR TWO PEOPLE	under $100	$100–$150	$151–$225	$226–$350	over $350

Prices are for a standard double in high season.

BEST BETS FOR TUCSON LODGING

Fodor's offers a selective listing of quality lodging experiences at every price range, from the city's best budget motel to its most sophisticated luxury hotel. Here, we've compiled our top recommendations by price and experience. The very best properties—in other words, those that provide a particularly remarkable experience in their price range—are designated in the listings with the Fodor's Choice logo.

Fodor'sChoice ★

Arizona Inn, p. 383
Casa Tierra, p. 391
Hacienda del Sol Guest Ranch Resort, p. 386
Hotel Congress, p. 381
Loews Ventana Canyon Resort, p. 386
White Stallion Ranch, p. 390

Best by Price

¢

Hotel Congress, p. 381
Quail's Vista Bed & Breakfast, p. 390

$

Adobe Rose Inn, p. 381
Casa Tierra, p. 391
Inn Suites Hotel & Resort, p. 381

$$

Peppertrees B&B Inn, p. 383
Windmill Inn, p. 387

$$$

Arizona Inn, p. 383
Hacienda del Sol Guest Ranch Resort, p. 386
Omni Tucson National Resort, p. 389
Westward Look Resort, p. 390

$$$$

JW Marriott Starr Pass, p. 391
Loews Ventana Canyon Resort, p. 386

Best By Experience

BEST B&BS

Casa Tierra, p. 391
Peppertrees B&B Inn, p. 383
Royal Elizabeth B&B Inn, p. 381

BEST DUDE RANCHES

Circle Z Ranch, p. 434
Tanque Verde Ranch, p. 385
White Stallion Ranch, p. 390

BEST RESORTS

JW Marriott Starr Pass, p. 391
Loews Ventana Canyon Resort, p. 386
Westin La Paloma, p. 386

BEST SPAS

Canyon Ranch, p. 385
Miraval, p. 389

BIGGEST (BY ROOM COUNT) HOTELS

Loews Ventana Canyon Resort, p. 386
Westin La Paloma, p. 386
Hilton Tucson El Conquistador, p. 387
JW Marriot Starr Pass Resort & Spa, p. 391

MOST KID-FRIENDLY

Hilton Tucson El Conquistador, p. 387
Tanque Verde Ranch, p. 385
Westin La Paloma, p. 386
White Stallion Ranch, p. 390

MOST ROMANTIC

Arizona Inn, p. 383
Hacienda del Sol, p. 386
JW Marriott Starr Pass, p. 391

DOWNTOWN TUCSON

¢ **⚞ Hotel Congress.** This hotel built in 1919 has been artfully restored to
Fodor'sChoice its original Western version of art deco. The gangster John Dillinger was
★ almost caught here in 1934—apparently his luggage, filled with guns and
ammo, was suspiciously heavy. Each room has a black-and-white tile
bath and the original iron bed frames. The convenient location downtown means it can be noisy, so make sure you don't get a room over the
popular Club Congress unless you plan to be up until the wee hours.
A great place to stay for younger or more adventurous visitors, it's the
center of Tucson's hippest scene. **Pros:** convenient location; good restaurant; funky and fun. **Cons:** no air-conditioning (just evaporative cool-
ing, which isn't very effective during July and August); no elevator (all
guest rooms are upstairs); noise from nightclub. ⊠ *311 E. Congress St.,
Downtown* ☎ *520/622–8848 or 800/722–8848* ⊕ *www.hotelcongress.
com* ↪ *40 rooms* ⚒ *In-room: no TV, no a/c, Wi-Fi. In-hotel: restaurant,
bar, no-smoking rooms* ☐ *AE, D, MC, V* ⊹ *B5.*

$ **⚞ Inn Suites Hotel & Resort.** Just north of the El Presidio district of Down-
town, this hotel—the term "resort" is a bit of a misnomer—is next to
Interstate 10 but quiet nevertheless. The large, peach-and-green South-
western-theme rooms, circa 1980, face an interior grassy courtyard
with a sparkling pool and *palapas* (thatched open gazebos). Free daily
extras such as a breakfast buffet, newspaper, and happy-hour cocktails
make this a haven in the center of the city. **Pros:** free breakfast and
cocktails; affordable. **Cons:** little character; long walk to downtown
restaurants. ⊠ *475 N. Granada Ave., Downtown* ☎ *520/622–3000
or 877/446–6589* ⊕ *www.innsuites.com* ↪ *265 rooms, 35 suites* ⚒ *In-
room: refrigerator, Wi-Fi. In-hotel: restaurant, bar, pool, no-smoking
rooms* ☐ *AE, D, DC, MC, V* ⓘ *BP* ⊹ *B5.*

$$ **⚞ The Royal Elizabeth Bed and Breakfast Inn.** Fans of Victoriana will
adore this B&B in the Armory Park historic district. The inn, built in
1878, is beautifully furnished with period antiques, and its six rooms
are quite spacious. Gracious hosts Jeff and Charles take turns in the
kitchen, preparing two-course breakfasts that might include chiles rel-
lenos, a wild-mushroom frittata, or a fresh-fruit soufflé. **Pros:** large and
well-appointed rooms; perks for business travelers (Internet confer-
ence calling in-room); a sense of privacy as well as B&B camaraderie.
Cons: pricey for downtown, neighbors aren't very lively (next door to
a funeral home). ⊠ *204 S. Scott Ave., Downtown* ☎ *520/670–9022*
⊕ *www.royalelizabeth.com* ↪ *6 rooms* ⚒ *In-room: DVD, Wi-Fi. In-
hotel: pool, no-smoking rooms* ☐ *AE, D, MC, V* ⓘ *BP* ⊹ *B5.*

UNIVERSITY OF ARIZONA

$–$$ **⚞ Adobe Rose Inn.** This 1933 adobe home offers six rooms of varying sizes and amenities. Two have beehive fireplaces and stained-glass
windows, two have kitchenettes, and one is an upstairs suite with its
own balcony. In the historic Sam Hughes neighborhood just east of the
university, the well-maintained inn is within easy walking distance of
shops, restaurants, and two major bus lines. Breakfast dishes like Southwestern soufflés or blueberry pancakes, always served with fruit and

Loews Ventana Canyon Resort

Arizona Inn

White Stallion Ranch

muffins, are enjoyed in a dining room overlooking the bougainvillea-draped pool area. **Pros:** sumptuous breakfasts; homelike yet private. **Cons:** some rooms are small; a long walk (about a mile) to the University Boulevard and 4th Avenue sights. ⊠*940 N. Olsen Ave., University* ☎*520/318–4644 or 800/328–4122* ⊕*www.aroseinn.com* ↙*6 rooms* ⌂*In-room: Wi-Fi, kitchen (some). In-hotel: pool, no kids under 10, no-smoking rooms* ☰*AE, D, MC, V* ⎛⎞*BP* ✛*C4.*

$$$
Fodor's Choice
★
Arizona Inn. Although near the university and many sights, the beautifully landscaped lawns and gardens of this 1930 inn seem far from the hustle and bustle. The spacious rooms are spread over 14 acres in pink adobe-style casitas—most have private patios and some have fireplaces. The resort also has two luxurious two-story houses with their own heated pools and full hotel service. The main building has a library, a fine dining restaurant, and a cocktail lounge where a jazz pianist plays. **Pros:** unique historical property, emphasis on service. **Cons:** rooms may not be modern enough for some, close to U of A Medical Center but long walk (1½ mi) from the main campus. ⊠*2200 E. Elm St., University* ☎*520/325–1541 or 800/933–1093* ⊕*www.arizonainn.com* ↙*70 rooms, 16 suites, 3 casitas* ⌂*In-room: Internet. In-hotel: 2 restaurants, room service, bar, tennis courts, pool, gym, laundry service, no-smoking rooms* ☰*AE, DC, MC, V* ✛*C3.*

$–$$
Catalina Park Inn. Classical music plays softly in the living room of this beautifully restored 1927 neoclassical house. The original art nouveau tile work and a butler's pantry are among many charming architectural details, and all rooms are spacious and quite private. You might be tempted to fill your suitcase with the papaya and lime scones that are part of breakfast. **Pros:** rooms are large, quiet, and well equipped for a small property, with DVDs and phones; comfortable beds. **Cons:** West University location is not as bucolic as east of campus. ⊠*309 E. 1st St., University* ☎*520/792–4541 or 800/792–4885* ⊕*www.catalina parkinn.com* ↙*6 rooms* ⌂*In-room: Wi-Fi, DVD. In-hotel: no kids under 10, no-smoking rooms* ☰*AE, D, MC, V* ☉*Closed July and Aug.* ⎛⎞*BP* ✛*B4.*

$$
Peppertrees B&B Inn. This restored 1905 Victorian is just west of the U of A campus. Two contemporary-style guesthouses at the rear of the tree-shaded main house have full kitchens, separate phone lines, private patios, and washers and dryers. The antique-filled main house (furnished with pieces from innkeeper Jill Light's family in England) has several guest rooms and a separate one-bedroom apartment. Light prepares elaborate breakfasts, served in rooms or in the lovely garden, and dinner is available on request. **Pros:** comfortably furnished and meticulously clean; very convenient. **Cons:** often booked far in advance. ⊠*724 E. University Blvd., University* ☎*520/622–7167 or 800/348–5763* ⊕*www.peppertreesinn.com* ↙*3 rooms, 1 suite, 2 guesthouses* ⌂*In-room: kitchen (some), Wi-Fi. In-hotel: no-smoking rooms* ☰*D, MC, V* ⎛⎞*BP* ✛*B4.*

$$
Tucson Marriott University Park. With the University of Arizona less than a block from the front door, the Marriott is an ideal place to stay when visiting the campus. This clean, contemporary hotel has a lush atrium lobby area that can be enjoyed from the restaurant and bar, and

7

the university shopping district's cafés, pubs, and stores are all within a short stroll. **Pros:** excellent location; clean. **Cons:** generic rooms; uninspired restaurant. ✉*880 E. 2nd St., University* ☎*520/792–4100 or 888/236-2427* ⊕*www.marriotttucson.com* ↘*234 rooms, 16 suites* ⚭*In-room: refrigerator (some), Wi-Fi. In-hotel: restaurant, room service, bar, pool, gym, laundry service, executive floor, no-smoking rooms* ⊟*AE, D, DC, MC, V* ✛*B4.*

CENTRAL TUCSON

$$ 🖭**Doubletree Hotel at Reid Park.** A sprawling, 1970s-era hotel and conference center, the Doubletree sits directly across the street from Tucson's best municipal golf course (Randolph Park) and Reid Park, which houses the city zoo, a lake with paddleboats, and numerous play areas. A pleasant jogging-walking trail encircles both parks. The hotel property is well tended though generic-looking. **Pros:** attractive gardens; close to recreation and restaurants. **Cons:** large, older property; small rooms. ✉*445 S. Alvernon Way, Central* ☎*520/881–4200 or 800/222–8733* ⊕*www.doubletree.com* ↘*295 rooms* ⚭*In-room: Wi-Fi. In-hotel: 2 restaurants, room service, bar, tennis courts, pool, gym, laundry service, no-smoking rooms* ⊟*AE, D, DC, MC, V* �ⓄⅠ*BP* ✛*D5.*

¢ 🖭**Extended Stay America.** If you're seeking convenience and value (and don't mind a certain blandness), this modern chain property will suffice. All rooms have kitchenettes, queen or king-size beds, and recliner chairs, but don't expect a view or coffee in the lobby. Crossroads Shopping Center, where there are restaurants, a Starbucks, a grocery store, shops, and a cinema, is only two blocks away. **Pros:** central location; cheap. **Cons:** no pool; some road noise. ✉*5050 E. Grant Rd., Central* ☎*520/795–9510 or 800/398–7829* ⊕*www.extendedstayhotels.com* ↘*120 rooms* ⚭*In-room: kitchen, refrigerator, Wi-Fi. In-hotel: laundry facilities, no-smoking rooms* ⊟*AE, D, MC, V* ✛*E4.*

$ 🖭**Varsity Clubs of America.** This sports-theme time-share facility also doubles as a hotel, so it may have some or all of its suites available for rental at any given time. Home to the Diamondbacks and the Rockies teams during spring training, it enjoys a handy and surprisingly quiet location. One- and two-bedroom suites have whirlpool tubs and full kitchens, but alternatives to cooking include the Stadium Sports Grill downstairs or any of the several restaurants within walking distance. **Pros:** apartment style; pleasant common areas include a billiards room, cozy library with fireplace, and a putting green. **Cons:** little curb appeal; bland decor in suites. ✉*3855 E. Speedway Blvd., Central* ☎*520/318–3777 or 888/594–2287* ⊕*www.ilxresorts.com* ↘*59 suites* ⚭*In-room: kitchen, Wi-Fi. In-hotel: restaurant, pool, gym, no-smoking rooms* ⊟*AE, D, MC, V* ✛*D3.*

EASTSIDE

¢–$ 🖭**Ramada Inn Foothills.** Families and business travelers stay in this Ramada on the northeast side of town, not really in the Foothills but fairly close to Sabino Canyon. An attractive stucco building with a Spanish tile roof and a fake bell tower, the hotel has serviceable, if generic, rooms and small suites. Free passes to a local health club are available. **Pros:** free breakfast buffet and happy-hour food and drink, walk to shops and restaurants. **Cons:** rooms are bland, no on-site restaurant. ⊠6944 E. Tanque Verde Rd., Eastside ☎520/886–9595 or 888/666–7934 ⊕www.ramadafoothillstucson.com ⤳52 rooms, 61 suites ⚙In-room: refrigerator, Wi-Fi. In-hotel: pool, laundry facilities, no-smoking rooms ⊟AE, D, DC, MC, V ⧀BP ⊹F4.

$$ ⌦**The SunCatcher.** The four rooms in this B&B are decorated in honor of four groups who settled the Old West: cowboys, Native Americans, Spanish, and Asians. Some have fireplaces and Jacuzzi tubs, and can be reconfigured as suites for families. The spacious common room has a sunken seating area and a mesquite-wood bar where happy-hour snacks are served. It's a comfortable retreat after a day of sightseeing or hiking—trailheads into Saguaro National Park East are just down the road. **Pros:** quiet escape from civilization; all rooms have separate entrances; resident pets to play with include a zebra, a potbelly pig, and a miniature horse. **Cons:** on the far east side of town. ⊠105 N. Avenida. Javelina, Eastside ☎520/885–0883 or 877/775–8355 ⊕www.suncatchertucson.com ⤳4 rooms ⚙In-room: DVD, Wi-Fi. In-hotel: pool, no-smoking rooms ⊟AE, D, MC, V ⧀BP ⊹H4.

$$$$ ⌦**Tanque Verde Ranch.** The most upscale of Tucson's guest ranches and
⏏ one of the oldest in the country, the Tanque Verde sits on 640 beautiful acres in the Rincon Mountains next to Saguaro National Park East. Rooms in one-story casitas have tasteful Western-style furnishings, fireplaces, and picture-window views of the desert. Breakfast, lunch and dinner buffets are huge, and barbecues add variety. Horseback excursions are offered for every skill level (lessons are included in rates), and children can participate in daylong activity programs, leaving parents to their leisure. **Pros:** authentic Western experience; loads of all-inclusive activities. **Cons:** expensive; at the eastern edge of town. ⊠14301 E. Speedway Blvd., Eastside ☎520/296–6275 or 800/234–3833 ⊕www.tanqueverderanch.com ⤳49 rooms, 23 suites, 2 casitas ⚙In-room: no TV. In-hotel: tennis courts, pools, gym, bicycles, children's programs (ages 4–11), no-smoking rooms ⊟AE, D, MC, V ⧀FAP ⊹H4.

$–$$ ⌦**Tucson Hilton East.** This high-rise, corporate-type hotel and conference center is set back from a main road on the suburban east side of town. An airy atrium lobby takes advantage of the view of the Santa Catalina Mountains; better yet, push "6" in the glass elevator and ascend for spectacular vistas. Rooms are spacious and well tended, but not particularly distinctive. **Pros:** comfortable and unpretentious, quiet. **Cons:** in a sleepy part of town, very generic-looking. ⊠7600 E. Broadway Blvd., Eastside ☎520/721–5600 or 800/774–1500 ⊕www.tucsoneast.hilton.com ⤳225 rooms, 8 suites ⚙In-room: Wi-Fi. In-hotel: restaurant, bar, pool, gym, no-smoking rooms ⊟AE, D, DC, MC, V ⊹G5.

CATALINA FOOTHILLS (NORTH)

$$$$ ⌦**Canyon Ranch.** The Canyon Ranch draws an international crowd of well-to-do health seekers to its superb spa facilities on 70 acres in the desert foothills. Two activity centers include an enormous spa complex and a Health and Healing Center, where dietitians, exercise

physiologists, behavioral-health professionals, and medical staff attend to body and soul. Just about every type of physical activity is possible, from Pilates to guided hiking, and the food is plentiful and healthy. Rates include all meals, activities, taxes, and gratuities. There's a four-night minimum. **Pros:** a stay here can be a life-changing experience; gorgeous setting. **Cons:** very pricey; not family-friendly. ⊠*8600 E. Rockcliff Rd., Foothills* ☎*520/749–9000 or 800/742–9000* ⊕*www. canyonranch.com* ☞*240 rooms* ♿*In-room: refrigerator, Wi-Fi. In-hotel: restaurant, tennis courts, pools, gym, spa, laundry facilities, airport shuttle, no kids under 12, no-smoking rooms* ▭*AE, D, MC, V* �📷*AI* ✛*G2.*

$$-$$$
Fodor's Choice
★

🖥**Hacienda del Sol Guest Ranch Resort.** This 32-acre hideaway in the Santa Catalina foothills is part guest ranch, part resort, and entirely gracious. It's a charming and lower-price alternative to the larger resorts. Designed in classic Mexican hacienda style, this former finishing school for girls was converted to a guest ranch during World War II and attracted stars like Clark Gable, Katharine Hepburn, and Spencer Tracy. The best rooms are the west-facing casitas with fireplaces and private porches, where you can watch the sun set over the Tucson Mountains. **Pros:** outstanding restaurant and bar, buildings and landscaping are stunningly beautiful. **Cons:** some rooms are dark, not as kid-friendly as other resorts. ⊠*5601 N. Hacienda del Sol Rd., Foothills* ☎*520/299–1501 or 800/728–6514* ⊕*www.haciendadelsol.com* ☞*22 rooms, 8 suites* ♿*In-room: refrigerator, Wi-Fi. In-hotel: restaurant, pool, no-smoking rooms* ▭*AE, D, MC, V* ✛*E1.*

$$$-$$$$
☾
Fodor's Choice
★

🖥**Loews Ventana Canyon Resort.** This is one of the most luxurious and prettiest of the big resorts, with dramatic stone architecture and an 80-foot waterfall cascading down the mountains. Rooms, facing either the Catalinas or the golf course and city, are modern and elegantly furnished in muted earth tones and light woods; each bathroom has a miniature, flat-screen TV and a double-wide tub. Dining options include everything from poolside snacks at Bill's Grill to fine Continental cuisine at the Ventana Room. The scenic Ventana Canyon trailhead is steps away, and there's a free shuttle to nearby Sabino Canyon. **Pros:** this place has everything: great golf, full spa, hiking, and even a kids' playground. **Cons:** some rooms overlook the parking lot. ⊠*7000 N. Resort Dr., Foothills* ☎*520/299–2020 or 800/234–5117* ⊕*www.loewshotels. com* ☞*384 rooms, 14 suites* ♿*In-room: refrigerator, Wi-Fi. In-hotel: 4 restaurants, room service, bar, golf courses, tennis courts, pools, gym, spa, bicycles, children's programs (ages 4–12), no-smoking rooms* ▭*AE, D, DC, MC, V* ✛*E1.*

$$$-$$$$
☾

🖥**Westin La Paloma.** Popular with business travelers and families, this sprawling resort offers views of the Santa Catalina Mountains above and the city below. It specializes in relaxation with an emphasis on fun: the huge pool complex has an impressively long waterslide, as well as a swim-up bar and grill for those who can't bear to leave the water. Kids' programs, including weekly "dive-in movies," make for a vacation the whole family can enjoy. The highly acclaimed Janos restaurant is on-site. **Pros:** top-notch golf, tennis, and spa; plush rooms; Janos/J Bar. **Cons:** so big it can feel crowded at pool areas and mazelike going to and

Downtown Tucson is close to the Catalina foothills, which fill with blooms in the springtime.

from guest rooms. ✉ *3800 E. Sunrise Dr., Foothills* ☎ *520/742–6000 or 888/625–5144* ⊕ *www.starwood.com* ⤶ *455 rooms, 32 suites* ⚿ *In-room: refrigerator, Wi-Fi. In-hotel: 4 restaurants, room service, bars, golf courses, tennis courts, pools, gym, spa, children's programs (ages 6 mos–12 yrs), no-smoking rooms* ⊟ *AE, D, DC, MC, V* ⊕ *D1.*

$$ 🔅 **Windmill Inn at St. Philip's Plaza.** This all-suites hotel is in a chic shopping plaza filled with glitzy boutiques, galleries, and good restaurants. Each 500-square-foot suite has a small sitting area, wet bar, two TVs, and three telephones (local calls are free). A few dollars extra will buy you a view of the pool and fountain rather than the parking lot. Complimentary coffee, muffins, juice, and a newspaper are delivered to your door; additional breakfast goodies are set up in the lobby. **Pros:** so many shops and restaurants to walk to, so little time; bicycles are available for treks along the adjacent Rillito River Path. **Cons:** sure, it's a suite, but both rooms are small. ✉ *4250 N. Campbell Ave., Foothills* ☎ *520/577–0007 or 800/547–4747* ⊕ *www.windmillinns.com* ⤶ *122 suites* ⚿ *In-room: refrigerator, Wi-Fi. In-hotel: pool, bicycles, laundry facilities, no-smoking rooms* ⊟ *AE, D, DC, MC, V* ⊚ *BP* ⊕ *C2.*

NORTHWEST TUCSON

$$$ 🔅 **Hilton Tucson El Conquistador.** A huge copper mural of cowboys and cacti, and a wide view of the Santa Catalina Mountains grace the lobby of this golf and tennis resort. A friendly upscale property, it draws families and conventioneers, some taking advantage of low summer rates for the excellent sports facilities, the spa, and the pool complex with a 140-foot waterslide. Rooms are either in private one-bedroom casitas

Dude Ranches: Where the West Is Still Wild

If you think Tucson has gone the way of sprawling, suburban development like Phoenix has to the north, well, you're partly right. Many of the wide-open spaces that inspired the lyrics of old cowboy songs have become housing tracts, golf courses, and shopping malls. But a sliver of the rugged and free-spirited ranching life that shaped the American West is alive and well on the outskirts of town, where urban cowboys and cowgirls come to fulfill their dreams at dude ranches, also called guest ranches.

Riding is the preferred activity on the ranch. Slow, fast, mountain, and all-day rides are offered, and some ranches allow you to help groom and feed the horses. As you ride up into Saguaro National Park or the Coronado National Forest, wranglers give sage advice on horsemanship and tell tales (some tall) of their most harrowing cattle drives. For those who don't saddle up, there are activities including birding and nature walks, mountain hikes, tennis, and swimming. Afterward, you can soak in the hot tub, get a massage, or laugh with new friends about the day's adventures over margaritas.

After a day of riding or hiking, or maybe just sitting outside with a book, guests find a warm welcome at happy hour, dinner, and around the campfire. Lodges are outfitted with comfortable couches, crackling

fireplaces, board games, and Western saloon-type bars (one even has saddles for barstools). Ranch stays are popular for family vacations, but the ranch experience also draws many single travelers who can easily find camaraderie in this setting.

Though accommodations are a bit more rustic than at resort hotels, there are arguably more comforts, and the dude-ranch experience eliminates many stresses often associated with more traditional vacations: since all meals and activities are included, you have fewer decisions to make about structuring your day (will it be the mountain ride or team penning?), and no anxiety about choosing a restaurant or dealing with crowds.

Two ranches are in the Tucson area and one is just a bit further southeast. The large and luxurious **Tanque Verde Ranch,** on the eastern edge of town, has two swimming pools (one indoor), a tennis pro, and lavish buffet meals. The **White Stallion Ranch,** adjacent to Saguaro National Park West, has challenging riding as well as massages and a fitness center. The owners live and work on this 3,000-acre cattle ranch, the setting for the *High Chaparral TV series.* The smaller and more rustic **Circle Z Ranch,** in Patagonia (⇨ *See Southern Arizona chapter),* takes riders through the picturesque Patagonia-Sonoita Creek Reserve.

or in the main hotel building, and more than half of them have kiva-style fireplaces. **Pros:** great variety of on-site activities, even horseback riding; low-key. **Cons:** huge place; location is farther northwest than other resorts, adding on driving time to restaurants and in-town sights. ✉ *10000 N. Oracle Rd., Northwest* ☎ *520/544–5000 or 800/325–3525* ⊕ *www.hiltonelconquistador.com* ✎ *328 rooms, 57 suites, 43 casitas* ⚒ *In-room: refrigerator, Wi-Fi. In-hotel: 5 restaurants, bar, golf courses,*

*tennis courts, pools, gym, spa, bicycles, children's programs (ages 4–12),
no-smoking rooms* ▭AE, D, DC, MC, V ⚓C1.

$ ⛶**La Posada Lodge and Casitas.** This 1960s motor lodge has been reborn
as a charming Santa Fe–style boutique hotel. Though most rooms in the
three-story building have Saltillo-tile floors and hand-painted Mexican
headboards, a few are whimsically decorated with blue-and-lime-green–
checkered bedspreads and curtains, along with kitschy furniture and lava
lamps, as a tribute to the hotel's past life. Upper-floor rooms have balconies with mountain and city views. A full breakfast is included. **Pros:**
good location, good restaurant. **Cons:** service is inconsistent; rooms
are not large. ✉*5900 N. Oracle Rd., Northwest* ☎*520/887–4800 or
800/810–2808* ⊕*www.laposadalodge.com* ⤳*72 rooms* ♿*In-room:
kitchen (some), refrigerator, Wi-Fi. In-hotel: restaurant, room service,
bar, pool, gym, no-smoking rooms* ▭*AE, MC, V* ⫶○⫶*BP* ⚓*B1.*

$$ ⛶**Marriott TownePlace Suites.** With full kitchens in all of its studio, one-
bedroom, and two-bedroom suites, this property is suitable for short
or extended stays. In fact, the longer you stay, the lower your nightly
rate. Its location is handy, yet the interior hallways and the way the
buildings are set back from the road make for a quiet retreat. Some
suites have a view of the neighboring par-3, executive golf course. **Pros:**
convenient location; well-equipped units. **Cons:** no restaurant; kind of
sterile-looking. ✉*405 W. Rudasill Rd., Northwest* ☎*520/292–9697 or
800/257–3000* ⊕*www.towneplacesuites.com* ⤳*77 suites* ♿*In-room:
kitchen, Wi-Fi. In-hotel: pool, laundry facilities, no-smoking rooms*
▭*AE, MC, V* ⫶○⫶*CP* ⚓*B1.*

$$$$ ⛶**Miraval.** Giving Canyon Ranch a run for its money, this New Age
health spa 30 mi north of Tucson has a secluded desert setting and
beautiful Southwestern rooms. Most of the spa services and wellness
programs, based primarily on Eastern philosophies, help you get in
touch with your inner self. Whether you prefer to be pampered with
a hot stone massage or seaweed body mask, participate in fitness and
nature activities, or walk a labyrinth, it's all here. All gratuities and
meals, including tasty buffets (with calories and fat content noted), are
included. **Pros:** very posh getaway in the middle of nowhere, tranquil.
Cons: very posh attitude makes some uncomfortable, extremely expen-
sive. ✉*5000 E. Via Estancia Miraval, Catalina* ☎*520/825–4000 or
800/825–4000* ⊕*www.miravalresort.com* ⤳*102 rooms* ♿*In-room:
safe, refrigerator, Wi-Fi. In-hotel: 2 restaurants, bar, tennis courts,
pools, gym, spa, bicycles, laundry facilities, laundry service, no-smoking
rooms* ▭*AE, D, DC, MC, V* ⫶○⫶*FAP* ⚓*C1.*

$$$ ⛶**Omni Tucson National Golf Resort & Spa.** Perfect for couples with differ-
ing ideas on how to spend a vacation, Tucson National is both a premier
golf resort (it hosts the Tucson Open) and a full-service European-style
spa, where you can be coiffed, waxed, and wrapped to your heart's con-
tent. Most of the rooms, although not technically suites, are spacious
with separate sitting areas. Some casitas have full kitchens and dining
rooms. Although this resort is a little farther from central Tucson than
others, it's still convenient to shopping and restaurants in the thriving
Northwest area. **Pros:** outstanding golf; friendly, relaxed environment.
Cons: tucked away in Northwest Tucson, too sedate for some. ✉*2727*

Much of the city's cultural activity takes place at or near the **Tucson Convention Center** (✉260 S. Church St., Downtown ☎520/791–4101, 520/791–4266 box office ⊕www.tucsonconventioncenter.org), which includes the Music Hall and the Leo Rich Theater. Dance, music, and other kinds of performances take place at the University of Arizona's **Centennial Hall** (✉1020 E. University Blvd., University ☎520/621–3341 ⊕www.uapresents.org).

One of Tucson's hottest rock-music venues, the **Rialto Theatre** (✉318 E. Congress St., Downtown ☎520/798–3333 ⊕www.rialtotheatre.com), was once a silent-movie theater but now reverberates with the sounds of jazz, folk, and world-music concerts, although the emphasis is on hard rock. Another recently refurbished old movie palace, the art deco **Fox Theatre** (✉17 W. Congress St., Downtown ☎520/547–3040 ⊕www. foxtucsontheatre.org), hosts film festivals and folk-rock concerts.

Each season brings visiting opera, theater, and dance companies to Tucson. Tickets to many events can be purchased through **Ticketmaster** (☎520/321–1000 ⊕www.ticketmaster.com), which has outlets at most Fry's Marketplace stores around town.

DANCE

Tucson shares its professional-ballet company, **Ballet Arizona** (☎888/ 322–5538 ⊕www.balletaz.org), with Phoenix. Performances, from classical to contemporary, are held at the Music Hall in the Tucson Convention Center. The city's most established modern dance company, **Orts Theatre of Dance** (✉300 E. University Blvd., University ☎520/624–3799 ⊕www.otodance.org), incorporates trapeze flying into their dances. Outdoor and indoor performances are staged throughout the year.

MUSIC

A Wednesday-night chamber-music series is hosted by the **Arizona Friends of Chamber Music** (☎520/577–3769 ⊕arizonachambermusic.org) at the Leo Rich Theater in the Tucson Convention Center from October through April. They also have a music festival the first week of March. The **Arizona Opera Company** (☎520/293–4336 ⊕www.azopera. com), based in Tucson, puts on five major productions each year at the Tucson Convention Center's Music Hall. The **Arizona Symphonic Winds** (⊕www.azsymwinds.org) has a spring–summer schedule of performances, many of which are held outdoors at Udall Park in Northeast Tucson. Performances are usually at 7 PM, but you need to arrive at least an hour early. From May through September the **Tucson Pops Orchestra** (☎520/722–5853 ⊕www.tucsonpops.org) gives free concerts each Saturday evening at the De Meester Outdoor Performance Center in Reid Park. Arrive about an hour before the music starts (usually at 7 PM) to stake your claim on a viewing spot.

The **Tucson Symphony Orchestra** (✉443 S. Stone Ave., Downtown ☎520/882–8585 box office, 520/792–9155 main office ⊕www.tucson symphony.org), part of Tucson's cultural scene since 1929, holds concerts in the Music Hall in the Tucson Convention Center and at sites in the Foothills and the Northwest as well.

Tucson's small but vibrant jazz scene encompasses everything from afternoon jam sessions in the park to Sunday jazz brunches at resorts in the Foothills. Call the **Tucson Jazz Society** (☎ *520/903–1265*) for information.

POETRY

The first weekend in April brings the **Tucson Poetry Festival** (☎ *520/256–4206* ⊕ *www.tucsonpoetryfestival.org*) and its four days of readings and related events, including workshops, panel discussions, and a poetry slam. Such internationally acclaimed poets as Jorie Graham and Sherman Alexie have participated.

The **University of Arizona Poetry Center** (⊠ *1508 E. Helen St., University* ☎ *520/626–3765* ⊕ *www.poetrycenter.arizona.edu*) runs a free series open to the public. Check during fall and spring semesters for info on scheduled readings.

THEATER

Arizona's state theater, the **Arizona Theatre Company** (⊠ *Temple of Music and Art, 330 S. Scott Ave., Downtown* ☎ *520/622–2823 box office, 520/884–8210 company office* ⊕ *www.aztheatreco.org*), performs classical pieces, contemporary drama, and musical comedy at the historic Temple of Music and Art from September through May. It's worth coming just to see the beautifully restored historic Spanish colonial–Moorish-style theater; dinner at the adjoining Temple Café is a tasty prelude.

The University of Arizona's **Arizona Repertory Theatre** (⊠ *1025 N. Olive St., University* ☎ *520/621–1162* ⊕ *www.uatheatre.org*) has performances during the academic year. **Borderlands Theater** (⊠ *40 W. Broadway, Downtown* ☎ *520/882–7406* ⊕ *www.borderlandstheater. org*) presents new plays about Southwest border issues—often multicultural and bilingual—at venues throughout Tucson, usually from late June through April.

☺ Children of all ages love the clever melodramas at the **Gaslight Theatre** (⊠ *7010 E. Broadway Blvd., Eastside* ☎ *520/886–9428* ⊕ *www.the gaslighttheatre.com*), where hissing at the villain and cheering the hero are part of the audience's duty. **Invisible Theatre** (⊠ *1400 N. 1st Ave., Central* ☎ *520/882–9721* ⊕ *www.invisibletheatre.com*) presents contemporary plays and musicals.

NIGHTLIFE

BARS AND CLUBS

In addition to the places listed below, most of the major resorts have late spots for drinks or dancing. The Westward Look Resort's Lookout Bar, with its expansive view and classic rock band on Friday and Saturday nights, is a popular spot for dancing. The bars at Westin La Paloma, Hacienda del Sol, and Loews Ventana have live acoustic music on weekends.

BLUES AND JAZZ
Boondocks (⊠ *3306 N. 1st Ave., Central* ☎ *520/690–0991*) is the unofficial home of the Blues Heritage Foundation, hosting local and touring singer-songwriters. A jazz combo plays Thursday–Saturday nights and for Sunday brunch on the lovely patio of **Acacia** (⊠ *4340 N. Campbell Ave., St. Philip's Plaza, Foothills* ☎ *520/232–0101*). **Old Pueblo Grille** (⊠ *60 N.*

Alvernon Way, Central ☎520/326–6000) has live jazz on Sunday nights. **Ric's Café** (✉5605 *E. River Rd.*, *Northeast* ☎520/577–7272) features jazz musicians in the courtyard on Friday and Saturday nights.

COUNTRY AND WESTERN An excellent house band gets the crowd two-stepping on Tuesday through Saturday nights at the **Maverick** (✉6622 *E. Tanque Verde Rd.*, *Eastside* ☎520/298–0430).

GAY AND LESBIAN BARS **Ain't Nobody's Bizness** (✉2900 *E. Broadway Blvd.*, *Central* ☎520/318–4838) is the most popular lesbian bar in town. **IBT's (It's 'Bout Time)** (✉616 *N. 4th Ave.*, *University* ☎520/882–3053) is Tucson's most popular gay men's bar, with rock and disco DJ music and drag shows Wednesday and Saturday nights. Expect long lines on weekends.

The **Cactus Moon Café** (✉5470 *E. Broadway Blvd.*, *Central* ☎520/748–0049), catering to a mostly yuppie crowd, offers a standard mix of Top 40, hip-hop, and modern country, often with free appetizer buffets during happy hour. The **Chicago Bar** (✉5954 *E. Speedway Blvd.*, *Central* ☎520/748–8169) is a good place to catch blues, reggae, and rock.

ROCK AND MORE **Club Congress** (✉*Hotel Congress, 311 E. Congress St.*, *Downtown* ☎520/622–8848) is the main Friday venue for cutting-edge rock
★ bands, with a mixed-bag crowd of alternative rockers, international travelers, and college kids. Saturday brings a more outrageous crowd dancing to an electronic beat. **El Parador** (✉2744 *E. Broadway, Central* ☎520/881–2744) has a live salsa band Friday and Saturday night, with dance lessons Friday at 10 PM.

★ The **Nimbus Brewing Company** (✉3850 *E. 44th St.*, *Southeast* ☎520/745–9175) is the place for acoustic blues, folk, and bluegrass, not to mention good, cheap food and microbrew beer.

Plush (✉340 *E. 6th St., at 4th Ave.*, *University* ☎520/798–1298) hosts alternative-rock bands like Camp Courageous and Greyhound Soul, as well as local performers with a loyal following. You can go totally retro at the **Shelter** (✉4155 *E. Grant Rd.*, *Central* ☎520/326–1345), a former bomb shelter decked out in plastic 1960s kitsch, lava lamps, and JFK memorabilia, which plays Elvis videos and music by the likes of Burt Bacharach and Martin Denny.

CASINOS

After a long struggle with the state of Arizona, two Native American tribes operate casinos on their Tucson-area reservations west of the airport. They are quite unlike their distant and much grander cousins in Las Vegas and Atlantic City. Don't expect much glamour, ersatz or otherwise: these casinos are more like glorified video arcades, though you can lose money much faster. You'll be greeted by a wall of cigarette smoke (the reservation is exempt from antismoking laws) and the wail of slot machines, video poker, blackjack, roulette, and craps machines. The only "live" gaming is keno, bingo, blackjack, and certain types of poker. No one under age 21 is permitted.

The Pascua Yaqui tribe's **Casino of the Sun** (✉7406 *S. Camino de Oeste, off W. Valencia Rd. about 5 mi west of I–19, Southwest* ☎520/883–1700 or 800/344–9435 ⊕*www.casinosun.com*) has slot and video-gambling machines, high-stakes bingo, and live poker. A few miles west of the Casino of the Sun is their newer, larger facility, **Casino del Sol** (⊠ *5655 W. Valencia, Southwest* ☎ *520/883–1700 or 800/344–9435* ⊕ *www. casinodelsol.com*), with live poker and blackjack, bingo, slots, and an above-average Italian restaurant. An adjacent 4,600-seat outdoor amphitheater books entertainers like Bob Dylan and James Taylor. Free shuttle buses operate from points all over Tucson; call for a schedule. The Tohono O'odham tribe operates the **Desert Diamond Casinos** (⊠ *7350 S. Old Nogales Hwy., 1 mi south of Valencia, just west of the airport, South* ⊠ *I–19 at Pima Mine Rd., South* ☎ *520/294–7777 or 866/332–9467* ⊕ *www.desertdiamondcasino.com*), which has an indoor concert venue, one-armed bandits, and video poker in addition to live keno, bingo, and Stud High, Texas Hold'em, Omaha, and Stud Lo poker.

SHOPPING

Much of Tucson's retail activity is focused around malls, but shops with more character and some unique wares can be found in the city's open plazas: St. Philip's Plaza (River Road and Campbell Avenue), Plaza Palomino (Swan and Fort Lowell roads), Casas Adobes Plaza (Oracle and Ina roads), and La Encantada (Skyline Drive and Campbell Avenue).

The 4th Avenue neighborhood near the University of Arizona—especially between 2nd and 9th streets—is fertile ground for unusual items in the artsy boutiques, galleries, and secondhand-clothing stores. For in-town deals, the outlet stores at the Foothills Mall in northwest Tucson score high marks.

MALLS AND SHOPPING CENTERS

Broadway Village (⊠ *2926 East Broadway Blvd., at Country Club Rd., Central*), Tucson's first shopping center, was built in 1939. Although small by today's standards, this outdoor complex and neighboring strip of shops houses a few interesting stores such as Zocalo for colonial Mexican furniture, Yikes! for fabulous off-the-wall toys, and Picante for Mexican clothing and crafts.

★ **Casas Adobes Plaza** (⊠ *Oracle and Ina Rds., southwest corner, Northwest* ⊕ *www.casasadobesplaza.com*) originally served the ranchers and orange-grove owners in this once remote part of town, now the city's fastest-growing area. It's an outdoor, Mediterranean-style shopping center with a Whole Foods grocery store, the superb Wildflower and Blue Fin restaurants, a gelato shop, upscale pizzas at Sauce, Starbucks, and diverse boutiques and gift shops.

Foothills Mall (⊠ *7401 N. La Cholla Blvd. at Ina Rd., Northwest* ☎ *520/ 742–7191* ⊕ *www.shopfoothillsmall.com*) has a Barnes & Noble Superstore, a Saks Fifth Avenue outlet store, and many other outlets including Samsonite, Nike, and Adidas. A 16-screen cineplex, video arcade, and several restaurants round out the place.

La Encantada (⊠ *Skyline Dr. and Campbell Ave., Foothills* ☎ *520/299– 3566*), the newest outdoor mall, has close to 50 stores (and six restaurants) decidedly aimed at affluent consumers. North, a nouvelle Italian bistro, and Ra Sushi are the standout eateries. Trendy tenants include

Local ceramics and other arts and crafts are popular in Tucson and the nearby town Tubac.

Crate & Barrel, Pottery Barn, Coach, and Tiffany & Co., plus a huge gourmet grocery that also serves casual meals.

The Lost Barrio (⊠ *Park Ave. and 12th St., south of Broadway, Central* is a cluster of 10 shops in an old warehouse district; Southwestern and ethnic art, furniture, and funky gifts (both antique and modern) are specialties.

Old Town Artisans Complex (⊠ *186 N. Meyer Ave., Downtown* ☎ *520/623–6024*), across from the Tucson Museum of Art, has a large selection of Southwestern wares, including Native American jewelry, baskets, Mexican handicrafts, pottery, and textiles.

Park Place (⊠ *5870 E. Broadway Blvd., Eastside* ☎ *520/747–7575*) is a busy enclosed mall with an extensive food court, a 20-screen cineplex, and more than 120 stores, including Macy's and Borders.

Plaza Palomino (⊠ *2980 N. Swan Rd., at Fort Lowell Rd., Central* ☎ *520/795–1177*), an outdoor mall, has unique shops, galleries, and clothing boutiques. On Saturday you can sample locally grown produce, baked goods, salsas, and tamales at the farmers' market. The Red Sky Cafe is also here.

St. Philip's Plaza (⊠ *4280 N. Campbell Ave., at River Rd., Foothills* ☎ *520/886–7485*) has more than a dozen chic boutiques and galleries arranged around a series of Spanish-style outdoor patios. The restaurants Vivace and Acacia are located here, too.

Tucson Mall (⊠ *4500 N. Oracle Rd., at Wetmore Rd., Central* ☎ *520/293–7330*), an indoor mall on the Westside, has Dillard's, Macy's, JCPenney, and more than 200 specialty shops. For tasteful Southwestern-style T-shirts, belts, jewelry, and prickly-pear candies, check out the shops on "Arizona Avenue," a section of the first floor that's devoted to regional items.

SPECIALTY SHOPS

ART GALLERIES If you're seeking work by regional artists, you might want to drive down to Tubac, a community 45 mi south of Tucson (⇨ *See Side Trips Near Tucson*). **Art Life in Southern Arizona** (☏*520/797–1271* ⊕*artlifearizona. com*), published annually, lists galleries and artists statewide.

Dinnerware Contemporary Arts (⊠*264 E. Congress St., Downtown* ☏*520/792–4503*), a nonprofit, membership gallery, focuses on artists of Southern Arizona in various media, including painting, sculpture, digital art, and furniture.

Etherton Gallery (⊠*135 S. 6th Ave., Downtown* ☏*520/624–7370*) specializes in photography but also represents artists in other mediums.

Gallery Row at El Cortijo (⊠*3001 E. Skyline Dr., at Campbell Ave., Foothills*) is a complex of galleries that collectively represent regional and national artists working in all mediums, including Native American, Western, and contemporary painting, crafts, and jewelry.

Madaras Gallery (☏*520/615–3001*), at El Cortijo, has the bright watercolor prints of cacti and animals by the popular local artist Diana Madaras.

Obsidian Gallery (⊠*St. Philip's Plaza, 4340 N. Campbell Ave., Suite 90, Central* ☏*520/577–3598*) has exquisite glass, ceramic, and jewelry pieces.

CACTI **B&B Cactus Farm** (⊠*11550 E. Speedway Blvd., Eastside* ☏*520/721–4687*), which you'll pass en route to Saguaro National Park East, has a huge selection of cacti and succulents. They ship anywhere in the country.

★ **Native Seeds/Search** (⊠*526 N. 4th Ave., University* ☏*520/622–5561*), dedicated to preserving native crops and traditional farming methods, sells 350 kinds of seeds as well as Native American crafts.

JEWELRY **Abbott Taylor** (⊠*6383 E. Grant Rd., Eastside* ☏*520/745–5080*) creates custom designs in diamonds and other precious stones.

Beth Friedman (⊠*Joesler Village, 1865 E. River Rd., Suite 121, Foothills* ☏*520/577–6858*) sells unsurpassed designs in silver and semiprecious stones. The store also carries an eclectic selection of ladies' apparel, fine art, and home furnishings.

MEXICAN AND SOUTHWEST CRAFTS **Antigua de Mexico** (⊠*3235 W. Orange Grove Rd., Northwest* ☏*520/742–7114*) sells well-made furniture and crafts that you are not likely to find elsewhere in town.

Del Sol (⊠*435 N. 4th Ave., University* ☏*520/628–8765*) specializes in Mexican folk art, jewelry, and Southwest-style clothing.

NATIVE AMERICAN ARTS AND CRAFTS San Xavier Plaza, across from San Xavier mission and also part of the Tohono O'odham reservation, is a good place to find vendors and stores selling the work of this and other area tribes. Other shops are listed below.

Bahti Indian Arts (⊠*St. Philip's Plaza, 4300 N. Campbell Ave., Foothills* ☏*520/577–0290*) is owned and run by Mark Bahti, whose father, Tom, literally wrote the book on Native American art, including an early definitive work on kachinas. The store sells high-quality jewelry, pottery, rugs, art, and more.

7

Admission Fees Admission to Saguaro is $10 per vehicle and $5 for individuals on foot or bicycle; it is good for seven days from purchase. Annual passes cost $25.

Admission Hours The park opens at 7 AM and closes at sunset. It is in the mountain time zone.

Permits Obtain a required backcountry permit for $6 nightly per campsite from the Saguaro East Visitor Center up to two months in advance.

Visitor Information Saguaro National Park (⊠ *3693 S. Old Spanish Trail, Tucson, AZ* ☎ *520/733–5158 Saguaro West, 520/733–5153 Saguaro East* ⊕ *nps. gov/sagu*).

EXPLORING

Saguaro National Park is filled with its namesake cacti standing sentinel in the desert. Known for their height (often 50 feet) and arms reaching out in weird configurations, these slow-growing giants can take 15 years to grow a foot high and up to 75 years to grow their first arm. The cacti can live up to 200 years and weigh up to two tons. In late spring (usually May), the succulent's top is covered with tiny white blooms—the Arizona state flower. The cacti are protected by state and federal laws, so don't disturb them.

SCENIC DRIVES

Unless you're ready to lace up your hiking boots for a long desert hike, the best way to see Saguaro National Park is from the comfort of your car.

Bajada Loop Drive. This 6-mi drive winds through thick stands of saguaros and offers two picnic areas and a few short hikes, including one to a rock-art site. Although the road is unpaved and moderately bumpy, it's a worthwhile trade-off for access to some of the park's densest desert growth. It's one way between Hugh Norris Trail and Golden Gate Road, so if you want to make the complete circuit, travel counterclockwise. The road is susceptible to flash floods during the monsoon season (July and August), so check road conditions at the visitor center before proceeding. ⊠*Saguaro West.*

★ **Cactus Forest Drive.** This paved 8-mi drive provides a great overview of all Saguaro East has to offer. The one-way road, which circles clockwise, has several turnouts that make it easy to pull over and admire the scenery; you can also stop at two picnic areas and three easy nature trails. Repaved in 2006, Cactus Forest Drive now offers more scenic pullouts, new roadside displays, and wider bicycle lanes. This road is open from 7 AM to sunset daily. ⊠*Saguaro East.*

HISTORIC SITE

Manning Camp. The summer home of Levi Manning, onetime Tucson mayor, was a popular gathering spot for the city's elite in the early 1900s. The cabin can be reached via one of several challenging high-country trails: Douglas Spring Trail to Cow Head Saddle Trail (12 mi), Turkey Creek Trail (7.5 mi), and Tanque Verde Ridge Trail (15.4 mi).

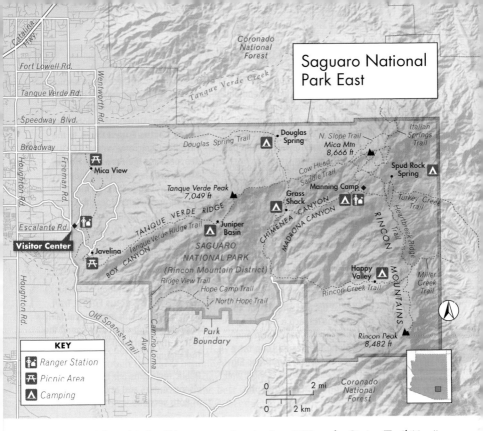

The cabin itself is not open for viewing. ⊠*Douglas Spring Trail (6 mi) to Cow Head Saddle Trail (6 mi), Saguaro East.*

SCENIC STOP

☪ **Signal Hill.** The most impressive petroglyphs, and the only ones with explanatory signs, are on the Bajada Loop Drive in Saguaro West. An easy 5-minute stroll from the signposted parking area takes you to one of the largest concentrations of rock carvings in the Southwest. You'll have a close-up view of the designs left by the Hohokam people between AD 900 and 1200, including large spirals some believe are astronomical markers. ⊠*4½ mi north of visitor center on Bajada Loop Dr., Saguaro West.*

VISITOR CENTERS

Red Hills Visitor Center. Take in gorgeous views of nearby mountains and the surrounding desert from the center's large windows and shaded outdoor terrace. A spacious gallery is filled with educational exhibits, and a lifelike display simulates the flora and fauna of the region. A 15-minute slide show, "Voices of a Desert," offers a poetic, Native American perspective of the saguaro. Park rangers and volunteers provide maps and suggest hikes to suit your interests. A nicely appointed gift shop and bookstore add to the experience. ⊠*2700 N. Kinney Rd., Saguaro West* ☎*520/733–5158* ☉*Daily 9–5.*

Saguaro National Park Flora and Fauna

The saguaro may be the centerpiece of Saguaro National Park, but more than 1,200 plant species, including 50 types of cactus, thrive in the park. Among the most common cacti here are the prickly pear, barrel cactus, and teddy bear cholla—so named because it appears cuddly, but rangers advise packing a comb to pull its barbed hooks from unwary fingers.

For many of the desert fauna, the saguaro functions as a high-rise hotel. Each spring the Gila woodpecker and gilded flicker create holes in the cactus and then nest there. When they give up their temporary digs, elf owls, cactus wrens, sparrow hawks, and other avians move in, as do dangerous Africanized honeybees.

You may not encounter any of the park's six species of rattlesnake or the Gila monster, a venomous lizard, but avoid sticking your hands or feet under rocks or into crevices. Look where you are walking; if you do get bitten, get to a clinic or hospital as soon as possible. Not all snakes pass on venom; 50% of the time the bite is "dry" (non-poisonous).

Wildlife, from bobcats to jackrabbits, is most active in early morning and at dusk. In spring and summer lizards and snakes are out and about, but tend to keep a low profile during the midday heat.

Desert vegetation. While walking this trail, keep in mind that it is the only off-road trail for bicyclists. ⊠ *Saguaro East.*

Cactus Garden Trail. This 100-yard paved trail in front of the Red Hills Visitor Center is wheelchair accessible, and has resting benches and interpretive signs about common desert plants. ⊠ *Saguaro West.*

☾ **Desert Discovery Trail.** Learn about plants and animals native to the region on this paved path in Saguaro West. The ½-mi loop is wheelchair accessible, and has resting benches and ramadas (wooden shelters that supply shade for your table). ⊠ *1 mi north of Red Hills Visitor Center, Saguaro West.*

☾ **Desert Ecology Trail.** Exhibits on this ¼-mi loop near the Mica View picnic area explain how local plants and animals subsist on a limited supply of water. ⊠ *2 mi north of Saguaro East Visitor Center.*

Freeman Homestead Trail. Learn a bit about the history of homesteading in the region on this 1-mi loop. Look for owls living in the cliffs above as you make your way through the lowland vegetation. ⊠ *2 mi south of Saguaro East Visitor Center at Javelina picnic area.*

Signal Hill Trail. This ¼-mi trail in Saguaro West is an easy, rewarding ascent to ancient petroglyphs carved a millennium ago by the Hohokam people. ⊠ *4½ mi north of Red Hills Visitor Center on Bajada Loop Dr., Saguaro West.*

MODERATE

Douglas Spring Trail. This challenging 6-mi trail leads almost due east into the Rincon Mountains. After a half-mile through a dense concentration of saguaros you reach the open desert. About 3 mi in is Bridal Wreath

Saguaro cactus are easy to anthropomorphize because of their giant "arms."

Falls, worth a slight detour in early spring when melting snow creates a larger cascade. Blackened tree trunks at the Douglas Spring Campground are one of the few traces of a huge fire that swept through the area in 1989. ⊠ *Eastern end of Speedway Blvd., Saguaro East.*

Hope Camp Trail. Well worth the 5.6-mi round-trip trek, this Rincon Valley Area hike offers gorgeous views of the Tanque Verde Ridge and Rincon Peak. ⊠ *From Camino Loma Alta trailhead to Hope Camp, Saguaro East.*

Sendero Esperanza Trail. You'll follow a sandy mine road for the first section of this 6-mi trail in Saguaro West, then ascend via a series of switchbacks to the top of a ridge where you'll cross the Hugh Norris Trail. Descending on the other side, you'll meet up with the King Canyon Trail. The Esperanza ("Hope") Trail is often rocky and sometimes steep, but rewards include ruins of the Gould Mine, dating back to 1907. ⊠ *1½ mi east of the intersection of Bajada Loop Dr. and Golden Gate Rd., Saguaro West.*

Sweetwater Trail. In Saguaro West, this one-way trail is the only footpath with access to Wasson Peak from the western side of the Tucson Mountains. The trailhead is located at the western end of El Camino del Cerro Road. After climbing 3.4 mi it ends at King Canyon Trail. Long and meandering, this little-used trail allows more privacy to enjoy the natural surroundings than some of the more frequently used trails. ⊠ *Saguaro West.*

Valley View Overlook Trail. On clear days you can spot the distinctive slope of Picacho Peak from this 1½-mi trail in Saguaro West. Even on an over-

EXPLORING

The site where **Tumacácori National Historic Park** now stands was visited by missionary Father Eusebio Francisco Kino in 1691, but the Jesuits didn't build a church here until 1751. You can still see some remnants of this simple structure, but the main attraction is the mission of San José de Tumacácori, built by the Franciscans around 1799–1803. A combination of circumstances—Apache attacks, a bad winter, and Mexico's withdrawal of funds and priests—caused the remaining inhabitants to flee in 1848. Persistent rumors of wealth left behind by both the Franciscans and the Jesuits led treasure seekers to pillage the site; it still bears those scars. The site was finally protected in 1908, when it became a national monument.

Information about the mission and the Anza trail is available at the visitor center, and guided tours are offered daily (more in winter than in summer). A small museum displays some of the mission's artifacts, and sometimes fresh tortillas are made on a wood-fire stove in the courtyard. In addition to a Christmas Eve celebration, costumed historical high masses are held at Tumacácori in spring and fall. An annual fiesta the first weekend of December has arts and crafts and food booths. ⊠ *1891 E. Frontage Rd., I–19, Exit 29, Tumacácori* ☎ *520/398–2341* ⊕ *www. nps.gov/tuma* ⊠ *$3* ⊙ *Daily 9–5.*

EN ROUTE Across the street from the Tumacácori National Historic Park, **The Santa Cruz Spice Factory** (⊠ *1868 E. Frontage Rd. Tumacacori* ☎ *520/398–2591*) packs and sells various spices if you'd like to take a taste of the Southwest home. A little museum, tasting area, and store are open Monday through Saturday.

WHERE TO STAY

$–$$ 🏨 **Esplendor Resort.** This isolated hotel and conference center has a historic, rather than hokey, Western feel, with a working blacksmith on-site and an elongated bar reminiscent of a Tombstone saloon. Some rooms continue the theme with cowhide headboards, tepee bed canopies, or whimsical bordello furnishings. Horseback riding is a popular activity here, but most guests come for the excellent golf course, the splendid views, and the isolation. **Pros:** a sense of leaving the world behind. **Cons:** mediocre restaurant; golf, tennis, and stables are across the highway (shuttle bus provided). ⊠ *1069 Camino Caralampi, off I–19 at Rio Rico Rd. (Exit 17), Rio Rico* ☎ *520/281–1901 or 800/288–4746* ⊕ *www. esplendor-resort.com* ⤳ *166 rooms, 14 suites* ⚇ *In-room: refrigerator, Wi-Fi. In-hotel: restaurant, bar, golf course, tennis courts, pool, gym, laundry service, no-smoking rooms* ⊟ *AE, D, MC, V.*

Southern Arizona

WORD OF MOUTH

"We spent a week in Tucson and drove to Bisbee and Tombstone for a day . . . the drive was as much a pleasure as the destination. We toured the mine, ate at the Bisbee Grille and walked around, then drove back to Tombstone . . . It's very touristy but that's OK. (Get it, OK, like corral.)"

—elizabeth_reed

WELCOME TO SOUTHERN ARIZONA

TOP REASONS TO GO

★ **Tour Kartchner Caverns:** The underground world of a living "wet" cave system is a rare and wonderful sensory experience. You'll see a multicolor limestone kingdom and probably feel "cave kiss" droplets grace your head; just *don't touch anything.*

★ **Hike in the Chiricahuas:** Stunning "upside-down" rock formations, flourishing wildlife, and relatively easy trails make for great hiking in this unspoiled region. The 3.4-mi Echo Canyon Loop Trail is a winner.

★ **Explore Bisbee:** Board the Queen Mine Train and venture into the life of a copper miner at the turn of the last century. Afterward, check out the narrow, hilly town's Victorian houses and thriving shops.

★ **Stargaze at Kitt Peak:** Clear skies and dry air provide ideal conditions for stargazing; the evening observation program, with top-notch telescopes and enthusiastic guides, is an excellent introduction to astronomy.

The Nature Conservancy's Patagonia-Sonoita Creek Preserve

1 Southeast Arizona. Old West history, colorful limestone caverns, bizarre hoodoo formations, sweeping "Sky Islands," Arizona's wine country, rolling grasslands, a world-renowned birding paradise, and rustic ranch retreats create a perfect mix of historical adventure and outdoor recreation.

GETTING ORIENTED

Southern Arizona ranges from the searing deserts surrounding Organ Pipe Cactus National Monument and the town of Yuma in the southwest to the soaring "Sky Islands"—steep hills that rise from the desert floor into the clouds—and rolling grasslands in the southeast. Towns are few and far between in the southwestern corner of the state, where the desert and dry climate rule. In stark contrast, the varied terrain in the southeastern region ranges from pine-forested mountains and cool canyons to desert grasslands and winding river valleys. A complex network of highways links the many communities situated in this part of the state, where the next town or attraction is just over the hill, making the decision on which way you want to go next the hardest part of traveling.

8

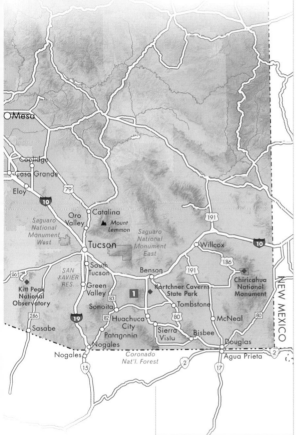

2 Southwest Arizona. The historical Yuma Territorial Prison, Yuma Crossing Historic Park, national wildlife refuges, Colorado River recreation, and Organ Pipe Cactus National Monument keep visitors busy in this remote desert region.

Kitt Peak Telescope

SOUTHERN ARIZONA PLANNER

When to Go

As you might expect, the desert areas are popular in winter, and the cooler mountain areas are more heavily visited in summer. Southern Arizona has developed seasonal travel, causing area hotels to adopt high-season (winter and spring) and low-season (summer and early fall) prices. In general, however, prices tend to be lower here than in the north. If you're seeking outdoor adventure, spring and fall are the best times to visit this part of the state. The region is in full bloom by late March and early April, and spring and fall are the peaks of birding season.

Getting Here and Around

Tucson is the major starting point for exploring both the southwest region and the southeast corner of the state. Yuma's remote location on the California–Arizona border makes it a destination in itself, and while it can be reached on a lengthy 3-hour drive from Tucson or Phoenix, it is most easily accessed through Yuma International Airport.

The best way to explore southeastern Arizona is on a leisurely road trip. The intricate network of highways in the San Pedro Valley provides looping access to the many scenic vistas and Old West communities, which makes the drive an integral part of the adventure. In stark contrast, a drive through the southwestern portion of the state is filled with long stretches of desert broken infrequently with tiny towns and intermittent gas stations. If you're heading west, pack a lunch, a few games, and plenty of music for entertainment along the way.

A car is essential in southern Arizona. The best plan is to fly into Tucson, which is the hub of the area, or Phoenix, which has the most flights. You can rent a car from several national companies at Yuma International Airport.

Amtrak trains run three times a week from Tucson to Benson and Yuma.

Making the Most of Your Time

The diverse geography of the region and the driving distances between sights require that you strategize when planning your trip. With Tucson as a starting point, the rolling hills and grasslands of Sonoita and Patagonia are little more than an hour away, as are the underground marvels in Kartchner Caverns (to the southeast) and the starry skies above Kitt Peak Observatory (to the southwest). You can explore the Old West of Tombstone, Bisbee, and the surrounding ghost towns in one day, or more leisurely in two. If you're heading to the cactus-studded hillsides at Organ Pipe Cactus National Monument, leave yourself at least a full day to explore the monument and the nearby town of Ajo. A trek through the stunning Chiricahua rock formations calls for an overnight stay, since the area is a 2½-hour drive southeast of Tucson.

What to Do and Where to Do It

Recreation in Cochise County centers on historic and natural treasures. History buffs can walk the streets of the Old West in Tombstone, revisit the infamous shootout at the OK Corral, and peek into the "birdcages" of a historic brothel. For a look at the mineral wealth that built Bisbee, take a tour of the Copper Queen Mine and visit the historic sights in this two-canyon town. Natural beauty and some of the best birding in the world draw flocks of visitors to southeastern Arizona's "Sky Islands," Coronado National Forest, and Chiricahua National Monument. Military might takes center stage at the remote ruins found at the Fort Bowie National Historic Site and at the active outpost of historic Fort Huachuca. Organ Pipe Cactus National Monument is worth the trip if you have a day to spare. If you're out this way, you may also want to visit the revitalized downtown district and historic highlights in Yuma.

Local Food and Lodging

There are plenty of chain hotels found throughout the southern region of Arizona, especially along the interstate highways, but why settle for boring basics in this beautiful and historic corner of the state? For the best experiences, seek out an old-fashioned room in a historic hotel, a rustic casita at a working cattle ranch, or a spacious suite in a stunning bed-and-breakfast. There are a few scattered dude ranches in the sweeping grasslands to the south. It's usually not hard to find a room any time of the year, but keep in mind that prices tend to go up in high season (winter and spring) and down in low season (summer through early fall).

In southern Arizona cowboy fare is more common than haute cuisine. There are exceptions, though, especially in the wine-growing area of Sonoita and in the trendy town of Bisbee, both popular for weekend outings from Tucson. And, as one would expect, Mexican food dominates menus.

Festivals and Events

Jan. Wings Over Willcox. This birding extravaganza is highlighted by the morning flights of thousands of wintering sandhill cranes lifting off from the Willcox Playa. ☎ *520/384–2272* ⊕ *www.wingsoverwillcox.com*

Feb. Cochise Cowboy Poetry and Music Gathering. In Sierra Vista, this festival showcases Western culture, history, and folklore. ☎ *520/417–6960* ⊕ *www.cowboypoets.com*

Oct. The Rex Allen Days. A rodeo and Western music and dance fill the first weekend in October, in Willcox. ☎ *520/384–2272* ⊕ *www.rexallendays.com*

Helldorado Days. The third weekend of October, history comes alive in Tombstone with gunfights in the streets, a parade, and an 1880s fashion show. ☎ *888/457–3929* ⊕ *www.tombstone.org*

8

WHAT IT COSTS					
	¢	$	$$	$$$	$$$$
Restaurant	under $8	$8–$12	$13–$20	$21–$30	over $30
Hotel	under $70	$70–$120	$121–$175	$176–$250	over $250

Restaurant prices are per person for a main course at dinner. Hotel prices are for a standard double in high season, excluding taxes and service charges.

Updated by
Mara Levin

Southern Arizona can do little to escape its cliché-ridden image as a landscape of cow skulls, tumbleweed, dried-up riverbeds, and mother lodes—but it doesn't need to. Abandoned mining towns and sleepy Western hamlets dot a lonely landscape of rugged rock formations, deep pine forests, dense mountain ranges, and scrubby grasslands.

South of Sierra Vista, just above the Mexican border, a stone marker commemorates the spot where the first Europeans set foot in what is now the United States. In 1540, 80 years before the pilgrims landed at Plymouth Rock, Spanish conquistador Don Francisco Vásquez de Coronado led one of Spain's largest expeditions from Mexico along the fertile San Pedro River valley, where the little towns of Benson and St. David are found today. They had come north to seek the legendary Seven Cities of Cíbola, where Native American pueblos were rumored to have doors of polished turquoise and streets of solid gold. The wealth of the region, however, lay in its rich veins of copper and silver, not tapped until more than 300 years after the Spanish marched on in disappointment. Once word of this cache spread, these parts of the West quickly became much wilder: fortune seekers who rushed to the region came face-to-face with the Chiricahua Apaches, led by Cochise and Geronimo, while Indian warriors battled encroaching settlers and the U.S. Cavalry sent to protect them.

Although the search for mineral booty in southeastern Arizona is more notorious, the western side of the state wasn't untouched by the rage to plunder. The leaching plant built by the New Cornelia Copper Company in 1917 transformed the sleepy desert community of Ajo into one of the most important mining districts in the state. Interest in going for the gold in California gave rise to the town of Yuma: the Colorado River had to be crossed to get to the West Coast, and Fort Yuma was established in part to protect the Anglo ferry business at a good fording point from Indian competitors. The Yuma tribe lost that battle, but another group of Native Americans, the Tohono O'odham, fared better in this part of the state. Known for a long time as the Papago—or "bean eaters"—they were deeded a large portion of their ancestral homeland by the U.S. Bureau of Indian Affairs.

SOUTHEAST ARIZONA

From the rugged mountain forests to the desert grasslands of Sierra Vista, the southeast corner of Arizona is one of the state's most scenic regions. Much of this area is part of Cochise County, named in 1881 in honor of the chief of the Chiricahua Apache. Cochise waged war against troops and settlers for 11 years, and was respected by Indian and non-Indian alike for his integrity and leadership. Today Cochise County is dotted with small towns, many of them smaller—and tamer—than they were in their heyday. Cochise County encompasses six, and part of the seventh, of the 12 mountain ranges that compose the 1.7-million-acre Coronado National Forest.

In the valleys between southeastern Arizona's jagged mountain ranges you'll discover the 19th-century charm of Bisbee—Queen of the Copper Camps. You can explore the eerie hoodoos and spires of Chiricahua National Monument and walk in the footsteps of the legendary Apaches, who valiantly stood against the U.S. Army until Geronimo's final surrender in 1886. This is also where you can travel through the grassy plains surrounding Sonoita and Elgin—the heart of Arizona's wine country.

A trip to this historically and ecologically important corner of the state will also take you to Fort Huachuca, the oldest continuously operating military installation in the Southwest; to southeastern Arizona's "Sky islands," the lush microclimates in the Huachuca and Chiricahua mountains where jaguars roam and migratory tropical birds flit through the canopy; and to historic mining and military towns, the tenacious survivors of the Old West—including Bisbee, Sierra Vista, and Tombstone.

TOMBSTONE

28 mi northeast of Sierra Vista via AZ 90, 24 mi south of Benson via AZ 80.

When prospector Ed Schieffelin headed out in 1877 to seek his fortune along the arid washes of San Pedro Valley, a patrolling soldier warned that all he'd find was his tombstone. Against all odds, his luck held out: he evaded bands of hostile Apaches, braved the harsh desert terrain, and eventually stumbled across a ledge of silver ore. The town of Tombstone was named after the soldier's offhand comment.

The rich silver lodes from the area's mines attracted a wide mix of fortune seekers ranging from prospectors to prostitutes and gamblers to gunmen. But as the riches continued to pour in, wealthy citizens began importing the best entertainment and culture that silver could purchase. Even though saloons and gambling halls made up two out of every three businesses on Allen Street, the town also claimed the Cochise County seat, a cultural center, and fancy French restaurants. By the early 1880s

$ ✕**Nellie Cashman's.** In 1882 a generous Tombstone pioneer opened a

AMERICAN   boardinghouse and restaurant catering to hard-rock miners. Named the "Angel of the Mining Camp," this kind-hearted entrepreneur was as well known for her hearty meals as for her good deeds. Today her spirit lives on at Nellie Cashman's—an 1880s-style restaurant decked out in cheery mismatched tablecloths and historical photographs. This homey favorite serves basic American food, including biscuits and gravy, chicken-fried steak, and hefty hamburgers. The strawberry-rhubarb pie is worth the trip alone. ✉*131 S. 5th St.* ☎*520/457–2212* ▭*AE, D, MC, V.*

WHERE TO STAY

$ ⊞**Holiday Inn Express.** Nestled into a hill just outside of town, this newer two-story property offsets basic rooms with spectacular views of the mountains and desert valley. The rooms are Western-theme, of course, and every night an old Western movie is screened in the dining room. **Pros:** clean, modern; nightly movie with free popcorn. **Cons:** very long walk (or 5-minute drive) into town; no elevator (request a ground-floor room if you don't want to climb stairs). ✉*580 W. Randolph Way* ☎*520/457–9507 or 888/465–4329* ⊕*www.hitombstone.com* ⟿*60 rooms, 7 suites* ⌂*In-room: refrigerator (some). In-hotel: pool, laundry facilities, Wi-Fi, no-smoking rooms* ▭*AE, D, MC, V* ⦿*BP.*

$–$$ ⊞**Legends Bed & Breakfast.** Five blocks from the hubbub of Allen Street, this plain but serviceable hacienda, circa 1980—not 1880—has views of the Dragoon Mountains from the sun porch and hot tub. Two guest rooms furnished with Victorian antiques share a bath, and two larger rooms with fireplaces have private baths. Two separate common areas add to the comfortable feel of the place. **Pros:** convenient to sights, quiet. **Cons:** not much of the Wild West theme here; hot tub is directly off one of the bedrooms. ✉*210 N. 9th St.* ☎*520/457–3858* ⊕*www. legendsbandb.com* ⟿*4 rooms* ⌂*In-room: no TV (some). In-hotel: no-smoking rooms* ▭*AE, D, MC, V* ⦿*BP.*

$ ⊞**Tombstone Boarding House Bed & Breakfast.** This friendly B&B is actu-

★   ally two meticulously restored 1880s adobes that sit side by side: guests sleep in one house and go next door for a hearty country breakfast. The spotless rooms, all with private entrances, have period furnishings collected from around Cochise County. Even if you don't stay here, the Lamplight Room restaurant is worth a visit. **Pros:** historic property, good breakfast included. **Cons:** small rooms, small bathrooms. ✉*108 N. 4th St.* ▵*Box 906, 85638* ☎*520/457–3716 or 877/225–1319* ⊕*www.tombstoneboardinghouse.com* ⟿*5 rooms* ⌂*In-room: no phone, no TV. In-hotel: restaurant, some pets allowed, no-smoking rooms* ▭*D, MC, V* ⦿*BP.*

NIGHTLIFE

★   If you're looking to wet your whistle, stop by the **Crystal Palace** (✉*436 E. Allen St., at 5th St.* ☎*520/457–3611*), where a beautiful mirrored mahogany bar, wrought-iron chandeliers, and tinwork ceilings date back to Tombstone's heyday. Locals come here on weekends to dance to live country-and-western music. Another hopping bar is **Big Nose Kate's Saloon** (✉*Allen St. between 4th and 5th Sts.* ☎*520/457–3107* ⊕*www. bignosekate.com*). Occasionally an acoustic concert livens things up

A visit to Tombstone is not complete without witnessing the recreated gunfight at the O. K. Corral.

even more at this popular pub, once part of the original Grand Hotel, built in 1881. Saloon girls encourage visitors to get into the 1880s spirit by dressing up in red-feather boas and dusters.

SHOPPING

Several curio shops and old-time photo emporiums await in the kitschy collection of stores lining Allen Street. Given the town's bloody history, it's not surprising that guns aren't permitted in most of the establishments, ★ but it's worth visiting **G. F. Spangenberg Pioneer Gun Shop** (⊠ *17 S. 4th St., at Allen St.* ☏*520/457–3227*), which opened in 1880. Wyatt Earp, Virgil Earp, Doc Holliday, the Clantons, and the McLowrys all purchased weapons at this shop, which still sells period firearms. Get into the spirit of the Old West by renting or purchasing 1880s-style costumes at **Madame Mustache** (⊠*419 E. Allen St., at 5th St.* ☏*520/457–3815*). **Silver Hills Trading Co** (⊠*504 E. Allen St.* ☏*520/457–3335*) offers everything from Native American jewelry to Southwestern souvenirs. Well-stocked **Tombstone Old West Books** (⊠*401 E. Allen St.* ☏*520/457–2252*) has a wide selection of books about Cochise County and the Old West.

BISBEE

★ *24 mi south of Tombstone.*

Like Tombstone, Bisbee was a mining boomtown, but its wealth was in copper, not silver, and its success continued much longer. The gnarled Mule Mountains aren't as impressive as some of the other mountain ranges in southern Arizona, but their rocky canyons concealed one of the richest mineral sites in the world.

Bird-watchers flock to Ramsey Canyon Preserve for rare eco-systems where deserts meet mountains.

$ ✕ **Velvet Elvis Pizza Co.** There aren't too many places where you can enjoy
PIZZA   a pizza heaped with organic veggies, a crisp salad of organic greens
★   tossed with homemade dressing, freshly pressed juice (try the beet-,
apple-, and lime-juice concoction), organic wine, and microbrewed or
imported beer while surrounded by images of Elvis *and* the Virgin Mary.
Owner Cecilia San Miguel uses a 1930s dough recipe for the restaurant's delightful crust, and you can pick up some pizza sauce in the gift
shop if you want to try your hand at pizza making at home. They also
have fabulous fruit pies. ⊠ *292 Naugle Ave.* ☎ *520/394–2102* ⊕ *www.
velvetelvispizza.com* ▭ *MC, V* ☯ *Closed Mon.–Wed.*

$ ✕ **Wagon Wheel Saloon.** The Wagon Wheel's restaurant, serving ribs,
AMERICAN   steaks, and burgers, is a more recent development, but the cowboy bar,
with its neon beer signs and mounted moose head, has been around
since the early 1900s. This is where every Stetson-wearing ranch hand
in the area comes to listen to the country jukebox and down a longneck,
maybe accompanied by some jalapeño peppers. ⊠ *400 W. Naugle Ave.*
☎ *520/394–2433* ▭ *MC, V.*

WHERE TO STAY

$$$$ ⊡ **Circle Z Ranch.** Rimmed by giant sycamore, ash, and cottonwood trees
☙   and surrounded by the Patagonia–Sonoita Creek Preserve, this seasonal
guest ranch served as a setting in the movie *Red River* and in several
episodes of *Gunsmoke*. Rooms in the adobe-style buildings have hardwood floors and area rugs, and antique Monterey pine chests. Riders
from beginner through advanced can be accommodated on adventurous, scenic trails. All meals, riding, and amenities are included. **Pros:**
excellent dude ranch experience in a lush, rather than desert, setting;

laid-back and friendly staff and guests. **Cons:** all-inclusive is pricey; three-night minimum stay. ✉*AZ 82, 4 mi southwest of town* ☐*Box 194, Sonoita 85624* ☎*520/394–2525 or 888/854–2525* ⊕*www.circlez. com* ⌂*24 rooms* ⚐*In-room: no a/c, no phone, no TV. In-hotel: restaurant, tennis court, pool, no-smoking rooms* ▭*MC, V* ⊙*Closed mid-May–Oct.* ¶◎*AI.*

$ ⚏**Duquesne House Bed & Breakfast/Gallery.** Built as a miners' board-
★ inghouse at the turn of the 20th century, this adobe home has rooms painted in pastel Southwest colors, lovingly and whimsically detailed by a local artist, and decorated with hand-stitched quilts and Mexican folk art. All the rooms are suites, with sofabeds in the sitting rooms, and have private entrances. Breakfast is served in your room or in the Santa Fe–style great room. A tiered backyard garden with hammocks adds to the tranquillity. **Pros:** quiet location only one block from town; cheerful, contemporary interior. **Cons:** few amenities. ✉*357 Duquesne Ave.* ☐*Box 772, Sonoita 85624* ☎*520/394–2732* ⌂*4 suites* ⚐*In-room: Wi-Fi, no TV* ▭*No credit cards* ¶◎*BP.*

NIGHTLIFE

If you're looking for some weekend rock 'n' roll fun in this sleepy section of the state, stop by **La Mision de San Miguel** (✉*335 McKeown Ave.* ☎*520/394–0123* ⊕*www.lamisionpatagonia.com* ⊙*Closed Mon.– Thurs.*). Inside a replica of a Spanish-colonial church, this tongue-in-cheek venue offers a smoke-free environment, a diverse mix of live country, bluegrass, flamenco, acoustic, and rockabilly music, and dancing into the wee hours.

SHOPPING

Patagonia is quickly turning into a shopping destination in its own right. Unlike the trendy shops in nearby Tubac, the stores here have reasonable prices in addition to small-town charm. Some of the artist spaces are open only by appointment. **Creative Spirit Gallery** (✉*317 McKeown Ave.* ☎*520/394–9186*) features jewelry, paintings, photography, quilts, and pottery by more than 60 local artists. **Global Arts Gallery** (✉*315 McKeown Ave.* ☎*520/394–0077*) showcases everything from local art and antiques to Native American jewelry, Middle Eastern rugs, and exotic musical instruments. At **High Spirits Flutes** (✉*714 Red Rock Ave.* ☎*520/394–2900 or 800/394–1523* ⊕*www.highspirits.com*) you can pick up Odell Borg Native American flutes. Shirley and Bill Ambrose sell decorative gourds and horseshoe art at their studio **Lil' Bit of Everything** (✉*567 Harshaw Ave.* ☎*520/394–2923*), by appointment only. **Mariposa Books & More** (✉*317 McKeown Ave.* ☎*520/394–9186*) shares quarters with the visitor center, and has a nice selection of new and used books on topics ranging from cooking to regional history. **Painted House Studio** (✉*355 McKeown Ave.* ☎*520/394–2740*) has an intriguing collection of hand-painted pieces including chairs, hutches, bowls, pillows, and birdhouses. The studio is open by appointment. The **Shooting Star Pottery** (✉*370 Smelter Ave.* ☎*520/394–2752*) displays clay pieces created by the village potter Martha Kelly by appointment only—or you can check out the mosaics Kelly and her students completed at the Patagonia Community Arts Center just off AZ 82.

8

CLOSE UP

Geronimo: No Bullet Shall Pass

The fearless Apache war shaman Geronimo, known among his people as "one who yawns," fought to the very last in the Apache Wars. His surrender to General Nelson Miles on September 5, 1886, marked the end of the Indian Wars in the West. Geronimo's fleetness in evading the massed troops of the U.S. Army and his legendary immunity to bullets made him the darling of sensationalistic journalists, and he became the most famous outlaw in America.

When the combined forces of the U.S. Army and Mexican troops failed to rout the powerful shaman from his territory straddling Arizona and Mexico, General Miles sent his officer Lieutenant Gatewood and relatives of Geronimo's renegade band of warriors to persuade Geronimo to parley with Miles near the mouth of Skeleton Canyon, at the edge of the Peloncillo Mountains. After several days of talks, Geronimo and his warriors agreed to the presented treaty and surrendered their arms.

Geronimo related the scene years later: "We stood between his troopers and my warriors. We placed a large stone on the blanket before us. Our treaty was made by this stone, as it was to last until the stone should crumble to dust; so we made the treaty, and bound each other with an oath." However, the political promises quickly unraveled, and the most feared of Apache medicine men spent the next 23 years in exile as a prisoner of war. He died on February 17, 1909, never having returned to his beloved homeland, and was buried in the Apache cemetery in Fort Sill, Oklahoma.

In 1934 a stone monument was built on State Route 80 in Apache, Arizona, as a reminder of Geronimo's surrender in 1886. The 16-foot-tall monument lies 10 mi northwest of the actual surrender site in Skeleton Canyon, where an unobtrusive sign and a pile of rocks mark the place where the last stone was cast.

in French and German, advise guests on hiking and birding activities at the Monument, 12 miles north; you'll see plenty of wildlife—from deer to Mexican Blue Jays—roaming their lush 27-acre property. **Pros:** excellent value, tranquil, convenient to Chiricahuas. **Cons:** hosts take vacation in late Spring—be sure to call ahead. ⊠ *13097 S. Hwy 181, Pearce* ☎ *520/824–3127* ⊕ *www.dreamcatcherbnb.com* ⇆ *5 rooms* ⌂ *In-room: refrigerator (some), no TV (some). In-hotel: Internet terminal, some pets allowed, no-smoking rooms* ⊟ *No credit cards* ⏇ *BP.*

$$$ ⌕ **Grapevine Canyon Ranch.** Nestled deep in the Dragoon Mountains'
★ Grapevine Canyon, this historic cattle ranch spurs the imagination with hair-raising tales of marauding Apache Indians and pioneering homesteaders. This natural stronghold once used by Chiricahua Indians led by Geronimo and Cochise is tamer these days, but the striking high-desert terrain and scattered cienegas (marshes) still provide enticing opportunities for adventurous exploration. Adjacent is a working cattle ranch, where visitors get the chance to watch—and, in some cases, participate in—day-to-day cowboy activities. Rooms are decorated in a mix of country and Southwestern-style furnishings—and all have spacious

The Remote Chiracahuas are filled with dramatic "upside-down" or "standing-up" volcanic rock formations.

decks and porches. Rates include riding, meals, and all activities. **Pros:** authentic dude ranch with outstanding riding. **Cons:** expensive; way out yonder; three-night minimum. ✉ *Highland Rd.* ✉ *Box 302, Pearce 85625* ☎ *520/826–3185 or 800/245–9202* ⊕ *www.gcranch.com* ➟ *12 rooms* ⚷ *In-room: no phone, refrigerator, no TV, Wi-Fi. In-hotel: pool, no kids under 12* ⊟ *D, MC, V* ⍢ *FAP.*

$ ⛺ **Portal Peak Lodge.** This barracks-style structure just east of Chiricahua National Monument near the New Mexico border is notable less for its rooms (clean and pleasant but nondescript) than for its winged visitors: the elegant trogon, 14 types of hummingbird, and 10 species of owl are among the 330 varieties of birds that flock to nearby Cave Creek Canyon. **Pros:** cheap; decks outside each room; on-site restaurant and store. **Cons:** basic lodging; isolated setting on east side of Chiricahuas. ✉ *1215 Main St.* ✉ *Box 364, Portal 85632* ☎ *520/558–2223* ⊕ *www. portalpeaklodge.com* ➟ *16 rooms* ⚷ *In-room: Wi-Fi, no phone. In-hotel: restaurant, no-smoking rooms* ⊟ *AE, D, MC, V.*

$$$–$$$$ ⛺ **Sunglow Guest Ranch.** Named after the ghost town of Sunglow, this lodge consists of nine casitas decked out in Southwestern style with fireplaces. Breakfast and dinner are served in a cozy dining room with a wraparound porch, and lunches can be packed for you (for an extra fee). There are no horses to ride, but you can borrow mountain bikes to explore the trails in Coronado National Forest, which borders the property on three sides. Birding and hiking are popular, and "star parties" attract astronomers, as this remote region offers some of the blackest skies around and perfect conditions for stargazing. **Pros:** very isolated, good for retreats. **Cons:** very isolated—it's still a 30-minute drive to hike in the Chiricahuas. ✉ *14066 S. Sunglow Rd., Pearce* ☎ *520/824–3334*

or 866/786–4569 ⊕*www.sunglowranch.com* ⟳4 *1-room casitas, 4 2-room casitas, 1 2-bedroom casita* ⟳*In-room: no phone, refrigerator, no TV. In-hotel: restaurant, Wi-Fi, bicycles, some pets allowed, no-smoking rooms* ⊟*AE, D, MC, V* ⍾O⍾*MAP* ⊙*Closed June–Aug.*

FORT BOWIE NATIONAL HISTORICAL SITE

8 mi northwest of Chiricahua National Monument.

GETTING HERE AND AROUND

Take AZ 186 west from Chiricahua National Monument; 5 mi north of junction with AZ 181, signs direct you to road leading to fort. Upon entering the site, you'll drive down a winding gravel road to a parking lot, where a challenging trail leads 1½ mi to the historic site.

EXPLORING

It's a bit of an outing to **Fort Bowie National Historical Site,** the site of Arizona's last battle between Native Americans and U.S. troops in the Dos Cabezas (Two-Headed) Mountains, but history buffs will find it an interesting diversion with the added benefit of high-desert scenic beauty. Once a focal point for military operations—the fort was built here because Apache Pass was an important travel route for Native Americans and wagon trains—it now serves as a reminder of the brutal clashes between the two cultures. The fort itself is virtually in ruins, but there's a small ranger-staffed visitor center with historical displays, restrooms, and books for sale.

Points of interest along the trail, indicated by historic markers, include the remnants of an Apache wickiup (hut), the fort cemetery, Apache Springs (their water source), and the **Butterfield stage stop,** a crucial link in the journey from east to west in the mid-19th century that happened to be in the heart of Chiricahua Apache land. Chief Cochise and the stagecoach operators ignored one another until sometime in 1861, when hostilities broke out between U.S. Cavalry troops and the Apache. After an ambush by the chief's warriors at Apache Pass in 1862, U.S. troops decided a fort was needed in the area, and Fort Bowie was built within weeks. There were skirmishes for the next 10 years, followed by a peaceful decade. Renewed fighting broke out in 1881. Geronimo, the new leader of the Indian warriors, finally surrendered in 1886. ⊠*3203 S. Old Fort Bowie Rd., Apache Pass Rd., 26 mi southeast of Willcox* ☎*520/847–2500* ⊕*www.nps.gov/fobo* ⍾*Free* ⊙*Daily 8–4:30.*

WILLCOX

26 mi northwest of Fort Bowie National Historical Site on AZ 186.

The small town of Willcox, in the heart of Arizona ranching country, began in the late 1870s as a railroad construction camp called Maley. When the Southern Pacific Railroad line arrived in 1880, the town was renamed in honor of the highly regarded Fort Bowie commander, General Orlando B. Willcox. Once a major shipping center for cattle ranchers and mining companies, the town has preserved its rustic charm; the downtown area looks like an Old West movie set. An elevation of 4,167 feet means moderate summers and chilly winters, ideal for growing apples, and apple pie fans from as far away as Phoenix make pilgrimages to sample the harvest.

EXPLORING

Don't miss the mile-high apple pies and hand-pressed cider at **Stout's Cider Mill** (⊠*1510 N. Circle I Rd.* ☎*520/384–3696*). Pick your own apples just outside of town at **Apple Annie's Orchards** (⊠*2081 W. Hardy Rd.* ☎*520/384–2084*) from late August to early October.

If you visit in winter, you can see some of the more than 10,000 sandhill cranes that roost at the **Willcox Playa**, a 37,000-acre area resembling a dry lake bed 12 mi south of Willcox. They migrate in late fall and head north to nesting sites in February, and bird-watchers migrate to Willcox the third week in January for the annual Wings over Willcox bird-watching event held in their honor.

Outside Willcox is the headquarters for the **Muleshoe Ranch Cooperative Management Area** (⊠*6502 N. Muleshoe Ranch Rd.* ☎*520/507–5229* ⊕*www.nature.org* ⊙*Mar. and Apr., daily 8–5; June–Aug., weekends 8–5; Sept.–Feb. and May, Thurs.–Mon. 8–5*), nearly 50,000 acres of riparian desert land in the foothills of the Galiuro Mountains that are jointly owned and managed by the Nature Conservancy, the U.S. Forest Service, and the U.S. Bureau of Land Management. It's a 30-mi drive on a dirt road to the ranch—it takes about an hour—but the scenery, wildlife, and hiking are worth the bumps. The varied terrain of mesquite bosques, desert grasslands, and rocky canyons is home to a diverse array of wildlife, including desert tortoise, javelina, mule deer, hognose skunk, Montezuma quail, and great horned owl. You might also catch a glimpse of roaming bands of coatimundi—unusual looking omnivores resembling land-bound monkeys. Backcountry hiking and mountain-biking trips can be arranged by the ranch, and overnight accommodations are available *(see below)*. Guided 1-mi nature hikes are held on Saturdays at 8 AM from September through May. To reach the ranch, take Exit 340 off Interstate 10, turn right on Bisbee Avenue, and continue to Airport Road, turn right again, and after 15 mi take the right fork at a junction just past a group of mailboxes and continue to the end of the road.

The **Rex Allen Arizona Cowboy Museum,** in Willcox's historic district, is a tribute to Willcox's most famous native son, cowboy singer Rex Allen. He starred in several rather average cowboy movies during the 1940s and '50s for Republic Pictures, but he's probably most famous as the friendly voice that narrated Walt Disney nature films of the 1960s. Check out the glittery suits the star wore on tour—they'd do Liberace proud. A special family rate is $5. ⊠*150 N. Railroad Ave.* ☎*520/384–4583 or 877/234–4111* ⊕*www.rexallenmuseum.org* ☎*$2* ⊙*Daily 10–4.*

Learn about the fierce Chiricahua Apaches and the fearless leaders Cochise and Geronimo at the **Chiricahua Regional Museum and Research Center,** located in downtown Willcox. Other interesting tidbits about the area can be found in displays featuring the U.S. Cavalry, a nice collection of rocks and minerals, and relics of the famed Butterfield Overland Stage Route. One oddity the museum points out is that the memoirs of Civil War general Orlando Willcox, for whom the town was named, don't even mention a visit to Arizona. ✉ *127 E. Maley St.* ☎ *520/384–3971* 🍽️*$2* ⊙*Mon.–Sat. 10–4.*

WHERE TO EAT AND STAY

¢   ✗ **Salsa Fiesta Mexican Restaurant.** You can't miss the bright neon lights of

MEXICAN   this little restaurant, just south of Interstate 10 at Exit 340 in Willcox. The interior is cheerful and clean, with tables, chairs, and walls painted in a spicy medley of hot pink, purple, turquoise, green, and orange. The menu consists of Mexican standards, and the salsa bar runs the gamut from mild to super-hot. There is a modest selection of domestic and Mexican beers, and takeout is available. ✉ *1201 W. Rex Allen Dr.* ☎ *520/384–4233* ⊟ *AE, D, MC, V* ⊙ *Closed Tues.*

$–$$ 🏨 **Muleshoe Ranch.** This turn-of-the-20th-century ranch is run by the Arizona chapter of the Nature Conservancy. Five casitas with kitchens sit in the pristine grassland foothills of the Galiuro Mountains, four around a courtyard hacienda-style. The fifth, a stone cabin set off by itself for more privacy, is the only unit open to families with children. The ranch has a visitor center, 22 mi of hiking trails, a guided, ¾-mi nature walk on Saturday at 9 AM, and private natural hot springs. There's a two-night minimum stay. **Pros:** good hiking, good value for groups, hot springs. **Cons:** no services nearby, and closest town is Willcox (30 mi away). ✉ *6502 N. Muleshoe Ranch Rd.* ☎ *520/212–4295* ⊕ *www.nature.org* 🔑*5 units* 🔌 *In-room: no a/c (some), no phone, kitchen, no TV* ⊟ *AE, D, MC, V* ⊙ *Closed June–Aug.*

TEXAS CANYON

Fodor's Choice   *16 mi southwest of Willcox off I–10.*

★   A dramatic change of scenery along Interstate 10 will signal that you're entering Texas Canyon. The rock formations here are exceptional—huge boulders appear to be delicately balanced against each other.

EXPLORING

Texas Canyon is the home of the **Amerind Foundation** (a contraction of "American" and "Indian"), founded by amateur archaeologist William Fulton in 1937 to foster understanding about Native American cultures. The research facility and museum are housed in a Spanish colonial–style structure designed by noted Tucson architect H.M. Starkweather. The museum's rotating displays of archaeological materials, crafts, and photographs give an overview of Native American cultures of the Southwest and Mexico. The adjacent Fulton–Hayden Memorial Art Gallery displays an assortment of art collected by William Fulton. Permanent exhibits include the work of O'odham women potters, an exquisite collection of Hopi kachina dolls, prized paintings by acclaimed Hopi artists, Pueblo pottery ranging from prehistoric pieces to modern ceramics, and archaeological exhibits on the Indian cultures of the prehistoric Southwest. The museum's gift shop has a superlative selection of Native American art, crafts, and jewelry. ✉ *2100 N. Amerind Rd., 1 mi southeast of I–10, Exit 318, Dragoon* ☎ *520/586–3666* ⊕ *www.amerind.org* 🎫*$5* ⊙ *Tues.–Sun. 10–4.*

WHERE TO STAY

\$\$–\$\$\$ ⚎ **Triangle T Guest Ranch.** Enjoy the romance of the Old West at this historic ranch situated on 160 acres of prime real estate in Texas Canyon. Although the cozy casitas offer Western charm, the big draw to this rustic ranch is the immediate access to the startling and stunning rock formations found in the canyon. Campsites with full hook-ups are available for $30. **Pros:** horseback riding (extra fee) and hiking trails; good base for exploring the region. **Cons:** expensive for this area; isolated. ✉ *Dragoon Rd., at Exit 318 off I–10* ⌂ *Box 218, Dragoon 85609* ☎ *520/586–7533* ⊕ *www.triangletguestranch.com* ⌖ *11 casitas* ♿ *In room: no phone, no TV, kitchen (some), Wi-Fi. In-hotel: restaurant, pool, bar, some pets allowed, no-smoking rooms* ▭ *MC, V.*

BENSON

12 mi west of Texas Canyon and 50 mi southeast of Tucson via I–10.

Back in its historic heyday as a Butterfield stagecoach station, and later as the hub of the Southern Pacific Railroad, Benson was just a place to stop on the way to somewhere else. That started to change with the 1974 discovery of a pristine cave beneath the Whetstone Mountains west of Benson, culminating 25 years later with the opening of Kartchner Caverns State Park, one of the most remarkable living cave systems in the world.

GETTING HERE AND AROUND

Amtrak runs trains from Tucson east to the Benson depot three times a week. The Benson Visitor Center is in the train depot. Benson Taxi offers transport services in the Benson area.

ESSENTIALS

Transportation Contacts Benson Taxi (✉ *Benson* ☎ *520/586–1294*). **Benson train station** (✉ *4th St. at San Pedro Ave., Benson*).

EXPLORING

Though the city is undergoing some modern development, you can see the story of Benson's past at the little **San Pedro Valley Arts and Historical Society Museum** (✉ *180 S. San Pedro Ave. at E. 5th St.* ☎ *520/586–3070*), a free museum open Tuesday through Saturday (but closed in August). Exhibits include a re-creation of an old-fashioned grocery store and railroad paraphernalia.

As you pass Benson on Interstate 10, watch for Ocotillo Avenue, Exit 304. Take a left and drive about 2¼ mi, where a mailbox with a backward sw signals that you've come to the turnoff for **Singing Wind Bookshop.** Make a right at the mailbox and drive ¼ mi until you see a green gate. Let yourself in, close the gate, and go another ¼ mi to the shop. If you don't see Winifred Bundy, who also runs the ranch, ring the gong out front. She knows just about every regional author around, so this unique bookshop-on-a-ranch has signed copies of books on just about any Southwestern topic. This chatty bibliophile also frequently shar her love of the area with visitors, throwing in choice tidbits ab obscure sights and her literary friends' favorite haunts. She doesn't

8

DID YOU KNOW?

Abandoned mining gear, like this ore loading chute, is all that remains of some of Southern Arizona's former boom towns. Copper, silver, and gold have all attracted miners at different times.

credit cards, though. ⊠*700 W. Singing Wind Rd.* ☎*520/586–2425* ⊙*Daily 9–5.*

WHERE TO EAT

$$

STEAK

★

✕**Chute-Out Steakhouse & Saloon.** Don't be deceived by the unassuming exterior of this stucco steak house and bar a block from Benson's main street. Once inside this warm and welcoming place, you'll understand why it's so popular. The food is excellent, and the service is efficient and friendly. Mesquite-grilled steaks, ribs, chicken, and seafood, fresh-baked breads and desserts, and salads (the house dressing is superb) make this spot well worth the visit. ⊠*161 S. Huachuca St.* ☎*520/586–7297* ▭*AE, D, MC, V* ⊙*No lunch.*

$

AMERICAN

✕**Palatiano's.** The kitchen at this family-friendly roadhouse, a local favorite, turns out traditional diner fare—including great burgers and fries—as well as pastas, Italian-style entrées, and Greek specialties like moussaka and spanikopita. In the center of the no-frills dining room there's a big salad bar, too—unusual in these parts. ⊠*601 W. 4th St.* ☎*520/586–3523* ▭*AE, MC, V* ⊙*No dinner Sun.*

¢

MEXICAN

★

✕**Ruiz's Mexican Food & Cantina.** In this part of the world the name is pronounced "Reese." This homey spot on the main drag has been in operation since 1959, serving a daily stream of customers, morning to night, hungry for green-corn tamales, chiles rellenos, *topopo* (deep-fried tortilla) salads, and other specialties. The handmade Sonoran-style dishes all originate from the owner's family recipes, giving the food a truly authentic flair rarely found on this side of the border. The adjoining bar hosts live bands on weekends. ⊠*687 W. 4th St.* ☎*520/586–2707* ▭*MC, V.*

WHERE TO STAY

$–$$

☺

★

🖃**Astronomers Inn.** You don't have to be an astronomer to enjoy this hilltop lodging on the grounds of the private Vega-Bray Observatory, but eight powerful telescopes are available for your universe-viewing pleasure. The B&B reflects the owners' delight in science: the comfortable rooms have such gadgets as lamps that simulate lightning and decorations (visible in black light) that resemble constellations painted on the ceiling. A special section in the science room is dedicated to kids. Astronomers travel from Tucson to the observatory on clear evenings to lead an evening of observation and science classes. The inn also has a 2-mi nature trail, and two ponds for boating. **Pros:** stargazing; country setting a few miles east of town. **Cons:** too focused on the stars for some. ⊠*1311 Astronomers Rd., 2 mi southeast of I–10, Exit 306* ☎*520/586–7906* ⊕*www.astronomersinn.com* ⬎*5 rooms* ⚹*In-room: kitchen (some), Wi-Fi. In-hotel: no-smoking rooms* ▭*D, MC, V* ⊚|*BP.*

$–$$

🖃**Holiday Inn Express.** The closest lodging to Kartchner Caverns State Park, this modern motel sits just off Interstate 10 at the "Kartchner Corridor," a few miles west of Benson. It has the comfort and amenities you'd expect, but with a Southwestern elegance rarely found in chain properties around the area. Rooms have coffeemakers and hair dryers, and a Continental breakfast is included. **Pros:** clean; friendly; convenient location. **Cons:** just off the highway; not particularly serene or scenic. ⊠*630 S. Village Loop* ⊕*Box 2252, Benson 85602* ☎*520/586–8800*

8

Kitt Peak National Observatory is open to visitors during the day, but it's easy to enjoy the night sky here.

path tunnel, which goes down hundreds of feet into the mountain. Kitt Peak scientists use these high-power telescopes to conduct vital solar research and observe distant galaxies.

The visitor center has exhibits on astronomy, information about the telescopes, and hour-long guided tours ($4 per person) that depart daily at 10, 11:30, and 1:30. Complimentary brochures enable you to take self-guided tours of the grounds, and there's a picnic area about 1½ mi below the observatory. The observatory buildings have vending machines, but there are no restaurants or gas stations within 20 mi of Kitt Peak. The observatory offers a nightly observing program ($46 per person) except from July 15 to September 1; reservations are necessary. ⊠ *AZ 386, Pan Tak* ☎ *520/318–8726, 520/318–7200 recorded message* ⊕ *www.noao.edu* ◻ *$2* ⊙ *Visitor center daily 9–3:45.*

SELLS

32 mi southwest of Kitt Peak via AZ 386 to AZ 86.

The Tohono O'odham Reservation, the second-largest in the United States, covers 4,400 square mi between Tucson and Ajo, stretching south to the Mexican border and north almost to the city of Casa Grande. To the south of Kitt Peak, the 7,730-foot Baboquivari Peak is considered sacred by the Tohono O'odham as the home of their deity, I'itoi ("elder brother"). Less than halfway between Tucson and Ajo, Sells—the tribal capital of the Tohono O'odham—is a good place to stop for gas or a soft drink. Much of the time there's little to see or do

BORDER TOWN SAFETY: NOGALES, MEXICO

⚠Drug-related violence in Mexico—especially near the U.S. border—has increased to the point that the U.S. government has strongly discouraged travel in and around Mexico border towns.

Before planning a trip to Nogales check ⊕www.state.gov/travel for updates and details.

Nogales used to draw tourists and locals, who would park on the American side and walk across the border to Mexico. Though shopping bargains and cheap bars are enticing, safety issues have changed in recent years.

If you must cross, bring your passport, remain alert, and stay in the central area on Avenida Obregón, which begins a few blocks west of the border entrance and runs north-south.

in Sells, but in winter an annual rodeo and fair attract thousands of Native American visitors.

EXPLORING

For traditional Indian and Mexican food like fry bread, tacos, and chili, try the **Papago Cafe** (⊠*AZ 86, near Chevron Station* ☏*520/383–3510*). At the Sells Shopping Center, the good-size market **Basha's Deli & Bakery** (⊠*Topawa Rd.* ☏*520/383–2546*) can supply all the makings for a picnic.

AJO

90 mi northwest of Sells.

"Ajo" (pronounced *ah*-ho) is Spanish for garlic, and some say the town got its name from the wild garlic that grows in the area. Others claim the word is a bastardization of the Indian word *au-auho,* referring to red paint derived from a local pigment.

For many years Ajo, like Bisbee, was a thriving Phelps Dodge Company town. Copper mining had been attempted in the area in the late 19th century, but it wasn't until the 1911 arrival of the Calumet & Arizona Mining Company that the region began to be developed profitably. Calumet and Phelps Dodge merged in 1935, and the huge pit mine produced millions of tons of copper until it closed in 1985. Nowadays Ajo is pretty sleepy; the town's population of 4,000 has a median age of 51, and most visitors are on their way to or from Rocky Point, Mexico.

At the center of town is a sparkling white Spanish-style plaza. The shops and restaurants that line the plaza's covered arcade today are rather modest. Unlike Bisbee, Ajo hasn't yet drawn an artistic crowd—or the upscale boutiques and eateries that tend to follow. Chain stores and fast-food haven't made a beeline here either—you'll find only one Dairy Queen and a Pizza Hut in this remote desert hamlet.

8

EXPLORING

You get an expansive view of Ajo's ugly gash of an open-pit mine, almost 2 mi wide, from the **New Cornelia Open Pit Mine Lookout Point.** Some of the abandoned equipment remains in the pit, and mining operations are diagrammed at the volunteer-run visitors' shelter, where there's a 30-minute film about mining. ⊠*Indian Village Rd.* ☏*520/387–7742* *Free* ⊙*Call for hrs.*

The **Ajo Historical Society Museum** has collected a mélange of articles related to Ajo's past from local townspeople. The displays are rather disorganized, but the historical photographs and artifacts are interesting, and the museum is inside the territorial-style St. Catherine's Indian Mission, built around 1942. ⊠*160 Mission St.* ☏*520/387–7105* *Donations requested* ⊙*Oct.–Apr., daily noon–4.*

The 860,000-acre **Cabeza Prieta National Wildlife Refuge,** about 10 minutes from Ajo, was established in 1939 as a preserve for endangered bighorn sheep and other Sonoran Desert wildlife. A permit is required to enter, and only those with four-wheel-drive vehicles, needed to traverse the rugged terrain, can obtain one from the refuge's office. ⊠*1611 N. 2nd Ave., Ajo* ☏*520/387–6483* ⊕*www.fws.gov/refuges* *Free* ⊙*Office weekdays 7:30–4:30, refuge daily dawn–dusk.*

WHERE TO EAT AND STAY

$ ✕**Ranch House Restaurant.** Carnivores will find plenty of good eatin'—
AMERICAN like rib eyes, T-bones, pork chops, and the epitome of country-style cooking, chicken-fried steak—at this unassuming roadhouse decorated in (you guessed it) a cowboy theme. The lower-priced lunch menu emphasizes burgers, bratwursts, and sandwiches. Portions are generous, and the service is friendly. ⊠*661 N. 2nd Ave.* ☏*520/387–6226* ⊟*AE, MC, V* ⊙*Closed Sun.*

$ 🏠**Guest House Inn Bed & Breakfast.** Built in 1925 to accommodate visiting Phelps Dodge VIPs, this lodging is a favorite for birders: guests can head out early to nearby Organ Pipe National Monument or just sit on the patio and watch the quail, cactus wrens, and other warblers that fly in to visit. Rooms are furnished in various Southwestern styles, from light Santa Fe to rich Spanish colonial. **Pros:** pleasant hosts, well-preserved home. **Cons:** no TV. ⊠*700 Guest House Rd.* ☏*520/387–6133* ⊕*www. guesthouseinn.biz* ⇆*4 rooms* ⚬*In-room: no phone, refrigerator, no TV, Wi-Fi. In-hotel: no-smoking rooms* ⊟*DC, MC, V* ⦿*BP.*

ORGAN PIPE CACTUS NATIONAL MONUMENT

32 mi southwest of Ajo.

GETTING HERE

From Ajo, backtrack to Why and take AZ 85 south for 22 mi to reach the visitor center.

SAFETY AND PRECAUTIONS

Be aware that Organ Pipe has become an illegal border crossing hot spot. Migrant workers and drug traffickers cross from Mexico under cover of darkness. At this writing, much of Puerto Blanco Drive has been closed indefinitely to the public. A two-way road that only travels

5 of the 53 mi on Puerto Blanco Drive is open, but the rest of the road will remain closed due to continuing concerns over its proximity to the U.S.–Mexico border. Even so, park officials emphasize that tourists have only occasionally been the victims of isolated property crimes—primarily theft of personal items from parked cars. Visitors are advised by rangers to keep valuables locked and out of plain view and not to initiate contact with groups of strangers whom they may encounter on hiking trails.

EXPLORING

Organ Pipe Cactus National Monument, abutting Cabeza Prieta National Wildlife Refuge but much more accessible to visitors, is the largest habitat north of the border for organ-pipe cacti. These multi-armed cousins of the saguaro are fairly common in Mexico but rare in the United States. Because they tend to grow on south-facing slopes, you won't be able to see many of them unless you take one of the two scenic loop drives: the 21-mi **Ajo Mountain Drive** or the 53-mi **Puerto Blanco Drive,** both on winding, graded, one-way dirt roads.

A campground at the monument has 208 RV (no hookups) and tent sites. Facilities include a dump station with potable water, flush toilets, grills, and picnic tables. ⊠ *AZ 85* ☎ *520/387–6849* ⊕ *www.nps.gov/ orpi* 🖃 *$8 per vehicle* ⊙ *Visitor center daily 8–5.*

YUMA

170 mi northwest of Ajo.

Today many people think of Yuma as a convenient stop between Phoenix or Tucson and San Diego—and this was equally true in the relatively recent past. It's difficult to imagine the lower Colorado River, now dammed and bridged, as either a barrier or a means of transportation, but until the early part of the 20th century this section of the great waterway was a force to contend with. Records show that since at least 1540 the Spanish were using Yuma (then the site of a Quechan Indian village) as a ford across a relatively shallow stretch of the Colorado.

Three centuries later, the advent of the shallow-draft steamboat made the settlement a point of entry for fortune seekers heading through the Gulf of California to mining sites in eastern Arizona. Fort Yuma was established in 1850 to guard against Indian attacks, and by 1873 the town was a county seat, a U.S. port of entry, and an army depot.

The steamboat shipping business, undermined by the completion of the Southern Pacific Railroad line in 1877, was finished off by the building of Laguna Dam in 1909. During World War II Yuma Proving Ground was used to train bomber pilots, and General Patton readied some of his desert war forces for battle at classified areas near the city. Many who served here during the war returned to Yuma to retire, and the city's economy now relies largely on tourism. The population swells during the winter months with retirees from cold climates who park their homes on wheels at one of the many RV communities. One fact may explain this: according to National Weather Service statistics, Yuma is the sunniest city in the United States.

Crested Saguaros at Organ Pipe National Monument are found alongside the monument's namesake cacti and other succulent plants.

¢ ✕**Lutes Casino.** Packed with locals at lunchtime, this large, funky res-
SOUTHWESTERN taurant and bar claims to be the oldest pool hall and domino parlor
★ in Arizona. It's a great place for a burger and a brew. The "Especial"
combines a cheeseburger and a hot dog and adds a generous dollop of
Lutes' "special sauce." ⊠*221 S. Main St.* ☏*928/782–2192* ⊕*www.
lutescasino.com* ⊟No credit cards.

$$ ✕**River City Grill.** This hip downtown restaurant is a favorite dining spot
AMERICAN for locals and visitors. It gets a bit loud on weekend nights, but the
★ camaraderie of diners is well worth it. Owners Nan and Tony Bain dish
out a medly of flavors drawing on Mediterranean, Pacific Rim, Indian,
and Caribbean influences. For starters you can sample everything from
Vietnamese spring rolls to curried mussels. Entrées include delicacies
like grilled wild salmon, rack of lamb, and such vegetarian dishes as
ricotta-and-spinach ravioli. ⊠*600 W. 3rd St.* ☏*928/782–7988* ⊕*www.
rivercitygrill.com* ⊟*AE, D, DC, MC, V* ⊘*No lunch weekends.*

WHERE TO STAY

$ ▥**Best Western Coronado Motor Hotel.** This Spanish tile–roofed motor
hotel was built in 1938 and has been well cared for. Bob Hope used to
stay here during World War II, when he entertained the gunnery troops
training in Yuma. Yuma Landing Restaurant & Lounge is on-site with
an impressive collection of historical photos. **Pros:** convenient to AZ
8, and a short walk from historic downtown area; retro property; full
breakfast at restaurant. **Cons:** some highway noise in rooms. ⊠*233 S.
4th Ave.* ☏*928/783–4453 or 800/528–1234* ⊕*www.bwcoronado.com*
⇰*86 rooms* ♿*In-room: refrigerator, DVD, Wi-Fi. In-hotel: restaurant,
bar, pool, laundry facilities* ⊟*AE, D, DC, MC, V* ⦿*BP.*

$$ ⓣ **Clarion Suites.** One wing of this sprawling hotel surrounds a well-manicured courtyard with a fountain; another faces the pool and Cabana Club, where the complimentary breakfast and happy-hour drinks are served. This is an all-suites property, and each accommodation has a separate sitting area with a desk. **Pros:** spacious, quiet. **Cons:** unimpressive location, no restaurant. ⊠ *2600 S. 4th Ave.* ☎ *928/726–4830 or 800/333–3333* ⊕ *www.clarionyuma.com* ⟲ *164 suites* ⟲ *In-room: refrigerator. In-hotel: bar, pool, laundry facilities, Wi-Fi, airport shuttle* ⊟ *AE, D, DC, MC, V* ⓘ *BP.*

$$$ ⓣ **Shilo Inn.** The full kitchens offered in the suites make this an excellent ⓒ place for families to stay. Rooms are spacious and most have views of the courtyard and pool. A sauna, steam room, and good-size fitness center give this property more amenities than most in the area. **Pros:** full breakfast served in the restaurant, across the street from the Yuma Palms Shopping Center. **Cons:** pricey for a standard room. ⊠ *1550 S. Castle Dome Rd.* ☎ *928/782–9511 or 800/222–2244* ⊕ *www. shiloinns.com* ⟲ *120 rooms, 15 suites* ⟲ *In-room: refrigerator, Wi-Fi. In-hotel: restaurant, bar, pool, gym, some pets allowed* ⊟ *AE, D, DC, MC, V* ⓘ *BP.*

SHOPPING

Art studios, antiques shops, and specialty boutiques have taken advantage of downtown Yuma's face-lift. The retail outlet of **The Bard Date Company** (⊠ *245 S. Main St.* ☎ *928/341–9966*) is a great place to sample and purchase all grades of the high-fiber, fat-free fruit, including delicious date shakes. **Colorado River Pottery** (⊠ *67 W. 2nd St.* ☎ *928/343–0413*) features handcrafted bowls, vases, and dishes. **Prickly Pear** (⊠ *324 S. Main St.* ☎ *928/343–0390*) is packed with an assortment of gourmet sauces, turquoise jewelry, imported dishes, hand-carved furniture, and wall art.

IMPERIAL NATIONAL WILDLIFE REFUGE

30 mi north of Yuma.

GETTING HERE AND AROUND

From Yuma, take U.S. 95 north and follow the signs to the refuge. It's about a forty-minute drive, and between January and March look for army paratroopers taking practice jumps as you pass the Yuma Proving Ground.

EXPLORING

ⓒ A guided tour is the best way to visit the 25,765-acre **Imperial National Wildlife Refuge,** created by backwaters formed when the Imperial Dam was built. Something of an anomaly, the refuge is home both to species indigenous to marshy rivers and to creatures that inhabit the adjacent Sonoran Desert—desert tortoises, coyotes, bobcats, and bighorn sheep. Mostly, though, this is a major bird habitat. Thousands of waterfowl and shorebirds live here year-round, and migrating flocks of swallows pass through in spring and fall. During those seasons, expect to see everything from pelicans and cormorants to Canada geese, snowy egrets, and some rarer species. Canoes can be rented at Martinez Lake Marina, 3.5 mi southeast of the refuge headquarters. It's best to visit from mid-

October through May, when it's cooler and the ever-present mosquitoes are least active. Kids especially enjoy the 1.3-mi Painted Desert Nature Trail, which winds through the different levels of the Sonoran Desert. From an observation tower at the visitor center you can see the river, as well as the fields being planted with rye and millet, on which the migrating birds like to feed. Call ahead to arrange a guided tour. ⊠ *Martinez Lake Rd., Box 72217, Martinez Lake* ☎ *928/783–3371* ⊕ *refuges.fws. gov* ⊡ *Free* ⊙ *Visitor center Apr.–Oct., weekdays 7:30–4; Nov.–Mar., weekdays 7:30–4, weekends 9–4.*

Northwest Arizona and Southeast Nevada

WORD OF MOUTH

"When we arrived in Oatman the burros were all waiting there to welcome us. Literally, they were all hovering around the 'Welcome to Oatman' sign. Great photo op, too."

—ellen_griswold

WELCOME TO NORTHWEST ARIZONA AND SOUTHEAST NEVADA

TOP REASONS TO GO

★ **Get Wet:** Boating, fishing, and water adventure top the list of favorite activities on the cool Colorado River and the adjoining lakes of Havasu, Mohave, and Mead.

★ **Experience a Slice of England:** Pass under or over London Bridge in Lake Havasu City.

★ **Drive the Open Road:** Get your kicks on legendary Route 66 and cruise the longest remaining stretch of the Mother Road from Seligman to Kingman.

★ **Take a Walk on the Wild Side:** For Vegas-style gambling and glitz spend some quality play time in the twin riverside cities of Laughlin, Nevada, and Bullhead City, Arizona.

★ **Hike Hualapai:** Take a break from the desert and climb the cool climes of Hualapai Mountain Park—the highest point in western Arizona.

Laughlin, Nevada's casinos are just over the Colorado River.

1 Northwest Arizona. Take a drive down memory lane on the longest remaining stretch of historic Route 66—roll down the windows and watch the sweeping desert views pass you by. Along the way, check out the funky little ghost towns of Oatman and Chloride and make a splash in the cool blue waterways of Lakes Mohave, Mead, and Havasu.

2 Southeast Nevada. Laughlin attracts laid-back gamblers and elite entertainers looking for all of the glitz and glamour of Las Vegas without the high prices and large crowds. Take a quick jaunt into Nevada for a look at the monumental Hoover Dam and a hand or two of blackjack in a riverside casino.

Rt. 66 is a classic American route for road trips.

GETTING ORIENTED

In the far northwestern corner of Arizona, Kingman is a good base for the wide range of activities found in the Arizona communities of Lake Havasu City and Bullhead City as well as Laughlin, Nevada. Kingman is the largest city out in this neck of the woods and acts as the Mohave County seat. The Colorado River flows out of the Grand Canyon to the north and then sweeps directly south, serving as the western border of the state of Arizona and supplying the lifeblood to the otherwise desolate desert region. Created from dams on the mighty Colorado River, Lakes Mead, Mohave, and Havasu provide a common link in the tristate area by offering some of the best water recreation around.

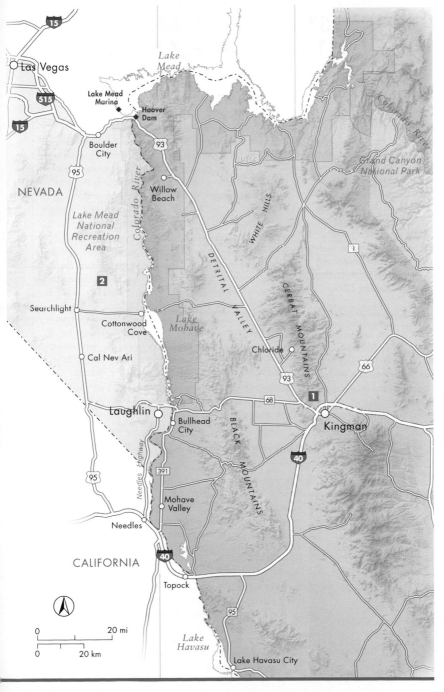

Las Vegas

Lake
Mead

Colorado River

Lake Mead
Marina

Hoover
Dam

93

Boulder
City

95

NEVADA

Grand Canyon
National Park

Willow
Beach

Lake Mead
National
Recreation
Area

Colorado River

WHITE HILLS

DETRITAL VALLEY

GERBAT MOUNTAINS

1

2

Searchlight

Cottonwood
Cove

Lake
Mohave

Chloride

93

66

Cal Nev Ari

68

1

9

Laughlin

Bullhead
City

Kingman

BLACK MOUNTAINS

40

391

Needles Highway

95

Mohave
Valley

Needles

CALIFORNIA

40

Topock

95

Lake
Havasu

Lake Havasu City

0   20 mi

0   20 km

NORTHWEST ARIZONA AND SOUTHEAST NEVADA PLANNER

When to Go

Unlike many destinations, the communities in northwestern Arizona don't have distinct high and low seasons. The arid climate and clear winter skies attract "snowbirds," retirees flocking south to escape the harsh northern climes. On the flip side, the hot, sunny summer months attract sports enthusiasts looking to cavort in the cool, blue waterways—despite searing temperatures topping 120°F.

Lake Havasu City plays host to hordes of college revelers during spring break in March and Kingman fills up fast during the annual Route 66 Fun Run in May. Things simmer down a bit during the spring and fall months—but not much! Overall, expect crowded weekends during the busy summer months and sold-out rooms during sporting events and fishing tournaments.

Getting Here and Around

Kingman and Laughlin/Bullhead City are accessible by air but most visitors drive to this corner of the state—after all, the road to Kingman is the longest remaining stretch of Route 66. At first glance, the countryside seems stark and remote, but there are many surprises along the way, including the strange-looking Joshua tree, the defining plant of the Mojave Desert. There are no traffic jams and navigation is as easy as travel in a one-stoplight town.

Historic Route 66 crosses east–west and lies north of Interstate 40, which also crosses the region. U.S. 93 is the main route for north–south travel. All of these roads are in excellent condition. On Interstate 40 high winds occasionally raise enough blowing dust to restrict visibility. In winter, ice may be present on the stretch of Interstate 40 between Kingman and Seligman, as well as on sections of Route 66. When signage warns of ice ahead, heed the warnings and slow down. Most of the county roads are improved dirt roads, but washboard sections may surprise you, so take your time and drive no faster than prudence dictates.

Fuel up while you're in this part of Arizona—all grades of gasoline can be as much as 30¢ to 50¢ per gallon less in Kingman and Bullhead City than in Laughlin.

Making the Most of Your Time

Kingman is an ideal base for exploring Lake Mead National Recreation Area, the ghost towns of Oatman and Chloride, and the forested Hualapai Mountain Park. You'll need at least a day to enjoy water sports on Lake Mead, whereas an hour or two is enough to explore the funky little ghost towns. Even though Lake Havasu is only an hour away from Kingman, visitors heading down to those sandy shores can get the most out of their trip by staying at one of the local resorts. Water activities dominate the scene here, but if you have an extra hour or two consider a side trip to London Bridge, a birding expedition at Havasu National Wildlife Refuge, or a foray into the quaint shops in English Village. If gambling is on your list of things to do, you can just hop across the Colorado River to Laughlin and spend hours or days reveling in the glitz and glitter.

What to Do and Where to Do It

Three of North America's deserts—the Mohave, Sonoran, and Chihuahuan—converge along the sinuous shores of the mighty Colorado River as it winds along Arizona's western border into Mexico. With more than 1,000 mi of shoreline and three large reservoirs—Lake Mead, Lake Mohave, and Lake Havasu—Arizona's west coast offers warm weather and cool waters perfect for a wide array of year-round water sports including boating, kayaking, water-skiing, sailing, scuba diving, and fishing. For the best canoeing and kayaking, head to Topock Gorge on the Colorado River. Lake Havasu has the best swimming beaches and sailing. Fishermen will want to launch a boat on Lake Mead or Lake Mohave.

Local Food and Lodging

Motel chains make up the most abundant and affordable lodging options in the major communities of Kingman, Lake Havasu City, and Bullhead City, and a few historic hotels break up the modern mix. The swanky resorts at Lake Havasu City and the glittery casinos in Laughlin provide upscale rooms for visitors seeking more refined relaxation. Staying in a houseboat on Lake Havasu or Lake Mead puts a decidedly different twist on water recreation. Best of all, these floating rooms with a view can be maneuvered into countless coves and inlets, allowing for peaceful solitude rarely found on the busy beaches and popular waterways.

Dining in this remote corner of the state is generally as casual as the lodging options. You're more likely to find a 1950s diner, a taqueria, or a family-owned café than a five-star dining establishment. For the most part you'll find home-cooked American favorites and "South of the Border" specialties. For the best in fine dining, head across the Colorado River to the casinos in Laughlin, Nevada, where you'll find a sophisticated medley of gourmet restaurants serving everything from seafood to steaks.

WHAT IT COSTS

	¢	$	$$	$$$	$$$$
Restaurant	under $8	$8–$12	$13–$20	$21–$30	over $30
Hotel	under $70	$70–$120	$121–$175	$176–$250	over $250

Restaurant prices are per person for a main course at dinner. Hotel prices are for a standard double in high season, excluding taxes and service charges.

Festivals and Events

May Route 66 Fun Run. This three-day event is a 40-mi drive along the longest remaining section of the "Mother Road." ☎ *928/753–5001* ⊕ *www. azrt66.com.*

July Solar Egg Frying Contest. In Oatman, this yearly Independence Day celebration takes place at high noon. Accompanying the cook-off are Old West gun fights and other entertainment and food. ☎ *928/768–6222* ⊕ *www.oat mangoldroad.org.*

Sept. Andy Devine Days. The festival honors the film and television actor with a parade and rodeo. ☎ *928/753–6106* ⊕ *www.kingmantourism.org.*

Oct. London Bridge Days. Lake Havasu City heats up with a weeklong Renaissance festival, a parade, and British-theme contests. ☎ *928/855–5655* ⊕ *www. golakehavasu.com.*

What Time Is It?

Remember that Arizona does not observe daylight saving time, but the neighboring states of Nevada and California do. When scheduling interstate travel, double-check all times to avoid confusion and missed connections.

9

Updated by
Carrie Frasure

Northwestern Arizona and southeastern Nevada comprise a unique blend of deserts, mountains, and 1,000 mi of shoreline. Despite the superficial aridity of much of the landscape, the region bubbles with an abundance of springs and artesian wells. Without these water sources seeping from the rocks and sand, this wide-open region would never have developed into the major crossroads it is today.

The defining feature of the region is the Colorado River. Since the late Pleistocene epoch when Paleo-Indians first set foot in the river that was once described as "too thick to drink and too thin to plow," the Colorado has been a blessing and a barrier. Prehistoric traders from the Pacific Coast crossed the river at Willow Beach on their way to trade shells for pelts with the Hopi Indians and other Pueblo tribes farther east. When gold was discovered in California in 1848, entrepreneurs built ferries up and down the river to accommodate the miners drawn to the area by what Cortez called "a disease of the heart for which the only cure is gold." Prosperity followed, particularly for Kingman.

Every spring the snowmelt of the Rocky Mountain watershed of the Colorado River rushed through high basaltic canyons like water through a garden hose and washed away crops and livestock. Harnessing such a powerful river required no ordinary dam. In 1935, notched into the steep and narrow confines of Black Canyon on the border separating Arizona and Nevada, 727-foot high Hoover Dam took control of the Colorado River and turned its power into electricity and its floodwaters into the largest man-made reservoir in the United States: Lake Mead.

Today, hundreds of thousands of vehicles travel through northwestern Arizona and southeastern Nevada every day. For many who view the area through the glass of their air-conditioned vehicles, the landscape is a daunting vision of opaque and distant mountains shimmering in the heat rising from the sun-baked pavement. But for those who pull over and step into the clean open air, northwestern Arizona and southeastern Nevada offer an enchanting blend of past and present, earth and sky, river and wind.

NORTHWEST ARIZONA

Towns like Kingman hark back to the glory days of the old Route 66, and the ghost towns of Chloride and Oatman bear testament to the mining madness that once reigned in the region. Water-sports fans, or those who just want to laze on a houseboat, will enjoy Lake Havasu, where you'll find the misplaced English icon, the London Bridge, or Lake Mead, one of the best fishing spots in the state.

KINGMAN

188 mi northwest of Phoenix, 149 mi west of Flagstaff via I–40.

The highway past Kingman may seem desolate, but the mountains that surround the area offer outdoor activities in abundance, especially along the Colorado River. Water sports play a big part in the area's recreation because about 1,000 mi of freshwater shoreline lie within the county along the Colorado River and around Lakes Havasu, Mohave, and Mead—all of which are within a one hour drive of this major stopping point for fishing and boating aficionados. And for those interested in the region's mineral wealth, the nearby "ghost" towns of Chloride and Oatman offer a glimpse of the Old West.

GETTING HERE AND AROUND

Amtrak's *Southwest Chief* stops in Amtrak and in Needles, California, which is 25 mi south of Bullhead City/Laughlin.

ESSENTIALS

Transportation Contacts Kingman Cab (☏ *928/753–1222*). **Yellow Cab** (☏ *928/753–4444 or 928/718–9000*).

EXPLORING

The **Powerhouse** building is a great first stop for visitors. A **Tourist Information and Visitor Center** (⊕ *www.kingmantourism.org* ☏ *928/ 753–6106*) has the usual brochures to acquaint you with local attractions. Pick up a walking tour guidebook, which highlights 27 historic sights including Locomotive Park—home to the 1928 steam locomotive Engine No. 3759. Inside the visitor center, the **Historic Route 66 Museum** (⊕ *www.azrt66.com* ☏ *928/753–9889* ◓ *$4*) provides a nostalgic look at the evolution of the famous route that started as a footpath followed by prehistoric Indians and evolved into a length of pavement that reached from Chicago, Illinois, to Santa Monica, California. The first weekend of May each year, the Historic Route 66 Association of Arizona holds the three-day Route 66 Fun Run, a 40-mi drive that attracts classic car buffs. Admission to the Historic Route 66 Museum also includes a visit to the Mohave Museum of History and Arts and the Bonelli House. **Memory Lane,** also inside the Powerhouse, is a store crammed with kitschy offerings that run the gamut of Route 66 memorabilia, including magnets, beer mugs, earrings, luggage, T-shirts, shot glasses, and signs. ✉ *The Powerhouse, 120 W. Andy Devine Ave.* ☉ *Daily 9–5.*

History buffs will enjoy a visit to the **Bonelli House,** an excellent example of Anglo-Territorial architecture featuring a facade of light-gray

9

quarried stone and whitewashed wood accents, a very popular style in the early 1900s. It is one of 62 buildings in the Kingman business district listed on the National Register of Historic Places and contains period pieces including a large wall clock that was once the only clock in Kingman. ⊠ *430 E. Spring St.* ☎ *928/753–1413* ⊠ *$4 includes admission to Historic Route 66 Museum and the Mohave Museum of History and Arts* ☉ *Weekdays 11–3.*

The **Mohave Museum of History and Arts** includes an Andy Devine Room with memorabilia from Devine's Hollywood years and, incongruously, a portrait collection of every president and first lady. The museum has an exceptional library collection of research materials related to the region. There's also an exhibit of carved Kingman turquoise, displays on Native American art and artifacts, and a diorama depicting the mid-19th-century expedition of Lt. Edward Beale, who led his camel-cavalry unit to the area in search of a wagon road along the 35th parallel. You can follow the White Cliffs Trail from downtown to see the deep ruts cut into the desert floor by the wagons that came to Kingman after Beale's time. ⊠ *400 W. Beale St.* ☎ *928/753–3195* ⊕ *www.mohavemuseum.org* ⊠ *$4 includes admission to Historic Route 66 Museum and the Bonelli House* ☉ *Weekdays 9–5, Sat. 1–5.*

ANDY DEVINE

Kingman's most famous citizen is Andy Devine (1905–77). The raspy-voiced Western character actor appeared in more than 400 films, most notably as the comic cowboy sidekick "Cookie" to Roy Rogers in 10 films. He also played "the Cheerful Soldier" in *The Red Badge of Courage* and was in several John Wayne flicks, including *The Man Who Shot Liberty Valance* (he played the hapless sheriff Linc Appleyard), *Stagecoach*, and *Island in the Sky*. On the last weekend of September each year, Kingman celebrates its favorite son with a rodeo (⊕ *www.kingmanrodeo.com*), parade, and community fair.

Fodor's Choice ★ You haven't truly hiked in northwestern Arizona until you've hiked in **Hualapai Mountain Park**. A 15-mi drive from town up Hualapai Mountain Road leads to the park's more than 2,300 wooded acres, with 16 mi of developed and undeveloped hiking trails, picnic areas, ATV trails, rustic cabins, and RV (full hookups) and tent areas. Along the park's trail system you'll find a striking variety of plant life such as prickly pear cactus and Arizona walnut. Abundant species of birds and mammals such as the piñon jay and the Abert squirrel live here, and pristine stands of unmarred aspen mark the higher elevations. Any of the trails can be hiked in about three hours. The **Hayden Peak Trail** is a branch of a 16-mi trail system, which links with many other trails at a high elevation. The popular **Aspen Peak Trail** is shorter, 2 mi one way. If you can only visit one place and do one thing in northwestern Arizona, hiking in Hualapai Mountain Park should be it. Trail maps are available at the park office. ⊠ *6250 Hualapai Mountain Rd.* ☎ *928/681–5700, 877/757–0915 for cabin reservations* ⊕ *www.mcparks.com* ⊠ *$5.*

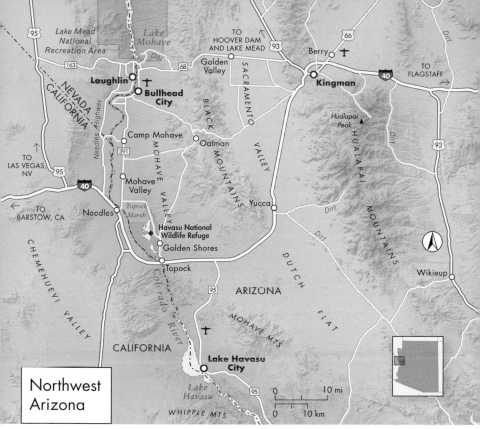

Northwest Arizona

OFF THE
BEATEN
PATH

Chloride. The ghost town of Chloride, Arizona's oldest silver-mining camp, takes its name from a type of silver ore mined here. During its heyday, from 1900 to 1920, some 75 mines operated in the area: silver, gold, lead, zinc, molybdenum, and even turquoise were mined here. About 360 folks live in Chloride today; there is one restaurant, one saloon, a grocery store, an inn, and two RV parks. Sights include the old jail, Chloride Baptist Church, the Jim Fritz Museum, and the Purcell Galleries of Fine Art. Western artist Roy Purcell painted the large murals on the rocks on the edge of town—10 feet high and almost 30 feet across, they depict a goddess figure, intertwined snakes, and Eastern and Native American symbols. Outdoors enthusiasts can take advantage of the miles of hiking trails and explore the mineral-rich hills with excellent rockhounding opportunities. Mock gunfights in the streets mark high noon on Saturdays. On the last Saturday of June the entire town turns out for Old Miner's Day—the biggest event of the year featuring a parade, bazaar, bake sale, and a family-friendly contests. The marked turnoff for Chloride is about 12 mi north of Kingman on U.S. 93. For more information, contact the **Chloride Chamber of Commerce** (✉ *4940 Tennessee* ☎ *928/565–2204* ⊕ *www.chloridearizona.com*).

⚠ **Experts believe there are more than 200,000 abandoned mines in Arizona, many in the rich mineral regions such as the one surrounding Chloride. Give**

A Short History of Old Route 66

In 1938 the 2,400 mi of roadway connecting Chicago and Los Angeles was declared "continuously paved." U.S. Route 66 was transformed from a hodgepodge string of local roads—most of them dirt in summer and mud in winter—connecting one isolated small town to another, into an "all-weather" highway that would enable commerce and the military to travel the route. And just as the road crews changed the landscape to accommodate the roadbed, Route 66 changed the social landscape as communities adapted to the new road.

The needs of the traveler were met by the new ideas of the gas station, the diner, and the motel—and nostalgic

glimpses of those icons and that culture can still be found. In Seligman, for example, you can stop at Delgadillo's Snow Cap Drive-in for a "small soda" and a chance to admire vintage automobiles. In Hackberry you can pose for pictures with vintage cars, kitschy signs, and highway memorabilia while sipping sarsaparilla from a bottle of Route 66 Beer. If you take Exit 139 from Interstate 40, 5 mi west of Ash Fork, you'll find yourself at the beginning of the longest remaining continuous stretch of Route 66. It will take you almost 160 mi through Seligman, Peach Springs, Truxton, Valentine, Hackberry, Kingman, and Oatman, and on to the Colorado River near Topock.

wide berth to mine entrances and shafts, which are often unstable and can cave in without warning.

★ **Grand Canyon West Ranch.** Sprawling at the base of Spirit Mountain, this historic 106,000-acre working cattle ranch takes guests on an adventure to the Old West. Corriente cattle still roam the hills and their cowboy caretakers guide horseback tours and horse-drawn wagon rides through the rugged countryside. Tap Duncan (a member of the Hole-in-the-Wall Gang) lived here, and Andy Devine supposedly spent some time working here. The ranch now offers rustic cabins, home-cooked meals, horseback riding, wagon rides, and a helicopter tour of Grand Canyon West. Take U.S. 93 north from Kingman 40 mi and turn right onto Pearce Ferry Road. Follow the paved road for 27 mi, then turn right onto the unpaved Diamond Bar Ranch Road. The Grand Canyon West Ranch is 7 mi farther on the right side of the road. Located just 14 mi southwest of Grand Canyon West, the ranch is a popular stopping-off point for day-trippers seeking spectacular canyon views in this remote region. Call ahead to arrange your visit. ⊠ *3750 E. Diamond Bar Ranch Rd., Meadview* ⚲*Reservations essential* ☎*702/736–8787 or 800/359–8727* ⊕*www.grandcanyonwestranch.com.*

EN
ROUTE

Traveling north from Kingman, keep an eye out for the strange-looking namesakes of the **Joshua Tree Forest** (*Yucca brevifolia*). This native of the dry Mojave Desert isn't a tree, but actually a member of the lily family. Standing as tall as 40 feet, the alien-looking plant can be recognized by its gangly limbs ending in dense clumps of dark green, bayonet-shaped leaves. Mormon emigrants traveling through the area in the mid-19th century named the towering plants after the biblical figure Joshua. From

Northwest Arizona is full of interesting pit stops off of Historic Route 66.

February through March, Joshua trees blossom in clusters of creamy white blossoms. The trees don't branch until after they bloom, and, because they rely on perfect conditions to flower, they don't necessarily bloom every year.

Grand Canyon Caverns and Inn. Nestled among rolling, juniper-covered hills 60 mi east of Kingman on Historic Route 66, the full extent of this dry cave is still unknown. Daily tours begin on the half hour with an elevator descent to the main floor of the caverns, 210 feet below ground. These caves were formed in the limestone bed of a sea that covered northern Arizona more than 37 million years ago. The ¾-mi walking tour takes 45 minutes. For an additional fee, spelunkers can take the extended, two-hour Explorers Tour (reservations required). In the rodeo arena behind the 48-room hotel, area cowboys often hold calf-roping competitions that are a hoot to watch, and free to boot. ⊠ *Rte. 66, Mile Marker 115* ☎ *928/422–3223 or 928/422–4565* ⊕ *www.gccaverns.com* ☜ *$14.95* ⊙ *Mar.–Oct., daily 8–6; Nov.–Feb., daily 10–5.*

WHERE TO EAT

$ ✕ **El Palacio of Kingman Mexican Restaurant.** Out of the way but worth
MEXICAN the effort, this casual restaurant with a Mexican motif is at the north end of town, near the intersection of Bank Street and Northern Avenue. Locals love El Palacio's Mexican favorites and Southwestern specialties—and what many believe are the best chiles rellenos in the county. A comprehensive drink menu includes a selection of Mexican beers, tropical margaritas, and chilled sangria. ⊠ *401 E. Andy Devine Ave.* ☎ *928/718–0018* ⊕ *www.serranoent.com* ☰ *AE, D, MC, V.*

$$$ ✕**Hubb's Bistro.** The bustling eatery in the historic Brunswick Hotel
CONTINENTAL caters to most tastes and does a wonderful job with everything from
steaks to seafood. Menu favorites include sautéed pork loin, Alaskan
king crab, and lobster tail. The stamped-tin ceiling, historic photos, and
antiques add a touch of elegance. An extensive wine list and multina-
tional beer selections add to the flavor-filled experience. ⊠*315 E. Andy
Devine Ave.* ☎*928/718–1800* ⊕*www.hotel-brunswick.com/bistro-bar.
html* ⊟*AE, D, MC, V* ⊘*Closed Sun. No lunch.*

$ ✕**Mr. D'z Route 66 Diner.** This popular spot serves up road food with a
AMERICAN '50s flair for breakfast, lunch, and dinner. The jukebox spins favorites,
☙ and tributes to Elvis and Marilyn Monroe adorn the walls in this old-
fashioned diner decked out in bright turquoise and hot pink. Expect
low prices and large servings of your favorite burgers and milk shakes.
⊠*105 E. Andy Devine Ave.* ☎*928/718–0066* ⊟*AE, MC, V.*

WHERE TO STAY

$ ⊞**Best Western–Kings Inn & Suites.** Conveniently located at the intersec-
tion of Interstate 40 and Highway 93, this hotel's clean, spacious rooms
are within close proximity to Lake Mead, Hualapai Mountain Park,
Laughlin, and the ghost towns of Chloride and Oatman. The minisuites
offer comfy beds and a sitting area. **Pros:** several restaurants are within
walking distance; a great base for exploring the region; hot breakfast
included. **Cons:** basic rooms with few amenities; traffic can be heard
from the highway. ⊠*2930 E. Andy Devine Ave.* ☎*928/753–6101 or
800/750–6101* ✍*101 rooms* ⚭*In-room: refrigerator, Wi-Fi. In-hotel:
pool, gym, laundry facilities, Wi-Fi, some pets allowed, no-smoking
rooms* ⊟*AE, D, DC, MC, V* ❖|*CP.*

¢ ⊞**Brunswick Hotel.** This hotel opened its doors in 1909 and was the first
three-story building in town. Rooms have antique furnishings, and the
early-1900s ambience is coupled with courtesy and today's amenities,
including a business center. Budget-minded guests can save a few dol-
lars by staying in the hotel's Cowboy and Cowgirl rooms, which share
a bathroom. **Pros:** only Kingman hotel with in-house bar and restau-
rant; large wraparound porch offers prime people-watching. **Cons:** train
noise bothers light-sleepers; standard rooms are small and basic. ⊠*315
E. Andy Devine Ave.* ☎*928/718–1800* ⊕*www.hotel-brunswick.com*
✍*18 rooms, 9 with shared bath, 6 suites* ⚭*In-room: no TV (some),
Wi-Fi. In-hotel: restaurant, room service, bar, laundry facilities, Inter-
net terminal, some pets allowed, no-smoking rooms* ⊟*AE, D, MC,
V* ❖|*CP.*

**EN
ROUTE**
A worthwhile stop on your way from Kingman to Lake Havasu, the
ghost town of **Oatman** is reached via old Route 66. It's a straight shot
across the Mojave Desert valley for a while, but then the road narrows
and winds precipitously for about 15 mi through the Black Mountains.
This road is public, but beyond a narrow shoulder, the land is privately
owned and heavily patrolled by private security thanks to still-active
gold mines throughout these low but rugged hills.

Oatman's main street is right out of the Old West; scenes from a num-
ber of films, including *How the West Was Won,* were shot here. It still
has a remote, old-time feel: many of the natives carry side arms, and

they're not acting. You can wander into one of the three saloons or visit the **Oatman Hotel,** where Clark Gable and Carole Lombard honeymooned in 1939 after they were secretly married in Kingman. Several times a day, resident actors entertain visitors with mock gunfights on the main drag.

Several curio shops and eclectic boutiques line the length of Main Street. Get in the spirit of the Old West with the leather jackets, Western gun holsters, and moccasins offered at the **Leather Shop of Oatman** (⊠ *162 Main St.* ☎ *928/768–3833*). Browse through a nice selection of Indian jewelry and Southwestern art at the **Ore House** (⊠ *194 Main St.* ☎ *928/768–3839*). **Main Street Emporium** (⊠ *150 S. Main St.* ☎ *928/788–3298*) offers a wide array of handcrafted items including Western-theme wall art, handwoven blankets, and cholla cactus candles.

The burros that often come in from nearby hills and meander down the street, however, are the town's real draw. A couple of stores sell hay to folks who want to feed these "wild" beasts, which at last count numbered about a dozen and which leave plenty of evidence of their visits in the form of "road apples"—so watch your step. For information about the town and its attractions, contact the **Oatman Chamber of Commerce** (☎ *928/768–6222* ⊕ *www.oatmangoldroad.org*).

LAKE HAVASU CITY

60 mi southwest of Kingman.

If there's an Arizona Riviera, this is it. Lake Havasu has more than 45 mi of lake shoreline, and the area gets less than 4 inches of rain annually, which means it's almost always sunny. Spring, winter, and fall are the best times to visit; in summer, temperatures often exceed 100°F. You can rent everything from water skis to Jet Skis, small fishing boats to large houseboats. The lake area has no fewer than 13 RV parks and campgrounds, about 125 boat-in campsites, and hundreds of hotel and motel rooms for additional creature comforts. There are golf and tennis facilities, as well as fishing guides who'll help you find, and catch, the big ones.

Learn about the purchase and reconstruction of London Bridge at the exhibit showcased at the Lake Havasu City Visitor Center, which is also a great place to pick up other information on area attractions.

GETTING HERE AND AROUND

In Lake Havasu City call Arizona Road Runner Shuttle for local and regional transportation. River City Shuttle offers service from Lake Havasu to several Laughlin casinos including Harrahs, River Palms, Golden Nugget, Pioneer, Tropicana Express, Colorado Belle, Edgewater, Aquarius, and Riverside Resort.

ESSENTIALS

Transportation Contacts Arizona Road Runner Shuttle (⊠ *2760 Sweetwater* ☎ *928/854–9333* ⊕ *www.arizonaroadrunnershuttle.com*). **River City Shuttle** (☎ *928/854–5253 or 888/948–3427* ⊕ *www.rivercityshuttle.com*).

Visitor Info Lake Havasu City Visitor Center (⊠ *420 English Village* ☎ *928/855–5655* ⊕ *www.golakehavasu.com*).

9

In Lake Havasu City, boaters combine recreation with a bit of English history as they pass under the London Bridge.

campsites ($23) with access to electricity and water, and public restrooms with showers.

With a boat, you have more options: you can find a quiet, secluded cove or beach to swim or fish. If you have a need for speed, you can plane up and down the lake with or without a skier in tow.

If you don't have the equipment or the vessel necessary to enjoy your water sport, you can rent one from a number of reputable merchants. You can rent everything from Jet Skis to pontoon boats, by the day or by the week, at **Sand Point Marina and RV Park** (✉ *7952 S. Sand Point Resort Rd.* ☎ *928/855–0549* ⊕ *www.sandpointresort.com*). **Arizona Water Sports** (✉ *655 Kiowa Ave.* ☎ *928/453–5558 or 800/393–5558* ⊕ *www.arizonawatersports.com*) rents Jet Skis, jet boats, ski boats, and pontoon boats.

WHERE TO EAT

$ ✗ **Barley Brothers Brewery and Grill.** In the Island Mall adjacent to the Eng-
AMERICAN lish Village and the London Bridge, Barley Brothers offers casual dining and a microbrewery specializing in ales on tap. Try the award-winning JennaGrace Hefeweizen and the Kickstart Oatmeal Stout along with such tasty morsels as wood-fired shrimp flatbread and German sausage from the comprehensive appetizer menu. For dinner, the standard salads, rotisserie chicken, burgers, and sandwiches are complemented by specials such as baby back ribs, Jamaican barbecue salmon, and savory porterhouse steaks. ✉ *1425 McCulloch Blvd.* ☎ *928/505–7837* ⊕ *www.barleybrothers.com* ▤ *AE, D, MC, V.*

¢ ✗ **Chico's Tacos.** The grill is always hopping at this taqueria, which spe-
MEXICAN cializes in grilled fish, chicken, and carne asada. This fast-food joint may

not be fancy, but this restaurant serves up some of the best Mexican food in town. The menu features such south-of-the-border standards as tacos, enchiladas, flautas, burritos, and fajitas. Best of all, the six different salsas at the salsa bar add a bit of spice to the mix. ⊠*1641 McCulloch Blvd.* ☎*928/680–7010* ▭*D, MC, V.*

$
AMERICAN

✗**Juicy's River Café.** This is a favorite hangout for the local folks who know good food when they taste it. The cozy café is small and fills up fast, especially for breakfast. Be prepared to wait on Sunday mornings at this neighborhood restaurant. The varied menu includes corned beef and cabbage, meatloaf, pot roast and vegetables, and homemade soups and desserts. Great service is paired with reasonable prices. ⊠*25 N. Acoma Blvd.* ☎*928/855–8429* ▭*D, MC, V.*

$$$
AMERICAN
★

✗**Shugrue's.** The Sedona Shugrue's is the original, but this branch is true to its name. More relaxed then the original, this restaurant still ranks among the top restaurants in Lake Havasu City. Shugrue's features hand-cut steaks, fresh seafood, salads, and other well-prepared American fare. The baked desserts are worth saving room for. Be sure to request a table with a bridge view. ⊠*1425 McCulloch Blvd.* ☎*928/453 1400* ▭*AE, MC, V.*

WHERE TO STAY

$

🏨**Havasu Springs Resort.** On a low peninsula reaching into Lake Havasu, the four hotels of this resort maximize your options. The closest accommodations to the lake are at the Marina Hotel, which overlooks the inner harbor. For more sweeping views try the accommodations at the Lakeview Motel, which offers a panoramic vista of the surrounding desert. Those looking for a central location can book a room at the Poolside Motel. And for longer stays and larger families, Vista Suites features full kitchens, one- and two-bedroom suites, cozy yards, barbecue facilities, and excellent views of the lake and the outer harbor. In addition to standard hotel rooms, the resort also offers suites and apartments. **Pros:** all-inclusive property; friendly staff; nice lakeside beachfront. **Cons:** chair shortage at the pool; rooms are run-down; RV traffic. ⊠*2581 AZ 95, Parker* ☎*928/667–3361* ⊕*www.havasu springs.com* ⇆*38 rooms, 4 suites, 3 apartments* ♿*In-room: kitchen (some). In-hotel: restaurant, bar, beachfront, water sports, golf course, tennis courts* ▭*AE, D, MC, V.*

$$$$
★

🏨**London Bridge Resort.** If you want to be close to the bridge, this hotel is a dependable choice. The decor is a strange mix of Tudor and Southwestern; other than that, studios are standard motel rooms with kitchenettes. The restaurant Martini Bay serves tapas and delectable main dishes like crab cakes, mussels, teriyaki salmon, and gold shrimp crouda (a shrimp "tower" with avocado and salsa). After dinner, you can stretch the night out at Kokomo Havasu, a 10,000-square-foot nightclub featuring multiple dance floors, five bars, and an outdoor swimming pool or at the high-energy dance club Style, the resort's newest nightclub. **Pros:** great views of London Bridge; suites come with sleeper sofas for extra guests; nightlife and business center. **Cons:** limited availability during the busy summer months; sales pressure from the resort's time-share options. ⊠*1477 Queen's Bay* ☎*928/855–0888 or 800/624–7939* ⊕*www.londonbridgeresort.com* ⇆*4 studios, 72 1-bedroom suites, 46*

9

2-bedroom suites ⅜In-room: kitchen, DVD, Wi-Fi. In-hotel: 3 restaurants, room service, bars, golf course, pools, gym, beachfront, laundry facilities, no-smoking rooms ═AE, D, MC, V.

HOUSEBOATS **Club Nautical Houseboats.** What houseboats lack in speed and maneuverability, they make up for in comfort and shade. Club Nautical has some of the most luxurious boats on the lake and the crew makes certain that boaters get the best instruction and tips for their travel into cool blue waters. ✉1000 McCulloch Blvd. ☎800/843–9218 ⊕www. lakehavasuhouseboatrental.com.

SOUTHEAST NEVADA

Laughlin, Nevada, and Bullhead City, Arizona, are separated by a unique state line: the Colorado River. It's an interesting juxtaposition of cities, with the casino lights of Laughlin sparkling across the river from Bullhead City. Sixty miles upstream, just southeast of Las Vegas, Boulder City is prim, languid, and full of historic neighborhoods, small businesses, parks, greenbelts—and not a single casino. Over the hill from town, enormous Hoover Dam blocks the Colorado River as it enters Black Canyon. Backed up behind the dam is incongruous, deep-blue Lake Mead, the focal point of water-based recreation for southern Nevada and northwestern Arizona and the major water supplier to seven southwestern states. The lake is ringed by miles of rugged desert country. Less than ½ mi downstream from the Hoover Dam and Lake Mead work continues on another engineering marvel—a bridge that will span the river canyon and link northwestern Arizona to southeastern Nevada, dramatically reducing traffic across Hoover Dam. It's set for completion in June 2010 (⊕ www.hooverdambypass.org).

BULLHEAD CITY, ARIZONA, AND LAUGHLIN, NEVADA

35 mi northwest of Kingman.

Laughlin is a unique state-line city separated from Arizona by the Colorado River. Its founder, Don Laughlin, bought an eight-room motel here in 1964 and basically built the town from scratch. By the early 1980s Laughlin's Riverside Hotel-Casino was drawing gamblers and river rats from northwestern Arizona, southeastern California, and even southern Nevada, and his success attracted other casino operators. Bullhead City has its small-town charms, but the lights of Laughlin are difficult to ignore. Today Laughlin is the state's third major resort area, attracting more than 3 million visitors annually. The city fills up, especially in winter, with both retired travelers who spend at least part of the winter in Arizona and a younger resort-loving crowd. The big picture windows overlooking the Colorado River lend a bright, airy, and open feeling particular to Laughlin casinos. Take a stroll along the river walk, then make the return trip by water taxi ($4 one way, $20 all day). Boating, using Jet Skis, fishing, and plain old wading are other options for enjoying the water.

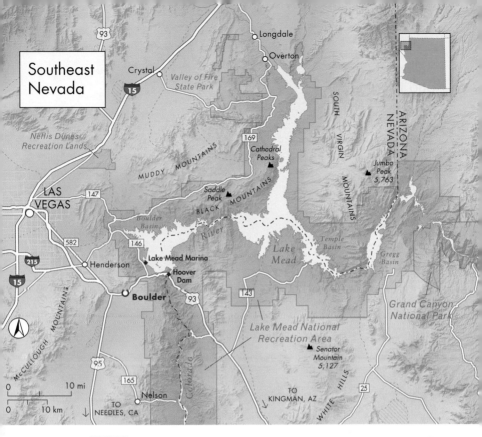

Southeast Nevada

TIMING
The state of Nevada is in the Pacific time zone, while Arizona is in the Mountain time zone. Arizona does not use daylight saving time, however. As a result, in summer Nevada and Arizona observe the same hours.

GETTING HERE AND AROUND
To get to Laughlin from Kingman, follow U.S. 93 for 35 mi.

Sun Country flies from 19 cities, including Seattle, Denver, Minneapolis–St. Paul, San Francisco, Phoenix, and Dallas–Ft. Worth as well as various destinations in Mexico and the Caribbean. Several hotel-casinos, like Harrah's, also sponsor charter flights.

Mills Tours, River City Shuttle, and Tri State Shuttle offer regular service from McCarran International Airport to Laughlin/Bullhead City. Reservations for all shuttle services are required. Individual hotel-casinos also sponsor bus trips from Las Vegas, Los Angeles, and other destinations.

Lucky Cab & Limo Company of Nevada services Laughlin and Bullhead City. For another approach in getting from casino to casino in Laughlin, hop aboard a water taxi with Americana River Ride or River Passage. Fares can be purchased at the casino dock ticket booths.

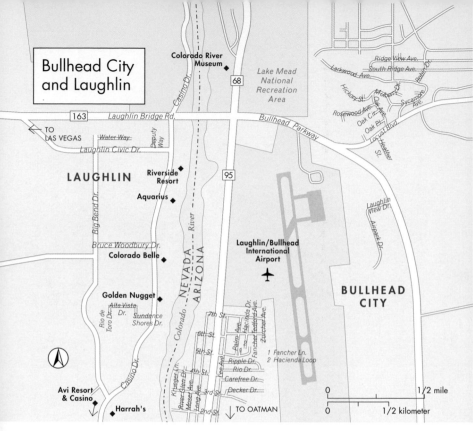

Bullhead City and Laughlin

Amtrak's *Southwest Chief* stops at Needles, California, which is 25 mi south of Laughlin, and at Kingman, Arizona, which is about 30 mi east of Laughlin. Amtrak provides bus service from Kingman to the Tropicana Express Laughlin.

ESSENTIALS

Airline Sun Country Airlines (☎ 800/359–6786 ⊕ www.suncountry.com).

Airport Laughlin/Bullhead International Airport (☎ 928/754–2134).

Bus Contacts Mills Tours (☎ 877/454–3734). **River City Shuttle** (☎ 928/854–5253 or 888/948–3427 ⊕ www.rivercityshuttle.com). **Tri State Shuttle** (✉ 1528 Alta Vista Rd., Bullhead City ☎ 800/801–8687 ⊕ www.tristate shuttle.net).

Rental Cars Avis-Airport (☎ 928/754–4686 ⊕ www.avis.com). **Enterprise-Airport** (☎ 928/754–2700 ⊕ www.enterprise.com). **Hertz-Airport** (☎ 928/754–4111 ⊕ www.hertz.com).

Taxis Americana River Ride (✉ Laughlin ☎ 928/754–3555). **Lucky Cab & Limo Company of Nevada** (✉ Laughlin ☎ 702/298–2299). **River Passage** (✉ Laughlin ☎ 702/299–0090).

Visitor Info Laughlin Chamber of Commerce (✉ 1585 S. Casino Dr. ☎ 702/298–2214 or 800/227–5245 ⊕ www.laughlinchamber.com). **Laughlin**

Visitors Information Center (✉ *1555 Casino Dr.* ☎ *702/298–3321 or 800/452–8445* ⊕ *www.visitlaughlin.com* ⊙ *Weekdays 8–5, weekends 8:30–5).*

EXPLORING

🔆 ★ Across the Laughlin Bridge, ¼ mi to the north, the **Colorado River Museum** displays the rich past of the tristate region where Nevada, Arizona, and California converge. There are artifacts from the Mojave Indian tribe, models and photographs of steamboats that once plied the river, rock and fossil specimens, and the first telephone switchboard used in neighboring Bullhead City. A military memorabilia collection formerly housed in the Ramada Casino is now housed at the museum. ✉ *2201 Highway 68, Laughlin* ☎ *928/754–3399* 🎫 *$2* ⊙ *Sept.–June, Tues.– Sun. 10–4.*

Searchlight Museum. Searchlight was once the biggest boomtown in southern Nevada, and this modern, one-room exhibit inside the town hall details the area's rich mining and railroad history. It also exposes the lives of its most famous couple, legendary silent-screen stars Rex Bell and Clara Bow. On the way to Laughlin from Las Vegas on U.S. 95, turn off at Cottonwood Cove Road, drive almost a mile to the end of town and turn left on Michael Wendell Way. ✉ *200 Michael Wendell Way, Searchlight* ☎ *702/297–1682* 🎫 *Free* ⊙ *Weekdays 1–5, Sat. 9–1.*

OFF THE BEATEN PATH

Christmas Tree Pass, a dirt road located 14 mi south of Searchlight on U.S. 95, leads into the Lake Mead National Recreation Area to an extensive petroglyph site in Grapevine Canyon. This side route runs 16 mi through a desert landscape sacred to several historical and modern native tribes. The pass cuts through the rough-cut Newberry Range near legendary Spirit Mountain. In addition to viewing the impressive collection of rock art etched on canyon boulders, you'll also get the chance to see desert wildflowers and blooming cacti in spring and early summer. The loop drive reconnects with U.S. 163 15 mi northwest of Laughlin.

9

WHERE TO EAT

$ | AMERICAN

✕ **Boiler Room Brew Pub.** Laughlin's only microbrewery pumps out 155,000 gallons of beer each year. Sample the handcrafted ales and stout, all of which pair nicely with the wood-fired specialty pizzas, gourmet hamburgers, and mesquite-grilled steaks. The pub is open daily for dinner, but lunch is only served on Saturday and Sunday. ✉ *Colorado Belle, 2100 S. Casino Dr., Laughlin* ☎ *702/298–4000 or 866/352–3553* ⊕ *www.coloradobelle.com* 🍴 *AE, D, DC, MC, V No lunch weekdays.*

$ | SEAFOOD ★

✕ **Joe's Crab Shack.** With a fun beachfront atmosphere and relaxing river views, this popular restaurant features fish-and-chips, seafood platters, Louisiana-style shrimp po'boy sandwiches, crab-stuffed shrimp, and heaping mounds of crab in a bucket. The seafood buffet, offered Monday to Friday 11–3, is the best buffet around. ✉ *Golden Nugget, 2300 S. Casino Dr.* ☎ *702/298–7143* ⊕ *www.joescrabshack.com* 🍴 *AE, D, DC, MC, V.*

$$$ | STEAKHOUSE

✕ **The Range Steakhouse.** Old Las Vegas makes an appearance at this eclectic eatery featuring such tasty fare as herb-encrusted rack of lamb, surf and turf, and veal scaloppine. Riverfront views and an extensive wine list add to the elegant experience. ✉ *Harrah's, 2900 S. Casino*

Dr., Laughlin ☎*702/298–6832* ⊕*www.harrahslaughlin.com* ▤*AE, D, DC, MC, V* ⊗*No lunch.*

\$\$ ✕**Saltgrass Steakhouse.** This casual eatery serves up Texas-sized portions
STEAKHOUSE of such favorites as certified Angus Beef steaks, herb-crusted prime rib, and barbecue baby back ribs. Other menu items include salads, sandwiches, hamburgers, chicken, and seafood. It's open for dinner daily and all day Sunday. ✉*Golden Nugget, 2300 S. Casino Dr., Laughlin* ☎*702/298–7153* ⊕*www.saltgrass.com* ▤*AE, D, MC, V* ⊗*No lunch Mon.–Sat.*

WHERE TO STAY

At each resort you visit, visit guest services for a player's card. These casino programs quickly rack up points for cash, discounts, and special offers.

¢ 🖭**Aquarius.** The old Flamingo Laughlin has shed its shabby image with extensive resortwide renovations and a new name. The fully renovated guest lobby and casino feature 1,500 slot and video-poker machines, a poker room, and a sports book. The spacious rooms, which were completely gutted in 2008, have been refitted and dressed up in clean, bright colors. **Pros:** business center; a 3,000-seat outdoor amphitheater hosting big-name entertainers; Colorado River views. **Cons:** construction noise; bland buffet; high hallway traffic. ✉*1900 S. Casino Dr.* ☎*702/298–5111 or 800/352–6464* ⊕*www.aquariuscasinoresort.com* ⇘*1,907 rooms, 82 suites* ♻*In-room: Wi-Fi. In-hotel: 3 restaurants, bars, tennis courts, pool, gym, laundry service, Wi-Fi, parking (paid), no-smoking rooms* ▤*AE, D, DC, MC, V.*

¢ 🖭**Avi Resort & Casino.** The only tribally owned casino in Nevada is
ⓒ run by the Fort Mojave tribe. The 25,000-square-foot casino houses
★ more than 1,000 slot and video-poker machines. The biggest draw, however, is the private white-sand beach where you can lounge or rent a watercraft from April through September. **Pros:** Sunday champagne brunch; 8-plex movie theater; KidQuest children's program. **Cons:** situated 10 mi south of the main drag; room refrigerators available on first-come, first-served basis (fee $10). ✉*10000 Aha Macav Pkwy.* ☎*702/535–5555 or 800/284–2946* ⊕*www.avicasino.com* ⇘*455 rooms, 29 spa suites* ♻*In-room: refrigerator (some), Wi-Fi. In-hotel: 7 restaurants, bar, golf course, pool, gym, beachfront, water sports, children's programs (ages 6 wks–12 yrs), laundry facilities, Internet, no-smoking rooms* ▤*AE, D, DC, MC, V.*

¢ 🖭**Colorado Belle.** This is a Nevada anomaly—a riverboat casino that's actually on a river. The 608-foot replica of a Mississippi paddle wheeler has nautical-theme rooms with views of the Colorado River. **Pros:** on-site market and gift shop; microbrewery; specialty candy shop. **Cons:** fee for in-room Wi-Fi ($10.99 for 24 hours); room refrigerators upon request for an additional fee ($7). ✉*2100 S. Casino Dr.* ☎*702/298–4000 or 866/352–3553* ⊕*www.coloradobelle.com* ⇘*1,119 rooms, 49 suites* ♻*In-room: kitchen (some), refrigerator (some), Wi-Fi. In-hotel: 5 restaurants, room service, bars, pools, gym, spa, beachfront, laundry service, Wi-Fi, no-smoking rooms* ▤*AE, D, DC, MC, V.*

¢ ▦ **Don Laughlin's Riverside Resort Hotel and Casino.** Town founder Don
☾ Laughlin still runs this northernmost joint himself. Check out the Los-
★ er's Lounge, with its graphic homage to famous losers, such as the
Hindenburg, the *Titanic*, and the like. And don't pass up Don's two
free classic-car showrooms, with more than 80 rods, roadsters, and tin
lizzies. **Pros:** charter flights to the resort from all over the country; family destination features an arcade, bowling center, 6-plex movie theater,
and supervised playtime at Don's Kid Kastle. **Cons:** hotel fills up fast in
the summer; incidental fees for Wi-Fi ($8.95 for 24 hours) and in-room
refrigerators ($8); rooms are basic and showing their age. ⊠ *1650 S.
Casino Dr.* ☏ *702/298–2535 or 800/227–3809* ⊕ *www.riversideresort.
com* ⇱ *1,400 rooms* ♿ *In-room: refrigerator (some), Wi-Fi. In-hotel:
6 restaurants, bar, pools, spa, children's programs (ages 3 mos–12 yrs),
laundry facilities, Wi-Fi, no-smoking rooms* ⊟ *AE, D, DC, MC, V.*

$ ▦ **Golden Nugget Laughlin.** A tropical atrium in this mini-version of the
Las Vegas Golden Nugget has two cascading waterfalls and more than
300 types of plants from around the world. Although this casino is
smaller than most of its local contemporaries, this resort is home to
two of the best restaurants in town and has one of the best player's club
cards around. **Pros:** local nightlife scene at Tarzan's nightclub; attached
parking garage; Sunday champagne brunch at Harlow's. **Cons:** limited
room availability; the only no-smoking area is in the slot section of
the casino. ⊠ *2300 S. Casino Dr.* ☏ *702/298–7111 or 800/950–7700*
⊕ *www.goldennugget.com* ⇱ *300 rooms* ♿ *In-room: Wi-Fi (some).
In-hotel: 3 restaurants, room service, bar, pool, laundry service, Wi-Fi,
no-smoking rooms* ⊟ *AE, D, DC, MC, V.*

$ ▦ **Harrah's.** This is the classiest joint in Laughlin: it comes with a private
sand beach and two casinos (one is no-smoking). Big-name entertainers such as Gary Allan perform in the Fiesta Showroom and at the
3,000-seat Rio Vista Outdoor Amphitheater and legendary artists such
as Tony Orlando perform at the indoor Fiesta Showroom. There's a
cocktail lounge in each of the casinos and another at the adults-only
pool. Card fans might also want to check out the World Series of Poker—themed poker room. **Pros:** separate family and adult towers and
pools; smoking and no-smoking casinos; air-charter flights from all
over the United States directly to resort for player card members. **Cons:**
pools fill up fast; long lines for guest services; incidental fees for Wi-Fi
($10.95 for 24 hours) and gym use ($5 per visit). ⊠ *2900 S. Casino
Dr.* ☏ *702/298–4600 or 800/427–7247* ⊕ *www.harrahs-laughlin.com*
⇱ *1,505 rooms* ♿ *In-room: Wi-Fi. In-hotel: 4 restaurants, room service, bars, pools, gym, spa, beachfront, water sports, laundry service,
Wi-Fi, no-smoking rooms* ⊟ *AE, D, MC, V.*

¢ ▦ **Pioneer Hotel and Gambling Hall.** You can spot this small (by casino
standards) motel by looking for the neon mascot, River Rick—he's
Vegas Vic's brother. Although other casinos stress the new, the Pioneer retains its laid-back Western theme with checkered tablecloths and
wagon-wheel light fixtures. **Pros:** refrigerators upon request; 10 designated pet rooms; Colorado River view rooms available. **Cons:** incidental
fees for Wi-Fi ($10 for up to three-night stay); no elevator in deluxe
and river-view buildings. ⊠ *2200 S. Casino Dr.* ☏ *702/298–2442*

9

or *800/634–3469* ⊕ *www.pioneerlaughlin.com* ⊃416 *rooms* ⟵*In-room: Wi-Fi. In-hotel: 2 restaurants, bars, pool, beachfront, some pets allowed, no-smoking rooms* ⊟*AE, D, MC, V.*

BOULDER CITY

76 mi northwest of Kingman.

In the early 1930s Boulder City was built by the federal government to house 5,000 construction workers on the Hoover Dam project. A strict moral code was enforced to ensure timely completion of the dam, and to this day, the model city is the only community in Nevada in which gambling is illegal. (Note that the two casinos at either end of Boulder City are just outside the city limits.) After the dam was completed, the town shrank but was kept alive by the management and maintenance crews of the dam and Lake Mead. Today it's a vibrant little Southwestern town.

GETTING HERE AND AROUND
It takes about 2 hours via U.S. 93 to get from Kingman to Boulder City.

ESSENTIALS
Visitor Info Boulder City Chamber of Commerce (⊠*465 Nevada Way, Boulder City* ☎*702/293–2034* ⊕*www.bouldercitychamber.com* ⊙*Weekdays 9–5*).

EXPLORING
★ Be sure to stop at the Dutch Colonial–style **Boulder Dam Hotel,** built in 1933. On the National Register of Historic Places, the 20-room bed-and-breakfast once was a favorite getaway for notables, including the man who became Pope Pius XII and actors Will Rogers, Bette Davis, and Shirley Temple. The **Boulder City/Hoover Dam Museum** (☎*702/294–1988* ⊕*www.bcmha.org* ⊠*$2* ⊙*Mon.–Sat. 10–5, Sun. noon–5*) occupies the first floor of the hotel. The museum has artifacts relating to the workers and construction of Boulder City and Hoover Dam. ⊠*1305 Arizona St., Boulder City* ☎*702/293–3510* ⊕*www.boulderdamhotel.com.*

HOOVER DAM

67 mi northwest of Kingman via U.S. 93.

GETTING HERE AND AROUND
Hoover Dam is about a 90 minute drive from Kingman via U.S. 93; it's about 15 minutes from Boulder City.

EXPLORING
In 1928 Congress authorized $175 million for construction of a dam on the Colorado River to control destructive floods, provide a steady water supply to seven Colorado River Basin states, and generate electricity. Considered one of the seven wonders of the industrial world, the art

Fodor's Choice deco **Hoover Dam** is 726 feet high (the equivalent of a 70-story building) and 660 feet thick (more than the length of two football fields) at
★ the base. Construction required 4.4 million cubic yards of concrete—enough to build a two-lane highway from San Francisco to New York. Originally referred to as Boulder Dam, the structure was later officially named Hoover Dam in recognition of President Herbert Hoover's role

the lake; breakfast, cocktail, and dinner-and-dancing cruises are available. Ninety-minute sightseeing cruises occur daily, and specialty cruises are scheduled on weekends. ✉ *Hemenway Boat Harbor, near Boulder Beach* ☎ *702/293–6180* ⊕ *www.lakemeadcruises.com* ✑ *$22–$58; reservations strongly recommended for specialty cruises* ☉ *Tours Nov.– Mar., daily noon and 2; Apr.–Oct., daily noon, 2, and 4.*

SCUBA DIVING AND SNORKELING   The creation of Lake Mead flooded a huge expanse of land, and, as a result, sights of the deep abound for scuba divers. The old Mormon town of St. Thomas, inundated by the lake in 1938, has many a watery story to tell. Wishing Well Cove has steep canyon drop-offs, caves, and clear water. Castle Cliffs and Virgin Basin both have expansive views of white gypsum reefs and submerged sandstone formations. In summer Lake Mead is like a bathtub, reaching 85°F on the surface and staying at about 80°F down to 50 feet below the surface. Divers can actually wear bathing suits rather than wet suits to do some of the shallower dives. But visibility—which averages 30 feet to 35 feet overall—is much better in the winter months before the late-spring surface-algae bloom obscures some of the deeper attractions from snorkelers. Be aware that Lake Mead's level has dropped because of low snowfall in the Rockies. This has had some effect on diving conditions; St. Thomas, for example, is now only partially submerged.

Outfitters American Cactus Divers (✉ *3985 E. Sunset Rd., Suite B, Las Vegas* ☎ *702/433–3483* ⊕ *www.americancactusdivers.com*). **Desert Divers Supply** (✉ *5720 E. Charleston Blvd., Las Vegas* ☎ *702/438–1000*).

UNDERSTANDING
ARIZONA

Arizona at a Glance

ARIZONA AT A GLANCE

FAST FACTS

Nickname: Grand Canyon State

Capital: Phoenix

Motto: Ditat Deus (God enriches)

State song: *Arizona*

State bird: Cactus wren

State flower: Saguaro cactus blossom (carnegiea gigantea)

State tree: Palo verde (cercidium)

Administrative divisions: 15 counties

Entered the Union: February 14, 1912 (48th state)

Population: 6.2 million

Population density: 45.2 people per square mi

Median age: 34.2

Infant mortality rate: 6.9 deaths per 1,000 births

Literacy: 18% had trouble with basic reading. Twenty-six percent spoke a language other than English at home, usually Spanish. Forty percent reported that they did not speak English "very well."

Ethnic groups: White 60%; Latino 29%; Native American 5%; African-American 4%; Asian 2%

Religion: Unaffiliated 60%; Catholic 19%; Christian 12%; Mormon 5%; Jewish 2%; other 2%

Come to this land of sunshine

To this land where life is young.

Where the wide, wide world is waiting,

The songs that will now be sung.

—opening lines of state song, Arizona, by Margaret Rowe Clifford

GEOGRAPHY AND ENVIRONMENT

Land area: 113,909 square mi

Terrain: Desert, with rocky mountains stretching across the southern area of the state. Along the Mogollon Rim that reaches in a crescent across the eastern third of the state, stands the largest ponderosa-pine forest in the world. The White Mountains of eastern Arizona receive more than 150 inches of snow annually, and the runoff provides much of the water that enables the desert communities to survive. Erosion by rivers has formed much of the state's geography, including the Grand Canyon and the Painted Desert

Highest point: Humphreys Peak, 12,655 feet

Natural resources: Cement, copper (Arizona leads the nation in production), gravel, molybdenum, pine and fir forests, sand

Natural hazards: Drought, earthquakes, floods, severe storms, wildfires

Environmental issues: Especially around Phoenix, air quality is bad enough that year-round monitoring is done for ground-level ozone pollution, carbon monoxide, and particulate matter; concern over how logging should be done in Arizona's pine forests; soil erosion from overgrazing, industrial development, urbanization, and poor farming practices; most of the state suffers from limited natural freshwater resources

Desert rains are usually so definitely demarked that the story of the man who washed his hands in the edge of an Arizona thunder shower without wetting his cuffs seems almost credible.

—Arizona: A State Guide (The WPA Guide to Arizona)

ECONOMY

GSP: $199.6 billion

Per-capita income: $30,239

Unemployment: 6.9%

Work force: 2.6 million; trade, transportation, and utilities 19%; government 17%; professional/business 15%; educational and health services 12%; leisure/hospitality 10%; construction 7%; financial 7%; manufacturing 7%; other 6%

Major industries: Cattle, dairy goods, manufacturing, electronics, printing and publishing, processed foods, aerospace, transportation, high-tech research and development, communications, construction, tourism, military

Agricultural products: Broccoli, cattle, cauliflower, cotton, dairy goods, lettuce, sorghum, wheat

Exports: $19.2 billion

Major export products: Electronic and electric equipment, industrial machinery and computers, fabricated metal products, scientific and measuring instruments, transportation equipment

The great pines stand at a considerable distance from each other. Each tree grows alone, murmurs alone, thinks alone. They do not intrude upon each other. The Navajos are not much in the habit of giving or of asking help. Their language is not a communicative one, and they never attempt an interchange of personality in speech. Over their forests there is the same inexorable reserve. Each tree has its exalted power to bear.

—Willa Cather (1873–1947), U.S. novelist, describing Navajo pine forests in northern Arizona.

DID YOU KNOW?

■ Yuma, Arizona, holds the world record for most sunshine. It gets an average of 4,055 hours, or more than 90%, of the 4,456 hours of sunshine possible in a year.

■ The Arizona or "Apache" Trout can only be found in the White Mountains of Arizona.

■ One of Arizona's most plentiful natural resources is molybdenum, an element linked with copper production. Molybdenum is used to make steel, as well as electrodes and catalysts.

■ During daylight saving time it's possible to drive in and out of time zones in Arizona in less than an hour. While the rest of the state sticks to Mountain Standard Time year-round, the state's Navajo Nation observes daylight saving, but the Hopi Reservation inside the Navajo goes along with the rest of Arizona.

■ César Chávez, who organized agricultural laborers across America, was born near Yuma, Arizona.

■ In 1930 Pluto was discovered by Clyde Tombaugh at Lowell Observatory in Flagstaff.

■ The Central Arizona Project Canal is 336 mi long and annually brings 1.5 million gallons of Colorado River water from Lake Havasu City, through the Phoenix metropolitan area, to Tucson.

■ The Hohokam, Arizona's earliest known inhabitants, were good at something crucial to Arizona today: irrigation. They built canals more than 10 mi long that channeled water to fields in the southern part of the state in about AD 300.

■ More than 10% of the nation's Native Americans live in Arizona.

Travel Smart Arizona

WORD OF MOUTH

"In the Southwest . . . the distances and the vistas are vast."

—Dutch

"Elevation is the key to understanding the climate. Northern/central Arizona sits upon a 6,000+ feet plateau—the same one the Grand Canyon cuts through. Phoenix is at the base of this plateau, with Sedona being part way up. As a result, only the extreme southern portion of Nevada and southern Arizona are truly that warm in the winter. The lower the altitude, the warmer the weather."

—LordBalfor

GETTING HERE AND AROUND

Most visitors to Arizona arrive either by car via one of the main east–west interstates, Interstate 40 or Interstate 10/8, or by air into the state's major airport in Phoenix. (Smaller numbers fly into Tucson.) Even visitors who fly in tend to rent cars; public transportation is limited and limiting, and this vast state is ideally suited for car touring. The state's highways are generally well maintained and have high speed limits (up to 75 MPH on some interstates), so traveling even significant distances by car isn't a great challenge.

▌ AIR TRAVEL

Despite its high passenger volume, long lines at the check-in counters and security checkpoints at Phoenix Sky Harbor are usually not a problem, although during busy periods (spring break, holiday weekends, and so on) you should anticipate long waits and arrive at the airport 30 to 60 minutes earlier than you would otherwise. Because Phoenix is the hub for Southwest and US Airways, it has direct flights to most major U.S. cities and a number of international destinations (Calgary, Cancun, Edmonton, London, Mexico City, Puerto Vallarta, San Jose [Costa Rica], Toronto, and Vancouver among them). Sample flying times from major cities are: one hour from Los Angeles, three hours from Chicago, and five hours from New York City.

Airlines and Airports Airline and Airport Links.com (⊕ www.airlineandairportlinks.com) has links to many of the world's airlines and airports.

Airline Security Issues Transportation Security Administration (⊕ www.tsa.gov) has answers for almost every question that might come up.

AIRPORTS

Major gateways to Arizona include Phoenix Sky Harbor International (PHX), about 3 mi southeast of Phoenix city center, and Tucson International Air Terminal (TUS), about 8½ mi south of the central business area.

Phoenix Sky Harbor International Airport is one of the busiest airports in the world for takeoffs and landings, but rarely suffers from congestion or lengthy lines. Its spacious, modern terminals are easily navigable, with plenty of dining options as well as free Wi-Fi. Sky Harbor's three passenger terminals are connected by inter-terminal buses that run regularly throughout the day.

Tucson International Airport has one terminal that has restaurants and free Wi-Fi. Although it services far fewer passengers per day than Sky Harbor, it does offer nonstop flights to a number of major metropolitan areas around the western half of the country (Atlanta and Charlotte are the only eastern cities with direct service).

Airport Information Phoenix Sky Harbor International (☎ 602/273-3300 ⊕ www.phx skyharbor.com). **Tucson International Airport** (☎ 520/573-8100 ⊕ www.tucsonairport.org).

FLIGHTS

Phoenix is a hub for Southwest Airlines and US Airways. These carriers offer the most direct flights in and out of Phoenix. Most of the nation's other major airlines also fly into Phoenix and have a few flights into Tucson as well.

Among the smaller airlines, AirTran flies from Phoenix to Atlanta and Milwaukee. Frontier connects Phoenix and Tucson with Denver. Hawaiian Airlines flies from Phoenix to Maui. Midwest Airlines connects Phoenix and Milwaukee. JetBlue has service from Phoenix to New York. Sun Country Airlines flies from Phoenix and Tucson to Minneapolis. Canada's WestJet connects Phoenix with Edmonton, Calgary, and Winnipeg.

Within Arizona, US Airways Express/ Mesa Airlines (part of US Airways) flies from Phoenix to Flagstaff and Yuma.

Service also has an extensive list of B&Bs and other lodgings, and can also help with vacation packages, guided tours, and golf vacations. Mi Casa Su Casa offers properties in a range of styles, from adobe haciendas in areas like Sedona and Tucson to pine cabins in the White Mountains.

Reservation Services Arizona Association of Bed and Breakfast Inns (☎ *No phone* ⊕ *www.arizona-bed-breakfast.com*). **Arizona Trails Reservation Service** (☎ *480/837-4284 or 888/799-4284* ⊕ *www.arizonatrails.com*). **Bed & Breakfast.com** (☎ *512/322-2710 or 800/462-2632* ⊕ *www.bedandbreakfast.com*) also sends out an online newsletter. **Bed & Breakfast Inns Online** (☎ *615/868-1946 or 800/215-7365* ⊕ *www.bbonline.com*). **BnB Finder.com** (☎ *212/432-7693 or 888/547-8226* ⊕ *www.bnbfinder.com*). **Mi Casa Su Casa** (☎ *480/990-0682 or 800/456-0682* ⊕ *www.azres.com*).

DUDE-GUEST RANCHES

Guest ranches afford visitors a close encounter with down-home cooking, activities, and culture. Most of the properties are situated around Tucson and Wickenburg, northwest of Phoenix. Some are resort-style compounds where guests are pampered, whereas smaller, family-run ranches expect *everyone* to join in the chores. Horseback riding and other outdoor recreational activities are emphasized. Many dude ranches are closed in summer. The Arizona Dude Ranch Association provides names and addresses of member ranches and their facilities and policies.

Information The Arizona Dude Ranch Association (☎ *520/823-4277* ⊕ *www.azdra.com*).

■ COMMUNICATIONS

INTERNET

As in all major U.S. cities, high-speed Internet and Wi-Fi connections are ubiquitous at hotels throughout the state, even in remote areas (although sometimes there's a fee of $5 to $15 per day). There are also connections at cafés, restaurants, and other businesses. In more remote areas you'll find fewer ways to get online, but usually a local café or motel has Wi-Fi.

Contacts Cybercafes (⊕ *www.cybercafes. com*) lists more than 4,000 Internet cafés worldwide.

■ EATING OUT

Two distinct cultures—Native American and Sonoran—have had the greatest influence on native Arizona cuisine. Chiles, beans, corn, tortillas, and squash are common ingredients for those restaurants that specialize in regional cuisine (cactus is just as tasty but less common). Mom-and-pop *taquerias* are abundant, especially in the southern part of the state. In Phoenix, Tucson, Sedona, and increasingly Flagstaff, Bisbee, Prescott, and some smaller but sophisticated parts of the state, you'll find hip, intriguing restaurants specializing in American and Southwestern cuisine, as well as some excellent restaurants specializing in such ethnic cuisines as Thai, Chinese, Japanese, and the like.

RESERVATIONS AND DRESS

Regardless of where you are, it's a good idea to make a reservation if you can. In some places (some of Scottsdale's top restaurants, for example) it's expected. We only mention them specifically when reservations are essential (there's no other way you'll ever get a table) or when they are not accepted. For popular restaurants, book as far ahead as you can (often 30 days), and reconfirm as soon as you arrive. (Large parties should always call ahead to check the reservations policy.) We mention dress only when men are required to wear a jacket or a jacket and tie.

Online reservation services make it easy to book a table before you even leave home. OpenTable covers most states, including 20 major cities, and has limited listings in Canada, Mexico, the United Kingdom, and elsewhere. DinnerBroker has restaurants throughout the United States as well as a few in Canada.

Contacts DinnerBroker (⊕ *www.dinnerbroker. com*). OpenTable (⊕ *www.opentable.com*).

WINES, BEER, AND SPIRITS

Although Arizona is not typically associated with viticulture, the region southeast of Tucson, stretching to the Mexico border, has several microclimates ideal for wine growing. The iron- and calcium-rich soil is similar to that of the Burgundy region in France, and, combined with the temperate weather and lower-key atmosphere, has enticed several independent and family-run wineries to open in the past few decades in the Elgin, Sonoita, and Nogales areas, with a somewhat more nascent crop of them having begun to develop in northern parts of the state, around Sedona and Verde Valley. Microbreweries have sprung up throughout the state in recent years, with a number of good ones in Phoenix, Tucson, and Flagstaff.

In Arizona you must be 21 to buy any alcohol. Bars and liquor stores are open daily, including Sunday, but must stop selling alcohol at 2 AM. In many municipalities, including Phoenix and Flagstaff, smoking is prohibited in restaurants and bars. You'll find beer, wine, and alcohol at most supermarkets. Possession and consumption of alcoholic beverages is illegal on Native American reservations.

Contacts Arizona Wine Growers Association (⊕ *www.arizonawine.org*). Callaghan Vineyards (☎ *520/455-5322* ⊕ *www. cal laghanvineyards.com*). Sonoita Vineyards (☎ *520/455-5893* ⊕ *www.sonoitavine yards.com*). The Village of Elgin Winery (☎ *520/455-9309* ⊕ *www.elginwines.com*).

▌ HEALTH

ANIMAL BITES

Wherever you're walking in desert areas, particularly between April and October, keep a lookout for rattlesnakes. You're likely not to have any problems if you maintain distance from snakes that you see—they can strike only half of their length, so a 6-foot clearance should allow

you to remain unharmed, especially if you don't provoke them. If you are bitten by a rattler, don't panic. Get to a hospital within two to three hours of the bite. Try to keep the area that has been bitten below heart level, and stay calm, as increased heart rate can spread venom more quickly. Keep in mind that 30% to 40% of bites are dry bites, where the snake uses no venom (still, get thee to a hospital). Avoid night hikes without rangers, when snakes are on the prowl and less visible.

Scorpions and Gila monsters are really less of a concern, since they strike only when provoked. To avoid scorpion encounters, look before touching: never place your hands where you can't see, such as under rocks and in holes. Likewise, if you move a rock to sit down, make sure that scorpions haven't been exposed. Campers should shake out shoes in the morning, since scorpions like warm, moist places. If you're bitten, see a ranger about symptoms that may develop. Chances are good that you won't need to go to a hospital. Children are a different case, however: scorpion stings can be fatal for them. Always try to keep an eye on what they may be getting their hands into to avoid the scorpion's sting. Gila monsters are relatively rare and bites are even rarer, but bear in mind that the reptiles are most active between April and June, when they do most of their hunting. Should a member of your party be bitten, it is most important to release the Gila monster's jaws as soon as possible to minimize the amount of venom released. This can usually be achieved with a stick, an open flame, or immersion of the animal in water.

DEHYDRATION

This underestimated danger can be very serious, especially considering that one of the first major symptoms is the inability to swallow. It may be the easiest hazard to avoid, however; simply drink every 10–15 minutes, up to a gallon of water per day in summer. Always carry a water bottle,

FOR INTERNATIONAL TRAVELERS

CURRENCY

The dollar is the basic unit of U.S. currency. It has 100 cents. Coins are the penny (1¢); the nickel (5¢), dime (10¢), quarter (25¢), half-dollar (50¢), and the very rare golden $1 coin and even rarer silver $1. Bills are denominated $1, $5, $10, $20, $50, and $100, all mostly green and identical in size; designs and background tints vary. You may come across a $2 bill, but the chances are slim.

CUSTOMS

U.S. Customs and Border Protection (⊕ www.cbp.gov).

DRIVING

Driving in the United States is on the right. Speed limits are posted in miles per hour (usually between 55 MPH and 70 MPH). Watch for lower limits in small towns and on back roads (usually 30 MPH to 40 MPH). Most states require front-seat passengers to wear seat belts; many states require children to sit in the back seat and to wear seat belts. In major cities rush hour is between 7 and 10 AM; afternoon rush hour is between 4 and 7 PM. To encourage carpooling, some freeways have special lanes, ordinarily marked with a diamond, for high-occupancy vehicles (HOV)—cars carrying two people or more.

Highways are well paved. Interstates—limited-access, multilane highways designated with an "I–" before the number—are fastest. Interstates with three-digit numbers circle urban areas, which may also have other limited-access expressways, freeways, and parkways. Tolls may be levied on limited-access highways. U.S. and state highways aren't necessarily limited-access, but may have several lanes.

ELECTRICITY

The U.S. standard is AC, 110 volts/60 cycles. Plugs have two flat pins set parallel to each other.

EMBASSIES

Australia (☎ 202/797–3000 ⊕ www. austemb.org). **Canada** (☎ 202/682–1740 ⊕ www.canadianembassy.org). **United Kingdom** (☎ 202/588–7800 ⊕ www. britainusa.com).

EMERGENCIES

For police, fire, or ambulance, dial 911 (0 in rural areas).

HOLIDAYS

New Year's Day (Jan. 1); Martin Luther King Day (3rd Mon. in Jan.); Presidents' Day (3rd Mon. in Feb.); Memorial Day (last Mon. in May); Independence Day (July 4); Labor Day (1st Mon. in Sept.); Columbus Day (2nd Mon. in Oct.); Thanksgiving Day (4th Thurs. in Nov.); Christmas Eve and Christmas Day (Dec. 24 and 25); and New Year's Eve (Dec. 31).

MAIL

You can buy stamps and aerograms and send letters and parcels in post offices. Stamp-dispensing machines can occasionally be found in airports, bus and train stations, office buildings, drugstores, and convenience stores. U.S. mailboxes are stout, dark blue steel bins; pickup schedules are posted inside the bin (pull down the handle to see them). Parcels weighing more than a pound must be mailed at a post office or at a private mailing center.

Within the United States a first-class letter weighing 1 ounce or less costs 44¢.

To receive mail on the road, have it sent c/o General Delivery at your destination's main post office (use the correct five-digit ZIP code). You must pick up mail in person within 30 days, with a driver's license or passport for identification.

DHL (☎ 800/225–5345 ⊕ www.dhl.com). **Federal Express** (☎ 800/463–3339 ⊕ www. fedex.com). **Mail Boxes, Etc./The UPS Store** (☎ 800/789–4623 ⊕ www.mbe.com). **United**

States Postal Service (⊕ *www.usps.com*). Passports and Visas

Visitor visas aren't necessary for citizens of Australia, Canada, the United Kingdom, or most citizens of European Union countries coming for tourism and staying for fewer than 90 days. If you require a visa, the cost is $100, and waiting time can be substantial, depending on where you live. Apply for a visa at the U.S. consulate in your place of residence; check the U.S. State Department's special Visa Web site for further information.

VISA INFORMATION
Destination USA (⊕ *www.unitedstatesvisas. gov*).

PHONES
Numbers consist of a three-digit area code and a seven-digit local number. Within many local calling areas you dial only the seven digits; in others you dial "1" first and all 10 digits—just as you would for calls between area-code regions. The same is true for calls to numbers prefixed by "800," "888," "866," and "877"—all toll-free. For calls to numbers prefixed by "900" you must pay—usually dearly.

For international calls, dial "011" followed by the country code and the local number. For help, dial "0" and ask for an overseas operator. Most phone books list country codes and U.S. area codes. The country code for Australia is 61, for New Zealand 64, for the United Kingdom 44. Calling Canada is the same as calling within the United States, whose country code, by the way, is 1.

For operator assistance, dial "0." For directory assistance, call 555–1212 or occasionally 411 (free at many public phones). You can reverse long-distance charges by calling "collect"; dial "0" instead of "1" before the 10-digit number.

Instructions are generally posted on pay phones. Usually you insert coins in a slot (usually 25¢–50¢ for local calls) and wait for a steady tone before dialing. On long-distance calls the operator tells you how much to insert; prepaid phone cards, widely available in various denominations, can be used from any phone. Follow the directions to activate the card (there's usually an access number, then an activation code), then dial your number.

CELL PHONES
The United States has several GSM (Global System for Mobile Communications) networks, so multiband mobiles from most countries (except for Japan) work here. Unfortunately, it's almost impossible to buy a pay-as-you-go mobile SIM card in the United States—which allows you to avoid roaming charges—without also buying a phone. That said, cell phones with pay-as-you-go plans are available for well under $100. The cheapest ones with decent national coverage are the GoPhone from Cingular and Virgin Mobile, which only offers pay-as-you-go service.

Cingular (☎ *888/333–6651* ⊕ *www. cingular.com*). **Virgin Mobile** (☎ *No phone* ⊕ *www.virginmobileusa.com*).

and replenish frequently, whether hiking, walking in the city, or at an outdoor sports or arts event.

HYPOTHERMIA

Temperatures in Arizona can vary widely from day to night—as much as 40°F. Be sure to bring enough warm clothing for hiking and camping, along with wet-weather gear. It's always a good idea to pack an extra set of clothes in a large, waterproof plastic bag that would stay dry in any situation. Exposure to the degree that body temperature dips below 95°F produces the following symptoms: chills, tiredness, then uncontrollable shivering and irrational behavior, with the victim not always recognizing that he or she is cold. If someone in your party is suffering from any of this, wrap him or her in blankets and/or a warm sleeping bag immediately and try to keep him or her awake. The fastest way to raise body temperature is through skin-to-skin contact in a sleeping bag. Drinking warm liquids also helps.

SUN EXPOSURE

Wear a hat and sunglasses and put on sunblock to protect against the burning Arizona sun. And watch out for heatstroke. Symptoms include headache, dizziness, and fatigue, which can turn into convulsions and unconsciousness and can lead to death. If someone in your party develops any of these conditions, have one person seek emergency help while others move the victim into the shade and wrap him or her in wet clothing (is a stream nearby?) to cool him or her down.

▍HOURS OF OPERATION

Most museums in Arizona's larger cities are open daily. A few are closed on Monday, and hours may vary between May and September (off-season in the major tourist centers of Phoenix and Tucson). Call ahead when planning a visit to lesser-known museums or attractions, whose hours may vary considerably. Major attractions are open daily.

Most retail stores are open 10 AM to 6 PM, although stores in malls tend to stay open until 9 PM. Those in the less-populated areas are likely to have shorter hours and may be closed on Sunday. Shopping centers are also often open Sunday from noon to 5 or later.

▍MONEY

ITEM	AVERAGE COST
Cup of Coffee	$2.50
Glass of Wine	$6
Glass of Beer	$4
Sandwich	$6
One-Mile Taxi Ride in Phoenix	$6.50
Museum Admission	$8

Prices throughout this guide are given for adults. Substantially reduced fees are almost always available for children, students, and senior citizens.

CREDIT CARDS

Throughout this guide, the following abbreviations are used: **AE**, American Express; **D**, Discover; **DC**, Diners Club; **MC**, MasterCard; and **V**, Visa.

It's a good idea to inform your credit-card company before you travel, especially if you're going abroad and don't travel internationally very often. Otherwise, the credit-card company might put a hold on your card owing to unusual activity—not a good thing halfway through your trip. Record all your credit-card numbers—as well as the phone numbers to call if your cards are lost or stolen—in a safe place, so you're prepared should something go wrong. Both MasterCard and Visa have general numbers you can call (collect if you're abroad) if your card is lost, but you're better off calling the number of your issuing bank, since Master-Card and Visa usually just transfer you to your bank; your bank's number is usually printed on your card.

Reporting Lost Cards American Express (☎ 800/992–3404 in the U.S. or 336/393–1111 collect from abroad ⊕ www.americanexpress.com). **Din-ers Club** (☎ 800/234–6377 in the U.S. or 303/799–1504 collect from abroad ⊕ www.dinersclub.com). **Discover** (☎ 800/347–2683 in the U.S. or 801/902–3100 collect from abroad ⊕ www.discovercard.com). **Mas-terCard** (☎ 800/622–7747 in the U.S. or 636/722–7111 collect from abroad ⊕ www.mastercard.com). **Visa** (☎ 800/847–2911 in the U.S. or 410/581–9994 collect from abroad ⊕ www.visa.com).

▌ PACKING

Pack casual clothing and resort wear for a trip to Arizona. Stay cool in cotton fabrics and light colors. T-shirts, polo shirts, sun-dresses, and lightweight shorts, trousers, skirts, and blouses are useful year-round in all but the higher-elevation parts of the state, where cooler temperatures mandate warmer garb. Bring sun hats, swimsuits, sandals, and sunscreen—essential warm-weather items. Bring a sweater and a warm jacket in winter, necessary during December and January throughout the state, particularly in the high country—anywhere around Flagstaff and in the White Mountains. And don't forget jeans and sneakers or sturdy walking shoes; they're important throughout the year.

SHIPPING SPORTING EQUIPMENT

Arizona is a wonderful destination for all kinds of equipment-intensive sports, from skiing to cycling to golfing. If you're driving here, lugging your gear isn't much of a hassle. But travelers arriving by plane may find hauling bags of clubs, mountain bikes, and skis a bit daunting. Sports Express specializes in shipping gear. The service isn't cheap, but it is highly reliable and convenient.

Contacts Sports Express (☎ 800/357–4174 ⊕ www.sportsexpress.com).

▌ SAFETY

Arizona's track record in terms of crime is not unlike that of other U.S. states, if a little higher than average in Phoenix and Tucson. In these big cities you should take the same precautions you would anywhere—be aware of what's going on around you, stick to well-lighted areas, and quickly move away from any situation or people that might be threatening. In both of these cities it's easy to find yourself driving into a less-than-savory neighborhood with little notice; if you feel uneasy about your surroundings, turn around and go back the way you came.

Check the U.S. government travel advisory before you plan a trip to the Mexico border towns. Visitors should take extra precautions.

Safety Transportation Security Administra-tion (TSA ⊕ www.tsa.gov). **U.S. Department of State** (⊕ travel.state.gov).

▌ TAXES

Arizona state sales tax (called a transaction privilege tax), which applies to all purchases except food in grocery stores, is 5.6%. Individual counties and munici-palities then add their own sales taxes, which add another few percentage points, depending on where you are. Phoenix and Tucson both levy city sales taxes of 2%, and Flagstaff taxes purchases at a rate of 1.72%. When added to county taxes, the total sales tax in Phoenix goes up to 8.3%; in Tucson, to 8.1%; and in Flagstaff, to 8.44%. Total sales taxes throughout the state range from 7.6% to 10.7%. Sales taxes do not apply on Indian reservations.

▌ TIME

Arizona is in the Mountain Time Zone, but Nevada, next door, is in the Pacific Time Zone. Arizona does not use Daylight Saving Time, though, and as a result, from spring through fall Nevada and Arizona observe the same hours. ▇**TIP➜** The Navajo Nation does observe Daylight Saving Time, however, so it's always the same time on Navajo territory as in Mountain Time Zone areas outside Arizona.

Time Zones Timeanddate.com (⊕ *www.time anddate.com/worldclock)* can help you figure out the correct time anywhere.

▌ TIPPING

The customary tip for taxi drivers is 15%–20%, with a minimum of $2. Bellhops are usually given $2 per bag in luxury hotels, $1 per bag elsewhere. Hotel maids should be tipped $2 per day of your stay. A doorman who hails a cab can be tipped $1–$2. You should also tip your hotel concierge for services rendered; the size of the tip depends on the difficulty of your request, as well as the quality of the concierge's work. For an ordinary dinner reservation or tour arrangements, $3–$5 should do; if the concierge scores seats at a popular restaurant or show or performs unusual services (getting your laptop repaired, finding a good pet-sitter, etc.), $10 or more is appropriate.

Waiters should be tipped 15%–20%, though at higher-end restaurants a solid 20% is more the norm. Many restaurants add a gratuity to the bill for parties of six or more. Ask what the percentage is if the menu or bill doesn't state it. Tip $1 per drink you order at the bar, though if at an upscale establishment, those $15 martinis might warrant a $2 tip.

▌ TOURS

ARCHAEOLOGY

The Archaeological Conservancy offers a number of tours covering significant sites around the country, including a few trips that involve sites in Arizona. Based in southwestern Colorado, Crow Canyon Archaeological Center has a few different trips that touch on portions of Arizona. These vary year to year, but have included Hiking in Carrizo Mountain Country, Hopi Kachina Workshops, Backcountry Archaeology in Northeastern Arizona, and Rock Art in Arizona. Utah's Southwest Ed-Ventures can work with you to customize your own trip through Arizona's Hopi and Navajo regions, and they also offer a number of scheduled group trips that touch on Arizona.

Contacts Archaeological Conservancy (☎ *505/266–1540* ⊕ *www.americanarchae ology.org).* **Crow Canyon Archaeological Center** (☎ *970/565–8975 or 800/422–8975* ⊕ *www.crowcanyon.org).* **Southwest Ed-Ventures** (☎ *435/587–2156 or 800/525–4456* ⊕ *www.sw-adventures.org).*

BICYCLING

A number of companies offer extensive bike tours that cover parts of the Southwest. Backroads organizes a nine-day Utah and northern Arizona national parks journey. Scottsdale-based AOA Adventures offers a variety of bike trips throughout the state. Timberline Adventure has biking tours of Arizona's White Mountains.▇**TIP➜**Most airlines accommodate bikes as luggage, provided they're dismantled and boxed.

Contacts AOA Adventures (☎ *480/945–2881 or 866/455–1601* ⊕ *www.aoa-adventures. com).* **Backroads** (☎ *510/527–1555 or 800/462–2848* ⊕ *www.backroads.com).* **Timberline Adventures** (☎ *303/368–4418 or 800/417–2453* ⊕ *www.timbertours.com).*

GOLF

Golfpac organizes golf vacations all over the world, Phoenix, Scottsdale, and Tucson being among its most popular destinations.

Contacts Golfpac (☎ 888/848–8941 ⊕ www. golfpactravel.com).

HIKING

Scottsdale-based AOA Adventures offers multiday hiking and biking tours through some of the state's most dramatic scenery, from the Grand Canyon to Havasupai. Vermont-based Boundless Journeys has wonderful hiking tours that take in the Grand Canyon region as well as Bryce and Zion in Utah.

Contacts AOA Adventures (☎ 480/945–2881 or 866/455–1601 ⊕ www.aoa-adventures. com). Boundless Journeys (☎ 800/941–8010 ⊕ www.boundlessjourneys.com).

NATIVE AMERICAN HISTORY

You can explore a number of parts of the state important to indigenous peoples— Sedona, the Grand Canyon, Hopi Country, Antelope Canyon, Canyon de Chelly—on walking, float-trip, and Jeep tours offered by Native American Journeys.

Contacts Native American Journeys (☎ 928/284–4735 ⊕ www.nativeamerican journeys.com).

NATURAL HISTORY

Consider booking a trip through Smithsonian Journeys if you're keen on experiencing the Grand Canyon with knowledgeable guides. Victor Emanuel Nature Tours is another excellent tour operator, offering four different tours (three in summer, one in winter) that emphasize bird-watching. Off the Beaten Path has a variety of tours in northern Arizona and elsewhere in the southwest.

Contacts Off the Beaten Path (☎ 406/586–1311 or 800/445–2995 ⊕ www. offthebeatenpath.com). Smithsonian Journeys (☎ 202/357–4700 or 877/338–8687 ⊕ www.smithsonianjourneys.org). Victor Emanuel Nature Tours (☎ 512/328–5221 or 800/328–8368 ⊕ www.ventbird.com).

RIVER-RAFTING

Rafting on the Colorado River through the Grand Canyon is a once-in-a-lifetime experience for many who try it. Numerous reliable companies offer rafting tours through the canyon, including Action Whitewater Adventures, OARS, and World Wide River Expeditions.

Contacts Action Whitewater Adventures (☎ 801/375–4111 or 800/453–1482 ⊕ www. riverguide.com). OARS (☎ 209/736–4677 or 800/346–6277 ⊕ www.oars.com). World Wide River Expeditions (☎ 435/259–7515 or 800/231–2769 ⊕ www.worldwideriver.com).

■ VISITOR INFORMATION

For local tourism information, see specific chapters and towns. Many of Arizona's Native American reservations have Web sites and helpful information. Some require permits for visiting certain areas.

Visitor Info Arizona Office of Tourism (☎ 602/364–3700 or 866/275–5816 ⊕ www. arizonaguide.com).

Native American Contacts Arizona Commission of Indian Affairs (☎ 602/542–3123 ⊕ www.indianaffairs.state.az.us). Gila River Indian Community (☎ 520/562–9500 ⊕ www.gric.nsn.us). Inter Tribal Council of Arizona: Hopi Tribe (☎ 928/734–2441 ⊕ www.itcaonline.com/tribes_hopi. html). Navajo Nation Tourism Office (☎ 928/810–8501 ⊕ www.discovernavajo. com). Salt River Pima-Maricopa Indian Community (☎ 480/850–8000 ⊕ www.saltriver.

pima-maricopa.nsn.us). **Tohono O'odham Nation** (☎ *520/383–2028* ⊕ *www.itcaonline. com/tribes_tohono.html*). **White Mountain Apache Nation** (☎ *928/338–4346 or 877/338–9628* ⊕ *www.wmat.nsn.us*).

ONLINE RESOURCES

Information of particular interest to outdoorsy types can be found on the Web site for Arizona State Parks, which has links to the many beautiful state-operated reserves throughout Arizona. The site for the National Park Service has links to the several national parks in Arizona. Of course, the Grand Canyon is the most famous of Arizona's parks, and you can find out much more about the park at the Canyon, The Great Outdoor Recreation Page is another font of information for hikers, skiers, and the like.

There are a handful of excellent general-interest sites related to travel in Arizona. A very good bet is the *Arizona Republic*–sponsored AzCentral.com, which provides news, reviews, and travel information on the entire state, with a particular emphasis on Phoenix. Alternative newsweeklies are another helpful resource, among them the Phoenix *New Times*. For the southern part of the state, look for *Tucson Weekly*. In Flagstaff and north-central Arizona, check out Flagstaff Live.

Contacts Arizona State Parks (⊕ *www. azstateparks.com*). **National Park Service** (⊕ *www.nps.gov*). **The Canyon** (⊕ *www. thecanyon.com*). The **Great Outdoor Recreation Page** (⊕ *www.gorp.com*). **AzCentral. com** (⊕ *www.azcentral.com*). **Phoenix New Times** (⊕ *www.phoenixnewtimes.com*). **Tucson Weekly** (⊕ *www.tucsonweekly.com*). **Flagstaff Live!** (⊕ *www.flaglive.com*).

INDEX

A

"A" Mountain (Sentinel Peak), *347*
Abyss, The, *150*
Accommodations, *497–498*
Actors Theatre of Phoenix, *114*
Adobe Village and Graham Inn 🖭, *228–229*
Adventure tours, *362, 475*
Agate Bridge, *333*
Agate House, *332–333, 335*
Agave, *450*
'Ahakhav Iribal Preserve, *474*
Air tours, *144, 158–159, 287*
Air travel, *493–494*
airports, *38, 493*
Grand Canyon, 147
North-Central Arizona, 201
Northeast Arizona, 286, 287
Northwest Arizona and Southeast Nevada, 479
Phoenix, Scottsdale, and Tempe, 38
Southern Arizona, 456
Tucson, 344
Ajo, *453–454*
Ajo Historical Society Museum, *454*
Ajo Mountain Drive, *455*
AJ's Fine Foods (shop), *124*
Alan Bible Visitors Center, *487*
Alpine, *325–327*
Amerind Foundation, *444*
Amsterdam (gay club), *119*
Andy Devine Days, *465*
Antelope Canyon, *293–294*
Antelope Canyon tours, *293–294*
Antiques and collectibles, shopping for, *123, 312–313*
Apache Cultural Museum, *307*
Apache-Sitgreaves National Forest, *328*
Apache Trail, *135–136, 138–142*
Arboretum, *136, 139*
Archaeology tours, *139–140, 321–322, 504*
Arcosanti, *134*
Arizona Center, *44*
Arizona Doll and Toy Museum, *43*
Arizona Grand Resort 🖭, *101*
Arizona Historical Society's Museum, *351–352*
Arizona Inn 🖭, *383*

Arizona Mining and Mineral Museum, *44*
Arizona Museum of Natural History, *55*
Arizona Opera Company, *392*
Arizona Science Center, *44*
Arizona Snowbowl, *202, 209*
Arizona-Sonora Desert Museum, *18, 342, 359*
Arizona State Museum, *352*
Arizona State University, *54–55*
Arizona State University Art Museum, *54–55*
Arizona Theatre Company, *114, 393*
Armory Park, *347*
Art galleries and museums.
⇨*See* Museums and Art galleries
Art Walk, *50*
Arts and crafts, shopping for, *123–124, 268, 271, 275, 277, 397–398*
Asarco Mineral Discovery Center, *408*
Astronomers Inn 🖭, *447*
ASU Karsten Golf Course, *58*
ASU Memorial Union, *54*
Avi Resort & Casino 🖭, *482*
Axis/Radius (dance club), *119*
AZ 88 ✕, *83*

B

Babbitt Brothers Building, *202, 204*
Bacavi, *272*
Backpacking, *224*
Bajada Loop Drive, *400, 402*
Ballet Arizona, *392*
Ballooning
North-Central Arizona, 224
Phoenix, Scottsdale, and Tempe, 56–57
Tucson, 362
Barrio Historico, *347*
Bars and lounges
gay and lesbian, 119-120, 394
Phoenix, Scottsdale, and Tempe, 116–117
Tucson, 393–394
Baseball, *362*
Basha's Deli & Bakery, *453*
Basis ✕, *76*
Bear Wallow Wilderness Area, *327*

Bed and breakfasts, *291, 429, 435, 497–498*
Bell Rock, *219–220*
Benson, *445, 447–448*
Besh-Ba-Gowah Archaeological Park, *139–140*
Best Western Grand Canyon Squire Inn 🖭, *190–191*
Betatakin, *283*
Bicycling
Eastern Arizona, 309–310, 325
Grand Canyon, 144, 159, 170, 179
North-Central Arizona, 208, 225–226
Phoenix, Scottsdale, and Tempe, 57
Tours, 504
Tucson, 362–363, 402–403
Bill Williams River National Wildlife Refuge, *474*
Biltmore Fashion Park, *121*
Biosphere 2 Center, *361*
Bird Cage Theater, *423*
Bird-watching
Grand Canyon, 144
North-Central Arizona, 223, 236–237
Northwest Arizona, 474
Southern Arizona, 427, 428, 437, 439, 449–450, 459–460
Tucson, 363–364, 403, 410
Bisbee, *414, 425–430*
Bisbee Mining and Historical Museum, *427*
Bisbee Visitors Center, *426*
Bitter Springs, *285*
Black Canyon Trail, *238*
Black Mesa, *275*
Black Theater Troupe, *114*
Blair's Dinnebito Trading Post, *292*
Blue Mesa Trail, *335*
Blue Range Primitive Area, *327*
Blue Vista, *325*
Bluegrass Festival, *247*
Blues, Jazz, and Rock, *117*
Boat tours, *295, 475*
Boating, *18, 144, 237, 250, 295, 462, 487*
Bonelli House, *467–468*
Boot Hill Graveyard, *420–421, 423*
Boulder City, NV, *484*
Boulder City Chamber of Commerce, *484*

Photo Credits: 1 and 2-3, Kerrick James. 5, Christophe Testi/Shutterstock. Chapter 1: Experience Arizona: 8-9, gary718/Shutterstock. 10, Wilde Meyer Gallery. 11 (left and right), Metropolitan Tucson Convention & Visitors Bureau. 13, Aramark Parks & Destinations. 14 (top left), National Park Service. 14 (bottom left), Mike Norton/Shutterstock. 14 (right) and 15 (left and top center), Kerrick James. 15 (top right), Katrina Brown/Shutterstock. 15 (bottom right), Daniel Gratton/Shutterstock. 16, Kerrick James. 17 and 18, Metropolitan Tucson Convention & Visitors Bureau. 19 (left), luchschen/Shutterstock. 19 (right), Paul Markow/Rancho de los Caballeros. 20 and 21, Royal Palms Resort and Spa. 22, Arizona Biltmore Resort & Spa. 26-27, Christophe Testi/Shutterstock. 28, Anton Foltin/Shutterstock. 29, Geir Olav Lyngfjell/Shutterstock. 30 (left), Wendy Holden/iStockphoto. 30 (right), Kerrick James. 31, Alexander Hafemann/iStockphoto. 32, Paul B. Moore/Shutterstock. 33, Kerrick James. Chapter 2: Phoenix, Scottsdale and Tempe: 35, Kerrick James. 36, John C. Russell/Four Seasons Hotels & Resorts. 37, Barbara Kraft/Four Seasons Hotels & Resorts. 40, Paul Markow/Rancho de los Caballeros. 42 and 53, Kerrick James. 60, JW Marriott Desert Ridge Resort. 74 and 75, Royal Palms Resort and Spa. 106 (top), Reddie Henderson. 106 (bottom left), Arizona Grand Resort. 106 (bottom right), Sanctuary on Camelback Mountain, Scottsdale. 107 (top), The Westin Kierland Resort & Spa. 107 (bottom left), JW Marriott Desert Ridge Resort. 107 (bottom right), Barbara Kraft/Four Seasons Hotels & Resorts. 111, Kerrick James. 114, Stuart Pearce/age fotostock. 123, Wilde Meyer Gallery. 132 (top), The Boulders Resort & Golden Door Spa. 132 (bottom), Mark Boisclair Photography. 137 and 141, Kerrick James. Chapter 3: Grand Canyon National Park: 143 and 145 (top and bottom), National Park Service. 148, Nickolay Stanev/Shutterstock. 153, poutnik/Shutterstock. 158, National Park Service. 171, Kerrick James. 178, Mark Lellouch/National Park Service. 188, Kerrick James. Chapter 4: North-Central Arizona: 195, Kerrick James. 196, Tom Grundy/Shutterstock. 197 (top), sochigirl/Shutterstock. 197 (bottom), Tom Grundy/Shutterstock. 198, FloridaStock/Shutterstock. 200, David M. Schrader/Shutterstock. 207, Kerrick James. 212, Zack Frank/Shutterstock. 221 and 227, Kerrick James. 230, Lindy Drew. 239, Kerrick James. 240, LouLouPhotos/Shutterstock. Chapter 5: Northeast Arizona: 249, Kerrick James. 250 (left), Sourav and Joyeeta Chowdhury/Shutterstock. 250 (right), Katrina Brown/Shutterstock. 251 (top and bottom), Aramark Parks & Destinations. 254, Robcsee/Shutterstock. 260-61, 270, 280, 285, 288, and 292, Kerrick James. 296, CAN BALCIOGLU/Shutterstock. Chapter 6: Eastern Arizona: 299, Kerrick James. 300 (left), Jim Parkin/Shutterstock. 300 (right), George Burba/Shutterstock. 301 (top), Mike Norton/Shutterstock. 301 (bottom), Zack Frank/Shutterstock. 304, Jeffrey M. Frank/Shutterstock. 311, 316, 323, 329, and 332, Kerrick James. 336, Sebastien Burel/Shutterstock. Chapter 7: Tucson: 341, 342, 343 (top and bottom), and 346, Metropolitan Tucson Convention & Visitors Bureau. 351 and 363, Kerrick James. 374, Metropolitan Tucson Convention & Visitors Bureau. 382 (top), Loews Ventana Canyon. 382 (bottom left), Arizona Inn. 382 (bottom right), White Stallion Ranch. 387, 396, and 405, Metropolitan Tucson Convention & Visitors Bureau. Chapter 8: Southern Arizona: 413, Kerrick James. 414 (top), Kevin Cole/wikipedia.org. 414 (bottom), Mark Godfrey/The Nature Conservancy. 415 (top and bottom), Metropolitan Tucson Convention & Visitors Bureau. 416, Mark Godfrey/The Nature Conservancy. 417 and 418, Metropolitan Tucson Convention & Visitors Bureau. 425, Kerrick James. 434, Mark Godfrey/The Nature Conservancy. 441, wikipedia.org. 446, Kerrick James. 452, Metropolitan Tucson Convention & Visitors Bureau. 458, Kerrick James. Chapter 9: Northwest Arizona and Southeast Nevada: 461, Kerrick James. 462 (left), cloki/Shutterstock. 462 (right), Bruce Grubbs/Shutterstock. 464, Joe Mercier/Shutterstock. 466, Kerrick James. 471, Rolf Hicker Photography/Alamy. 476 and 485, Kerrick James.